TEXAS CRIMINAL PROCEDURE
AND EVIDENCE

ASPEN SELECT SERIES

TEXAS CRIMINAL PROCEDURE AND EVIDENCE

Amanda Peters
Helen & Harry Hutchens Research Professor
Professor of Law
South Texas College of Law Houston

 Wolters Kluwer

About Wolters Kluwer Legal & Regulatory U.S.

Wolters Kluwer Legal & Regulatory U.S. delivers expert content and solutions in the areas of law, corporate compliance, health compliance, reimbursement, and legal education. Its practical solutions help customers successfully navigate the demands of a changing environment to drive their daily activities, enhance decision quality and inspire confident outcomes.

Serving customers worldwide, its legal and regulatory solutions portfolio includes products under the Aspen Publishers, CCH Incorporated, Kluwer Law International, ftwilliam.com and MediRegs names. They are regarded as exceptional and trusted resources for general legal and practice-specific knowledge, compliance and risk management, dynamic workflow solutions, and expert commentary.

About Wolters Kluwer Legal & Regulatory U.S.

For Bret

Summary of Contents

Contents

Chapter 3: Warrantless Searches

Chapter 4: Jurisdiction, Venue, and Charging Instruments

Chapter 5: Bail

Chapter 6: The Grand Jury and Examining Trials

Chapter 7: Pretrial Matters

Chapter 8: Plea Negotiations

Chapter 9: Discovery

Chapter 10: Statements

Chapter 11: Jury Selection

Chapter 12: Trial

Chapter 13: Punishment

Chapter 14: Post-Conviction Relief

Chapter 15: Evidence

Introduction

I would like to highlight several features of this book, tell you about myself, and thank several people. I'll talk about the book first.

The practice questions that appear in this book are modeled after real bar exam questions that have appeared on the Texas Criminal Procedure & Evidence portion of the Texas Bar Exam. *Every single question* that has been asked since July of 2000 is accounted for in this book. In writing this book, I became a student of the bar exam. I included all questions in the book, documented when they were asked, and taught every subject needed to master all questions. Some questions are followed with tips on how to answer them. My goal was to educate students on criminal procedure and evidence and prepare them to take the corresponding portion of the bar exam. As bar exam scores drop statewide, students need more assistance with bar topics during law school. This book was designed to give students more points on the bar exam.

While every subject tested is accounted for by the text, there are areas of criminal procedure that have not been tested, but nevertheless were included in this book. Though 85-90% of the text is bar related, students need to understand important practice points and areas of law that may be tested in the future or that round out partially tested topics.

The cases in this book were carefully selected. I spent a considerable amount of time searching for cases that taught students well and were written in plain English. This was a challenging task. Cases include only necessary text, as do statutes, rules, and any other sources of law included in this book. Again, the goal was to focus on what students need to know, not to examine material exhaustively. Professors sometimes forget what it is like to learn an area of law from scratch. This book was written with the novice in mind. Even with simple instruction, students must comprehend and memorize a large amount of procedural and substantive law to master the topics in this book.

You'll notice the cases in the text include the full name of the defendant. We need to remember these cases involved people whose lives were impacted by the laws, procedures, and systems put in place to enforce criminal laws.

It doesn't take long for a writer to reveal who she is through her writing. My written communication style is casual, concise, and direct. I was a Technical Writing major and a Communications minor. I was trained to consider who my reader is and to meet my reader's needs. My hope is that the readers of this text – students and professors alike – find the reading easy. My aim was to write a straightforward, simplified book.

Finally, I'd like to tell you about my legal career. The Harris County District Attorney's Office in Houston, Texas offered me a job during my third year of law school. I worked there for eight years. I spent five years in the Trial Bureau litigating misdemeanor and felony cases. I then spent three years writing appellate briefs in the Appellate Division. I left the office to work as a criminal defense attorney in Houston and Galveston, where I represented clients in trial and appellate courts for three years. I left practice to teach at South Texas College of Law, which is where I still work. I was grateful to represent victims as a prosecutor, to represent clients as a criminal defense attorney, and I am grateful to teach and mentor law students as a professor.

Writing this book reminded me that my first legal love was criminal law and procedure. It's easy to be reminded of the passions and interests that bring law students to law school when you work in one. I have always loved criminal law and procedure. I hope that is apparent from reading this book.

I have a few people I would like to thank. Jovani Diaz, a cheerful, hard-working, detail-oriented former student of mine, provided research assistance with the first draft of this book. My former boss, Alan Curry, Appellate Division Chief of the Harris County District Attorney's Office, read several chapters of this book and provided much needed feedback and encouragement. I could not have written this book without the understanding, love, encouragement, and help of my husband Bret and our children Simon, Faith, Isaac, and Samuel Peters. To Bob, Linda, and Chris Dowlen, along with Bill and Monya Peters, I love you and thank you too for your understanding and encouragement while I wrote this book. God has blessed me with such a wonderful family. Thank you all.

Chapter 1
Arrest

Introduction

The Fourth Amendment to the U.S. Constitution mandates that no arrest warrant shall issue unless it is supported by probable cause.[1] In both the federal system and in Texas, there is a clear preference for "the warrant process in which police officers present their facts to a neutral magistrate to decide if there is probable cause to issue that warrant."[2] Why are magistrate-reviewed arrest warrants preferred over warrantless arrests made by police officers? The U.S. Supreme Court explained as follows:

> The point of the Fourth Amendment, which often is not grasped by zealous officers, is not that it denies law enforcement the support of the usual inferences which reasonable men draw from evidence. Its protection

---

[1] U.S. CONST. amend IV.
[2] *Rodriguez v. State*, 232 S.W.3d 55, 59 (Tex. Crim. App. 2007).

1

consists in requiring that those inferences be drawn by a neutral and detached magistrate instead of being judged by the officer engaged in the often competitive enterprise of ferreting out crime.[3]

Put yourself in the shoes of a peace officer. The peace-keeping function of this job necessarily involves searching for criminal activity and putting an end to it. However, while crime prevention and community safety are important, so are the legal safeguards designed to protect the public from overreaching law enforcement officers.

Though arrests pursuant to warrants are preferred, federal and Texas legislatures have carved out a number of exceptions to the warrant requirement. The general rule in federal law and in Texas is that a warrantless arrest is unreasonable per se unless it fits into one of the limited exceptions to the arrest warrant requirements.[4] This chapter will discuss arrest, arrest warrants, exceptions to the arrest warrant requirement, and the process that follows an arrest.

———————◆———————

What Is an Arrest?

An arrest takes place "when [a person] has been actually placed under restraint or taken into custody by an officer or person executing a warrant of arrest, or by an officer or person arresting without a warrant."[5] An arrest is a seizure of a person. While arrest may seem straightforward, it isn't always. It is important to explore the different levels of police encounters and then revisit the definition of *arrest*.

There are generally three levels of interaction between police officers and civilians. First, officers may have a consensual encounter with a person. Imagine an officer is investigating an act of vandalism and in so doing looks for a suspect who fits a specific description. The officer might ask a passerby in the area, "Have you seen a tall, skinny, white male in his 20s with a shaved head and a brown goatee wearing a yellow shirt and black pants? We have reason to suspect he vandalized a neighbor's car, and we would like to speak

---

[3] *Johnson v. United States*, 333 U.S. 10, 13 (1948).
[4] *Torres v. State*, 182 S.W.3d 899, 901 (Tex. Crim. App. 2005) (quoting *Minnesota v. Dickerson*, 508 U.S. 366, 372 (1993)).
[5] TEX. CODE CRIM. PROC. ANN. art. 15.22 (West 2016).

with him." The passerby is not a suspect, is not being detained, and is not under arrest. Officers do not need to suspect the person of a crime to initiate a conversation, nor is the passerby legally required to participate in the conversation.

The second level of interaction is an investigative detention. Officers may detain a person to investigate potential criminal activity if they have reasonable suspicion. "Reasonable suspicion exists if the officer has specific, articulable facts that, when combined with rational inferences from those facts, would lead him to reasonably conclude that a particular person actually is, has been, or soon will be engaged in criminal activity."[6] Reasonable suspicion is analyzed by courts by considering the totality of the circumstances.[7] Texas courts explain the distinction between the consensual encounter, defined in the previous paragraph, and detention supported by reasonable suspicion as follows:

> [C]onsensual confrontations are acceptable so long as a reasonable person would feel free to disregard the police and go about her business. However, when the citizen yields to a display of authority under circumstances in which a reasonable person would believe that she was not free to leave, an investigative detention has occurred.[8]

The test between the two then is whether the person feels free to leave. A consensual encounter can become an investigative detention.

There are other legally permissible brief detentions. Officers may detain a person for officer safety, to make sure the detainee has no weapons that could be used to hurt the officer during an encounter or investigation. As part of this type of detention, officers may pat the person down to ensure that he has no knife in a pocket or no gun in a waistband. While the officer is checking for weapons, the person is not free to leave. There are a few names for this brief detention: a *Terry* stop, a pat down, or a frisk.[9]

Terry, the namesake for this type of search, is worth mentioning briefly. In *Terry*, an experienced officer noticed three men acting suspiciously outside of a store; he believed they were preparing to rob it.[10] After observing the men for many minutes, he decided to approach them, identify himself, and

---

[6] *Castro v. State*, 227 S.W.3d 737, 741 (Tex. Crim. App. 2007).
[7] *Brodnex v. State*, 485 S.W.3d 432, 437 (Tex. Crim. App. 2016).
[8] *Lewis v. State*, 412 S.W.3d 794, 799 (Tex. App.—Amarillo 2013, no pet.).
[9] The "*Terry* stop" gets its name from *Terry v. Ohio*, 392 U.S. 1 (1968).
[10] *Id.* at 6.

investigate. Believing they might be armed, he patted them down on the exterior of their clothes and discovered two of the men had guns.[11] He confiscated the guns and arrested the men for carrying concealed weapons.[12]

The U.S. Supreme Court was asked to address "whether it is always unreasonable for a policeman to seize a person and subject him to a limited search for weapons unless there is probable cause for an arrest."[13] After thoughtfully balancing officer safety and the intrusion of individual rights, the Court held:

> where a police officer observes unusual conduct which leads him reasonably to conclude in light of his experience that criminal activity may be afoot and that the persons with whom he is dealing may be armed and presently dangerous, where in the course of investigating this behavior he identifies himself as a policeman and makes reasonable inquiries, and where nothing in the initial stages of the encounter serves to dispel his reasonable fear for his own or others' safety, he is entitled for the protection of himself and others in the area to conduct a carefully limited search of the outer clothing of such persons in an attempt to discover weapons which might be used to assault him.[14]

Terry's significance was and is enormous. The *Terry* Court recognized for the first time that there are degrees of intrusiveness in search and seizure and degrees of police encounters. Because the Court found the brief detention and frisk in that case was less intrusive than an arrest or a full-blown body search, the Court set out a less-than-probable-cause reasonableness standard. The standard has come to be known as *reasonable suspicion*, and it is the requisite for investigative stops and detentions.

Detentions should only be brief, long enough to investigate what has raised the officer's suspicions that a crime is occurring or has occurred. An investigative detention implies that the obtrusive act is for the purpose of actually investigating. Thus, where no investigation is undertaken, the detention cannot be considered investigatory and rises to the level of an arrest.[15] Furthermore, when an officer has concluded an investigation, say for issuing a traffic ticket, continued detention without further reasonable

---

[11] *Id.* at 7.

[12] *Id.*

[13] *Id.* at 15.

[14] *Id.*

[15] *Burkes v. State*, 830 S.W.2d 922, 925 (Tex. Crim. App. 1991).

suspicion for an additional criminal act exceeds the scope of the first detention, making it unlawful.[16]

Let's return to the hypothetical vandalism scenario. Suppose the witness to the vandalism saw two people run from the scene but could only offer a detailed description of the goateed suspect. Remember that the vandals spray painted a car. Now imagine the conversation between the officer and the passerby concerning the whereabouts of the goateed suspect. What if the passerby does not fit the description of the suspect but appears to be concealing something from the officer's view? Imagine that just as the officer is aware the person is trying to hide something, he hears sounds consistent with a spray paint can: an aerosol "shhhh" and the internal metal rattling that a shaken spray paint can makes. At this point, based upon the officer's personal knowledge of the sound of spray paint cans, the fact the car was vandalized with spray paint, and the fact the crime occurred moments earlier nearby, the officer would be justified in detaining the passerby for further investigation. He now possesses articulable facts to warrant a detention based on reasonable suspicion, but he does not yet have probable cause to arrest the passerby for vandalism. In order to do that, he must conduct a more thorough investigation.

The third and final level of police-civilian interaction is arrest. Officers have the authority to arrest when they have probable cause to believe a crime has occurred and the arrestee is the person who committed the crime. The Texas Court of Criminal Appeals explained the probable cause requirement as follows:

> Under Texas law, a police officer must have both probable cause with respect to the person being arrested, plus statutory authority to make that arrest. To establish probable cause to arrest, the evidence must show that "'at that moment [of the arrest] the facts and circumstances within the officer's knowledge and of which he had reasonably trustworthy information were sufficient to warrant a prudent man in believing that the arrested person had committed or was committing an offense.'" There is, of course, a significant difference between the notion that there is probable cause to believe that someone has committed an offense and probable cause to believe that this particular person has committed an offense.

16 *St. George v. State*, 237 S.W.3d 720, 726 (Tex. Crim. App. 2007).

Probable cause to arrest must point like a beacon toward the specific person being arrested.[17]

While a consensual encounter is not detention and detention is not arrest, sometimes what feels like an arrest to a defendant is characterized as a detention by the officer. In other words, officers and defendants may view encounters differently. Texas appellate courts consider several factors relevant in determining whether someone was arrested or merely detained, which may include, but aren't limited to:

- whether the officer actually conducted an investigation;
- whether the accused was handcuffed, detained at gunpoint, or transported to another location;
- whether the number of police officers far outnumbered the citizens at the scene;
- whether the officers used threatening language;
- whether the officers prevented the accused's vehicle from leaving the scene;
- whether the officers used physical force against the accused; and
- whether the accused was detained for a long period of time.[18]

Yes answers to all but the first factor in the list may lead to a conclusion that the encounter was an arrest, whereas more no answers may lead a court to classify the encounter as a detention. Accurately labeling an encounter requires an in-depth factual analysis. A changed fact or an altered timeline may skew the outcome when it comes to arrest analysis. The following case illustrates the analysis courts must conduct to determine whether police-citizen contact amounted to an encounter, a detention, or an arrest.

———————◆———————

[17] *Parker v. State*, 206 S.W.3d 593, 596-97 (Tex. Crim. App. 2006).
[18] *Carter v. State*, 150 S.W.3d 230, 237 (Tex. App.—Texarkana 2004, no pet.).

Leonard L. Martinez v. State
304 S.W.3d 642
(Tex. App.—Amarillo 2010, pet. ref'd)

In his motion to suppress, Appellant asserted he was illegally arrested without probable cause. As a result, he sought to suppress all evidence derived from the seizure.

At the suppression hearing, Sergeant Mark Wims of the Lubbock Burglary Unit, testified that, on April 24, 2007, he received a call reporting a burglary at 2705 86th Street. That call implicated three Hispanic males and a maroon Ford Expedition in the burglary. The SUV's description was similar to a particular SUV linked to Leonard Martinez, Junior, a burglary suspect that his unit had been investigating for several months. The ongoing investigation by the Burglary Unit linked Appellant, Martinez Junior (his son), and a maroon Ford Expedition with a dent on the rear hatch, to a house located at 2810 65th Street.

At approximately 11:30 a.m., Detective Bobby Thompson, Property Crime Division, received Sergeant Wims's call reporting a burglary involving three Hispanic males and a maroon Expedition that could be located at 2810 65th Street. Detective Thompson proceeded to the location in an unmarked car. When he didn't locate the Expedition, he parked in a lot across from the residence at the intersection of 65th and Canton Streets. Sergeant Wims also proceeded to that location as did other officers responding to his call. Sergeant Wims was aware Detective Thompson was on location looking for the vehicle.

At approximately 12:27 p.m., Detective Thompson spotted a maroon SUV driven by a Hispanic male. After the SUV drove through the intersection, he pulled behind and turned on his flashing lights. The SUV then pulled into the driveway at 2810 65th Street and stopped.

In conformance with his training and experience, Detective Thompson treated the stop as a "high risk felony stop" because burglary suspects have been known to be armed. From a vantage point behind his car door and engine firewall, Detective Thompson drew his weapon and ordered the occupants out of the SUV. The driver exited and joined two passengers on the opposite side of the SUV. Detective Thompson then ordered the three men to lie down on the ground. Uncertain whether anyone was inside, he covered the front of the house and the SUV until Officer Richard Calderon arrived and handcuffed the three men. The officers then patted them down, separated them, and placed them in the back seats of different patrol cars for safety reasons. Detective Thompson testified they were not under arrest but detained for further investigation. After the scene was secured, Detective Thompson looked inside the SUV to make certain there were no other passengers and observed a Sony PlayStation and video camera lying in the front floorboard on the passenger side of the vehicle.

Detective Thompson then spoke to each of the three men without warning them of their rights against self-incrimination. He asked their identities, where they lived, what they were doing at the residence, and whether there was anyone in the house. Appellant asserted he did not live at the residence but owned the SUV. Appellant also stated he loaned the SUV to his son whom he had just picked up. Appellant explained the PlayStation and video camera were in the vehicle "when he got there."

When questioned by Detective Thompson, Martinez Junior indicated Appellant and Daniel Trevino, the third passenger in the SUV, picked him up about eight minutes before the stop. He claimed the PlayStation and video camera were in the SUV when *Appellant* picked him up. [The third occupant,] Trevino[,] refused to speak with Detective Thompson.

[Next,] Candra Fulford, the victim who reported the burglary, was brought to the location of the stop. She placed Martinez Junior and the SUV at the scene of the burglary. Based upon surveillance connecting Appellant, Martinez Junior, the Ford Expedition and the residence at 2810 65th Street to a burglary investigation, the victim's identification of Martinez Junior and the Expedition as being involved in the Fulford burglary, the suspects' conflicting stories regarding their prior activities, and the items found in the SUV, the three men were placed under arrest and the SUV impounded.

When the SUV's contents were inventoried, Detective Thompson found a receipt in the video camera bag from Royal Caribbean International to Myrna Porras. Later that day, he arranged to meet Porras at her home. When she arrived, Porras determined that her house had been burglarized that morning while she was at work. She also identified the video camera, PlayStation, and jewelry taken from Trevino's pockets as belonging to her. ...

Appellant contends Detective Thompson effected an unlawful arrest by drawing his service weapon, ordering him out of the SUV onto the ground, handcuffing him, and placing him in the backseat of a patrol car because Detective Thompson lacked probable cause to arrest him for burglary at that time. As a result, Appellant asserts the trial court should have suppressed all evidence obtained by the officers after Appellant was stopped.

The Fourth Amendment does not forbid all seizures, just unreasonable seizures; and, for purposes of constitutional analysis, both investigative detentions and arrests are seizures of a citizen by law enforcement officers. The differences between the two are the degrees of intrusion involved and the different legal justifications required of each.

An investigative detention occurs when an officer lacks probable cause to arrest but nonetheless possesses a reasonable suspicion: that is, the officer is able to point to specific, articulable facts that, taken together with rational inferences from those facts, reasonably warrant the detention. The articulable facts used by the officer must create some reasonable suspicion that some activity out of the ordinary is occurring, or has occurred, some suggestion to connect the detainee with the unusual activity, and some indication the unusual activity is related to criminal activity. An arrest, on the other hand, is a greater restraint upon a person's freedom to leave or move than is a temporary detention which also restrains a person's freedom. "If the degree of incapacitation appears more than necessary to simply safeguard the officers and assure the suspect's presence during a period of investigation, this suggests the detention is an arrest."

The standard for distinguishing between an arrest and investigative detention is not always clear because the distinction between these seizures rests on a fact-specific inquiry rather than clearly delineated criteria. By definition, "[a] person is arrested when he has been actually placed under restraint or taken into custody by an officer or person executing a warrant of arrest, or by an officer or person arresting without a warrant." This "restraint of liberty" standard, however, is not adequate when distinguishing between an arrest and a detention because it is a characteristic common to both. Whether a person is under arrest or subject to a temporary investigative detention is a matter of degree and depends on the length of the detention, the amount of force employed, and whether the officer actually conducts an investigation.

During an investigative detention, an officer may employ the force necessary to effect the reasonable goals of the detention: investigation, maintenance of the status quo, and officer safety. An officer may conduct a limited pat-down search of the outer clothing for weapons during an investigative detention if the officer fears for his safety or that of others.

Police officers are not required to use the "least intrusive means" to verify or dispel their suspicions; however, if the force utilized exceeds that reasonably necessary to effect the goal of the stop, this force may transform an investigative detention into a full-blown arrest.

Because an officer's safety may be threatened by a passenger's access to weapons in an automobile, an officer may, as a matter of course, order a passenger lawfully stopped to exit the vehicle and lie down on the ground pending completion of the stop. *See Smith v. State*, 813 S.W.2d 599, 601 (Tex. App.—Houston [14th Dist.] 1991, pet. ref'd) (investigative detention not transformed into an arrest when officer requested that suspect exit his car, lie on the ground, and submit to a pat-down for officer safety reasons). Furthermore, approaching a vehicle with a service weapon drawn does not transform an investigative detention to an arrest. *See Marsh v. State*, 684 S.W.2d 676, 679 (Tex. Crim. App. 1984) (one officer approaching driver's side of vehicle with a rifle drawn, while another officer approached the passenger's side of vehicle with his gun in hand).

Likewise, the use of handcuffs does not automatically convert an investigative detention into an arrest; and there is no bright line rule that handcuffing a suspect always constitutes an arrest. Ordinarily handcuffing a suspect is more consistent with a full-blown arrest than it is with an investigatory detention; however, an officer may resort to handcuffs without transforming an investigative detention into an arrest when he or she is reasonably concerned for safety or to maintain the status quo. ... *Balentine*, 71 S.W.3d at 771 (investigative detention did not evolve into an arrest simply because appellant was escorted to patrol car and handcuffed); *Rhodes*, 945 S.W.2d at 116–118 (appellant required to exit vehicle and handcuffed); *Mays v. State*, 726 S.W.2d 937, 944 (Tex. Crim. App. 1986), *cert. denied*, 484 U.S. 1079 (1988) (frisked and handcuffed); ...*Morris*, 50 S.W.3d at 97-98 (removed from truck at gunpoint, placed on ground, and handcuffed behind back); ...*Salazar v. State*, 805 S.W.2d 538, 540 (Tex. App.—Fort Worth 1991, pet. ref'd) (removed from car, hands on head, handcuffed, and patted-down).

In the absence of a reasonable safety concern or need to maintain the status quo, however, [the] officers' use of force to secure a suspect has been held to constitute an arrest. *See Amores v. State*, 816 S.W.2d 407, 411–12 (Tex. Crim. App.1991) (arrest where handcuffed and no investigation performed). ...*Akins v. State*, 202 S.W.3d 879, 888 (Tex. App.—Fort Worth 2006, pet. ref'd) (arrest where car boxed in, approached with guns drawn, placed on ground, and handcuffed in absence of any necessity to maintain officer safety or status quo); *Moore*, 25 S.W.3d at 386–87 (forgery suspect handcuffed in absence of officer safety concern); *Gordon v. State*, 4 S.W.3d 32, 37 (Tex. App.—El Paso 1999, no pet.) (handcuffed and placed in backseat of patrol car solely to keep suspect out of house while K–9 search performed); *Rodriguez v. State*, 975 S.W.2d 667, 675-77 (Tex. App.—Texarkana 1998, pet. ref'd) (boxed in car, removed suspect at gunpoint, had him lie face down in parking lot, and performed no investigation); *Flores v. State*, 895 S.W.2d 435, 441 (Tex. App.—San Antonio 1995, no pet.) (removed from car at gunpoint assuming spread-eagle position with hands on roof of car, officer testified suspect was not free to leave, and no evidence of officer safety concerns).

In evaluating whether police conduct during an investigatory detention is reasonable, common sense and ordinary human experience govern over rigid criteria. Whether a detention is an actual arrest or an investigative detention depends on the reasonableness of the intrusion under all the facts. Reasonableness is measured by balancing the nature of the intrusion into an individual's Fourth Amendment interests against the public interest of legitimate government interest at stake … and must be judged from the perspective of a reasonable officer at the scene, rather than with the advantage of hindsight. Allowances must be made for the fact that officers must often make quick decisions under tense, uncertain, and rapidly changing circumstances. Additional factors to consider in determining the reasonableness of the detention include the nature of the crime under investigation, the degree of suspicion, the location of the stop, the time of day, the number of suspects present, and the reaction of each suspect. The officer's opinion, while not determinative, is another factor to be considered. Also very important is whether the officers actually conducted an investigation after seizing the suspect.

Based on the information known to the officers investigating the burglary at the Fulford residence… and the observations of Detective Thompson, we find the police acted within constitutional parameters of a reasonable investigative detention. Appellant's detention was reasonably related in scope to the circumstances that justified the interference at the outset and lasted only so long as was reasonably necessary to include, or exclude, him as a suspect. After obtaining conflicting responses to questions related to their prior whereabouts and ownership of property in the SUV, Appellant was detained until Fulford and Velasquez could be brought to the scene. After

Fulford and Velasquez placed the maroon SUV and Martinez Junior at the Fulford residence at the time of the burglary, sufficient probable cause for arrest existed, and Appellant was arrested.

We find the duration of the stop was reasonable and the officers diligently pursued a means of investigation that was likely to dispel or confirm their suspicions as quickly as possible. *See Josey*, 981 S.W.2d at 840-41 (ninety minute detention reasonable). The SUV was stopped at approximately 12:30 p.m. By 1:23 p.m., the SUV and Martinez Junior had been identified, and the three men arrested were in the process of being transported to jail. During this period of time, the officers stopped Appellant, secured the scene, identified the three men, questioned them regarding their whereabouts and ownership interest in the SUV, concluded the identification process with Fulford and Velasquez, arrested the three men, and inventoried the SUV's contents.

The force Detective Thompson employed during the detention was also reasonable under the circumstances. Detective Thompson acted alone when he stopped an SUV anticipated to contain at least three suspects in a felony burglary. The SUV's windows were tinted and [the SUV] stopped at its destination, a house with two windows facing the street [with] curtains drawn. In his experience and training, he treated the stop as a "high risk felony stop" because burglars are known to be armed. He was also concerned for his safety because he did not know how many occupants were in the SUV, whether they had weapons, and whether there were persons in the house that might also be armed.

We find Detective Thompson's need for officer safety and to maintain the status quo during the investigative detention reasonable. He was outnumbered at the outset and attempting to initiate an investigation in an open area where he could easily be targeted from the SUV's tinted windows or the residence linked to the suspects. After he secured the area, he conducted an investigation appropriate to an investigative detention. He held Appellant only so long as was necessary to eliminate or verify him as a suspect. After Fulford and Velasquez identified the SUV and Martinez Junior, the three men were arrested and the SUV impounded. The entire detention took a little less than an hour. On this record, we find Appellant's detention was reasonable under the circumstances, and the trial court did not abuse its discretion in denying Appellant's motion to suppress evidence due to an illegal arrest.

Notes and Questions

1. A person is arrested when "he has been actually placed under restraint or taken into custody by an officer or a person executing a warrant of arrest," by an officer arresting a suspect without a warrant, by a magistrate requesting that an officer arrest a suspect, or by a citizen.[19] Thus, four forms of arrest are statutorily authorized: one by a police officer with a warrant, one by a police officer without a warrant, one by a magistrate without a warrant, and one by a citizen without a warrant.

2. Arrest does not necessarily mean a person is handcuffed and placed in a patrol car after being told by the officer that the person is under arrest for committing a specific crime, though this is often how arrest is depicted on film. Texas courts have a wider view of arrest. For example, one court stated that "submission to an officer's show of authority will also constitute an arrest."[20] As broad as this may sound, courts still look into multiple factors, as the *Martinez* court did above, in determining whether an arrest has taken place.

———◆———

Arrest Warrant Requisites

An arrest warrant is a magistrate's written order that allows a peace officer or some other specifically named person to seize the body of a person accused of a criminal offense.[21] The arrest warrant forces the person to deal with the consequences of the alleged criminal action. The accused may be required to enter a plea, pay a fine, or stand trial as a result of the arrest. Regardless of the consequences or the decisions made by the prosecutor or the accused following the arrest, a valid arrest warrant results in the seizure of a person and his detention until he bonds out of jail and answers to the crime in court.

---

[19] TEX. CODE CRIM. PROC. ANN. art. 15.22 (West 2016).
[20] *McCraw v. State*, 117 S.W.3d 47, 52 (Tex. App.—Fort Worth 2003, pet. ref'd).
[21] TEX. CODE CRIM. PROC. ANN. art. 15.01 (West 2016).

An arrest warrant must begin with the words "in the name of The State of Texas" and have the following components:

1. Specifically state the name of the arrestee if known, and if not known, give a specific description of him;
2. State the crime the person is accused of committing; and
3. Be signed by the magistrate, with the magistrate's office being made clear in the body of the warrant or through his signature.[22]

An officer or a prosecutor drafts the arrest warrant. A magistrate may issue a warrant when a person "make[s an] oath before the magistrate that another has committed some offense against the laws of the State."[23] This sworn oath is called a *complaint*; it serves as the basis for a magistrate to issue an arrest warrant. A legally valid complaint must contain the following information:

1. It must state the known name of the accused or, if the name is unknown, give a reasonably detailed description of her;
2. It must state the criminal offense the accused committed and that the affiant (the person swearing that this information is true) believes the accused committed this offense;
3. It must state as definitely as possible the time and the place where the crime was committed; and
4. It must be signed by the affiant.[24]

The second requirement amounts to probable cause to believe the accused committed the alleged crime. A complaint that does not meet this requirement will render the warrant it supports invalid, despite the fact that a magistrate ultimately signed the warrant or the warrant was properly executed. When a complaint is invalid, defense counsel can attack the validity of the warrant itself and the complaint that was used to secure the warrant.

After the warrant is drafted, edited, and finalized, the officer then takes it to the magistrate or the judge to be signed. The magistrate or the judge must make sure there is probable cause for the arrest. If it is not clear from the face of the warrant that a crime has been committed and the officer has probable cause to believe the suspect committed the crime, the magistrate

---

[22] TEX. CODE CRIM. PROC. ANN. art. 15.02 (West 2016).
[23] TEX. CODE CRIM. PROC. ANN. art. 15.03 (West 2016).
[24] TEX. CODE CRIM. PROC. ANN. art. 15.05 (West 2016).

will refuse to sign the arrest warrant, thus denying the officer an opportunity to arrest the suspect.

Capias and Summons

Capias warrants differ from arrest warrants in at least two ways. First, they are issued by a judge or a court clerk, not a law enforcement agency.[25] Second, their purpose is not to authorize the arrest of a person for committing a crime but to authorize an arrest as a consequence of an issue that has arisen while the case is pending. The capias directs a law enforcement officer to arrest the person immediately and bring her before the court.[26]

The Code states that a capias may be issued anytime between the setting of bail and before trial (*i.e.*, while the case is pending).[27] Here are some specific examples of when a capias may issue:

- When a charging instrument— whether complaint, information, or indictment— is filed;[28]
- When a defendant forfeits her bond;[29] or
- When a judgment and a sentence are rendered in the defendant's absence.[30]

Like arrest warrants, capias warrants must meet certain requirements. This is a list of what must appear on the face of the capias:

1. It must run in the name of "The State of Texas;"
2. It must name the person, or if name unknown, describe the person, who is to be arrested;
3. It must specify the offense the person committed and state that this act violates the penal laws of Texas;
4. It must name the court and the return time;
5. It must be dated and sworn to by the person issuing the capias.[31]

---

[25] TEX. CODE CRIM. PROC. ANN. art. 23.01(1) (West 2016).
[26] TEX. CODE CRIM. PROC. ANN. art. 23.01(2) (West 2016).
[27] TEX. CODE CRIM. PROC. ANN. art. 23.01(1) (West 2016).
[28] TEX. CODE CRIM. PROC. ANN. art. 23.03 and 23.04 (West 2016).
[29] TEX. CODE CRIM. PROC. ANN. art. 23.05 (West 2016).
[30] TEX. CODE CRIM. PROC. ANN. art. 43.04 (West 2016).
[31] TEX. CODE CRIM. PROC. ANN. art. 23.02 (West 2016).

There is yet another way to get a suspect to court: a summons. The Code describes a summons as follows:

> A summons may be issued in any case where a warrant may be issued, and shall be in the same form as the warrant except that it shall summon the defendant to appear before a magistrate at a stated time and place. The summons shall be served upon a defendant by delivering a copy to him personally, or by leaving it at his dwelling house or usual place of abode with some person of suitable age and discretion then residing therein or by mailing it to the defendant's last known address. If a defendant fails to appear in response to the summons a warrant shall be issued.[32]

A traffic ticket is a summons: it requests a suspect to appear in court; if the person fails to appear, an arrest warrant will be issued for the person.

These are the major differences between an arrest warrant, a capias, and a summons:

- An arrest warrant is issued by a law enforcement agency and signed by a magistrate. It gives an officer the authority to seize the defendant. The defendant is subsequently brought before a magistrate and then taken to jail.
- A capias is issued by a court with jurisdiction over a defendant. It authorizes an officer to bring the defendant to court.
- A summons is issued by a magistrate to a suspect directing him to appear before the magistrate. If the suspect does not appear, a warrant will be issued.

---------◆---------

Notes and Questions

1. An arrest warrant is not the only available legal document used to seize a person. A search warrant can provide for the seizure of persons.[33] If the magistrate had probable cause to believe "a person has committed some offense under the laws of this state, the search warrant may, in addition,

---

[32] TEX. CODE CRIM. PROC. ANN. art. 15.03 (West 2016).
[33] TEX. CODE CRIM. PROC. ANN. art. 18.02(a)(11) (West 2016).

order the arrest of such persons."[34] Thus, a combination arrest and search warrant is valid, but both must still be supported by probable cause.[35]

———————————◆———————————

Jurisdictional Authority to Arrest

In Texas, law enforcement officers are either employed by a city (*e.g.*, El Paso Police Department), by a county (*e.g.*, Dallas County Sheriff's Office), or by the State (*e.g.*, the Department of Public Safety). Most states have similar levels of government, even though the name for each level may be different (*e.g.*, Louisiana has parishes instead of counties). The officer's employer— the city, the county, or the state— defines the parameters of the officer's jurisdiction. An officer may make arrests in her employer's jurisdiction.

In limited circumstances, an officer may even arrest someone outside of her jurisdiction without an arrest.[36] This typically happens when the officer is off duty, is driving to or from work, or when a suspect crosses jurisdictions or evades detention. Officers are allowed to arrest someone who commits specified crimes in their presence even when the criminal act occurs outside of their employer's jurisdiction.[37] The specified crimes include all felonies, any crime that constitutes a breach of the peace, disorderly conduct (Chapter 42 of the Penal Code), and intoxication offenses (Chapter 49 of the Penal Code). For example, an officer outside of her jurisdiction could detain a person based upon reasonable suspicion if she believes the suspect is drunk driving.[38]

---

[34] TEX. CODE CRIM. PROC. ANN. art. 18.03 (West 2016); *Pecina v. State*, 516 S.W.2d 401, 403 (Tex. Crim. App. 1974) ("an arrest warrant incorporated within a search warrant is no different than an arrest warrant issued separate and independent of a search warrant. And it should be noted that the authority to arrest under an arrest warrant incorporated in a search warrant is not limited to the premises described in the search warrant.").

[35] *Pecina v. State*, 516 S.W.2d 401, 403 (Tex. Crim. App. 1974), *overruled on other grounds, Madden v. State*, 644 S.W.2d 735, 737–38 (Tex. Crim. App. 1983).

[36] TEX. CODE CRIM. PROC. ANN. art. 14.03(g) (West 2016).

[37] TEX. CODE CRIM. PROC. ANN. art. 14.03(d) (West 2016).

[38] *E.g., State v. Purdy*, 244 S.W.3d 591, 594 (Tex. App.—Dallas 2008, pet. ref'd).

The above scenarios apply to a warrantless arrest. What happens when there is an arrest warrant? An arrest warrant extends to every part of Texas; once a valid arrest warrant is issued in the state, it can be executed anywhere.[39] This means that though an arrest warrant may have originated in Amarillo, an officer who encounters the defendant in Abilene has permission to arrest her on the basis of that warrant.

◆

Challenging an Arrest Warrant

The lawfulness of the arrest is a critical question. If an arrest is unlawful, defense counsel will challenge the legality of the arrest and may even file a motion to suppress evidence seized following the arrest.

Both warrantless arrests and arrests with warrants are challengeable. Arrest warrants are challenged for a number of reasons. A warrant may fail to adequately describe the person who was ultimately arrested. In *Visor v. State*, the Court of Criminal Appeals was called upon to examine a combination search and arrest warrant that authorized the arrest of an "unknown black female."[40] Because several women fitting this description entered, exited, or were in the apartment while officers observed the location, there was no way of knowing whether the person described in the warrant was the person officers ultimately searched and arrested.[41] Therefore, the Court found the arrest warrant lacking and the subsequent arrest unlawful.[42]

The complaint used to support the arrest warrant contains direct evidence or a reasonable belief that the defendant committed the crime.[43] Witness or affiant credibility may become an issue. For example, an informant or snitch may seek a reduced sentence for a crime she is "working off" by providing information about the criminal activity of others. This snitch's motives are suspect. Some witnesses are deemed more credible than others: a Good Samaritan who places himself in harm's way, someone who witnesses the crime firsthand, or a third party who provides unsolicited

---

[39] TEX. CODE CRIM. PROC. ANN. art. 15.06 (West 2016).
[40] *Visor v. State*, 660 S.W.2d 816, 816 (Tex. Crim. App. 1983).
[41] *Id.* at 816-20.
[42] *Id.* at 820.
[43] TEX. CODE CRIM. PROC. ANN. art. 15.05 (West 2016).

details of the crime along with her own contact information and does not personally know any of the parties.[44] Judges may be called upon to have an in camera or private inspection of the witness's or informant's credibility and basis of knowledge.

Another challenge could be that the warrant fails to contain probable cause. That a magistrate found probable cause by signing it does not mean a subsequent judge will agree with the earlier probable cause finding. The warrant could fail to meet the statutory requirements in the bulleted list. In these instances, the defendant will likely contest the validity of the warrant following his arrest.

Attorneys may allege the warrant was executed unlawfully. Officers have several duties when they execute a warrant: they must take the arrestee to a magistrate without delay;[45] they must be careful with the force they use in effecting an arrest;[46] they should, in many instances, knock and announce their presence before making forcible entry into a home to arrest a person;[47] and officers must announce their position and their authority before arresting a person.[48] Most execution challenges fail to result in the suppression of evidence, but they are raised by defendants nonetheless.

When a warrant is challenged in court, the judge will look to the "four corners" of the document to determine its sufficiency.[49] The four corners rule means the court will not consider extraneous facts or evidence in analyzing whether the warrant was valid, only what is contained within the arrest warrant itself and the complaint.[50] Probable cause, the credibility of the affiant, the defendant's name or physical description, and any other necessary details must be sufficiently described within the four corners of the warrant and complaint.

The good faith exception that exists for search warrants also exists for arrest warrants. The exclusionary rule in Texas carves out an exception for evidence obtained "by a law enforcement officer acting in objective good

---

[44] *Garcia v. State*, 296 S.W.3d 180, 185 (Tex. App.—Houston [14th Dist.] 2009, no pet.).
[45] TEX. CODE CRIM. PROC. ANN. art. 15.16 (West 2005).
[46] TEX. CODE CRIM. PROC. ANN. art. 15.24 (West 2016).
[47] TEX. CODE CRIM. PROC. ANN. art. 15.25 (West 2016).
[48] TEX. CODE CRIM. PROC. ANN. art. 15.26 (West 2003).
[49] *Jones v. State*, 568 S.W.2d 847, 855 (Tex. Crim. App. 1978).
[50] *Black v. State*, 362 S.W.3d 626, 636–37 (Tex. Crim. App. 2012)

faith reliance upon a warrant issued by a neutral magistrate based on probable cause."[51] Courts in Texas have found objective good faith in cases where mistakes were made, but the officers objectively believed they were relying on valid warrants. For example, in *Dunn v. State*, a magistrate found probable cause to issue several warrants but failed to sign one.[52] The officers did not realize this until after they executed the warrant. When they did discover it, they immediately sought to remedy the mistake by taking the warrant back to the magistrate.[53] The Court of Criminal Appeals found that the officers acted in good faith.[54] In another case, *Durio v. State*, the defendant served time on outstanding warrants, but for some reason, the police department failed to recall them.[55] An officer acting reliably on the seemingly outstanding warrants arrested the defendant and in a search incident to arrest found cocaine in his pocket.[56] The court found that the officers objectively believed the warrants were outstanding, and as a result, the cocaine was admissible to support the possession of a controlled substance charge.[57] In sum, good faith and probable cause may overcome an invalid arrest warrant.

————————◆————————

Notes and Questions

1. When the defense files a motion to suppress, who carries the burden during the motion hearing? The answer depends on whether there was an arrest warrant. If there was an arrest warrant, the defense carries the burden of proving the arrest was unlawful. Why? In suppression issues, the defense generally carries the burden to prove a law violation or improper police conduct.[58] If the defendant establishes either, the burden then shifts to the State to rebut the evidence produced by the defense.[59]

---

[51] TEX. CODE CRIM. PROC. ANN. art. 38.23 (West 2016).
[52] *Dunn v. State*, 951 S.W.2d 478, 478–79 (Tex. Crim. App. 1997).
[53] *Id.*
[54] *Id.*
[55] *Durio v. State*, 807 S.W.2d 876, 877-78 (Tex. App.—Corpus Christi 1991, no pet.).
[56] *Id.* at 877.
[57] *Id.* at 878.
[58] *State v. Robinson*, 334 S.W.3d 776, 778-79 (Tex. Crim. App. 2011).
[59] *Id.* at 780.

When there is no warrant, the State carries the burden of establishing that the warrantless arrest fell into one of the exceptions and met the requirements of the exception. Why? Warrantless arrests are considered per se unreasonable.

2. Officers are permitted to use any force necessary to make an arrest, but they may not use excessive force or more force than is needed.[60]

––––––––––◆––––––––––

Exceptions to the Warrant Requirement

There is a preference that officers use an arrest warrant since it is monitored by a neutral and detached magistrate. However, "[a] police officer may arrest an individual without a warrant only if probable cause exists with respect to the individual in question and the arrest falls within one of the exceptions."[61] These exceptions are mostly found in Chapter 14, titled "Arrest without Warrant," of the Texas Code of Criminal Procedure. This section will closely examine each of the exceptions that apply to warrantless arrests.

As you read the warrantless arrest exceptions, note that they all require probable cause. The probable cause standard for arrest is necessary to ensure the rights guaranteed by the Fourth Amendment of the U.S. Constitution: no arrest warrant shall issue unless it is supported by probable cause. If no arrest warrant shall be put into effect without probable cause, then a warrantless arrest likewise must be supported by probable cause. All arrests must be supported by probable cause.

––––––––––◆––––––––––

Offenses Committed Within View of a Peace Officer

The first two articles within the warrantless arrest chapter permit an arrest when an officer, any other person, or a magistrate witnesses a felony or an offense against the public peace.[62] Additionally, officers may arrest an offender for any offense committed in their presence, which includes all

---

[60] TEX. CODE CRIM. PROC. ANN. art. 15.24 (West 2016).
[61] *Torres v. State*, 182 S.W.3d 899, 901 (Tex. Crim. App. 2005).
[62] TEX. CODE CRIM. PROC. ANN. art. 14.01 and 14.02 (West 2016).

traffic violations except for speeding and having an open container of alcohol in a vehicle.[63] The next case establishes what *within view* means.

State v. Ian Steelman
93 S.W.3d 102
(Tex. Crim. App. 2002)

A police officer may arrest an individual without a warrant only if (1) there is probable cause with respect to that individual and (2) the arrest falls within one of the statutory exceptions. One of those exceptions, Article 14.01(b), provides that "[a] peace officer may arrest an offender without a warrant for any offense committed in his presence or within his view." In *Beverly*, this Court explained that:

> The test for probable cause for a warrantless arrest under [article 14.01(b)] is whether at that moment the facts and circumstances within the officer's knowledge and of which he had reasonably trustworthy information were sufficient to warrant a prudent man in believing that the arrested person had committed or was committing an offense.[64]

An offense is deemed to have occurred within the presence or view of an officer when any of his senses afford him an awareness of its occurrence. However, the information afforded to the officer by his senses must give the officer reason to believe that a particular suspect committed the offense.

Consider again the facts and circumstances before the officers that night. There is an unsubstantiated, anonymous tip that someone at the Steelman residence is dealing drugs. The officers walk up to the house, peer into the house through a small crack in the window blind, and, by their own admission, observe no criminal activity. They then knock on the door. Ian steps out and closes his door. They smell the odor of marijuana in the air but not on Ian himself. Given those circumstances, what did the officers have probable cause to believe? Certainly they had probable cause to believe that someone, somewhere, was or had been smoking marijuana. But, did the mere smell of marijuana in the air give the officers probable cause to believe that

---

[63] TEX. CODE CRIM. PROC. ANN. art. 14.01(b) (West 2016); TEX. TRANSP. CODE ANN. § 543.004 (West 2016); *Owens v. State*, 861 S.W.2d 419, 420 (Tex. App.—Dallas 1993, no pet.) ("an officer may arrest and take into custody a person seen committing a traffic offense").

[64] *Beverly v. State*, 792 S.W.2d 103, 105 (Tex. Crim. App. 1990).

Ian possessed marijuana? No. This Court has recognized that "odors alone do not authorize a search without a warrant." Why, then, did the officers burst into the house? What offense, if any, did they observe Ian committing? The State argues that given the anonymous tip and the odor of burned marijuana, the officers had probable cause to believe an offense, possession of marijuana, had been committed in their presence. We disagree.

First of all, a mere anonymous tip, standing alone, does not constitute probable cause. In this case, the tip, that someone at the residence was dealing drugs, did not amount to anything. The tip was never substantiated, and none of the occupants were ever charged with drug dealing.

Second, the mere odor of burning marijuana did not give the officers probable cause to believe that Ian had committed the offense of possession of marijuana in their presence. The odor of marijuana, standing alone, does not authorize a warrantless search and seizure in a home. An arresting officer must have specific knowledge to believe that the person to be arrested has committed the offense.

[T]he officers in this case had no idea who was smoking or possessing marijuana, and they certainly had no particular reason to believe that Ian was smoking or possessing marijuana.

Given the evidence before it, the trial court in the instant case could have reasonably concluded that the arrest of Ian was not lawfully made without a warrant because the arresting officers did not have probable cause to believe that Ian had committed an offense in their presence. Since the officers had no authority to make a warrantless arrest under article 14.01(b), they had no authority (under article 14.05) to enter the residence without a warrant and conduct a search, and any evidence seized as a result of those illegalities was tainted and subject to suppression. Therefore, the Court of Appeals did not err in upholding the trial court's decision to grant the appellees' motion to suppress.

We affirm the judgment of the Court of Appeals.

———————◆———————

Notes and Questions

1. The offense within view exception is clear: when an officer witnesses a crime, she can arrest without a warrant. However, appellate courts have

interpreted this section broadly. The Court of Criminal Appeals explains the wider reach of this provision as follows:

> Under Article 14.01(b), "A peace officer may arrest an offender without a warrant for any offense committed in his presence or within his view." Probable cause for a warrantless arrest under Article 14.01(b) "may be based on [an officer's] prior knowledge and personal observations.... [A]n officer may rely on reasonably trustworthy information provided by another person in making the overall probable cause determination." Thus, all of the information to support probable cause does not have to be within an officer's personal knowledge. The ultimate question under Article 14.01(b) is "'whether at that moment the facts and circumstances within the officer's knowledge and of which he had reasonably trustworthy information were sufficient to warrant a prudent man in believing that the arrested person had committed or was committing an offense.'"[65]

Is the Court saying all that is necessary under this provision is mere probable cause, or is there something additional that sets Article 14.01 apart from an arrest supported by nothing more than probable cause?

———————◆———————

Citizen's Arrests

The same article that authorizes within view warrantless arrests for officers also authorizes within view warrantless arrests for citizens. Citizen arrests are rare, but there are limited instances when a lay person may arrest a suspect for an offense he witnesses, as the next case illustrates. As you read the next case, notice the differences between the officer within view exception and the citizen's arrest within view exception.

Lawrence Preston Miles v. State
241 S.W.3d 28
(Tex. Crim. App. 2007)

A tow-truck driver made a citizen's arrest of appellant for DWI after pursuing him through busy Houston streets late one night. Appellant was then charged with DWI and unlawfully carrying a weapon. He filed a motion to suppress under Article 38.23, the Texas exclusionary statute, and claimed

---

[65] *State v. Woodard*, 341 S.W.3d 404, 412 (Tex. Crim. App. 2011).

that evidence obtained as a result of this citizen's arrest should have been excluded because the tow-truck driver violated traffic laws when he pursued appellant. After the trial court denied the motion to suppress, appellant pleaded guilty and appealed the trial court's suppression ruling.

The evidence showed that Edward James, a limousine driver, was stopped at the corner of Westheimer and Loop 610 at 1:45 a.m., waiting for the light to change. Suddenly a purple Corvette ran into the car behind Mr. James, veered toward the curb, and finally "jagged" back to the left hitting the limousine. The Corvette ended up underneath the rear bumper of Mr. James's limousine. Appellant was driving the Corvette.

Mr. James and a couple of his clients, professional football players, got out of the limousine to inspect the damage. The football players said that appellant was drunk, and then they got back into the car. Mr. James asked appellant for his driver's license and proof of insurance. He noticed that appellant had alcohol on his breath, his speech was "blurry," his eyes were "wiggling" and red, his balance was unsteady, and "he was backing up and holding onto his car, propping himself up onto his car." Mr. James concluded that appellant was drunk. Appellant and Mr. James exchanged driver's license information, but appellant never gave Mr. James his insurance documentation. Mr. James asked him to wait until the police arrived, but after waiting for a while, appellant became very nervous. He said, "I'm going to have to go, I've got to go." Appellant got into his car and backed it up, tearing out part of the limousine's back bumper. Mr. James said that appellant ran the red light as he drove west down Westheimer at a high rate of speed.

Meanwhile, several tow-truck drivers had arrived at the accident scene. Joseph Moore was one of them. He noticed that the damage to the three cars wasn't too bad; they could all still be driven. He thought that the parties could resolve the accident without the need for police assistance. But there was a problem because appellant did not have the required insurance information. Appellant "was reluctant to cooperate and he seemed agitated at the fact that the limo driver wanted him to stay until the police arrived[.] [H]e wanted to leave and he seemed really testy about the limo driver pressing him for the information that he needed." Appellant appeared to be under the influence of something. "His speech was slurred. He was fumbling. He was agitated.... He didn't seem coordinated." Mr. Moore did not think it was safe for appellant to leave the scene, so he "made the decision based on public safety and his mannerisms that something needed to be done in an effort to try to stop him from harming anyone else or himself." Mr. Moore was especially concerned because he didn't think that appellant "ever looked to find out if any other traffic was coming" when he left the accident scene.

Mr. Moore and about five other wrecker drivers followed appellant in their trucks because they were "really uncomfortable with the fact that he was driving and at that time of night there was a lot of people on the road and [they] felt like he was a danger to himself and other people." They tried to stop him near the corner of Post Oak and Westheimer, but appellant put his Corvette into reverse, backed up, drove partially up on the curb and went around them. He then "whipped" into a parking lot and crossed it at 30 to 40 miles an hour, came back out onto the road, "never hit[ ] his brakes, almost sideswipe[d] a car and proceed[ed] westbound on Westheimer."

Mr. Moore followed as appellant took two left turns and went the wrong way down West Alabama into oncoming traffic. His driving was "[v]ery dangerous," so Mr. Moore followed with his "overhead lights on to alert people that we are coming the wrong way." Mr. Moore knew that he was taking a chance going down a one-way street, but "[m]y motive is public safety." Then appellant drove west in the east-bound lanes head-on into heavy traffic on Westheimer, so Mr. Moore crossed over the median and followed, going the right way. Appellant "whip[ped]" into a bar parking lot going "maybe 50 m.p.h." Mr. Moore followed, along with other wrecker drivers who had caught up. They "corralled" appellant in the parking lot. Mr. Moore got out and went up to appellant's Corvette, asked him to put the car in park and give up the keys. When appellant told him "to 'F' off," Mr. Moore reached in to take the keys "at which point I felt a cold object to the right temple of my head." It was a handgun. Mr. Moore slid down beside appellant's car and sidled to the rear of the car until the police arrived two or three minutes later.

At the motion to suppress hearing, the trial judge asked appellant to specify his legal issue, and defense counsel stated,

> The sole argument ... is whether the citizen who placed Mr. Miles under arrest had probable cause to do so, number one. Whether it violated a law in order to arrest Mr. Miles. Number three, whether a citizen has a right to pursue a person if the citizen believes that that person committed a breach of the peace.

After the trial judge denied the motion, appellant pled guilty and appealed those legal issues.

C. Texas Law Allows a Citizen's Arrest for DWI.

Under Texas law, neither officers nor citizens have an unfettered right to arrest a person. They may do so only under limited, statutorily-authorized, circumstances set out in Chapter 14 of the Code of Criminal Procedure. … [A] peace officer may arrest offenders for any misdemeanor committed within his view as well as any such felony, while citizens may arrest only for a felony or a misdemeanor that is "an offense against the public peace."

Professor Dawson has noted, "In one sense, of course, all criminal violations are offenses against the public peace." Such a broad interpretation of "public peace" would make Article 14.01(a) unnecessary. Under that broad interpretation, both officers and citizens would be able to arrest for any offense committed within their view or presence, but Article 14.01(b) explicitly limits such a right to peace officers. As Professor Dawson explains, Texas courts have developed two independent lines of cases interpreting what constitutes "offenses against the public peace" under Article 14.01(a). First, some cases have held that only those misdemeanor offenses listed in Title 9 of the Penal Code are "offenses against the public peace" under the citizen-arrest statute. Second, some cases have equated "offense against the public peace" with "breach of the peace." Under this second line of cases, a valid citizen's arrest for a misdemeanor required "some showing of actual or threatened violence." In *Woods v. State*, we quoted Corpus Juris which explained that the term "breach of the peace" included

> all violations of the public peace or order, or decorum; … a disturbance of the public tranquility by any act or conduct inciting to violence or tending to provoke or excite others to break the peace; a disturbance of public order by an act of violence, or by any act likely to produce violence, or which, by causing consternation and alarm disturbs the peace and quiet of the community.... Actual or threatened violence is an essential element of a breach of the peace.

We then concluded that whether a specific act constituted a breach of the peace depended upon the surrounding facts and circumstances in the particular case. In *Woods*, we held that the defendant did not have a right to arrest the deceased who had assaulted the defendant's wife because the deceased had already completed the assault and had left the scene. "There was nothing to suggest that the breach of the peace might be renewed or continued or that appellant's pursuit of [the] deceased was to prevent a renewal of the offense." Thus, in *Woods*, we reaffirmed our earlier rule of law:

> the right of a private individual to arrest without warrant for a breach of the peace, committed in his presence or view, is limited to the time the offense is committed or while there is continuing danger of its renewal, and does not include the right to pursue and arrest for the purpose of insuring the apprehension or future trial of the offender.

We have also indicated that some crimes are, by their very nature, offenses against the public peace. These include public drunkenness and driving while intoxicated. But, as Judge Davidson noted in his dissent in *McEathron v. State*, this may be too broad a position. One can imagine a scenario in which a person, though intoxicated, poses no threat to the public peace at the time that an officer or private citizen makes a warrantless arrest.

The statutory authorization for both officers and citizens to arrest for an "offense against the public peace" codifies an "exigent circumstances" exception to the warrant requirement. This exception to the warrant requirement is like that set out in Article 18.16 which allows "any person"—officer or citizen—to make a warrantless arrest to prevent the consequences of theft—the escape of the thief and the disappearance of the property stolen. Similarly, under Article 14.04, an officer may make a warrantless arrest when he has "satisfactory proof" to believe that a person has committed a felony offense and is about to escape. In all of these statutes, the Legislature codified a preference for arrests under warrant. But it also recognized that under some circumstances there is no time to procure a warrant. These exigent circumstances require an immediate arrest and include 1) offenses committed in the presence or view of an officer or citizen that pose a continuing threat to the public peace, 2) theft offenses in which the perpetrator may disappear along with the stolen property, and 3) escapes of felony offenders. One might even conclude that the statutory right to make a warrantless arrest under Article 14.03 when the offender is found in a "suspicious place" is yet another codification of the exigent circumstances exception to arrest under warrant.

Based on the history and purpose of Article 14.01(a), as well as precedent, we reaffirm the reasoning in *Woods* and conclude that a citizen may make a warrantless arrest of a person who commits a misdemeanor within the citizen's presence or view if the evidence shows that the person's conduct poses a threat of continuing violence or harm to himself or the public. It is the exigency of the situation, not the title of the offense, that gives both officer and citizen statutory authorization to protect the public from an ongoing threat of violence, harm, or danger by making a warrantless arrest.

With this general framework of Article 38.23(a) in mind, we turn to the circumstances in this particular case....

Appellant acknowledges that this Court has previously held that driving while intoxicated is a breach of the peace, but he claims that *Romo* confused "breaches of the peace" with "offenses against the public peace." This is a semantic difference without a legal distinction under Article 14.01(a). The relevant legal issue is whether (1) Mr. Moore had probable cause to believe that appellant was driving while intoxicated in his view, and (2) the evidence showed that appellant's commission of this offense, if not stopped, posed an ongoing threat of violence or harm to appellant or others.

In this case, the evidence shows that Mr. Moore clearly had probable cause to believe that appellant was driving while intoxicated on "something" when he left the scene of the accident. Mr. Moore was not alone in forming the opinion that appellant was intoxicated, and Mr. Moore was not alone in seeing that appellant left the scene at a high rate of speed. According to one witness, he ran a red light while leaving the scene. Such driving, especially while intoxicated, posed a danger to pedestrians and other drivers on the road. Indeed, appellant had already caused a three-car accident, so Mr. Moore's concern was well-founded. The evidence showed that there were numerous other cars traveling on Westheimer at this time of night. Mr. Moore testified that he pursued appellant "based on public safety" and because he thought "something needed to be done in an effort to stop him from harming anyone else or himself." Appellant's driving down Westheimer was "very dangerous." He "whipped" in and out of a parking lot at high speeds, almost sideswiped another car, and turned down West Alabama, a one-way-street, going the wrong way into oncoming traffic. Then he drove the wrong way into heavy traffic on Westheimer. Appellant's conduct indisputably posed a continuing danger to himself and others. This ongoing, potentially lethal conduct was, under any definition of the term, both a breach of the public peace and an offense against the public peace. Clearly, no one—neither citizen nor police officer—must obtain an arrest warrant before attempting to protect the public welfare from this type of reckless driving while intoxicated. These are precisely the type of exigent circumstances that the Texas Legislature envisioned when it explicitly authorized a citizen's arrest for an offense against the public peace. Thus, Mr. Moore was legally authorized to make a citizen's arrest of appellant under Article 14.01(a).

---◆---

Notes and Questions

1. What, if anything, does the *Steelman* case add to the within view statutory warrant exception for officers?

2. What, if anything, does the *Miles* case add to the statutory exception permitting citizen's arrest?

3. Article 14.02 permits an officer to arrest a person who commits a felony or a breach of the peace within the view of a magistrate. If the magistrate verbally orders the officer to arrest the offender, the officer may do so without a warrant.

---◆---

Article 14.03 Warrantless Arrests

Article 14.03 is a catch-all section of the Code that authorizes several categories of warrantless arrests from suspicious places arrests to felony arrests following a confession. This section will detail what is required to establish a valid arrest under each Article 14.03 exception.

Suspicious Places

Officers have the authority to arrest a person without a warrant if he is found in a suspicious place under circumstances that indicate he is guilty of a felony offense, disorderly conduct, breach of the peace, public intoxication, or is about to or has threatened to commit a criminal act.[66] This exception is probably the most amorphous, as the next case illustrates.

---

[66] TEX. CODE CRIM. PROC. ANN. art. 14.03(a)(1) (West 2016).

Bradley Robert Dyar v. State
125 S.W.3d 460
(Tex. Crim. App. 2003)

Article 14.03(a)(1) ... allows a lawful warrantless arrest when officers discover a person in a suspicious place and under circumstances which reasonably show an offense has been or is about to be committed . . . Texas legislative history is sparse with respect to the legislature's intent in passing this Article, and there is no definition of "suspicious places" given. Therefore, this Court is left to interpret Article 14.03(a)(1).

In *Lara v. State*,[67] this Court handed down the test to be applied to an Article 14.03(a)(1) analysis. In that case, the defendant was convicted of possession of a controlled substance and sentenced to life in prison. At trial, the officers testified that they observed the defendant running from a known drug house. They further testified that they apprehended the defendant and performed an initial search, and upon apprehending the remaining individuals, they read the defendant his rights. They then performed a second search of the defendant and found a capsule of heroin. On appeal, this Court affirmed the conviction, holding that there was no reversible error where, under all the circumstances observed by the officers and the facts known by them, they had probable cause and the defendant's arrest was authorized under Article 14.03(a)(1). This test has been repeated on many occasions by this Court and others.

In this case, the appellant was taken to the hospital before the police arrived at the scene of the accident. When Trooper Thompson arrived at the scene, he observed a single car accident where the appellant's vehicle had left the road and landed upside down. At the hospital, the trooper noticed that the appellant had slurred speech, red glassy eyes, a strong smell of alcohol and that many of the appellant's answers were unintelligible. Further, the appellant admitted to the trooper that he had been drinking and driving that night.

The Court of Appeals used the above factors in a totality of the circumstances test in deciding the legality of the appellant's warrantless arrest. The Court of Appeals held that Trooper Thompson reasonably inferred from those facts the alcohol was likely a factor in the accident. We agree.

[67] 469 S.W.2d 177, 179 (Tex. Crim. App. 1971).

The appellant, however, focuses on the hospital where the arrest occurred. He argues that a hospital is not a "suspicious place." The appellant asserts that under *Johnson*, a "suspicious place" is where the criminal activity occurred.

In *Johnson*,[68] this Court held that, since the appellant's arrest at the felony crime scene within two hours of the offense was based upon probable cause, the arrest was authorized under Article 14.03(a)(1). The fact that the appellant was at the scene of the crime two hours after the murder, was a factor in finding that the appellant was found in a suspicious place and was also a factor in determining probable cause. In *Johnson*, this Court stated, "Initially, we note that few, if any places are suspicious in and of themselves. Rather, additional facts available to an officer plus reasonable inferences from those facts in relation to a particular place may arouse justifiable suspicion."

In light of this, several examples of "suspicious places" are in order. In *Hamel v. State*,[69] the appellant had been under surveillance for suspicion of burglary and narcotics trafficking. The appellant was arrested for shoplifting after his car was stopped due to suspicion of shoplifting and contraband was found in plain view. This Court held that the defendant's car was a "suspicious place" under the facts because the appellant had previous convictions for selling heroin, for burglary, and was further known by the arresting officers as the subject of numerous burglary investigations. The appellant's behavior as the "wheel man" in front of the store was suspicious, as was the hurried, nervous and watchful behavior of the appellant and his companions, all of whom went into the store empty handed, but emerged carrying objects in their hands. Thus, this Court held that the arrest of the defendant was authorized under 14.03(a)(1).

In the case of *Douglas v. State*,[70] the appellant was arrested for murder after officers responded to calls of shots being fired and being advised by the caller of the appellant's location. The court held that the defendant's house was a suspicious place since (1) there was a dead body lying in the front yard, (2) the police were informed that the defendant was "in there [the house]," (3) [the] defendant had been seen near the body and had put something in a car

---

[68] *Johnson v. State*, 722 S.W.2d 417, 421 (Tex. Crim. App. 1986).
[69] *Hamel v. State*, 582 S.W.2d 424, 426 (Tex. Crim. App. 1979).
[70] *Douglas v. State*, 679 S.W.2d 790, 790 (Tex. App.—Fort Worth 1984, no pet.).

parked outside the house and (4) [the] defendant had run back into the house upon being seen by a witness. These circumstances were sufficient for the court to hold that the defendant, arrested inside his own home, was "in a suspicious place."

In *Thomas v. State*,[71] the appellant was arrested for burglary of a habitation with intent to commit theft. The court, while noting that "there is nothing inherently suspicious about members of a neighborhood walking down the street carrying something in broad daylight," held that since (1) one of the men was carrying a television set, (2) the men deposited some property in an abandoned house and (3) the arresting officer knew that at least one house in the neighborhood had been recently burglarized, the defendant was in a "suspicious place"—in this case, the street.

Finally, in *Sheffield v. State*,[72] the appellant was arrested for theft and possession of marijuana. The police were alerted to the presence of a suspicious person thought to have been involved in a theft from a dormitory on the previous day. Two officers saw the appellant enter a building and exit at a rapid pace with a wallet and some dollar bills in his hand. The appellant tried to conceal the wallet from the officers and then told the officers that he had found it in the grass. The court held that the defendant's actions prior to an investigatory stop combined with the police officers' knowledge of a recent theft in the area by a man matching defendant's description was sufficient to justify an arrest under 14.03(a)(1)—holding that the defendant's location had become a "suspicious place." *See also Johnson v. State*, 722 S.W.2d 417, 419–20 (Tex. Crim. App. 1986) (suspicions of police aroused by circumstances and actions of "maintenance man" who arrived to clean up mess from stabbing); *Battles v. State*, 626 S.W.2d 149, 150 (Tex. App.—Fort Worth 1981, no pet.) (defendant in "suspicious place" when found in complainant's house with gun in hand after call for discharge of firearms—defendant in view of police and homeowner directed police to defendant).

There are also several cases in which the courts have found a location not to be a "suspicious place." In *Amores v. State*,[73] the appellant was arrested for possession of cocaine. On appeal, he claimed that the evidence was illegally

[71] *Thomas v. State*, 681 S.W.2d 672, 673 (Tex. App.—Houston [14th Dist.] 1984, pet. ref'd).

[72] *Sheffield v. State*, 647 S.W.2d 413, 414 (Tex. App.—Austin), *pet. ref'd*, 650 S.W.2d 813 (Tex. Crim. App. 1983).

[73] *Amores v. State*, 816 S.W.2d 407, 410 (Tex. Crim. App. 1991).

seized through a warrantless arrest. This Court held that the appellant's initial detention was an arrest, not an investigative stop because the officer blocked the appellant's car, drew his revolver at the appellant, ordered him from the car at gunpoint, ordered him to lie face down and told him he would be shot if he did not obey orders.

The arresting officer testified that the facts known to him at the time of the arrest were the following: 1) the police received a telephone report of a burglary in progress involving a black male putting something in the trunk of a car; 2) the location of the reported burglary was at an apartment complex whose manager he knew to have called in numerous reports of criminal activity; 3) upon arriving at the scene within one minute of the report, he observed a black male sitting at the wheel of the car; 4) the car was backed into a parking space; 5) the black male was about to drive away as the officer drove into the lot; and 6) he knew that no "blacks" lived at these apartments at this time. The officer further acknowledged that, at the time he arrived on the scene, no burglary was occurring from his viewpoint and that, until the point at which he found the weapon in the appellant's car, he did not observe any violation of the law. This Court held that, where events are as consistent with innocent activity as with criminal activity, the arrest of a suspect based on those events is unlawful under Article 14.03(a)(1).

In *Hoag v. State*,[74] the officers placed the defendant under surveillance for the purpose of apprehending him in a burglary. Subsequently, the officers removed the defendant from his car at gunpoint and gave him *Miranda* warnings. After searching the defendant's car, they found stolen jewelry and arrested the defendant for burglary of a habitation. The defendant claimed that the jewelry was illegally seized through a warrantless arrest.

In that case, the arresting officers observed the appellant park his car and enter an apartment complex. When the appellant emerged from the complex, he was carrying a newspaper and a soft drink. The officers saw the appellant take something out of his pocket and put it on the floor of the car. Suspecting that a burglary had taken place, the officers checked the complex for signs that an apartment had been burglarized and found none.

This Court held that since the officers checked the apartment complex and failed to find any signs of burglary, there were no other circumstances which could have reasonably shown that the appellant had been guilty of

---

[74] 728 S.W.2d 375, 377 (Tex. Crim. App. 1987).

burglary. Therefore, the appellant was not in a suspicious place and the warrantless arrest [could] not be upheld under Article 14.03(a)(1).[75]

The appellant claims that in interpreting Article 14.03(a)(1), the courts have not given meaning to "suspicious places." That is a misconception.

In *Muniz v. State*, this Court interpreted Article 14.03(a)(1) as the functional equivalent of probable cause.[76] That interpretation, as stated, is overly broad. Although probable cause that the defendant committed the crime is one part of the test, it is not the complete test. However, this Court did apply the correct analysis in that case.

In *Muniz*, the appellant was found hiding in his brother's closet. A closet is not per se a suspicious place. However, the facts showed that on the night the victim disappeared, the appellant had been seen near the scene of the murder following a woman who matched the victim's description, he was seen wearing dirty, wet clothes and showing wounds from a struggle, and he asked a witness to deny having seen him. At this point, the appellant became a suspect in the murder.

A highway patrolman went to the house of the appellant's brother. The appellant's brother told the patrolman that he would turn over the appellant if he were in the house. The appellant's wife, who was also at the house, nodded towards the bedroom and the appellant was found hiding in the closet. This Court concluded that the appellant was arrested in a suspicious place.

In its analysis, this Court first looked at all the facts and circumstances known to the police officer which would reasonably show that the defendant had committed a crime listed in Article 14.03(a)(1). Next, this Court looked at all the facts and circumstances in relation to a particular place to show that the defendant was in a suspicious place. In other words, this Court used the totality of circumstances test to find first, probable cause that the defendant

---

[75] See also *Lowery v. State*, 499 S.W.2d 160, 164 (Tex. Crim. App. 1973) (court found that apartments were not a suspicious place because there was no evidence of how the officers knew appellant was at that location, nor was there evidence concerning his circumstances there); *Holland v. State*, 788 S.W.2d 112, 115 (Tex. App.—Dallas 1990, pet ref'd) (appellant's apartment was not a suspicious place where the appellant was found in the back room of his own apartment and no weapon was found, there were no stolen items present, and no contraband was in sight).
[76] *Muniz v. State*, 851 S.W.2d 238, 251 (Tex. Crim. App.) *cert. denied*, 510 U.S. 837 (1993).

committed the crime and second, to find that the defendant was in a suspicious place. Many of the facts supported both conclusions.

Then in *Johnson*, as discussed above, this Court held that, since the appellant's arrest at the felony crime scene within two hours of the offense was based upon probable cause, the arrest was authorized under Article 14.03(a)(1) of the Texas Code of Criminal Procedure. Again, this holding does not state the complete test, but this Court applied the complete test.

In its analysis, this Court stated that the circumstances within the knowledge of a peace officer which reasonably show that a particular person is guilty of a crime are the functional equivalent of probable cause to believe that a particular person has committed a crime. The appellant was arrested under circumstances which reasonably showed that he was guilty of the felony offense of murder. The question then became what is a suspicious place for the purposes of Article 14.03.

This Court found that the appellant was present at the crime scene within two hours of the murder, the appellant appeared nervous, he had blood on his pants and he admitted that the keys found at the murder scene belonged to him. The presence of the appellant was not contrived by law enforcement officials to circumvent the procurement of a warrant. Therefore, this Court held that the appellant's arrest was authorized under Article 14.03(a)(1).

In this case, Trooper Thompson arrived at the scene of the accident and was informed that the driver was taken to the hospital. This information would tend to make a hospital a suspicious place in which to seek the driver who was suspected of causing the accident.

At the hospital, soon after the accident, the trooper observed that the appellant had slurred speech, red glassy eyes, a strong smell of alcohol and that many of the appellant's answers were unintelligible. The appellant also admitted to drinking and driving.

Those facts in relation to the hospital make the hospital a "suspicious place." Those same facts also provided probable cause to believe that the appellant had been drinking and driving.

The determination of whether a place is a "suspicious place" is a highly fact-specific analysis. Review of the case law indicates that several different factors have been used to justify the determination of a place as suspicious. However, only one factor seems to be constant throughout the case law. The time frame between the crime and the apprehension of a suspect in a suspicious place is short. We are not setting any specific time limits today, but we are pointing out that the time between the crime and the apprehension of the suspect in a suspicious place is an important factor.

Conclusion

Reviewing courts in Texas have consistently used the totality of the circumstances test for deciding whether an arrest is proper under Article 14.03(a)(1). When the Legislature meets, after a particular statute or article has been judicially construed, without changing that statute or article, we presume the Legislature intended the same construction should continue to be applied. The Texas Legislature has not chosen to amend this Article after that interpretation by this Court. Therefore, we reaffirm today that the test under Article 14.03(a)(1) is a totality of the circumstances test. First, probable cause that the defendant committed a crime must be found and second, the defendant must be found in a "suspicious place." The judgment of the Third Court of Appeals is affirmed.

———————◆———————

Notes and Questions

1.   In a thoughtful concurring opinion to the *Dyar* case, Judge Cochran explained that this exception troubles the legal community and has questionable historical origins.[77] Judge Cochran stated,

> I agree with the majority in its implicit holding that "places" are not inherently suspicious; rather it is people and circumstances taken together that are sometimes suspicious. Just as the Fourth Amendment does not protect places, it protects people, any "place" may become suspicious when a person at that location and the accompanying circumstances raise a reasonable belief that the person has committed (or is about to commit) a crime and there is no time to obtain a warrant.[78]

In the end, Judge Cochran called for the legislature to create a more fact-specific, exigent-circumstances-type exception so law enforcement officers,

---

[77] *Dyar v. State*, 125 S.W.3d 460, 468–69 (Tex. Crim. App. 2003) (J. Cochran, concurring).
[78] *Id.* at 470.

judges, and lawyers could apply the suspicious places exception in a way that avoids potential Fourth Amendment violations.[79]

2.   Some appellate courts in Texas consider crime scenes suspicious places.[80] Courts have also applied the suspicious place exception to places near a crime scene or to places where things from a crime scene were moved.[81]

3.   If you were a prosecutor, how comfortable would you be with a case where the officer relied upon the suspicious place exception as the basis for her warrantless arrest? Why? Now put yourself in the place of defense counsel. Would you feel the same if this exception was the basis for the arrest? Why?

————————————◆————————————

Assault

Article 14.03(a)(2) addresses warrantless arrests for assault cases. This section permits arrests in the following instances:

1.   When the officer has probable cause;
2.   To believe an assault involving bodily injury to another person occurred; and
3.   The officer believes there is a danger of further bodily injury to that person if the suspect is not arrested.

---

[79] *Id.* at 468-71.

[80] *E.g., Lewis v. State*, 412 S.W.3d 794, 802 (Tex. App.—Amarillo 2013, no pet.) ("the scene of the hit-and-run accident was a suspicious place"); *Johnson v. State*, 722 S.W.2d 417, 421 (Tex. Crim. App. 1986), *overruled on other grounds, McKenna v. State*, 780 S.W.2d 797, 798 (Tex. Crim. App. 1989) (defendant appeared at crime scene two hours after crime was committed, which was a factor considered in suspicious place analysis).

[81] *E.g., Rysiejko v. State*, 782 S.W.2d 529, 533 (Tex. App.—Houston [14th Dist.] 1989, pet. ref'd) ("Where persons matching descriptions of burglary suspects carry what appears to be stolen property toward the location of a car known to have been involved in a burglary earlier in the day, the location of that car and those suspects becomes a suspicious place...."); *Goldberg v. State*, 95 S.W.3d 345, 363 (Tex. App.—Houston [1st Dist.] 2002, pet. ref'd) (vehicle that was at crime scene later found outside appellant's house made his house a suspicious place).

Bodily injury is defined in the Penal Code as "physical pain, illness, or any impairment of physical condition."[82] This includes any physical contact that hurts, such as a slap, scratch, or bruise.

───────◆───────

Violation of a Protective Order

There are two ways an officer can arrest a person for violating a protective order. The first is found in Article 14.03(a)(3). This provision permits an officer to arrest when she did not witness the violation, but she has probable cause to believe the person violated a standard protective order or a protective order issued on the basis of a sexual assault. Article 14.03(b) permits an officer to arrest a person she has probable cause to believe has violated either type of protection order when it was committed within the officer's view.

───────◆───────

Family Violence

Article 14.03(a)(4) permits an officer to arrest someone she has probable cause to believe has committed an act of family violence. *Family violence* involves assaulting a member of your household, whether or not that person is a blood relative or a romantic partner. Family violence includes dating violence, any form of abuse of a child, or

> an act by a member of a family or household against another member of the family or household that is intended to result in physical harm, bodily injury, assault, or sexual assault, or that is a threat that reasonably places the member in fear of imminent physical harm, bodily injury, assault, or sexual assault, but does not include defensive measures to protect oneself.[83]

If there is an assault of any kind on any member of the suspect's household, including sexual assaults, officers have the authority to make a warrantless arrest.

───────◆───────

---

[82] TEX. PENAL CODE ANN. §1.07(a)(8) (West 2011).
[83] TEX. FAM. CODE ANN. §71.004 (West 2015).

Interference with Emergency Request for Assistance

In some family violence cases, and occasionally in other types of cases, the defendant interferes with the victim's attempt to place a call for emergency assistance (*i.e.*, a 911 call). Interference with an emergency call is a crime.[84]

Article 14.04(a)(5) permits officers to arrest a suspect without a warrant when he has prevented another from making a request for emergency assistance, even when the crime was not committed in the officer's presence. In order to meet the requirements of this section, officers must establish that the defendant knowingly prevented a person from placing an emergency call or request assistance from a law enforcement agency, medical facility, or other agency whose primary purpose is to act as safety provider.[85] The basis for the emergency request can be fear of imminent assault or concern of imminent property destruction.[86]

---◆---

Confessions to Felony Offenses

Article 14.03(a)(6) grants officers the authority to arrest a person who gives a voluntary confession that is admissible under Article 38.21 when the confession establishes probable cause to believe the person committed a felony. Article 38.21 and its requirements for a valid confession, otherwise known as a *statement* in Texas, are described in more detail in Chapter 10 of this book. For now, understand that if a confession is admissible, and it establishes probable cause to believe the defendant committed a felony offense, the warrantless arrest of that defendant is permissible under this exception.

---◆---

[84] TEX. PENAL CODE ANN. §42.062 (West 2011).
[85] TEX. PENAL CODE ANN. §42.062(a) (West 2011).
[86] TEX. PENAL CODE ANN. §42.062(d) (West 2011).

Public Intoxication

Officers are permitted to arrest an adult they have probable cause to believe is publicly intoxicated.[87] The crime of public intoxication has two elements: (1) the defendant appears in a public place (2) while intoxicated to such an extent that the person is a danger to himself or to others.[88] The statute provides alternatives to arrest when officers have detained someone for public intoxication, which include placing the suspect with a responsible caregiver or dropping him off at a treatment center.[89] Whether an officer decides to arrest the intoxicated person, release him, or drop him off at a treatment facility is entirely within the officer's discretion.[90]

———◆———

Escape

The escape warrantless arrest statute appears in Article 14.04, but neither the name of the statute ("When Felony has been Committed") or its nickname (Escape) fully describe its requirements. Article 14.04 authorizes a warrantless arrest when "it is shown by satisfactory proof to a peace officer, upon the representation of a credible person, that a felony has been committed, and that the offender is about to escape, so that there is no time to procure a warrant."[91] This article allows the officer to pursue and arrest the suspect without an arrest warrant when there is not time to get one. Courts have considered factors in determining when an officer may objectively believe a person is attempting to escape such that a warrantless arrest is justifiable:

> [S]everal factors ... help ... indicate that a suspect may be committing, or have just committed, an offense, or that the suspect may be attempting to escape from the commission of the offense. These factors include furtive movements and gestures, flight at the approach of strangers or law officers, the place where a suspect is found and the direction in which he is traveling, and being on a public street instead of in a private residence. These factors

---

[87] TEX. CODE CRIM. PROC. ANN. art. 14.031(a) (West 2016).
[88] TEX. PENAL CODE ANN. §49.02 (West 2011).
[89] TEX. CODE CRIM. PROC. ANN. art. 14.031(a) (West 2016).
[90] *Id.*
[91] TEX. CODE CRIM. PROC. ANN. art. 14.04 (West 2016).

are strong indicia of *mens rea*, and when coupled with specific knowledge on the part of the officer relating the suspect to the evidence of the crime, are properly considered in the decision to make an arrest. When taken alone and by themselves, these factors may be as insufficient for this purpose as an inarticulate hunch on the part of the arresting officer. In each case, it is the combination of the knowledge of the arresting officer and other cooperating officers, the observations of the arresting officer, and the factors that indicate the commission of a crime and an attempt to escape therefrom which constitute a reasonable conclusion that there is probable cause to make an arrest without a warrant.[92]

The next case illustrates the importance of considering all of the above factors when it comes to making a warrantless arrest based upon the escape exception.

Dennis Dowthitt v. State
931 S.W.2d 244
(Tex. Crim. App. 1996)

[Appellant and his 16-year old son were charged with capital murder for raping and murdering two, young girls.]

Appellant argues that his arrest did not fall within one of the warrantless arrest exceptions found in Article 14....

The only potentially applicable warrantless arrest exception is the felony/escape rule found in Article 14.04. We have held that Article 14.04 must be strictly construed in the suspect's favor. One requirement of the statute is that the law enforcement officer must have "some evidence amounting to satisfactory proof ... that the defendant was about to escape." The escape requirement is obviously met where the suspect has previously fled or otherwise evidences an intention to flee. In interpreting ambiguous behavior by a suspect, "it is important to keep in mind the 'temporal proximity' of the actions of [the] suspect both to the commission of the crime, and to the suspect's discovery of the police investigation of him." But, satisfactory proof of escape is not established by the mere fact that a suspect travels from one place to another.

---

[92] *Pyles v. State*, 755 S.W.2d 98, 109 (Tex. Crim. App. 1988).

Moreover, we have emphasized that the escape requirement is not met merely because the police confront the suspect with their suspicions. Discovery of pursuit is but a factor in the overall picture, and the police/suspect confrontation is not sufficient in itself to constitute satisfactory proof of escape. When the proof of imminent escape consists solely of observations by law enforcement personnel, we have generally required that those observations include evidence of some act by the suspect tending to show an intent to escape. We held that the escape requirement was not met where a suspect had been warned earlier in the day that the police were looking for him but was nevertheless drinking at a bar at 12:30 a.m. The fact that the bar was going to close at 1:00 a.m., and the police did not know where to find the suspect after the bar closed, was not enough to show satisfactory proof of imminent escape. ...

After examining the record, we can find no act by appellant indicating an intent to escape. Appellant voluntarily appeared at the police station in the morning and after lunch. He remained at the station for questioning for six hours and then agreed to submit to a polygraph examination, which lasted another four hours. After the polygraph examination, he continued to participate in the police interrogation despite the lateness of the hour. In fact, appellant appears to have exhibited extraordinary patience with the police investigation. The officers did not have satisfactory proof of escape.

An exception to our general requirement of an act by the suspect indicating an intent to escape is found in *West v. State*, 720 S.W.2d 511 (Tex. Crim. App. 1986) (plurality opinion), *cert. denied*, 481 U.S. 1072 (1987). In *West*, police officers were called to the scene of a murder after witnesses had reported hearing loud noises in an apartment complex. After discovering the victim's body, one of the officers talked with the witnesses. After hearing the loud noises, the witnesses had seen a man, whose clothes were wet with blood, exit the victim's apartment. Another person believed she recognized the man described by the witnesses and led the police to his apartment. The police knocked on the door, which was opened by the suspect's companion. The police saw the suspect, eight feet away, wearing only a pair of shorts. After ascertaining that the suspect matched the description given by the witnesses, the police arrested him. We held that the warrantless arrest was proper under Article 14.04, despite the absence of any act by the suspect tending to show an intent to escape, because of the narrow circumstances present:

We hold that where, as in the instant case, officers who reasonably believe that further investigation of an offense may be necessary in order to justify the issuance of a warrant, and where those officers undertake that investigation lawfully and without impinging upon reasonable expectations of privacy, and where that investigation leads to the receipt of information which in combination with their other information constitutes probable cause to arrest the suspect, but that information is obtained in the presence of the suspect under circumstances which would lead the officers reasonably to believe that the suspect would take flight if given the opportunity to do so, the officers are authorized by Article 14 to arrest the suspect without first procuring a warrant.

In *West* the lack of an act by the suspect indicating intent to escape was excused because of the circumstances under which probable cause to arrest arose. The inference of intent to escape was reasonable, despite the lack of an overt act by the suspect.

In the present case, as in *West*, officers undertook their investigation lawfully, the investigation led to receipt of information establishing probable cause to arrest, and the information was obtained in the presence of the suspect. Were those the only requirements of *West*, appellant's arrest would have been justified. But *West* also requires that the circumstances be such that they would lead the officers reasonably to believe that the suspect would take flight if given the opportunity to do so.

The evidence in this case shows not just the lack of an overt act by appellant indicating intent to escape, but acts that contradict such an intent. Unless we are to hold that a warrantless arrest is justified under Art. 14.04 whenever probable cause to arrest develops in the presence of a suspect, we cannot disregard circumstances that negate an intent to escape. Given the particular circumstances present in this case, the police could not reasonably "believe that the suspect would take flight if given the opportunity to do so." Hence, Article 14.04 was not met, and appellant's arrest was illegal.

———————— ◆ ————————

Theft

Most warrantless arrest exceptions are confined to Chapter 14 of the Code. Theft is one of the few exceptions found outside of this chapter. Oddly enough, it appears in the Search Warrants chapter, perhaps because the statute authorizes the seizure of the person along with the suspected stolen goods.[93]

Any person is permitted to prevent a theft from occurring by seizing the stolen property openly and seizing the theft suspect.[94] Though the statute says the person making the arrest must have a reasonable ground to believe the property is stolen, courts believe that reasonable ground equates to probable cause.[95]

Typically, the person who detains or arrests a theft suspect is an employee of the store or the business where the theft took place. Stores employ loss prevention officers whose job is to monitor the stores, detect theft, recover stolen merchandise, and notify police when a shoplifter has been detained. Following the arrest, the suspect must be taken to a peace officer or a magistrate without delay.[96]

---------------◆---------------

Exigency and Hot Pursuit

The Code of Criminal Procedure has not recognized exigency, or hot pursuit, as a basis for warrantless arrest, but the U.S. Supreme Court[97] and Texas appellate courts have.[98] Thus, it is a common law exception to the requirement that officers have a warrant to arrest a person. The Dallas Court of Appeals explained exigency as it relates to warrantless arrest as follows:

> Exigent circumstances embrace situations in which real, immediate, and serious consequences will certainly occur if a police officer postpones

---

[93] TEX. CODE CRIM. PROC. ANN. art. 18.16 (West 2016).

[94] *Id.*

[95] *Aitch v. State*, 879 S.W.2d 167, 172 (Tex. App.—Houston [14th Dist.] 1994, pet. ref'd).

[96] TEX. CODE CRIM. PROC. ANN. art. 18.16 (West 2016).

[97] *Welsh v. Wisconsin*, 466 U.S. 740, 752–53 (1984) (exigent circumstances justify a warrantless arrest inside the home).

[98] *E.g., Winter v. State*, 902 S.W.2d 571, 574 (Tex. App.—Houston [1st Dist.] 1995, no pet.) (exigent circumstances supported defendant's arrest for DWI and evading arrest); *Waddy v. State*, 880 S.W.2d 458, 459–60 (Tex. App.—Houston [14th Dist.] 1994, pet. ref'd) ("hot pursuit" justified warrantless arrest for gun possession); *Duenez v. State*, 735 S.W.2d 563, 566 (Tex. App.—Houston [1st Dist.] 1987) (exigent circumstances supported arrest for unauthorized use of a motor vehicle); *Carter v. State*, 824 S.W.2d 767, 768–69 (Tex. App.—Waco 1992, no pet.) ("hot pursuit" exception justified defendant's warrantless arrest for felony DWI).

action to obtain a warrant. Exigent circumstances affecting the validity of a warrantless entry into a residence resulting in an arrest include the following: (1) a risk of danger to the police or the victim; (2) an increased likelihood of apprehending a suspect; (3) possible destruction of evidence or contraband; (4) hot or continuous pursuit; and (5) rendering aid or assistance to persons who the officer reasonably believes are in need of assistance. The validity of a warrantless seizure of a suspect in a constitutionally protected area is also determined by the seriousness of the offense. The warrantless entry of a constitutionally protected area to arrest or detain a suspect for a non-jailable offense is not permissible. However, if an offense, either a misdemeanor or a felony, is punishable by confinement and there are exigent circumstances, then it is serious enough to justify the warrantless entry of a constitutionally protected area.[99]

---◆---

Pretext Arrests

Officers can arrest a person for virtually any law violation they observe, including minor infractions such as walking in a street where a sidewalk is provided, not using a turn signal within the distance required under the Traffic Code, not having a light reflector on a bicycle, and jaywalking.[100] These bases for arrest are controversial in part because they disproportionately affect impoverished and minority populations and those who live in high-crime areas. When this happens, the officer is usually suspicious that a greater criminal offense has occurred or is occurring, and the minor infraction used to justify the basis for the arrest is merely an excuse or pretext.

Once a suspect is arrested, the officer may search her incident to arrest. The suspect's car may be towed and impounded, where it will be searched and all items found within inventoried. Officers know this. They recognize that if they can arrest the suspect for any offense, they may be able to search the person or the person's vehicle and find evidence of a greater crime. Pretext arrests are commonplace in criminal law. Many are based on traffic violations. For example, most driving while intoxicated cases begin, even when the officer believes the suspect is driving while intoxicated, with a

[99] *Randolph v. State*, 152 S.W.3d 764, 771–72 (Tex. App.—Dallas 2004, no pet.).
[100] TEX. CODE CRIM. PROC. ANN. art. 14.01 (West 2016).

traffic violation, such as not staying within a single lane of traffic or failing to make a complete stop at a stop sign. The next case illustrates that even when the officer suspects a greater criminal offense, he may arrest a suspect for a lesser offense.

Antonio Garcia v. State
827 S.W.2d 937
(Tex. Crim. App. 1992)

Appellee was charged with unlawful possession of a controlled substance. The trial court granted appellee's motion to suppress the cocaine after finding it was the fruit of a search based upon a "pretext stop." The State appealed the trial court's pretrial order. The El Paso Court of Appeals held the trial judge had "erred as a matter of law" by granting the motion to suppress, vacated the trial court's order, and remanded the case to the trial court. We granted appellee's petition to address the "pretext arrest" theory on which the court of appeals premised its holding. We will affirm.

The following facts are taken from the court of appeals' opinion:

On the afternoon of March 25, 1989, two uniformed El Paso police officers, Duran and Ruiz, were on routine patrol in their assigned district. They observed a tan Cadillac parked at the curb in front of 3717 Finley Street. The address was known to both officers as a frequent "shooting gallery" for drug offenders, as well as a frequent exchange point for stolen property. They had never seen this vehicle at or near the premises before. The officers were not in fact even aware of whether the driver of the vehicle was in that house. Nonetheless, their suspicions were aroused—albeit without sufficient reasonable, articulable facts to justify an investigative stop. They continued their patrol through the nearby streets. One hour later, they were again approaching the 3700 block of Finley, southbound on Latta Street. As they approached the intersection with Finley, they observed the Cadillac pass through the intersection in front of them, eastbound on Finley. Officer Duran testified that he started to follow the Cadillac ... and then saw the driver continue through the next intersection without stopping at a posted stop sign. ... Officer Duran pursued the Cadillac, employing both emergency lights and siren to signal the driver to stop. The Cadillac continued, [but] was stopped by vehicles waiting for a red light .... Duran ... approached the driver's window on foot, knocked on the glass and asked the driver to lower the window. The Appellee (the driver and sole occupant of the Cadillac) did not comply despite repeated requests.

Duran returned to the patrol vehicle and told Officer Ruiz to ask the drivers ahead of the Cadillac to remain in position, blocking Appellee's vehicle, while Duran called for backup. Ruiz walked ahead of the Cadillac. Appellee suddenly backed up even with the patrol vehicle and then accelerated forward at an angle toward Ruiz. Duran shouted a warning, drew his weapon and fired a shot into the passenger door on the Cadillac. Ruiz dodged out of the way. In moving forward, Appellee hooked his rear bumper on the front bumper of the patrol vehicle and began dragging the police unit down Paisano Drive. As the vehicles passed Ruiz, he dove into the passenger seat of the police unit. Duran pursued on foot initially, but was then given a ride by a civilian motorist. Appellee dragged the patrol vehicle approximately two hundred yards before stopping and fleeing on foot into an adjacent residential area. Duran resumed his foot pursuit. Appellee jumped a fence and entered the residence of an elderly woman who was outside. Duran pursued the Appellee inside and found him in a bathroom trying to dispose of several small plastic bags containing what appeared to be cocaine. Police searched appellee's vehicle and found cocaine. Appellee was charged with the instant offense, as well as with aggravated assault on a police officer. No traffic citations were issued to appellee.

The court of appeals noted that one of the trial court's findings of fact was that appellee committed the stop sign violation. Consequently, the court of appeals framed the "pretext arrest" issue as whether a trial court must suppress evidence seized during an objectively valid detention for a trivial offense, when the arresting officers had a preexisting suspicion of a greater offense at the time of the detention and took advantage of the occurrence of the trivial offense to enhance their investigative opportunities of the greater offense. After extensive discussion regarding the genesis of the "pretext arrest" doctrine, that court held that, given the actual occurrence of appellee's traffic offense, the officers' actions leading to the stop, search and seizure were proper, regardless of the existence of any preexisting suspicion or desire to stop appellee's automobile.

Appellee contends that recent decisions of the United States Supreme Court indicate the motivations and bad faith of government officials are relevant and important to a determination of whether a Fourth Amendment violation has occurred. In support of this proposition, appellee cites [several Supreme Court decisions]. These cases are not applicable as they are concerned with the scope of various searches by law enforcement officials, rather than actual pretext stop situations.

Appellee also argues that the purpose of the exclusionary rule is to deter willful or flagrant actions by the police. Appellee contends that since good faith is a consideration given weight in the Fourth Amendment context, bad faith should be considered as well. Appellee avers that the rule proposed by the court of appeals would dilute the deterrent effect of the federal exclusionary rule.

The term "pretext arrest," as used in the instant case, refers to an "objectively" valid stop for an allegedly improper reason. In other words, a pretext arrest occurs when an individual is validly stopped or arrested for one offense only because law enforcement officials desire to investigate that individual for a different offense—*i.e.*, an offense for which they do not have valid legal grounds to stop or arrest. The pretext arrest doctrine is not new to this Court. ...

[Several United States] Supreme Court cases demonstrate that the subjective reasons a law enforcement official may have for making an arrest or stop are irrelevant to a determination of the legality of that detention ... "Again and again, in precisely the present context, the Court has told us that where police officers are objectively doing what they are legally authorized to do ... the results of their investigations are not to be called in question on the basis of any subjective intent with which they acted."

Our research reveals that eleven of the twelve federal circuit courts have adopted an objective approach to determining the legality of so-called pretext arrests and stops, with only the Ninth Circuit Court of Appeals apparently still adhering to the wholly subjective analysis.... [We adopt] the prevailing, entirely objective approach adopted by a majority of the federal circuit courts.

The above-cited Supreme Court and federal court cases persuade us that, for Fourth Amendment purposes, the validity of an arrest or stop should be determined solely by analyzing objectively the facts surrounding the event. We discuss, briefly, two of the primary reasons why the objective approach clearly makes more sense, and is more reasonable in terms of application, than is an attempt to determine an officer's subjective reasons for a "pretext" detention.

First, an objective evaluation of the facts and circumstances surrounding a stop or arrest comports with the federal exclusionary rule and its deterrence rationale. The exclusionary rule was designed to prevent unlawful police conduct, and our Fourth Amendment jurisprudence has evolved around this core concept. "[T]he reason lies in the purpose of [the exclusionary] rule: to deter unlawful actions by police. Where nothing has been done that is objectively unlawful, the exclusionary rule has no application and the intent with which [police officers] acted is of no consequence." Expanding the exclusionary rule to cover pretext arrests

> would be defensible only if we felt it important to deter policemen from acting lawfully but with the plan—the attitude of mind—of going further and acting unlawfully if the lawful conduct produces insufficient results. We might wish that policemen would not act with impure plots in mind, but I do not believe that wish a sufficient basis for excluding, in the supposed service of the Fourth Amendment, probative evidence obtained by actions—if not thoughts—entirely in accord with the Fourth Amendment.[101]

It makes little sense to maintain the pretext arrest doctrine solely to deter the subjectively bad intentions of law enforcement personnel when these intentions do not ultimately manifest themselves in any objectively ascertainable Fourth Amendment violations. Thus, as long as the facts and circumstances show a valid and legal detention, it serves no actual Fourth Amendment function to attempt to unearth the subjective reasons for such detention.

Second, application of the subjective "pretext arrest" doctrine ...presupposes the ability to successfully determine a police officer's state of mind at the time of the detention. But the subjective intent of a police officer is neither easily nor consistently ascertained by courts....

[S]urely the catch is not worth the trouble of the hunt when courts set out to bag the secret motivations of police in this context. A subjective purpose to do something that the applicable legal rules say there is sufficient objective cause to do can be fabricated all too easily and undetectably....[102]

In light of overwhelming federal authority, ... [a]s long as an actual violation [of the law] occurs, law enforcement officials are free to enforce the laws and detain a person for that violation, regardless of whatever the usual practices or standards of the local law enforcement agency are and regardless

---

[101] *Massachusetts v. Painten*, 389 U.S. 560, 565 (1968) (White, J., dissenting).
[102] Anthony G. Amsterdam, *Perspectives on the Fourth Amendment*, 58 MINN. L. REV. 349, 436-437 (1974)

of the officer's subjective reasons for the detention. Thus, the appropriate limitation of an officer's discretion, under the Fourth Amendment, is the existence of a law and the actual commission of the offense; an officer's subjective intent is relevant only to a credibility determination of his stated reasons for stopping or arresting an individual.

In the instant case the record shows, and the trial court found, that appellee committed a stop sign violation. Therefore, the police officers' stop and detention of appellee for a traffic violation was reasonable under Fourth Amendment principles, notwithstanding their illicit motives, if any, for doing so. The judgment of the Court of Appeals is affirmed and this case is remanded to the trial court for proceedings consistent with this opinion.

——————————◆——————————

The Initial Appearance and the Arresting Magistrate's Duties

An arrestee, whether he is arrested with or without an arrest warrant,[103] must be brought before a magistrate "without unnecessary delay," but no more than 48 hours following his arrest.[104] Depending on the jurisdiction, this appearance before the magistrate may be called a preliminary hearing, an initial appearance, a preliminary initial appearance, a 15.17 hearing, or even an arraignment (though it should be distinguished from the arraignment described in Chapter 26 of the Texas Code of Criminal Procedure, which takes place when the defendant appears before the judge presiding over his case for the first time). This chapter will call it an "initial appearance."

The initial appearance should happen in the county of arrest before the magistrate who signed the arrest warrant, before a magistrate in the county of arrest where there was no warrant or the warrant issued from a different county, or in a county where it could happen "more expeditiously" than taking the person to the county where the warrant issued.[105]

---

[103] TEX. CODE CRIM. PROC. ANN art. 15.16 (West 2016) (magistrate warnings required for those arrested with a warrant); TEX. CODE CRIM. PROC. ANN. art. 14.06(a) (West 2016) (magistrate warnings required for those arrested without a warrant).

[104] TEX. CODE CRIM. PROC. ANN. art. 15.17(a) (West 2016).

[105] TEX. CODE CRIM. PROC. ANN. art. 14.06(a) and 15.17(a) (West 2016).

During the initial appearance, the magistrate "shall inform in clear language the person arrested, either in person or through the electronic broadcast system," the following legal information or warnings:

- the accusation against him,
- his right to retain counsel,
- his right to remain silent, and if he waives that right, the warning that he is not required to make any statement, and any statement he does make can and will be used against him,
- his right to have an attorney present during interviews with peace officers or prosecutors,
- his right to terminate the interview at any time,
- his right to have an examining trial, and
- his right to request the appointment of counsel if he cannot afford counsel.[106]

In addition to the warnings, magistrates are required to:

- make probable cause findings in warrantless arrest cases;[107]
- set bail;
- accommodate someone who is deaf or cannot speak English with interpreters;
- assist the arrestee in completing indigency forms; and
- appoint counsel to represent indigent defendants.[108]

Whether the appearance before the magistrate happens in person or through an electronic broadcast system, a recording of the warnings must be made and kept for a period of time.[109] Defense counsel can obtain a copy, if he requests it and pays for the cost to copy it.[110]

The initial appearance serves several important functions. In warrantless arrests, it guarantees a finding of probable cause will be made since one is not made by a magistrate in warrantless arrests. The U.S. Supreme Court has

---

[106] TEX. CODE CRIM. PROC. ANN. art. 15.17(a) (West 2016).
[107] TEX. CODE CRIM. PROC. ANN. art. 17.033(a)-(b) (West 2016).
[108] TEX. CODE CRIM. PROC. ANN. art. 15.17(a) (West 2016).
[109] *Id.* (when the pretrial hearing date ends, 91 days for misdemeanors, or 120 days for felonies).
[110] *Id.*

stated, "the detached judgment of a neutral magistrate is essential if the Fourth Amendment is to furnish meaningful protection from unfounded interference with liberty. Accordingly, we hold that the Fourth Amendment requires a judicial determination of probable cause as a prerequisite to extended restraint of liberty following arrest."[111] Therefore, an accused has a right to a probable cause finding early in the arrest process both in the federal system and in Texas.

In addition, the initial appearance ensures the accused receives notice of the charges, bail, and *Miranda* warnings ("You have the right to remain silent. Anything you say can and will be used against you in a court of law. You have the right to an attorney. If you cannot afford an attorney, one will be provided for you.").[112] It guarantees the accused is read other rights at an early stage of the criminal justice process where rights such as self-incrimination could be waived without fully understanding the implication of such a waiver. In sum, the magistrate's warnings protect the defendant's constitutional rights.

Challenges to the timing or the content of the initial appearance often arise when the accused seeks to suppress her confession based upon an alleged error that happened during the initial magistrate appearance. The next case illustrates what happens when the defendant challenges a statement based upon an alleged initial appearance error.

State v. Sharon Duke Vogel
852 S.W.2d 567
(Tex. App.—Dallas 1992, pet. ref'd)

Sharon Duke Vogel, appellee, is charged with the misdemeanor offense of driving while intoxicated. Appellee's motion to suppress was heard by the trial court which granted appellee's motion in part and denied it in part. The State appeals the trial court's ruling granting the motion in part and raises two points of error: (1) that the appellee failed to meet her burden to show a causal connection between the failure to take appellee before a Collin County magistrate and appellee's statements made on videotape after appellee's arrest; and (2) that the trial court erred by granting appellee an equitable remedy to an alleged violation of article 14.06 of the Texas Code of Criminal Procedure.

---

[111] *Gerstein v. Pugh*, 420 U.S. 103, 114 (1975).
[112] *Miranda v. Arizona*, 384 U.S. 436 (1966).

Facts

On February 21, 1991, in the early hours of the morning, appellee was arrested by Officer Charles Avery of the Dallas Police Department for the offense of driving while intoxicated. Appellee failed four field sobriety tests conducted by Avery. The arrest occurred within the Dallas city limits but within Collin County which borders Dallas County. In accordance with Dallas Police Department policy, appellee was taken to Lew Sterrett Criminal Justice Center in Dallas County.

After arriving at Lew Sterrett, appellee was taken to the video room where she was *"Mirandized,"* videotaped, and asked questions about her activities earlier that evening. Appellee waived her rights under *Miranda* and refused a request to take a breathalyzer test. Approximately four hours after she was arrested, appellee was taken before a Dallas County magistrate. Appellee was never taken before a Collin County magistrate.

At a motion-to-suppress hearing, appellee sought to suppress everything that occurred in Dallas County following the arrest because the police failed to take appellee before a Collin County magistrate. During the hearing, the trial court found this failure was a violation of article 14.06 of the Texas Code of Criminal Procedure and, as an equitable remedy, suppressed the audio portion of the videotape made at Lew Sterrett.

Failure to Take Before Collin County Magistrate

In its first point of error, the State contends that appellee failed to meet her burden to show a causal connection between the failure to take appellee before a Collin County magistrate and appellee's statements made on videotape after her arrest. The State further argues there is no showing that the validity of any admissions or statements made by the appellee was affected. Therefore, the trial court erred in suppressing the audio portion of the videotape. We agree.

Applicable Law

There are no cases in Texas concerning the particular issue in the instant case. However, there is case law pertaining to an accused not being taken before a magistrate. Article 14.06 of the Texas Code of Criminal Procedure states:

In each case enumerated in this Code, the person making the arrest shall take the person arrested or have him taken without unnecessary delay before the magistrate who may have ordered the arrest, before some magistrate of the county where the arrest was made without an order, or, if necessary to provide more expeditiously to the person arrested the warnings described by Article 15.17 of this Code, before a magistrate in a county bordering the county in which the arrest was made. The magistrate shall immediately perform the duties described in Article 15.17 of this Code.

The purpose of article 14.06 is to insure that the accused is presented before a magistrate to receive the article 15.17 warnings. Where there is a failure to carry an accused before a magistrate, a confession will be vitiated only when there is a causal connection between such failure and the making of the confession. The burden is on the defendant to show the delay was unreasonable and to show the causal connection between the confession and the delay.

Application of Law to Facts

We conclude that the trial court abused its discretion in partially granting the motion to suppress. This case concerns an article 14.06 violation where appellee was brought before a Dallas County magistrate instead of a Collin County magistrate. Appellee does not complain that she failed to receive the proper admonishments from the Dallas County magistrate. Further, she does not contend that the statements made on the videotape were a confession or that she was persuaded to make them. The record shows that the videotaping officer made it clear to appellee that she could refuse to answer any question or to end the interview completely. Appellee fails to demonstrate that she was harmed by the article 14.06 violation or to show that there was any causal connection between her failure to be taken before a Collin County magistrate and the making of the statements on the videotape.

The order granting the motion to suppress in part is reversed....

———————◆———————

Notes and Questions

1. When it comes to motions to suppress evidence based on delay or other violations of the statutory requirements, the defendant must prove a causal connection between the evidence obtained and the violation in order

to successfully suppress evidence. What happens when no probable cause determination has been made, and the clock has run?

Where no probable cause finding is made in a misdemeanor case within 24 hours, the arrestee is to be released on a $5,000 bond, and if she cannot afford that bond, she is to be released on personal bond.[113] Personal bond and surety bonds will be discussed in greater detail in Chapter 5, but for now, understand that a personal bond permits the defendant to be released on a promise to appear in court at the designated time. If the arrestee is charged with a felony and no probable cause determination is made within 48 hours, she is to be released on a $10,000 bond, and if she cannot afford this, she can be released on personal bond.[114] A violation of the "without unnecessary delay" requirement does not result in a dismissal of charges[115] or invalidate the indictment.[116]

───────────◆───────────

Practice Questions

Each chapter will include practice bar questions that mirror the topics covered in the chapter. These questions are not taken verbatim from the actual bar questions. Rather, they include the same concepts but are worded differently. Before each question, you'll see a notation that includes the month and the year the question appeared on a bar exam. For example, "(J-2012)" means a question similar to this one appeared on the July 2012 bar exam. If you see multiple notations, a similar question has appeared on multiple bar exams. These practice questions serve a dual purpose. First, they help you put the law you've learned in each chapter into practice. This is why they're called "practice questions." Second, they better prepare you for the Texas bar exam.

Arrest questions appear on the bar exam regularly. In some years, as many as three arrest questions have appeared on the exam, while in other years, bar examiners have asked no arrest questions, but in most years, there

---

[113] TEX. CODE CRIM. PROC. ANN. art. 17.033(a) (West 2016).
[114] *Id.*
[115] *Johnson v. State*, 379 S.W.2d 329, 332 (Tex. Crim. App. 1994) ("the failure to take appellant immediately before a magistrate would not vitiate the indictment").
[116] *Id.*

are one or two arrest questions per exam. These questions often ask examinees to apply arrest law to an arrest fact pattern. However, questions on this topic commonly cover arrest warrant requisites, magistrate duties and warnings, and whether an arrest was valid.

1. (J-2016) Defendant was arrested pursuant to a valid arrest warrant. Could the magistrate have issued a summons instead of an arrest warrant? Explain.

_____

_____

_____

_____

_____

2. (F-2016-1, J-2013, and F-2011) List three requisites of a valid arrest warrant.

_____

_____

_____

_____

_____

Note to students: The next question asks you to determine whether the arrest was valid. Before you attempt to answer it, please consider the following tips on how to answer arrest questions.

Every time the bar examiners have asked whether an arrest was valid, they have used a warrantless arrest fact pattern. Nearly half the time, the arrest was not supported by probable cause. In these fact patterns, examinees were told early in the question that the defendant committed the crime. However, in these scenarios, the officer arrested the defendant before he himself developed probable cause. I describe this behavior as *jumping the gun*, which is a track analogy that describes a runner who begins the race before the start gun fires. Officers sometimes jump the gun when they make arrests. The officer may have a hunch and may even have reasonable suspicion to investigate but is lacking probable cause to arrest, yet the officer arrests the suspect anyway. Students must separate what they know about the facts (that the defendant committed the crime because the bar exam question says so) from what the officer knows about the facts at the time of arrest. The bar examiner comments indicate many examinees reached the wrong conclusion when they answered arrest questions.

Bar examiners have used the following warrantless arrest exceptions in their fact patterns: offense within view, suspicious place, escape, and assault of a family member. Let's examine one example of a question involving a warrantless arrest exception. On the February 2004 bar exam, examiners characterized the fact pattern as possibly supporting the escape exception. In that instance, two elements of the exception were supported by the fact pattern (credible person and defendant committed a felony), whereas two elements were not satisfied by the facts (no time to procure a warrant and the suspect was about to escape). Bar examiners said that few examinees analyzed the escape exception.

The search and seizure bar exam questions require you to apply the law to a fact pattern. This can be difficult. How should you prepare to answer arrest questions? First, consider whether there was there a warrant. If there was a warrant, you must determine whether the facts support probable cause and whether the warrant meets the other statutory requisites. If there was not a warrant, you must determine whether an exception to the warrant requirement applies. Second, you need to know the applicable requirements that lead to a valid arrest. For example, in the escape exception, examinees had to know the elements to that exception, they had to list the elements in their answer, and they had to apply the elements to the facts in order to answer the question properly. You must do the same. Third, you need to delineate when the arrest took place and when officers had probable cause. Whether officers established probable cause in the end does not matter. They must develop probable cause before they arrest, not afterwards. Fourth, every time the bar examiners have asked whether an arrest was valid, the arrest was a warrantless arrest. When an arrest was unlawful in the bar exam facts, most of the time there was no warrant, no probable cause, and no crime committed within view. Be on the lookout for similar problems in a question. Using these four considerations, examine the following question, which is based on an actual case.[117] For more practice, go to the Board of Law Examiners website, and practice using the arrest questions from past bar exams.

3. (F-2016, J-2012, F-2012, J-2010, J-2008, J-2004, F-2004, J-2003, and F-2003) Confidential Informant tells Officers that Defendant has a reputation for buying and selling stolen property from his home. Officers set up surveillance outside Defendant's home. Over the course of several hours, they see people enter and exit, but they never see anyone carrying anything into or out of the home. A few hours later, they see a man pull into Defendant's driveway and honk his horn. Defendant exits the home. The driver opens the trunk of his car, lifts the top of a cloth bag, and opens it. Defendant looks inside the bag, shakes his head up and down, takes the bag, and walks towards the front door of his house.

    Officers decide it is time to act. They drive their surveillance vehicle to the end of the driveway and block the driver. They order Defendant and the driver to the ground verbally with their guns drawn and pointed at the men, place handcuffs on both men, *Mirandize* them both, and inform them that they are under arrest. They look in the bag and discover that the bag is full of electronic devices. Through their investigation, the officers determine the electronics were taken during recent home burglaries. Defendant is charged with the felony offense of theft for receiving stolen property. Was the arrest valid? Explain.

    _____

    _____

    _____

    _____

    _____

4. (J-2015, F-2013, and F-2011) When must a defendant appear before the magistrate following an arrest for a felony offense?

    _____

    _____

---

[117] *McVea v. State*, 635 S.W.2d 429 (Tex. App.—San Antonio 1982, pet. ref'd).

_____

_____

_____

5. (F-2015 and J-2010) How long does the magistrate have to make a probable cause finding following a felony arrest? What happens if this finding is not made within that time frame?

_____

_____

_____

_____

_____

6. (J-2014 and J-2009) Must an officer who plans to make an arrest and a search at the same time have both an arrest warrant and a search warrant? Explain.

_____

_____

_____

_____

_____

7. (J-2014 and F-2011) Defendant's arrest warrant is issued in Garza County. He is stopped for a traffic violation in Borden County. Is the officer in Borden County permitted to make an arrest based upon the Garza County arrest warrant? Explain.

_____

_____

_____

_____

_____

8. (J-2012) List three warnings a magistrate must give a defendant following arrest.

_____

_____

_____

_____

_____

9. (J-2011) What is a capias?

_____

_____

_____

_____

_____

10. (F-2009) Deputy is patrolling a roadway when he notices Defendant drive by with his window down and his long hair blowing in the wind. Deputy does not think men should have long hair, and in his experience, long-haired men are nothing but trouble. He stops Defendant. As he approaches the vehicle, he notices a screwdriver in the key ignition, which is a tell-tale sign of a stolen vehicle. He detains Defendant, runs a check on the car, and discovers it is indeed stolen. Prosecutor plans on calling Deputy to testify about what he saw when he approached the vehicle and about everything that happened after that.

What procedural step, if any, can you take to keep Deputy from testifying, and what argument, if any, can you make in order to succeed? Explain.

_____

_____

_____

_____

_____

11. (J-2002) What are the magistrate's duties following Defendant's arrest?

_____

_____

_____

_____

_____

———————————◆———————————

Chapter 2
Search Warrants and
Motions to Suppress Evidence

Introduction to Search Warrants

Most criminal cases begin with an arrest or a search. As a result, this book begins with search and arrest chapters then follows the criminal process in chronological order to its conclusion. The first chapters that address arrest and then search and seizure laws contain the most complex legal concepts. After these chapters, the material gets more procedural and less substantive. Let's begin exploring search and seizure law by examining search warrants.

The Fourth Amendment of the U.S. Constitution states that American citizens have the right "to be secure in their persons, houses, papers, and effects, against unreasonable searches and seizures," and this right "shall not be violated, and no warrants shall issue, but upon probable cause, supported by oath or affirmation, and particularly describing the place to be searched, and the persons or things to be seized."[1]

---

[1] U.S. CONST. amend. IV.

The primary objective of this amendment was to prohibit general warrants, which invaded the colonists' privacy by permitting officers to search for nothing in particular.[2] To this day, the Fourth Amendment dictates how police officers conduct investigations, search persons and property, and seize evidence.

There is a preference in the federal and Texas legal systems for searches with warrants.[3] Texas's Constitution protects against unreasonable searches and seizures and places limits on searches, just like the U.S. Constitution does.[4] Search warrant law implicates both federal and state law, but this chapter will focus on Texas procedure. The chapter will examine the requirements for search warrant affidavits and warrants and their execution as well as how to suppress evidence that was obtained in violation of the law.

———————————◆———————————

The Search Warrant Affidavit

A search warrant is "a written order, issued by a magistrate and directed to a peace officer, commanding him to search for any property or thing and to seize the same and bring it before such magistrate…pursuant to the order."[5] A search warrant consists of three documents: the search warrant affidavit, the search warrant, and the return. In order for the magistrate to find probable cause to authorize the search warrant, he must first know why the search warrant is needed. These facts appear in the search warrant affidavit.

You will see the word affiant appear in the affidavit and in court opinions describing the language of the affidavit. *Affiant* means the person who swears that everything in the affidavit is true, which is usually a law enforcement officer. However, the source of the affiant's facts alleged in the affidavit may come from a victim, a witness, a third party, an accomplice, or a confidential informant.

---

[2] *Hulit v. State*, 982 S.W.2d 431, 436 (Tex. Crim. App. 1998).
[3] *State v. McLain*, 337 S.W.3d 268, 271 (Tex. Crim. App. 2011).
[4] TEX. CONST. art. I, §9.
[5] TEX. CODE CRIM. PROC. ANN. art. 18.01(a) (West 2016).

Requisites of the Sworn Affidavit

While the search warrant permits the search and seizure of evidence of a crime, it is the affidavit that provides the factual basis for probable cause needed to authorize the search warrant. This is what the Code says about the affidavit:

> No search warrant shall issue for any purpose . . . unless sufficient facts are first presented to satisfy the issuing magistrate that probable cause does in fact exist for its issuance. A sworn affidavit setting forth substantial facts establishing probable cause shall be filed in every instance in which a search warrant is provided.[6]

The Texas Court of Criminal Appeals explained what probable cause is in the context of search warrants, as opposed to the arrest context: "Probable cause exists if, under the totality of the circumstances set forth in the affidavit before the magistrate, there is a 'fair probability' that contraband or evidence of a crime will be found in a particular place at the time the warrant is issued."[7] Once the magistrate finds the facts alleged within the affidavit establish probable cause, she signs the search warrant.[8]

Source Credibility

It is not enough that the facts in the affidavit establish probable cause. The source of information in the affidavit, whether it is an officer or a lay person, must be credible. Some search warrant affidavit sources are more credible than others. Police officers, witnesses, victims, or third parties are sources viewed with greater credibility by judges.[9]

The confidential informant (CI), also known as a "snitch," is a common source in some types of cases. Because CIs may be implicated in criminal activity themselves and may receive leniency for turning in others engaged in criminal activity, their motives and their credibility are viewed more skeptically. For CIs who have a successful track record, an officer's statement

---

[6] TEX. CODE CRIM. PROC. ANN. art. 18.01(b) (West 2016).
[7] *State v. Jordan*, 342 S.W.3d 565, 568-69 (Tex. Crim. App. 2011).
[8] TEX. CODE CRIM. PROC. ANN. art. 18.01(b) (West 2016).
[9] *E.g., State v. Anderson*, 917 S.W.2d 92, 96 (Tex. App.—Houston [14th Dist.] 1996, pet. ref'd) (rape victim and police officer who personally observed stolen property in defendant's home while he was searching for evidence of rape were credible sources of information).

in the affidavit that the CI is reliable and has given information that has led to past arrests is sufficient to establish credibility.[10] However, an officer who relies upon information provided by a first-time CI must indicate the informant is credible and must take steps to corroborate the information provided by the CI in order for a magistrate to sign the search warrant.

Here is how an officer conveyed the reliability of a first-time CI in *Bonds v. State*, which resulted in the defendant's conviction for possession with intent to deliver methamphetamine:

> In his supporting affidavit, [Sergeant Jeff] Ashburn described the suspected place and the items to be seized.... His affidavit also described his investigation.... As a commissioned peace officer with the Department of Public Safety for over ten years, the past twenty-six months of which he was assigned to the Narcotics Service, Ashburn stated that he is trained in the investigation of narcotics violations, the handling of witnesses, search warrant preparation, and the investigation of persons who derive substantial income from illegal importation, manufacture, distribution, and sale of illegal controlled substances. Ashburn's investigation began when a credible confidential informant told him in November 2007 that he had seen Bonds in possession of methamphetamine and had also seen methamphetamine in Bonds's home "located at Texas State Highway 59 and Barker Street in Bowie, Montague County, Texas." Ashburn then transported the confidential informant to Bonds's home, which Ashburn identified as "401 Barker Street, Bowie, Montague County, Texas." The confidential informant identified Bonds from a photographic line-up as the person with whom he "conducted a controlled purchase of methamphetamine."

> Ashburn further determined that, according to records maintained by the Texas Department of Public Safety, Bonds listed his address as 401 Barker Street .... Ashburn conducted a criminal-history search revealing Bonds's prior arrest for possession of marijuana and for possession of a penalty-group 1 controlled substance, and multiple arrests for possession of a penalty-group 1 controlled substance.... On [three days], Ashburn conducted garbage searches . . . [which] produced a number of melted glass smoking pipes containing drug residue which tested positive for cocaine and methamphetamine, plastic bags containing methamphetamine and cocaine residue, and a MasterCard application addressed to Bonds at 401 Barker Street .... With the assistance of other officers, Ashburn executed

---

[10] *State v. Duarte*, 389 S.W.3d 349, 357-58 (Tex. Crim. App. 2012).

the warrant and seized methamphetamine, other controlled substances, drug paraphernalia, and United States currency.[11]

Notice that the investigation began with the CI's allegation that Bonds was selling methamphetamine from his home. Sergeant Ashburn corroborated the CI's allegations, conducted his own investigation to ensure Bonds lived at that residence, and made sure there was a fair probability that evidence of the crime would be found when officers executed the warrant.

Ashburn also discussed his own extensive background in narcotics investigations. In a warrant that failed to tout the officer's experience, the Court of Criminal Appeals said the

> [b]est practice is for the affiant expressly to include an officer's experience, background information, and previous associations with contraband so that little is left to inference, and the magistrate has specifically articulated facts to evaluate. Otherwise, the officer/affiant risks denial of his warrant, suppression of evidence at trial, or reversal on appeal because the warrant lacks a substantial basis.[12]

Another possible affidavit source is the anonymous caller, who, like the first-time CI, lacks credibility to establish probable cause without corroboration.[13] Imagine that you are an officer who is dispatched to a country road where an anonymous 911 caller stated the driver of a tan pickup truck with license plate number KCR-4567 is driving while intoxicated. The caller suspects the driver is drunk because the driver is swerving all over the road. As an officer, you have no idea whether this is true, but you have an obligation to investigate, detect, and prevent criminal activity. You drive to the location, find the truck, wait for the driver to commit a traffic violation, activate your siren and lights once the driver does, stop the truck, detain the driver, perform field sobriety tests, and make your own determination as to whether the driver is intoxicated. Assume you want to obtain a search warrant to obtain a blood sample because the driver refuses to consent to a breath test. If you were to rely upon the 911 caller's assertions alone, the magistrate would refuse to sign the warrant, but if you were to explain that the 911 caller merely alerted the 911 dispatcher that there was a problem and

---

[11] 403 S.W.3d 867, 870 (Tex. Crim. App. 2013).
[12] *Davis v. State*, 202 S.W.3d 149, 157–58 (Tex. Crim. App. 2006).
[13] *Glass v. State*, 681 S.W.2d 599, 601 (Tex. Crim. App. 1984).

your investigation, detailed step-by-step in the search warrant affidavit, corroborated what the 911 caller suspected, the magistrate may sign it.[14]

In the above scenario, the 911 caller's credibility can be bolstered through facts verifying or corroborating what the source alleges to be true. Under Texas law, an affidavit for a search warrant based upon hearsay must satisfy the two-prong test that the magistrate is informed of the underlying circumstances which render the information reliable and that he is informed of specific factual allegations which render the source of the information reliable.[15]

Credibility is critical to the search warrant affidavit because the magistrate must have probable cause to authorize the warrant and must trust that the information alleged in the search warrant affidavit is true. No magistrate wants to sign a warrant that is based on false information or an untrustworthy source.

The Search Warrant

The affidavit provides the facts used to convince the magistrate there is probable cause to search and seize evidence. The search warrant, on the other hand, is the legal order directing law enforcement to conduct the search.[16] These two documents serve two distinct purposes: the affidavit is written to describe probable cause for the magistrate, whereas the search warrant is a legal document that authorizes officers to search and seize evidence. Because of their different purposes and contents, the affidavit and the search warrant have different legal requirements.

According to the Code, search warrants must include:

1. Language that the warrant is issued in "The State of Texas;"
2. A clear description of the thing to be seized and the place, the person, or the thing to be searched;

---

[14] It is also important to note that courts will afford greater credibility to citizen-informants, as opposed to the typical CI. *State v. Duarte*, 389 S.W.3d 349, 355-57 (Tex. Crim. App. 2012).
[15] *Eisenhauer v. State*, 684 S.W.2d 782, 785 (Tex. App.—Houston [1st Dist.] 1984), *rev'd on other grounds*, 754 S.W.2d 159 (Tex. Crim. App. 1988).
[16] TEX. CODE CRIM. PROC. ANN. art. 18.01(a) (West 2016).

3. A command to any peace officer acting within that jurisdiction to
    search the named place, person, or thing; and

4. The magistrate's signature and date.[17]

Particularity Requirement

The second item on the previous list requires that the search warrant
contain a clear description of the place to be searched and the thing to be
seized. Article I, Section 9 of the Texas Constitution echoes this requirement
by saying, "no warrant to search any place, or to seize any person or thing,
shall issue without describing them as near as may be." This is known as the
particularity requirement. General descriptions will not suffice. The Code states
that only "specifically described property or items may be seized."[18]

What would happen if search warrants were not detailed in their
descriptions of the places to be searched or the things to be seized? They
would become general warrants—the type of warrants the Framers sought to
prohibit when they wrote the Fourth Amendment. Consider a search warrant
a legal intrusion— a burglary or a forced entry by law enforcement officers—
of a home, a car, or a person. To protect the safety of officers and the safety
and privacy of the public, officers must carefully and accurately describe the
person, the place, or the thing to be searched and the evidence to be seized.

Officers sometimes fail to particularly describe the place to be searched
or the items to be seized, or they may search for items or in places not
included in the scope of the search warrant. The following case discusses the
particularity requirement in this context.

Gwin Long v. State
132 S.W.3d 443
(Tex. Crim. App. 2004)

Sgt. Scott Wilson, an undercover officer for the Texas Attorney General's
Special Crimes Unit conducted an investigation into illegal gambling
operations at appellant's business establishment, "Train's," which is located
in a rural area of Henderson County. Sgt. Wilson went to "Train's" one
evening to play eight-liner video gambling devices. He spoke with appellant,

---

[17] TEX. CODE CRIM. PROC. ANN. art. 18.04 (West 2016).
[18] TEX. CODE CRIM. PROC. ANN. art. 18.01(d) (West 2016).

who told him that successful players were no longer rewarded with Wal-Mart gift certificates, but they were entered into a weekly contest to win a dinner for two and $50.00 cash. Sgt. Wilson returned on several other days, continued playing the eight-liners, and saw others doing so as well.

Based upon his investigation, Sgt. Wilson drafted a lengthy and thorough affidavit and search warrant which authorized a search of the "Train's" premises as well as appellant's arrest. Other police officers executed this warrant, and they searched not only the business establishment of "Train's," but also another train car located in the same vicinity, and appellant's home which was a nearby red caboose. Neither of these structures was mentioned in the warrant or affidavit. The facts establishing probable cause to believe that appellant was operating a gambling business, owned gambling paraphernalia, and kept records of gambling activity specified activity only at the silver colored passenger train car. When they searched appellant's home, officers seized cash, bank records, Wal-Mart gift certificates, and the keys to the eight-liner machines.

At trial, appellant objected to the admission of any items seized from her home because the search warrant authorized a search only of "Train's." She claimed that the search of her home without either a warrant or exigent circumstances violated her Fourth Amendment rights. ... [T]he trial court allowed the admission of all items taken from appellant's home.... And [t]he jury convicted appellant of five gambling offenses....

One of the specific commands of the Fourth Amendment is that no warrant shall issue except one "particularly describing the place to be searched." The present warrant and affidavit, taken together, provide a remarkably specific description of the place to be searched. The affidavit begins with this description:

> THERE IS IN ... HENDERSON COUNTY, TEXAS, A SUSPECTED PLACE AND PREMISES DESCRIBED AND LOCATED AS FOLLOWS:

> An unnamed business establishment known locally as Train's is located at 1075 Pritchett Lane, Seven Points, Henderson County, Texas. The structure is a silver in color passenger train car. The passenger train car is located north, 8/10 of a mile from State Highway 334 on the west side of Pritchett Lane, Seven Points, Henderson County, Texas. In front of this silver in color passenger train car is a black mail box located on the west side of Pritchett Lane with the numbers "1075". This is the only silver in color

passenger train car located on Pritchett Lane 8/10 of a mile north of State Highway 334, Seven Points, Henderson County, Texas.

From this superb description, we can go to Henderson County and find that silver passenger train car. We also know that there is only one such train car. It is silver, it is a passenger car, and it is a business. It is not red, it is not a caboose, and it is not a home. In front of this solitary silver passenger train car business establishment is a black mail box with the numbers "1075" written on it. Finding that mail box will help us find the silver passenger car right behind it.

Are we now to conclude that the affiant, having set out such an exemplary description of the specific property to be searched, did not mean what he said? Instead, was he really seeking a warrant to search any and all structures near the described business, including appellant's home? The affiant officer testified at trial that he knew the red caboose was appellant's home, so if he had probable cause to search her separate home as well as her business establishment, why did he not say so? Then the neutral magistrate could have decided whether there was probable cause to believe that appellant kept gambling devices, paraphernalia and business records in her home as well as at the nearby business. To conclude that this description of the specific property to be searched includes, *sub silentio*, the right to search appellant's home subverts the objectives of the Fourth Amendment's Particularity Clause.

..."A search made under authority of a search warrant may extend to the entire area covered by the warrant's description." And, when courts examine the description of the place to be searched to determine the warrant's scope, they follow a common sense and practical approach, not a[n] ... overly technical one.

... [H]aving described the business establishment known as Train's with such detail and thoroughness, the officers clearly had a right to search every nook and cranny of that business establishment—the silver passenger-train car with the "open" sign above the door. Appellant's home, however, was not within that business area.

As the court of appeals in this case correctly noted, cases from all jurisdictions have ...held that if a search warrant/affidavit authorizes the search of a residence and its "premises," then the officers may generally search outlying structures within the curtilage of that residence. Similarly, a search warrant/affidavit that authorizes the search of a specific business would include the search of nearby rooms or outlying structures, such as storage sheds, garages, or garbage containers that would naturally serve some function for that business.

But private homes and public businesses are not fungible items for purposes of Fourth Amendment protection. Under the Fourth Amendment, appellant's humble little red caboose is her home; it is sacrosanct, and it is as worthy of full constitutional protection as is the grandest castle owned by the richest lord of the land. "'At the very core' of the Fourth Amendment 'stands the right of a man to retreat into his own home and there be free from unreasonable governmental intrusion.'" [19] Government intrusion into one's home is presumptively unreasonable under the Fourth Amendment unless the officers have a warrant to enter that home. A warrant to enter a nearby business establishment which is open to the public is not an "Open Sesame" for the home. United States Supreme Court Justice Robert Jackson eloquently articulated this constitutional position more than fifty years ago:

> Crime, even in the privacy of one's own quarters, is, of course, of grave concern to society, and the law allows such crime to be reached on proper showing. The right of officers to thrust themselves into a home is also a grave concern, not only to the individual but to a society which chooses to dwell in reasonable security and freedom from surveillance. When the right of privacy must reasonably yield to the right of search is, as a rule, to be decided by a judicial officer, not by a policeman or government enforcement agent.[20]

Before we hold that a search warrant for an alleged gambling business open to the public implicitly authorizes the search of the business owner's separate, private home, we should be certain that our understanding of the federal constitution is correct.

Neither the parties nor the court of appeals have cited a single case in which a reviewing court has held that the curtilage of a specifically described business enterprise includes the entirely distinct and separate structure of the home of that business owner. In this case, the red-caboose home is located approximately thirty feet from the silver-passenger-car business and is "blocked" by a tree. Furthermore, the business, as a gambling establishment, is obviously and explicitly "open" to the public; the red-caboose home is not.

---

[19] *Kyllo v. United States*, 533 U.S. 27, 31 (2001).
[20] *Johnson v. United States*, 333 U.S. 10, 14 (1948).

Furthermore, there is no evidence that appellant invited business customers into the red caboose for business purposes or that her home was otherwise accessible to those who visited the business. Except for mere physical proximity, there is no evidence in this record to suggest that the red-caboose home was an outbuilding within the curtilage of the silver-passenger-car business.

…Furthermore, we believe that a reasonable magistrate or officer, reading the description of "Train's" in the present search warrant/affidavit in a common-sense, practical manner, could not conclude that the warrant also authorized a search of appellant's red caboose home.

The State also argues that the officers could have reasonably believed, when they first arrived, that the red caboose really was a part of the "Train's" business enterprise and not appellant's home. There is, however, no evidence in the record that they did make this honest mistake. Further, such an initial mistake would not permit them to continue searching through the red caboose once they discovered that they had crossed over the threshold of a private home.

It was certainly reasonable for the affiant to conclude that business records relating to a gambling operation would "usually" be located "in an office area(s) of these businesses," or, perhaps on the person of the business owner. But he said nothing about the possibility or probability of finding such items in the business owner's home.

In sum, the affiant set out a great deal of information about the types of gambling machines and devices used in the public premises of "Train's" and his use of those public premises. No reasonable person reading this long, logical, and carefully drafted affidavit would conclude that appellant had a home nearby or that the affiant had probable cause to believe that she used her home as part of the business enterprise conducted at "Train's."

The Fourth Amendment Warrant Clause limits its authorization to the specific areas and things for which there is probable cause to search, thereby ensuring that:

> the search will be carefully tailored to its justifications, and will not take on the character of the wide-ranging exploratory searches the Framers intended to prohibit. Thus, the scope of a lawful search is "defined by the object of the search and the places in which there is probable cause to believe that it may be found. Just as probable cause to believe that a stolen lawnmower may be found in a garage will not support a warrant to search

an upstairs bedroom, probable cause to believe that undocumented aliens are being transported in a van will not justify a warrantless search of a suitcase."[21]

In the present case, there is no suggestion (much less facts amounting to probable cause) in the warrant or the affidavit that any of the gambling machines, paraphernalia, or business records that the officers were authorized to seize, would be found in appellant's home.

…We therefore reverse the [lower court's] decision and remand the case … for further proceedings consistent with this opinion.

———————◆———————

Notes and Questions

1. The affidavit must establish "a sufficient nexus between criminal activity, the things to be seized, and the place to be searched."[22] In the above case, the affiant created a nexus between the gambling business records and the business, but there was no nexus between the business records and the defendant's home set out in the affidavit that the magistrate signed. As a result, not only was Ms. Long's home not mentioned in the search warrant as the place to be searched, but there was no nexus between the things to be seized and Ms. Long's home.

2. One of the footnotes in the *Long* cases stated, "[W]hen the affidavit is attached to the warrant, these documents should be considered together as defining the place to be searched, but the description in the affidavit controls over the language in the warrant itself."[23]

———————◆———————

Items to Be Seized

A search warrant does not authorize general exploratory searches; in other words, officers may not obtain a warrant to search for nothing in particular. The Code restricts what officers may search for and seize pursuant

---

[21] *Maryland v. Garrison*, 480 U.S. 79, 84-85 (1987) (quoting *United States v. Ross*, 456 U.S. 798, 824 (1982)).
[22] *Bonds v. State*, 403 S.W.3d 867, 873 (Tex. Crim. App. 2013).
[23] *Long v. State*, 132 S.W.3d 443, 446 n. 11 (Tex. Crim. App. 2004).

to a search warrant. The Code permits officers to seize the following items only: contraband or illegal goods, fruits of crime or things obtained from the crime, instrumentalities or things used to commit a crime, people through arrest, and mere evidence.[24]

Mere evidence refers to "property or items, except the personal writings by the accused, constituting evidence of an offense or constituting evidence tending to show that a particular person committed an offense."[25] Officers may seize mere evidence when it is reasonably related to the offense officers are investigating.[26]

Warrants for mere evidence are considered *evidentiary warrants*. Because they have a tendency to be broader and vague, they resemble the dreaded general warrant the Fourth Amendment sought to prevent. For this reason, the legislature has created more stringent requirements to obtain them:[27]

1. A particular crime has been committed;
2. The property described in the warrant constitutes evidence the crime was committed; and
3. The property officers want to seize is located on the person, the place, or the thing to be searched.[28]

Only the specific items listed in an evidentiary search warrant may be seized.[29] This safeguard prevents an evidentiary search warrant from becoming a general warrant. The type of judge who can sign an evidentiary warrant is more restricted, as is the process for obtaining a subsequent evidentiary warrant.[30] In these ways, evidentiary search warrants for mere evidence are treated differently than search warrants that issue for contraband and fruits or instrumentalities of crime, for example.

Typographical Errors in the Warrant

As is possible with any typed document, search warrants may contain typographical errors. A warrant writer may inadvertently type the wrong date

---

[24] TEX. CODE CRIM. PROC. ANN. art. 18.02(a) (West 2016).
[25] TEX. CODE CRIM. PROC. ANN. art. 18.01(a)(10) (West 2016).
[26] *Joseph v. State*, 807 S.W.2d 303, 307 (Tex. Crim. App. 1991).
[27] *See generally* TEX. CODE CRIM. PROC. ANN. art. 18.01 (West 2016).
[28] TEX. CODE CRIM. PROC. ANN. art. 18.01(c) (West 2016).
[29] TEX. CODE CRIM. PROC. ANN. art. 18.01(d) (West 2016).
[30] TEX. CODE CRIM. PROC. ANN. art. 18.02(c)-(d) (West 2016).

or address while preparing the warrant. When this happens, defense counsel may raise a legal challenge that seeks to invalidate the warrant. Typically, courts look behind the warrant to examine the error and why it happened. Technical discrepancies in dates or times do not automatically invalidate a search warrant.[31] When it comes to descriptions of the place to be searched, appellate courts typically follow these rules:

> [T]echnical discrepancies in the descriptive portions of a search warrant will not automatically vitiate the warrant's validity. For many years, the Texas test for the sufficiency of the description [of a place to be searched] was whether the officer executing the warrant could, with reasonable effort, locate the premises and distinguish it from others in the community. While this continues as an element of search warrant review, the test has been fleshed out by later opinions addressing the goals of the warrant requirements. The first of these is to insure an adequate showing of probable cause. The second is to protect the privacy of innocent parties from mistaken execution of a defective warrant. The present constitutional test in federal court is the same. If the warrant is sufficient to enable the executing officer to locate and identify the premises intended to be searched, and the deficiencies in the description do not give rise to a reasonable probability that mistaken execution will take place at an unintended site, then the warrant is valid.[32]

Courts are generally gracious about typographical mistakes. These mistakes may occur in the street address of a property (15243 Broadway versus the real address of 12543 Broadway) or in the date the warrant was signed (January 1, 2015, versus the actual date of January 1, 2016), but the State must call witnesses to testify in a suppression hearing about the mistake; when the State fails to explain the error is merely typographical, the warrant may be deemed invalid.[33]

---

[31] *Green v. State*, 799 S.W.2d 756, 759 (Tex. Crim. App. 1990).

[32] *Olivas v. State*, 631 S.W.2d 553, 555-56 (Tex. App.—El Paso 1982, no pet.) (citations omitted).

[33] *E.g., Meeks v. State*, 851 S.W.2d 373, 377-78 (Tex. App.—Houston [1st Dist.] 1993, pet. ref'd) (because no testimony was proffered to explain a four-month gap between the date the affidavit was sworn and the date the search warrant was signed, evidence seized pursuant to that warrant should have been suppressed).

Executing the Warrant

Once a magistrate finds probable cause, it is up to the officers to execute or carry out the search pursuant to the warrant. Officers must comply with several Code-specific guidelines when executing warrants.

First, officers are required to execute warrants without delay after they are signed by the magistrate.[34] Practically speaking, the "life span of a search warrant"[35] is usually three days from the time it issues, not including the day of its issuance and the day of its execution.[36] If officers fail to search the premises in this limited time frame, they risk having the warrant declared invalid, the search unreasonable, and the seized evidence suppressed.[37] Why is there such a strict time line?

> In order to issue a warrant, a magistrate is required "to determine (1) that it is now probable that (2) contraband . . . will be on the described premises (3) when the warrant is executed." . . . A magistrate must be able to ascertain from the affidavit the closeness of time of the event that is the basis for probable cause sufficient to issue the warrant based on an independent judgment of probable cause. The facts attested to in the affidavit must be "so closely related to the time of the iss[uance] of the warrant as to justify a finding of probable cause at that time."[38]

In some instances, the magistrate may order officers to execute a warrant in a shorter time frame. Special search warrants (*e.g.*, warrants for wire taps or DNA specimens) may have longer life spans from the date they are signed.[39] Regardless, officers must carefully comply with the statutory or specially designated time frame.

Second, when officers attempt to execute a search warrant, they should announce their presence and give residents an opportunity to open the

---

[34] TEX. CODE CRIM. PROC. ANN. art. 18.06 (West 2016).

[35] *Williams v. State*, 965 S.W.2d 506, 507 (Tex. Crim. App. 1998).

[36] TEX. CODE CRIM. PROC. ANN. art. 18.06 and 18.07(a) (West 2016).

[37] *Green v. State*, 799 S.W.2d 756, 759 (Tex. Crim. App. 1990) ("When a search warrant is not executed within the time period provided by [the Code] . . . it [has no] . . . official force or effect. It follows that any search whose legality depends on the warrant is unauthorized.").

[38] *Jones v. State*, 338 S.W.3d 725, 736 (Tex. App.—Houston [1st Dist.] 2011), *aff'd*, 364 S.W.3d 854 (Tex. Crim. App. 2012) (citations omitted).

[39] TEX. CODE CRIM. PROC. ANN. art. 18.07(a)(1)-(2) (West 2016).

door.[40] This is known as the "knock-and-announce" rule. However, officers are not required to knock and announce when a threat of physical violence exists, their presence is already known to the occupants, evidence will be destroyed, or the announcement would be futile.[41] Furthermore, the rule can be waived by a magistrate who is persuaded entry is dangerous, must be accomplished by surprise, or exigent circumstances are involved.[42] The rule is not required if officers gain entry through deception or ruse (*e.g.*, they pose as deliverymen).[43] Even when officers fail to knock and announce their presence and their entry does not fit under any of the above exceptions, Texas courts have not found the violation necessitates suppression of the evidence seized.[44] This is because Texas courts fail to see a but-for causation between the officers' unlawful entry and the seizure of evidence that would have been permissibly seized through a legally valid search warrant.[45]

Third, officers must show the warrant to the owner of the premises at the time they execute the search.[46] If the owner is not there, officers may show the warrant to someone who is in possession of the premises; if there is no one on the premises, officers are required to leave a copy of the warrant behind to notify the owner and residents of the search.[47]

Fourth, recall that there are three parts to the warrant: the affidavit, the search warrant itself, and what is referred to as the inventory or return.[48] Officers are required to create a written inventory of the property they seized, sign the inventory, and provide a copy of the inventory to the owner.[49] If the

---

[40] *State v. Callaghan*, 222 S.W.3d 610, 612 (Tex. App.—Houston [14th Dist.] 2007, pet. ref'd); TEX. PENAL CODE ANN. §9.51(a)(2) (West 2011).
[41] *Burton v. State*, 339 S.W.3d 349, 362-63 (Tex. App.—Texarkana 2011, no pet.).
[42] *Id.*
[43] *Martinez v. State*, 220 S.W.3d 183, 189 (Tex. App.—Austin 2007, no pet.).
[44] *State v. Callaghan*, 222 S.W.3d 610, 614 (Tex. App.—Houston [14th Dist.] 2007, pet. ref'd).
[45] *Id.*
[46] TEX. CODE CRIM. PROC. ANN. art. 18.06(b) (West 2016).
[47] *Id.*
[48] *E.g., Gonzales v. State*, 743 S.W.2d 718, 719 (Tex. App.—Houston [14th Dist.] 1987, pet. ref'd) ("Photocopies of the affidavit for the search warrant, the search warrant and the return are in the record before us."); *Turner v. State*, 886 S.W.2d 859, 865 (Tex. App.—Beaumont 1994, pet. ref'd) ("With regard to the instant case, art. 18.06 does not require that the affidavit be served upon the owner of the premises to be searched, only the warrant and the written inventory.").
[49] TEX. CODE CRIM. PROC. ANN. art. 18.06(b) (West 2016).

owner is not present, officers can leave the inventory at the place they searched.[50] An officer must then take possession of the seized property and a copy of the inventory and "return" them, along with the original affidavit and search warrant, to the magistrate.[51]

When officers fail to execute the search warrant in a timely fashion, the warrant becomes invalid.[52] However, violations of most of the other procedures above do not generally render the search warrant void unless a defendant can establish prejudice.[53] Consider the following excerpt in a case where the officers failed to serve the defendant with a copy of the warrant at the time of the search:

> The two objectives of the law concerning search warrants are to insure that there is adequate probable cause to search and to prevent a mistake in the execution of the warrant against an innocent third party. These objectives are not furthered by a rigid application of the rules concerning warrants, thus we review technical discrepancies with a judicious eye for the procedural aspects surrounding issuance and execution of the warrant. In accordance with this general rule, it has been held that the failure of a police officer to deliver a copy of the search warrant to the defendant does not require suppression of the seized evidence absent a showing of prejudice. [Defendant] Green does not argue that the warrant was not issued before the search, nor does he suggest in this situation how the officer's failure to give him a copy of the warrant at the time of the search caused prejudice. In light of the circumstances surrounding the creation and execution of this search warrant, we find that the State's failure to provide a copy of the warrant at the time of the search is harmless error.[54]

———————————— ◆ ————————————

---

[50] *Id.*

[51] Tex. Code Crim. Proc. Ann. art. 18.10 (West 2016).

[52] *Green v. State*, 799 S.W.2d 756, 759 (Tex. Crim. App. 1990) ("When a search warrant is not executed within the time period provided by [the Code] . . . it [has no] . . . official force or effect. It follows that any search whose legality depends on the warrant is unauthorized.").

[53] *Pecina v. State*, 516 S.W.2d 401, 404 (Tex. Crim. App. 1974).

[54] *Green v. State*, 880 S.W.2d 198, 201 (Tex. App.—Texarkana 1994, no pet.).

Challenging the Search Warrant

Warrant errors may not be discovered until after the defendant has been charged with a crime and defense counsel has had time to examine the warrant. Perhaps the warrant was executed six days after it was signed by the magistrate, or the affidavit does not contain enough information to establish probable cause. If the warrant is deemed invalid by the trial judge, the evidence seized pursuant to that warrant may be suppressed at trial.

Burden of Proof

The defendant has the initial burden of producing evidence that rebuts the presumption that the police conduct was proper.[55] Where a search warrant is involved, the defendant must allege there was no warrant, which makes the search per se unreasonable, or that the warrant was invalid. Only when the defendant rebuts the presumption, alleges no warrant, or alleges a problem with the warrant does the burden shift to the State to prove the search or seizure was legally permissible.[56] The next case discusses the burden shifting involved when the defendant challenges the search.

State v. David Leonard Wood
828 S.W.2d 471
(Tex. App.—El Paso 1992, no pet.)

… David Leonard Wood was indicted for the offense of capital murder, for which the State seeks the death penalty. Specifically, the Defendant was indicted for causing the death of six women, between May and August 1987. The indictment alleges that one victim was stabbed with a sharp instrument, while the remaining five victims met their death [in an unknown way].

…[T]he State sought and obtained two identical search warrants to search a specific beige 1986 Nissan pickup truck which was under the control of the Defendant. The pertinent portions of the evidentiary search warrants read as follows:

3. It is the belief of Affiant that [Wood abducted, raped, and killed

---

[55] *State v. Robinson*, 334 S.W.3d 776, 778-79 (Tex. Crim. App. 2011).
[56] *Amador v. State*, 221 S.W.3d 666, 672-73 (Tex. Crim. App. 2007); *Illinois v. Gates*, 462 U.S. 213, 228-29 (1983).

G___ G___ and raped J___ B___].

4. There is located in the suspected vehicle, items concealed and kept constituting evidence of said offenses … described as the following: Clothing belonging to J___ B___ , cigarette butts, fingerprints, ligatures, and [a] knife belonging to David Wood.

The evidentiary search warrants were executed and the vehicle in question searched …. During such search of Defendant's vehicle, the following described property was found and seized:

One (1) pair men's black work boots with hair evidence
One checkered shirt with hair evidence
One small brush
One blue card
One purple colored doll
Three plastic baggies with vacuumed samples from 1986 NISSAN
One wooden cain [sic]

… Defendant filed a Motion to Suppress, seeking to exclude "fiber evidence" which purportedly linked the Defendant to the death of the six women named in the indictment. The Defendant did not attack the validity of the evidentiary search warrant; rather, he attacked the legality and reasonableness of the search by asserting violations of the Fourth Amendment of the United States Constitution and Article I, Section 9 of the Texas Constitution. Specifically, the Defendant alleged that the search exceeded the scope of the evidentiary search warrants in that the fiber evidence was not specifically listed in the warrants.

[T]he [trial court] sustained Defendant's Motion to Suppress and ordered that the evidence seized from the Defendant's 1986 beige Nissan pickup truck pursuant to the search warrants be suppressed. …

The State, in its brief, asserts that it did not need to present any evidence other than the warrants, and further, that the burden of proof lies with the Defendant to show that the items seized were outside the scope of the evidentiary search warrant. Moreover, the State, again in its brief, concedes that all the evidence seized pursuant to the execution of the evidentiary search warrant should be excluded, save and except the three plastic baggies with vacuumed samples from the Defendant's vehicle. The State, for the first time on appeal, maintains that the vacuumings were clearly a practical method of seeking cigarette butts and ligatures.

III. The Burden of Proof Applicable in Motions to Suppress Physical Evidence

When a defendant seeks to suppress evidence on the basis of a Fourth Amendment violation, the Court of Criminal Appeals has placed the burden of proof initially upon the defendant. ...As the movant ..., a defendant must produce evidence that defeats the presumption of proper police conduct and therefore shifts the burden of proof to the State. ...A defendant meets his initial burden of proof by establishing that a search or seizure occurred without a warrant. ...

In the instant case, the Defendant, and not the State, established the existence of a search and seizure. The Defendant, in its introduction of the two evidentiary search warrants in evidence, established that none of the items seized, in particular the fiber evidence, were sought by the evidentiary search warrants. Consequently, all the items seized were, in effect, seized without a valid warrant. As noted, the State concedes that all the evidence seized should be excluded, save and except the three plastic baggies with vacuumed samples from the Defendant's vehicle.

Once a defendant has established (1) that a search or seizure occurred and (2) that no warrant was obtained, the burden of proof shifts to the State. We find that by the introduction of the two evidentiary search warrants, each of which on its face reveals the seizure of items not specified in the evidentiary search warrants, that the Defendant met [his] initial burden. The burden of proof then shifted to the State to produce evidence of a warrant to support the seizure of the three plastic baggies. The State failed to produce a warrant to support such a seizure. Had the State produced evidence of a warrant to support the seizure of the three plastic baggies, the burden of proof would have shifted back to the defendant to show the invalidity of any such warrant. ...Insofar as the State failed to produce evidence of a warrant for the seizure of the three plastic baggies, it was incumbent upon the State to prove the reasonableness of the search or seizure. ...As noted above, the State for the first time on appeal, maintains that the vacuumings were clearly a practical method of seeking cigarette butts and ligatures; yet, the State failed to produce evidence that the items were properly seized pursuant to one of the many exceptions to the warrant requirement, or in the alternative, evidence as to the reasonableness of the search and seizure of the three plastic baggies or the contents thereof.

We find that the State, by its failure to introduce any evidence, failed to meet its burden of proof at the hearing on the Defendant's Motion to Suppress Evidence that the three plastic baggies were not obtained in violation of the Fourth Amendment, the Texas Constitution and other statutory provisions. ... Accordingly, we affirm the ruling of the trial court.

———————◆———————

Notes and Questions

1. Why do you suppose of all the items seized, the only piece of evidence the defendant contested at trial and on appeal was the fiber evidence?

2. Police officers obtained an evidentiary search warrant in the *Wood* case. Remember that when officers are executing this type of search warrant, they are limited to seizing only the items listed on the warrant. This is why the El Paso Court of Appeals deemed the seizure warrantless even though there was a search warrant in this case.

3. How did the State fail to meet its burden? If the State does fail, what is the consequence?

———————◆———————

Judicial Review of Search Warrants

When a defendant contests a search warrant's validity, trial and appellate courts are called upon to review the warrant. Judicial review requires the court to examine the warrant using the following legal concepts.

Totality of the Circumstances and the Four Corners Rule

When a defendant raises a challenge to the search warrant, the reviewing court looks at the totality of the circumstances. Consider what the Amarillo Court of Appeals said about the test and its limitations:

> [W]hether the facts in the affidavit are adequate to establish probable cause depends on the totality of the circumstances. And, they establish such cause when the totality of those circumstances justifies a conclusion that the object of the search is probably on the premises. Yet, one cannot forget that the totality of the circumstances to which we allude must appear in the

affidavit. This is so because the four corners of the affidavit comprise the field upon which we work.[57]

Thus, while a reviewing court looks at the totality of the circumstances to assess probable cause, it is limited to the facts alleged in the "four corners" of the search warrant affidavit. The four corners rule prohibits either party from bringing forth extraneous information for the judge to consider when it is not contained within the search warrant affidavit.

Franks *Hearing*

Normally, the defendant is not allowed to attack the accuracy of the statements contained within the affidavit or search warrant. Just as the State is prohibited from shoring up missing facts in a search warrant affidavit that are not contained within the four corners of the affidavit, a defendant may not call witnesses to rebut the facts alleged in an affidavit. There is a limited exception to the four corners rule when it comes to facial attacks by the defendant: where the affiant made material, knowing misrepresentations in the affidavit. When a defendant makes such an allegation, he is entitled to a *Franks* hearing, named after the well-known federal case, *Franks v. Delaware*, 438 U.S. 154 (1978).

In a *Franks* hearing, the defendant must prove by a preponderance of the evidence (1) the affiant made at least one false statement in the search warrant affidavit; (2) the false statement was made intentionally, knowingly, or with reckless disregard for the truth; and (3) the false statement was material.[58] In other words, but for the false statement, the warrant would lack probable cause.[59] This is a heavy burden. As a result, it is rare that defendants are able to prove the officer made intentional or reckless false statements about a material fact.

In many cases where a *Franks* hearing is held, the trial court finds that the mistakes, if any, in the affidavit are not material misrepresentations but accidents or unintentional mistakes. For example, in *Wise*, the officer said "several pills of an unknown substance" were contraband in the place to be searched, when those pills later turned out to be over-the-counter allergy

---

[57] *Cardona v. State*, 134 S.W.3d 854, 858 (Tex. App.—Amarillo 2004, pet. ref'd).
[58] *Wise v. State*, 223 S.W.3d 548, 555 (Tex. App.—Amarillo 2007, pet. ref'd).
[59] *Id.*

pills.[60] The officer testified at the *Franks* hearing that he relied on another officer's hearsay statement, was in a hurry to draft the search warrant before evidence could be destroyed, and did not have time to verify whether the pills were contraband.[61] The Court found his testimony credible.[62] Most *Franks* hearings end this way.

The policy reasons for this rule, however, are obvious. Magistrates must depend on the veracity of the affiant and the credibility of the sources of information contained within the affidavit. If an officer is lying about material facts, withholding information, or stretching the truth, the affiant's credibility is damaged, and the probable cause statement is suspect. In the rare case when a defendant is successful in proving the three *Franks* criteria, the warrant is rendered legally invalid, and the fruits of the search are deemed inadmissible.[63]

◆

Cell Phone Search Warrants

Most people have an expectation of privacy in the search data contained within their phone. However, the law related to searches of cell phones has been slow to catch up to the pace of technology. Both federal and Texas courts have recognized the wealth of information stored on cell phones and the expectation of privacy that the owner has in that information.

Recently, the Court of Criminal Appeals rejected the "argument that a modern-day cell phone is like a pair of pants or a bag of groceries, for which a person loses all privacy protection once it is checked into a jail property room."[64] Citing "the incredible amount of personal information stored and accessible on a cell phone," the Court recognized that a person has a legitimate expectation of privacy in a cell phone, and this expectation is one society is prepared to recognize.[65] (These expectations will be discussed in the next section of the chapter in more detail.) Likewise, the U.S. Supreme Court held that while officers are permitted to examine the outside of a

---

[60] *Id.* at 557.
[61] *Id.*
[62] *Id.*
[63] *Id.*
[64] *State v. Granville*, 423 S.W.3d 399, 402 (Tex. Crim. App. 2014).
[65] *Id.* at 405-08, 417.

phone, they are not free to examine the contents or data held within the device absent a search warrant.[66] The Supreme Court recognized, however, that warrantless searches may be permissible if there are exigent circumstances.[67]

In 2015, the Texas legislature added a provision to the Code that specifically prohibits police officers from searching a person's cell phone or other wireless communication device without obtaining a warrant.[68] There are a few, limited exceptions: (1) the owner consents to the search; (2) the phone has been reported stolen by the owner; (3) the officer reasonably believes it is in the hands of a fugitive who committed a felony, or there "exists an immediate life-threatening situation" that involves hostages or the threat of death or serious bodily injury.[69] These exceptions are very narrow. In most instances, officers are legally required to get a search warrant to examine the contents of the phone.

----◆----

Introduction to Evidence Suppression

When evidence of a crime or a person—through detention or arrest—is seized, the defendant may challenge the lawfulness of that seizure. If that seizure is deemed unlawful, the evidence may be suppressed or kept out at trial. Moreover, if the seizure led officers to other admissible evidence of the crime, that evidence may be viewed as tainted and likewise inadmissible. When a court suppresses evidence the State needs to prove the elements of a crime, the prosecutor may be unable to prove the case beyond a reasonable doubt and, therefore, may be forced to dismiss it. For these reasons, defendants frequently file motions to suppress evidence. This portion of the chapter will examine fundamental search and seizure concepts that lead to the suppression of evidence, the Texas exclusionary rule, exceptions to the rule, motions to suppress evidence, and appeals of motions to suppress evidence.

----◆----

[66] *Riley v. California*, 134 S. Ct. 2473, 2485-92 (2014).
[67] *Id.* at 2094.
[68] TEX. CODE CRIM. PROC. ANN. art. 18.0215 (West 2016).
[69] *Id.*

Core Suppression Concepts

In order to understand motions to suppress evidence, you must first understand several core concepts: standing, "fruit of the poisonous tree," and scope of search. The topics in this section will help you better understand the subjects that follow and motions to suppress evidence.

———————————◆———————————

Standing

At the core of search and seizure law is the issue of privacy. Each of us has expectations that our places and our things will be kept secure and private from unlawful government intrusion. You learned about standing to sue in the civil context in your first-year law school courses. Standing plays a role in criminal cases as well. Standing in the criminal procedure context starts with expectations of privacy or an examination of whether officers have trespassed upon a person's personal property rights.[70]

To challenge a search under the privacy theory, the defendant must have a legally protected expectation of privacy. There are two questions courts ask to establish whether this expectation of privacy exists. First, did the defendant have a subjective expectation of privacy in the searched place?[71] Second, was the defendant's expectation one society is willing to recognize as reasonable under the circumstances?[72] The first question is analyzed from a subjective standpoint, whereas the second question is examined from an objective perspective.

When it comes to the subjective expectation of privacy, courts typically find there is a lesser expectation of privacy when the place searched does not belong to the defendant, or the defendant was not in exclusive possession of the place. In other words, a defendant has a greater expectation of privacy in his own home or car than he does in someone else's home or car. However,

---

[70] After the decision of the U.S. Supreme Court in *United States v. Jones,* 132 S. Ct. 945 (2012), a search and seizure claim may be based upon a trespass theory of search (one's own personal effects have been trespassed), or a privacy theory of search (one's own expectation of privacy was breached). *Ford v. State,* 477 S.W.3d 321, 328 (Tex. Crim. App. 2015); *State v. Bell,* 366 S.W.3d 712, 713-14 (Tex. Crim. App. 2012).

[71] *Parker v. State,* 182 S.W.3d 923, 925-26 (Tex. Crim. App. 2006).

[72] *Id.*

courts carefully examine each case's circumstances individually and sometimes find reasonable subjective expectations of privacy in another's place, depending on the facts present in the case. Though this factor looks at the individual's expectation of privacy, it is examined from a reasonableness perspective by a trial judge or appellate court.

The second question relates to whether society is willing to recognize a privacy expectation in the place searched. Is society willing to recognize an expectation of privacy in your belongings when you are staying at a family member's home overnight? Courts have answered yes to this question.[73] Is society willing to recognize a reasonable expectation of privacy in a stolen vehicle exclusively possessed by the defendant? Courts have answered this question with a "no."[74] Is it reasonable to expect privacy in personal belongings you take through an airport and on a commercial flight? No, because it is objectively unreasonable to have a privacy right in a carry-on bag that you know or should know will be screened at the airport before you board your flight.[75]

You will see expectations of privacy, whether those expectations are reasonable, and whether they are likely to be recognized by society come up again and again in the cases in this chapter and in search and seizure jurisprudence.

------------◆------------

Notes and Questions

1. Prosecutors often argue that the defendant had no expectation of privacy in trash or abandoned property that is later used to link an accused to criminal activity. This is because it is objectively unreasonable for a person to claim a legitimate expectation of privacy in objects she no longer wanted and entrusted others to carry away.[76]

---

[73] *Villarreal v. State*, 935 S.W.2d 134, 144 (Tex. Crim. App. 1996) ("[P]rivacy in the place where we sleep is an interest society is willing to recognize, even if that privacy derives not from a place of one's own, but rather from the grace of extended family or friends.").

[74] *Hughes v. State*, 897 S.W.2d 285, 305 (Tex. Crim. App. 1994).

[75] *Turner v. State*, 132 S.W.3d 504, 508 (Tex. App.—Houston [1st Dist.] 2004, pet. ref'd).

[76] *Matthews v. State*, 431 S.W.3d 596, 608 (Tex. Crim. App. 2014) ("No person can reasonably expect privacy in property he abandons.").

2. Open fields or areas that lay outside the immediate vicinity of one's home are also areas with little or no subjective expectation of privacy. One court of appeals discussed the open fields doctrine as it related to the seizure of marijuana plants the defendant cultivated in his yard:

> The doctrine is based upon the premise that the Fourth Amendment accords "special protection . . . to the people in their 'persons, houses, papers and effects,' [but] is not extended to open fields." An "open field" need not be "open" or "a field" as those terms are commonly used. A fenced, thickly wooded area may be an open field for purposes of Fourth Amendment analysis. The term may be defined as "any unoccupied or undeveloped area outside the curtilage" of a dwelling. "Curtilage" is a common law concept referring to the area immediately adjacent to the home to which the intimate activity of home life extends. In this case, the first batch of marihuana seen by the officers was growing in an open garden approximately 25 feet from the [defendant Smith's] trailer. [The officer] could see the marihuana as he drove up. From the first garden, a second garden of marihuana could be seen. From the second garden, a third garden of marihuana could be seen. All the marihuana seized after Smith was taken into custody was being grown outside and in the open. Smith had no legitimate expectation of privacy concerning these gardens.[77]

———————◆———————

"Fruit of the Poisonous Tree"

Suppose a defendant challenges the officer's seizure of evidence. Assume there is a legitimate subjective and objective expectation of privacy in the evidence seized, but the officer violated the defendant's rights or the law in seizing the evidence, making the seizure unlawful. If the seizure of this evidence led to the discovery of more incriminating evidence, the defendant may argue the subsequently seized evidence is "fruit of the poisonous tree." In other words, but for the unlawfulness of the officer's conduct, the officer would not have found the incriminating evidence.

The defendant will argue all of the evidence—what was initially found and what was subsequently found—that followed the unlawful police action should be suppressed. In this way, the "fruit of the poisonous tree" doctrine

---

[77] *Smith v. State*, 722 S.W.2d 205, 208 (Tex. App.—San Antonio 1986, no pet.) (citations omitted).

applies to evidence directly and indirectly obtained from a law violation.[78] Fruit includes not just tangible evidence but arrests, oral statements, and witnesses—anything that could be used as evidence against the accused.

A diagram and a hypothetical scenario will help illustrate this concept. Imagine the blue arrow below represents a timeline, with the far left part of the arrow representing the beginning of a police-civilian encounter and the far right representing the conclusion of the officers' investigation.

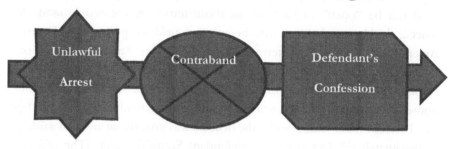

Assume that officers have not yet established probable cause to arrest or search the suspect, but sometime after their initial encounter, they arrest him anyway. The arrest is not supported by probable cause; therefore, it is unlawful. Because of the unlawfulness of the arrest, any evidence officers obtained due to the arrest may be considered "fruit of the poisonous tree." The evidence—in this case, contraband (illegal items) and the defendant's subsequent confession—may be challenged through a motion to suppress. The motion to suppress will allege that because officers acted unlawfully, a just consequence would be to exclude the evidence they found because of the unlawful arrest.

The purpose behind excluding unlawfully obtained evidence is that by rendering the evidence inadmissible, courts discourage unauthorized behavior by law enforcement officers. Not only does exclusion act to prevent unlawful conduct in future cases, but it also preserves the current defendant's Fourth Amendment and Texas legal rights against illegal arrests and seizures of evidence.

———————————— ◆ ————————————

[78] *Monge v. State*, 315 S.W.3d 35, 40 (Tex. Crim. App. 2010).

Scope of Search

While conducting a search, officers may exceed the scope of the search warrant. This typically happens when officers search beyond the parameters of the listed place in the warrant—as you saw in the *Long* case—or exceed the scope by seizing items not listed on the search warrant—as you saw in the *Wood* case. Scope issues may arise in cases with or without search warrants. This section will address scope problems in the search warrant context. Since there are two cases in this chapter addressing searches that exceeded the scope of the search warrant, let's examine a case where the defendant alleged a scope violation, but the court did not find one.

In *DeMoss v. State*, an officer received a tip that the defendant was using an illegal cable box to steal services from a local cable television company.[79] Based on this tip, he secured a search warrant to search the defendant's home for the illegal cable box.[80] When he did not find the box near the television, he extended the search to the entire house.[81] Inside a bedroom closet, he found a heavy shoebox; when he opened the shoebox, he discovered photos of the defendant engaged in sexual acts with a child.[82] The defendant was subsequently charged with the felony offense of aggravated sexual assault of a child.[83]

The San Antonio Court of Appeals was asked to determine whether the officer exceeded the scope of the search warrant by examining the contents of the shoe box in a bedroom closet when he was supposed to be looking for a cable television box. This is the test that the Court set out:

> A search is unreasonable and violates the protections of the Fourth Amendment if it exceeds the scope of the authorizing warrant. While the scope of the search warrant is governed by its terms, the search may be as extensive as is reasonably required to locate items described in the warrant. If the scope of the search is challenged because of the location where the items were found, the officer must show that he was properly in the place

---

[79] *DeMoss v. State*, 12 S.W.3d 553, 555 (Tex. App.—San Antonio 1999, pet. ref'd).
[80] *Id.*
[81] *Id.*
[82] *Id.*
[83] *Id.*

where the item was found, either on basis of the search warrant or under the authority of an exception to the warrant requirement.[84]

The Court then applied the above test to the facts and determined that because the box and its component parts could have fit in the shoebox, and the search warrant authorized the officer to search the home, the officer had reason to search the entire home, including any containers that were big enough to house the cable box or its component parts.[85] As long as officers have authority to search for items in a location, they may search the particular location and any area or container that may hold items listed on the search warrant.

Not only do scope issues appear in the context of search warrants, but they frequently arise in warrantless search contexts as well. When analyzing whether officers exceeded the scope of the search, one must consider the search warrant exception or the wording of the search warrant itself and determine whether the seizure fell within the confines or purpose of the exception or within the ambit of the search warrant itself. For example, once an officer has determined a suspect does not possess a weapon following a *Terry* frisk, any further search or removal of objects that are not weapons exceeds the scope and purpose of the frisk. Whatever is seized—drugs, contraband, etc.—exceeds the scope of the search and is thus subject to suppression.

———————————— ♦ ————————————

The Exclusionary Rule

Most people who are not familiar with criminal procedure would assume that if the prosecutor has incriminating evidence, it will be admitted against the defendant at trial. As you know from taking Evidence, however, not all evidence is admissible. Just as evidentiary rules may operate to prohibit the introduction of evidence, so too do exclusionary rules.

In order to discourage unlawful police conduct, the governments have created exclusionary rules, which prohibit the admission of unlawfully obtained evidence. The federal exclusionary rule applies to evidence

---

[84] *Id.* at 558.

[85] *Id.*

unlawfully seized by government agents.[86] The Texas rule, embodied in Texas Criminal Code of Procedure Article 38.23, is broader. It states,

> No evidence obtained by an officer *or other person* in violation of any provision of the Constitution or laws of the State of Texas, or of the Constitution or laws of the United States of America, shall be admitted in evidence against the accused on the trial of any criminal case.[87]

Why is Texas's exclusionary rule broader than the federal exclusionary rule? The answer dates back to the 1920s and the time of Prohibition when alcohol was banned in the United States:

> The Texas Legislature enacted an exclusionary rule broader than its federal counterpart precisely because of the . . . "widespread problem of vigilante-type private citizens [acting] in concert with the police conducting illegal searches for whiskey." Long before national Prohibition laws were enacted, Texas had created its own local-option liquor and prohibition laws. Enforcement of these local-option laws led to the formation of various citizen groups, including the "Law and Order League," whose members pledged to aid officers to enforce the laws, especially local-option laws, and to "'clean up' their town and county of crime[.]" Presumably, the Legislature foresaw that, if the exclusionary rule applied only to government officials or their agents, these "Law and Order League" members might well continue their illegal search-and-seizure operations without the participation or supervision of police officers. Then these vigilante members would hand over the illegally seized evidence, on a "silver platter," to government officers for use in criminal trials. To avoid the prospect of implicitly encouraging or condoning vigilante action by these citizen groups, the Legislature applied its statutory exclusionary rule to both law-enforcement officers and private persons.[88]

Prohibition may be long gone, but Texas's broad exclusionary rule remains intact. The provision related to the exclusion of evidence based on a citizen's law violation is still applicable. For example, in *Jenschke v. State*, the parents of an underage rape victim burglarized her rapist's truck to seize

---

[86] *Burdeau v. McDowell*, 256 U.S. 465, 475 (1921) ("The Fourth Amendment gives protection against unlawful searches and seizures, and ... its protection applies to governmental action. Its origin and history clearly show that it was intended as a restraint upon the activities of sovereign authority....").

[87] TEX. CODE CRIM. PROC. ANN. art. 38.23 (West 2016).

[88] *Miles v. State*, 241 S.W.3d 28, 34-35 (Tex. Crim. App. 2007).

evidence of the rape located in the truck's glove compartment box.[89] Because the Court of Criminal Appeals classified the parents' conduct as criminal, it ruled the evidence should have been excluded.[90]

The Texas exclusionary rule also suggests any law violation will result in suppression of evidence. However, not every law violation qualifies. For example, Texas appellate courts have held that violations of lawyer disciplinary rules,[91] statutory business name regulations,[92] and education code provisions[93] were not the type of law violations the exclusionary rule encompassed. The Court of Criminal Appeals explained that the purpose of the exclusionary rule is

> to protect a suspect's liberty interests against the overzealousness of others in obtaining evidence to use against them. Thus, unless someone's privacy or property interests are illegally infringed upon in the obtainment of evidence, the core rationale for providing this prophylactic measure is not met and its use is unwarranted. To expand the breadth of 38.23 to any and every violation of Texas "law"—beyond those that affect a defendant's privacy or property interests—is to ignore the basic premise under which the statute was created and would lead to absurd results.[94]

Here you see this expectation of privacy concept again. It lies at the center of search and seizure law. When courts can trace the unlawful conduct of officers to the defendant's expectations of privacy, the evidence obtained as a result of that unlawful activity is subject to exclusion.

———————————◆———————————

---

[89] 147 S.W.3d 398, 399 (Tex. Crim. App. 2004). The court suggested that the result might be different if the parents had acted with the intent to turn the seized evidence over to the police. *Id.* at 402 ("when a person who is not an officer or an agent of an officer takes property that is evidence of crime, without the effective consent of the owner and with the intent to turn over the property to an officer, the conduct may be non-criminal even though the person has intent to deprive the owner.").

[90] *Id.* at 403.

[91] *Pannell v. State*, 666 S.W.2d 96, 98 (Tex. Crim. App. 1984).

[92] *Roy v. State*, 608 S.W.2d 645, 651 (Tex. Crim. App. 1980).

[93] *Stockton v. State*, 756 S.W.2d 873, 874 (Tex. App.—Austin 1988, no pet.).

[94] *Chavez v. State*, 9 S.W.3d 817, 822-23 (Tex. Crim. App. 2000).

Exceptions to the Exclusionary Rule

There are a few, limited exceptions that apply to the exclusionary rule: the good faith exception, the independent source doctrine, and attenuation. These exceptions are narrow.

———————◆———————

Good Faith Exception

The good faith exception is the only one based in statutory law. It appears with the exclusionary rule in the same statute: Article 38.23 of the Texas Code of Criminal Procedure. Following the exclusionary rule, titled "Evidence not to be used", the statute says that it "is an exception[to the exclusionary rule] … that the evidence was obtained by a law enforcement officer acting in objective good faith reliance upon a warrant issued by a neutral magistrate based on probable cause."[95]

Federal and Texas have different good faith exceptions. An example will help illustrate the differences. Assume a rookie officer submits a search warrant affidavit to a magistrate believing the magistrate will find probable cause and issue a search warrant. The affidavit is missing a material fact objectively needed to establish probable cause. Both the officer and the magistrate overlook this, and the magistrate signs the warrant. The officer executes the warrant and seizes the contraband he expected to find. The defendant is arrested and charged with a crime. The defendant hires a lawyer to represent him. The lawyer reads the affidavit and the warrant and files a motion to suppress the evidence based upon a lack of probable cause.

Under federal law, as long as the officer was relying on what he reasonably and objectively believed to be a valid search warrant, the evidence may still be admissible under the good faith exception. *United States v. Leon*, 468 U.S. 897 (1984) created this federal good faith exception. The same is not true in Texas. The Texas good faith rule requires more than the federal good faith rule: actual probable cause. The practical effect of this narrow language is that the Texas good faith exception applies only to technical errors such as a missing magistrate's signature or an incorrect date on an otherwise valid search warrant supported by actual probable cause.[96] This is

---

[95] TEX. CODE CRIM. PROC. ANN. art. 38.23(b) (West 2016).
[96] *Dunn v. State*, 951 S.W.2d 478, 479 (Tex. Crim. App. 1997).

yet another area of criminal procedure where Texas limits the rights of the government and grants greater rights to criminal defendants.

—————————◆—————————

Independent Source Doctrine

The independent source doctrine is an exception based on common law. The independent source doctrine, according to the Texas Court of Criminal Appeals, was referred to for the first time by the U.S. Supreme Court in 1920.[97] The Texas Court of Criminal Appeals characterizes the doctrine as follows: "At its core, the independent source doctrine provides that evidence derived from or obtained from a lawful source, separate and apart from any illegal conduct by law enforcement, is not subject to exclusion."[98] The Court of Criminal Appeals has held that because the independent source doctrine applies to situations where there is no causal connection between the unlawful police conduct and the seized evidence, it does not run afoul of the language of Article 38.23's exclusionary rule.[99]

—————————◆—————————

Attenuation

Another common-law exception to the exclusionary rule is attenuation. The word *attenuate* means to reduce the force or effect of something. In the search and seizure context, it often refers to an intervening event that occurs between the officer's unlawful conduct and the evidence obtained following that conduct, thus "attenuating the taint" of the unlawful conduct. Attenuation is often raised when a voluntary confession follows an unlawful arrest, as illustrated by the following case. Though *Miranda* warnings and confessions, called "statements" in Texas, are discussed later in Chapter 10, the exclusionary rule and attenuation concepts in the next case are easy to understand.

---

[97] *Wehrenberg v. State*, 416 S.W.3d 458, 464 (Tex. Crim. App. 2013) (referencing *Silverthorne Lumber Company v. United States*, 251 U.S. 385, 392 (1920)).
[98] *Id.* at 465.
[99] *Id.* at 464-65, 470.

Abelino Monge v. State
315 S.W.3d 35
(Tex. Crim. App. 2010)

The record reflects that on July 14th a detective discovered a cell phone near the scene of a murder which had occurred two days earlier. The phone belonged to appellant and had been used to call and receive calls from the victim. It also had been used to call a third person, Margil Ochoa.

Detectives wearing plain clothes located appellant at his workplace on July 21st at 10:30 a.m. They invited appellant to accompany them to their office at the police station to answer some questions about the phone. Appellant advised the detectives that his phone had been stolen and agreed to accompany them. The detectives offered to give appellant a ride because appellant's car was in the shop. Appellant accepted the offer, was not handcuffed, and he rode in the front passenger seat of an unmarked police vehicle.

Appellant arrived at the station at 11:15 a.m. and was escorted to an interview room, where he was questioned. At 1:00 p.m., the detectives asked appellant for a DNA sample, and he agreed to provide one. The detectives advised appellant that he had not been charged with a crime and was free to leave.

Over the course of the afternoon appellant was provided with a chicken lunch and a smoke break. The detective also requested permission to search appellant's car and home and that appellant take a polygraph test. Appellant agreed to all the requests and failed the polygraph test. Appellant maintained his innocence, and questioning ended for the day at 6:10 p.m. Although free to leave, appellant instead went to sleep in the interview room.

Meanwhile, detectives had found Ochoa, the other man whose name was associated with the cell phone, and were questioning him in another room. Sometime between midnight and 4:13 a.m., Ochoa admitted that both he and appellant had been involved in the victim's murder and named appellant as the shooter.

At 7:00 a.m., a detective informed appellant that he was under arrest, placed him in handcuffs, and began working on the paperwork concerning appellant's arrest. A detective read appellant the *Miranda* rights at 8:44 a.m. and confronted him with Ochoa's confession. Appellant then confessed his involvement in the crime.

Before trial, appellant filed a motion to suppress his confession, contending that he was unlawfully arrested, that his subsequent confession was tainted under the doctrine of the "fruit of the poisonous tree," and that the state did not prove attenuation of the taint.

The trial court found that appellant's arrest was unlawful because the police officers failed to obtain an arrest warrant. ... However, the court denied appellant's motion to suppress because it also found that the taint of appellant's warrantless arrest had been attenuated. ... Appellant subsequently pled guilty to capital murder and was sentenced to life in prison.

Analysis

The Four Factor Test

...The "fruit of the poisonous tree" doctrine generally precludes the use of evidence, both direct and indirect, obtained following an illegal arrest. Here, the State does not challenge the illegality of appellant's warrantless arrest, which did not fit within any of the recognized exceptions to the warrant requirement. Instead, the State contends the nexus between the unlawful arrest and appellant's confession was so attenuated as to dissipate the taint of the prior illegality.

Evidence that is sufficiently attenuated from the unlawful arrest is not considered to have been obtained therefrom. The prosecution carries the burden of proving attenuation. In deciding whether appellant's confession, which was given following an illegal arrest, was sufficiently attenuated as to permit the use of the confession at trial, we are to consider the following factors:

1. whether *Miranda* warnings were given;
2. the temporal proximity of the arrest and the confession;
3. the presence of intervening circumstances; and
4. the purpose and flagrancy of the official misconduct.[100]

These four factors do not necessarily carry equal weight. No single factor is decisive. We examine each factor in turn and then consider the effect of the factors as a whole.

---

[100] See *Brown v. Illinois*, 422 U.S. 590, 603-04 (1975); *Bell v. State*, 724 S.W.2d 780, 788 (Tex. Crim. App. 1986).

Miranda Warnings

Miranda warnings are an important and necessary factor in determining whether the confession is obtained by exploitation of an illegal arrest. However, the fact that a *Miranda* warning has been given is not sufficient to break the causal connection between an illegal arrest and the confession. In this case, a *Miranda* warning was given to appellant before his confession, thus the first *Brown* factor weighs in favor of the state.

The Temporal Proximity of the Arrest

Temporal proximity is generally not a strong determining factor. Nevertheless, if there is a short period of time (under three hours) between the illegal arrest and the confession, this factor will weigh in favor of appellant. In this case, appellant was illegally arrested at the time he was implicated by Ochoa, was informed of his arrest at 7:00 a.m., and gave his confession approximately two hours later at 8:44 a.m. The short period of time between his illegal arrest and confession weighs in favor of appellant.

The Presence of Intervening Circumstances

The presence of an intervening circumstance is an important factor. Generally, "[a] confession obtained through custodial interrogation after an illegal arrest should be excluded unless intervening events break the causal connection between the illegal arrest and the confession so that the confession is sufficiently an act of free will to purge the primary taint."[101] However, the lack of intervening circumstances is not dispositive if other *Brown* factors weigh strongly in favor of the state.

Confrontation with significant evidence untainted by an illegal arrest may be an intervening circumstance if it breaks the causal connection between the arrest and the confession. However, in a particularly coercive atmosphere, such confrontation will not be sufficient to break the causal connection between an arrest and the confession.

…Appellant voluntarily went to the police station and submitted to a lengthy interrogation even though he was told that he was free to leave. After Ochoa gave a statement that implicated appellant in the murder, police officers had probable cause to believe that appellant was involved in the

---

[101] *Townsley v. State*, 652 S.W.2d 791, 789 (Tex. Crim. App. 1983).

murder, but they did not obtain a warrant before they arrested appellant. A distinction is that, instead of confessing after being confronted with his own earlier statements, appellant confessed immediately after being confronted with a confession by Ochoa that was untainted by appellant's illegal arrest. Appellant's subsequent confession flowed at least as much from being confronted with his co-defendant's untainted confession as from his arrest. In such circumstances, we hold that confrontation with Ochoa's confession was an intervening circumstance that weighs in favor of the state in this case.

Purpose and Flagrancy of Official Misconduct

Purpose and flagrancy of official misconduct "is one of the most important factors to be considered."[102] When official misconduct is the most flagrantly abusive, the standard for the state to prove attenuation is elevated to require the "clearest indications of attenuation."[103] Examples of such abusive conduct may include "reliance on factors in making an arrest which were so lacking in indicia of probable cause as to render belief in its existence entirely unreasonable; an arrest effectuated as a pretext for collateral objectives; or an arrest which is unnecessarily intrusive on personal privacy." Similarly, the taint may not be attenuated if the accused was arrested for no apparent justification and with the sole intent to extract a confession by exploitation. This contrasts with situations in which probable cause exists and failure to get an arrest warrant is a comparatively less serious misconduct.

As in all attenuation cases, there was official misconduct, specifically, failing to obtain a warrant before the arrest. However, none of the Bell examples of abusive conduct occurred in this case. Based on Ochoa's confession, the discovery of appellant's phone at the crime scene, and appellant's failing of a polygraph test, the detectives had probable cause to arrest appellant. Furthermore, the detective in charge testified that he chose not to procure a warrant because he misunderstood [the law] to mean that a warrant was unnecessary in the situation.

Appellant contends that police misconduct is further demonstrated by the fact that he was in the control of law enforcement for over 22 hours and received only one meal during that period. Additionally, appellant claims that

---

[102] *Bell v. State*, 724 S.W.2d 780, 788 (Tex. Crim. App. 1986).
[103] *Id.* at 789.

the detectives misled him by telling him he was being charged with "murder" instead of "capital murder."

Neither of those contentions have merit. The record reflects that appellant went to the station voluntarily and cooperated with police up until he was arrested approximately two hours before his confession on July 22; he was not held against his will for an extraordinary or coercive length of time. Furthermore, there is evidence that the detectives were civil and non-coercive while appellant was at the station and not in custody. The detectives gave appellant a ride to the station when told his car was in the shop, he rode in the front of the patrol car, they provided a lunch, they took smoke breaks with him, they provided a blanket when appellant got cold, and they maintained a sympathetic and non-coercive atmosphere even after the arrest.

...We therefore conclude that the fourth *Brown* factor weighs in favor of the state.

Conclusion

Three of the four *Brown* factors weigh in favor of the state. Weighing the factors together, we are satisfied that the confession in this case was sufficiently attenuated from the taint of the illegal arrest. We affirm the judgment of the court of appeals.

---◆---

Notes and Questions

1. Sixteen years before the *Monge* decision, the Court of Criminal Appeals harmonized the attenuation doctrine with Texas's exclusionary rule in this way:

> [T]he attenuation doctrine is applicable to Art. 38.23's prohibition against evidence "obtained" in violation of the law because evidence sufficiently attenuated from the violation of the law is not considered to be "obtained" therefrom. ... If the evidence is not "obtained" in violation of the law, then its admission into evidence is not in contravention of Art. 38.23. Thus, the attenuation doctrine is not an exception to Art. 38.23, but rather is a method of determining whether evidence was "obtained" in violation of the law, with "obtained" being included in the plain language of the statute.[104]

---

[104] *Johnson v. State*, 871 S.W.2d 744, 750-51 (Tex. Crim. App. 1994).

2. Notice that the Court declared the attenuation doctrine is not an exception to the exclusionary rule. While the Court may have done so, other courts, practitioners, and academics still consider it an exception.

3. An exception to the exclusionary rule under federal law is the inevitable discovery exception. However, this is not a recognized exception in Texas. This exception applies when the evidence was unlawfully obtained but police would have found it inevitably through lawful means. The Court of Criminal Appeals has explained why this federal exception is disfavored in Texas:

> The inevitable discovery doctrine assumes a causal relationship between the illegality and the evidence. It assumes that the evidence was actually "obtained" illegally. The doctrine then asks whether the evidence would have been "obtained" eventually in any event by lawful means. But the fact that evidence could have been "obtained" lawfully anyway does not negate the fact that it was in fact "obtained" illegally. Under Article 38.23 the inquiry regarding the possible legal attainment of the evidence should never be reached. Once the illegality and its causal connection to the evidence have been established, the evidence must be excluded.[105]

Therefore, unlike the other exceptions, there is no basis for the inevitable discovery exception in the language of the Texas exclusionary rule.[106] The Court of Criminal Appeals has suggested that if the Texas legislature would like to create an inevitable discovery exception in Texas, it must amend the language of Article 38.23 to include it.[107]

━━━━━━━━━━ ◆ ━━━━━━━━━━

Motions to Suppress Evidence

Think of a motion to suppress as a special objection to inadmissible evidence.[108] Defense attorneys have several options when it comes to requesting that incriminating evidence be suppressed by the court. First, defense counsel could make a plea to the prosecutor to exclude the evidence. Most prosecutors recognize that unlawfully obtained evidence must be excluded and are willing to dismiss the case, if required, on this basis or

[105] *State v. Daugherty*, 931 S.W.2d 268, 270 (Tex. Crim. App. 1996).
[106] *Garcia v. State*, 829 S.W.2d 796, 799-800 (Tex. Crim. App. 1992).
[107] *Id.*
[108] *Galitz v. State*, 617 S.W.2d 949, 952 n.10 (Tex. Crim. App. 1981).

proceed to trial without the objectionable evidence. Second, the defense attorney could file a motion to suppress at a pretrial hearing[109] or request a suppression hearing before or during trial. In this instance, the judge must decide whether to suppress the evidence.[110] Third, defense counsel may ask the jury to ignore the unlawfully obtained evidence. The jury has no authority to suppress the evidence or render it inadmissible, but it may choose not to consider the evidence during deliberations.[111]

If a defendant requests a motion to suppress through a pretrial hearing, the suppression issues can be considered through motion, affidavit, oral testimony, or in another manner subject to the discretion of the court.[112]

All of the three exclusion methods have one thing in common: the defense attorney is objecting to the evidence being considered by the factfinder.[113] In Texas, defendants may use one or more of these avenues; in other words, they are not limited to one suppression path.

Article 38.23 Jury Instruction

If defense counsel wants the jury to not consider the evidence, she must request an Article 38.23 jury instruction informing the jury that it has this option.[114] The language of the instruction tracks the language of the statute: "the jury shall be instructed that if it believes, or has a reasonable doubt, that the evidence was obtained in violation of the provisions of this Article, then … the jury shall disregard any such evidence so obtained."[115]

In order to get the instruction, the evidence must raise an issue of fact (not merely law) suggesting that the evidence was obtained unlawfully.[116] Furthermore, the facts must be disputed by the State, and the contested

---

[109] TEX. CODE CRIM. PROC. ANN. art. 28.01 §1(6) (West 2016).

[110] *Id.*

[111] *Bell v. State*, 881 S.W.2d 794, 802 (Tex. App.—Houston [14th Dist.] 1994, pet. ref'd).

[112] TEX. CODE CRIM. PROC. ANN. rt. 28.01 §1(6) (West 2016).

[113] *Vafaiyan v. State*, 279 S.W.3d 374, 383 (Tex. App.—Fort Worth 2008, pet. ref'd) ("A motion to suppress is only a specialized objection to the admissibility of that evidence.").

[114] *Id.*

[115] TEX. CODE CRIM. PROC. ANN. art. 38.23 (West 2016).

[116] *Madden v. State*, 242 S.W.3d 504, 510 (Tex. Crim. App. 2007); *Pierce v. State*, 32 S.W.3d 247, 251 (Tex. Crim. App. 2000) ("There is no issue for the jury when the question is one of law only.").

factual issue must be relevant to the alleged unlawfulness of the obtained evidence.[117]

Challenging the arrest, search, or seizure before a jury is risky. First, jurors are rarely knowledgeable about the law on evidence suppression. Even so, after being properly instructed by the court on the legal issues involved in a particular search and seizure dispute, jurors are qualified to judge whether policing or investigation procedures crossed appropriate lines. Second, in order to challenge the lawfulness of a search, the defense must raise a fact issue. This means that the defense must admit testimony or evidence, which may require the defendant to testify. Unlike a suppression hearing, where the defendant's testimony is limited to the issues surrounding the lawfulness of the search,[118] the defendant's testimony at trial is not limited and neither is cross-examination by the prosecutor.[119] Nevertheless, juries in Texas are called upon to set aside unlawfully obtained evidence, and sometimes they answer the defendant's call by ignoring it.

Burden of Proof

Who carries the burden of proof in a motion to suppress evidence? When a defendant seeks to suppress evidence, the defendant initially has the burden of proof.[120] What happens next depends on whether there is a warrant. If there is a warrant, the defendant must defeat the presumption that officers acted reasonably.[121] If there was no warrant, the burden of proof shifts to the State to establish by a preponderance of the evidence that the search or seizure was lawful.[122]

———————————◆———————————

Appealing Rulings on Motions to Suppress Evidence

Both the prosecutor and the defendant may appeal an unfavorable motion to suppress ruling. If the defense's motion to suppress is granted, it

---

[117] *Id.*

[118] *Franklin v. State*, 606 S.W.2d 818, 825 (Tex. Crim. App. 1978).

[119] *Id.* at 825-26.

[120] *Russell v. State*, 717 S.W.2d 7, 9-10 (Tex. Crim. App. 1986).

[121] *Id.*

[122] *Id.*; *Handy v. State*, 189 S.W.3d 296, 299 (Tex. Crim. App. 2006).

could undermine the State's case. If the motion to suppress is denied, the defendant may decide he would rather plead guilty than risk facing a harsher punishment at the hands of a judge or jury. At the request of a losing party, the trial judge is required to make specific findings of fact and conclusions of law on the suppression issue.[123] While the right to appeal is available to both parties, each party must go about it differently.

The Code permits the defendant to appeal "matters which have been raised by written motion filed prior to trial" even after he has pled no contest or guilty to the crime.[124] The Texas Rules of Appellate Procedure authorize an appeal of matters following a plea of guilt or no contest for motions filed and ruled on before trial.[125] Both of these legal provisions cover not only a defendant's right to appeal following a plea, but also a trial where the legality of the search and seizure was contested.

Typically, when a defendant ends his case by pleading guilty, he is asked to waive any right to appeal. Even a valid right to appeal a motion to suppress can be waived.[126] However, if the defendant follows the proper appellate procedure and does not waive his right to appeal the motion to suppress ruling, he may appeal an unfavorable ruling on his motion to suppress.

Notice that some of the cases in this chapter were appealed not by the defendant but by the State. This is not common; it is generally the defendant who appeals following a conviction. An appeal taken before a case is final, which is what happens when the State appeals an unfavorable ruling on a motion to suppress evidence, is called an "interlocutory appeal." *Interlocutory* means provisional, or an action taken between the beginning and end of a legal action, one that occurs before any lasting harm.

---

[123] *State v. Cullen,* 195 S.W.3d 696, 699 (Tex. Crim. App. 2006).
[124] TEX. CODE CRIM. PROC. ANN. art. 44.02 (West 2016); TEX. CODE CRIM. PROC. ANN. art. 26.13(a)(3) (West 2016) (when the defendant pleads guilty, "the trial court must give its permission to the defendant before the defendant may ... appeal ... except for those matters raised by written motions filed prior to trial").
[125] TEX. R. APP. P. 25.2(a)(2).
[126] *Marsh v. State,* 444 S.W.3d 654, 660 (Tex. Crim. App. 2014) ("[T]he record shows that Appellant knowingly and voluntarily waived his right to appeal the motion to suppress.").

The Code permits the State the right to appeal when the trial court grants a motion to suppress evidence, and jeopardy has not yet attached.[127] The State does not have to go forward with the trial but may immediately appeal the trial court's decision. The prosecutor has 20 days from the time the court makes its ruling to file the appeal.[128] The State is required to certify to the trial court (1) the appeal is not taken for purposes of delay, and (2) the evidence is of substantial importance to the case.[129]

———————◆———————

This next case pulls together many of the legal concepts discussed in this chapter: search warrants, probable cause, credibility of the affiant, the totality of the circumstances test, the four corners doctrine, standing, expectations of privacy, "fruit of the poisonous tree," motions to suppress, and the State's right to file an interlocutory appeal when the defendant's motion to suppress is granted by the judge. It is a good way to illustrate how all of these distinct legal search and seizure concepts are interconnected.

State v. Marli Shealyn Elrod
395 S.W.3d 869
(Tex. App.—Austin 2013, no pet.)

The State of Texas appeals a pretrial order granting, in part, Marli Shealyn Elrod's motion to suppress. In two points of error, the State contends that the trial court erred by concluding that Elrod had standing to contest the searches conducted by investigating detectives and by suppressing the evidence resulting from two of the complained-of searches. We affirm the trial court's order of suppression.

BACKGROUND

On March 17, 2011, deputies and emergency personnel responded to a 911 call concerning an infant child who had stopped breathing. Upon responding to the location, the "Yorkshire residence," deputies made contact

---

[127] TEX. CODE CRIM. PROC. ANN. art. 44.01(a)(5) (West 2016). The double jeopardy clause is discussed in more detail in Chapter 12.
[128] TEX. CODE CRIM. PROC. ANN. art. 44.01(d) (West 2016).
[129] TEX. CODE CRIM. PROC. ANN. art. 44.01(a)(5) (West 2016).

with Elrod who indicated that she was babysitting the child, Paige,[130] while the child's mother was away from the residence. She explained to the deputies that earlier in the day she had accidentally dropped Paige as she was putting Paige down for her nap when a dog bit her in the ankle. She said the child struck her head on the railing of the crib before falling to the floor where she landed on a stuffed animal toy. Elrod informed the deputies that she picked Paige up and calmed her. She indicated that after Paige stopped crying she was happy and even played with Elrod's 14–month old daughter. Elrod said she later put Paige back down for her nap. When she subsequently checked on her, she discovered the child was having difficulty breathing so she called for emergency help.

During the course of their investigation, sheriff's deputies obtained four separate search warrants. The first search warrant … was issued that same day, March 17, 2011, and authorized a search of the Yorkshire residence. During the execution of this search warrant, officers seized a laptop … and took photographs, measurements, and a video recording of the inside of the home. The second search warrant … was issued the following day, March 18, 2011, and authorized a search of the laptop seized from the home on March 17th. A third search warrant … was issued March 29, 2011, and authorized an additional search of the Yorkshire residence. During the execution of this search warrant, officers seized a baby crib and wooden chairs with booster seats attached, and took photographs of those items within the home. The fourth search warrant … was also issued March 29, 2011, and authorized a search of Elrod's cell phone.

Prior to trial, Elrod filed a motion to suppress all of the evidence obtained as a result of the execution of the four search warrants. At the pretrial hearing on the motion, the State argued that Elrod lacked standing to contest the searches. After hearing testimony from Elrod and argument from both parties, the trial court concluded that Elrod had standing. No further testimony was presented at the hearing. Elrod argued that the first search warrant lacked sufficient probable cause both to show that a crime had been committed or that evidence of a crime would be found at the residence. She next argued that, as a result of the invalidity of the first search warrant, the search of the laptop pursuant to the second search warrant was the fruit of

---

[130] "Paige" is a pseudonym used to replace the child's initials "P.E.," which appear in the original case.

the poisonous tree. She further argued that [the other three search warrants failed to state a crime had occurred or that evidence of a crime would be found in the places to be searched].

...[T]he trial court [eventually] granted Elrod's motion to suppress as to the first two search warrants ... and suppressed the evidence recovered from the searches pursuant to those warrants. The court concluded that the affidavit in support of the first search warrant lacked sufficient probable cause and, consequently, the second search warrant was "tainted by the fruit of the poisonous tree" because the laptop was recovered during the execution of the first search warrant. The trial court denied Elrod's motion as to the last two search warrants .... The State appeals the trial court's order.

DISCUSSION

In its first point of error, the State contends, as it did below, that Elrod lacks standing to contest the search of the Yorkshire residence because she failed to demonstrate a legitimate expectation of privacy in the residence. In its second point of error, the State argues that the trial court erred in suppressing the evidence recovered from the search of the Yorkshire residence and the laptop seized from the residence because the affidavits in support of those search warrants sufficiently set forth probable cause.

Standing

The State first urges that the trial court erred by concluding that Elrod had standing to contest the search of the Yorkshire residence or the laptop seized from the residence and thus to complain about the search warrants issued by the magistrate in this case.

Expectation of Privacy in Residence

The Fourth Amendment to the United States Constitution and Article I, Section 9 of the Texas Constitution protect individuals against unreasonable searches and seizures. The rights secured by the Fourth Amendment and Article I, Section 9 are personal. A defendant seeking to suppress evidence on the ground that it was obtained in violation of the Fourth Amendment or Article I, Section 9 must show that he personally had a reasonable expectation of privacy that the government violated. The defendant bears the burden of demonstrating standing to challenge the legality of the search by showing that he had a subjective expectation of privacy in the place invaded that society is prepared to recognize as reasonable.

In considering whether an appellant has demonstrated an objectively reasonable expectation of privacy, we examine the totality of the circumstances surrounding the search, including whether: (1) the defendant had a property or possessory interest in the place invaded; (2) he was legitimately in the place invaded; (3) he had complete dominion or control and the right to exclude others; (4) prior to the intrusion, he took normal precautions customarily taken by those seeking privacy; (5) he put the place to some private use; and (6) his claim of privacy is consistent with historical notions of privacy. This list of factors is not exhaustive, nor is any one factor dispositive of an assertion of privacy.

An "overnight guest" has a legitimate expectation of privacy in his host's home. However, the legitimate privacy expectation of an overnight guest does not extend to a casual visitor or guest who is merely present with the consent of the homeowner.

The State contends that Elrod lacked standing because she was only a babysitter and, as such, was simply a casual visitor or guest without the expectation of privacy of an overnight guest. However, Elrod's testimony at the suppression hearing established that she kept clothing and other personal property at the Yorkshire residence and that she and her daughter "often" spent the night in the home, "every weekend" from Friday through Sunday or sometimes Monday. In fact, she testified that the room where she and her daughter slept on those occasions was considered by her and those living in the home to also be "their" room. Her testimony also established that she had spent the night at the residence on March 16th, the night before she called for emergency help for Paige, and that when she called for help she was in the home caring for Paige and her child. Thus, the record reflects that as a frequent overnight guest and caretaker for children in the home, Elrod had a possessory interest in the residence and was legitimately in the home. Further, as the babysitter, Elrod had dominion and control over the residence and had the right, perhaps even the duty, to exclude others from the home.

In its argument, the State focuses on evidence that, according to the State, contradicts Elrod's testimony. First, Elrod previously lived full time at this residence but moved out over a year before this incident and expressed to detectives that she had no desire to move back in with her boyfriend. Second, she told investigating deputies that she had moved back in with her parents in Austin, Texas and on March 17th her parents' Austin residence was where she was receiving her mail and was the address listed on her driver's license. The State also asserts that Elrod was inconsistent in her testimony because she admitted on cross-examination that she told deputies that she and her daughter only spent the weekends at the Yorkshire residence on those weekends that the homeowners' son, her boyfriend, did not work.

None of this evidence, however, negates the fact that Elrod was a frequent overnight guest in the residence, with clothing and personal property in the home. At best, this testimony creates a conflict in evidence that the trial court was permitted to resolve in Elrod's favor. The trial judge is the sole trier of fact and exclusive judge of credibility of the witnesses and the weight to be given to their testimony. We defer to the trial court's factual findings .... Under the circumstances, the trial court could reasonably conclude that Elrod had a subjective expectation of privacy in the home that was objectively reasonable. ...

Probable Cause

The State next argues that the trial court erred by concluding that the magistrate lacked probable cause to issue the search warrants for the Yorkshire residence and the laptop seized from that residence. Consequently, the State contends that the trial court abused its discretion in suppressing the evidence recovered from those searches.

Probable Cause Affidavit

No search warrant may issue unless a sworn affidavit is first presented to the magistrate setting forth sufficient facts to show that probable cause exists for its issuance. The sworn affidavit must set forth facts sufficient to establish probable cause:

> (1) that a specific offense has been committed, (2) that the specifically described property or items that are to be searched for or seized constitute evidence of that offense or evidence that a particular person committed that offense, and (3) that the property or items constituting evidence to be searched for or seized are located at or on the particular person, place, or thing to be searched.

Probable cause for a search warrant exists if, under the totality of the circumstances presented to the magistrate, there is at least a "fair probability" or substantial chance" that contraband or evidence of a crime will be found at the specified location.

When reviewing a decision by a judge or magistrate to issue a search warrant, we apply a deferential standard of review because of the constitutional preference for law enforcement officials to obtain warrants rather than conduct warrantless searches. The facts submitted for the magistrate's probable cause determination are those contained within the four corners of the affidavit and are to be read in a common-sense and realistic manner. A magistrate may draw reasonable inferences from the facts stated in the affidavit. When in doubt about the propriety of the magistrate's conclusion, we defer to all reasonable inferences the magistrate could have made. Our inquiry, then, is whether there are sufficient facts stated within the four corners of the affidavit, coupled with inferences from those facts, to establish a fair probability that evidence of a particular crime will likely be found at a given location.

The affiant in this case was Detective Wayne E. Lehman. The affidavit filed by the detective in support of his request for a search warrant for the Yorkshire residence asserted his belief that evidence used in the commission of aggravated assault would be found at that location. To support this belief, the detective first included a description of Elrod's account of how Paige sustained her injuries. According to Lehman, Elrod explained that she accidentally dropped the child when she was putting her down for a nap because the dog bit her on the ankle. She further explained that Paige's head struck the railing of the crib as she fell to the floor where she landed on top of a stuffed animal toy. The detective then stated in his affidavit that he looked at photographs taken by a colleague at the hospital where, according to the detective's recitations, the child was "conscious and alert." The photos, attached to his affidavit, depict several bruises on the child's face. The detective then opined that the bruises on the child's face "did not appear to be consistent with [Elrod's] account of the incident."

There was no information in the affidavit about the detective's training and experience, his general knowledge of child abuse crimes, or his familiarity with injuries sustained in such crimes based on his training and experience. Nor did he detail the facts on which he based his belief that Elrod, or someone else, had somehow intentionally inflicted serious bodily injury to Paige. Simply put, the information the detective provided in the affidavit merely asserted that he did not believe Elrod's story. A mere conclusory statement will not suffice to show probable cause.

Although the detective stated in the affidavit that he sought evidence in connection with the offense of aggravated assault, the affidavit did not provide any basis from which it could be inferred that Paige was the victim of an aggravated assault. Nor did the affidavit contain any information indicating that Lehman would have any reason to believe that evidence relating to an aggravated assault would be found in the residence. There were no facts articulated to form a basis of belief that Paige's injuries were sustained in an aggravated assault, other than the detective's disbelief of Elrod's account based on his viewing of the photographs of the child. While the detective sought evidence of objects that "could cause blunt force trauma to an infant child's head," there were no facts set forth in the affidavit indicating that Paige suffered blunt force trauma to the head. The only information concerning the child's medical condition was the attached photographs depicting bruises on her face along with the recitation that these photographs were taken at the hospital where the child was conscious and alert. The detective also sought evidence of items that "could be used to suffocate or strangle an infant child," yet nowhere in the affidavit are there any facts suggesting that Paige was strangled or suffered injuries consistent with strangulation or suffocation. Finally, the detective also sought computer and digital evidence "which could be used for internet searches that could be researched to conceal or attempt to conceal said offense." However, the affidavit set forth no facts from which to infer that Elrod had used any such devices. The detective's belief that a computer device could be used for such purposes does not set forth facts from which to believe or infer that a computer device had been so used on this occasion.

Given the paucity of facts in the affidavit, we conclude that the magistrate did not have a substantial basis for determining that probable cause existed to search the Yorkshire residence. The affidavit lacked a substantial basis for determining that there was probable cause to believe that the offense of aggravated assault had been perpetrated or that there was evidence related to the commission of such offense in the Yorkshire residence. Accordingly, we hold that the trial court did not abuse its discretion in granting Elrod's motion to suppress the evidence obtained during the search of the Yorkshire residence pursuant to the first search warrant.

The "fruit of the poisonous tree" doctrine serves to exclude as evidence not only the direct products of Fourth Amendment violations, but also the indirect products. The evidence recovered from the laptop seized during the first search of the Yorkshire residence was the indirect product of an illegal search. Therefore, that evidence was properly subject to suppression based on the taint of the illegal search through which the laptop was obtained. Moreover, the affidavit in support of the search warrant for the laptop, while adding the offense of injury to a child as an offense believed to be committed, contained the same information, or lack thereof, as the first search warrant. It too failed to set forth sufficient facts from which a magistrate could determine that an offense had been perpetrated against Paige or that there was evidence related to the commission of such offense on the laptop. Again, the detective's mere suspicion that the laptop could have been used to research how to conceal a crime does not suffice to show probable cause. ...

CONCLUSION

We conclude that the trial court did not abuse its discretion in finding that Elrod had standing to challenge the complained-of searches or in finding that the first two search warrants lacked sufficient facts to show that probable cause existed for their issuance. Accordingly, we affirm the trial court's order of suppression.

———————◆———————

Practice Questions

The topics in this chapter appear frequently on the bar exam. Search and seizure questions appear in various formats. Most questions are preceded by a fact pattern, which requires examinees to make substantive arguments. Other questions ask examinees to list answers. Be prepared to carefully read (and re-read) the fact pattern and make legal arguments that may include substantive topics such as exceptions to the warrant requirement or standing. While most questions ask you to assume the role of defense counsel, some of these questions ask for arguments the prosecutor could make; this happens when the State has legal or factual arguments to support its position.

Search Warrants

1. (F-2016, F-2009, and J-2006) What document must be filed when a search warrant is requested, and what information must be included in it?

_____

_____

_____

_____

_____

2. (F-2012) Officer suspects Defendant of committing multiple arsons. He drafts a sworn affidavit for an evidentiary search warrant that would allow him to search Defendant's home for evidence indicating Defendant was a serial arsonist. In the sworn affidavit, he includes Defendant's correct home address and indicates that arson instrumentalities will be found in the home.

   Is Officer's affidavit for the evidentiary search warrant proper? Explain.

_____

_____

_____

_____

_____

3. (J-2011 and J-2002) What is required in Texas for a search warrant to be deemed legally valid? Explain.

_____

_____

_____

_____

_____

4. (J-2010) Defendant is arrested for the felony offense of human trafficking. Officer seizes Defendant's cell phone and begins to examine Defendant's call logs, text messages, photos, and recent Internet activity. Officer finds evidence that corroborates Defendant's involvement in human trafficking. The phone is kept in police custody as evidence of the charged offense. At trial, you learn Prosecutor plans on admitting evidence seized from Defendant's phone.

   What procedural step can you take to keep this evidence from being introduced at trial? What arguments will you make? Explain.

   _____

   _____

   _____

   _____

   _____

5. (J-2009 and J-2006) You ask to read the search warrant. In the warrant, Defendant's home is described as "a brown-colored apartment building located on a busy street on the east side of Dallas, Texas."

   Is this description sufficient? If it is not, what must you do to challenge the warrant, and what remedy will you seek? Explain.

   _____

   _____

   _____

   _____

   _____

6. (J-2009 and J-2002) Under Texas law, when do officers have the authority to break down a residential door to execute a search warrant? Explain.

   _____

   _____

   _____

_____

_____

7. (J-2008) Officer makes a knowingly false statement in his search warrant affidavit about his confidential informant's credibility; Officer knows informant is a compulsive liar. The magistrate does not know this about informant, so she issues a search warrant believing Officer's affidavit is truthful. One week after the warrant issues, Officer executes the warrant and finds contraband in Defendant's home.

    a. What procedural step can you take to challenge the issuance of the search warrant? What must you prove? What kind of relief will you seek? Explain.

_____

_____

_____

_____

_____

    b. Can you successfully challenge the execution of the search warrant, and if so, how? Explain.

_____

_____

_____

_____

_____

8. (J-2002) In June, Police Department received an anonymous tip that Defendant was engaged the sale of stolen goods from his home. Based on this information, Officer prepared a sworn affidavit and obtained a search warrant to search Defendant's home. Two days later, when Officers executed the warrant, they found no evidence of the suspected crime but instead discovered cocaine in Defendant's car, which was parked in his brother's driveway down the street. Defendant is charged with possession of a controlled substance.

Describe two arguments you can make in your motion to suppress the drugs.

_____

_____

_____

_____

_____

Suppression of Evidence

9. (J-2016 (warrantless seizure), J-2015 (search lacked probable cause and exceeded scope), F-2015 (warrantless search, no exception), J-2014 (warrantless search, no exception), J-2013 ("fruit of poisonous tree"), F-2013 (standing and "fruit of poisonous tree"), J-2012 (search incident to arrest and inventory search), F-2012 (standing and confession), F-2011 (inventory search), J-2010 (cell phone search and suppression of witness identification of defendant), F-2010 (confession and suppression of statement to witness), J-2009 (search warrant particularity), F-2009 (no reasonable suspicion, "fruit of poisonous tree," and confession), J-2008 (invalid search warrant), F-2008 (no warrant, reasonable suspicion, probable cause, or exception), J-2007 (identification of defendant), J-2006 (invalid search warrant), J-2004 (no probable cause or warrant, "fruit of poisonous tree"), J-2003 (confession), J-2002 (anonymous tip and search exceeded scope of warrant), J-2001 (motion to suppress defendant's invocation of rights on video), J-2000 (identification and confession):

    Officer suspects Defendant is engaging in organized crime. Officer knocks on Defendant's apartment door. When Defendant opens the door, Officer enters the apartment without a search warrant, looks in each room in the apartment, sees contraband in one of the rooms, detains Defendant, and calls for a search warrant using the evidence he saw in the home as the basis for the warrant. When Officer obtains the search warrant, he seizes the contraband pursuant to the warrant.

What procedural step can you take to prevent the evidence and the officer's testimony about what he saw in the home from being admitted at trial? What will you argue? Explain.

_____

_____

_____

_____

_____

Note: When bar examiners ask what procedural step you should take to keep evidence from the fact finder, the answer is usually to file a motion to suppress the evidence. If you look through all of the motion to suppress questions over the years, you'll see that some of them resulted from unlawful actions, whereas others were pursuant to a valid warrant or an exception to the warrant requirement, which is the subject of the next chapter.

Many times, bar examiners ask what arguments you could make in addition to taking the procedural step. Bar examiner comments suggest that examinees forget to include either the step or the argument that supports exclusion of the evidence. Examiners have also noted examinees' erroneous answer that the inevitable discovery exception applies. Remember that Texas law differs from federal law in several key areas. On the Texas Criminal Procedure and Evidence portion of the bar exam, unless you are asked to compare Texas law to federal law (which has happened only twice, early in the exam's history), you need to relate only Texas, not federal law.

10. (J-2014 and F-2012) The State has offered a plea bargain, and Defendant is considering it. If Defendant enters a plea for the sentence Prosecutor is offering, will he be barred from appealing Judge's denial of his motion to suppress? Explain.

_____

_____

_____

_____

_____

11. (F-2013 and F-2012) Defendant and Friend attended a party where Defendant got into a fight with Victim. Defendant walked to Friend's car, retrieved a gun, and threatened to kill Victim. Someone called 911. Police responded and found Defendant and Friend nearby. Everyone else had already left the party. Officer asked Defendant what happened. Defendant admitted to Officer that he threatened Victim with a gun but did not kill him. Before Defendant is placed under arrest for aggravated assault with a deadly weapon, Officer conducted a warrantless search of Friend's car and found the gun inside.

    You file a motion to suppress the gun. What argument could Prosecutor make in response to your motion?

    _____

    _____

    _____

    _____

    _____

12. (F-2008) Judge denied your motion to suppress evidence. Can the jury at Defendant's trial still consider whether the evidence was obtained unlawfully? What procedural step, if any, should you take to have the jury consider this issue? Explain.

    _____

    _____

    _____

    _____

    _____

13. (J-2006 and J-2002) Can Prosecutor appeal a successful motion to suppress? What requirements, if any, must the State meet in order to do so? Explain.

    _____

    _____

    _____

Chapter 3
Warrantless Searches

Introduction

Searches with warrants are legally preferred over searches without them.[1] The Texas Constitution protects against unreasonable searches and seizures and places limits on warrantless searches.[2] As the Texas Court of Criminal Appeals states, "Fourth Amendment analysis of warrantless searches rests heavily on a simple notion: 'It remains a cardinal principle that searches conducted outside the judicial process, without prior approval by judge or magistrate, are per se unreasonable under the Fourth Amendment—subject only to a few specifically established and well-delineated exceptions.'"[3] This chapter will address these exceptions.

———————◆———————

---

[1] *State v. McLain*, 337 S.W.3d 268, 271 (Tex. Crim. App. 2011).
[2] TEX. CONST. art. I, §9.
[3] *State v. Villarreal*, 475 S.W.3d 784, 820 (Tex. Crim. App. 2014) (quoting *California v. Acevedo*, 500 U.S. 565, 580 (1991)).

Warrantless Searches

There are a number of exceptions to the search warrant requirement. Some are so frequently used that warrantless searches are commonplace. Nevertheless, the U.S. Supreme Court has stated that the search warrant exceptions "have been jealously and carefully drawn,"[4] and the Austin Court of Appeals echoes this sentiment by describing Texas's search warrant exceptions as "carefully crafted."[5] In order for the warrantless search to be upheld in court, the State has the burden to prove that the warrantless search fell within one of these delineated exceptions.[6] The search warrant exceptions that follow, many illustrated by a case, explain these narrow exceptions.

————————◆————————

Consent

Many legal rights, including Fourth Amendment protections, can be waived when the accused gives officers his consent to search. This consent waives the accused's right to have a search warrant issue upon probable cause, and it also likely waives the ability to contest the search at trial or on appeal. Officers frequently obtain consent from suspects to search a car, a house, or personal belongings. Even when a suspect knows he has contraband and officers may find it, he still may feel compelled to consent to the search.

However, just because a defendant acquiesces to a search does not make it a consensual search. These are some of the factors courts examine when determining objectively whether the defendant consented to the search freely:

1. whether, and to what extent, officers exhibited a show of force, including a display of weapons;
2. whether the actions of the officers could be classified as flagrant misconduct;
3. whether the police threatened to obtain a search warrant if the suspect did not acquiesce, or whether the police claimed a right to search;

---

[4] *Jones v. United States,* 357 U.S. 493, 499 (1958).
[5] *Ramirez v. State,* 105 S.W.3d 730, 743 (Tex. App.—Austin 2003, no pet.).
[6] *Wilson v. State,* 621 S.W.2d 799, 804 (Tex. Crim. App. 1981).

4. whether police first gave the suspect *Miranda* warnings ("You have the right to remain silent. Anything you say can and will be used against you in a court of law. You have the right to an attorney. If you cannot afford an attorney, one will be provided for you.");[7]

5. whether the arrest was made in order to obtain consent;

6. whether the suspect knew that he could refuse to allow a search;

7. whether consent was offered by the suspect or was in response to a police request; and

8. the suspect's education, intelligence, and physical condition at the time consent was given.[8]

Notice that several of these factors, if present, would point to the officers' attempt to break the will of the defendant through force or threat. No one fact, however, is dispositive. Courts examine the totality of circumstances to determine whether consent was voluntary, as illustrated by the following case.

Michael Moss v. State
878 S.W.2d 632
(Tex. App.—San Antonio 1994, pet. ref'd)

[Three law enforcement officers, DPS pilot Gene Matocha, DPS agent James Walker, and Kendall County Deputy Sheriff Hugo Boehm were looking from the air via helicopter] for a methamphetamine (speed) lab and a "chop shop," a stolen car operation. Their search for these locations was unsuccessful. ... As the helicopter rose out of the canyon ... Matocha, with a naked-eye observation, spotted marihuana growing in a garden "about a quarter of a mile to our right front." The fenced garden was about thirty to forty yards behind a house in an isolated area, an "extremely private location."

The observation necessitated a closer look to make a positive identification of the substance. Matocha circled and brought the helicopter down to "about 100 feet" over the garden and made a positive identification of about twenty growing marihuana plants. The helicopter circled and Matocha made a second pass over the garden area. Photographs were taken. Ground units, across the county at Comfort, were then called. At first, as the helicopter circled, there was no response from the house. Then a man (later

---

[7] *Miranda v. Arizona*, 384 U.S. 436 (1966).

[8] *Gallups v. State*, 104 S.W.3d 361, 366 (Tex. App.—Dallas 2003), *aff'd*, 151 S.W.3d 196 (Tex. Crim. App. 2004).

identified as appellant) came out of the house, looked up, and then walked to the front gate that he appeared to lock. He then returned to the house. Fearing that the marihuana would disappear, Matocha decided to land the helicopter. ... The ground units arrived in about twenty minutes. Matocha observed the ground units summon appellant to his front gate by use of loud speakers. The two units "went in."

...Appellant told Walker that the marihuana was grown only for appellant's personal use and that there were not many plants. He asked that "no big deal be made of it." Walker stated that he asked for and received appellant's consent to search. Appellant then voluntarily led the officers to the garden and to the shed. In the garden, the officers found twenty marihuana plants about four feet tall growing among Johnson grass and sunflower plants. Four male marihuana plants were found in the cloth-covered shed. Walker testified that appellant later signed a written consent form authorizing a search of the residence, but no contraband was found there.

Appellant testified that he lived on the thirty-five acre tract in the Alamo Springs Subdivision with his wife and three children, ages five, eight, and twelve years; that he was a self-employed furniture designer and builder; and that on the morning of August 14, 1990, he was preparing lunch for the children while his wife was at work.

At the time in question, appellant heard a helicopter and then saw it come in over his garden at about thirty-five feet and drop to about twenty feet below the level of the trees behind the garden. The helicopter flew in circles over the house and garden for about thirty to forty minutes. The wind turbulence of the helicopter flattened what tomato and other vegetable plants he had left in the garden and broke off the limbs of his fruit and other trees on the property. Appellant stated that the noise of the helicopter scared his children, who began to cry and became somewhat disoriented.

Appellant related that ground units arrived and that he was called out of his house by the use of bullhorns. Appellant came out of the house dressed in gym shorts and a tank top followed by his five-year-old daughter, who was scared to leave his side. Appellant stated that Deputy Leifeste had a drawn sawed-off shotgun pointed at him and his child and was screaming at him. Another officer was behind a car door with a pistol drawn, holding it with both hands. The officers screamed at him to get away from the child and to keep his hands up. The officers demanded admission to the property. When appellant asked if they had a search warrant, the officers said that they did not have one, but told appellant: "Well, it won't make any difference whether we have a search warrant or not. We can get one, so you might as well cooperate and open your gate, because the only difference it will be is about an hour and a half to two hours' difference." Appellant was then told that he could not return to the house to take care of the other two children as he was under arrest. Appellant was then instructed: "You can stand right here with us, if you want, but the helicopter is going to stay on top of your house and your garden and we're going to stand here with you and your five-year-old daughter until we get a search warrant."

When asked if he consented to having the officers enter his property, appellant stated that he did so "under duress."

George MacNaughton testified that he had been out jogging on the morning in question when a silver and blue helicopter came in over his property level with the roof line of his two story house; that the helicopter stayed in the area about five minutes; and that helicopter flight knocked items off the wall in his house and frightened his child.

... Grace Marie Butcher, who lived about a mile from appellant, testified that on the morning of August 14, 1990, a blue and gray helicopter flew over her trailer house for about five minutes at an altitude of about twenty feet, touching the top of the trees. Her children were scared and running in circles. She described the incident as a horrifying experience.

... Bill Moss, appellant's brother, testified that a gray-blue helicopter came over his house in the Alamo Springs Subdivision on the morning of August 14, 1990, at about thirty to thirty-five feet. When a neighbor later called about speeding vehicles that had been seen in the subdivision, Bill Moss telephoned appellant's house. Appellant's twelve-year-old daughter told him that the police were all over the place and "they had a gun on my dad." The daughter was "crying out of control."

In the instant case, ... the officers did not ... use their observations [of the marijuana plants from the air] as the basis for a search warrant based on probable cause. Here, the plot thickens. The pilot testified that when appellant came out of his house, apparently locked his front gate, and returned to the house, she and the other officers became fearful that if they left the scene the marihuana would disappear. The attempt to land the helicopter was ill-fated, and it continued to circle the area for some twenty to forty minutes. It was during this prolonged circling that there was noise, wind, turbulence, and the children became upset. There can be little question that at this point there was warrantless intrusion on appellant's property that violated appellant's reasonable expectation of privacy, albeit there was no seizure.

... [T]he officers ... should have maintained control of the premises while a search warrant was obtained instead of proceeding with a full warrantless search and seizure of evidence .... [U]nless the State had a right to rely upon another exception to the rule requiring both a warrant and probable cause, a search warrant should have been secured.

When a search is conducted pursuant to a valid consent to search, another exception arises. Consent must be freely and voluntarily given to be considered effective. The burden of proof is upon the State to show by clear and convincing evidence that the consent was freely and voluntarily given. The consent must be positive and unequivocal, and police must not have employed duress or coercion, actual or implied, in obtaining permission to search. Consent must not be physically or psychologically coerced. Whether consent to a search was in fact voluntary is a question of fact to be determined from the "totality of the circumstances."

Consent may be ineffective if induced by a show of force by police or other coercive surroundings at the time the consent is given. The display of weapons is a coercive factor that sharply reduces the likelihood of freely given consent. "This is certainly true when the person from whom the consent is being sought has just been arrested at gunpoint, but it is likewise the case when the person merely answers the door to find officers with guns drawn."

The fact that a person is under arrest does not, in and of itself, prevent a free and voluntary consent from being given. Custody is merely one of the factors to be considered. The burden of proving that consent was freely given cannot be discharged by showing no more than acquiescence to a claim of lawful authority. While a warning that an individual does not have to consent to a search and has the right to refuse is not required or essential, the showing of a warning is of evidentiary value in determining whether a valid consent was given. Likewise, the lack of any warning, though not required, is also probative on the issue of consent. An otherwise voluntary consent is not vitiated by the fact an officer asserts that he could seek or would obtain a search warrant if consent is refused. A threat to seek a warrant cannot always be said to be without probative effect.

In the instant case, the undisputed evidence shows that appellant was "bullhorned" from his residence by armed officers and placed under arrest. Agent Walker arrived on the scene some four minutes later. He was the only State witness to testify as to consent. There was no showing that appellant was given *Miranda* warnings or advised of his right to refuse to consent. Walker testified that he asked for appellant's consent to search and that appellant consented. Appellant testified he was arrested with guns pointed at him and his five-year-old daughter, as one officer screamed at him. When he asked about a search warrant, the armed officers told him that they could get one within two hours, but he and his five-year-old daughter would have to stay where they were until the warrant was secured, and that appellant could not return to the house to take care of his other two children. Appellant admitted that he consented but claimed that it was under duress. Walker could not remember whether the other officers had their guns drawn when he arrived. The officers in the ground units were not called to testify. We conclude, as a matter of law, that the State did not sustain its burden of proof by showing by clear and convincing evidence that the consent was freely and voluntarily given.

---◆---

Notes and Questions

1. In light of the burden of proof, what is significant about the fact the State called only one witness to testify about consent, and this one witness could not remember details about the encounter?

2. Consent need not be given verbally. In *Gallups v. State*, 104 S.W.3d 361, 367-69 (Tex. App.—Dallas 2003), *aff'd*, 151 S.W.3d 196 (Tex. Crim. App. 2004), the Court held the defendant's hand motion of waving officers into his home after officers requested to enter, amounted to consent to search the residence.

3. Others with common authority over the property can consent to a search. For example, a suspect's spouse may consent for police to search a residence.[9] A child's consent to search or seize evidence, on the other hand,

---

[9] *White v. State*, 21 S.W.3d 642, 646 (Tex. App.—Waco 2000, pet. ref'd) (wife "had common authority over the premises to be searched" because she lived in the residence for over a month).

is not sufficient to waive an adult's reasonable expectation of privacy.[10] The voluntariness of a third-party's consent is examined using a totality of circumstances test.

4. Refusal to consent does not give officers probable cause to search or arrest.[11] Probable cause to search "exists when reasonably trustworthy facts and circumstances within the knowledge of the officer on the scene would lead a man of reasonable prudence to believe that the instrumentality of a crime or evidence pertaining to a crime will be found."[12] Refusal to consent, without more, does not amount to probable cause.

5. In the *Moss* case, officers threatened to obtain a search warrant but never did. Suppose instead they unlawfully searched the premises and, based on what they discovered, obtained a search warrant. Would the search pursuant to the warrant have been lawful? When confronted with this issue, the Austin Court of Appeals held, once "a search warrant is issued on the basis of an affidavit containing unlawfully obtained information, the evidence seized under the warrant is admissible only if the warrant clearly could have been issued on the basis of the untainted information in the affidavit."[13]

6. It is good practice for officers to use a written consent form when a suspect verbally authorizes a search. After the defendant has consented and before the search begins, officers should inform the defendant of his *Miranda* rights, inform him he has the right to refuse to grant consent, and have him sign the form indicating he is waiving these rights. Some law enforcement agencies require officers to use a form such as this when obtaining a suspect's consent. Others do not. Why might officers prefer not to use a consent-to-search form, even when an informative consent waiver may later be used as evidence that consent was voluntarily given?

————————◆————————

[10] *Reynolds v. State*, 781 S.W.2d 351, 355 (Tex. App.—Houston [1st Dist.] 1989, pet. ref'd) ("We simply acknowledge the right to privacy in the bedroom area of one's own home, and under these facts, we refuse to entrust that precious right to the judgment of a 12-year-old boy.").
[11] *Smith v. State*, 243 S.W.3d 722, 724 n. 2 (Tex. App.—Texarkana 2007, pet. ref'd).
[12] *Washington v. State*, 660 S.W.2d 533, 535 (Tex. Crim. App. 1983).
[13] *Pitonyak v. State*, 253 S.W.3d 834, 848 (Tex. App.—Austin 2008, pet. ref'd).

Search Incident to Arrest

You have probably watched television shows, whether real or fictional, where an officer handcuffs a suspect, reads him his rights, and empties his pockets before he places him in the patrol car. When officers place someone under arrest, so long as the arrest is supported by probable cause and is otherwise lawful, officers have the right to search without a warrant. This is called *search incident to arrest,* but in order for the search to be lawful, what precedes it— a stop or an arrest— must be lawful. The *Barrow* case illustrates this search warrant exception.

Jerry Don Barrow v. State
241 S.W.3d 919
(Tex. App.—Eastland 2007, pet. ref'd)

The jury convicted Jerry Don Barrow of tampering with physical evidence and assessed his punishment at five years confinement. In two issues, he contends … his counsel was ineffective for not requesting a proper jury instruction on illegally obtained evidence. We affirm.

Midland Police Officer Chris Lummus was performing surveillance on King's Sandwich Shop in Midland because of suspected drug activity when he saw two males engaged in apparent drug trafficking. A vehicle approached the shop, and one of the males squeezed between the driver's door and the driver. After what appeared to be a drug transaction, the two went back to the shop and the vehicle drove away. Officer Lummus decided to follow the vehicle. When the driver failed to stop properly at an intersection, Officer Lummus initiated a traffic stop.

Officer Lummus identified the driver as Barrow. When Officer Lummus approached the vehicle, he saw white specks on Barrow's left arm and on his steering wheel. He thought these might be crack cocaine, and he asked Barrow to exit the vehicle. He suspected that Barrow had something in his mouth because he would not open his mouth fully and because of the way in which he spoke. Officer Lummus asked Barrow to open his mouth, which Barrow did momentarily. Officer Lummus observed a white rock-like object that appeared to be crack cocaine. Officer Lummus asked Barrow to spit it out. Barrow initially refused to do so. When Barrow eventually opened his mouth, there was no foreign object present. Officer Lummus believed Barrow had swallowed the object, and he placed him under arrest.

Barrow filed a pretrial motion to suppress. Barrow contended that he was unlawfully detained and asked the trial court to suppress any evidence obtained in connection with his detention. Barrow's motion was supported by his affidavit in which he stated that he was never presented with a warrant or advised of his rights and that he would have invoked his right to remain silent had he known of his right to do so. The trial court also received an affidavit from Officer Lummus describing his surveillance of the shop and Barrow's arrest. The trial court denied the motion to suppress, and the jury ultimately found Barrow guilty of tampering with physical evidence.

Barrow complains that his trial counsel was ineffective for failing to request a jury instruction pursuant to [the Texas exclusionary rule,] Article 38.23. When the trial court determines that evidence was obtained illegally, it must exclude that evidence from the jury's consideration. However, if there are disputed fact questions concerning the legality of a seizure, Article 38.23 requires the trial court to instruct the jury:

> [I]f [it] believes, or has a reasonable doubt, that the evidence was obtained in violation of ... any provisions of the Constitution or laws of the State of Texas, or the Constitution or laws of the United States of America, ... then and in such event, the jury shall disregard any such evidence so obtained.

…Barrow does not challenge the legality of the traffic stop …. Nor does Barrow identify what evidence the jury would have disregarded had it received an Article 38.23 instruction. Presumably, Barrow believes that a properly instructed jury would have determined that he was illegally stopped and disregarded the State's entire case. However, Barrow has failed to identify a fact question that would have justified an instruction. Officer Lummus testified that he stopped Barrow after observing him commit a traffic violation. Barrow never disputed Officer Lummus's statement that he failed to properly stop at an intersection. Barrow points to several instances in which trial counsel objected to the legality of the stop, but this is not the same as presenting conflicting evidence. The jury was presented with undisputed evidence that Officer Lummus stopped Barrow after observing him commit a traffic violation.

Because Officer Lummus properly stopped Barrow, the subsequent search was proper. …[P]olice may conduct a search incident to an arrest following a traffic stop. They may order passengers to exit their car pending completion of the stop, ... as well as search the person of the individual being arrested.... Officer Lummus's observation of the rock-like substance in Barrow's mouth after stopping him for a traffic offense falls within the scope of a valid search incident to an arrest. Barrow has failed to establish that he was entitled to an Article 38.23 instruction; therefore, we cannot conclude that his trial counsel was ineffective for not requesting one. Barrow's second issue is overruled.

————————◆————————

Notes and Questions

1. Notice that the above case repeats what you learned in the previous two chapters on arrest and search warrants: when there is a material fact issue in dispute on the legality of the officers' actions, the jury may, in its factfinder capacity, be asked to resolve the conflict. If the jurors find the stop was unlawful, they may disregard the evidence seized following that stop pursuant to Texas's exclusionary rule found in Article 38.23. Here, however, there was no factual issue in dispute; the defense did not contest the legality of the stop at Barrow's trial. Therefore, the judge never gave the jury a 38.23 instruction.

2. You may be tempted to think of a search traditionally: the search of pockets, a purse, a home, or a car. You should think of searches more broadly. *Barrow* illustrates that even the search of a mouth is a search that, when conducted without a warrant, must fall into one of the warrantless search exceptions.[14]

3. Not only may officers search a defendant incident to arrest, but they may also search the area surrounding the defendant at the time of the arrest. When a person is arrested following a traffic stop, this rule applies to the driver's area and passenger area of the car—the area within arm's reach of the arrestee. In addition, officers may search containers located in that area. However, the U.S. Supreme Court has more recently held that a warrantless automobile search incident to arrest is constitutional only when (1) the arrestee is within reaching distance of the vehicle during the search, or (2) the police have reason to believe that the vehicle contains evidence relevant to the crime of arrest.[15]

---

[14] See also *State v. Villarreal,* 475 S.W.3d 784 (Tex. Crim. App. 2014) (conducting the same analysis regarding a search for a suspect's blood).

[15] *Arizona v. Gant,* 556 U.S. 332, 343 (2009).

Terry Frisks

Another common search, not incident to arrest but incident to brief detentions, is the *Terry* frisk, pat down, or weapons search. This limited-in-scope search exists for officer safety. It derives its namesake from the well-known federal case, *Terry v. Ohio*, 392 U.S. 1 (1968), which was discussed in Chapter 1.

In *Terry*, an experienced officer noticed three men who appeared to be preparing to rob a store.[16] After observing the men for many minutes, he decided to approach them, identify himself, and investigate; believing they might be armed, he patted the exterior of their clothes and discovered guns on two of the men.[17] He confiscated the guns and arrested the men for carrying concealed weapons.[18]

The U.S. Supreme Court was asked to address whether it is always unreasonable for a policeman to seize a person and subject him to a limited search for weapons unless there is probable cause for an arrest.[19] After thoughtfully balancing officer safety and the intrusion of individual rights, the Court held:

> where a police officer observes unusual conduct which leads him reasonably to conclude in light of his experience that criminal activity may be afoot and that the persons with whom he is dealing may be armed and presently dangerous, where in the course of investigating this behavior he identifies himself as a policeman and makes reasonable inquiries, and where nothing in the initial stages of the encounter serves to dispel his reasonable fear for his own or others' safety, he is entitled for the protection of himself and others in the area to conduct a carefully limited search of the outer clothing of such persons in an attempt to discover weapons which might be used to assault him.[20]

When officers can quickly tell while conducting a frisk that they have found a weapon because of the way it feels (*e.g.*, a gun), they may remove the weapon and proceed with their investigation. The purpose for a frisk is officer safety, not to search for and seize contraband. Therefore, when

---

[16] *Terry*, 392 U.S. at 6.
[17] *Id.* at 6-7.
[18] *Id.* at 7.
[19] *Id.* at 15.
[20] *Id.* at 30.

officers do not believe the object in the suspect's pocket or under his clothing is a weapon, they are not permitted to remove, seize, or further inspect that object, that is, unless it is immediately apparent to the officer that the object is another type of contraband.[21]

To illustrate this point, suppose an officer working security at a bar is told by a patron that a man is acting suspiciously in a bathroom stall. Concerned for his safety, the officer briefly detains the man and pats him down. While he is patting the man down for weapons, he feels what he believes to be a baggie with pills in the man's shirt pocket. Suppose he then removes the baggie, discovers the pills are ecstasy, and arrests the man for possession of a controlled substance. Is this search justifiable under *Terry*? No, it is not. No officer would mistake a bag of pills for a weapon. In this instance, once the officer ascertained there were no weapons on the suspect, the basis for the frisk was over. If he developed an independent basis for probable cause to arrest him, he could have searched the man incident to that arrest. However, he may not rely on *Terry* for the search and seizure of the drugs because the search exceeded the scope of *Terry*, which permits a weapons frisk on the sole basis of officer safety.

———————◆———————

Protective Sweeps

Just as officers are permitted to do a weapons pat-down for protection, officers likewise are permitted to "sweep" through the home to make sure no one inside will harm them or use a weapon against them. Protective sweeps are an extension of the *Terry* search.

A protective sweep is permissible "when the officer reasonably believes that the area to be swept harbors an individual posing a danger to the persons present at the scene."[22] The purpose of this kind of search is to secure the premise to protect investigating officers.

In *Beaver v. State*, 942 S.W.2d 626, 628–29 (Tex. App.—Tyler 1996, pet. ref'd), officers had an arrest warrant for the defendant. Before they executed

---

[21] *Griffin v. State*, 215 S.W.3d 403, 410 (Tex. Crim. App. 2006) (citing *Minnesota v. Dickerson*, 508 U.S. 366, 375-76 (1993) (articulating the so-called "plain-feel" doctrine)).

[22] *Mondragon-Garcia v. State*, 129 S.W.3d 674, 677 (Tex. App.—Eastland 2004, pet. struck).

it, they watched his home from a nearby shop, where they saw several people entering and exiting. When the officers executed the arrest warrant at the home, they performed a protective sweep lasting about one minute to make sure others weren't inside. During the sweep, they saw items associated with methamphetamine distribution. They did not seize these items but were subsequently able to obtain a search warrant and seize this contraband. The defendant challenged the search and seizure on appeal. In upholding it, the Tyler Court of Appeals said,

> The officers detained Appellant prior to arrest only long enough to conduct a protective sweep for their own safety. The officers had observed individuals walking in and out of the Appellant's mobile home behind the radiator shop. The officers went to the mobile home to execute the warrant for Appellant's arrest and told Appellant they were going to perform a protective sweep to determine what other persons might be in the mobile home and if those persons were armed. The sweep was cursory and limited only to open areas.

Permissible protective sweeps should be limited in time and scope, focusing on places where people could hide, looking for weapons or people who could harm officers. Protective sweeps that are longer in duration, more exhaustive in nature, or extend to places where people or weapons could not fit are not justifiable under this exception. For example, the Eastland Court of Appeals held that an officer's decision to look under a mattress for a person was unreasonable and exceeded the scope of the protective sweep.[23]

Protective sweeps do not just apply to homes. They also apply to automobiles. Officers may sweep the passenger compartment of a car or any reachable area, such as an unlocked glove compartment, if they have reason to believe the detainee has a weapon in the vehicle. The Austin Court of Appeals explains why:

> [O]ne purpose for permitting *Terry* searches of automobiles is "to make sure there [are] no weapons in a lungeable area, so that when we allow him back in the car, the officers are safe." Nonetheless, before such a search is undertaken, the officer conducting the search must have a reasonable basis

---

[23] *Id.*

for believing that the suspect is dangerous and may gain control of a weapon when he reenters the vehicle.[24]

However, when there is no indication the driver or the passengers of the vehicle are armed, or there is no reasonable suspicion the vehicle houses weapons that occupants can access, a weapons search of the vehicle is unlawful.[25]

———————◆———————

Plain View Doctrine

Plain view is less of a search exception and more of a doctrine. Why? When officers see evidence of a crime in plain view—in the open—they have obviously not searched to find it. Calling this a search exception is therefore a bit of a misnomer. Nevertheless, academics and practitioners place it among the search warrant exceptions because no warrant is required to seize what is seen in plain view. Perhaps it should be called the "plain view seizure exception."

The Amarillo Court of Appeals described the doctrine as follows:

> This "plain view" seizure doctrine allows an officer to seize an item during a warrantless search if (1) the officer sees an item in plain view at a vantage point where he has the right to be, and (2) it is immediately apparent that the item seized constitutes evidence—that is, there is probable cause to associate the item with criminal activity. Because such an officer is legitimately on the private premises, and so long as he has not exceeded the authority granted him . . . that legitimizes his presence in the first place, he may seize any item in plain view that probable cause tells him is contraband.[26]

Rarely is the seized item something seemingly innocuous, though this too may happen. In *State v. Dobbs*,[27] officers spotted golf clubs and clothing while

———————

[24] *Horton v. State*, 16 S.W.3d 848, 853–54 (Tex. App.—Austin 2000, no pet.)(quoting *Michigan v. Long*, 463 U.S. 1032, 1050–51 (1983)).

[25] *Id.* at 854 ("[T]he State failed to prove that the officers had specific, articulable facts that reasonably warranted a belief that appellant's car contained a weapon or that appellant himself was dangerous.").

[26] *Shadden v. State*, 431 S.W.3d 623, 629 (Tex. App.—Amarillo 2014, pet. ref'd) (citations omitted).

[27] 323 S.W.3d 184, 185 (Tex. Crim. App. 2010).

executing a valid search warrant on the defendant's premises. Upon further investigation, officers discovered these items were stolen. The Court was asked to interpret the "immediately apparent" part of the doctrine outlined above. It held that

> viewing officers must have probable cause to believe an item in plain view is contraband before seizing it. So long as the probable cause to believe that items in plain view constitute contraband arises while the police are still lawfully on the premises, and their "further investigation" into the nature of those items does not entail an additional and unjustified search of (*i.e.*, a greater physical intrusion than originally justified), or presence on (*i.e.*, a longer intrusion than originally justified), the premises, we see no basis to declare a Fourth Amendment violation. Supreme Court precedent does not dictate that we construe "immediately apparent" necessarily to mean "quickly apparent." Rather, "immediately apparent" in this context means without the necessity of any further search.[28]

Plain view seizures are a commonly invoked exception to the warrant requirement.

———————◆———————

Notes and Questions

1.   There are many types of plain searches beyond plain view. *Terry* frisks involve "plain feel": The officer must be able to determine that it is a weapon by feeling it before she can seize it.

There are also "plain smell" searches. Marijuana has a unique smell that is immediately recognizable. However, even when officers smell marijuana, they must have probable cause to search or be able to justify the search under one of the warrant exceptions.[29] Nevertheless, the smell of marijuana may justify reasonable suspicion to detain a person and investigate further.

———————◆———————

---

[28] *Id.* at 189.
[29] *State v. Steelman*, 93 S.W.3d 102, 108 (Tex. Crim. App. 2002) ("This Court has recognized that 'odors alone do not authorize a search without a warrant.'").

Inventory or Administrative Searches

Inventory searches are conducted as a matter of standardized policy or routine. Their purpose is not a design to uncover evidence of crime, though sometimes they may. There are a number of types of inventory or administrative searches. For example, when a car is impounded or when a person is booked into jail, personal belongings are inventoried and are temporarily stored in a secure location. These searches protect the person's property and the entity storing the property. Other forms of administrative searches occur at airports, checkpoints, along borders, or in closely regulated businesses or industries. These administrative searches occur as a matter of policy or security.[30] That incriminating evidence may be found during these searches does not invalidate their general permissibility.

The following case illustrates the automobile inventory search, which is invoked when a person is arrested and the contents of the vehicle are inventoried, and the vehicle is towed and impounded until the person is released from jail. Pay particular attention to the policy reasons for this exception, its requirements, and the unique nature of automobile searches that the Court of Criminal Appeals considered in its analysis.

Oscar Romeo Benavides v. State
600 S.W.2d 809
(Tex. Crim. App. 1980)

This is an appeal from a conviction for the offense of murder....

On April 25, 1977, Dallas police officers were dispatched to a Dallas residence where they found the appellant and his wife on the garage floor. They both had been shot; appellant's wife was dead and the appellant had a stomach wound. A handgun and spent cartridges were found at the scene. Appellant was taken to a nearby hospital. The police, after asking appellant's half-brother what kind of vehicle appellant drove, ascertained the location of appellant's automobile. The automobile was locked and legally parked about two blocks away from the premises where the appellant and his wife's body were found. The automobile was impounded and prior to its being towed it was searched and an inventory was made. The search was made without a

---

[30] *E.g., Gibson v. State,* 921 S.W.2d 747, 757-58 (Tex. App.—El Paso 1996, pet. ref'd); *City of Los Angeles v. Patel,* 135 S. Ct. 2443, 2452-55 (2015).

warrant and there is no evidence of probable cause for the search. Certain items were discovered in the search but only the purported suicide note was admitted in evidence. The note was offered as part of the prosecution's case in chief and it was important to the State's theory of murder and attempted suicide. Admitting the note in evidence was not harmless error.

The State's sole contention is that the note was properly obtained pursuant to an inventory search as approved in *South Dakota v. Opperman*, 428 U.S. 364 (1976). In *Opperman*, the Supreme Court upheld the practice of police securing and inventorying an automobile's contents pursuant to a standard procedure when an automobile was impounded. The procedures, the Court stated, were developed to protect the owner's property while it was in police custody, to protect the police against claims or disputes over lost or stolen property, and to protect the police against potential danger. However, before any need arises to inventory the contents of an automobile there must be a lawful impoundment. The Supreme Court stated in *Opperman*:

> The (police) were indisputably engaged in a caretaking search of a lawfully impounded automobile. The inventory was conducted only after the car had been impounded for multiple parking violations. The owner, having left his car illegally parked for an extended period and thus subject to impoundment, was not present to make other arrangements for the safekeeping of his belongings. The inventory itself was prompted by the presence in plain view of a number of valuables inside the car. ... [T]here is no suggestion whatever that this standard procedure . . . was a pretext concealing an investigatory police motive.[31]

Therefore, before an inventory search can be upheld as lawful there must be an inquiry into the lawfulness of the impoundment.

The automobile has been subject to less stringent warrant requirements for searches and seizures than other "effects" protected under the Fourth Amendment. The reasons for this are twofold. First, the inherent mobility of an automobile creates circumstances of such exigency that as a matter of practical necessity strict enforcement of the warrant requested is impossible. Second, there is a lesser expectation of privacy with respect to an automobile. ... Nonetheless automobiles are "effects" and within the scope of the Fourth Amendment... "The word 'automobile' is not a talisman in whose presence the Fourth Amendment fades away and disappears." Thus in

[31] 428 U.S. at 375.

order for an impoundment of an automobile to be lawful, the seizure of the automobile must be reasonable under the Fourth Amendment.

The Supreme Court in *Opperman* and in decisions since then has failed to earnestly discuss what is necessary for an impoundment of an automobile to be considered a reasonable seizure. Still the Court in *Opperman* did mention two bases for a lawful impoundment. The Court stated:

> In the interest of public safety and as part of what the court has called 'community caretaking functions' automobiles are frequently taken into police custody. Vehicle accidents present one such occasion. To permit the uninterrupted flow of traffic and in some circumstances to preserve evidence, disabled or damaged vehicles will often be removed from the highway or street at the behest of police engaged solely in caretaking and traffic control activities. Police will also frequently remove and impound automobiles which violate parking ordinances and thereby jeopardize both the public safety and the efficient movement of vehicle traffic. The authority of police to seize and impound from the streets vehicles impeding traffic or threatening public safety and convenience is beyond challenge.[32]

Besides removal from an accident scene or impoundment for parking violations as stated above, the police may lawfully impound vehicles in other circumstances. Thus where the owner or driver requests or consents to the impoundment, the seizure would be reasonable. The impoundment is lawful if the automobile is stolen or the police have a reasonable belief that it is stolen. If the vehicle is abandoned, a hazard, or so mechanically defective that it creates a danger to others using public streets or highways it may be lawfully impounded. An automobile may be impounded if the driver is arrested for being intoxicated while in the vehicle and no other person is available to drive the vehicle or otherwise safeguard the vehicle. Police may impound a vehicle if they are authorized to do so under a statute. Also, an automobile may be impounded if the driver is removed from his automobile and placed under custodial arrest and no other alternatives are available other than impoundment to insure the protection of the vehicle.

While the cases cited above do not include every basis that an impoundment has been upheld, they are indicative of the grounds that most jurisdictions would agree upon to allow impoundments. We now turn to the merits of the case.

---

[32] 428 U.S. at 368–69.

The police officer who authorized the impoundment stated that it was impounded for "protective custody" and that he was reasonably sure that it belonged to the appellant. He stated further that it was standard operating procedure to take the vehicle of an accused into custody when the accused had been arrested. Also he stated that there were no valuables in plain view but a key ring with keys on it was visible under the dashboard. While there is some confusion as to whether the appellant had been formally charged when the impoundment took place we conclude that that is not controlling in these facts and circumstances. What is controlling is that the only reason given for the impounding of the vehicle was its "safekeeping."

We conclude that neither *Opperman* nor any Supreme Court decision authorizes this kind of seizure. The mere arrest of a defendant cannot be construed to authorize the seizure of his automobile when the arrest took place two or more blocks away from the automobile. There was no evidence that the car was impeding the flow of traffic or that it was a danger to public safety. The vehicle was legally parked in a residential area and it was locked.

The State contends that a local ordinance prohibits a vehicle from being parked in one position on a street for over twenty-four hours. Further they argue that since the appellant was seriously wounded and under arrest he would be unable to take any action in moving his car the police were justified in impounding the vehicle for its own protection. This argument is without merit. First of all, no violation of the ordinance had yet occurred. We cannot agree that a pre-violation seizure of an automobile is permissible. Furthermore there was no testimony that it was standard procedure to impound a vehicle for this violation or whether the issuance of a citation was the usual procedure. Also while the appellant himself may not have been able to attend to the vehicle he may have been able to instruct someone to do it for him. Finally, there was no basis stated why the police were reasonably concerned with the protection of the appellant's property.

While it may have been standard police procedure to impound the vehicle of a person who is arrested we conclude that the Fourth Amendment protection against seizures cannot be whittled away by a police regulation. For such a procedure there must be some reasonable connection between the arrest and the vehicle. In the case … none existed. Nor was there any other reasonable ground given for the impoundment. We, therefore, hold that the impoundment of appellant's automobile and the subsequent search were unlawful.

Notes and Questions

1. Law enforcement agencies have vehicle inventory policies that help officers know when it is permissible to inventory a vehicle's contents following the driver's arrest. Courts look to these policies when the search is challenged. Consider what the U.S. Supreme Court said in *Florida v. Wells*, 495 U.S. 1, 5 (1990):

> The facts of this case demonstrate a prime danger of insufficiently regulated inventory searches: police may use the excuse of an "inventory search" as a pretext for broad searches of vehicles and their contents. In this case, there was no evidence that the inventory search was done in accordance with any standardized inventory procedure.

Not only do courts look to ensure a law enforcement officer followed her employer's inventory policy, but they also may be critical of the policy itself. An overbroad policy may permit the search of every vehicle under any circumstance. Evidence discovered following a search pursuant to an overbroad inventory policy may be suppressible.

2. The State has the burden of establishing the warrantless search was legally permissible. According to a Houston Court of Appeals, the State "may satisfy its burden by showing that (1) the driver was arrested, (2) no alternatives other than impoundment were available to insure the automobile's protection, (3) the impounding agency had an inventory policy, and (4) the policy was followed."[33] The Court added that police officers do not have to investigate whether there are alternatives to impoundment, but that alternatives may, in fact, exist that the officer is immediately aware of at the time the driver is arrested.[34]

3. The *Benavides* opinion lays out several sets of principles that should be considered when examining the lawfulness of automobile inventory searches.

   a. What are reasons the police department is permitted to impound and inventory a vehicle?
   b. What are reasonable alternatives to impounding a vehicle that may be available to officers? Must officers exhaust those reasonable alternatives before they impound a vehicle?
   c. Who is protected by an inventory policy?
   d. If there is an inventory policy, how closely must it be followed?

---

[33] *Garza v. State*, 137 S.W.3d 878, 882 (Tex. App.—Houston [1st Dist.] 2004, pet. ref'd).
[34] *Id.*

4. Why did the State carry the burden of proving the search was proper in the *Benavides* case? Who carries the burden in a motion to suppress hearing or at trial when the search was conducted pursuant to a search warrant? Who carries the burden when officers seized evidence in a warrantless search?

5. Inventory searches and seizures happen in other contexts for the same reason: to protect the property from being stolen and to protect the entity holding the property from claims of theft or to protect the entity from harm. For example, hospitals and prisons conduct inventory searches. Think back to television shows and movies you've watched where a soon-to-be released inmate is given an envelope with items he wore or had on his person when he was incarcerated. These items were seized through an inventory search when the inmate was booked into jail. If you observe a criminal court docket, you see an inventory search and seizure happen daily as the bailiff takes a person into custody following a guilty plea or verdict. The property the bailiff seizes from a defendant in the courtroom is inventoried, stored in the jail, and returned to the defendant once he is released from jail.

6. Border checkpoint searches are another form of administrative searches. In *Gutierrez v. State*, 22 S.W.3d 75, 77-83 (Tex. App.—Corpus Christi 2000, no pet.), the appellate court stated, "Border patrol checkpoint operations are conducted pursuant to statutory authorizations empowering border patrol agents to interrogate those believed to be aliens as to their right to be in the United States." Thus, when the defendant exhibited nervous behavior, it was permissible for officers to search his vehicle thoroughly, as was customary at the checkpoint.

7. DWI checkpoints are a different matter altogether. They are deemed a "suspicionless search" with the goal of detaining people and detecting crime.[35] Officers most commonly use these types of roadblocks to find people who are driving while intoxicated. Courts generally weigh the public's interest in the roadblock against the individual's right to privacy, using three factors: (1) the state's interest in preventing accidents caused by drunk drivers; (2) the effectiveness of the DWI roadblock in preventing accidents; and (3) the level of the intrusion on road-blocked driver's privacy.[36] The Court of Criminal Appeals has held that these types of seizures are unconstitutional unless they are part of an "authorized statewide procedure" overseen by a

---

[35] *Holt v. State*, 887 S.W.2d 16, 18 (Tex. Crim. App. 1994).
[36] *Id.*

"politically accountable governing body" with constitutional policies in place.[37] To date, these criteria have not been met. Thus, while DWI checkpoints are permitted in other states, they are not currently carried out in Texas.

————————◆————————

The Automobile Exception

Automobiles are treated differently than searches of homes. The automobile exception to the warrant requirement permits a warrantless search of a vehicle when officers have probable cause to believe it contains contraband. There are at least two reasons for this exception.

First, vehicles by their very nature are mobile. A car containing incriminating evidence can be driven away or easily hidden. Officers have less time to obtain a search warrant for a vehicle given its mobility. Therefore, courts permit more relaxed standards when it comes to automobiles when an officer has probable cause to believe it contains contraband.

Second, owners of cars have a lower expectation of privacy in the contents than an owner of a house. Think about the last time you walked through a parking lot. If you wanted to, you could have peered inside every automobile to see personal items within. When an officer conducts a traffic stop and approaches your window to ask for your license and insurance, he can see most of the vehicle's interior. When you take your car to be inspected, to the mechanic, or allow passengers to ride with you, others are given access to the interior of your automobile and can see its contents. For all of these reasons, automobiles are viewed differently by courts.

Many other warrantless search exceptions are applicable to automobile searches as well, as you see in the next case.

Arturo Lopez v. State
223 S.W.3d 408
(Tex. App.—Amarillo 2006, no pet.)

Presenting a sole issue, appellant asserts the trial court erred in overruling his motion to suppress evidence based on lack of probable cause to search the locked gas compartment of his vehicle. We affirm.

---

[37] *Id.* at 19.

... While on patrol one evening, Officer Jeffrey Coffey stopped appellant because his car displayed blue turn signals in violation of the Transportation Code. ...Coffey approached the driver's side and asked appellant for his driver's license and insurance card; he had neither. A check revealed no outstanding warrants and that appellant possessed a Texas identification card, but no Texas driver's license. While in the process of issuing a citation to appellant, Officer Coffey approached the passenger's side of the car to determine if the passenger could take custody of the vehicle once the stop was completed.

Initially, the passenger gave a false name. He quickly admitted doing so and was arrested for failure to identify himself and placed in the back of the patrol car. Appellant and the child in the back seat were asked to exit the car to conduct a search incident to the passenger's arrest. Coffey began with a search of the driver's side and, as he proceeded around the rear of the vehicle to the passenger's side, observed a "tiny bit" of a plastic baggie in the crease around the gas cap compartment located on the rear driver's side.

Believing he had probable cause, Coffey entered the car and pulled the release lever to disengage the gas cap cover without appellant's consent. He observed but did not remove at that time the plastic baggie containing what appeared to be a white powder located inside the gas compartment. The record at the suppression hearing does not demonstrate when, or under what circumstances, the baggie was seized.

... [A]ppellant challenges the denial of his motion to suppress asserting a lack of probable cause to search the locked gas compartment. He maintains the search was constitutionally invalid as either a search incident to the passenger's arrest or a search pursuant to the automobile exception. The State contends the seizure of the narcotics was legitimate under both the automobile exception and the plain view doctrine. The discrete question presented for our review is whether the officer had probable cause to open the locked gas cap compartment without consent or a search warrant.

Search Incident to Arrest

A search incident to arrest is limited to an arrestee's person and the area in his immediate control to prevent him from obtaining possession of a weapon or concealing or destroying evidence.... In *New York v. Belton*, 453 U.S. 454, 459–60, (1981), to establish a workable rule regarding the definition of the area within an arrestee's immediate control, the Court held that when an officer makes a lawful custodial arrest of the occupant of a vehicle, he may, contemporaneously incident to that arrest, search the passenger compartment of the vehicle. A lawful search also includes the contents of containers found within the passenger compartment of the vehicle.[38]

According to Coffey's testimony on direct examination, after the passenger was arrested and placed in the patrol car, he began his search of the interior of the car on the driver's side. During cross-examination, Coffey indicated an intent to search the passenger's immediate wingspan. No incriminating evidence was discovered in the interior of the car. It was after this search that Coffey noticed the plastic baggie in the crease of the gas cap compartment and investigated further to discover the cocaine. Coffey testified the gas cap compartment was located outside the vehicle on the rear driver's side. Concluding that *Chimel* and *Belton* do not validate the search of the gas cap compartment, we next consider the automobile exception to warrantless searches.

Automobile Exception

In 1925, the Supreme Court established the automobile exception to the Fourth Amendment's warrant requirement in *Carroll v. United States*, 267 U.S. 132 (1925). It held that a warrantless search of a vehicle stopped by officers with probable cause to believe the vehicle contained contraband did not run afoul of the Fourth Amendment. *Carroll* distinguished a search of dwellings or structures with a search of movable vessels and rationalized that mobility justified a warrantless search. The Court then addressed under what circumstances a warrantless search was reasonable and concluded probable cause was necessary. ...

Then, in *Chambers v. Maroney*, 399 U.S. 42 (1970), the Court found no distinction, given probable cause, between carrying out an immediate search of a vehicle without a warrant or seizing and holding the vehicle and conducting a delayed search. In *Chambers*, witnesses to an armed robbery described the vehicle, its four occupants, and some of their clothing to officers. Shortly after details were broadcast over the police radio, officers stopped a vehicle answering the description. The occupants were arrested

---

[38] The breadth of a search of a vehicle incident to arrest was later limited by the Supreme Court in *Arizona v. Gant*, 556 U.S. 332 (2009).

and the vehicle was driven to the police station and thoroughly searched. Evidence material to the robbery was discovered and introduced at trial.

The Supreme Court reasoned that probable cause is determined at the time of the stop and if an immediate search is valid, so too is a later search. The justification to conduct a warrantless search does not vanish once the vehicle is immobilized.

In 1982, the Supreme Court clarified the scope of a *Carroll* automobile search and held that officers may conduct a search of a vehicle that is as thorough as a magistrate could authorize in a warrant describing the place to be searched. *See United States v. Ross*, 456 U.S. 798, 800 (1982). Ross was stopped by officers based on a reliable informant's tip that he was selling narcotics stored in the trunk of his car. A warrantless search of the interior of the car revealed a bullet in the front seat and a pistol in the glove compartment. Ross was arrested and handcuffed. Thereafter, a detective took his keys and opened the trunk of the car to reveal a closed brown paper bag which the detective opened to discover a number of bags containing white powder, later determined to be heroin. He replaced the bag, closed the trunk, and drove the car to the police station. In addition to the brown paper bag, a thorough search revealed a red zippered leather pouch which contained $3,200 in cash.

The Court explained that the scope of a warrantless search of a vehicle is defined by the object of the search and the places in which there is probable cause to believe it may be found. It held that if probable cause exists to believe contraband is concealed in a lawfully stopped vehicle, officers are justified in conducting a probing search of compartments and containers within the vehicle whose contents are not in plain view and which may conceal the object of the search.

A different line of cases developed regarding luggage, bags, and other closed containers under *United States v. Chadwick*, 433 U.S. 1 (1977). In *Chadwick*, federal agents had probable cause to believe that marihuana was contained in a 200 pound padlocked footlocker being transported by train. The locker was carried through the train station to a waiting car. As the defendants lifted the locker into the trunk of the car, they were arrested. The locker was seized, removed to a secure place, and searched without a warrant. The Court recognized that a person's expectation of privacy in luggage is substantially greater than in a vehicle. It rejected the argument that the search of the footlocker was analogous to a warrantless search of an automobile because it also had mobile characteristics and instead, reaffirmed the principle that closed containers and packages may not be searched without a warrant.

The *Chadwick* rule was extended to a suitcase being transported in the trunk of a car in *Arkansas v. Sanders*, 442 U.S. 753 (1979). Officers received a tip that the defendant would be arriving at the airport with a suitcase containing marihuana. They observed the defendant place his suitcase in the trunk of a taxi, enter the taxi, and drive away. Officers pursued and stopped the taxi and seized and searched the suitcase without a warrant. The Court was presented with the task of determining whether the search of the suitcase fell under the *Chadwick* or *Chambers/Carroll* rules. The Court found no justification for applying the automobile exception and, instead, emphasized the heightened expectation of privacy in personal luggage and concluded its presence in a car did not diminish the owner's expectation. It held the warrant requirement of the Fourth Amendment applied to personal luggage taken from an automobile.

The dichotomy presented over the years was that if probable cause existed to search a car, then the entire car, including any closed containers could be searched, but if probable cause existed only as to a container in a car, the container could be held but not searched without a warrant. Presented with the discrepancy between the *Chadwick* and *Ross* rules and the confusion for law enforcement ... the Court revisited the different lines of cases and held the Fourth Amendment does not compel separate treatment for an automobile search that extends only to a container within the car.

The Court re-examined the privacy protections of the *Chadwick-Sanders* line of cases and concluded any protection was minimal because more than likely a warrant would be forthcoming to search the container that had been seized. It interpreted *Carroll* as providing one clear-cut rule to govern automobile searches and eliminated the warrant requirement for closed containers. That rule is that, given probable cause to believe the presence of contraband or evidence, officers may search an automobile and the containers within it without a warrant.

The foundation for a warrantless search of an automobile is probable cause. Probable cause has been defined as the sum total of layers of information, and not merely individual layers and considerations that a reasonable and prudent man acts upon. It exists when facts and circumstances within the officer's knowledge or about which he has reasonably trustworthy information are sufficient to warrant a person of reasonable caution to believe that an offense was or is being committed. Additionally, probable cause is determined by the totality of the circumstances.

According to the testimony at the suppression hearing, appellant had purchased the car just two weeks earlier from a neighbor and had been in possession of it for one week. Officer Coffey testified he was working with the Violent Crime Reduction Task Force and that in his knowledge and experience, appellant was stopped in a high crime area for narcotics. Regarding the "tiny bit" of a plastic baggie in the crease of the gas cap compartment, Coffey testified his suspicion was aroused because there was no reason for a baggie to be in that location. Based on his training and experience, he knew the gas cap compartment was an area used for concealing narcotics.

On cross-examination, Coffey testified his search of the interior of the car revealed no incriminating evidence. Additionally, he testified that neither appellant nor the passenger appeared to be under the influence. The record establishes that no furtive gestures were made, and there was no attempt to conceal anything at the time of the stop. Coffey admitted he had nothing articulable to suspect narcotics.

Based on Coffey's testimony that appellant was stopped in a high crime area for narcotics and that in his experience a car's gas cap compartment is an area for concealing them, he had probable cause to believe an offense was being committed.

Plain View Doctrine—Gas Cap Compartment

Moreover, based on the following analysis, under the plain view doctrine, the officer had probable cause that the plastic baggie presented incriminating evidence. ...

It is well established that under certain circumstances officers may seize evidence in plain view without a warrant. Plain view alone, however, is never enough to justify the warrantless seizure of evidence. Two requirements must be satisfied. They are: (1) the officer must have a prior justification or otherwise properly be in a position from which he can view the area, and (2) it must be immediately apparent to the officer that the item may be evidence of a crime, contraband, or otherwise subject to seizure.

The plain view doctrine involves no invasion of privacy and, thus, cannot be considered an exception to the Fourth Amendment warrant requirement. *Texas v. Brown*, 460 U.S. 730, 738–39 (1983). If an item is in plain view, neither its observation nor its seizure involves any invasion of privacy.

In *Brown*, the Court was confronted with the "immediately apparent" requirement and noted the phrase "was very likely an unhappy choice of words, since it can be taken to imply that an unduly high degree of certainty as to the incriminatory character of evidence is necessary for an application of the 'plain view' doctrine." Brown was stopped as part of a routine driver's license checkpoint. As the officer shined his flashlight into the car, he noticed Brown take his hand out of his right pants pocket. Between his two middle fingers he was holding an opaque, green party balloon, knotted about one-half inch from the top. He let the balloon fall to the seat beside his leg and reached across to open the glove compartment to look for his license. The officer noticed small plastic vials containing loose white powder and an open bag of party balloons in the glove compartment. After Brown was asked to exit the vehicle, the officer picked up the green party balloon and noticed a powdery substance within the tied-off portion. After Brown was arrested, the officers discovered other contraband.

The Court of Criminal Appeals concluded the officer had to *know* that "incriminating evidence was before him when he seized the balloon." The Supreme Court, however, concluded the opaque texture of the balloon was irrelevant and its distinctive character spoke volumes as to its contents, especially to the trained eye of the officer. Also, the officer testified he had knowledge that balloons tied in the manner of the one possessed by Brown were used to package narcotics. Other evidence from Brown's car suggested he was involved in possession of contraband. Without resolving whether probable cause was required to invoke the plain view doctrine, the Court decided that what was required to satisfy the immediately apparent prong was a "practical, nontechnical" probability that incriminating evidence was involved.

…The fact that an item comes lawfully within an officer's plain view cannot, alone, supplant the requirement of probable cause.

Here, Officer Coffey was lawfully in a position from which to view the tiny bit of the plastic baggie. His prior justifications for the search were a valid traffic stop and a search incident to the passenger's arrest. He was in the process of issuing a citation to appellant when he noticed the baggie conspicuously located in the crease of the gas cap compartment. The immediately apparent prong does not require actual knowledge by the officer of incriminating evidence. It is not essential that the officer's belief be correct or more likely true than false.

The Court of Criminal Appeals has recognized that certain objects not inherently suspicious can become so under certain circumstances. *See generally Gonzales v. State*, 648 S.W.2d 684, 686 (Tex. Crim. App. 1983) (balloons containing heroin); *Sullivan v. State*, 626 S.W.2d 58, 59 (Tex. Crim. App. 1981) (a partially unzipped pouch exposing a dark brown bottle and a clear plastic bag containing a white powder); ... *Duncan v. State*, 549 S.W.2d 730, 732 (Tex. Crim. App. 1977) (recognizing the popularity of plastic bags as containers for narcotics, but declining to hold that the bag itself, without more, is contraband). Accordingly, a plastic baggie, under suspicious circumstances, can provide probable cause to invoke the plain view doctrine.

As previously noted, the evidence established that appellant was stopped in a high crime area for narcotics. Officer Coffey, in his experience, could conceive of no other reason for a plastic baggie to be visible in the crease of the gas cap compartment other than to conceal narcotics. Given the facts and circumstances within his knowledge, Coffey had probable cause to believe the plastic baggie presented evidence of a crime sufficient to satisfy the immediately apparent prong.

The act of opening the locked gas cap compartment on his own volition because he knew it was a common hiding area for narcotics is analogous to the officer in Brown knowing that balloons are frequently used to carry narcotics. The tip of the baggie exposed in the crease of the gas cap compartment was in plain view just as the knotted balloon was in Brown. Neither the baggie nor the balloon showed any contraband until further investigation based on probable cause. We conclude that under the plain view doctrine, the search of the gas cap compartment was constitutionally valid. The trial court did not abuse its discretion in denying appellant's motion to suppress. Appellant's sole issue is overruled.

Accordingly, the trial court's judgment is affirmed.

———————◆———————

Notes and Questions

1. There are many categories of automobile searches. Can you craft a rule for each of the following, based upon the *Lopez* case?

    a. The automobile exception to the warrant requirement.

    b. Delayed searches of vehicles.

    c. Compartment searches.

    d. Container searches.

2. While the automobile exception treats vehicles differently due to their mobility and lack of privacy, based upon *Lopez*, are the requirements for warrantless searches the same in an automobile and elsewhere? In other words, do the legal requirements for plain view apply equally to the car here as they would for other places?

---◆---

Emergency, Exigency, and Hot Pursuit

Policing can be dangerous, and at critical times, officers may not have time to obtain a search warrant. Courts recognize a handful of emergency circumstances that produce limited opportunities to bypass the warrant requirement: exigent circumstances, emergency doctrine, and hot pursuit. These searches are permissible when officers are objectively faced with an emergency and have probable cause to support the search.

Several underlying reasons justify relaxing the warrant requirement when exigent circumstances exist: the inability to get a warrant given the urgent circumstances, the possibility the suspect will get away or evidence will be destroyed, and the dangers present if officers are forced to wait before they search. Courts must weigh these circumstances against the accused's privacy rights, as the next case illustrates.

Richard Brimage v. State
918 S.W.2d 466
(Tex. Crim. App. 1996)

[Appellant worked with Mary Beth Kunkel and her boyfriend, Michael Beagly. Appellant asked Kunkel to come to his house to pick up some tools for Beagly. When she arrived, Appellant and his roommate physically attacked, restrained, sexually assaulted, and then killed Kunkel. When Beagly found Kunkel's car parked in an unusual place, he filed a missing person report.

At some point after the police began to investigate her disappearance,] the investigation began to focus on appellant. The police knew of his acquaintance with Kunkel; knew that appellant had quit his job without notice; and knew that Kunkel's car had been found … near appellant's residence. Throughout the two days of the investigation neither the police nor appellant's former employers were able to contact him. The police had also been told that the month before appellant had attempted to sexually assault another woman.

…[P]olice officers acted on their suspicions and went to appellant's home on West Richard. When no one answered their knocks at the front door, the officers explored the outside of the house, peering through the windows and checking for unlocked doors. The officers found all the doors and windows locked, the garage door down and the lights out. The officers left the West Richard residence satisfied that no one was home. It was at this point that Captain George Gomez, Jr., a detective with the Kingsville Police Department, assumed supervision of the investigation.

That afternoon, Gomez contacted Roy C. Turcotte, a local attorney and a relative of appellant. Gomez told Turcotte that he suspected appellant was involved in Kunkel's disappearance and that he wanted to talk to either appellant or his parents. Gomez also asked Turcotte for permission to search the residence on West Richard Street. Turcotte told Gomez that he would find out how to contact appellant's parents. He also expressly told Gomez that he did not have the authority to consent to a search of the Brimage residence.

After his telephone conversation with Turcotte, Gomez was called out to the Rodeway Plaza Inn, a local motel. He was told appellant had stayed in room 119 the night before and had not been seen since. The owner of the motel provided Gomez with appellant's room registration card and his suitcase, which had been removed from his room earlier in the day. Inside appellant's suitcase, Gomez found a … woman's bra, a pair of women's underwear, pieces of what appeared to have been women's pajama bottoms, a jaggedly cut piece of red cloth that appeared to be blouse material, and a pair of large scissors. Gomez testified that both the red cloth and the scissors were "blood stained." Gomez returned to the police station with the suitcase.

Gomez was met at the station by Turcotte and the Honorable Max Bennett of the 319th District Court in Corpus Christi. Bennett is appellant's maternal uncle. Turcotte had called Bennett earlier and told him of police suspicion of appellant. Bennett had then driven to Kingsville, and the two attorneys had broken into appellant's home. At the police station, the two men told Gomez of their break-in and that there was evidence of "violence" or a "violent act" at the residence. Gomez asked Bennett for permission to search the house, and Bennett replied, "Yes, you need to get in there." Without securing a warrant, the police did just that.

Within an hour, the police entered appellant's house and began an exhaustive search of the premises. They found the master bedroom in a state of disarray. Clothing and other items littered the floor and the bed. A jewelry box had been knocked over. A heavy blanket had been placed over a window otherwise screened by both venetian blinds and drapes. Some of the clothing in the room had been cut up, and blood had been splattered in several places. Not long after the search began, the police found Kunkel's body in the trunk of a car in the garage. ...The search was suspended at approximately 2:00 o'clock that morning, and the house was secured. The police returned the following day to collect more evidence—again, without a warrant.

Based in part on the evidence obtained from the search of the West Richard residence, Kingsville police obtained an arrest warrant for appellant. On Thursday morning, ... that warrant was executed .... [Appellant confessed to the crime and his confession, along with the evidence the police obtained during the searches, was admitted at trial.]

...[At the motion to suppress hearing,] [n]either Gomez nor Bennett characterized the police search of the Brimage home as a response to an "emergency" situation. ...

Both Gomez and Bennett testified that they did not discuss securing a search warrant for the Brimage residence prior to the search of the house by the police. When asked whether he, as a district judge, was "concerned about entering a house on a search for evidence in a criminal case without a search warrant," Bennett replied that he was not, explaining, "I was prepared to accept the consequences of doing something I thought was necessary.... I was not concerned about those legal aspects at all. I was not functioning as a lawyer or as a judge."

...It is generally accepted that "the Fourth Amendment does not bar police officers from making warrantless entries and searches when they reasonably believe that a person within is in need of immediate aid." This exception is commonly referred to as the emergency doctrine.

This so-called emergency doctrine is nothing more than a specific application of the exigent circumstances exception to the Fourth Amendment's warrant requirement. Whether the circumstances surrounding the officers' warrantless entry and search [are] characterized as exigent or that of an emergency, both may serve to exempt the officers' actions from the warrant requirement of the Fourth Amendment. Under the emergency doctrine, the exigency which may render the warrantless entry and search reasonable is the officers' "need to act immediately to protect or preserve life or to prevent serious injury."

As is true of every warrantless search of a residence, the burden of proof is on the State to justify the search. In order to justify the search of a residence under the emergency doctrine, the State must show 1) that the officers had probable cause to search the residence, and 2) that obtaining a search warrant was impracticable because the officers reasonably believed there was an immediate need to act in order to protect or preserve life or to prevent serious bodily injury. This is not to say that the State must prove an actual emergency existed at the time of the officer's warrantless entry. The State need only show that the facts and circumstances surrounding the entry and search were such that the officers reasonably believed that an emergency existed which made obtaining a search warrant impracticable. Courts must use an objective standard of reasonableness in assessing the officers' belief that such an emergency actually existed.

The State argues that the warrantless search of appellant's home is justified because the police believed that the missing girl might be in the house and that she might be injured or in need of assistance. The facts developed at the pre-trial hearing, however, do not bear this out. Quite to the contrary, the police characterized the search as "evidentiary" in nature. The decision to search the residence was arrived at almost casually, based entirely on the "consent" granted by Bennett. The police were not expecting to find a body at the house, much less an alive and injured victim in need of assistance. We therefore reject the State's argument.

… Having found that the search of appellant's home was illegal, and that evidence obtained in that search was admitted against him at trial in violation of Article 38.23, … and that the error in admitting the evidence was not harmless beyond a reasonable doubt, we reverse appellant's conviction and remand the cause to the trial court.

————————◆————————

Notes and Questions

1. When officers are in immediate and continuous pursuit, also known as "hot pursuit," of a suspect who is fleeing detention or arrest, they may enter the place where the suspect has fled and search for him without waiting to obtain a warrant.[39] Hot pursuit is considered an exigent circumstance.

2. The *Brimage* Court reiterates that even though the doctrines that fall under this category—emergency, exigency, and hot pursuit—do not require a warrant, they still require probable cause.

————————◆————————

Community Caretaking

Officers are not always investigating crimes or chasing down suspects. Police officers wear many hats. An officer may help direct traffic at a nearby school. That same officer, two hours later, may rescue a child who has fallen in a river. Both of these situations involve caring for the community and its members as a public servant.

What happens when the officer performing in either capacity inadvertently discovers evidence of criminal activity? The following case addresses this question.

Laurin Stuart Laney v. State
117 S.W.3d 854
(Tex. Crim. App. 2003)

We granted discretionary review to determine whether the "community caretaking function" exception to the warrant requirement applies to the warrantless entry and search of a private residence. While this term has been used in various contexts, we take this opportunity to clarify its use and hold that, as part of the police officer's community caretaking functions to protect and preserve life and prevent substantial injury, an officer may enter and

---

[39] *Yeager v. State*, 104 S.W.3d 103, 109 (Tex. Crim. App. 2003).

search a private residence without a warrant for the limited purpose of serving those functions when it is objectively reasonable.

Shortly after midnight, on May 25, 1999, Harris County Sheriff's deputies responded to a call involving a disturbance between neighbors in appellant's mobile home park. As the deputies were speaking with some of the neighbors about the incident, appellant came out of his trailer, approached the officers, and explained that he had turned off the electricity to a neighbor's trailer in retaliation for the neighbor's turning off his electricity. The deputies placed appellant in the back of their patrol car for their safety pending possible charges for criminal mischief. While the deputies continued their investigation, one of the deputies, Brian Quiser, noticed two young boys come out of appellant's darkened trailer onto the front porch. Deputy Quiser asked appellant if the children were his; he replied they were not. When Quiser made eye contact with the children, both walked back into the trailer. Quiser then asked appellant if he had ever been arrested, and appellant informed him he had been arrested for indecency with a child.

Quiser walked over to the trailer to speak with the boys. At the suppression hearing, Quiser testified that since appellant was detained and possibly going to jail, it was his responsibility to get the children out of the trailer and find out who their parents were. As Quiser approached the trailer, one of the boys came out and stood there with the door open. When asked where the other child was, the boy told Quiser the other child was his brother, Joey, and that he was in the back bedroom. Quiser told the boy to stay on the porch and proceeded to enter the trailer. He called Joey's name, but there was no response. With his flashlight on, Quiser moved toward one of the back bedrooms where he found Joey sitting on the bed. While scanning the room with his flashlight, he noticed a piece of paper lying on a shelf by itself. The paper had photographic reproductions of what appeared to be eleven- to twelve-year-old boys engaging in deviant sexual contact. Quiser did not touch the paper, but instead led Joey out of the trailer. Quiser immediately informed his supervisor, Deputy Garrett DeMilia, that he had found something in the trailer. DeMilia testified that they both then proceeded back into the trailer and went directly to the bedroom where the paper with the photographs was located. As with Quiser, DeMilia testified that he did not touch the paper. DeMilia then called his supervisors and detectives to come to the scene. Upon arrival, the deputies obtained appellant's consent to search the trailer. During the subsequent search, the deputies seized the paper along with a floppy disk that turned out to contain similar images.

At the hearing on appellant's motion to suppress, the State argued that the community caretaking function exception to the warrant requirement applied to Quiser's warrantless entry and search of appellant's trailer. Following a hearing on the motion, the trial court made the following oral findings:

> That the police went out there to investigate the incident involving turning off the electricity. The defendant was lawfully detained for the purposes of investigating this situation between the defendant and the neighbor regarding the disconnecting of the electricity. That the police officers ... observed two young boys come out of defendant's trailer, who appeared to be between the ages of ten and twelve. And that upon seeing the officers, they ran back into the apartment. The defendant told the officers that they were not his sons, told the officers he had been twice previously convicted of the offense of indecency with a child, and it is the court's opinion that the police officers were absolutely unequivocally, without question, entitled to enter the defendant's trailer in order to conduct a search for the remaining child who they did not have possession of. One of the boys was outside the trailer told the officers, my brother is inside. I think it would be absolutely incredible, totally outrageous to have required police officers to have obtained a search warrant under those circumstances to secure the possession of a child .... There's no doubt, no question exigent circumstances existed, allowing the officers to enter the trailer to secure the ... child ... [T]he court is of the opinion ... the pornographic material [was] in plain view.

... While we ... recognize the existence of the community caretaking function in Texas, we emphasize its narrow applicability. Only in the most unusual circumstances will warrantless searches of private, fixed property, or stops of persons located thereon, be justified under the community caretaking function, given the greater expectation of privacy inherent with respect to residences and other private real property.

... "A police officer has 'complex and multiple tasks to perform in addition to identifying and apprehending persons committing serious criminal offenses.'" They do so acting out of "concern for the safety of the general public...." ... These "community caretaking functions" include, among others, the duty to "reduce the opportunities for the commission of some crimes through preventive patrol and other measures," "aid individuals who are in danger of physical harm," "assist those who cannot care for themselves," and "resolve conflict." And while not all of these community caretaking functions will justify a warrantless entry and search of a private residence, the Supreme Court has recognized that, "[t]he need to protect or preserve life or avoid serious injury is justification for what would be otherwise illegal absent an exigency or emergency." Therefore, the Court has held, "[T]he Fourth Amendment does not bar police officers from making warrantless entries and searches when they reasonably believe that a person within is in need of immediate aid."

…The notion that officers act pursuant to their "community caretaker functions" serves as a basis for three separate doctrines created by the Supreme Court:

1. the emergency aid doctrine;
2. the automobile impoundment and inventory doctrine; and
3. the community caretaking doctrine, or public servant doctrine.

The common thread in each of these three exceptions to the warrant and probable cause requirements is the officer's purpose.

The emergency doctrine is not the same as the community caretaking doctrine….

The distinction between the emergency doctrine and the community caretaking doctrine … is a narrow, but critical one. Under the emergency doctrine, the officer has an immediate, reasonable belief that he or she must act to "protect or preserve life or avoid serious injury." [Under the community caretaking doctrine], the officer "might or might not believe there is a difficulty requiring his general assistance." … Therefore, while both doctrines are based on an officer's reasonable belief in the need to act pursuant to his or her "community caretaking functions," the emergency doctrine is limited to the functions of protecting or preserving life or avoiding serious injury.

…[W]e now turn to clarifying the use of the term "exigency" as it relates to the emergency doctrine. The emergency doctrine is considered synonymous with the exigent circumstances doctrine. "The exigent circumstances doctrine applies when the police are acting in their 'crime-fighting' role." …[T]he emergency doctrine applies when the police are acting … in their limited community caretaking role to "protect or preserve life or avoid serious injury."

We now turn to the problem of applying the proper doctrine. In this case, the State argued in the trial court that the community caretaking exception applied. The trial court found, "There's no doubt, no question exigent circumstances existed, allowing the officers to enter the trailer to secure the person." The court of appeals analyzed the case under what it labeled a community caretaking doctrine …. This being an emergency doctrine case, however, the proper standards are those set forth by this Court regarding the emergency doctrine…

"We have used an objective standard of reasonableness in determining whether a warrantless search is justified under the Emergency Doctrine." This objective standard looks at the police officer's conduct and "takes into account the facts and circumstances known to the police at the time of the search." Furthermore, we look to ensure that the warrantless search is "strictly circumscribed by the exigencies which justify its initiation." If the emergency doctrine applies, the police may seize any evidence that is in plain view during the course of their legitimate emergency activities.

Although we disapprove of the court of appeals' analysis …, we nonetheless agree with the court's conclusion that Deputy Quiser's actions in entering the home to ensure the well-being of the young child were reasonable under the circumstances. Quiser's actions were "totally divorced from the detection, investigation, or acquisition of evidence relating to the violation of a criminal statute." The appellant had already been detained for suspicion of committing criminal mischief. Quiser did not enter appellant's trailer to continue his investigation of that offense. Instead, he saw two young boys, not belonging to the appellant, emerge from appellant's darkened trailer sometime after midnight, and then witnessed one of the boys run back into the trailer. Quiser testified that because the appellant was going to jail, it was his responsibility to get the boy out of the trailer and find out who his parents were. Arguably, the deputies would have been criminally liable for leaving the child behind. *See* TEX. PENAL CODE ANN. § 22.041 (West 2003) (abandoning or endangering child). Under the circumstances, Deputy Quiser's actions were reasonable.

More important to the emergency doctrine's application, there was an immediate, objectively reasonable belief on Deputy Quiser's part that he needed to act to protect the life of the child and prevent him from incurring serious injury. Although there was no immediate threat to the child's safety or well-being, had the boy been left alone in the trailer while deputies took appellant away, there would have been a substantial risk of harm to the child. Furthermore, Deputy Quiser's search was "strictly circumscribed" by the exigencies which justified its initiation. After the boy ran back in the trailer, Quiser called out for him but there was no response. Quiser then proceeded directly to where he was told the boy was—the back bedroom. When he found the boy there, he also saw the pornographic photos in plain view. Rather than expand his search for pornographic material, he immediately took the child out of the room. Based on these circumstances, we find that the emergency doctrine applies. Accordingly, the deputies were not required to secure a warrant to enter and search appellant's residence.

We do not intend our holding today to be interpreted to necessarily allow police officers to make warrantless entries and searches every time there is a need to protect or preserve life or prevent serious injury. Instead, the courts should carefully apply the objective standard of reasonableness when determining whether an officer's warrantless entry and search is justified under the emergency doctrine....

The judgment of the Court of Appeals is affirmed.

JOHNSON, J., filed a concurring opinion.

I concur in the judgment of the Court. The court of appeals' opinion did not mention that the record shows that the officers knew before they arrested appellant that the two boys were the sons of appellant's girlfriend. There is no indication that officers made any attempt to contact the mother before entering appellant's home to retrieve the second boy. This makes the legality of the first entry a much closer case.

We do not know whether the boys' mother knew of appellant's prior convictions. We do know that the boys were not at their own home and it was after midnight. The officers faced a situation in which, through ignorance of appellant's prior sexual offenses or disregard of the dangers posed by a sexual predator, the boys' mother allowed them to be alone with appellant. It was not unreasonable for the officers to believe that it was important to retrieve the second boy from appellant's home.

I am troubled, however, by the second warrantless and unconsented-to entry. Whether the officers touched anything during the entry is not the issue. The boys were safe, and no other emergency existed. There was no legal justification for the second entry. The opinion of the Court should not be read to condone such improper entries and searches.

Notes and Questions

1. Do you agree more with the majority decision or the concurrence? Why?

2. Can you, based upon the above decision, distinguish the officer's role in the following circumstances?

    a. An emergency role

    b. A community caretaking role

    c. An exigent circumstances role

Scope

Scope must be analyzed in every search, whether it was executed with or without a warrant. In the warrantless search context, scope may arise in virtually any of the warrantless search exception contexts detailed in this chapter. For example, in *Gutierrez v. State*, 221 S.W.3d 680, 686 (Tex. Crim. App. 2007), officers were permitted to search the defendant's residence for a recently stolen computer under the exigent circumstances exception, but they exceeded the scope of that search when they called for a narcotics team to search the remainder of his home for contraband.[40] In *Campbell v. State*, 864 S.W.2d 223, 226 (Tex. App.—Waco 1993, pet. ref'd), officers exceeded the scope of a *Terry* frisk by searching the contents of a film canister and vial. In *State v. Clouse*, 839 S.W.2d 459, 463 (Tex. App.—Beaumont 1992, no pet.), a law enforcement agent exceeded the scope of the administrative search of a junk yard by searching vehicles on the property instead of what was authorized by law, which was the junk yard's business documents.

Scope issues are frequently raised in the consent context. The *Weaver* case illustrates the test courts use when they examine the scope of consent.[41] In *Weaver*, police were looking for a fugitive named Bear who was known to hang out at the defendant's welding shop. They asked Weaver if they could look around the shop for Bear, and he consented. They did not find Bear. When officers asked to search Weaver's van, he said, "No." A sergeant ordered a drug dog to sniff outside the van; when the dog indicated drugs were inside the van, officers searched the van and found methamphetamines

---

[40] *Gutierrez v. State*, 221 S.W.3d 680, 683-86 (Tex. Crim. App. 2007).
[41] *State v. Weaver*, 349 S.W.3d 521, 531-32 (Tex. Crim. App. 2011).

and drug paraphernalia. The Texas Court of Criminal Appeals held the subsequent dog sniff and search of the van exceeded the scope of the defendant's consent, stating:

> [In this case,] the officers had finished looking for the specific individual and had achieved the ostensible purpose of their entry. And … Mr. Weaver unequivocally said "No," to a further search of his van.

> The legal question is, what would "the typical reasonable person have understood by the exchange between the officer and the suspect?" We think that it was objectively unreasonable for the officers to conclude that Mr. Weaver's act of objecting to the van search indicated… his consent for the officers to remain standing beside his van while one officer went back out to the patrol car and retrieved a drug dog to run around his van. A typical reasonable person would have understood—from Mr. Weaver's refusal of consent to search the van—that he had had enough. It would be unreasonable for that typical person, having heard an unequivocal "No," to think that he had "positive and unequivocal" consent, not only to remain standing beside the van on the non-public premises, but also to retrieve yet another unwelcome intruder. There is certainly no indication in the record that Mr. Weaver consented for the officers to bring the drug dog from the patrol car to the van parked at his loading dock. From these facts, the trial judge could have concluded that the consent to search for "Bear" was lawful at its inception, but … [t]he officers had completed their stated mission. Thus, when Mr. Weaver unequivocally said "No" to any further search of his van, the officers violated the Fourth Amendment by remaining on his private business premises and bringing in a drug dog without legal authorization.[42]

When analyzing warrantless search scope issues, it is important to examine whether the search has parameters (*e.g.*, in a protective sweep, officers are limited to looking for persons or weapons that may place them in danger while they are on the premises investigating), whether the officers exceeded those parameters, and whether they discovered evidence as a result of exceeding the scope of the search. If so, defense counsel may argue that the evidence should be suppressed.

———————————◆———————————

---

[42] *Id.*

Practice Questions

Like warrantless arrest bar questions, warrantless search bar questions require examinees to apply the law to a specific fact pattern. Warrantless search and seizure questions almost always ask examinees to consider taking a procedural step—filing a motion to suppress—and then ask what arguments can be made. While many bar questions build upon only one area of law, warrantless search and seizure questions may also build upon detentions or arrests, motions to suppress, the exclusionary rule, "fruit of the poisonous tree," and search warrant law. In order to answer these questions, you will need to rely on the legal concepts in this chapter and earlier chapters of this book.

Most warrantless search and seizure questions draw upon the initial fact pattern bar examiners provide. Be prepared to carefully read and re-read the fact pattern and make legal arguments based upon that fact pattern. Bar examiners often inform examinees—almost as a third-party observer who sees all—that a crime has been committed and the defendant committed it. More often than not, the defendant is guilty of the charged offense. It is easy, therefore, for examinees to assume the officer knows what they know and to impart reasonable suspicion or probable cause when the officer has not yet developed either. As a result, when examinees are asked about the lawfulness of the arrest, search, or seizure, they must objectively look at the facts the officer knows, not the facts they know.

As you contemplate your answer, consider the following:

- Did officers have probable cause to search or arrest? Look at what the officer knew at the time of the arrest or search, not what you know now.
- Was there a search warrant?
- If there was no search warrant, does a valid exception apply?
- If the search was conducted pursuant to an exception, were the officer's actions before the search lawful?
- When you consider the timeline from the start of police contact on, can you identify whether there was an unlawful act, and if so, when it occurred on the timeline? If there was an unlawful act, does that render the evidence seized "fruit of the poisonous tree"?

- Bar examiners have yet to ask about attenuation, but they may in the future. Was the taint of the unlawful act attenuated by some intervening circumstance?
- Was the scope of the search permissible?
- Should the evidence be suppressed? If so, what is your legal argument to support a motion to suppress?

Remember that if there is no warrant and no exception, then the search is per se unreasonable. Many warrantless search and seizure questions involve standing, unlawful stops, detentions, or searches; the actions of the officer render the evidence seized fruit of the poisonous tree. The following exceptions have been tested on previous exams: search incident to arrest, vehicle inventory searches, the automobile exception, and jail inventory searches.

Now it's time to put into practice what you learned in this chapter, in Chapter 1, and in Chapter 2 by answering the following questions.

1. (J-2016, F-2013, and F-2012) Defendant works as a salesman at a car lot. Unbeknownst to the owner and his manager, Defendant sells cocaine from the car lot too. He has agreed to sell one kilogram of cocaine to undercover Officer at the car lot. When Officer arrives, he pretends to be shopping for cars with Defendant. After a few minutes of fake car shopping, the two go inside the car lot office where Officer intends to pay Defendant in exchange for the cocaine. As they walk towards the office, Officer notifies a tactical unit that they are getting ready to exchange the money for the cocaine. Once inside, Officer hands the money to Defendant as Defendant retrieves a bag behind his desk that conceals the kilo of cocaine. He places the bag of cocaine on the floor beside Officer's feet in the middle of the car lot office. Next, the tactical unit enters the building and, without a warrant, arrests Defendant and seizes the cocaine in the bag.[43]

---

[43] This fact pattern is based upon the facts of *Martinez v. State*, 880 S.W.2d 72 (Tex. App.—Texarkana 1994, no pet.).

What procedural step, if any, can you take to prevent Prosecutor from introducing the drugs? What can Prosecutor argue in response to the step you take? Explain.

_____

_____

_____

_____

_____

2. (J-2015, F-2008, and J-2004) Victim's convenience store is robbed. The robber stole cash from the register and lotto tickets. Victim gives the following description to police: "he has brown hair, blue eyes, is normal height, and he was driving a light-colored SUV." One hour later, Officer finds the Defendant, who fits this description. He handcuffs Defendant, pats him down, sticks his hands in Defendant's pocket, and finds a lotto ticket. He arrests Defendant and then searches his SUV. In it, he finds a bag of money and stolen lotto tickets in the SUV's back seat.

Prosecutor plans on admitting the money and lotto tickets into evidence. What procedural step can you take to prevent the money and lotto tickets from being admitted at trial? What arguments will you make? Explain.

_____

_____

_____

_____

_____

3. (F-2015) Defendant leaves young Child at home while she goes to a bar. Neighbor hears Child screaming and comes over to see what is wrong. She discovers Child pulled a pot of boiling water from the stove and is seriously burned. Neighbor calls police, screaming, "We need someone over here now!" before hanging up the phone. Officer responds and knocks on the door. After no one answers the door, he enters the home and begins to search. He finds Defendant's car keys, her purse, and a

receipt in the laundry room that establishes Defendant was at the bar at the time Child was injured. He confiscates the receipt. Defendant is charged with the felony offense of Injury to a Child. Prosecutor wants to enter receipts into evidence to prove that Defendant was at a bar when the injury occurred.

What can you do to prevent this testimony from being admitted and what is your best argument?

_____

_____

_____

_____

_____

4. (J-2014) Defendant has an unusual machete in his garage. Several people have looked at it and inquired about it over the years. One night, Friend learns that police are looking for a man who has randomly attacked people with a machete. Friend calls Crime Stoppers, reports Defendant owns a machete, and that Defendant keeps the machete in his garage.

When Detective arrives at Defendant's house, he opens the garage door, goes inside, inspects the machete, and then leaves the garage. Later that day, Detective arrests Defendant for aggravated assault with a deadly weapon.

Prosecutor plans on calling Detective to testify about what he saw when he entered the garage. What can you do to prevent this testimony from coming in at trial? What is your argument?

_____

_____

_____

_____

_____

5. (J-2013) Detective is investigating a phishing scam whereby scammers attempt to trick email recipients to disclose personal identifying information that is used to steal the person's identity. Detective's investigation leads him to Defendant. Detective goes to Defendant's home to question him.

   When Defendant answers the door, Officer walks into the apartment and begins looking for evidence of the phishing scam. On the kitchen table, he finds a computer, numerous identification cards with Defendant's picture (but with different names) and several credit cards with different names, but he does not seize any of this evidence. He leaves the apartment, quickly gets a search warrant, and returns to the apartment where he then seizes this evidence.

   Prosecutor intends to introduce the evidence Officer seized pursuant to the search warrant. What procedural step can you take to prevent this testimony and evidence from being admitted at trial? What will you argue?

   _____

   _____

   _____

   _____

   _____

6. (J-2012) Defendant is lawfully arrested for the felony offense of driving while intoxicated. Before Officer places Defendant in the patrol car, he frisks him and finds methamphetamine in his shirt pocket. Defendant's Wife is the only passenger in the car. She is not intoxicated. After Officer places Defendant in the patrol car, he calls a tow truck and begins to inventory the car. When Wife exclaims she can drive the car home, Officer tells her that Police Department has a policy that states, "All automobiles may be searched and all contents seized and inventoried in order to uncover evidence of crimes." In the trunk of the car, Officer finds a larger amount of methamphetamine. Defendant is subsequently charged with felony DWI and possession of a controlled substance. Prosecutor plans to introduce the methamphetamine into evidence at Defendant's trial.

a. You object to the methamphetamine found in his pocket coming into evidence on the ground that it was seized following an unlawful search. How should the Court rule on your objection? Explain.

_____

_____

_____

_____

_____

b. What procedural step can you take to prevent Prosecutor from admitting the methamphetamine found in Defendant's trunk into evidence? What will you argue? Explain.

_____

_____

_____

_____

_____

7. (F-2011) Victim's home was burglarized. Victim reported several pieces of jewelry, including a unique men's platinum and black diamond ring and an antique woman's opal bracelet, stolen. Detective forwarded a list of the jewelry, along with detailed descriptions, to all local pawn shops. Pawn Shop Owner notifies police that the opal bracelet arrived in his store earlier this morning, and Defendant pawned it. After investigating further, Officer obtains an arrest warrant and arrests Defendant.

Following routine booking procedures, Jailor inventories Defendant's personal belongings, including the stolen platinum ring that was inside his pants pocket. Prosecutor intends to introduce both the bracelet and the ring into evidence at trial. You file a motion to suppress the ring, arguing that Defendant did not consent to the seizure of his things, nor did Officer have a search warrant.

How should Judge rule? Explain.

_____

_____

_____

_____

_____

———————————◆———————————

Chapter 4
Jurisdiction, Venue, and Charging Instruments

Introduction

A *charging instrument* is a legal document used to charge the defendant with violating the criminal law. It places the defendant on notice as to what crime he committed. An *indictment* is a charging instrument used in felony cases and in some misdemeanor cases. An *information* is a charging instrument used in jailable misdemeanor cases. Indictments will be the charging instrument discussed most frequently in this chapter.

The Texas Constitution states:

An indictment is a written instrument presented to a court by a grand jury charging a person with the commission of an offense. An information is a written instrument presented to a court by an attorney for the State charging a person with the commission of an offense. ... The presentment of an indictment or information to a court invests the court with jurisdiction of the cause.[1]

As you see from the constitutional provision, the charging instrument is more than a piece of paper that makes a legal accusation. There is a process to creating it that differs depending on the level of crime committed. Once the charging instrument is lawfully obtained and filed, the State has a role in pursuing the case, and the court has jurisdiction over the defendant until that case is resolved.

This chapter will examine all things related to the charging process: the jurisdiction of criminal courts in Texas, proper venue, changes of venue, the procedures surrounding the charging process, and the legal requirements of charging instruments.

———————◆———————

Jurisdiction

In order for a court to send a defendant to jail, place her on probation, place bond conditions on her, set bail, or otherwise control the outcome of the case or the defendant's behavior while the case is pending, it must have jurisdiction over the case and the person. Courts in Texas possess subject matter jurisdiction over the type of case and personal jurisdiction over the defendant, which begins with the filing of the charging instrument.

There are a number of criminal courts in Texas, reflected by the diagram on the following page. The information within each box explains the type of case over which the court has jurisdiction. The arrows that appear beneath the boxes signify the direction of appeals from lower courts to higher courts.

———————◆———————

[1] TEX. CONST. art. V, §12 (b).

Court of Criminal Appeals

The highest appellate criminal court with discretionary, statewide jurisdiction. It has final review over all Class A and B misdemeanor and non-capital felony cases and original jurisdiction over death penalty cases.

Article 4.04

Courts of Appeals

Texas has 14 intermediate appeals courts with regional jurisdiction. They mandatorily review all Class A and B misdemeanor appeals and non-death penalty felony cases.

Article 4.03

District Courts

These trial courts have jurisdiction over all felony cases and any lesser-included offenses (LIO) of felonies, even if the LIO is a misdemeanor offense.

County Courts

Trial courts with jurisdiction over Class A and B misdemeanors and mandatory appellate review of Class C misdemeanors.

Articles 4.05 and 4.06

Articles 4.07 and 4.08

Municipal Courts

City courts with jurisdiction over Class C misdemeanors. These courts have jurisdiction when a city law enforcement agency (*e.g.*, El Paso Police Department) arrests.

Article 4.14

Justice Courts

County courts with jurisdiction over Class C misdemeanors. They have jurisdiction when a county or state law enforcement agency (*e.g.*, Tarrant County Sheriff, Constable, or Department of Public Safety) arrests.

Articles 4.11, 4.12 and 4.1

Venue

It is important to distinguish venue from jurisdiction. Venue refers to where the criminal case begins, whereas jurisdiction refers to the authority of the court over the type of case. For example, Harris County would be the appropriate venue for a misdemeanor theft that occurred in Houston, a city that sits within the geographic boundaries of Harris County. However, a district court in Harris County would never have jurisdiction to hear a Class B shoplifting misdemeanor case because district courts do not have jurisdiction to hear misdemeanor cases.[2]

Most of the statutes on venue appear in Chapter 13 of the Code of Criminal Procedure. Chapter 13 contains numerous special venue provisions, which fall into two categories: (1) crime-specific statutes that address venue (*e.g.*, in a forgery case, the defendant may be prosecuted in the county where she forged the document or in the counties where the forged document was deposited or collected);[3] and (2) fact-specific statutes that address venue given a specific fact pattern (*e.g.*, in a murder case, where venue is appropriate when the victim is injured in one county but dies in another).[4]

There are two basic issues related to venue: whether a case is tried in the correct county and whether, due to prejudice, a case tried in the right county should be moved to another county or venue. The first of these concepts involves the issue of proper venue whereas the second issue deals with changing the venue. We will address these concepts in order below.

The general rule is that venue is appropriate in a county where any part of the crime was committed. A hypothetical kidnapping case helps illustrate this general rule. Assume a defendant kidnapped his ex-girlfriend from Uvalde County, drove her through Zavala County, and hid her in his home in Maverick County before police arrested him. The crime of kidnapping requires the State to prove the defendant intentionally or knowingly abducted another person.[5] Since his abduction began when he kidnapped her and continued until his arrest, his trial could take place in any of the three counties where an element of kidnapping occurred. There is also a specific

---

[2] The only exception to this rule is when it is a misdemeanor involving official misconduct. TEX. CODE CRIM. PROC. ANN. art. 4.05 (West 2016).

[3] TEX. CODE CRIM. PROC. ANN. art. 13.02 (West 2016).

[4] TEX. CODE CRIM. PROC. ANN. art. 13.07 (West 2016).

[5] TEX. PEN. CODE ANN. §20.03 (West 2011).

kidnapping venue statute that says a defendant can be prosecuted in the county where the kidnapping began or in the county or counties where the victim was taken during the kidnapping.[6] Many of the crime-specific statutes apply the same general venue rule: venue is appropriate where any element of the crime took place. In this instance, if you follow the general rule, the proper venue would be any of the above three counties; if you follow the crime-specific rule, venue would be appropriate in any of the three counties. This outcome is not always true, but it generally is.

The prosecutor must prove venue by a preponderance of the evidence.[7] Venue does not have to be proved beyond a reasonable doubt, as it is not an element of an offense. The prosecutor can prove venue through direct or circumstantial evidence.[8] It is presumed that venue is proved in the trial court, unless the record affirmatively shows otherwise or venue becomes an issue at trial.[9]

Most of the time, determining where the crime occurred is easy. However, there are instances when it is difficult or impossible. The next case examines a rule that the legislature created when the place where the crime occurred is unknown, as well as several crime-specific venue statutes for homicide, theft, and kidnapping—all of which were raised by the evidence the State presented at trial.

Jedidiah Isaac Murphy v. State
112 S.W.3d 592
(Tex. Crim. App. 2003)

[Defendant was charged with capital murder and sentenced to death.]

In his twelfth point of error, appellant claims the evidence was insufficient to prove venue. At the close of the State's case, appellant sought a directed verdict on the ground that the evidence was insufficient to prove venue in Dallas County. Appellant's motion for a directed verdict was denied. The jury was charged that venue was proper in any one of the following counties:

1. in the county in which the offense was committed, or

---

[6] TEX. CODE CRIM. PROC. ANN. art. 13.12 (West 2016).
[7] TEX. CODE CRIM. PROC. ANN. art. 13.17 (West 2016).
[8] *E.g., Braddy v. State*, 908 S.W.2d 465, 467 (Tex. App.—Dallas 1995, no pet.).
[9] TEX. R. APP. P. 44.2(c)(1).

2. where the property is stolen in one county and removed by the offender to another, in the county where the defendant took the property or in any other county through or into which he may have removed the same, or

3. if a person receives an injury in one county and dies in another by reason of such injury, in the county where the injury was received or where the death occurred, or in the county where the dead body is found, or

4. in the county in which the kidnapping offense was committed, or in any county through, into, or out of which the person kidnapped may have been taken.

However, if an offense has been committed within this State and it cannot readily be determined within which county or counties the commission took place, trial may be held in the county in which the defendant resides, in the county in which he was apprehended, or in the county to which he was extradited.

Appellant objected to the charge, arguing that venue should be limited to the county where the homicide occurred. Appellant's objections were overruled. Appellant ... alleges ... that the evidence is insufficient to prove venue in Dallas County.

Under Article 13.18, if venue is not specifically stated, then the proper county for prosecution is the county in which the offense was committed. In this appeal, appellant reasons that since there is no statute specifically governing capital murder cases, Article 13.18 applies. Applicant argues that "the county in which the offense was committed" in a capital murder case should be the county in which the homicide occurred. He further argues that if venue were so restricted, the evidence would be insufficient to prove the homicide occurred in Dallas County.

The State need prove venue only by a preponderance of the evidence. Art. 13.17. We recently explained the effect and purpose of special venue provisions:

In Texas, if the Legislature has not specified venue for a specific type of crime, then "the proper county for the prosecution of offenses is that in which the offense was committed." Special venue statutes, however, expand the number of counties in which an offense may be prosecuted. These special venue statutes have been enacted for various reasons, such as: 1) the difficulty of proving precisely where the offense was committed; 2) the location where evidence of the crime is found; 3) the effect that a crime may have upon several different counties; or 4) the effect that the actor may have upon various counties. Texas venue statutes are a species of codified "substantial contacts" jurisdiction; thus, for venue to lie, the defendant, his conduct, his victim, or the fruits of his crime must have some relationship to the prosecuting county. The Legislature has specified the types of contacts that satisfy this "substantial contacts" threshold for various offenses.[10]

While some of the special venue statutes expressly apply to identifiable penal code offenses, other special venue provisions apply by virtue of the particular facts of the case rather than the specifically charged offense. ... There is no special venue statute expressly applicable to the prosecution of a capital murder. Nor is there any statute providing that in capital murder cases, venue occurs only where the homicide takes place. Any number of the special venue provisions may apply to a given capital murder case, depending upon its facts.

In the instant case, the victim was last seen alive in Collin County. In his confession, appellant stated that he was drinking at a bar called Bleachers. There was evidence that Bleachers Sports Grill is a bar located in Dallas County. According to his confession, appellant left Bleachers and hitched a ride with the victim "on the road beside Bleachers on [his] way to [Interstate] 635." Detective Myers testified that the area from Bleachers to 635 is located in Dallas County. Appellant's confession further states that appellant and the victim were driving toward 635 when he asked the victim to stop and get into the trunk, and he then shot her. The admission suggests that this occurred somewhere in the same area as the abduction—between Bleachers and 635, within Dallas County. Appellant thereafter drove around in the victim's car to various locations in Collin and Dallas Counties, using the victim's credit cards and attempting to use her ATM card. The medical examiner testified that although the gunshot wound was fatal, the victim could have lived for several minutes or longer after the shooting. The victim's body was discovered in a creek in Van Zandt County. Finally, the evidence showed that at the time of the offense, appellant's residence was in Dallas County.

---

[10] *Soliz v. State*, 97 S.W.3d 137, 141 (Tex. Crim. App. 2003).

Venue will stand if it is sufficient under any one of the venue provisions the jury was instructed upon . . . Article 13.19 provides that if an offense is committed within the state but "cannot readily be determined within which county or counties the commission took place," trial can be held in the county in which the defendant resides, the county where he is apprehended, or the county to which he is extradited. This provision was made a part of the trial court's charge. Given the difficulty of determining exactly where the offense occurred, a rational jury could have relied on this provision and concluded venue was proper in Dallas County, the county of appellant's residence. Point of error twelve is overruled.

———————————◆———————————

Notes and Questions

1. Notice that the jury charge in the above case contained a rule that applies in cases where the location of the crime cannot be determined, based upon the facts: "[I]f ... it cannot readily be determined within which county or counties the commission took place, trial may be held in the county in which the defendant resides, in the county in which he was apprehended, or in the county to which he was extradited."[11] Again, this rule only applies when it cannot be determined where the crime occurred.

2. Article 21.06 states that "[w]hen the offense may be prosecuted in either of two or more counties, the indictment may allege the offense to have been committed in the county where the same is prosecuted, or in any county or place where the offense was actually committed."

While this fact scenario is uncommon, might it lead to forum shopping? Could a law enforcement agency pick the county with better prosecutors? Could it place the case in the most conservative, law-enforcement prone county, hoping for a harsher sentence from the judges or resident jurors?

3. When offenses are committed outside of the state or partially within the state, venue is appropriate where the defendant is found or where at least one element of the crime occurred.[12] When crimes occur on or near county or city lines, venue is appropriate in either locale.[13]

---

[11] *Murphy v. State*, 112 S.W.3d 592, 604 (Tex. Crim. App. 2003).
[12] TEX. CODE CRIM. PROC. ANN. art. 13.01 (West 2016).
[13] TEX. CODE CRIM. PROC. ANN. art. 13.04 (West 2016); TEX. CODE CRIM. PROC. ANN. art. 13.045 (West 2016).

Change of Venue

Not all cases can be tried in the county where the crime occurred due to pretrial publicity or bias within the community. Most often the bias is directed at defendants, but it can be directed at other persons involved in the case, such as the elected district attorney, a witness, or the victim. There may be extreme community favor towards a party, making it impossible to receive a fair trial. When the fairness of the trial is compromised, the Texas Code of Criminal Procedure permits the judge to change the venue of the trial.

The judge has the authority to move the trial to an adjoining county when she perceives that either party is likely unable to receive a fair trial.[14] The judge may hear evidence on the matter. The judge may even move the trial to a nonadjacent county after giving the parties a hearing and ten days' notice.[15] The judge may also consider the convenience of the parties or issues that affect justice in changing venue.[16] Parties can and sometimes do agree to change the trial venue.

The Code permits the State to request a change of venue where circumstances exist that favor the accused or where someone's safety or life may be in danger if the trial is not moved.[17] More often, it is the defendant who requests a change of venue.

If the defendant wishes to have his trial moved, he must file a written motion to change venue.[18] The defendant's motion must include his own sworn affidavit and two or more affidavits from credible residents of the county explaining why he cannot receive a fair trial there. All of these affidavits must address the prejudice the defendant faces if his trial takes place in the current venue and must articulate evidence that demonstrates there is "a dangerous combination against him instigated by influential persons" which prevents him from receiving a fair trial.[19]

---

[14] TEX. CODE CRIM. PROC. ANN. art. 31.01 (West 2016).

[15] However, if the defendant contests moving the trial to a nonadjacent county, and it can be shown later that a trial within the county or in an adjoining county would have sufficed, it is reversible error. TEX. CODE CRIM. PROC. ANN. art. 31.03 (West 2016).

[16] TEX. CODE CRIM. PROC. ANN. art. 31.03(b) (West 2016).

[17] TEX. CODE CRIM. PROC. ANN. art. 31.02 (West 2016).

[18] TEX. CODE CRIM. PROC. ANN. art. 31.03 (West 2016).

[19] TEX. CODE CRIM. PROC. ANN. art. 31.02(a)(2) (West 2016).

Determining whether venue should be changed depends on what the public has heard about the case, whether that has created bias, and whether the court can nevertheless assemble a jury that is fair and impartial to both sides. A judge won't know how pervasive bias is until she hears from jurors during voir dire. For this reason, the judge is authorized to wait until voir dire concludes before deciding whether to grant or deny a motion to change venue.[20]

The State has the right to controvert the evidence the defendant offers in support of his motion. The State may submit controverting affidavits from people with knowledge and credibility who dispute the defendant's allegations that he cannot receive a fair trial.[21] Once the State offers controverting affidavits, the burden shifts back to the defendant to establish he cannot receive a fair trial.[22] The court then must determine whether the affidavits are credible and grant or deny the motion.[23] It is extremely difficult to overturn the court's decision because the standard for review on appeal is abuse of discretion, which is most deferential to the trial court's decision.

If the State fails to produce controverting evidence or consents to the change of venue, the judge must grant the defendant's motion.[24] In the next case, however, that did not happen. Before reading the *Freeman* case, it is important to understand the decision-making process when there is a change of venue requested on the basis of pretrial publicity. It is not enough for a defendant to illustrate that his case garnered significant pretrial media attention. "To justify a change of venue based upon media attention, a defendant must show that the publicity was pervasive, prejudicial, and inflammatory."[25] In making her decision, the judge may consider the extent and type of publicity the case received, the evidence presented at the motion hearing, and the testimony of people reporting for jury service.[26] This next case illustrates the difficult burden a party who requests a change of venue carries.

---

[20] *Foster v. State*, 779 S.W.2d 845, 852-55 (Tex. Crim. App. 1989).

[21] TEX. CODE CRIM. PROC. ANN. art. 31.04 (West 2016).

[22] *Alvarado v. State*, 709 S.W.2d 339, 341 (Tex. App.—Houston [14th Dist.] 1986, pet. ref'd).

[23] TEX. CODE CRIM. PROC. ANN. art. 31.01–.04 (West 2016).

[24] TEX. CODE CRIM. PROC. ANN. art. 31.03(c) (West 2016); *Clarke v. State*, 928 S.W.2d 709, 718 (Tex. App.—Fort Worth 1996, pet. ref'd).

[25] *Gonzalez v. State*, 222 S.W.3d 446, 449 (Tex. Crim. App. 2007).

[26] *Id.*

James Garrett Freeman v. State
340 S.W.3d 717
(Tex. Crim. App. 2011)

[Appellant, James Garrett Freeman, was convicted of capital murder and sentenced to death. On the night of the murder, Freeman was caught poaching animals by a game warden. After he evaded arrest at high speeds, he shot and killed a game warden who was attempting to apprehend him. Other officers were dispatched to the scene, and appellant shot at them with an AK–47 assault rifle. The case received significant media attention in the small county where it occurred: Wharton County. It was the first death penalty case the county tried since 1979. The Wharton County District Attorney asked Kelly Siegler, a well-known, successful, and aggressive retired prosecutor from Harris County, to help him try the case. Her participation in the case generated even more media attention; she would later create and star in a hit TNT television series named "Cold Justice."]

In his first point of error, appellant alleges that the trial court erred in denying his requested change of venue because he could not obtain a fair and impartial trial in Wharton County. Appellant states that "[t]he single most important issue in this entire case was the trial court's refusal to recognize reality and move this high profile case out of Wharton County." He alleges that "despite extraordinary evidence of the difficulty of obtaining a fair trial," the trial court erroneously denied appellant's Motion for Change of Venue.

Appellant complains that the pretrial publicity began to taint the Wharton County jury pool almost immediately after the offense. According to appellant, because Wharton County has a small population of around 40,000 residents, local publicity and gossip concerning the offense was extensive. Appellant points out that the community quickly hosted fund-raisers and created a memorial fund to help the victim's widow. Appellant theorizes that the organizers' true intentions were to keep the victim's death fresh in the minds of the public, thus prejudicing the jury pool. He also alleges that false rumors from "known and trusted sources" quickly spread throughout the community.

Appellant also complains that the State's response to the Motion for Change of Venue exacerbated the prejudice against him. After appellant filed his motion and supporting affidavits, the State began collecting controverting affidavits. Appellant claims that in doing so, the State further publicized the murder. Appellant takes issue with the number of controverting affidavits collected and the manner in which some were collected. The State collected 372 controverting affidavits, which appellant characterizes as "an overt attempt to influence the judicial process" … Appellant argues that this large number of controverting affidavits is evidence of a prejudice in the county because there was a concerted public effort to influence the process and keep the trial in Wharton County.

Appellant additionally complains that thirteen of the fifty-one notaries who validated the affidavits also signed controverting affidavits themselves. Further, he complains that one of the notaries was an elected constable who was involved in the chase preceding the offense and ultimately testified during trial. This notary collected twenty affidavits while in uniform, which appellant argues "means that elected and other County officials were actively involved in collecting these affidavits and were asking people to try to keep the trial in Wharton County."

Appellant further complains that the sheer size of the venire pool evidenced the community prejudice against him. The trial court ultimately requested two special venires of 600 people each, for a total of 1,200 potential jurors. The Appellant characterizes the size of the first special venire as evidence that the trial court was "suspicious" of whether appellant could receive a fair trial. Appellant claims that the need for a second special venire was further proof that he could not receive a fair trial in Wharton County.

The initial qualification of the venire was held on September 9, 2007, and fewer than 200 of the 600 called appeared in person. Twenty-nine potential jurors were excused before the venire was seated. The trial court conducted group voir dire with 162 qualified jurors. Only 28 of the 162 had not read about the case in the newspaper. At the conclusion of the trial court's voir dire, 121 potential jurors remained to complete questionnaires. Of those, 62 potential jurors were questioned in individual voir dire. Eleven jurors were seated from this panel, and the trial court requested an additional 600–person special venire from which to seat the twelfth juror and two alternate jurors. The trial court conducted group voir dire of the second special venire with 161 qualified jurors. Only fifteen had not heard about the case. Following the trial court's group voir dire, 84 potential jurors remained to fill out questionnaires. The remaining juror and two alternate jurors were chosen from this panel following the individual voir dire of eight potential jurors.

Appellant argues that the large number of potential jurors who had some knowledge of the case, as well as the need to call 1,200 potential jurors, was indicative of the fact that he could not receive a fair trial in Wharton County.

Article 31.03(a) of the Texas Code of Criminal Procedure provides that a change of venue may be granted if the defendant establishes that:

1. [T]here exists in the county where the prosecution is commenced so great a prejudice against him that he cannot obtain a fair and impartial trial; and
2. [T]here is a dangerous combination against him instigated by influential persons, by reason of which he cannot expect a fair trial.

Appellant's primary argument, as understood by the Court, concerns the pervasiveness and the inflammatory nature of local pretrial publicity. He claims that the pretrial publicity poisoned the jury pool, which denied him the opportunity of a fair trial, and thus, it was erroneous for the trial court to deny his motion. We review a trial court's ruling on a motion for change of venue for abuse of discretion. If the trial court's decision falls within the zone of reasonable disagreement, it will be upheld. The two primary means for discerning whether publicity is pervasive are a hearing on the motion to change venue and the voir dire process. In this case, the trial court used both.

At the hearing on the motion to change venue, appellant introduced into evidence four articles about the offense published by local newspapers: *Siegler Shares Thoughts on Emotions of Trials, Public Seating to be Limited during Freeman Murder Trial, Siegler Now Able to Focus on Trial Without Playing Politics,* and *Former Harris County ADA Joins Prosecution Team For Freeman Trial.* He also introduced lists of law enforcement officers who attended Hurst's funeral, a transcript of the radio broadcast of the funeral, a list of contributions made to memorial funds honoring Hurst, and copies of thirty-two controverting affidavits that were faxed to the District Attorney's office from the El Campo Police Department and seven that were faxed to the District Attorney's office from El Campo High School. Appellant did not present evidence of how many people heard the radio broadcast. Similarly, he did not present evidence as to how many people read the newspaper coverage of the case. During the hearing, appellant agreed that the shooting of a game warden would likely create statewide, and not just local, publicity. The trial court pointed out that whether a potential juror had contributed to a memorial fund was a matter that could be investigated during voir dire.

In regard to the voir dire process, appellant argues that the number of jurors who were unable to serve on the jury in this case shows the extent to which local pretrial publicity permeated the community. Out of 323 members of the two special venires, 280 were familiar with the case. Appellant reasons that the high percentage of special venire members who had heard about the case is reason enough to consider the entire community "poisoned" by the pretrial publicity.

Appellant's conclusion, however, does not comport with this Court's precedent. In the past, this Court has found that trial courts acted within their discretion in not granting a motion for a change of venue even where a large portion of the venire had seen publicity about the case. *See, e.g.,* [*Gonzalez v. State*, 222 S.W.3d 446, 450 (Tex. Crim. App. 2007)] (121 of 180 venire members were familiar with the case); *Von Byrd v. State*, 569 S.W.2d 883, 890-91 (Tex. Crim. App. 1978) (69 of 109 venire members were familiar with the case). We have also found no abuse of discretion even when many of the venire members stated that they had formed an opinion that they could not set aside. *See, e.g., Gonzalez,* 222 S.W.3d at 450 (58 of the 180 venire members indicated that they could not set aside their opinions).

The trial court heard responses from prospective jurors regarding their knowledge of the case and their ability to be fair and impartial. The trial court was within its discretion to believe prospective jurors' statements that they were not unduly influenced and could deliver a fair verdict. That there were a large number of venire members who had heard of the case, or who could not set aside their opinions about the case, does not establish that pretrial publicity permeated the community to such an extent that it was impossible to seat a fair and impartial jury. The trial court's decision to deny the Motion for Change of Venue was not outside the zone of reasonable disagreement.

Regarding appellant's brief claim of a "dangerous combination against him," he has presented nothing other than speculation to convince this Court that the trial court abused its discretion in denying his Motion for Change of Venue on this basis. Appellant's complaint ... is not persuasive and is not supported by the record. Point of error one is overruled.

———————◆———————

Notes and Questions

1. As stated earlier, that the jurors have heard about the case does not mean they are prejudiced about the case. Having said that, news channels feature many local crime stories on a daily basis. Think about the crime reports you have seen relayed on the after-work news channel: are they pro-defendant, pro-State, or neutrally reported? Might the way a story is covered in the news prejudice potential jurors?

2. According to the *Murphy* Court, what "two primary means for discerning whether publicity is pervasive" should a trial court consider while contemplating a motion to change venue?

3. The *Freeman* Court stated that the defendant failed to offer proof of how many people in Wharton County read news articles or watched TV broadcasts about the case. Is it possible for parties moving for a change of venue to produce such evidence? Do you believe the evidence Freeman and his attorneys produced was, as the Court described, "speculation"?

4. Considering the deferential abuse-of-discretion standard, what court—trial or appellate—is in a better position to discern whether the moving party can receive a fair trial in the present location?

5. The party requesting a change of venue cannot control where the case is moved if venue is granted.[27]

6. Motions to change venue must be filed seven days before the pretrial hearing.[28] If the judge overrules the motion at the pretrial hearing, the moving party may renew the motion during voir dire.[29] If the moving party fails to file the motion seven days before the pretrial hearing, she may not subsequently raise a change of venue except by permission of the trial court upon a showing of "good cause."[30]

———————◆———————

---

[27] *E.g., De La Garza v. State*, 650 S.W.2d 870, 874 (Tex. App.—San Antonio 1983, pet. ref'd) ("Appellant was not entitled to select the county for trial").
[28] TEX. CODE CRIM. PROC. ANN. art. 28.01, §1(7) and §2 (West 2016).
[29] *Id.*
[30] *Id.*

Charging Documents

Nearly all criminal cases start the same way. Initially, law enforcement officers interview witnesses, victims, and defendants to discover whether a crime occurred. During their investigation, officers ascertain whether there is enough evidence to prove each element of the criminal offense. Once they determine there is enough evidence, in some counties, they may contact the local county or district attorney's office to seek a formal charge,[31] whereas in other counties, the practice may require officers to initiate charges through a complaint filed with the magistrate.[32]

Regardless of who accepts the charge, the officer, the magistrate, or the prosecutor must ensure there is probable cause to support every element of the charged offense. If the evidence is lacking, charges should be declined.[33]

The *charging instrument* is the legal document that formally charges the defendant with committing a criminal offense. This document is one of the first documents created in any criminal case. One purpose is to inform the accused of the facts surrounding the offense charged so he may prepare a defense.[34] It is through the felony indictment, misdemeanor information (used for Class A and B misdemeanors), or misdemeanor complaint (used for Class C misdemeanors), that the defendant learns what crime she is alleged to have committed and how she committed it. The charging instrument also vests a court with criminal jurisdiction over the defendant and the cause of action.

In addition to alleging all of the essential elements of the charged offense, the law requires that the charging instrument include specific pieces of information. The following charts summarize each document's statutorily required contents.

---

[31] In the case of Class C misdemeanors, however, officers do not need an attorney's approval to issue a citation.

[32] TEX. CODE CRIM. PROC. ANN. arts. 2.05 and 15.04 (West 2016).

[33] *E.g.*, ABA Standards for Criminal Justice, Prosecution Function and Defense Function 3–3.9 (a) and (f) (3d ed. 1990) (a prosecutor must have probable cause to believe a crime was committed and must not charge more crimes than the evidence warrants).

[34] *Chapa v. State*, 420 S.W.2d 943, 944 (Tex. Crim. App. 1967).

Statutory Requirements for a Class C Misdemeanor Complaint[35]
1. It must be in writing.
2. It must begin with the following language: "In the name and by authority of the State of Texas."
3. It must state the name of the accused, if known, and if not known, give some reasonably definite description of him.
4. It must show that the accused has committed some offense against the laws of the State, either directly or that the affiant has good reason to believe, and does believe, that the accused has committed such offense.
5. It must state the date the offense occurred as definitively as possible.
6. It must be signed by the affiant by writing his name or affixing his mark.
7. It must be filed in the jurisdiction where the crime was committed (city for municipal courts, county for justice courts).
8. It must conclude with "Against the peace and dignity of the State" or, if a city ordinance was violated, it must end with the words, "Contrary to the said ordinance."

---

[35] TEX. CODE CRIM. PROC. ANN. art. 45.019 (West 2016).

Statutory Requirements for a Class A or B Misdemeanor Information[36]
1. It must begin with the following language: "In the name and by authority of the State of Texas."
2. It must be presented by a proper officer.
3. It must be presented to a court with jurisdiction to hear the case.
4. It must include the name of accused or if name unknown, a definite description of accused.
5. The date of crime must precede the date of presentment and otherwise comply with the statute of limitations.
6. The elements of the offense must be written plainly and intelligibly.
7. It must conclude with the words "Against the peace and dignity of the State."
8. It must include a signature of the district or county attorney.

Statutory Requirements for a Felony Indictment[37]
1. The indictment must begin with the phrase "In the name and by authority of the State of Texas."
2. It must be presented in a district court that sits in the same county as the grand jury who issued the indictment.
3. It must state the name of the accused or a detailed description of him, if his name is unknown.
4. The place where the crime was committed must be within the court's geographical jurisdiction.
5. The crime must have occurred before the presentment of the indictment, and the timing of the charge must otherwise comply with the statute of limitations.
6. The offense must be written in plain English.
7. It must conclude with the words "Against the peace and dignity of the State."
8. It must be signed by the grand jury foreman.

---

[36] TEX. CODE CRIM. PROC. ANN. art. 21.21 (West 2016); TEX. CONST. art. V, §12 ("An information is a written instrument presented to a court by an attorney for the State charging a person with the commission of an offense.").

[37] TEX. CODE CRIM. PROC. ANN. art. 21.02 (West 2016); TEX. CONST. art. V, §12 ("An indictment is a written instrument presented to a court by a grand jury charging a person with the commission of an offense.").

If a prosecutor fails to include all of these elements, the defendant could object to the indictment through a motion to quash the charging instrument. When a motion to quash is granted, the court loses its jurisdiction, and the defendant is free to leave.[38] However, the prosecutor may recharge the defendant so long as he acts within the statute of limitations.[39]

To protect against missing requirements, most counties and municipalities in Texas have computer databases with charges that include all of the above statutory requirements. The prosecutor uses the database—adding language to include the manner and means—to fashion the charging instrument. The overwhelming majority of charging instruments meet the statutory requirements. However, no person, government agency, or computer produces error-free charging instruments every time. Occasionally, these documents, like other typed or computer-generated documents, contain errors, with legal consequences that may affect the case.

———————————◆———————————

Notes and Questions

1. A criminal case may originate with a complaint. The Code states that in misdemeanor cases, "the attorney shall … prepare an information based upon such complaint" and that in felony cases, the attorney shall "file the complaint with a magistrate of the county."[40] Another provision of the Code states that a complaint "charges the commission of an offense."[41] The Court of Criminal Appeals stated in *State v. Drummond*[42] that "the term 'complaint' is used in three different contexts: (1) as a prerequisite to an information;[43] (2) to obtain an arrest warrant, issue a summons, or authorize further detention of a suspect after a warrantless arrest;[44] and (3) as the sole charging instrument in municipal and justice courts."[45]

---

[38] TEX. CODE CRIM. PROC. ANN. art. 28.04 (West 2016); *Wilson v. State,* 792 S.W.2d 477, 481 (Tex. App.—Dallas 1990, no pet.).
[39] TEX. CODE CRIM. PROC. ANN. art. 28.04 (West 2016).
[40] TEX. CODE CRIM. PROC. ANN. art. 2.05 (West 2016).
[41] TEX. CODE CRIM. PROC. ANN. art. 15.04 (West 2016).
[42] No. PD-1238-15, ____ S.W.3d ____ (Tex. Crim. App. Sept. 28, 2016).
[43] TEX. CODE CRIM. PROC. ANN. art. 21.22 (West 2016).
[44] TEX. CODE CRIM. PROC. ANN. arts. 15.03-15.05 (West 2016) (magistrate may issue warrant or summons); *Green v. State,* 872 S.W.2d 717, 721 (Tex. Crim. App.

2.   When a complaint is used as a prerequisite to an information, the complaint contains a sworn affidavit made by a credible person charging the defendant with an offense.[46] When a complaint is used to secure a person's arrest or detention, that arrest or detention may be for a felony or misdemeanor offense.[47] In other words, though a complaint is limited to a misdemeanor offense in the first category above, it is not limited to misdemeanor offenses in the context of arrests or detentions. Finally, complaints are the charging instruments used for Class C misdemeanors.

3.   What is the purpose of a felony complaint? The Code makes clear a complaint charges an offense, yet the Court of Criminal Appeals has stated it does not amount to a charging instrument for a felony offense in a felony court.[48] The Court described a felony complaint as, "the initial step of an action instituted to secure [an accused's] conviction and punishment."[49] In felony cases, it is filed with a magistrate who issues an arrest warrant.[50] In sum, a felony complaint filed with a court is a legal document used to initiate the criminal process against an accused or, if it is filed with a magistrate, it may be used to secure an arrest warrant.

———————◆———————

Notice

Remember that one of the fundamental purposes of the charging instrument is to provide the defendant with notice of the crime for which she has been charged. The next case examines how much notice is due.

1994) (defendant arrested without a warrant is entitled to a prompt probable-cause determination).

[45] TEX. CODE CRIM. PROC. ANN. arts. 45.018(a) (West 2016) (defining a complaint as a sworn allegation charging the accused with commission of an offense) and 45.019 (setting forth the formal requirements of a complaint to charge a defendant in justice and municipal courts).

[46] TEX. CODE CRIM. PROC. ANN. arts. 2.04 and 21.12 (West 2016).

[47] TEX. CODE CRIM. PROC. ANN. arts. 15.03-15.05 (West 2016).

[48] TEX. CODE CRIM. PROC. ANN. art. 15.04 (West 2016); *Rios v. State*, 718 S.W.2d 730, 732 (Tex. Crim. App. 1986).

[49] *Ex Parte Clear*, 224 S.W.2d 224, 228 (Tex. Crim. App. 1978); *Ex Parte Ward*, 560 S.W.2d 660, 662 (Tex. Crim. App. 1978).

[50] *Ex Parte Clear*, 224 S.W.2d at 226.

State v. Stephen Gregory Barbernell
257 S.W.3d 248
(Texas Crim. App. 2008)

Stephen Gregory Barbernell was charged with DWI. The court of appeals affirmed the trial judge's decision to grant Barbernell's motion to quash [the information] due to the State's failure to allege which definition of "intoxicated" that it intended to prove at trial. The court reasoned that intoxication is an act or omission and that the definitions of "intoxicated" provide for different means of commission. Because we hold that the definitions of "intoxicated" do not describe an act or omission, we reverse and vacate the judgment of the court of appeals and remand this case to the trial court.

I. Procedural History

Barbernell was charged by information with the misdemeanor offense of driving while intoxicated under Texas Penal Code, Section 49.04... [which] defines the offense of DWI and reads, in part, as follows: "A person commits an offense if the person is intoxicated while operating a motor vehicle in a public place." Section 49.01(2), Texas Penal Code, sets out two definitions of "intoxicated."

"Intoxicated" means:

(A) not having the normal use of mental or physical faculties by reason of the introduction of alcohol, a controlled substance, a drug, a dangerous drug, a combination of two or more of those substances, or any other substance into the body; or

(B) having an alcohol concentration of 0.08 or more.

The information charging Barbernell alleged: "on or about April 30, 2005, in Montgomery County, Texas, Stephen Gregory Barbernell ..., while operating a motor vehicle in a public place, was then and there intoxicated[.]"

Barbernell moved to quash the information because the State failed to allege the definition of "intoxicated" set out in Section 49.01(2) that it intended to prove at trial.

In support of his motion, Barbernell relied on our 1991 decision in *State v. Carter*, which held that the State must allege which definition of intoxicated... [it] intends to prove at trial. Barbernell claimed that the information failed to provide him with adequate notice of the manner and means (*i.e.*, the definition of "intoxicated" that the State intended to prove) in which he committed the offense. In response, the State argued that our 2004 opinion in *Gray v. State* establishes that the definitions of "intoxicated" are not elements of DWI. After a brief hearing, the trial judge granted Barbernell's motion to quash. The State then timely filed a notice of appeal.

II. Court of Appeals

In the Beaumont Court of Appeals, … the court …held that the element of "intoxicated" is an act or omission and that the definitions of "intoxicated" provide different manner or means to commit intoxication. Due to the State's failure to allege the definition of "intoxicated" that it intended to prove at trial, the court held that the information did not sufficiently notify Barbernell of the charged offense. As a result, the court affirmed the trial judge's decision to grant Barbernell's motion to quash.

In a concurring opinion, …Justice Horton stated that he believed that the State was correct in asserting that the definitions of "intoxicated" are evidentiary matters, as opposed to manner and means of commission, and therefore do not need to be alleged in the charging instrument.

Notice

The Texas and United States Constitutions grant a criminal defendant the right to fair notice of the specific charged offense. "The charging instrument must convey sufficient notice to allow the accused to prepare a defense." Toward that end, Chapter 21 of the Texas Code of Criminal Procedure governs charging instruments and provides legislative guidance concerning the requirements and adequacy of notice.

With respect to the information, Article 21.21 sets out what facts must be included in an information and states, in part, "[t]hat the offense [must] be set forth in plain and intelligible words[.]" Additionally, an information must include everything that is necessary to be proved. An information is sufficient if it

> charges the commission of the offense in ordinary and concise language in such a manner as to enable a person of common understanding to know what is meant, and with that degree of certainty that will give the defendant

notice of the particular offense with which he is charged, and enable the court, on conviction, to pronounce the proper judgment[.]

We have recognized that in most cases a charging instrument that tracks the statutory text of an offense is sufficient to provide a defendant with adequate notice. When a statutory term or element is defined by statute, the charging instrument does not need to allege the definition of the term or element. Typically the definitions of terms and elements are regarded as evidentiary matters. But in some cases, a charging instrument that tracks the statutory language may be insufficient to provide a defendant with adequate notice. This is so when the statutory language fails to be completely descriptive. The statutory language is not completely descriptive "when the statutes define a term in such a way as to create several means of committing an offense, and the definition specifically concerns an act or omission on the part of the defendant." In such cases, "more particularity is required to provide notice." Thus, "if the prohibited conduct is statutorily defined to include more than one manner or means of commission, the State must, upon timely request, allege the particular manner or means it seeks to establish."...

[T]he definitions of "intoxicated" describe two types of DWI offenses, a "loss of faculties" offense and a "per se offense." The "loss of faculties" offense...

> may be established by proving the defendant drove or operated a motor vehicle in a public place while not having the normal use of his mental faculties, or while not having the normal use of his physical faculties, because of the introduction into his body of (1) alcohol; (2) a controlled substance; (3) a drug; or (4) a combination of two or more of those substances.

In contrast, ... the "per se" offense "may be established by proving the defendant drove or operated a motor vehicle in a public place while having an alcohol concentration [higher than the legal limit] ... in his blood, breath, or urine."

... Section 1.07 defines the elements of the offense as "the forbidden conduct, the required culpability, the required result, and the negation of any exception to the offense." The type of intoxicant does not constitute any of these, and "[t]he mere fact that the DWI statute separately defines intoxication does not automatically elevate the intoxicant to the status of an element of the offense."

... [I]t would be bad public policy to hold that the specific type of intoxicant is an element of DWI because a defendant could obtain an acquittal if the State, at trial, ultimately proves that the defendant used another type of intoxicant than the one alleged in the charging instrument. The DWI statute... does not focus on the act of becoming intoxicated; it focuses on the act of the defendant while intoxicated.

IV. Analysis

... The State asserts that a person's state of intoxication is not an act or omission; instead, it is the defendant's condition and a circumstance that accompanies the defendant's act of operating a motor vehicle. In response, Barbernell argues that ... the court of appeals was correct in affirming the trial judge's ruling.

... In analyzing whether a charging instrument provides adequate notice, ...courts must engage in a two-step analysis. First, a court must identify the elements of an offense. As recognized in *Gray*, the elements, defined by the Legislature, include: the forbidden conduct, the required culpability, if any, any required result, and the negation of any exception to the offense. Next, as to the second inquiry, when the Legislature has defined an element of the offense that describes an act or omission, a court must ask whether the definitions provide alternative manners or means in which the act or omission can be committed. If this second inquiry is answered in the affirmative, a charging instrument will supply adequate notice only if, in addition to setting out the elements of an offense, it also alleges the specific manner and means of commission that the State intends to rely on at trial.

The shortcomings of [our previous holdings that DWI manner and means are elements of the offense] have not gone unnoticed by legal scholars. Criminal law experts Professors Dix and Dawson have criticized this opinion, stating that the Court "took considerable liberties with the concept of 'behavior' or conduct constituting an offense." In their view,

> [t]he State's choice between the methods of proving intoxication does not in any sense determine what acts, conduct or 'behavior' of the accused that the State will rely on. Rather, the choice concerns the type of evidence the State will rely upon to show particular conduct by the accused—'driving' or

'operating' a vehicle—performed while a particular circumstance—intoxication—existed.

Having determined that [our opinion]... evolved from a flawed analysis, we now reevaluate the notice issue according to the dictates of our precedent. With the understanding that "intoxicated" is an element of DWI and that Section 49.01(2) sets out two definitions for "intoxicated," we ask whether the definitions of "intoxicated" concern an act or omission and create two different manners and means of committing DWI. Our recent examination of the definitions of "intoxicated" in *Bagheri v. State* leads us to conclude that the answer to this question is "no."

Echoing the sentiments of Professors Dix and Dawson, in *Bagheri*, we held that the definitions "set forth alternative means by which the State may prove intoxication, rather than alternate means of committing the offense." We then explained, "The conduct proscribed by the Penal Code is the act of driving while in a state of intoxication. That does not change whether the State uses the per se definition or the impairment definition to prove the offense." These statements make clear that the definitions of "intoxicated" are purely evidentiary matters; therefore, they do not need to be alleged in a charging instrument to provide a defendant with sufficient notice.

... A charging instrument that pleads the offense of DWI provides adequate notice when it sets out the elements of the offense as provided in Section 49.04.

Thus, in this case, the information, though it did not allege either definition of "intoxicated," provided Barbernell with adequate notice, and the court of appeals erred to conclude otherwise.

V. Conclusion

After reevaluating our analysis in *Carter*, we hold that the definitions of "intoxicated" in Section 49.01(2) are evidentiary and therefore do not need to be alleged in a charging instrument. Therefore, a trial court should not quash a DWI information charging a defendant with DWI due to the State's failure to allege the definition of "intoxicated" that it intends to prove at trial. The judgment of the court of appeals is reversed and vacated, and the cause is remanded to the trial court.

————————◆————————

Notes and Questions

1. *Barbernell* is an interesting case from the prosecutor's perspective. The defendant argued the State was required to prove which intoxication definition it relied upon, and the trial judge agreed by granting his motion to quash. In many cases where a breath or blood sample is taken, the district or county attorney's office alleges both loss of normal use and alcohol concentration. In this case, the prosecutor alleged neither. Why do you think the prosecutor refused to amend the charging instrument and instead appealed the trial court's decision? Would you have taken the same risk were you the prosecutor? Why or why not?

2. Notice requires that a defendant understand what he has allegedly done from the face of the charging instrument. Imagine a defendant is guilty of the charged crime. Does he need a detailed account of the offense, or will minimal details suffice to put him on notice for the crime for which he is being prosecuted?

3. Now imagine an innocent defendant, a person who did not commit the crime. Would this defendant need more information about the details of the charged crime to prepare a defense? Is there a fundamental criminal procedure problem with viewing guilty defendants as needing less information in a charging instrument than innocent defendants? Given the presumption of innocence for all defendants, what should the standard for notice be?

4. Consider the following statement from the Court of Criminal Appeals:

> It has long been held that [notice of the nature and cause of the accusation] must come from the face of the indictment. Indeed, the accused is not required to look elsewhere . . . And it is not sufficient to say that the accused knew with what offense he was charged. The inquiry must be whether the charge, in writing, furnished that information in plain and intelligible language.[51]

5. A motion to quash is limited to attacking the form or the substance of the charging instrument, not the underlying facts of the case.

---

[51] *Riney v. State*, 28 S.W.3d 561, 565 (Tex. Crim. App. 2000) (internal citations omitted).

The indictment must be specific enough to inform the defendant of the nature of the accusations against him so that he may prepare a defense. ... A motion to quash should be granted only when the language concerning the defendant's conduct is so vague or indefinite as to deny the defendant notice of the acts he allegedly committed.... In the pretrial setting, there is neither constitutional nor statutory authority for a defendant to test, or for a trial court to determine, the sufficiency of evidence to support or defeat an element alleged in the indictment. Therefore, a motion to quash the indictment cannot be used to argue that the prosecution is unable to prove one of the elements of the crime.[52]

---◆---

Components

A charging instrument must include the statutory requirements listed earlier in this chapter, it must allege all essential elements of the charged offense,[53] and it must provide notice to the accused.[54] Like all documents, occasionally the charging instrument contains errors, omits information, or otherwise fails to give the defendant notice of the charged crime. These errors present problems for the State, especially when they are not caught until after the trial begins. It is the prosecutor's duty to verify the charging document before the day trial begins.

The next case illustrates what, at a minimum, the charging instrument must include for constitutional purposes.

---◆---

Neil Cook v. State
902 S.W.2d 471
(Tex. Crim. App. 1995)

Appellant was convicted by a jury of theft over $20,000.00. ... [T]he trial judge assessed punishment at ten years confinement and ordered restitution ... The Court of Appeals affirmed. We granted appellant's petition for discretionary review to determine whether the charging

---

[52] *Turner v. State*, 435 S.W.3d 280, 286–87 (Tex. App.—Waco 2014, pet. ref'd.).
[53] *Yuncevich v. State*, 626 S.W.2d 784, 785 (Tex. Crim. App. 1982).
[54] TEX. CODE CRIM. PROC. ANN. art. 21.02(7) (West 2016) ("The offense must be set forth in plain and intelligible words.").

instrument was so deficient as to not invest the trial court with jurisdiction. We will reverse.

I.

We set out the charging instrument below:

IN THE NAME AND BY AUTHORITY OF THE STATE OF TEXAS, the Grand Jury of Bexar County, State of Texas, duly organized, empaneled and sworn as such at the March term, A.D., 1991, of the 186th Judicial District Court of said County, in said Court, at said term, do present in and to said Court that in the County and State aforesaid, and anterior to the presentment of this indictment, and on or about the 1ST day of June 1987, hereinafter referred to as defendant, with intent to deprive the owner, namely: ELIZABETH K. PRICE, of property, namely: LAWFUL CURRENCY OF THE UNITED STATES OF AMERICA, said property being other than real property which had A VALUE of Twenty Thousand Dollars ($20,000.00) or more, without the effective consent of the owner;

[Signed by Grand Jury Foreperson]

On direct appeal, appellant contended his conviction was void because the charging instrument was constitutionally deficient because it omitted appellant's name .... We granted appellant's petition for discretionary review to determine whether a charging instrument which fails to charge "a person" still constitutes an indictment as contemplated by [the Texas Constitution].

The Texas Constitution guarantees to defendants the right to indictment by a grand jury for all felony offenses. Tex. Const. art. I, § 10. [This section] provides in pertinent part:

Rights of accused in criminal prosecutions
In all criminal prosecutions the accused ... shall have the right to demand the nature and cause of the accusation against him, and to have a copy thereof ... and no person shall be held to answer for a [felony] criminal offense, unless on an indictment of a grand jury....

An indictment serves two functions. First, it provides notice of the offense in order to allow a defendant to prepare a defense. Second, an indictment serves a jurisdictional function. The filing of an indictment is essential to vest the trial court with jurisdiction over a felony offense. Jurisdiction vests only upon the filing of a valid indictment in the appropriate court.

Art. V, § 12(b) defines an "indictment" as "a written instrument presented to a court by a grand jury charging a person with the commission of an offense." Therefore, to comprise an indictment within the definition provided by the constitution, an instrument must charge: (1) a person; (2) with the commission of an offense. ... We therefore hold that the definition of an indictment provided by art. V, § 12(b) establishes constitutional requisites for an indictment. ...If the charging instrument fails to charge "a person" then it is not an indictment and does not vest the trial court with jurisdiction. Moreover, because a valid indictment is essential for jurisdiction, it is not subject to waiver.

In the instant case, the charging instrument wholly failed to charge "a person." Thus, the charging instrument did not meet the first prong of the constitutional definition of art. V, § 12(b). Consequently, the charging instrument was not an indictment as required by art. V, § 12(b) and art. I, § 10, and did not vest the trial court with jurisdiction. Therefore, appellant's conviction is void.

The judgment of the Court of Appeals is reversed and we remand this cause to the trial court with instructions to dismiss the prosecution in this cause.

———————◆———————

Notes and Questions

1. If merely charging a person with a crime is sufficient to deem a document an indictment pursuant to the Constitution, why include the other statutory requirements? For example, what purpose(s) does including the date serve? Why include the county or city where the crime occurred? What is the reason for requiring the affiant, the person swearing the information the drafting attorney is relying upon, is credible? What purposes do these facts serve, if they are not constitutionally essential, to the charging instrument?

———————◆———————

Amendments and Abandonments

There are two ways a prosecutor can alter the charging instrument language once the document is complete: through amendment or abandonment. Both are physical alterations the prosecutor makes to the face of the charging instrument. The Court of Criminal Appeals explained amendments as follows:

> An amendment is an alteration to the face of the charging instrument which affects the substance of the charging instrument. For example, in *Sodipo v. State*, we found the alteration of a cause number in an enhancement paragraph was an amendment. In *Hillin v. State*, the alteration of a weapon in an aggravated assault indictment was an amendment. In *Beebe v. State*, the addition of the manner and means of committing an offense was an amendment. In *Garcia v. State*, the alteration of the alleged date was an amendment. In *McCoy v. State*, the addition of a complainant was an amendment. The Court of Appeals in *Hilton v. State* found the alteration of the indictment from "two facsimile machines" to "one facsimile machine" was an amendment. In *Hinojosa v. State*, deleting "delivery" and replacing it with "possession" was an amendment.[55]

As you can see, amendments are alterations to the indictment that affect what the State must prove at trial—a date, an element, the charged manner and means. Several restrictions apply to amendments:

1. The prosecutor must seek the trial court's approval to make the amendment and must amend with the court's supervision;[56]
2. The prosecutor must notify the defendant;
3. The amendment must be done before the date the trial begins;
4. If the defendant requests time to respond to the amendment, the court shall grant the defendant not less than ten days, unless the defendant requests a shorter period of time;
5. A prosecutor may amend after trial begins but only if the defendant does not object;
6. An indictment or information may not be amended over the defendant's objection if the amendment charges the defendant with an additional or different offense or if the defendant's substantial rights are prejudiced.[57]

---

[55] *Eastep v. State*, 941 S.W.2d 130, 132–33 (Tex. Crim. App. 1997), *overruled on other grounds, Riney v. State*, 28 S.W.3d 561 (Tex. Crim. App. 2000), and *Gollihar v. State*, 46 S.W.3d 243 (Tex. Crim. App. 2001) (citations omitted).
[56] TEX. CODE CRIM. PROC. ANN. art. 28.11 (West 2016).
[57] TEX. CODE CRIM. PROC. ANN. art. 28.10 (West 2016).

Two of these requirements— (4) ten days' notice and (6) charging a new offense—require greater explanation. A hypothetical scenario helps explain both requirements.

Suppose that a felony trial is set for Monday, July 1. Imagine the prosecutor finalizes trial preparation on Thursday, June 27 and while doing so discovers an error in the charging instrument for the first time. Assume the indictment's manner and means is not supported by the evidence.

The prosecutor notifies the court and defense counsel on Friday, June 28 that she wishes to amend the indictment. Defense counsel requests the full ten days' notice, which is common practice. As a result, the judge cannot go forward with trial on Monday, July 1 as originally planned. To accommodate defense counsel's request, the trial must now be moved to July 8, at the earliest, since defense counsel was notified on June 28 and has requested the full ten days to respond to the new indictment.

Now suppose that after speaking with witnesses and accumulating evidence, the prosecutor realizes the charge itself must change from one felony offense to another felony offense governed by an entirely different statute. Can the prosecutor change the crime through an amendment to the indictment? The Code indicates that she can if the defendant does not object.[58] If the defendant objects that changing the crime through amendment deprives him the right to a grand jury probable cause determination, the indictment cannot be amended.[59] In this instance, the prosecutor would be required to dismiss the case and seek a new indictment based upon the new charge.

Abandonments are not the same as amendments. The Court of Criminal Appeals characterized abandonments as follows:

> We have recognized three situations where altering the charging instrument constitutes an abandonment: (1) abandonment of one or more of the alternative means in which an offense may be committed...; (2) abandonment of an allegation in the charging instrument if the effect of such abandonment is to reduce the prosecution to a lesser included

---

[58] TEX. CODE CRIM. PROC. ANN. art. 28.10(c) (West 2016).

[59] *Id.*; *Flowers v. State*, 815 S.W.2d 724, 729 (Tex. Crim. App. 1991) ("an amendment ... [changing the] charge [to] a different occurrence or incident than that originally alleged in the indictment ... [would implicate] the substantial rights of a defendant [who] would be prejudiced in part because he has been denied any grand jury review of the offense as required by Art. I, §10").

offense...; or, (3) abandonment of surplusage. ... Such alterations are abandonments and, therefore, do not invoke the requirements of ... [amendment articles] 28.10 and 28.11.[60]

In these instances, the prosecutor is free to abandon the language in a charging instrument by physically altering the charging instrument without the need for notice or approval from the judge or the defendant.

———————————— ◆ ————————————

Challenges

While the prosecutor has obligations in creating this document, so too does the defendant in challenging it, which the Court of Criminal Appeals discusses in the following case. It is important to note before reading *Teal* that it is a felony offense to harbor a fugitive the defendant knows has a warrant for a felony offense. In contrast, a person who harbors a fugitive without knowing he has a felony warrant is guilty of a misdemeanor offense.[61]

———————————— ◆ ————————————

Wilbert James Teal v. State
230 S.W.3d 172
(Tex. Crim. App. 2007)

Appellant was indicted for the offense of hindering apprehension. The indictment failed to allege that appellant knew that Curtis Brown, the person whose apprehension appellant was hindering, was a fugitive for Failure to Register as a Sex Offender. The court of appeals held that the district court never acquired subject-matter jurisdiction to try the case because the indictment alleged only a misdemeanor. We granted the State's Petition for Discretionary Review to determine whether "the court of appeals erred in holding that the indictment presented in this case was insufficient to vest the district court with subject-matter jurisdiction." We hold that...the indictment sufficed to vest jurisdiction in the district court....

---

[60] *Eastep v. State*, 941 S.W.2d 130, 135 (Tex. Crim. App. 1997), *overruled on other grounds*, *Riney v. State*, 28 S.W.3d 561 (Tex. Crim. App. 2000), and *Gollihar v. State*, 46 S.W.3d 243 (Tex. Crim. App. 2001) (citations omitted).
[61] TEX. PENAL CODE ANN. §38.05 (West 2011).

On June 8, 2004, Lufkin police received a Crimestopper's tip that a fugitive, Curtis Brown, was staying at appellant's house. When police officers arrived at his house, appellant was sitting on the front porch with his front door open. Officer Burfine told appellant that they were looking for Brown, a fugitive with outstanding parole violator and sex offender warrants. He informed appellant that both of these were felony warrants. Officer Burfine told appellant that they had information that Brown was in the house. Appellant said that he had seen Brown the night before, but that he had not seen Brown that day. He repeatedly denied that Brown was in the house, and he refused to allow the police to enter his house.

Meanwhile, Officer Smith heard noises from the rear of the house, so he went to check and discovered Brown attempting to flee. Officer Smith arrested Brown. The officers also found another man who had an outstanding sexual assault warrant when they searched appellant's house.

Appellant was indicted for the offense of hindering apprehension. The indictment alleged that appellant

> ... then and there intentionally, with intent to hinder the arrest, prosecution, or punishment of Curtis Brown for the offense of Failure to Comply with Registration as a Sex Offender, did harbor or conceal Curtis Brown by stating to peace officers that Curtis Brown was not present at said residence occupied by defendant at a time when Curtis Brown was then and there present....

As soon as the jury was empaneled, appellant objected to the indictment and argued that the district court did not have jurisdiction because the indictment alleged only a misdemeanor, not a felony. The trial court overruled his objection. After hearing the evidence, the jury convicted appellant and sentenced him to two years in prison.

On appeal, appellant argued that the evidence was legally and factually insufficient and that the jury instructions were erroneous. The court of appeals, however, *sua sponte* addressed the issue of whether the trial court had subject matter jurisdiction. A two-justice majority of the court of appeals stated that the indictment failed to allege "that Teal had knowledge of Brown's felony fugitive status so as to facially charge a third degree felony under section 38.05, and vest the district court with subject-matter jurisdiction." Because the charging instrument did not charge an offense that fell within the district court's jurisdiction, the court of appeals concluded that the district court should have transferred the indictment to a county court with misdemeanor jurisdiction. Justice Gaultney dissented and stated that the indictment did vest the district court with jurisdiction. Relying on the Texas Constitution and this Court's decision in *Studer v. State*,[62] Justice Gaultney concluded that the indictment was valid because "[a]n indictment vests the court with jurisdiction even if it fails to allege an element of the offense."

The Texas Constitution requires that, unless waived by the defendant, the State must obtain a grand jury indictment in a felony case. Absent an indictment or valid waiver, a district court does not have jurisdiction over that case. An indictment also provides a defendant with notice of the offense and allows him to prepare a defense. Further, the "constitutional guarantee is intended to provide the accused an impartial body which can act as a screen between the rights of the accused and the prosecuting power of the State."

Before 1985, defects of form and defects of substance in an indictment had very different results. Failure to object to a defect of form waived any error on appeal, but the failure to object to a defect of substance did not waive error on appeal. The reasoning was that an indictment that contained a substantive defect was "void" and therefore insufficient to invoke the jurisdiction of the court. Under this reasoning, a defendant could attack a felony conviction based on a substantively defective indictment on appeal, even though he had not objected at trial. Defendants could "lie behind the log," and either plead guilty or take their chances at trial and, if convicted, then raise a claim of a "void" indictment in a later appeal or application for habeas corpus relief. Numerous decisions from this Court exhaustively debated the fine technical distinctions between defects of form and those of substance, and numerous decisions from this Court reversed convictions years after the fact for defects of substance in the indictment.

In 1985, the citizens of Texas and their legislature resoundingly rejected this hypertechnical case law both by Constitutional amendment and by statute. The voters amended the Texas Constitution to include the definition of an indictment. An indictment, as now defined by the Texas Constitution, is "a written instrument presented to a court by a grand jury charging a person with the commission of an offense."

As part of the same reform package, the legislature amended several provisions of the Code of Criminal Procedure to ensure that indictment

---

[62] *Studer v. State*, 799 S.W.2d 263 (Tex. Crim. App. 1990).

defects could be objected to and repaired pretrial, but that these defects would not invalidate an otherwise valid conviction if not raised before trial.

Additionally, the legislature amended article 28.10 to ensure that the State had ample opportunity to repair indictment defects and that the defendant received the requisite notice of indictment changes, as well as an opportunity to respond to them:

(a) After notice to the defendant, a matter of form or substance in an indictment or information may be amended at any time before the date the trial on the merits commences. On the request of the defendant, the court shall allow the defendant not less than 10 days, or a shorter period if requested by the defendant, to respond to the amended indictment or information.

(b) A matter of form or substance in an indictment or information may also be amended after the trial on the merits commences if the defendant does not object.

(c) An indictment or information may not be amended over the defendant's objection as to form or substance if the amended indictment or information charges the defendant with an additional or different offense or if the substantial rights of the defendant are prejudiced.

The legislature's purpose in amending the constitution and the statutes was to change the focus from "whether a defect is fundamental [*i.e.* a defect of substance or not]" to "whether the defendant brought the defect to the court's attention." And the legislature intended the constitutional provision and statutes to work together. That is, indictments charging a person with committing an offense, once presented, invoke the jurisdiction of the trial court and jurisdiction is no longer contingent on whether the indictment contains defects of form or substance. The 1985 statutes clearly mandate that defendants must object to errors in the form or substance of an indictment "before the date on which the trial on the merits commences[.]" Thus, Texas law now requires the defendant to object to any error in the indictment before the day of trial and certainly before the jury is empaneled. [In past decisions, we have been] clear: raise indictment defects before the date of trial.... [A] defect in a charging instrument is waived unless raised prior to trial."

| Texas Criminal Procedure and Evidence

The "fatally flawed indictment" issue was raised again in *Cook v. State*, in which the charging instrument did not charge "a person." ... *Cook* held that, because the charging instrument failed to charge a person, it did not meet one of the two requirements of an indictment, and therefore, it was not an indictment at all and did not vest any trial court with jurisdiction.

Studer and *Cook* are "book-end" cases. *Studer* held that the defendant must object to any indictment defects before the date of trial or forfeit any complaint about its sufficiency thereafter. *Cook* held that the Texas Constitution requires that an indictment allege that (1) a person, (2) committed an offense. Without both of those elements the charging instrument is not an indictment and does not vest the district court with jurisdiction.

The proper test to determine if a charging instrument alleges "an offense" is whether the allegations in it are clear enough that one can identify the offense alleged. If they are, then the indictment is sufficient to confer subject matter jurisdiction. Stated another way: Can the trial court (and appellate courts who give deference to the trial court's assessment) and the defendant identify what penal code provision is alleged and is that penal code provision one that vests jurisdiction in the trial court? With this background, we turn to the present case.

Appellant alleges that the present indictment was missing one of the elements that raises the offense of Hindering Apprehension from a misdemeanor to a felony:

In order for the State to prosecute Appellant for the third degree felony offense of hindering apprehension in district court the State had to additionally allege and prove that the person, in the present case Curtis Brown, who was allegedly being harbored or assisted was facing arrest, charge or had been convicted of a felony and that Appellant had knowledge that the person (Curtis Brown) who he was allegedly harboring or assisting had been convicted of a felony.

Appellant further argues that "[e]ven though the indictment in the instant case did state that Curtis Brown did have felony fugitive status for failure to comply with Registration as a Sex Offender it failed to additionally allege that Appellant had knowledge of Curtis Brown's felony fugitive status." Thus, appellant contends that the indictment was defective because it did not explicitly state that appellant knew that Curtis Brown was a felon. This defect, he contends, was jurisdictional and thus it "may be raised at any time [because] .... [j]urisdiction is a systemic requirement that cannot be waived or conferred by consent and which may be considered at any time."

The State responds that it did allege that appellant was harboring a fugitive, and "it is clear that the State intended to prosecute the defendant for the felony offense of Hindering Apprehension, by including the language 'with intent to hinder the arrest, prosecution, or punishment' of Curtis Brown for the offense of Failure to Comply with Registration as a Sex Offender." This offense is itself a felony, which, the State argues, clearly indicates its intent to prosecute appellant for the felony offense of Hindering Apprehension.

After *Studer* and *Cook*, courts must now look to the indictment as a whole, not to its specific formal requisites. Constitutionally, district courts have jurisdiction over a felony when an indictment charging a person with an offense is signed by the grand jury foreman and presented to the district court. In *Duron v. State*, this Court held that "a written instrument is an indictment or information under the Constitution if it accuses someone of a crime with enough clarity and specificity to identify the penal statute under which the State intends to prosecute, even if the instrument is otherwise defective." We stated that "all that *Studer* and *Cook* require to satisfy the mandate of Art. V, § 12 [is] that an indictment charge 'the commission of an offense.' This is true whether an indictment fails to allege one element of an offense..."

Implicit within both *Studer* and *Cook* is that "the offense" charged must be one for which the trial court has subject-matter jurisdiction. Although the "indictment" provision of the constitution explicitly speaks only of the two requirements of "a person" and "an offense," the constitution also sets out the subject-matter jurisdiction of Texas courts. An indictment must also satisfy the constitutional requirement of subject-matter jurisdiction over "an offense."

Thus, the complete test for the constitutional sufficiency of a particular charging instrument goes slightly further than that expressly set out in *Studer* and *Cook*: Can the district court and the defendant determine, from the face of the indictment, that the indictment intends to charge a felony or other offense for which a district court has jurisdiction? Suppose, for example, that a named person is indicted for the offense of speeding. The constitutional requirements of an indictment are met—a named person and an offense— but district courts do not have subject-matter jurisdiction over speeding offenses, regardless of how "perfect" the wording of the charging instrument might be. Thus, the indictment, despite whatever substantive defects it contains, must be capable of being construed as intending to charge a felony.

The element that was missing in this indictment was whether appellant knew that Brown was a felony fugitive. This is one of the two *mens rea* requirements for Hindering Apprehension. We have previously upheld the validity of the indictment in several cases, including *Studer* itself, in which the *mens rea* allegation was missing or defective. In this case, the indictment, as a whole, was sufficient to vest the district court with subject-matter jurisdiction and give the defendant notice that the State intended to prosecute him for a felony offense. It alleged whom appellant was hiding (Brown); it stated the offense Brown was hiding from (a felony); it alleged that appellant told police that Brown was not present. Because Brown was alleged to be a fugitive "for the offense of Failure to Comply with Registration as a Sex Offender" which is a felony, the district court could conclude, from the face of the charging instrument, that the State intended to charge a felony hindering apprehension offense. It certainly was a defective indictment because it omitted one of the two elements that raise hindering apprehension from a misdemeanor to a felony, but it was nonetheless sufficient to vest jurisdiction—it charged "an offense" and one could fairly conclude from the face of the charging instrument that the State intended to charge a felony offense. If appellant was confused about whether the State did or intended to charge him with a felony, he could have and should have objected to the defective indictment before the date of trial.

Appellant did not object to the substance of the indictment until right *after* the jury had been empaneled. His failure to make a timely objection before the date of trial was exactly the type of action that the citizens of Texas summarily rejected in voting for the 1985 constitutional amendment and the Texas Legislature prohibited in enacting the 1985 enabling statutes. Appellant forfeited any right to object to indictment defects thereafter, and the court of appeals should not have *sua sponte* reversed appellant's conviction on this basis. Therefore, we vacate the judgment of the court of appeals and remand the case to that court.

Notes and Questions

1. In *Teal*, failing to object and preserve error at the appropriate time resulted in the defendant's inability to raise that error for the first time on appeal. Thus, defense counsel must object to the charging instrument before the trial starts. Prosecutors, on the other hand, must check every charging instrument well in advance of trial to ensure it is error free. Failing to do so could result in a delay of trial or worse.

2. How can you reconcile the differences between the holdings in *Cook*, where the defendant prevailed on appeal, and *Teal*, where the defendant lost on appeal, when both charging instruments were missing information that should have been included?

3. There are limitations to what defense counsel can expect from filing a motion to quash the indictment. It should be used to attack errors within the indictment, not to argue the merits of the case. The Court of Criminal Appeals has stated, "[A] motion to quash an indictment ... , like any pretrial motion, cannot be used to 'argue that the prosecution could not prove one of the elements of the crime.' ... [A] pretrial proceeding should not be a 'mini-trial' on the sufficiency of the evidence to support an element of the offense."[63]

———————◆———————

Errors

The charging document may be the most important document for the prosecution. Its drafting is entirely within the control of the prosecutor. Nevertheless, errors are more common than they should be.

One area of charging instrument error is form or substance error. "Matters of substance include essential elements of the offense charged, the time and place where the offense took place, and prior convictions when a repeat offense is charged. Matters of form include such items as the caption of the indictment and the number and term of the court."[64]

---

[63] *Lawrence v. State*, 240 S.W.3d 912, 916 (Tex. Crim. App. 2007) (citations omitted).
[64] *Peterson v. State*, 732 S.W.2d 22, 25 (Tex. App.—San Antonio 1987, pet. granted).

If form or substance errors exist, the defendant may challenge the charging instrument. The defendant can file a written motion to quash, a motion to set aside, or a motion to dismiss the indictment or information. While these names may be used interchangeably, in practice, most attorneys call it a motion to quash.[65] The judge may grant or deny the motion. If the motion is granted, the prosecutor is forced to dismiss the case. The prosecutor may then recharge the defendant, either by seeking a re-indictment or by amending the charging instrument. In most cases, substance and form errors can be corrected through a new indictment or information. In rare cases, no amount of amending or abandoning the charging language will help. This may occur when the facts initially seem to support a criminal charge but, upon further investigation, do not, or when what is charged is not actually criminal conduct.

———————◆———————

Variances

It is one thing to have an indictment that fails to include required information, whether the omission is fatal or not. It is another to plead information that the prosecutor cannot prove at trial. For example, the prosecutor may plead facts or select a manner and means that does not match the testimony or evidence admitted at trial. If the prosecutor is unable to prove all elements of the crime, as pled, it may be a fatal variance.

Variances are something every criminal attorney experiences on occasion. What happens to the case when there is a variance? The following case answers this question.

———————◆———————

---

[65] TEX. CODE CRIM. PROC. ANN. art. 27.10 (West 2016); *State v. Salinas*, 982 S.W.2d 9, 10 n. 1 (Tex. App.—Houston [1st Dist.] 1997, pet. ref'd) (the names of these motions are used interchangeably in the Code, but a motion to dismiss is typically used to challenge substance defects whereas a motion to quash may be more appropriately used to challenge notice).

Perry Montez Johnson v. State
364 S.W.3d 292
(Tex. Crim. App. 2012)

The question in this case is whether a variance between the allegations in the charging instrument and the proof at trial renders the evidence legally insufficient to support the conviction. Because the variance in this case involves a non-statutory allegation that does not affect the "allowable unit of prosecution," the variance cannot render the evidence legally insufficient to support a conviction. We shall affirm the judgment of the court of appeals.

Appellant was indicted for various counts of aggravated assault. The count at issue in the present case charged that appellant did then and there "intentionally or knowingly cause serious bodily injury to [the victim] by hitting her with his hand or by twisting her arm with his hand." The victim testified that appellant threw her against the wall and that hitting the wall caused her to fall to the floor and break her arm.

On appeal, appellant claimed that this variance between pleading and proof rendered the evidence legally insufficient to support his conviction. The court of appeals disagreed, holding that the variance was "not material because it only concerned the method by which appellant caused the serious bodily injury."

The standard for determining whether the evidence is legally sufficient to support a conviction is "whether, after viewing the evidence in the light most favorable to the prosecution, any rational trier of fact could have found the essential elements of the crime beyond a reasonable doubt." In *Malik v. State*, we articulated the modern Texas standard for ascertaining what the "essential elements of the crime" are; they are "the elements of the offense as defined by the hypothetically correct jury charge for the case." The hypothetically correct jury charge is one that at least "accurately sets out the law, is authorized by the indictment, does not unnecessarily increase the State's burden of proof or unnecessarily restrict the State's theories of liability, and adequately describes the particular offense for which the defendant was tried." We have described the law "as authorized by the indictment" to be "the statutory elements of the offense ... as modified by the charging instrument," but we have said also that the hypothetically correct jury charge does not necessarily have to track exactly all of the charging instrument's allegations.

A variance in pleading and proof can occur in two different ways. First, a variance can involve the statutory language that defines the offense. This can happen when a statute specifies alternate methods by which an offense could be committed, the charging instrument pleads one of those alternate methods, but the State proves, instead, an unpled method. For example, the retaliation statute makes it a crime to threaten a "witness" or "informant." The first type of variance occurs if the State pleads only "witness" in the charging instrument and proves only the unpled element of "informant" at trial. Second, a variance can involve a non-statutory allegation that is descriptive of the offense in some way. For example, the charging instrument pleads "Mary" as the victim, but the State proves "John" at trial. Or the charging instrument pleads the offense was committed with a knife, but the State proves at trial that a baseball bat was used.

With respect to the first type of variance between pleading and proof, this Court has held… that the failure to prove the statutory language pled renders the evidence legally insufficient to support the conviction…

[I]n contrast to our treatment of statutory allegations, for non-statutory allegations we tolerate some variation in pleading and proof. We tolerate "little mistakes" that do not prejudice the defendant's substantial rights but we will not tolerate a variance that really amounts to a failure to prove the offense alleged. What is essential about variances with respect to non-statutory allegations is that the variance should not be so great that the proof at trial "shows an entirely different offense" than what was alleged in the charging instrument. For example, in a murder prosecution, the victim's name need not be proved with exactness, but the State must prove that the victim alleged in the indictment is the same person as the victim proved at trial. If the State has alleged the murder of "Dangerous Dan" but has proved, instead, the murder of "Little Nell," then the State has proved a different murder than it has alleged, and an acquittal is required.

The key to this conclusion is that each victim is an allowable unit of prosecution for the offense of murder. If there are multiple murder victims, the State may obtain multiple murder convictions. So, the murder of one individual is a different offense from the murder of a different individual. But some types of facts—such as the method by which a murder is committed—do not relate at all to the allowable unit of prosecution. The State could allege "poisoning, garroting, shooting, stabbing, or drowning," of a single individual, and those different acts would simply be alternate methods of committing a single offense. With only one victim, there can be only one murder, regardless of how that murder is committed.

… [A] variance could involve a non-statutory allegation that has nothing to do with the allowable unit of prosecution and, therefore, cannot be a basis for saying that the proved offense is different from the one that was pled. "Stabbing with a knife" and "bludgeoning with a baseball bat" are two possible ways of murdering Dangerous Dan, but they do not constitute separate offenses. These methods of committing murder do describe an element of the offense: the element of causation. But murder is a result-of-conduct crime. What caused the victim's death is not the focus or gravamen of the offense; the focus or gravamen of the offense is that the victim was killed. Variances such as this can never be material because such a variance can never show an "entirely different offense" than what was alleged.

In the present case, appellant was charged with aggravated assault by causing serious bodily injury. The variance in this case involves the charged acts of "hitting the victim with his hand" and "twisting the victim's arm with his hand" versus the proved act of "throwing the victim against the wall." All of these acts describe the causation element of the offense, but none of them are used to describe the injury suffered by the victim. What caused the victim's injury is not the focus or gravamen of this offense. The aggravated assault offense at issue is a result-of-conduct crime with the focus or gravamen being the victim and the bodily injury that was inflicted. "The precise act or nature of conduct in this result-oriented offense is inconsequential." Had the State pled and proved different injuries, a question might arise as to whether the difference between what was pled and what was proved was significant enough to be material. Separate crimes of aggravated assault could be based upon separately inflicted instances of bodily injury. But the act that caused injury does not define or help define the allowable unit of prosecution for this type of aggravated-assault offense, so the variance at issue cannot be material.

To summarize, variances can be classified into three categories, depending upon the type of allegation that the State has pled in its charging instrument but failed to prove at trial. First, a variance involving statutory language that defines the offense always renders the evidence legally insufficient to support the conviction (i.e. such variances are always material). Second, a variance involving a non-statutory allegation that describes an "allowable unit of prosecution" element of the offense may or may not render the evidence legally insufficient, depending upon whether the variance is material (i.e. such variances are sometimes material). Finally, other types of variances involving immaterial non-statutory allegations do not render the evidence legally insufficient. The variance in the present case falls within the third category.

We affirm the judgment of the court of appeals.

————————◆————————

Notes and Questions

1. Make sure that you understand the types of variances described above and the outcomes for each type.

2. The court discusses one type of variance leading to legally insufficient evidence. "If, upon the trial of a case in a justice or municipal court, the state fails to prove a prima facie case of the offense alleged in the complaint, the defendant is entitled to a directed verdict of 'not guilty.'"[66] If the trial judge grants the defendant's motion for directed verdict at the close of the State's case-in-chief, the judge verbally commands or directs the jury to return a "not guilty" verdict. This can be confusing for the jury, especially when it is tasked to be the factfinder. It is also quite embarrassing for a prosecutor to fail to elicit evidence or testimony regarding all elements, thereby acquitting the defendant. Unfortunately, this mistake happens more often than it should in courthouses around Texas. Remember that the State always carries the burden of proving up the case. When it fails, the defendant must be set free through the charge's dismissal or acquittal.

3. Prosecutors should plead conservatively and strategically and read every charging instrument carefully well in advance of trial to ensure a successful prosecution. Defense attorneys should also read the charging document carefully well in advance of trial and move for a directed verdict in every case where the evidence fails to support an element of the crime.

————————◆————————

---

[66] TEX. CODE CRIM. PROC. ANN. art. 45.032 (West 2016).

4. Jurisdiction, Venue, and Charging Instruments | 215

Counts

In federal courts, it is common to see one charging instrument with many counts or offenses charged. In Texas courts, this rarely occurs.

The Penal Code authorizes a prosecutor to include more than one count in a charging instrument if the charges arise out of the same criminal episode. The Texas Penal Code defines a single criminal episode as

> the commission of two or more offenses, regardless of whether the harm is directed toward or inflicted upon more than one person . . . [if] the offenses are committed pursuant to the same transaction or ... constitute a common scheme or plan; or the offenses are the repeated commission of the same or similar offenses.[67]

The act of charging more than one offense in a single charging instrument is called joinder, not to be confused with joinder of offenses at trial, which involves trying multiple cases arising out of the same criminal episode during a single trial. That type of joinder will be discussed in Chapter 12.

Texas courts have held that indictments charging a person with numerous counts of sexually assaulting more than one child,[68] committing aggravated robbery and rape within minutes of each other,[69] and sexually assaulting children with a four-year gap between count dates[70] all met the

---

[67] TEX. PENAL CODE ANN. §3.01 (West 2011).
[68] *Schmitt v. State*, No. 12-01-00306-CR, 2003 WL 22411210, at *2 (Tex. App.—Tyler Oct. 22, 2003, no pet.) (fact that count one alleged first child sexual assault occurred in 1996 whereas second occurred in 1997 was still a single criminal episode due to the fact that child testified sexual assaults occurred repeatedly between 1996 and 1998).
[69] *Kela v. State*, 786 S.W.2d 81, 82 (Tex. App.—San Antonio 1990, pet. ref'd).
[70] *Casey v. State*, 349 S.W.3d 825, 830-31 (Tex. App.—El Paso 2011, pet. ref'd).

single criminal episode standard. Neither statutory nor case law imposes a time limit on a "criminal episode" when repeated commissions of the same or similar offenses are alleged.[71]

---◆---

Notes and Questions

1.   Each count represents a separate offense. Moreover, a prosecutor may allege different manners and means to prove a single count.[72] For example, in an aggravated assault felony indictment, a prosecutor may allege a single count of aggravated assault but use two manner and means paragraphs to allege serious bodily injury and use of a deadly weapon. Regardless of the number of counts or the various manner and means paragraphs, trial courts must carefully sort out verdict forms to ensure the jury's verdict is unanimous and there are no more convictions than counts.

2.   According to the Penal Code,

> When the accused is found guilty of more than one offense arising out of the same criminal episode prosecuted in a single criminal action, a sentence for each offense for which he has been found guilty shall be pronounced ... [and with few exceptions,] the sentences shall run concurrently.[73]

A defendant may also elect to sever the offenses, but if she does so, it is within the judge's discretion to run the sentences concurrently or consecutively.[74] Like joinder of trials, severances of trials (versus severances of counts or offenses) will be discussed in more detail in Chapter 12.

---◆---

[71] TEX. PENAL CODE ANN. §3.01 (West 2011); *Guidry v. State*, 909 S.W.2d 584, 585 (Tex. App.—Corpus Christi 1995, pet. ref'd).
[72] TEX. CODE CRIM. PROC. ANN. art. 21.24(b) (West 2016).
[73] TEX. PEN. CODE ANN. §3.03 (West 2011).
[74] TEX. PEN. CODE ANN. §3.04 (West 2011).

Dismissals

Just as charges can be brought against an accused, they can also be dismissed. The general rule is the power to dismiss rests with the State. In *State v. Marmolejo*, the State appealed after a justice of the peace negotiated a plea with the defendant in one case in exchange for a dismissal in another.[75] The Court stated,

> In the absence of specific authority, a trial court cannot dismiss a prosecution except on the motion of the prosecuting attorney. There is no constitutional, statutory, or common law authority of which this Court is aware permitting a trial court to dismiss a prosecution on its own motion pursuant to a plea bargain negotiated by defense counsel and the court.[76]

Not only was the justice of the peace at fault for negotiating a plea with the defendant, but also for dismissing cases pursuant to the plea agreement. This is the State's job, not the judge's.

If the prosecutor desires to dismiss a case, she must file a motion to dismiss and present it to the trial court. The Code provides that the prosecutor may dismiss a case with the trial court's permission at any time by filing documents explaining the reason for the dismissal.[77] The name for this dismissal motion is a *nolle prosequi*, which is a Latin phrase meaning "we shall no longer prosecute." In practice, attorneys may refer to it as a "*nolle*" (which rhymes with *Molly*), or as a motion to dismiss.

The image on the following page is a copy of a motion to dismiss that was filed in a Harris County district court. This form is used by Harris County prosecutors to dismiss charges in that county. It is presented by the prosecutor, who signs the motion, and then it is given to the judge, who grants the motion by signing it. Once granted, the judgment entered is a dismissal, which ends the defendant's criminal case.[78]

---

[75] *State v. Marmolejo*, 855 S.W.2d 275, 276 (Tex. App.—Austin 1993, no pet.).
[76] *Id.*
[77] TEX. CODE CRIM. PROC. ANN. art. 32.02 (West 2016).
[78] *Id.*

OFFENSE: DWl 3rd

CAUSE NO. ██████████

THE STATE OF TEXAS

VS.

██████████

IN THE ██ DISTRICT COURT
IN COUNTY CRIMINAL COURT AT LAW NO.____
OF
HARRIS COUNTY, TEXAS

MOTION TO DISMISS

TO THE HONORABLE JUDGE OF SAID COURT:

NOW COMES the State of Texas, by and through her District Attorney, and respectfully requests the Court to dismiss the above entitled and numbered criminal action for the following reason:

- ☐ The Defendant was convicted in another case.
- ☐ In custody elsewhere.
- ☐ Old case, no arrest.
- ☐ Missing witness.
- ☐ Request of complaining witness.
- ☐ Motion to suppress granted.
- ☐ Co-Defendant tried, this Defendant testify.
- ☒ Insufficient evidence.
- ☐ Co-Defendant convicted, insufficient evidence this Defendant.
- ☐ Case refiled as cause no. _____
- ☐ Other.

EXPLANATION:

No SFSTs + retrograde to possible .067 ± .01

WHEREFORE, PREMISES CONSIDERED, it is requested that the above entitled and numbered cause be dismissed.

Respectfully submitted,

_____
Assistant District Attorney
Harris County, Texas

ORDER

The foregoing motion having been presented to me on this the ____ day of October, A.D.20 14 and the same having been considered, it is, therefore, ORDERED, ADJUDGED, and DECREED that said above entitled and numbered cause be and the same is hereby dismissed.

_____
JUDGE ____ DISTRICT COURT
COUNTY CRIMINAL COURT AT LAW NO. _____
HARRIS COUNTY, TEXAS

White-Original   Yellow-Defendant's Copy   Pink-State's Copy

11-167-(06/00)

The Court of Criminal Appeals has delineated a few limited exceptions to the general rule that it is the prosecutor alone who has power to dismiss a case:

> [W]e acknowledge that a court has the power to dismiss a case without the State's consent in certain circumstances, such as when a defendant has been denied a speedy trial, when there is a defect in the charging instrument [through a motion to quash], or, pursuant to Article 32.01, when a defendant is detained and no charging instrument is properly presented. The power to dismiss in these circumstances is authorized by common law or statute and does not give rise to a [trial court's] general right to dismiss in contravention of the general rule [that it is prosecutors who typically hold the power to dismiss a case].[79]

Though a trial court possesses limited dismissal powers, the judge may grant the defense's motion to dismiss an invalid charging instrument, a motion to quash an indictment, or find no probable cause in a case, which forces the State to dismiss the case. A judge may not issue a dismissal based upon a pretrial belief that the State will be unable to prove the crime beyond a reasonable doubt. "It is for the prosecutor, as the officer charged with the responsibility for preparing and prosecuting criminal suits, to decide whether a prosecution is sustainable."[80]

The general rule and the limited exceptions are understood more fully when you consider the roles of the prosecutor and the trial court. Prosecutors work for the State of Texas, even though they are paid by the county where they are employed. When there is a criminal law violation, it is "against the peace and dignity of the State." It is the State's duty, through the prosecutor, to charge and prosecute crimes, and it is the State's responsibility to dismiss them.

The judge, on the other hand, manages dockets, acts as fact-finder and evidence gatekeeper, determines the applicable law, assesses punishments,

---

[79] *State v. Johnson*, 821 S.W.2d 609, 612 n. 2 (Tex. Crim. App. 1991). See also *State v. Terrazas*, 962 S.W.2d 38, 40 (Tex. Crim. App. 1998) (trial court may have authority to dismiss case without State's consent when defendant has suffered demonstrable prejudice and there is no other way to neutralize that prejudice); *State v. Frye*, 897 S.W.2d 324, 330-31 (Tex. Crim. App. 1995) (trial court may have authority to dismiss case without State's consent in some situations in which defendant's Sixth Amendment rights have been violated).

[80] *State v. Nolan*, 808 S.W.2d 556, 560 (Tex. App.—Austin 1991, no pet.) (trial court erred at motion to suppress hearing by dismissing cases due to insufficient evidence).

and pronounces judgments. Though the cases are assigned to the judge's court, they do not belong to the judge but to the State. This explains why the general rule permits the State to dismiss, not the judge.

————————◆————————

Practice Questions

In recent years, bar examiners have included two to three questions on the topics covered in this chapter. The topic of charging instruments is the most asked topic in this chapter, venue is the second-most asked topic, and jurisdiction is the least asked topic. This section groups questions on these three topics together.

Jurisdiction Questions

1. (J-2015) Defendant is charged with a state jail felony. Which of the following courts have jurisdiction over his case: (a) a municipal court, (b) a county court, or (c) a district court? Explain.

   _____

   _____

   _____

   _____

   _____

2. (J-2011) Does a district court have jurisdiction over a misdemeanor lesser-included-offense of a case that was originally filed as a felony?

   _____

   _____

   _____

   _____

   _____

3. (J-2009) Prosecutor is deciding whether to charge Defendant with the felony offense of robbery (where the evidence is weak) or with the misdemeanor charge of theft of property, valued at $250 (which is a

stronger case). The robbery is a second-degree felony. The misdemeanor is punishable by up to 180 days in jail and a maximum fine of $2000.

What courts have jurisdiction over the robbery trial, and what courts have jurisdiction over the theft trial? Explain.

_____

_____

_____

_____

_____

Venue Questions

4. (J-2015, J-2014, J-2012, F-2009, J-2004, and F-2003) The defendant lives in Travis County. He kidnaps his victim at gunpoint from Travis County and drives her through Hays and Comal Counties on the way to Bexar County. He is caught and arrested in Comal County, where police find Victim unharmed.

    Where may or must the Defendant's prosecution for aggravated kidnapping take place?

_____

_____

_____

_____

_____

5. (J-2014) Who must establish whether venue is proper or improper, and what is the required standard of proof?

_____

_____

_____

_____

_____

6. (J-2011 and J-2000) You decide to file a motion to change venue because you fear the Defendant cannot get a fair trial in the county.

   When must you file your motion? What happens if your motion is untimely filed?

   _____

   _____

   _____

   _____

   _____

7. (J-2010) Defendant is a national celebrity who allegedly commits a crime in his hometown, where he is beloved. Prosecutor believes her evidence is strong, but jurors will not convict Defendant in light of the fact that there has been widespread effort and attention to get the District Attorney to drop charges.

   What procedural step, if any, can Prosecutor take to solve this problem? If Prosecutor can do something, what must she show to succeed? Explain.

   _____

   _____

   _____

   _____

   _____

8. (F-2008 and J-2000) Defendant is charged with the felony offense of possession of a controlled substance (heroin) with intent to deliver. He was selling heroin to teens near Lake Conroe in Montgomery County. That night, the lead news story featured Defendant's mug shot and the Montgomery County's sheriff's department's announcement that it was initiating a new campaign against local heroin dealers. Interest in the case and campaign soared in the community.

What procedural step, if any, can you take to protect Defendant's right to a fair trial? What documents must you file in support of this step? What must the evidence show in order for you to succeed? Explain.

_____

_____

_____

_____

_____

Charging Instruments Questions

9. (J-2016 and F-2011) Defendant and Co-defendant are charged in the same indictment as parties to a burglary. Is the grand jury legally required to charge them using two separate indictments? Explain.

_____

_____

_____

_____

_____

10. (J-2016, J-2015, F-2014, F-2013, F-2012, F-2010, J-2008, F-2007, and F-2001) You read Defendant's indictment and realize the State has failed to allege a criminal offense.

    What procedural step should you take to make the Court aware of this error? When must you do this?

_____

_____

_____

_____

_____

11. (F-2016, F-2015, and J-2010) You represent a parent accused of injuring her three children. In a single indictment, the grand jury charges

Defendant with three counts of injury to a child, alleging each child's injury in a separate count.

Is the State permitted to charge her with three crimes in one indictment under these circumstances? Explain.

_____

_____

_____

_____

_____

12. (F-2016) List three requirements of an indictment.

_____

_____

_____

_____

_____

13. (F-2016, J-2013, and F-2011) Before trial, Prosecutor moves to amend the indictment to allege a different crime. You object to Prosecutor's motion to amend. How should the Judge rule? Explain.

_____

_____

_____

_____

_____

14. (J-2014, F-2010, and J-2001) What is an indictment? List two ways in which an indictment differs from an information.

_____

_____

_____

_____

_____

15. (F-2014 and J-2010) Does Defendant have a right to a grand jury indictment? If Defendant decides to plead guilty without seeking a grand jury indictment, what charging instrument will be used instead of an indictment?

_____

_____

_____

_____

_____

16. (F-2014) What specific words are used to begin and end an indictment?

_____

_____

_____

_____

_____

17. (J-2013) What is a felony complaint?

_____

_____

_____

_____

18. (J-2012) In the process of investigating Defendant's case, you discover a witness who will testify that Defendant is not guilty of the crime charged.

Is there any procedural step that you can take to have the Court dismiss the indictment based upon insufficient evidence or actual innocence? Explain.

_____

_____

_____

_____

_____

19. (F-2012, J-2008, F-2007, J-2005, F-2004, F-2002, and F-2001) A grand jury indicts Defendant. The indictment reads as follows:

In the Name and by the Authority of the State of Texas:

The Grand Jury hereby charges that on June 14, 2012, Doug Davis did then and there intentionally and knowingly commit the offense of aggravated robbery by exhibiting a deadly weapon in the course of committing theft and placing the Complainant Jack Smith, in fear of imminent bodily injury.

Suzanne Robertson

Foreperson of the Grand Jury

Identify three defects in this indictment. Explain.

_____

_____

_____

_____

_____

Note: Charging instruments in bar questions like this one are usually missing several components from the list of indictment requirements but are often missing the culpable mental state or an essential element of the crime itself as well. Examinees are expected to spot and list all errors, including substantive errors, in the charging instrument.

———————◆———————

Chapter 5
Bail

Introduction

After a defendant is arrested, she may be required to post a bail bond to get out of jail while her case is pending. The words *bail* and *bond* are often used interchangeably, but they actually mean different things. Bail is the money required to be released from jail pending resolution of the case. The Texas Code of Criminal Procedure defines bail as the "security given by the accused that he will appear and answer before the proper court."[1] A *bail bond* is a "written undertaking entered into by the defendant and the defendant's sureties."[2]

The U.S. Constitution's Eighth Amendment does not guarantee citizens the right to bail, but it does state that if bail is granted, it shall not be excessive.[3] Bail "is excessive if set in an amount greater than is reasonably necessary to satisfy the government's legitimate interests."[4] The government is interested in seeing the person appear in court to answer the charge against

---

[1] TEX. CODE CRIM. PROC. ANN. art. 17.01 (West 2016).
[2] TEX. CODE CRIM. PROC. ANN. art. 17.02 (West 2016).
[3] U.S. CONST. amend. VIII.
[4] *Ex parte Beard*, 92 S.W.3d 566, 573 (Tex. App.—Austin 2002, pet. ref'd).

him. Thus, bail should be just high enough to secure the defendant's presence in court.

Bail is granted in the overwhelming majority of cases. The U.S. Supreme Court has stated that "[i]n our society, liberty is the norm, and detention prior to trial or without trial is the carefully limited exception."[5] This is true in Texas as well.[6] The purpose of bail is not to keep a defendant in custody pending the case's resolution. If it were, it would be a punishment enacted against a person who is still presumed innocent. In most cases, the defendant will be eligible for release from jail on some form of bond.

— — — — — — ◆ — — — — — —

Types of Bond

Bond types and bail amounts vary. Defendants often hire bondsmen to post their bail. This type of bond is called a *surety bond*. A *surety* is someone other than the defendant who promises to pay the bail on the defendant's behalf and is liable for the amount of bail if the defendant fails to appear in court. A hypothetical scenario helps illustrate how a surety bond works.

Assume Andrew is charged with a felony offense, and his bail is set at $5,000. Andrew does not have $5,000. If Andrew can raise $500, which is ten percent of the total bail amount, he can hire a bondsman to pay the remaining $4,500. The $500 is nonrefundable to Andrew; it is a percentage of the total bail amount, usually 10 percent, paid as a fee to secure the bondsman's services. If Andrew appears in court, the bail is returned to the surety, and the bondsman makes $500 from the transaction. None of the money that Andrew paid the bondsman and none of the money that the bondsman paid on Andrew's behalf is returned to Andrew; it all goes to the bondsman. If Andrew does not appear in court, his bail will be revoked, and the $5,000 the bondsman gave to the court on Andrew's behalf will be forfeited to the county government. The surety agreement ensures that in the event the bond is revoked, the defendant will pay the full amount back to the bondsman.

---

[5] *United States v. Salerno*, 481 U.S. 739, 755 (1987).
[6] TEX. CONST. art. I, §13.

A second type of bond is a cash bond.[7] A *cash bond* is paid by the defendant in full without employing a surety. If the defendant appears in court when required, his cash bond is fully refundable. Using the same hypothetical above, if Andrew was able to pay the $5,000 himself, and if he went to court every time, the full amount would be refunded to him at the close of his case. A defendant who is able to pay a cash bond gets it all back once the case is resolved, whereas the defendant who uses a surety to post bail loses the fee that he paid to the bondsman.

A third type of bond is a *personal bond*. This type of bond does not involve a surety or a cash bond. Instead, it is the defendant's oath by signature that he will appear in court.[8] It is in the judge's discretion to grant a personal bond.[9] A personal bond is more likely to be granted when the defendant has not committed a serious crime and has a good reputation within and established ties to the community. However, there is a growing movement to increase the number of personal bonds granted, not just in Texas but across the nation. Some nonprofit advocacy groups argue that the inability to pay bail disproportionately affects the poor, jails are unnecessarily overcrowded with pretrial detainees, most detainees would better serve themselves, their families, and their communities outside of jail, and few countries outside of the United States employ the use of bondsmen. Some communities in the United States—Washington, D.C. is one of them—have almost entirely done away with bail and bondsmen. These communities have had success with pretrial monitoring and personal bond; however, they are in the minority of jurisdictions in the United States that do so. Regardless of the type of bond or the amount of bail, the bond lasts for the duration of the case unless the judge states otherwise.[10]

———————◆———————

[7] TEX. CODE CRIM. PROC. ANN. art. 17.02 (West 2016).
[8] TEX. CODE CRIM. PROC. ANN. art. 17.04(3) (West 2016).
[9] TEX. CODE CRIM. PROC. ANN. art. 17.03 (West 2016).
[10] TEX. CODE CRIM. PROC. ANN. art. 17.09 (West 2016).

Rules for Setting Bail

Most defendants will be bailable. The Code contains a number of rules that judges must consider in setting bail, which appear verbatim in the Code as follows:

1. The bail shall be sufficiently high to give reasonable assurance that the undertaking will be complied with.
2. The power to require bail is not to be so used as to make it an instrument of oppression.
3. The nature of the offense and the circumstances under which it was committed are to be considered.
4. The ability to make bail is to be regarded, and proof may be taken upon this point.
5. The future safety of a victim of the alleged offense and the community shall be considered.[11]

The next case demonstrates an appellate court's application of the above rules to the facts of a specific defendant's case and circumstances.

———————◆———————

Bruce Glenn Milner v. State
263 S.W.3d 146
(Tex. App.—Houston [14th Dist.] 2006, no pet.)

In his sole point of error, appellant argues that the evidence was legally insufficient to deny his request to reduce bail [from $500,000] and that the trial court abused its discretion in denying appellant's request to reduce bail.

A. Nature of the Offense

To determine whether the trial court abused its discretion, we consider the rules found in article 17.15 of the Texas Code of Criminal Procedure. The record reflects that the State indicted appellant for intentionally or knowingly causing the death of his wife with a firearm, a first degree felony. The offense carries a sentence of 5 to 99 years or life and a fine not to exceed $10,000. The State also indicted appellant for attempting to intentionally or knowingly cause the death of his mother-in-law with a deadly weapon.

---

[11] TEX. CODE CRIM. PROC. ANN. art. 17.15 (West 2016).

Attempted murder is a second degree felony. The offense of attempted murder carries a sentence of 2 to 20 years and a fine not to exceed $10,000. The State also included two enhancement paragraphs that could qualify appellant as an habitual offender, thus elevating appellant's punishment range. In that instance, the minimum sentence appellant could receive, if convicted, is 25 years.

In other murder cases, $500,000 for bail has been held not to be excessive. *See Ex parte Davis*, 147 S.W.3d 546 (Tex. App.—Waco 2004, no pet.) (reversing trial court's bail amount of $1,000,000 for murder and rendering bail at $500,000 for one defendant and $750,000 for a co-defendant); *Ex parte White*, 01–02–00480–CR, 2002 WL 1933721 (Tex. App.—Houston [1st Dist.] Aug. 22, 2002, no pet.) (*not designated for publication*) (affirming the trial court's reduction of bail from $500,000 to $475,000 for defendant charged with murdering his wife); *Ex parte Simpson*, 77 S.W.3d 894 (Tex. App.—Tyler 2002, no pet.) (affirming $600,000 bail for capital murder when appellant was charged with brutal and violent crime and posed a threat to community); *Ex parte Chavfull*, 945 S.W.2d 183 (Tex. App.—San Antonio 1997, no pet.) (holding that $750,000 bail is not excessive for defendant charged with murdering an individual with a firearm because violent nature of crime and threat to community).

Here, the nature of the offense reflects that appellant allegedly shot and killed his wife and shot his mother-in-law multiple times, all in front of his children. Based on the serious nature of the crime and the substantial penalty if convicted, the trial court could have reasonably concluded that the nature of the offense did not favor a bail reduction.

B. Sufficient Bail to Assure Appearance but Not Oppress

Other than living in Harris County for a very short period, appellant has always lived in Brazoria County. At the time of the offense, appellant, age 35, was studying automotive technology at Brazosport College. Prior to taking classes, he worked as a contractor. Appellant has two children, ages six and seven. Appellant's children currently reside at his mother's home in Oyster Creek. Appellant also has additional family members in Brazoria County and a cousin who lives in San Antonio. Appellant owns no real estate and no personal property, such as automobiles, airplanes, or boats. Although appellant previously worked as a contractor, he testified that he owns no tools. Appellant also testified that he had no bank accounts that contained any funds and no savings accounts.

This evidence indicates that, other than being near his two children and other family members, appellant does not have a reason to remain in Brazoria County, if released on bail. Before his arrest, appellant was not employed, he owns no property in the area, and he has no checking or savings accounts. Before his arrest, appellant led police on a high-speed chase, which demonstrates he could be a flight risk. Thus, the trial court may have concluded that a reasonably high bail is necessary to have assurance that appellant will appear at trial. In addition, the record contains nothing to indicate that the trial court rendered its decision for the purpose of forcing appellant to remain incarcerated pending trial.

C. Ability to Make Bail

To show that he is unable to make bail, a defendant generally must show that his funds and his family's funds have been exhausted. *Ex parte Willman*, 695 S.W.2d at 754; *see also Richardson v. State*, 181 S.W.3d 756, 760 (Tex. App.—Waco 2005, no pet.) (considering funds of appellant's father and brother). Unless he has shown that his funds and those of his family have been exhausted, a defendant must usually show that he made an unsuccessful effort to furnish bail before bail can be determined to be excessive. If both the defendant and his family indicate a financial inability to procure a surety bond, the court will not require him "to do a useless thing."

The ability or inability of an accused to make bail, however, even indigency, does not alone control in determining the amount of bail. If the ability to make bond in a specified amount controlled, the role of the trial court in setting bond would be completely eliminated and the accused would be in the position to determine what his bond should be.

Here, appellant testified that he owned no real estate and no personal property such as automobiles, airplanes, or boats. He also testified that he had no bank accounts that contained any funds, no savings accounts, and no financial instruments. When the State asked appellant whom he contacted regarding the $500,000 bond, appellant stated, "I haven't contacted anybody." Appellant's mother, Evelyn Jean Morrison, testified that she called a bonding company and learned that she had to post 10 percent of the total bond. She testified that she had no means of acquiring $50,000. She is currently supporting appellant's two children. She and her husband, Carl Morrison, own their home and have a mortgage. She stated that the value of her home is about $70,000 and that she still owes $40,000. She has no other property except some property that they sold in which they are now the note owner. She receives $450 in monthly income on the note. She retired from Dow chemical after 30 years of service and now receives a $3,100 monthly retirement check from Dow before taxes. She owns a 1999 Ford Taurus free and clear, but owes $5,000 on a 1999 Honda Odyssey van. Her husband teaches flight instruction on ultralight airplanes, but he cannot currently give lessons. She has $2,000 in a checking account, but no savings accounts or certificates of deposit. She has a 401k retirement account worth about $90,000.

The evidence shows that appellant himself made no effort to determine whether he could obtain a bond to make bail. Nevertheless, his testimony indicates that he does not have the financial resources to make the bond. Appellant's family does not have the financial resources to pay for the bond in cash, but the trial court may have determined that appellant's mother could obtain a bond in light of the value of her 401k account and that no attempt had been made to determine whether appellant could obtain a bond on the basis of his family's resources. Thus, the trial court could have determined that the evidence supports maintaining the present bail amount. Even if appellant had established that he could not make bail, however, this element would not control over all other considerations.

D. Future Safety of Victim and Community and Other Factors

Finally, article 17.15 of the Code of Criminal Procedure requires that "[t]he future safety of a victim of the alleged offenses and the community shall be considered." Additional factors to consider in reviewing a bond decision include appellant's work record, family ties, length of residency, past criminal record, conformity with the conditions of any previous bond, other outstanding bonds, and aggravating factors involved in the offense.

Although no specific evidence was introduced, one of appellant's alleged victims, his mother-in-law, could be at risk if appellant makes bail. Also, when appellant's own mother was asked if appellant could live with her and the children if appellant were released on bond, appellant's mother stated, "I've got a lot of conflicting thoughts in my head about that." This evidence supports maintaining the present bail amount.

Moreover, appellant's record and the gravity and nature of the charges against him indicate that he presents a risk to the safety of the community. We have already considered what little information the record provides on appellant's work record, family ties, and length of residency. Thus, we turn to appellant's past criminal record. Appellant admitted that he was convicted of burglary and received a seven-year sentence, but he had to serve only four years. Appellant admitted that he went to the penitentiary for a burglary that occurred in Brazoria County. He also went to prison for aggravated assault that occurred in Harris County. He recalled being arrested for making a terroristic threat against his mother in 1989. He also admitted that he had been arrested twice for unlawfully carrying a weapon, once in Harris County and once in Brazoria County. He was convicted for possession of marihuana in 2000 in Houston. He also was arrested in 2003 for terroristic threats, an offense of which he was acquitted. Prior to the time the current indictment alleges appellant murdered his wife, appellant's wife had obtained a protective order against appellant. Appellant admitted that he was also charged with evading arrest after the alleged shooting of his wife. None of these factors favors a bail reduction.

Appellant did present evidence that he had complied with past conditions of bail from a charge of terroristic threat in which the jury found him not guilty. He also has a total of $30,000 in bail for two other offenses. Appellant's past compliance with his conditions of bail and the additional $30,000 in bail would favor a reduction in bail. However, based on the totality of these other factors, the trial court could have determined that the evidence supports maintaining the present bail amount.

Conclusion

Given appellant's extensive criminal history, the lack of evidence of his connections to Brazoria county, the violent nature of the alleged crimes, appellant's potential as a flight risk, and the safety of the victim, appellant's children, and the community, we conclude that the trial court did not abuse its discretion in refusing to reduce bail. We affirm the order of the trial court.

————————◆————————

As you can see from this case, judges have discretion in bail decisions, but this discretion should be carefully employed. Judges must balance the protection of the community, the victim, and the witnesses with the defendant's interest to remain free pending the resolution of his case. In balancing these interests, judges consider the type of crime, facts of the alleged offense, defendant's criminal history, defendant's ability to make bail, defendant's work record, family ties, residency, ability to conform to previous bond conditions, and any outstanding cases and/or bonds the defendant has.[12] Judges must make sure bail is high enough to secure the defendant's presence in court but not too high as to be oppressive.

A defendant who is unable to make bond may face difficult consequences. These consequences include a greater likelihood the defendant will plead guilty, even if he is not; negative financial consequences due to lost income or employment; increased familial poverty and/or failure to pay child support; increased risk of eviction or repossession of property; and most importantly, increased difficulty in preparing his defense.

In an effort to treat similarly situated defendants the same, most counties have created a bail schedule. Judges can vary from the bail schedule as needed, but many do not. Below, you will see the felony bail schedule for Harris County, which includes Houston and its surrounding municipalities.

Harris County District Court Bail Schedule

Offense	Bail
Capital felonies	No Bond
Murders not specified below	$50,000
First-degree felonies not specified below	$20,000
Second-degree felonies not specified below	$10,000
Felony DWI not specified below	$10,000
Third-degree felonies not specified below	$5,000
Fourth-degree (state jail) felonies not specified below	$2,000

---

[12] *Milner v. State*, 263 S.W.3d 146, 148 (Tex. App.—Houston [14th Dist.] 2006, no pet.).

Repeat Offenders	Bail
Habitual (*i.e.*, a defendant facing a felony offense following at least two prior felony convictions, which is Texas's three strikes law)	No bond
First-degree felony with previous conviction	$30,000
Second-degree felony with previous conviction	$20,000
Felony DWI with prior felony DWI conviction	Double bound amount for each previous felony DWI conviction
Third-degree felony with previous conviction	$10,000
Fourth-degree (state jail) felony with prior conviction	$5,000
Fourth-degree (state jail) felony with more than one prior conviction	$15,000
Defendant on Bail for any Felony Charge with:	**Bail**
First-degree felony	No bond
Second-degree felony	No bond
Third-degree felony	No bond
Fourth-degree (state jail) felony	No bond
Particular Situations	**Bail**
Multiple counts	Separate standard bail for each offense in the transaction
Person on felony probation for any grade of felony	No bond
Any 3g offense or offense where the use of a deadly weapon is alleged[13]	$30,000.00
Person with deportation history or undocumented presence in United States	$35,000.00
Motion to revoke probation	No bond
Motion to adjudicate guilt	At the judge's discretion
Large quantities of a controlled substance or stolen property	Double the value of a large controlled substance or property

---

[13] The phrase "3g offense" refers to any crime listed in Article 42.12 § 3g of the Code of Criminal Procedure. A defendant convicted of these more serious or violent crimes (*e.g.*, capital murder, murder, aggravated offenses, sexual assaults, human trafficking, etc.) may not receive probation from a judge and is required to serve more time incarcerated before becoming parole eligible.

Notes and Questions

1. What competing policies and interests do you see in the above bail schedule? In what ways does it protect the community? How does it promote the administration of justice and fairness? Is the bail schedule punitive in any way?

2. What arguments can you make for and against using the nature of the offense in determining bail when the defendant is presumed innocent at the time she is charged?

3. Bail may be set by more than one person during more than one point in time while the case is pending. For example, the magistrate should set bail at the time the defendant makes an appearance immediately following his arrest.[14] Though the Code does not prescribe it, bail may be set or adjusted at the defendant's initial appearance in the court where she faces charges. The judge could set bail at the defendant's examining trial.[15] Finally, the judge can set bail following indictment.[16] Bail may be reconsidered, revoked, or adjusted while the case is pending as needed.[17]

———————◆———————

Denying Bail

In limited instances, a defendant is nonbailable or may be held without bail for a period of time. The first type of nonbailable defendant is one who faces a charge of capital murder where the State seeks the death penalty. In Texas, every prisoner "shall be bailable unless for capital offenses when the proof is evident."[18] The State has the burden of establishing that the proof is evident.[19] This is satisfied when the State proves the defendant committed capital murder, that the jury will not only convict the defendant of the crime, but also sentence him to death.[20] In these cases, the defendant will not be released on bail pending trial.

---

[14] TEX. CODE CRIM. PROC. ANN. art. 15.17 (West 2016).
[15] TEX. CODE CRIM. PROC. ANN. art. 16.01 (West 2016).
[16] TEX. CODE CRIM. PROC. ANN. art. 23.03(a) (West 2016).
[17] TEX. CODE CRIM. PROC. ANN. art. 17.091 (West 2016).
[18] TEX. CODE CRIM. PROC. ANN. art. 1.07 (West 2016).
[19] *Ex parte Wilson*, 527 S.W.2d 310, 311 (Tex. Crim. App. 1975).
[20] *Id.*

There are instances when a defendant may be held without bail for a period of time before becoming bailable. A judge is allowed to "no bond" a defendant who is: (1) a habitual felon (one who has previously been convicted of two felonies); (2) a person charged with a felony who commits a felony while on bond; (3) a prior felon who commits an aggravated felony offense or who uses a weapon in the course of committing the subsequent felony; or (4) a sexual or violent offense committed by someone who is "under the supervision of a criminal justice agency of the State."[21] Regarding the last category, the Texas Constitution defines violent crimes as murder, aggravated assault with a deadly weapon, aggravated kidnapping, and aggravated robbery.[22] It defines sexual crimes as sexual assault, aggravated sexual assault, and indecency with a child.[23] In each of these cases, the safety of the community takes precedence over the defendant's right to be free.

In order to hold the defendant without bail in the above instances, the judge must hold a hearing within seven days of the defendant's arrest.[24] The judge can only hold the defendant without bond for 60 days before she must set bail.[25] While using bail as a "seed[] of preventive detention" is "abhorrent to the American system of justice,"[26] the 60-day unbailable period gives the judge time to have a hearing and determine the best course of action for releasing what may be a dangerous, repeat, or violent offender.

A defendant charged with family violence can also be held without bond for 48 hours while the State gets a magistrate's order for emergency protection (MOEP). This gives the prosecutor time to meet with and gather information from the victim, incorporate that information into a legal document signed by a magistrate in an effort to protect the victim from future threats or violence, and serve it on the defendant.[27]

Finally, bail may be denied due to violating a condition of bond. The Texas Constitution states that a defendant accused of a felony or a family violence crime who is released on bail and violates a condition may have bail revoked or forfeited pending trial "if a judge or magistrate ... determines by

---

[21] TEX. CONST. art. I, §11a.
[22] Id.
[23] Id.
[24] Id.
[25] Id.
[26] Taylor v. State, 667 S.W.2d 149, 152 (Tex. Crim. App. 1984).
[27] TEX. CODE CRIM. PROC. ANN. art. 17.152 (West 2016).

a preponderance of the evidence at a subsequent hearing that the person violated a condition of release related to the safety of a victim of the alleged offense or to the safety of the community."[28]

———————————◆———————————

Release Due to Delay

When a defendant has been arrested without a warrant, the magistrate must determine whether there was probable cause to arrest the defendant.[29] That determination must be made within 24 hours for defendants accused of committing misdemeanors and within 48 hours for defendants accused of committing felonies. If the magistrate has not made a probable cause finding in that time frame, the defendant must be given no more than a $5,000 bond in a misdemeanor case or no more than a $10,000 bond in a felony case. If the defendant is unable to make that bond, the statute requires he be released on a personal bond. The State may seek an extension for 72 hours if it can state why the magistrate has not been able to make the probable cause determination.

What happens when, for whatever reason, the State is not ready for trial, and the defendant sits in jail unable to make bail? The following case explores the answer to this question.

———————————◆———————————

Ex parte Michael Rowe v. State
853 S.W.2d 581
(Tex. Crim. App. 1993)

Before the trial court, the appellant sought release from pretrial detention based upon Article 17.151 ... and the State not being ready for trial of the felony charges. It was undisputed that appellant had been arrested on murder and aggravated assault allegations. The State stipulated that appellant had not been indicted within the 90 days. Appellant sought habeas relief, specifically release upon a personal bond. However, the trial court refused and instead reduced the bond on each charge by $1,000 (murder from $10,000 to $9,000,

---

[28] TEX. CONST. art. I, §11b.
[29] TEX. CODE CRIM. PROC. ANN. art. 17.033 (West 2016).

aggravated assault from $4,000 to $3,000, aggravated assault from $4,000 to $3,000). Appellant appealed the decision of the trial court.

The Fourteenth Court of Appeals affirmed the trial court's decision. The court of appeals focused upon one of the prosecutor's explanations for not indicting appellant within the 90-day period of Article 17.151, that being appellant had wanted to testify before the grand jury. It considered such to be invited error and specifically held "that a delay in indicting, that is caused by the accused's request to testify before the grand jury, will not be held against the State or entitle the accused to a personal recognizance bond." Appellant's petition for discretionary review asserts that the court of appeals erred in holding such.

Article 17.151 provides that if the State is not ready for trial within 90 days after commencement of detention for a felony, the accused "must be released either on personal bond or by reducing the amount of bail required[.]" Thus the trial court has two options: release upon personal bond or reduce the bail amount. However, there is nothing in the statute indicating that the provisions do not apply if the delay was based upon the accused's request to testify before the grand jury. In fact, Article 17.151 contains no provisions excluding certain periods from the statutory time limit to accommodate exceptional circumstances. Thus we hold that the court of appeals erred in concluding that appellant's request to testify before the grand jury somehow removed him from the protections of Article 17.151.

Although the trial court denied the request for personal bond, it interpreted appellant's motion as also requesting a reduction in bond. At the conclusion of a hearing on September 28, 1992, the judge lowered the bonds in each of the cases in which appellant was charged.

Counsel argues that appellant cannot make any bond, and at a subsequent hearing on October 2, 1992, introduced testimony to that effect. The State argued to the contrary and elicited testimony as to pending criminal charges in the State of Oklahoma and that appellant had resided in Texas only two weeks prior to the date of the instant offense. The trial court stated into the record, "I also have to make sure that the bail is of such an amount that we'll see [appellant] in court to answer the allegations."

Conclusion

The trial court's action in reducing the bonds did not comply with the dictates of Article 17.151. The record does not support the trial court's decision to reduce each bond by $1,000.00 rather than release appellant on personal bond. The record reveals that appellant could not make any bond. We therefore grant appellant's petition for discretionary review and remand this cause to the trial court with directions to release appellant on personal bond.

———————◆———————

Notes and Questions

1. Did the judge have a legitimate community safety concern given the type of crimes the defendant allegedly committed? Consider again the wording of Article 17.151:

> A defendant who is detained in jail pending trial of an accusation against him must be released either on personal bond or by reducing the amount of bail required, if the state is not ready for trial of the criminal action for which he is being detained within ... 90 days from the commencement of his detention if he is accused of a felony.

Do safety concerns matter given the clear directive of Article 17.151?

2. If the State is concerned about the defendant being released on a personal bond under Article 17.151, what must it do?

———————◆———————

Challenging the Amount of Bail

The defendant's ability or inability to make bail does not alone control the amount of bail the judge may set. As seen in the *Milner* case, the court will examine the defendant's assets, income, and property, along with that of his family members', and consider many other factors before setting bail. But what happens when bail is set and the defendant requests that it be lowered?

A defendant who cannot make bail may seek to have it reduced by filing a writ of habeas corpus, as you saw in the last two cases.[30] The Latin phrase "*habeas corpus*" means "you have the body." When a lawyer files a writ of habeas corpus, the lawyer is asking for a court to order the release of the prisoner from custody. The writ, if granted, commands the person who has

---

[30] TEX. CODE CRIM. PROC. ANN. art. 11.24 (West 2016).

custody over the prisoner (*e.g.*, the constable, sheriff, or warden) "to produce [the prisoner] at a time and place named in the writ and show why he is being held in custody or under restraint."[31] In the case of bail, the remedy sought by a writ of habeas corpus is to produce the detainee and show why he is being held in custody for an amount of bail he cannot pay.

The requisites for a written writ of habeas corpus are set out in the Code. The writ must name the person who is being illegally restrained against his liberty and the person restraining him; it must contain a copy of the legal document restraining him, or it should state the copy is unavailable; if the defendant is illegally restrained without a legal document, the writ must state that he is illegally confined or restrained against his liberty; the writ must include a prayer for relief; and it must be made on oath that all allegations in the writ are true.[32] These requirements apply to all writs of habeas corpus, not just those requesting bail reductions.

A lawyer filing a writ of habeas corpus is entitled to request a hearing.[33] The judge is required to notify the State about the requested bail reduction hearing.[34] At the hearing, the defendant must produce evidence that bail, as set, is excessive.[35] The defendant should testify about unsuccessful attempts to make bail, her financial and property holdings, and what amount of bail she could meet.[36] The defendant should not fear being asked questions about the offense at this hearing, since questions are limited to the ability to make bail unless the defendant discusses the offense.[37] If the defendant's proof sustains the request for reduction, it may result in a reduced amount.

Although the defendant carries the burden of proof, the court should hear evidence neutrally.[38] However, where the defendant vaguely asserts, without specificity, that she cannot afford bail, the court will generally deny

---

[31] Tex. Code Crim. Proc. Ann. art. 11.01 (West 2016).

[32] Tex. Code Crim. Proc. Ann. art. 11.14 (West 2016).

[33] Tex. Code Crim. Proc. Ann. art. 17.091 (West 2016).

[34] *Id.*

[35] *E.g., Ex parte Rubac*, 611 S.W.2d 848, 849 (Tex. Crim. App. 1981).

[36] *E.g., Holliman v. State*, 485 S.W.2d 912, 914 (Tex. Crim. App. 1972) (the record should reflect what bail amount the defendant can pay); *Ex parte Lee*, 461 S.W.2d 407 (Tex. Crim. App. 1970) (trial court's decision to deny reduction request affirmed on appeal where defendant offered no proof of unsuccessful attempts to pay bail).

[37] *Ex parte Homan*, 963 S.W.2d 543 (Tex. App.—Tyler 1996, pet. dism'd).

[38] *Ex parte Davis*, 574 S.W.2d 166, 168 (Tex. Crim. App. 1978) ("presumptions are not to be indulged against the applicant").

the defendant's request to reduce bail.[39] The defendant must be transparent about what bail amount she can afford and proffer evidence to support her contention that the current bail amount is too high.

———————————◆———————————

Judicially Imposed Conditions

Magistrates and judges are authorized by law to condition a defendant's release on bail. This means that if the defendant wishes to remain free on bail, she must abide by the judicially imposed conditions attached to that bail. While conditions may be put in place to protect others, conditions are sometimes imposed to protect the defendant from her own dangerous, foolish, or criminal actions while on bond. Defense attorneys may welcome conditions, though they would be hard pressed to admit this to their clients. That is because defendants usually dislike conditions due to their expense, inconvenience, and burden. Nevertheless, they are designed to keep defendants out of legal and personal trouble while they remain free on bail.

In the next case, pay close attention to the three criteria by which bail conditions are judged on appeal.

Ex Parte Allen-Pieroni
___ S.W.3d ___, 2016 WL 762724
(Tex. App.—Waco Feb. 24, 2016, no pet.)

Appellant Bonnie Allen-Pieroni (Bonnie) appeals the trial court's denial of her petition for writ of habeas corpus to amend bond conditions. In her petition, Bonnie challenged the trial court's imposition of bond conditions requiring that she be subject to electronic monitoring and to home confinement. After an evidentiary hearing, the trial court denied relief.

Asserting seven issues, Bonnie complains that the trial court abused its discretion by imposing the bond conditions and that the home-confinement condition unreasonably infringes on several constitutional rights.

---

[39] *E.g., Cooley v. State*, 232 S.W.3d 228 (Tex. App.—Houston [1st Dist.] 2007, no pet.) (defendant's attempt to get his bail reduced from $750,000 to $90,000 failed because other testimony established defendant was a millionaire, whereas his wife's misleading testimony suggested only her bank accounts were insufficient to make his bond).

Background

Bonnie was arrested for the offenses of possession of a weapon in a prohibited place, a third-degree felony, and evading arrest, a Class A misdemeanor, each arising out of the same incident of her allegedly carrying a pistol in her purse while going through the metal detector at the Johnson County courthouse. Despite allegedly attempting to flee when the pistol was noticed, she was immediately arrested and taken to the Johnson County Jail and held without bond until a psychological evaluation of her was done. The results of the evaluation showed that Bonnie did not represent a threat to herself or others.

After receiving the results of the psychological evaluation, the trial court set bail at $5,000 on the weapon charge and at $1,500 on the evading-arrest charge; it further imposed bond conditions that Bonnie not be released until an electronic-monitoring device was attached to her ankle and that she be confined to her home at all times. Another condition, which Bonnie does not challenge, is that she not have any weapons.

In her habeas petition and supporting brief, Bonnie asserted that the bond conditions of home confinement and electronic monitoring were unreasonable and oppressive and violated her statutory and constitutional rights. She requested that the bond conditions be deleted altogether or, alternatively, that the trial court amend the bond conditions to allow her to travel to her attorney's office as needed to prepare her defense, to work as a real-estate agent, to attend church services, and to leave her home when in the company of her husband, a former peace officer.

At the evidentiary hearing on her habeas petition, Bonnie presented several witnesses from all aspects of her life: her family, her church, her employment, her friends, and her neighbor. Collectively, these witnesses testified that Bonnie is not a flight risk and that she is not a threat to others. She also presented evidence that the trial court has not imposed the bond conditions of electronic monitoring and home confinement on any other defendant in those cases currently on the court's docket, including those involving serious, violent offenses. The trial court even stated on the record that it has imposed this condition less than five times in seventeen years. An employee from the company responsible for installing and monitoring the GPS monitor on Bonnie testified that electronic monitoring coupled with "24/7" house arrest is typically reserved for individuals charged with serious offenses like murder or sexual assault. The State did not present any witnesses or exhibits.

At the conclusion of the hearing, Bonnie argued for the removal of the bond conditions of electronic monitoring and home confinement or, alternatively, that the electronic monitoring remain a condition but that she be placed on a curfew. In denying relief, the trial court stated that Bonnie was in an ongoing custody dispute with her ex-husband and father to her three minor children in the same trial court. The trial court referred to a prior incident in which Bonnie allegedly exhibited a gun to her ex-husband while picking up her children from him and a subsequent order from the trial court for both parents to turn over to their attorneys any weapons that each parent may have. The trial court explained that its decision to order these bond conditions and to not grant habeas relief was based on these events.

Standard of Review and Applicable Law

The primary purpose of pretrial bail is to secure the defendant's attendance at trial, and the power to require bail, including the power to set conditions to bail, should not be used as an instrument of oppression. Article 17.15 of the Code of Criminal Procedure provides a framework for setting a defendant's bail:

1. The bail shall be sufficiently high to give reasonable assurance that the undertaking will be complied with.
2. The power to require bail is not to be so used as to make it an instrument of oppression.
3. The nature of the offense and the circumstances under which it was committed are to be considered.
4. The ability to make bail is to be regarded, and proof may be taken upon this point.
5. The future safety of a victim of the alleged offense and the community shall be considered.

Factors to be considered in applying the above framework include the possible length of sentence for the alleged offense; the nature and any aggravating factors of the offense; the applicant's employment record, family and community ties, and length of residence in the jurisdiction; the applicant's conformity with previous bond conditions; and the applicant's prior criminal record.

To secure a defendant's attendance at trial, a magistrate may impose any reasonable bond condition related to the safety of a victim of the alleged offense or to the safety of the community.[40] One such statutorily permitted condition is "home confinement and electronic monitoring."[41] Bond conditions, however, must not unreasonably impinge on an individual's constitutional rights.[42] Therefore, courts must be mindful that one of the purposes of release on bail pending trial is to prevent the infliction of punishment before conviction. "The trial court's discretion to set the conditions of bail is not ... unlimited. A condition of pretrial bail is judged by three criteria: it must be reasonable; it must be to secure the defendant's presence at trial; and it must be related to the safety of the alleged victim or the community."[43]

We review a trial court's imposition of bond conditions for an abuse of discretion. The appellant bears the burden of showing that the trial court abused its discretion in imposing the specific condition.

Analysis

Bonnie has no criminal record; she is employed, has minor children, and has longtime and strong ties to the community. Except for possibly the charge of evading arrest, nothing in the record shows that she is a flight risk. Neither charged offense involved violence or threats of violence.

In explaining his denial of Bonnie's request for habeas relief on the bond conditions, the trial court recounted his experience with Bonnie in her contentious child-custody proceeding with her ex-husband, beginning with the trial court's viewing of a video of the incident where Bonnie exhibited a gun to her ex-husband while picking up her children. The trial court then stated:

> Because of that concern I asked her under oath if she had any weapons and she said yes, she had one. This was August 28th. I ordered that that weapon and any other weapon she may have, any other guns she may have, be turned over to her attorney and that her attorney file an affidavit stating that the gun had been turned over to him. He filed that affidavit stating that her

---

[40] TEX. CODE CRIM. PROC. ANN. art. 17.40(a) (West 2016).
[41] TEX. CODE CRIM. PROC. ANN. art. 17.44 (West 2016).
[42] *Ex parte Anderer*, 61 S.W.3d 398, 402 (Tex. Crim. App. 2001).
[43] *Ex parte Anunobi*, 278 S.W.3d 425, 427 (Tex. App.—San Antonio 2008, no pet.) (citing *Anderer*, 61 S.W.3d at 401–02).

only gun had been turned over to him. I did the same thing for Mr. Pieroni as well. And then it wasn't two months—less than two months later that allegedly Ms. Pieroni—excuse me, Ms. Thomas allegedly came into the courthouse allegedly with a gun in her purse and then allegedly tried to run when she was called on it and was allegedly caught outside the courthouse. That is grave concern to me if that is accurate.

I'm singling out the alleged conduct in this case that concerns me gravely. Now if and when this issue is appealed to the Tenth Court of Appeals and the Tenth Court of Appeals saying, Judge Neill, you overreact, we're going to remove this bond condition, I'll remove it, but until that time it's going to stay in place.

We repeat that courts must be mindful that one of the purposes of release on bail pending trial is to prevent the infliction of punishment before conviction. And the power to require bail, including the power to set conditions to bail, should not be used oppressively. Finally, a "trial court's discretion to set the conditions of bail is not ... unlimited." We understand and share the trial court's concern with the combination of guns and a contentious child-custody proceeding. And while we further understand the trial court's frustration with Bonnie's alleged (and thus far unexplained) possession of a gun after ordering the surrender of guns by both parents, that potentially contemptuous conduct should be addressed in the child-custody proceeding, not by an assessment of the most extreme bond condition of home confinement.

Conclusion

Accordingly, after our review of the record under the applicable law set out above, we hold the trial court abused its discretion by denying habeas relief on the home-confinement bond condition. We therefore sustain Bonnie's first issue. We reverse in part the trial court's order denying habeas relief and delete the home-confinement condition. We otherwise affirm the trial court's imposition of electronic monitoring.

In their briefing and at oral argument, both Bonnie and the State have alternatively suggested that a reasonable bond condition in place of the home-confinement condition would be the imposition of home curfew. We agree, and we further agree with Bonnie's suggestion of a home curfew "from the hours of 8 p.m. to 8 a.m. each day." Therefore, we modify the trial court's bond-conditions order and impose on Bonnie a home curfew from the hours of 8 p.m. to 8 a.m. each day. This case is remanded to the trial court for further proceedings as may be necessary.

——————————◆——————————

The *Allen-Pieroni* court makes it clear that not every bond condition a judge may impose is reasonable. It examined general conditions of bond; in other words, the bond conditions were not unique to the charge the defendant faced in criminal court. The Code also contemplates crime-specific bond conditions.

Crime-Specific Conditions of Bail

There are many statutorily defined conditions of release, some of which relate to specific crimes. For example, consider bond conditions unique to driving while intoxicated (DWI) cases. The judge may place an ignition interlock device on the defendant's vehicle, which requires the defendant to provide a breath sample before her car will start.[44] The judge may impose no-drinking and no-drug conditions or random drug and alcohol testing as a condition of bond.[45] If the defendant tests positive for drugs or alcohol or provides a breath sample that indicates alcohol consumption, she risks revocation of her bond as they are conditions she must meet in order to remain free. However, were a defendant charged with shoplifting, it would be unreasonable to place a guardian interlock device on her car. Such a condition would not protect the community nor would it ensure the defendant's presence at trial. Thus, it would not meet the three criteria for bail conditions.

Here are other bond conditions authorized by law:

1. Conditions designed to protect children complainants from speaking, seeing, or residing with a defendant who allegedly abused them.[46]
2. In prostitution cases, both for the buyer and the seller of sex, HIV and AIDS testing may be required as a condition for release, for the purpose of educating the person undergoing the testing about his or her health.[47]

---

[44] TEX. CODE CRIM. PROC. ANN. art. 17.441 (West 2016).
[45] TEX. CODE CRIM. PROC. ANN. art. 17.44 (West 2016).
[46] TEX. CODE CRIM. PROC. ANN. art. 17.41 (West 2016).
[47] TEX. CODE CRIM. PROC. ANN. art. 17.45 (West 2016).

3. In stalking, domestic assault, or harassment cases, a magistrate will likely impose a condition that the defendant have no contact with the victim.[48]

4. In sexual assault cases, a judge may require the defendant to provide a sample of DNA to local law enforcement officials to compare with DNA samples taken from victims of rape statewide.[49]

These are just some examples of crime-specific conditions of bond. This list does not include all conditions, just a few to illustrate the fact that certain types of cases warrant specific bond conditions.

There are many other general, non-crime-specific conditions that judges may impose in an effort to protect others from wrongdoing while the defendant is on bond. Common, yet reasonable non-crime-specific conditions include abiding by curfews, wearing an electronic monitor, obeying the law, and submitting to drug and alcohol treatment.

If the defendant violates a condition of bond, the judge must set a hearing, listen to evidence, and if she finds by a preponderance of the evidence that the defendant violated the condition, she may revoke the defendant's bond, immediately return the defendant to jail, and set a new bail with new or additional conditions.[50]

----------◆----------

Notes and Questions

1. The best way to challenge a bond condition is through a writ of habeas corpus, as illustrated by the *Allen-Pieroni* case.

2. Suppose a husband is charged with assaulting his wife. Despite the assault, the complainant still wants to live with her husband while the case is pending, even though the judge has ordered them not to have contact with one another until the case is resolved through a condition, a protective order, or a no-contact order. If the husband and the wife ignore this condition, what affect might this have on the defendant's bond? What practical and legal advice would you give this defendant if you were his counsel?

---

[48] TEX. CODE CRIM. PROC. ANN. art. 17.46 (West 2016); TEX. CODE CRIM. PROC. ANN. art. 17.49 (West 2016).
[49] TEXAS CODE CRIM. PROC. ANN. art. 17.47 (West 2016).
[50] TEX. CODE CRIM. PROC. ANN. art. 17.40 (West 2016).

3.   Conditions of bond are expensive, and the defendant bears the burden of paying for them. If the defendant wants to be free from detention, there is a price not only for various electronic devices (*e.g.*, ignition interlock, electronic monitoring) but also for drug and alcohol testing and the county employees' salaries who do the testing. Even when the conditions themselves do not cost the government money, they may nevertheless place a financial burden on the defendant. For example, if a couple in a domestic violence case must live in separate residences while the case is pending, there may be a cost-of-living expense increase that affects the household finances. In other words, in addition to paying for an attorney, the defendant may be saddled with condition expenses he never anticipated.

Indigency and Bail

Indigent defendants may qualify to have an attorney appointed to represent them. "[T]he court or the courts' designee may not consider whether the defendant has posted or is capable of posting bail" in determining whether the defendant should be appointed counsel, "except to the extent that it reflects the defendant's financial circumstances" in general.[51] In sum, the court can consider income, assets, property, dependents, and other factors in deciding whether the accused should be given appointed counsel, but it shall not make the decision solely on the defendant's ability to post bail.[52]

Forfeiture and Revocation

Bail is aimed at ensuring the defendant's presence in court when ordered to appear. A defendant's case could potentially be pending for weeks or months. Attorneys may reset the case, requiring the defendant to appear numerous times for any number of reasons. For example, the prosecutor

---

[51] TEX. CODE CRIM. PROC. ANN. art. 26.04(m) (West 2016) (emphasis added).
[52] *Padilla v. State*, No. 03-02-00345-CR, 2003 WL 21401256, at *4 (Tex. App.—Austin June 19, 2003, pet. ref'd).

may need to further investigate the case before determining whether to offer a plea bargain. The defense attorney may need to give the defendant time to pay her fees for representation. The judge may require a progression of settings before a defendant can set her case for trial. There are numerous reasons why the defendant may be ordered to come to court several times before the case is resolved. So long as the judge, the attorneys, and the defendant agree to reset the case, the defendant must come to court each time the case appears on the trial court docket.

Judges may revoke bail when a defendant fails to appear in court. Before every docket begins, each appearing person's name is called aloud by the judge, the bailiff, the court coordinator, or another employee of the court. Each defendant's name is called at the door of the courthouse or the courtroom, and if the defendant does not appear "within a reasonable time" after his name is called, the bond is forfeited.[53] These forfeited bail monies are used by counties to improve roads and fund government projects; they may amount to millions of dollars in larger counties, depending on the annual number of bond forfeitures. In fact, many larger counties employ lawyers whose only job is to litigate bond forfeitures.

If the defendant has a valid excuse for not appearing in court when required (*e.g.*, sickness or an emergency), he must appear before the judge and explain his circumstances. A defendant may have a valid reason for not appearing in court, and revocation in this instance may be unjust.[54] However, some defendants intentionally or knowingly fail to appear in court. These defendants may be charged with the additional crime of bail jumping or failure to appear in court.[55] If they jump bail, a warrant will issue for the new crime, the bond for the first crime will be forfeited, and the judge has the authority to require a cash bond for any subsequently posted bail.[56]

There are other instances when a bond may be revoked. For instance, when the defendant commits a new criminal offense while he is on bail, his original bail will be revoked, and the judge will set a new bail amount with new or additional conditions of bond.

---

[53] TEX. CODE CRIM. PROC. ANN. art. 22.02 (West 2016).
[54] TEX. CODE CRIM. PROC. ANN. art. 22.13 (West 2016) (sickness is a valid excuse for not appearing in court as is a failure to appear that "arose from no fault on [the defendant's] part").
[55] TEX. PENAL CODE ANN. §38.10 (West 2011).
[56] TEX. CODE CRIM. PROC. ANN. art. 23.05 (West 2016).

———————◆———————

Practice Questions

Bar examiners have asked about types of bond, conditions of bail, connections between indigence and appointed lawyers, writs of habeas corpus, delays in setting bail, rules for setting bail, and the processes for challenging and denying bail. Examinees may also be placed in the role of defense counsel and may be asked to make arguments for their client's bail reduction.

Bail-related questions have appeared on more than half of bar exams. In the past decade, there has been at least one bar question devoted to bail in most exams. On some exams, bar examiners have not asked any questions related to bail, whereas in other exams, they have asked as many as three questions per exam.

1. (J-2016 and F-2014) Defendant has been charged with fraud. Prosecutor asks the Judge to hold Defendant without bail.

   Can Defendant be denied bail?

   _____

   _____

   _____

   _____

   _____

2. (J-2016, J-2013, and F-2010) What is bail? What is a bail bond? How does a bail bond differ from a personal bond?

   _____

   _____

   _____

   _____

   _____

3. (J-2015) Can Defendant, who is charged with a felony offense, be released from jail if he has no money to pay a cash bond or pay a surety? Explain.

    _____

    _____

    _____

    _____

    _____

4. (F-2015, F-2009, J-2004, and J-2000) The defendant is arrested for abusing her elderly mother. She works as a secretary at a marketing firm and owns her own home and car in the county where she is being tried. She has never been arrested before. All of her extended family lives in town. At her examining trial, you argue that she cannot post the $50,000 bail but can afford a $20,000 bail.

    What procedural step can you take to seek a bail reduction and what argument(s) can you make on her behalf?

    _____

    _____

    _____

    _____

    _____

5. (J-2014, F-2011, F-2009, J-2005, F-2005, and J-2001) Name three rules a trial court must consider when fixing the amount of bail?

    _____

    _____

    _____

    _____

    _____

6. (J-2013 and F-2003) Defendant, who is charged with sexually abusing Child, has a bail originally set at $100,000. You, acting as Defense Counsel, file a writ of habeas corpus, and after the hearing, the Court reduces the bail to $25,000. Defendant is ordered by the Court not to directly communicate with or go near Child, which poses a problem since Defendant lives with Child's family. You believe the Court lacks the authority to impose such a condition because it would require Defendant to move out of his home.

Is this a valid bond condition under Texas law? Explain.

_____

_____

_____

_____

_____

7. (F-2013, F-2012, and J-2004) The Judge denies Defendant's bail even though he has no criminal record.

What procedural step can you take to challenge denial of bail? Name two requisites of this procedural step?

_____

_____

_____

_____

8. (F-2013, F-2009, and J-2005) Defendant is released from custody after she posts bail. Judge denies her request for appointed counsel on the ground that if she could afford to post bail, she can hire her own attorney.

What is the general rule when it comes to indigency and bail? Is there any exception to this rule? Explain.

_____

_____

_____

_____

_____

9. (J-2011) Defendant is charged with a felony offense.

    What facts, if any, in Defendant's criminal history would allow a Court to deny him bail?

    _____

    _____

    _____

    _____

    _____

10. (J-2010) You represent Defendant, who is a juvenile charged with a criminal offense. Magistrate would like to release Defendant without using a surety but is concerned Defendant will not obey his parents or will be on the streets at night.

    What type of bond is Magistrate considering? What kinds of conditions can Magistrate attach to the bond to relieve her concerns about releasing Defendant? Explain.

    _____

    _____

    _____

    _____

    _____

11. (J-2009 and F-2006) Judge refuses to set Defendant's bail. You plan on filing an application for a writ of habeas corpus.

What is this? Who is it directed to? Who grants or denies it? What is the remedy?

_____

_____

_____

_____

_____

12. (J-2008) Defendant was arrested for aggravated robbery; bail was set at $50,000. Four months later, Defendant is still in jail because she cannot afford to post bail. She asks whether you can get her bail reduced. Prosecutor tells you he is not prepared to announce that he is ready for trial.

Is there a legal basis for the Court to reduce Defendant's bail under these circumstances? Explain.

_____

_____

_____

_____

_____

13. (F-2008) Defendant is charged with possession of cocaine. He is released on bond under the condition that he not go near any residence or school where children are present. He has asked you, his Defense Counsel, to challenge this condition so he can be around his two young siblings.

What, if any, basis is there to challenge this bond condition? Explain.

_____

_____

_____

_____

_____

Chapter 6
The Grand Jury and Examining Trials

Introduction

The Texas Constitution guarantees defendants the right to indictment by a grand jury for all felony offenses.[1] Defendants may waive this right, yet most do not. Defendants also have the right to an examining trial.[2] However, this right is rarely exercised and often waived. Both of these procedures are explored in this chapter. This chapter will examine the purpose and policy reasons for grand juries before turning to more mechanical aspects about how grand jurors are selected and how the grand jury functions. The chapter will conclude by discussing the purposes and process for examining trials.

———————————◆———————————

[1] TEX. CONST. art. I, §10.
[2] TEX. CODE CRIM. PROC. ANN. art. 15.17 (West 2016).

The Grand Jury

There are two kinds of juries in Texas: *petit juries* and *grand juries*. Petit (French for "small") juries serve a role as factfinder in misdemeanor and felony trials. Grand ("large") juries are those whose primary function is to investigate and make probable cause determinations in felony cases. Defendants accused of felony offenses have a right to be indicted by a grand jury. In Texas, "[n]o person shall be held to answer for a felony unless on indictment of a grand jury."[3] As a result, every felony in Texas must be presented to a grand jury for indictment unless the defendant waives this right. The waiver process will be discussed later in this chapter.

The charging decision typically begins with law enforcement officers who make an arrest or suspect a person has committed a crime. In many jurisdictions, their arrest or investigation does not lead to a criminal charge without a prosecutor's assistance. How does a prosecutor seek a grand jury indictment? Prosecutors present felony cases to the grand jury. They do this by giving the grand jurors records and reports associated with the case, discussing the case with the grand jurors, calling witnesses, and answering questions. The grand jurors also have powers to investigate cases independently, if they want. The grand jury has several options after the prosecutor's presentment:

- Request more time to investigate the matter;
- "True bill" the indictment, which means that the grand jury found probable cause to believe the defendant committed a crime;[4]
- "No bill" the indictment, which means that the grand jury did not find probable cause to believe the defendant committed a crime;
- Indict the defendant on a different criminal charge than the one requested by the prosecutor; or

---

[3] TEX. CODE CRIM. PROC. ANN. art. 1.05 (West 2016).

[4] The terms *true bill* and *no bill* do not appear in the statutes. These words are assigned meaning in the practice and in the common law. *E.g., Sledge v. State*, 903 S.W.2d 105, 108 (Tex. App.—Fort Worth 1995), *aff'd*, 953 S.W.2d 253 (Tex. Crim. App. 1997) ("The grand jury must inquire into the offense and, if nine jurors vote a true bill, return an indictment, which is the written statement of a grand jury accusing the person named in the indictment of some act or omission constituting an offense.").

- Take no action, which means that the grand jurors did not vote to either return a true bill or a no bill after having concluded their investigation.

A no bill does not necessarily connote a lack of probable cause. Prosecutors and grand juries sometimes determine that in the interest of justice, even though probable cause may exist to charge the defendant with a particular criminal offense, it is not just to do so. Furthermore, if one grand jury no bills a case, the case may be presented to another grand jury or re-presented to the same grand jury following more investigation. In the end, it is the grand jury who must decide whether to indict.

———————————◆———————————

The History and Purpose of the Grand Jury

We will begin our discussion about the grand jury by examining its function. The following case gives a short, yet detailed history of the grand jury. It highlights all grand jury duties, which extend beyond finding probable cause in felony cases.

Peggy Marie Taylor v. State
735 S.W.2d 930
(Tex. App.—Dallas 1987, no pet.)

The role of the grand jury as an important instrument of effective law enforcement necessarily includes an investigatory function with respect to determining whether a crime has been committed and who committed it. To this end it must call witnesses, in the manner best suited to perform its task. A grand jury investigation is not fully carried out until every available clue has been run down and all witnesses examined in every proper way to find if a crime has been committed. It is only after the grand jury examines the evidence that a determination of whether the proceeding will result in an indictment can be made. Without thorough and effective investigation, the grand jury would be unable either to ferret out crimes deserving of prosecution, or to screen out charges not warranting prosecution.

The grand jury has always occupied a high place as an instrument of justice in our system of criminal law—so much so that it is enshrined in the Constitution. The grand jury is an English institution brought to this country by the early colonists and incorporated in the Constitution by the Founders. There is every reason to believe that our constitutional grand jury was intended to operate substantially like its English progenitor. The basic purpose of the English grand jury was to provide a fair method for instituting criminal proceedings against persons believed to have committed crimes. Grand jurors were selected from the body of the people, and their work was not hampered by rigid procedural or evidentiary rules. In fact, grand jurors could act on their own knowledge and were free to make their presentments or indictments on such information as they deemed satisfactory. Despite its broad power to institute criminal proceedings the grand jury grew in popular favor with the years. It acquired an independence in England free from control by the Crown or judges. Historically, the grand jury has been regarded as a primary security to the innocent against hasty, malicious and oppressive persecution; it serves the invaluable function in our society of standing between the accuser and the accused to determine whether a charge is founded upon reason or was dictated by an intimidating power or by malice and personal ill will. The grand jury's historic functions survive to this day. Its responsibilities continue to include both the determination whether there is probable cause to believe a crime has been committed and the protection of citizens against unfounded criminal prosecutions. The grand jury's operation generally is unrestrained by the technical procedural and evidentiary rules governing the conduct of criminal trials.

The grand jury occupies a similarly high place of importance in the Texas system of justice as it does in the federal system as stated by the Supreme Court of the United States. Indeed, each of the pronouncements by the United States Supreme Court are as true of the Texas grand juries as they are of federal grand juries. The integrity and independence of our grand jury system must be protected from unwarranted intrusion by the prosecutor. Under Texas law, the grand jury has the authority to conduct their own investigations, to subpoena evidence and witnesses, to fail to return indictments sought by the district attorney, and to indict on matters as to which the district attorney has presented no evidence and sought no indictment. They summon witnesses and the like and determine for themselves whether there are sufficient facts to justify an indictment.

————————————◆————————————

The *Taylor* decision states that one of the primary functions of the grand jury is to investigate, hear testimony through its subpoena power, and indict or not indict. Additionally, the grand jury "shall inquire into all offenses liable for indictment" whether these inquiries are presented by the prosecutor or not.[5] In this way, grand juries can function on their own or at the bequest of the prosecutor presenting cases to the grand jury.

While it is the district attorney who organizes the presentations and houses and oversees grand jury proceedings,[6] the grand jury is an independent body. It is common knowledge that most grand juries do what the prosecutor asks most of the time. If the prosecutor asks the grand jury to indict, it is usually because there is evidence and probable cause to believe the defendant committed the crime. If the prosecutor does not want the grand jury to indict, the grand jury may follow the prosecutor's request to no bill the case. Occasionally, there are "runaway grand juries," who investigate matters not on the agenda and refuse to follow the prosecutor's suggestions. However, the overwhelming majority of grand jurors follow most of the prosecutor's recommendations.

———————————◆———————————

Grand Jury Evidence

One of the roles of the grand jury is that of investigator. Grand jurors can investigate virtually anything they want to, so long as it is an offense for which a person can be indicted. They are not limited to investigations that are included on the agenda of cases the prosecutor brings them. To this end, the Code of Criminal Procedure dictates what kind of evidence they can consider and how they may conduct their investigations.

Evidence Before the Grand Jury

The Texas Rules of Evidence do not apply to grand jury proceedings.[7] This means that hearsay and other typically inadmissible evidence can be considered by the grand jury during its investigation.

---

[5] TEX. CODE CRIM. PROC. ANN. art. 20.09 (West 2016).
[6] TEX. CODE CRIM. PROC. ANN. art. 20.03-04 (West 2016).
[7] TEX. R. EVID. 101(d)(1)(B).

Grand jury indictments may not be attacked by a defendant on the basis that evidence was presented to the grand jury that would be inadmissible at trial. The U.S. Supreme Court justified the law this way:

> If indictments were to be held open to challenge on the ground that there was inadequate or incompetent evidence before the grand jury, the resulting delay would be great indeed. The result of such a rule would be that before trial on the merits a defendant could always insist on a kind of preliminary trial to determine the competency and adequacy of the evidence before the grand jury. This is not required by the Fifth Amendment. An indictment returned by a legally constituted and unbiased grand jury, . . . if valid on its face, is enough to call for trial of the charge on the merits."[8]

The suspect/defendant or his counsel may present evidence for the grand jury to consider. Likewise, this evidence does not have to comport with the rules of evidence. Even though it is prohibited in federal practice,[9] in Texas, defense attorneys may write a letter to the grand jury or submit a packet of information that offers the defense's perspective about the case. Some defense attorneys find this practice effective because it may lead to a no bill. Others find it risky because it leaves a record of the defense or, if the defendant testifies, a record of his testimony, which may be used for impeachment later. Obviously, these are considerations defense counsel should discuss with a client who wants to present evidence to the grand jury.

Questioning Witnesses

The grand jury foreman and the prosecutor have the authority to subpoena or summon a witness anywhere in the State to appear and give testimony or produce documents or records.[10] The summons does not have to reveal what or who is being investigated.[11] A witness who evades the summons can be held in contempt of court by the judge.[12] The witness may also be attached—in other words, arrested—and brought to the court or grand jury involuntarily.[13]

---

[8] *Costello v. United States*, 350 U.S. 359, 363 (1956).
[9] 18 U.S.C. §1504 (2012).
[10] TEX. CODE CRIM. PROC. ANN. art. 20.10–.11 (West 2016).
[11] TEX. CODE CRIM. PROC. ANN. art. 20.02(a) (West 2016).
[12] TEX. CODE CRIM. PROC. ANN. art. 20.14 (West 2016).
[13] TEX. CODE CRIM. PROC. ANN. art. 20.12 (West 2016).

Once a witness is brought before the grand jury, if the criminal investigation is uncertain as to who committed the crime or how it was committed, the witness must be informed of the subject matter of the investigation and questioned.[14] The grand jury has the right to compel testimony for all questions except those that would elicit self-incriminating answers.[15]

If a witness refuses to testify before the grand jury or answer a specific question the witness or the suspect deems incriminating, the judge must review the question(s) asked and determine whether to compel the witness to testify.[16] If the witness persists in refusing to answer the question(s) after the judge has ordered him to do so, the witness can be fined and jailed for contempt of court until he testifies.[17] The Court of Criminal Appeals parsed the roles of the judge and the grand jury when it comes to the reluctant witness as follows:

> The mere refusal by a witness, to answer questions propounded by a grand jury, without more, is not contempt. The grand jury has no power or authority to find or hold one in contempt for such refusal. The grand jury must go to the court for recourse. The court may compel the witness to answer by so ordering. Upon refusal by the witness, the court may then punish the witness for violating the court's order. [I]t is ... the court alone which has the power to compel testimony before the grand jury. In terms of a nexus between the court and the grand jury, the independent fact-finding and ultimate charging determination may depend in large part on the enforcement powers of the court.

Therefore, once the court orders the witness to answer before the grand jury, then a violation of such order constitutes contempt of the court. While the act of refusal—the violation of the specific order—occurs before the grand jury, the contempt is the violation of the court's order, and is, thus, contempt of the court.[18]

Witnesses who evade a summons, who refuse to appear, who appear and refuse to testify, and who disobey a judge's order to answer a non-incriminating question may face charges of contempt of court. Unless

---

[14] TEX. CODE CRIM. PROC. ANN. art. 20.18 (West 2016).

[15] *Andino v. State*, 645 S.W.2d 615, 619 (Tex. App.—Austin 1983, no pet.).

[16] TEX. CODE CRIM. PROC. ANN. art. 20.15 (West 2016).

[17] *Id.*; *Ex parte Kyler*, 906 S.W.2d 657, 658 (Tex. App.—Austin 1995, no writ).

[18] *Ex parte Joseph Edone*, 740 S.W.2d 446, 448-49 (Tex. Crim. App. 1987).

exempted from a judge for an incriminating question, witnesses must testify before a grand jury when they are asked to do so.

Questioning Suspects and Defendants

It is another matter altogether when the grand jury subpoenas the defendant or the suspect to testify.[19] The defendant does not have a right to appear before the grand jury.[20] He also does not have the right to cross examine the witnesses who testify against him.[21] If and when the grand jury subpoenas him, he must appear. This is different from a criminal trial, where the defendant cannot be compelled to testify. He must be given adequate time to hire a lawyer or apply to have counsel appointed to represent him.[22] He must be given sufficient time to talk to his attorney before questioning begins; counsel may remain outside the grand jury room to advise the defendant but may not be in the room during questioning,[23] unless the prosecutor approves.[24]

The Code contemplates a two-part process when the grand jury questions the defendant.[25] The first part involves informing the defendant about why he is there.[26] The second part requires the grand jury to warn the defendant before he testifies.[27] Each part requires several steps, which are detailed below.

Before questioning, the grand jury must first inform the defendant about:

- the offense that the person is suspected of committing,
- the county where the crime was committed, and
- when the crime was committed.[28]

---

[19] TEX. CODE CRIM. PROC. ANN. art. 20.17 (West 2016).
[20] *Moczygemba v. State*, 532 S.W.2d 636, 638 (Tex. Crim. App. 1976).
[21] *Id.*
[22] TEX. CODE CRIM. PROC. ANN. art. 20.17 (West 2016).
[23] *Id.*; TEX. CODE CRIM. PROC. ANN. art. 20.011 (West 2016).
[24] TEX. CODE CRIM. PROC. ANN. art. 20.04 (West 2016).
[25] TEX. CODE CRIM. PROC. ANN. art. 20.17 (West 2016).
[26] *Id.* at (a).
[27] *Id.* at (b)-(c).
[28] TEX. CODE CRIM. PROC. ANN. art. 20.17 (West 2016).

Second, the grand jury must warn the defendant of his rights before he testifies, both in writing and orally.[29] The warnings are the same in both the written and oral forms:

- Your testimony is under oath;
- Material questions answered falsely may lead to aggravated perjury charges;
- You have the right to remain silent when answering questions that would incriminate you;
- You have the right to be advised by your lawyer, who will wait outside chambers, about answering incriminating questions;
- Anything you say can be used against you now and in future proceedings; and
- You have the right to retain or be appointed counsel to advise you how to answer questions that might incriminate you.[30]

The suspect/defendant's statement shall be recorded, either by a stenographer or by audio recording.[31] A statement or admission made by a defendant who appears voluntarily during grand jury questioning is admissible at trial.[32]

Immunity Granted in Exchange for Witness Testimony

In the course of investigating a matter or determining probable cause, the grand jury may want to hear from a witness or co-defendant. If summoned, this person is required to appear before the grand jury. If the person believes that the grand jurors' questions elicit self-incriminating answers, the witness may have grounds to refuse to testify. The prosecutor has an option of offering the witness immunity in exchange for testimony. If offered and accepted, the person cannot be prosecuted for the testimony she offers unless she commits perjury by giving false testimony to the grand jury. If she fails to appear before the grand jury, she will be held in contempt and could face a fine or jail time until she willingly appears.

---

[29] TEX. CODE CRIM. PROC. ANN. art. 20.17(b) (West 2016).
[30] TEX. CODE CRIM. PROC. ANN. art. 20.17(c) (West 2016).
[31] TEX. CODE CRIM. PROC. ANN. art. 20.012 (West 2016).
[32] TEX. CODE CRIM. PROC. ANN. art. 38.22 § 5 (West 2016); *Yarbrough v. State*, 617 S.W.2d 221, 226 (Tex. Crim. App. 1981).

Immunity agreements specifically aimed at grand jury witnesses or defendants take two forms. The first is broader: transactional immunity. This kind of immunity protects the witness or the defendant from prosecution for the crime that is being investigated. In other words, the person is immune from prosecution for the entire criminal transaction that she testifies about. The second type—use immunity—is narrower. Here, the prosecutor can use evidence or testimony from others to prosecute the witness for her criminal participation but cannot use the witness's own statements proffered to the grand jury. The following cases examine the policy reasons for granting witnesses immunity and the Fifth Amendment rights that are implicated when a witness or suspect gives incriminating evidence against himself.

Juan Figueroa Andino v. State
645 S.W.2d 615
(Tex. App.—Austin 1983, no pet.)

[W]hen the [grand jury's] question is asked [to the witness and]… the witness interposes his privilege [to remain silent], the grand jury has two choices. If the desired testimony is of marginal value, the grand jury can pursue other avenues of inquiry; if the testimony is thought sufficiently important, the grand jury can seek a judicial determination as to the bona fides of the witness' Fifth Amendment claim … in which case the witness must satisfy the presiding judge that the claim of privilege is not a subterfuge. If in fact "'there is reasonable ground to apprehend danger to the witness from his being compelled to answer,'" … the prosecutor must then determine whether the answer is of such overriding importance as to justify a grant of immunity to the witness.

If immunity is sought by the prosecutor and granted by the presiding judge, the witness can then be compelled to answer, on pain of contempt, even though the testimony would implicate the witness in criminal activity.... Immunity is the Government's ultimate tool for securing testimony that otherwise would be protected; unless immunity is conferred, however, testimony may be suppressed, along with its fruits, if it is compelled over an appropriate claim of privilege. … On the other hand, when granted immunity, a witness once again owes the obligation imposed upon all citizens—the duty to give testimony—since immunity substitutes for the privilege.

Ex parte Mark Edward Shorthouse,
Ex parte Anna Marie Shorthouse,
Ex Parte Lewis Crowell, and
Ex Parte Helen Crowell
640 S.W.2d 924
(Tex. Crim. App. 1982)

On January 14, 1982, all the applicants were called to testify before the grand jury. They did not appear or testify.

On January 15, 1982, the district attorney applied for and obtained immunity for each of the applicants from the district judge. The immunity applications stated the grand jury was presently considering indictments … against each named individual and other parties and the individual named in each of the immunity applications was a party to an offense … and was a material witness against other individuals [to the offense of engaging in organized crime], and should be granted testimonial immunity.

[Section] 71.04, provides:

(a) A party to an offense under this Chapter may be required to furnish evidence or testify about the offense.

(b) No evidence or testimony required to be furnished under … this section nor any information directly or indirectly derived from such evidence or testimony *may be used* against the witness in any criminal case, except a prosecution for aggravated perjury or contempt."

The orders granting immunity read in pertinent part:

It is therefore Ordered that (applicant) pursuant to Section 71.04, Texas Penal Code appear before the Bastrop County Grand Jury at Bastrop, Texas on January 20, 1982, at 9:00 o'clock a.m., where he is ordered to furnish evidence and testify about such offense. It is further Ordered that no evidence or testimony furnished by (applicant), nor any information directly or indirectly derived from such evidence or testimony may be used against (applicant) in any criminal case, except in a prosecution for aggravated Perjury or Contempt.

…On January 20, 1982, each of the applicants was called to testify before the grand jury, and each refused to testify and invoked their privilege against self-incrimination. On January 22, 1982, motions for contempt were filed by the district attorney and on January 25, 1982, the district court ordered each of the applicants to appear before the grand jury on February 8, 1982 and testify pursuant to the immunity granted.

Thereafter on February 8, 1982, the court conducted a hearing, determined that the applicants had refused to testify before the grand jury on February 8th despite the grants of immunity, that the questions propounded were proper questions... and held the applicants in contempt of court for their refusal to testify.

Applicants attack the contempt orders on a number of grounds. ... We turn first then to applicants' contention that . . . § 71.04, fails to provide sufficient protection of the privilege against self-incrimination as established by Article I, § 10 of the Texas Constitution and the [case] law of this state. Applicants argue that it is well established . . . that any grant of immunity must serve to absolutely prohibit prosecution for the offense about which the required testimony relates. Applicants thus contend that only absolute, complete, full or transactional immunity is permissible under Texas law and that the testimonial or use and derivative use immunity authorized by . . . § 71.04 is unauthorized and unconstitutional. We do not agree.

In Kastigar v. United States, 406 U.S. 441 (1972), the Supreme Court of the United States upheld the federal constitutionality of a statute, 18 U.S.C. § 6002, that provides for derivative use or testimonial immunity. The Court held:

> The statute's explicit proscription for the use of any criminal case of 'testimony (or other information directly or indirectly derived from such testimony or other information)' is consonant with Fifth Amendment standards. We hold that such immunity from use and derivative use is co-extensive with the scope of the privilege of self-incrimination, and therefore is sufficient to compel testimony over a claim of the privilege. While a grant of immunity must afford protection commensurate with that afforded with the privilege, it need not be broader. Transactional Immunity, which accords full immunity from prosecution for the offense for which the compelled testimony relates, affords the witness considerably broader protection than does the 5th Amendment privilege.

It is clear why the applicants do not rely upon the Fifth Amendment and its interpretation by the United States Supreme Court. It is the applicants' contention that the self-incrimination privilege of Article I, § 10 of our State Constitution is broader than that of the Fifth Amendment and has so been interpreted by Texas courts. ...

[T]he privilege against self-incrimination embodied in Article I, § 10 of our State Constitution is not to be given a broader construction than that of the Fifth Amendment, United States Constitution.

. . . We therefore hold that immunity from use and derivative use of testimony . . . is sufficient to compel testimony over a claim of the privilege.

———————◆———————

Notes and Questions

1. When does a witness's right to remain silent trump the grand jury's power to investigate crimes and compel testimony?

2. What steps must the judge take in order to ensure that the rules of criminal procedure are followed before holding a witness in contempt for failure to testify to the grand jury?

———————◆———————

Waiving Indictment

The defendant may waive a grand jury indictment in any noncapital felony case.[33] For a waiver of an indictment to be valid, it must: (1) be in writing; (2) be knowingly, intelligently, and voluntarily given by the accused; (3) while represented by counsel.[34] A pro se defendant, someone representing himself, may not waive indictment. If the waiver meets all of the statutory requirements, the prosecutor may proceed on a felony information, rather than on an indictment.[35]

Why might a defendant waive indictment? One reason is to plead guilty before the grand jury indicts him. Grand juries may take up to 90 days to indict a defendant. If the defendant wants to plead guilty before that time, she must wave indictment.

———————◆———————

---

[33] TEX. CODE CRIM. PROC. ANN. art. 1.141 (West 2016).
[34] *Id.*
[35] *Id.*

The Secrecy of Grand Jury Proceedings

It is important to note that "[t]he proceedings of the grand jury shall be secret."[36] The Code of Criminal Procedure contains many provisions designed to ensure grand jury secrecy. The following case discusses the shroud of secrecy and the policy reasons for it in more depth.

Jack R. Stern v. State
869 S.W.2d 614

(Tex. App.—Houston [14th Dist.] 1994, writ denied)

This is an appeal from a judgment removing Jack R. Stern from the office of District Attorney for Fort Bend County. Relators alleged incompetence and official misconduct under the Texas Removal Statute as grounds for Mr. Stern's removal. The crux of the complaint against Jack Stern is twofold: (1) he publicly released transcripts of grand jury testimony, and (2) he abused a grand jury witness. This combined conduct forms the bedrock upon which the removal action was founded. After trial, the jury returned a verdict removing Stern from office for official misconduct and incompetent behavior. ... We affirm.

...District attorneys have a clearly defined statutory and a common law duty to keep grand jury testimony secret.

Article 19.34 swears grand jurors to secrecy. Article 19.36 swears bailiffs to secrecy. Article 20.02 provides a penalty for grand jurors and bailiffs who reveal anything that transpires before them during the course of their official duties. Article 20.16 swears witnesses to secrecy and imposes a penalty upon any witness who reveals the content of his testimony, or any other matter that occurs before the grand jury in his presence. Article 20.03 permits an attorney for the state to appear. Article 20.04 also provides that only grand jurors and the state's attorney have a right to question witnesses. Thus, the attorney for the accused is not entitled to attend the sessions, he is not entitled to cross-examine witnesses, he is not even entitled to be present when the accused is being questioned. No one, other than a witness or the state's attorney may address the grand jury about a matter that is before it. The accused, or the attorney for the accused, may, on their own initiative,

---

[36] TEX. CODE CRIM. PROC. ANN. art. 20.02(a) (West 2016).

address the grand jury only if the state's attorney permits. The public is not allowed to attend grand jury sessions.

Viewing the scheme of the Code as a whole, grand jury proceedings, including the taking of testimony, are secret. Moreover, article 20.02 clearly proclaims that any grand juror or bailiff who divulges "anything transpiring before them in the course of their official duties" shall be in contempt of court. Not only are "deliberations" included within the ambit of the rule of secrecy, but anything that takes place before the bailiffs and grand jurors, including testimony. Texas courts have uniformly followed this rule. Any communication made to the grand jury in the regular performance of its duties is secret.

A prosecuting attorney is the servant of the grand jury. Among his many duties, the prosecuting attorney takes custody of evidence that is submitted for the grand jury's consideration. It must always be remembered, however, that evidence and testimony presented to the grand jury remains in the possession of that institution even though it is physically held by officials who take custody of such records and files. As such, these matters are not subject to public disclosure, and where the grand jury members have no authority to disclose, their servants have no authority to disclose.

The policy reasons for secrecy are compelling. It ensures the utmost freedom to the grand jury in its deliberations. It prevents other persons subject to indictment, or their friends, from importuning the grand jurors; no undue influence should be permitted to sway its counsels or govern its action. Moreover, grand jurors should be free from the apprehension that someone may disclose subsequently their opinions and votes. The requirement of confidentiality also prevents subornation of perjury or tampering with the witnesses who may testify before the grand jury and later appear at the trial of those indicted. Further, secrecy encourages free and untrammeled disclosures by persons who have information with respect to the commission of crimes. Witnesses can give evidence without fear of reprisal from an accused or any other person. Confidentiality also protects the innocent accused who is exonerated from disclosure of the fact that he has been under investigation. Such a consideration is particularly important in light of the fact an elected official's reputation may be irreparably harmed by public disclosure even though investigation of the allegations reveals no basis for prosecution. It also saves persons who have been cleared by the grand jury from the expense of standing trial where there was no probability of guilt.

Additionally, the requirement saves the public the trouble, expense, and disgrace of having matters disclosed that no longer have any merit. Finally, grand jury secrecy also prevents the escape of those whose indictment is contemplated.

Texas courts have permitted the veil of grand jury secrecy to be pierced in only a few instances. Evidence of what transpired before a grand jury is admissible only when, in the judgment of the court, it becomes material to the administration of justice that disclosure be allowed. ... *Hines v. State*, 39 S.W. 935, 936 (1897) (grand jury testimony admissible to impeach witness or prove perjury); *Spangler v. State*, 55 S.W. 326, 329 (1900) (grand jury testimony may be used to refresh memory of witness); *Addison v. State*, 211 S.W. 225, 225 (1919) (grand jury testimony may be disclosed to show circumstances in which grand jury secrets became known); *Rothschild v. State*, 7 Tex. Ct. App. 519, 537 (1880) (veil of grand jury secrecy may be pierced to determine whether jury was made up of required number of persons); *Trevinio v. State*, 11 S.W. 447, 447 (1889), *overruled on other grounds by Singleton v. State*, 346 S.W.2d 328, 330 (1961) (grand jury secrecy may be pierced to determine whether unauthorized person was present when the jurors were deliberating or voting); *Euresti v. Valdez*, 769 S.W.2d 575, 582 (Tex. App.—Corpus Christi 1989, no writ) (grand jury testimony may be divulged to prove elements of malicious prosecution). We find it compelling that in each instance in which disclosure may be obtained, it may only be obtained by judicial order. We find no case in the jurisprudence of this state that suggests a prosecutor, court reporter, or any other individual, may unilaterally disclose the contents of grand jury testimony while a grand jury investigation is in progress.

Appellant urges that there has long been a distinction between "deliberations" and the taking of testimony by the grand jury ... We do agree that such a distinction has been made; however, the distinction relates specifically to times when a party to a law suit or criminal proceeding may gain access to events that occurred before the grand jury. Although each of the cases appellant relies on provides examples of when the veil of grand jury secrecy may be pierced, and to what extent, none of them suggests that testimony before the grand jury is not secret, but that discussions and voting are secret. In fact, the cases stand for the opposite proposition: all these events are secret except in specifically enumerated instances.

The Texas Code of Criminal Procedure places great importance upon maintaining the secrecy of what transpires before the grand jury. Standing behind the Code is the common law rule that the proceedings of the grand jury are secret. We hold that prosecutors have both a clear statutory and a common law duty to keep secret the proceedings of the grand jury. By publicly disclosing transcripts of testimony given before the grand jury, Stern intentionally failed, refused, or neglected to perform a duty imposed upon him by law. This was evidence that Jack Stern engaged in official misconduct. The trial court did not err in denying Stern's motions for directed verdict, . . . and new trial.

. . . In conclusion, we wish to point out that we are not holding that prosecutors may never discuss, in general terms, grand jury proceedings. In fact, most prosecutors discuss what they expect to prove or plan to investigate. To pull such a cloak of absolute secrecy about grand jury proceedings would be futile in this era of mass communication where it is easily known which witnesses are appearing before the grand jury, the reason for their appearance, and even what they are likely to discuss. The requirement of secrecy should be imposed only to the extent that it contributes to the effectiveness of the grand jury as that institution carries out its investigative and screening functions. Beyond that, however, the requirement of confidentiality serves no purpose. What set Jack Stern's conduct apart is that he disclosed transcripts of actual grand jury testimony after that institution refused to indict a prominent county official for perjury. Stern's conduct defeated at least four primary goals of the grand jury: (1) protection from disclosure of the person under investigation who is later exonerated; (2) keeping grand jurors free from outside pressures; (3) securing to the grand jurors freedom from the apprehension that someone may disclose subsequently their opinions and votes; and, (4) protection of witnesses from the fear of reprisal. Had Stern not divulged the grand jury testimony, the public would never had known of the accusations against Sheriff Hillegeist; his reputation would have remained untarnished. Stern's disclosures also amounted to an attempt to influence the grand jurors through the media. Furthermore, prominent members of Hillegeist's political party who were also members of the grand jury would not have been placed in a position where members of the public could speculate on the reasons the grand jury refused to indict the sheriff. Finally, the witnesses who testified, employees of the sheriff's department, would not have had to fear the possibility, however remote, of reprisal.

———————◆———————

Notes and Questions

1. What are the roles and parameters of the prosecutor's involvement with the grand jury?

2. Ultimately, who does the grand jury serve? With that answer in mind, where do the loyalties of the grand jury reside?

3. Prosecutors rarely act as Jack Stern did. Most prosecutors are incredibly deferential to grand jurors. Consider the following excerpt from John Brewer, former grand jury division chief in Harris County (Houston) who wrote an article that was published in the Texas District and County Attorneys Association's publication, *The Prosecutor*:

> On occasion, a grand jury will look to the prosecutor for guidance regarding its decisions. Although most prosecutors steer away from flat-out telling the grand jury what they think should be done (*i.e.*, "Please no-bill this case"), there doesn't seem to be any admonition in the code stopping us. I think the real reason is wariness on the part of the prosecutor to be seen as controlling the grand jury or infringing upon its independence. Such straightforward requests from a prosecutor can often upset the sensibilities of a grand jury, resulting in questions like, "Why are you using us to get rid of the case? Why didn't you dismiss it?" The reality is that we may be "allowing" them to dispose of a case that ultimately we would have to dismiss. Is that OK, or should we be taking the responsibility of filling out the [dismissal] ourselves? I can say that I have done both many a time. It seems to me that both prosecutors and grand juries have the responsibility of disposing of "bad" cases. Their responsibility starts at determining if probable cause exists but also includes a healthy dash of "how do we feel about this particular case in our county?"[37]

Brewer reflects a belief that many prosecutors hold: the grand jury is an independent body, and the prosecutor must respect it and give it a level of deference. Prosecutors do not want to appear bossy or demanding. Many prosecutors like to take problematic factual or legal cases to the grand jury; the process permits another decision-making body to help make difficult

---

[37] John L. Brewer, *Grand Jury: Where the Community Meets the Law*, 43 THE PROSECUTOR (November-December 2013), available at http://www.tdcaa.com/journal/grand-jury-where-community-meets-law.

decisions in difficult cases. When the grand jury no bills a difficult case, it relieves the prosecutor from the political consequences that follow a dismissal.

◆

Who May Be Present During Proceedings?

The actual proceedings—the prosecutor's presentation, the questioning of witnesses, the deliberations—are addressed in detail by the Code. The grand jurors have a room secured by a bailiff where they hear testimony and deliberate.[38] The only people permitted to be in the room when they are hearing evidence are:

- Grand jurors;
- Bailiffs;
- The attorney representing the State of Texas;
- Witnesses being examined;
- Interpreters, if necessary;
- A court reporter; and
- Someone operating video teleconferencing equipment in the event the witness is testifying from a remote location.

Aside from these individuals, no one else is permitted to be in the room. A defendant may attack the validity of the indictment based upon the presence of an unauthorized person only if the person was in the room while the grand jury was deliberating.[39]

The attorney representing the State may question witnesses, advise grand jurors how to interrogate witnesses, and appear in the room with the grand jurors at any time except when they are deliberating or voting.[40]

Only grand jurors can be in the room when the grand jury deliberates or votes. Only the attorney for the State and the grand jurors can question witnesses; no other attorney or member of the public (except a testifying

---

[38] TEX. CODE CRIM. PROC. ANN. art. 20.01 (West 2016).
[39] TEX. CODE CRIM. PROC. ANN. art. 20.011 (West 2016).
[40] TEX. CODE CRIM. PROC. ANN. arts. 20.03 and 20.04 (West 2016).

witness) can address the grand jury about a case it is considering.[41] However, defense counsel may appear before the grand jury if the State's attorney permits it.[42] This is not a common practice. If defense counsel is present to support or advise his client, he usually waits outside the grand jury room.

Other states permit defense counsel to be in the grand jury room during questioning of the defendant.[43] What are reasons for or against such a policy? Can you think of a structured way to permit defense counsel in the grand jury room that would not derail or upset its function and role as investigator?

Who May Grand Jurors Consult?

Grand jurors are rarely law-trained. Because they are almost always laypersons, they may have legal questions or need to consult a law-trained person when it comes to probable cause determinations. After all, they are making a probable cause determination without any formal legal training that experienced law-enforcement agents, prosecutors, magistrates, and judges make on a daily basis. Therefore, the Code permits grand jurors to send for the State's attorney when they need advice,[44] or go as a group to the judge or make a written request for the judge's advice. If the grand jury goes to the judge, it must preserve secrecy about the case it is inquiring about when it discusses the case with the judge.[45]

Who Drafts and Signs the Indictment?

It is the prosecutor who drafts the indictment and presents it to the grand jury.[46] Indictments are delivered to the grand jury foreperson, who

---

[41] TEX. CODE CRIM. PROC. ANN. art. 20.04 (West 2016); *San Antonio Express-News v. Roman*, 861 S.W.2d 265, 267 (Tex. App.—San Antonio 1993, no writ); *Mason v. State*, 322 S.W.3d 251, 253-54 (Tex. Crim. App. 2010) (police officer was not permitted to be in grand jury room to question eyewitness).

[42] TEX. CODE CRIM. PROC. ANN. art. 20.04 (West 2016).

[43] *E.g.*, ARIZ. R. CRIM. PROC. 12.6 (1993) (permits suspect or target of investigation to be advised by counsel before appearing and while offering testimony to the grand jury); COLO. REV. STAT. §16-5-204 (IV)(d) (2012) (any witness may have counsel present during questioning); MINN. R. CRIM. PROC. 18.03 (2009) (witness given immunity may be advised by counsel during grand jury testimony).

[44] TEX. CODE CRIM. PROC. ANN. art. 20.05 (West 2016).

[45] TEX. CODE CRIM. PROC. ANN. art. 20.06 (West 2016).

[46] TEX. CODE CRIM. PROC. ANN. art. 20.20 (West 2016).

signs them officially; the prosecutor must include any witness names who testified before the grand jury on the indictment.[47]

When Can the Defendant Access Information About the Grand Jury?

Typically, a court reporter transcribes testimony during questioning. The testimony is thus preserved and may be used in future proceedings. A witness's statement before the grand jury is only discoverable to defense counsel after that witness has testified on direct examination.[48] If the defendant desires to discover grand jury testimony or evidence before direct examination, he must demonstrate a particularized need for it.[49] Absent such a showing, he is not entitled to discover it. Furthermore, only on a "showing of good cause" can the court disclose the identifying information about a grand juror to a party in the proceeding.[50]

It is very difficult to meet the "particularized need" or "good cause" requirements. For example, where it was alleged that the prosecutor withheld evidence favorable to the accused from the grand jury,[51] or where a witness gave conflicting testimony to the grand jury and petit jury and the prosecutor refused to allow the defense access to the prior inconsistent statement,[52] Texas appellate courts ruled the trial court did not abuse its discretion in finding that the defendants failed to establish a particularized need.

---◆---

Grand Jury Selection

The earlier parts of this chapter examined the duties and the responsibilities of the grand jurors and the secrecy of their proceedings. Now that you know what they do, you need to know how they are chosen.

Grand jurors are selected from the pool of those who report for petit jury duty.[53] This pool is created through random selection of individuals who

---

47 *Id.*
48 TEX. R. EVID. 615(a) and (f)(3).
49 TEX. CODE CRIM. PROC. ANN. art. 20.02(d) (West 2016).
50 TEX. CODE CRIM. PROC. ANN. art. 19.42 (West 2016).
51 *In re Grand Jury Proceedings*, 129 S.W.3d 140, 141 (Tex. App.—San Antonio 2003, pet. dism'd).
52 *Bynum v. State*, 767 S.W.2d 769, 781–83 (Tex. Crim. App. 1989).
53 TEX. CODE CRIM. PROC. ANN. art. 19.01(b) (West 2016).

are registered to vote in Texas and those with driver's licenses. Typically, district judges share responsibility in gathering members of a grand jury; in counties with multiple district courts, there are just a handful of grand juries at any one time, though there may be a greater number of district court judges. The grand jury will be associated with the court's judicial number (*e.g.,* the grand jury for the 180th District Court). When it is a judge's turn to put together a grand jury, she will summon a group of potential jurors from the regular jury pool and ask whether any of them would be willing to serve as grand jurors and whether they are qualified to do so.[54]

Grand jurors serve a term that lasts approximately 90 days.[55] These grand jurors meet each week, usually two days per week. The workdays may be short or full, depending on the number of cases schedule to be heard. As you can imagine, few people are able to serve this long and this frequently due to work or personal obligations.

Grand Jury Qualifications

In order to be qualified to serve as a grand juror in Texas, the person must:

- Be a citizen of Texas, a resident of the county in which they serve, and be qualified to vote in the county, even if they are not actually registered to vote in that county;
- Be of sound mind and good moral character;
- Be able to read and write;
- Not have been convicted of misdemeanor theft or felony crimes or be under indictment or currently facing charges for those crimes;
- Not be closely related to anyone else serving on the same grand jury;
- Not have served as a grand juror in the year before the current grand jury service begins; and

---

[54] TEX. CODE CRIM. PROC. ANN. art. 19.01(b) and 19.21-23 (West 2016).
[55] But see TEX. CODE CRIM. PROC. ANN. art. 19.07 and 19.41 (West 2016) (grand jury term can be extended to give grand jurors time to conclude and investigation, and grand jury can be discharged and reassembled during the term).

- Not be a complainant—a victim—in any case appearing before the grand jury.[56]

Assembling the Grand Jury

When 14 grand jurors, 12 members and 2 alternates, have been qualified, the judge will impanel the grand jury.[57] Once the grand jury is impaneled, the judge must instruct the grand jurors about their duties and administer an oath asking them to promise to be diligent, keep the proceedings secret, and act honorably and without malice as they carry out their duties.[58]

Among the 12 primary grand jurors, a foreperson is selected; if the foreperson is not present when the grand jury is meeting, another foreperson must be appointed.[59] There must be at least nine grand jurors present to make a quorum; a quorum is necessary in order to discharge any duty or exercise any right given to a grand jury.[60] This includes making a probable cause determination on a case. If a grand jury indicts a defendant with fewer than nine grand jurors present, the defendant can attack the validity of the indictment by filing a motion to set aside the indictment.[61]

———————◆———————

Notes and Questions

1. Not only does the district court who empanels the grand jury play a role in its members' selection, but it also continues to supervise the grand jury it assembles. The Court of Criminal Appeals described the district court's role as follows:

> [T]he grand jury is very connected to the court which impaneled it. The court exercises supervisory power over the grand jury whether by impaneling, re-assembling, qualifying, quashing subpoenas, or aiding investigation. The grand jury "is more frequently characterized as 'an arm of the court by which it is appointed'", rather than as an autonomous entity.

---

[56] TEX. CODE CRIM. PROC. ANN. art. 19.08 and 19.18 (West 2016).
[57] TEX. CODE CRIM. PROC. ANN. art. 19.26 (West 2016).
[58] TEX. CODE CRIM. PROC. ANN. art. 19.34, 19.35 (West 2016).
[59] TEX. CODE CRIM. PROC. ANN. art. 19.34, 19.39 (West 2016).
[60] TEX. CODE CRIM. PROC. ANN. art. 19.40 (West 2016).
[61] TEX. CODE CRIM. PROC. ANN. art. 27.03 (West 2016).

Given the relation and function of the court to the grand jury, this characterization is quite accurate ....

[The Code] gives the district court jurisdiction, power and authority over one not otherwise subject to the power of the court. Art. 20.15 states:

> When a witness, brought in any manner before a grand jury, refuses to testify, such fact shall be made known to the attorney representing the State or to the court; and the court may compel the witness to answer the question, if it appear[s] to be a proper one, by imposing a fine not exceeding five hundred dollars, and by committing the party to jail until he is willing to testify.

> The court thus aids the investigation of the grand jury under the authority of Art. 20.15. However, the court also exerts some "control" or supervision over the grand jury .... The court decides if the question propounded before the grand jury is proper, and, thus, decides whether or not to aid the investigation of the grand jury by then compelling an answer. Without the action of the court the grand jury is powerless to enforce its investigative duty to gain testimony from a witness and decide on the presentment of an indictment. In this sense, the court acts independently and in a supervisory role (deciding whether to compel an answer) as well as jointly with the grand jury ....

> A grand jury is clothed with great independence in many areas, but it remains an appendage of the court, powerless to perform its investigative function without the court's aid.... [62]

Challenging the Grand Jury

The Code outlines the way grand jurors should be selected. Grand jurors are supposed to represent the community and act fairly and honestly in carrying out their duties.[63] What if they are not representative of the community, were chosen in violation of the law, or are biased? There is a process for challenges should these concerns arise.

---

[62] *Ex parte Edone*, 740 S.W.2d 446, 448 (Tex. Crim. App. 1987) (citations omitted).
[63] TEX. CODE CRIM. PROC. ANN. art. 19.34 (West 2016).

A defendant may want to challenge the grand jury's composition or challenge a specific grand juror for several reasons. There are two statutorily articulated reasons given to challenge the grand jury array. The first is that they were chosen by some method not articulated in the Code, and the second is that the sponsoring judge acted corruptly in summoning them.[64]

The Code also anticipates challenges to the grand jurors individually. Grand jurors can be challenged for any of the following reasons:

- The juror is insane;
- The juror is medically unfit for jury service, or is legally blind or unable to hear testimony and presentations;
- The juror is a witness in or a target of a pending grand jury investigation;
- The juror served on a petit jury in a former trial of the same alleged conduct or offense that the grand jury is investigating;
- The juror has a bias or prejudice in favor of or against the person accused or suspected of committing an offense that the current grand jury is investigating;
- The juror, based upon hearsay or another reason, has already concluded the guilt or the innocence of the person accused and would influence the juror's vote on the presentment of the indictment;
- The juror is a close relative (within the third degree by consanguinity or affinity) of the suspect or the victim;
- The juror has a bias or prejudice against the law that was violated in the present case;
- The juror is not qualified; or
- The juror is also the prosecutor bringing the accusation against the person making the challenge.

Any person may challenge the grand jury as a group or an individual grand juror before the grand jury has been impaneled.[65] Since most suspects and defendants will not know who is serving on the grand jury prior to their arrest and charge, there is a way to challenge the grand jury after it has been

---

[64] TEX. CODE CRIM. PROC. ANN. art. 19.30 (West 2016).
[65] TEX. CODE CRIM. PROC. ANN. art. 19.27 (West 2016).

impaneled. The defendant must challenge the grand jury at the first opportunity he has through a motion to quash the indictment.[66] The Code states that a defendant may challenge the grand jury as illegally impaneled by filing a motion to quash the indictment if he shows he had no earlier opportunity to challenge the array at the time it was impaneled.[67] If the defendant waits to challenge it when he could have done so earlier, his motion will fail.[68] In sum, he must raise the challenge as soon as possible through a motion to quash.

The following case illustrates the typical complaint defendants raise when challenging the array: discrimination in grand jury selection.

Joe Long Jr. v. State
340 S.W.2d 58
(Tex. Crim. App. 1960)

The offense is receiving and concealing stolen property; the punishment, 2 years.

In view of our disposition of this case, a recitation of the facts will not be deemed necessary.

… Another serious question is presented by this record which we have concluded calls for a dismissal of this prosecution. It was established that the then-existing grand jury in the 30th Judicial District of the same county had deliberated on the charge against appellant, as well as two or three others, and had returned no bills. Following this, the jury commission, which appointed the grand jury who returned the instant indictment, was appointed. A member of such jury commission talked to "two or three" prospective grand jurors and had his business partner, who was "concerned" about the failure of the 30th District grand jury to indict appellant and others, talk to two other prospective grand jurors. It is these conversations which have caused us deep concern. In each of them the man who later became a grand juror was asked, when being approached by the jury commissioner and his partner, about whether or not he would be willing to serve, why a new grand

---

[66] *Muniz v. State*, 672 S.W.2d 804, 807–08 (Tex. Crim. App. 1984).
[67] TEX. CODE CRIM. PROC. ANN. art. 27.03 (West 2016). *Cf. State v. Hart*, 342 S.W.3d 659, 666-67 (Tex. App.—Houston [14th Dist.] 2011, pet. ref'd) (attorney should have filed a motion to set aside the indictment, not a motion for new trial after alleging grand juror misconduct).
[68] *Id.*

jury was needed when one was already in existence, and in each case the prospective grand juror was informed that the existing grand jury had refused to indict appellant. It was after this information was given the prospective grand juror that he agreed to serve if selected and did in fact serve. This conduct on the part of the jury commission in question was in direct violation of the [law].

This Court and the Supreme Court of the United States from time to time have been called upon to quash grand jury indictments because of discriminatory practices on the part of jury commissioners in the selection of grand jurors. These cases usually arose when the discrimination was racial. ...

The rule announced, however, is by no means limited to racial discrimination, but includes all fact situations where discrimination is practiced against the accused for any reason.

Here, the instant facts are deemed sufficient to support the conclusion that ...the grand jury commission selected prospective grand jurors with the view that those selected would return an indictment against this appellant.

We have concluded that the learned trial court fell into error in failing to sustain appellant's motion to quash the indictment.

The judgment is reversed and the prosecution is dismissed.

———————◆———————

Notes and Questions

1. The grand jury in the *Long* case was selected through the "key man" system, which was abolished in 2015. There used to be two ways to select grand jurors. In addition to obtaining grand jurors in the way you obtain a petit juror, Texas used a "key man" system. This system was highly controversial. It permitted a commissioner to select grand jurors. As you saw in the *Long* case, this system was subject to abuse.

2. If a defendant wants to challenge the entire array, he must file a motion to quash the indictment.[69] A defendant who fails to assert the challenge through a motion to quash waives the right to challenge the grand jury array.

---

[69] *Ex parte Covin*, 277 S.W.2d 109, 112 (Tex. Crim. App. 1955).

3. Discrimination challenges to the grand jury array have rarely been successful.[70] In one instance where such a challenge was effective, the Amarillo Court of Appeals held "once appellant established the underrepresentation of his [race] over a significant period of time by use of the gross population statistics, thereby evidencing a prima facie case of discriminatory purpose, the State had the burden to rebut the case."[71] It failed to offer any evidence to dispel the defendant's evidence.[72] Therefore, the Court declared the indictment void, and the prosecution was dismissed.[73]

————————◆————————

Setting Aside the Indictment

Defense counsel may challenge the substance of the indictment (*e.g.*, because it fails to allege a crime) or the form of the grand jury's indictment based upon the way the grand jury indicted the defendant. A defendant can challenge the form of the indictment, specifically related to the grand jury itself, on the following grounds:

- Fewer than nine grand jurors (the number needed for a quorum) voted on the indictment;
- An unauthorized person was in the room when the grand jury deliberated;
- The grand jury was illegally impaneled.[74]

In these instances, the defendant must file a written motion to set aside the indictment; he carries the burden to prove one of the above violations occurred.[75] Any issues of fact related to the motion, in this instance, must be determined by the judge, not a petit jury.[76]

————————◆————————

---

[70] *Cerda v. State*, 644 S.W.2d 875, 879 (Tex. App.—Amarillo 1982, no pet.).

[71] *Id.*

[72] *Id.*

[73] *Id.*

[74] TEX. CODE CRIM. PROC. ANN. art. 27.03 (West 2016).

[75] *Ray v. State*, 561 S.W.2d 480, 481 (Tex. Crim. App. 1977)

[76] TEX. CODE CRIM. PROC. ANN. arts. 27.03, 20.04, and 27.10 (West 2016).

Examining Trials

We will now turn our attention to examining trials. Examining trials are a type of preliminary hearing. Not every jurisdiction regularly schedules them. Whether examining trials ever take place in the courthouse depends largely on the practice and desire of local judges and members of the bar. Some counties routinely schedule them, whereas other counties may rarely, if ever, schedule them. Nevertheless, the examining trial is an unusual and unique criminal procedure in Texas.

———————————◆———————————

The Threefold Purpose of Examining Trials

Only defendants charged with felony offenses may request an examining trial.[77] The examining trial's purpose is threefold: (1) to determine whether probable cause exists; (2) to set bail; and (3) to take the testimony of witnesses, which may include any voluntary statement the suspect wants to make.[78]

The primary purpose of the examining trial is to determine whether there is probable cause to believe the defendant committed the charged offense. When an examining trial concludes, the presiding judge will determine whether the defendant should face charges or be released. The judge must make a probable cause finding within 48 hours of the examining trial's conclusion, or her inaction will result in a finding of no probable cause, and the defendant will be released from custody.[79]

The examining trial's probable cause requisite is mandated by the Texas legislature.[80] The initial probable cause finding, made by a magistrate following arrest, is required by the Fourth Amendment of the U.S. Constitution.[81] Together, these two findings (and additional probable cause

---

[77] TEX. CODE CRIM. PROC. ANN. art. 16.01 (West 2016).

[78] *State ex rel. Holmes v. Salinas*, 784 S.W.2d 421, 424 (Tex. Crim. App. 1990).

[79] TEX. CODE CRIM. PROC. ANN. art. 16.17 (West 2016).

[80] *Id.*

[81] U.S. CONST. amend IV ("The right of the people to be secure in their persons, houses, papers, and effects, against unreasonable searches and seizures, shall not be violated, and no Warrants shall issue, but upon probable cause, supported by Oath or affirmation, and particularly describing the place to be searched, and the persons or things to be seized.").

findings made by the officer at the scene, the magistrate who signs an arrest or search warrant, and the prosecutor screening the case) serve as checks and balances on the decision to charge the defendant with a crime and restrain the defendant's liberty.

A secondary purpose of examining trials is to determine bail. The presiding magistrate or judge will set or adjust bail if the offense is bailable.[82] Finally, a third purpose of examining trials is to provide both sides with informal discovery. The defendant's testimony at his examining trial can be used against him.[83] A witness who testifies at the examining trial and who testifies again at trial can be impeached with any sworn testimony given at the examining trial, if the proper impeachment predicate is laid.[84]

However, for a witness's testimony to be admitted without her presence at a subsequent hearing or trial, the attorney proffering that evidence has a substantial burden to overcome. The witness has to be unavailable—out of state or deceased—for examining trial testimony to be admitted later.[85] Furthermore, the Court of Criminal Appeals stated, after discussing the defendant's constitutional right to confront witnesses against him,

> In seeking to reproduce testimony of [an unavailable trial] witness given at a prior examining trial, the State has the burden of establishing clearly and satisfactorily that the testimony was given under oath, that it was competent, that the accused on trial is the same accused who was present, as an accused, at the examining trial and that the accused had adequate opportunity through counsel to cross-examine the deceased witness. Supplementing this constitutional test that does not otherwise alter or modify them are the statutory standards of Article 39.01: that the deposition be duly taken before an examining trial and reduced to writing and certified according to law; that is, when a statement of facts taken by a court reporter is, according to Article 16.09, ... authenticated by State and defense counsel and approved by the presiding magistrate, and delivered to the clerk of the trial court.[86]

In practice, it would be difficult for most attorneys to meet all of the above requirements, which means that the testimony at the examining trial in

---

[82] TEX. CODE CRIM. PROC. ANN. arts. 16.01 (West 2016).

[83] TEX. CODE CRIM. PROC. ANN. art. 38.22 § 5 (West 2016).

[84] *Weaver v. State*, 472 S.W.2d 518, 520 (Tex. Crim. App. 1971).

[85] TEX. CODE CRIM. PROC. ANN. art. 39.01 (West 2016).

[86] *Russell v. State*, 604 S.W.2d 914, 920-21 (Tex. Crim. App. 1980).

the unavailability of the testifying witness would likely not be admissible at a subsequent trial or hearing.

———————————◆———————————

Notes and Questions

1. Examining trials are rare in Texas. In fiscal year 2014-2015, Texas justices of the peace, acting as magistrates, conducted 1,183 examining trials statewide.[87] In 2015, the State filed 196,316 new felony offenses; this number does not account for felony cases pending when the year began. Though the time frames for these statistics vary slightly, the numbers reflect that just over one-half of 1 percent of defendants proceed to an examining trial.

There are several plausible reasons why examining trials are so infrequently used across the State. First, probable cause determinations may be made by several individuals, eliminating the need for an examining trial. The magistrate may find probable cause following arrest, a prosecutor may assess probable cause at the time she accepts charges or drafts an arrest warrant, and the trial judge overseeing the defendant's case may assess probable cause at the defendant's first appearance in court. Thus, probable cause may have already been determined on multiple occasions by the time a defendant requests an examining trial.

Second, bail is usually set at the time of arrest or when the magistrate arraigns the defendant.[88] This too lessens the need for the examining trial. Third, courts at all levels are busier than ever before. Judges do not want to have unnecessary or duplicative proceedings. Fourth, prosecutors do not like examining trials for the informal discovery they provide. Fifth, defense attorneys do not want their clients testifying, which could be used against them by the prosecutor or as impeachment evidence at trial. While none of these reasons diminish the defendant's right to have an examining trial, they explain why the procedure is unpopular. Finally, many district attorney offices quickly indict cases; this practice eliminates the defendant's right to

---

[87] Justice Courts Activity Detail, 3 (2016), available at http://www.txcourts.gov/media/1252949/3-Justice_Court_Activity_Detail-2015.pdf.

[88] See TEX. CODE CRIM. PROC. ANN. arts. 14.06, 15.17, and 17.033 (West 2016).

have an examining trial.[89] For all of these reasons and more, examining trials will likely continue to be infrequently used.

———————◆———————

The Examining Trial Procedure

Upon arrest, the magistrate must inform the defendant that he has the right to an examining trial.[90] Only defendants charged with felony offenses have a right to an examining trial.[91] At the examining trial, witnesses are called to testify. If a witness is unavailable, a magistrate may postpone the examining trial at the request of either party.[92]

If the defendant wants to testify, he may do so voluntarily (he may not be compelled to testify), but the magistrate must provide warnings to the accused before the witnesses testify.[93] He must be warned that (1) he has a right to make a statement about the charges made against him, (2) he cannot be compelled to make a statement, but (3) if he does make a statement, it may be used as evidence against him.[94] The accused must also offer his testimony before any other witness testifies.[95] If he does not want to be under oath, he may write out his testimony and sign it; his testimony need not be sworn.[96]

All of the witnesses must testify in the presence of the defendant, and they may be questioned on both direct or cross examination by both the prosecutor and the defense attorney.[97] As in a jury trial, the defendant retains his right to confront the witnesses against him. Likewise, the same rules of evidence that apply to a regular trial apply to an examining trial.[98] For

---

[89] The right to an examining trial terminates upon the return of an indictment. See *White v. State,* 576 S.W.2d 843, 844 (Tex. Crim. App. 1979); TEX. CRIM. PROC. CODE ANN. art. 16.01 (West 2016).

[90] TEX. CODE CRIM. PROC. ANN. art. 15.17 (West 2016).

[91] TEX. CODE CRIM. PROC. ANN. art. 16.01 (West 2016).

[92] TEX. CODE CRIM. PROC. ANN. arts. 16.02 and 16.14 (West 2016).

[93] TEX. CODE CRIM. PROC. ANN. art. 16.03 (West 2016).

[94] *Id.*

[95] TEX. CODE CRIM. PROC. ANN. art. 16.04 (West 2016).

[96] *Id.*

[97] TEX. CODE CRIM. PROC. ANN. arts. 16.06 and 16.08 (West 2016).

[98] TEX. CODE CRIM. PROC. ANN. art. 16.07 (West 2016).

example, hearsay would not be admissible at a jury trial, so it would not be admissible during the examining trial.

———————————◆———————————

Waiving or Losing the Right to an Examining Trial

The accused may also waive her right to an examining trial. She can do this by failing to request one or by making an untimely request.[99] Unless the defendant or her attorney requests an examining trial before the grand jury returns an indictment, she waives the right to have one.[100] "The return of a true bill by the grand jury satisfies the principal purpose and justification for [the examining trial:] that there is probable cause to believe the accused committed the crime charged."[101]

———————————◆———————————

Practice Questions

Grand jury questions appear with regularity on bar exams. While some bar exams have no grand jury questions, most have at least one, and some have as many as three. These questions are among the most varied. Grand jury questions tend to take slightly different forms each time they are asked.

Examining trial questions, on the other hand, are asked on nearly half of all bar exams. These questions typically ask the examinee to explain the purposes for an examining trial, the evidentiary rules that apply to examining trials, or to determine, based upon a fact pattern, whether a person has waived the right to have an examining trial.

Grand Jury Questions

1. (J-2016, F-2013, and J-2010) Defendant believes the police misinterpreted what happened in his case. He insists on being heard by the grand jury.

———————————

[99] *Markle v. State*, 715 S.W.2d 113, 114 (Tex. App.—Texarkana 1986, pet. ref'd).
[100] *Id.*
[101] *Manning v. State*, 681 S.W.2d 792, 793 (Tex. App.—Houston [14th Dist.] 1984, no pet.).

Does he have this right? Can he also demand that his defense attorney be there to give him advice on how to answer questions? Explain.

_____

_____

_____

_____

_____

2. (J-2016) During deliberations, two grand jurors begin to argue about the facts of a case. They call for Prosecutor to come in and determine who is right.

Is Prosecutor permitted by law to mediate the dispute under these circumstances?

_____

_____

_____

_____

_____

3. (F-2016, J-2013, and J-2009) Describe how grand jurors are selected.

_____

_____

_____

_____

_____

4. (J-2015, J-2012, and F-2008) Defendant is charged with committing a crime against Mayor's mother. Mayor is attempting to influence who sits on the grand jury that hears Defendant's case.

What, if any, procedural step can you take given these facts and when must you take it? Explain.

_____

_____

_____

_____

_____

5. (F-2015, J-2010, and J-2004) Can Defendant waive a grand jury indictment? If so, how? Are there any exceptions?

_____

_____

_____

_____

_____

6. (F-2015 and F-2004) Can Judge compel a reluctant witness to answer questions before the grand jury, and if so, what is the process? What, if any, rights does that witness have?

_____

_____

_____

_____

_____

7. (J-2014) Name three, non-grand-jury participants who may be present in the room with the grand jurors before they deliberate.

_____

_____

_____

_____

_____

8. (J-2014 and J-2011) How many jurors serve on a grand jury? What number must agree to indict a defendant? Who drafts the indictment? Explain.

_____

_____

_____

_____

9. (F-2014 and J-2013) If the defendant agrees to cooperate with the prosecutor and testify before the grand jury, who may question him when he appears before the grand jury?

_____

_____

_____

_____

_____

10. (F-2014 and J-2008) Prosecutor has asked Defendant to cooperate by testifying before the grand jury.

Name three warnings Defendant must be given before he testifies.

_____

_____

_____

_____

_____

11. (F-2013) Under what circumstances may a party discover the grand jurors' names and personal contact information?

_____

_____

_____

_____

_____

12. (F-2013) What is the procedure Prosecutors must follow when presenting cases to grand juries?

_____

_____

_____

_____

_____

13. (F-2011) After the grand jury is selected, the grand jurors seek legal advice from Prosecutor about how to proceed in their investigation of Defendant. Prosecutor counsels them.

Did the grand jurors break the law by asking Prosecutor for legal advice? Explain.

_____

_____

_____

_____

_____

14. (J-2009 and J-2005) Is Defendant permitted discovery of grand jury transcriptions pretrial? If so, what must he prove in order to receive them? Explain.

_____

_____

_____

_____

_____

15. (F-2007, J-2006, F-2004, and F-2002) Defendant does not want to testify before the grand jury.

If the grand jury nevertheless desires to hear Defendant's side of the story, can it compel him to appear? What rights, if any, does Defendant have in this situation? Explain.

_____

_____

_____

_____

_____

16. (F-2004) Officers in Denton County are aware of a drug ring in the area. However, they have not been able to determine its whereabouts. After a routine traffic stop, police discover a large amount of narcotics on Snitch, who tells them she is part of the ring and will reveal her supplier if she is given immunity. Snitch leads police to your client, Defendant, alleging he is her supplier of drugs. The grand jury is now considering an indictment against Defendant.

If Snitch testifies before the grand jury, does she have any rights or obligations regarding her appearance?

_____

_____

_____

_____

_____

17. (F-2001) Is there any situation that would permit you to appear before the grand jury and present evidence on Defendant's behalf? Explain.

_____

_____

_____

_____

_____

Examining Trial Questions

18. (J-2016, J-2014, and F-2011) At Defendant's examining trial, Prosecutor calls Witness to testify. You object to a hearsay statement Witness makes; Prosecutor replies, "Evidentiary rules do not apply to examining trials." Later, when you request to cross examine Witness, Prosecutor objects, stating: "This is not a jury trial, Your Honor, so Defense Counsel is not permitted to cross-examine Witness."

How should Judge rule on both of these issues? Explain.

_____

_____

_____

_____

_____

19. (F-2016) List three rights that Defendant has at his examining trial.

_____

_____

_____

_____

_____

20. (F-2015, F-2014, J-2007, F-2005, F-2004, J-2003, J-2002, and J-2000)
    Defendant's bail is so high he cannot bond out of jail. He asks you to get
    his bail reduced. In the meantime, the grand jury indicts Defendant. You
    request an examining trial.

    What is the purpose of an examining trial? Explain whether Defendant is
    entitled to an examining trial under these circumstances.

    _____

    _____

    _____

    _____

    _____

21. (J-2013) What warning(s) must Judge give Defendant before any
    witnesses testify at his examining trial?

    _____

    _____

    _____

    _____

    _____

22. (J-2012) The jailors leave Defendant at the jail instead of bringing him to
    observe his own examining trial.

    Can Magistrate conduct the examining trial without Defendant being
    present? Explain.

    _____

    _____

    _____

    _____

    _____

23. (J-2012 and F-2008) As Defendant's attorney, you request an examining
    trial. Defendant wants to make a voluntary statement but does not want
    to be placed under oath.

Is Defendant permitted to give an unsworn statement at the examining trial?

_____

_____

_____

_____

_____

24. (J-2011) Defendant tells you, after his initial appearance, that his arrest was due to a mistake on the law enforcement officers' part. He says he heard from someone in jail that there is a procedure where the judge can dismiss the case against him early in the criminal justice process.

    Is Defendant permitted to have the judge assess the truth of the accusation made against him? If so, what is the procedure, and what determination will be made? Explain.

_____

_____

_____

_____

_____

Note: This question is problematic. There is no procedure that would allow a judge to dismiss a charge for this reason. The bar examiner comments indicate they expected examinees to discuss the purpose of and judicial findings following an examining trial or other procedures that would result in some judicial review of the underlying charge. None, however, would result in the judge dismissing the charge. The only party who can dismiss a charge is the State; however, if the judge finds no probable cause, the State has no choice but to dismiss the case.

25. (F-2008) During Prosecutor's direct examination of Deputy at Defendant's examining trial, she testifies she cannot remember what Defendant was wearing when he fled from the scene of the crime. Before Defendant's jury trial, Deputy retires and moves out of state.

Can you introduce Deputy's examining trial testimony into evidence at the jury trial, and if so, under what conditions?

_____

_____

_____

_____

_____

26. (J-2005) Which courts have jurisdiction to hold examining trials? If Defendant chooses to make a voluntary statement at his examining trial, when must he do so?

_____

_____

_____

_____

_____

———————◆———————

Chapter 7
Pretrial Matters

Introduction

After a defendant has been charged with a crime and arrested, he will begin appearing in court until his case is resolved either through dismissal, a guilty plea, or a trial. The defendant may make several appearances in court while his case is pending. The defendant's case is set on a court's docket, and it may reappear periodically until final resolution. Judges and attorneys may refer to these appearances as *settings*.

Much is going on behind the scenes during these settings. The prosecutor may be calling witnesses to gather more facts, waiting on toxicology reports, or evaluating the case for trial. The defendant may be weighing the plea offer or building his defense. The defense attorney may be investigating her client's case or requesting settings to give the defendant time to pay her legal fees. Because everyone is working on multiple cases, and resolving legal matters take time, the prosecutor, defense counsel, and judge will typically agree to multiple settings, or resets.

Judges employ staff who coordinate these resets and manage their dockets. The court clerk keeps a record of these settings, and bondsmen guarantee the defendant will appear in court for each setting. During these settings, attorneys may file motions, invoke rights, or raise concerns. This chapter will discuss several issues that may be raised before trial and the documents filed during this stage. This chapter will discuss the right to counsel, statute of limitations, competency, insanity, subpoenas, continuances, and judicial recusal.

———————————◆———————————

Right to Counsel

Defendants have a federal and state constitutional right to assistance of counsel at critical stages of the criminal process.[1] "Whether a particular stage is critical turns on an assessment of the usefulness of counsel to the accused at that time."[2] The well-known federal case on this issue, *Gideon v. Wainwright*, explains the Sixth Amendment right to counsel.

Clarence Earl Gideon v. Wainwright
372 U.S. 335 (1963)

Petitioner was charged in a Florida state court with having broken and entered a poolroom with intent to commit a misdemeanor. This offense is a felony under Florida law. Appearing in court without funds and without a lawyer, petitioner asked the court to appoint counsel for him, whereupon the following colloquy took place:

> The COURT: Mr. Gideon, I am sorry, but I cannot appoint Counsel to represent you in this case. Under the laws of the State of Florida, the only time the Court can appoint Counsel to represent a Defendant is when that person is charged with a capital offense. I am sorry, but I will have to deny your request to appoint Counsel to defend you in this case.

---

[1] *Upton v. State*, 853 S.W.2d 548, 553 (Tex. Crim. App. 1993); U.S. CONST. amend. VI; TEX. CONST. art. I, §10.
[2] *Massingill v. State*, 8 S.W.3d 733, 736 (Tex. App.—Austin 1999, no pet.).

The DEFENDANT: The United States Supreme Court says I am entitled to be represented by Counsel.

Put to trial before a jury, Gideon conducted his defense about as well as could be expected from a layman. He made an opening statement to the jury, cross-examined the State's witnesses, presented witnesses in his own defense, declined to testify himself, and made a short argument "emphasizing his innocence to the charge contained in the Information filed in this case." The jury returned a verdict of guilty, and petitioner was sentenced to serve five years in the state prison. Later, petitioner filed in the Florida Supreme Court this habeas corpus petition attacking his conviction and sentence on the ground that the trial court's refusal to appoint counsel for him denied him rights "guaranteed by the Constitution and the Bill of Rights by the United States Government."

The Sixth Amendment provides, "In all criminal prosecutions, the accused shall enjoy the right ... to have the Assistance of Counsel for his defence." We have construed this to mean that in federal courts counsel must be provided for defendants unable to employ counsel unless the right is competently and intelligently waived....

[I]n our adversary system of criminal justice, any person haled into court, who is too poor to hire a lawyer, cannot be assured a fair trial unless counsel is provided for him. This seems to us to be an obvious truth. Governments, both state and federal, quite properly spend vast sums of money to establish machinery to try defendants accused of crime. Lawyers to prosecute are everywhere deemed essential to protect the public's interest in an orderly society. Similarly, there are few defendants charged with crime, few indeed, who fail to hire the best lawyers they can get to prepare and present their defenses. That government hires lawyers to prosecute and defendants who have the money hire lawyers to defend are the strongest indications of the wide-spread belief that lawyers in criminal courts are necessities, not luxuries. The right of one charged with crime to counsel may not be deemed fundamental and essential to fair trials in some countries, but it is in ours. From the very beginning, our state and national constitutions and laws have laid great emphasis on procedural and substantive safeguards designed to assure fair trials before impartial tribunals in which every defendant stands equal before the law. This noble ideal cannot be realized if the poor man charged with crime has to face his accusers without a lawyer to assist him. A defendant's need for a lawyer is nowhere better stated than in the moving words of Mr. Justice Sutherland in *Powell v. Alabama*:

> The right to be heard would be, in many cases, of little avail if it did not comprehend the right to be heard by counsel. Even the intelligent and educated layman has small and sometimes no skill in the science of law. If charged with crime, he is incapable, generally, of determining for himself whether the indictment is good or bad. He is unfamiliar with the rules of evidence. Left without the aid of counsel he may be put on trial without a proper charge, and convicted upon incompetent evidence, or evidence irrelevant to the issue or otherwise inadmissible. He lacks both the skill and knowledge adequately to prepare his defense, even though he have a perfect one. He requires the guiding hand of counsel at every step in the proceedings against him. Without it, though he be not guilty, he faces the danger of conviction because he does not know how to establish his innocence.[3]

…The judgment is reversed and the cause is remanded to the Supreme Court of Florida for further action not inconsistent with this opinion.

———————◆———————

Notes and Questions

1. The *Gideon* Court concluded that the Sixth Amendment right to counsel was applicable to the states via the Fourteenth Amendment.[4] Thus, states and judges must ensure that when an offense is jailable, and the defendant cannot afford to hire his own attorney, counsel is appointed. In Texas, a criminal defendant is entitled to appointed counsel if he is indigent and is charged with any jailable offense, which is any offense other than a Class C misdemeanor.[5]

2. Clarence Gideon asked for a lawyer because he could not afford one. However, some defendants choose to represent themselves regardless of whether they are able to hire a lawyer. "[A] trial court may not force an accused to accept an attorney if he wishes to waive representation and defend himself."[6] Most judges will discourage a defendant who works *pro se*

---

[3] *Powell v. Alabama*, 287 U.S. 45, 68-69 (1932).
[4] *Gideon v. Wainwright*, 372 U.S. 335, 343 (1963).
[5] TEX. CODE CRIM. PROC. ANN. art. 26.04(b)(3) (West 2016).
[6] *Ex Parte Bain*, 568 S.W.2d 356, 361 (Tex. Crim. App. 1978).

(Latin for "on behalf of themselves"). Ultimately, however, a defendant has the right to defend himself. Nevertheless, *pro se* defendants rarely fare well in court against a law-trained adversary, nor do they understand the law or legal procedures required to master litigation. Clarence Gideon, though convicted by the jury, should have had some satisfaction that the United States Supreme Court said that he "conducted his defense about as well as could be expected from a layman."

---◆---

Duties of Appointed Counsel

When a defendant has satisfied the Court that he cannot afford to hire an attorney—by filling out paperwork related to his income and finances—the Court must appoint counsel to represent him. The Code permits judges to monitor and exercise authority over the attorneys they appoint.[7]

Appointed counsel is perceived by society at large as a lesser attorney who is less zealous and not as capable as hired counsel. In some instances, this may be true, but many appointed counsel in Texas are excellent attorneys who are more qualified than their hired counterparts. In fact, some counties require appointed attorneys or public defenders to have years of experience, a significant number of trials, and pass a difficult exam before they are appointable. There is no comparable standard for hired defense counsel; they may represent a defendant on a serious charge or a complicated case even when they are inexperienced or lack a proper work ethic to carry out the task.

Judges in Texas are required to create countywide procedures for the appointment of counsel in indigent cases.[8] The procedures are supposed to ensure that criminal defendants meet with counsel before judicial proceedings begin, attorneys perform their jobs well, and appointments be "allocated among qualified attorneys in a manner that is fair, neutral, and nondiscriminatory."[9]

---

[7] TEX. CODE CRIM. PROC. ANN. art. 26.04 (West 2016).
[8] *Id.*
[9] TEX. CODE CRIM. PROC. ANN. art. 26.04(b)(3), (5), and (6) (West 2016).

While the judge has an obligation to ensure qualified attorneys are appointed in a fair and neutral way, the appointed attorney likewise has legal obligations. The Code states appointed counsel shall:

1. make every reasonable effort to contact the defendant not later than the end of the first working day after the date on which the attorney is appointed and to interview the defendant as soon as practicable after the attorney is appointed;

2. represent the defendant until charges are dismissed, the defendant is acquitted, appeals are exhausted, or the attorney is permitted or ordered by the court to withdraw as counsel for the defendant after a finding of good cause is entered on the record;

3. with respect to a defendant not represented by other counsel, before withdrawing as counsel for the defendant after a trial or the entry of a plea of guilty ... advise the defendant of the defendant's right to file a motion for new trial and a notice of appeal[,] . . . assist the defendant in requesting the prompt appointment of replacement counsel; and . . . if replacement counsel is not appointed promptly and the defendant wishes to pursue an appeal, file a timely notice of appeal.[10]

The judge may remove appointed counsel from the case for failing to meet with his client as required in subsection (1) above.[11] Judges may remove an attorney who is a repeat offender from the county appointment list altogether.[12] Judges must be careful not to remove an attorney over the objection of the defendant for anything other than a failure to meet the statutory expectations set out above:

> Although an indigent defendant does not have the right to counsel of his own choosing, once counsel is appointed, the trial judge is obliged to respect the attorney-client relationship created through the appointment. The attorney-client relationship between appointed counsel and an indigent defendant is no less inviolate than if counsel is retained. There must be some principled reason, apparent from the record, to justify a trial judge's *sua sponte* replacement of appointed counsel under these circumstances.[13]

---

[10] TEX. CODE CRIM. PROC. ANN. art. 26.04(j)(1)-(4) (West 2016).
[11] TEX. CODE CRIM. PROC. ANN. art. 26.04(k) (West 2016).
[12] *Id.*
[13] *Buntion v. Harmon*, 827 S.W.2d 945, 949 (Tex. Crim. App. 1992).

The entire article that governs the appointment process, appointed counsel's obligations, and removal of appointed counsel for failure to timely meet and investigate the defendant's case is limited to appointed, not retained counsel.[14] Thus, judges do not have the legal authority to remove a hired attorney who fails to meet the expectations of appointed attorneys set out in the Code.

Experts and Investigators for Indigent Defendants

In the course of representing a defendant who wants a trial, an attorney may recognize the need to hire an investigator or expert. Investigators are particularly useful in tracking down witnesses, scouring through police records, and piecing together evidence. An expert is particularly useful in cases involving forensic evidence and scientific or medical testimony. An expert may not only testify about these issues at trial but may help defense counsel cross-examine the State's expert witnesses. In other words, investigators and experts help the defense attorney do his job better.

Investigators and experts need to be paid for their services. How does a defendant who is indigent afford to pay them? The State of Texas permits indigent defendants funds to hire investigators or experts, so long as the fees are reasonable, and the court approves the expense.[15] An appointed attorney who needs an investigator or an expert must make a request to the trial court by filing a motion for an investigator or a motion for expert assistance.

Defendants may need investigators and experts to build a meaningful defense. "[A]n indigent [defendant] is entitled to 'meaningful access to justice', which means that he should have 'access to the raw materials integral to the building of an effective defense', thus ensuring 'a proper functioning of the adversary process.'"[16] When a defendant is denied a defense due to a court's refusal to pay for investigators or experts, it raises due process concerns. In a case where the defendant requested a psychiatrist to aid in his defense and was denied one, the Court of Criminal Appeals stated:

---

[14] *Harville v. State*, 591 S.W.2d 864, 869 (Tex. Crim. App. 1978); *Banks v. State*, 494 S.W.2d 839, 840 (Tex. Crim. App. 1973).

[15] TEX. CODE CRIM. PROC. ANN. art. 26.05(a) and (h) (West 2016).

[16] *Williams v. State*, 958 S.W.2d 186, 192 (Tex. Crim. App. 1997) (quoting *Rey v. State*, 897 S.W.2d 333, 337 (Tex. Crim. App. 1995)).

In an adversarial system, due process requires at least a reasonably level playing field at trial. In the present context that means more than just an examination by a "neutral" psychiatrist. It also means the appointment of a psychiatrist to provide technical assistance to the accused, to help evaluate the strength of his defense, to offer his own expert diagnosis at trial if it is favorable to that defense, and to identify the weaknesses in the State's case, if any, by testifying himself and/or preparing counsel to cross-examine opposing experts.[17]

A defendant making a motion for expert assistance is entitled, upon request, to make his motion *ex parte* (without the prosecutor present) so that she is not in the position of revealing her defensive theories to the State.[18]

---◆---

Pretrial Hearings

Assume in a hypothetical case that the defendant is indigent, he has been appointed counsel, and his case is currently pending before a felony district court. The defendant wants to plead not guilty and requests a jury trial. Before the trial date, the Judge may set his case for a pretrial hearing.[19] This hearing is designed to resolve evidentiary, administrative, and procedural matters before the case proceeds to trial. The issues addressed at this hearing concern motions and pleadings.

The defendant, the defendant's attorney, and the State must appear at the place and on the date the court orders for the hearing.[20] The defendant is required to attend any and all pretrial hearings.[21] The trial court can give notice of the hearing by announcing it in open court with defense counsel and the defendant present, by personal service, or by mail.[22]

The pretrial hearing shall address the following matters:

- Arraignment, if necessary;
- Appointment of counsel, if necessary;

---

[17] *DeFreece v. State*, 848 S.W.2d 150, 159 (Tex. Crim. App. 1993).
[18] *Id.* at 194.
[19] TEX. CODE CRIM. PROC. ANN. art. 28.01 §1 (West 2016).
[20] *Id.*
[21] *Id.*
[22] TEX. CODE CRIM. PROC. ANN. art. 28.01 §2 (West 2016).

- Pleadings of the defendant;
    - A plea of guilty, not guilty, or no contest;
    - An application for probation;
    - Trial election (whether the trial will be before the judge or the jury and which of these two will assess punishment); and
    - Any other motions or pleadings to be filed.[23]
- Special pleas;
    - Double jeopardy[24]
- Challenges to the form or substance of the indictment;
- Motions for continuance, if known;
- Motions to suppress evidence;
- Motions for change of venue;
- Motions for discovery;
- Entrapment as a defense; and
- Motions for the appointment of an interpreter.[25]

This list is not exhaustive. Any number of motions or other administrative issues that need to be addressed before the trial date could or should be raised at the pretrial hearing. For example, defendants planning on raising insanity as a defense should file a motion 20 days before trial, but if the court sets a pretrial hearing, the defendant is required to give the State notice of its intent to raise insanity as a defense during the pretrial hearing.[26]

The Code requires that the Court give the parties ten days' notice to raise and file pleadings, and it also requires the pleadings be filed seven days before the hearing.[27] When the court complies with the required ten days' notice, any matters not raised at the pretrial hearing or filed within seven days prior to the hearing will not be permitted to be raised or filed unless the court excused the party's lateness for good cause shown.[28] In this way, the

---

[23] TEX. CODE CRIM. PROC. ANN. art. 27.02 (West 2016).
[24] TEX. CODE CRIM. PROC. ANN. arts. 27.02(2) and 27.05 (West 2016).
[25] *Id.*
[26] TEX. CODE CRIM. PROC. ANN. art. 46C.051(c) (West 2016).
[27] TEX. CODE CRIM. PROC. ANN. art. 28.01 §2 (West 2016).
[28] *Id.*

court maintains some discretion over late filings or issues raised after the pretrial hearing.[29]

The defendant not only has a right to be present at the hearing but to testify as well.[30] The defendant's testimony at the hearing cannot be used against her at trial.[31] This is because the testimony at the pretrial hearing is limited to the issues raised at the hearing and cannot be used to violate the defendant's Fifth Amendment right against self-incrimination at trial.[32] However, if the defendant makes inconsistent statements at the hearing and trial, her pretrial testimony can be used to impeach her at trial.[33]

Also, cross-examination at a hearing is limited to the matters raised by the testimony offered at the hearing.[34] For example, a motion to suppress hearing is limited to the suppression issues raised by defense counsel in the motion and testified to by the defense witnesses. This means the prosecutor may be prohibited from asking questions of the witnesses that would otherwise be permissible questions to ask at trial.

----------◆----------

[29] *Saathoff v. State*, 908 S.W.2d 523, 525 (Tex. App.—San Antonio 1995, no pet.).
[30] TEX. CODE CRIM. PROC. ANN. art. 28.01 §1 (West 2016).
[31] *Nelson v. State*, 765 S.W.2d 401, 402-03 (Tex. Crim. App. 1989).
[32] *Franklin v. State*, 606 S.W.2d 818, 825 (Tex. Crim. App. 1978); *Williams v. State*, 607 S.W.2d 577, 579 (Tex. Crim. App. 1980). The defendant's Fifth Amendment rights are discussed in more detail in the Chapter 12.
[33] *Castillo v. State*, 899 S.W.2d 391, 395 (Tex. App.—Houston [14th Dist.] 1995, no pet.); *Manns v. State*, 122 S.W.3d 171, 192 (Tex. Crim. App. 2003) (the impeachment exception "'leaves defendants free to testify truthfully on their own behalf; they can offer probative and exculpatory evidence to the jury without opening the door to impeachment by carefully avoiding any statements that directly contradict the suppressed evidence'") (quoting *James v. Illinois*, 493 U.S. 307, 314 (1990)).
[34] *Franklin v. State*, 606 S.W.2d 818, 825 (Tex. Crim. App. 1978) ("When the appellant testified for limited purposes at the pretrial hearings the State was properly restricted in its interrogation and cross-examination of the appellant").

Statutes of Limitations

While statutes of limitations could be addressed within the charging instruments chapter, the time to raise an issue related to the timing of the charge is at the pretrial hearing. Therefore, statutes of limitations will be discussed in this chapter.

The primary reason for statutes of limitations is to discourage litigation of stale claims. These statutes encourage parties to investigate and try cases promptly, while evidence is fresh. Most prosecutors dislike trying older cases because an older case, by virtue of its staleness, may produce reasonable doubt. Listed below are the statutes of limitations in Texas.[35]

Offense category	Limitation Period
Any kind of murder, manslaughter, aggravated sexual assault, sexual offenses against children, hit and run fatalities, and human sexual trafficking of children and minors	No limitation
Probate theft, public servant theft, forgery, elder abuse, rape, arson, human trafficking of adults, and forced prostitution	10 years
Financial crimes, Medicaid fraud, and bigamy	7 years
Theft, robbery, kidnapping, burglary, child abandonment or endangerment, and insurance fraud	5 years
Sexual performance of a child, kidnapping of a child, and burglary where the intent was to commit a crime against a child	20 years from the victim's 18th birthday
Human labor trafficking of children, injury to children, compelling prostitution of children, and bigamy where the spouse was a minor at the time of marriage	10 years from the victim's 18th birthday
All other felonies not mentioned above	3 years
All misdemeanor offenses	2 years

---

[35] TEX. CODE CRIM. PROC. ANN. arts. 12.01, 12.02, and 12.03 (West 2016).

Unless otherwise stated above, for attempted crimes, conspiracy to commit crimes, criminal solicitation, or aggravated crimes, the limitations period is the same as for the offense the person was trying to commit.[36]

To calculate time, you must determine the date when all elements for the crime were completed and the date when the indictment or information was acted upon and received or filed in court.[37] You then consider the time between those two dates to determine whether the statute of limitations has run.[38] For example, if the crime is a misdemeanor offense, and the time between the date when the crime was completed and the date when the information was filed in court is less than two years, the statute of limitation has not run, and the offense may be prosecuted.

Mental Competency

All defendants have the right to be competent throughout the criminal justice process.[39] The Code deems a person incompetent if he does not have (1) "sufficient present ability to consult with [his] lawyer with a reasonable degree of rational understanding" or (2) "a rational as well as factual understanding of the proceedings against" him.[40] The Code states, "A defendant is presumed competent to stand trial and shall be found competent to stand to trial unless proved incompetent by a preponderance of the evidence."[41] The defendant bears the burden of proof.[42]

While the defendant is the one who must prove he is incompetent to stand trial, any number of persons may develop and raise competency concerns about a particular defendant. Defense counsel may question competency after the initial interview, the prosecutor may question it after reading the offense report, or the magistrate may develop concerns during arraignment. Mentally ill persons who regularly cycle in and out of jail are often identified by jailers following arrest. Any and all of these people may

---

[36] TEX. CODE CRIM. PROC. ANN. art. 12.03 (West 2016).
[37] TEX. CODE CRIM. PROC. ANN. art. 12.04, 12.06, and 12.07 (West 2016).
[38] TEX. CODE CRIM. PROC. ANN. art. 12.04 (West 2016).
[39] *Casey v. State*, 924 S.W.2d 946, 948-49 (Tex. Crim. App. 1996).
[40] TEX. CODE CRIM. PROC. ANN. art. 46B.003 (West 2016).
[41] TEX. CODE CRIM. PROC. ANN. art. 46B.003(b) (West 2016).
[42] *Hall v. State*, 160 S.W.3d 24, 38 (Tex. Crim. App. 2004).

bring issues of mental competency to the trial court's attention. As soon as the judge is made aware of these concerns, she must conduct an informal investigation looking for evidence of incompetency.[43] "A suggestion of incompetency is the threshold requirement for an informal inquiry … and may consist solely of a representation from any credible source that the defendant may be incompetent."[44]

Once the judge determines there is evidence of mental incompetence, the judge must halt proceedings and order a mental competency evaluation of the defendant.[45] Evaluations are done by qualified psychologists or psychiatrists who work for the county or in the jail, but they may be performed by an expert of the defendant's choosing.[46] The evaluation is often completed before the next court setting. The evaluation will either conclude that the defendant is incompetent or meets the competency standard.

After the defendant has been evaluated, the court is statutorily required to hold a competency hearing (which is like a mini-trial), unless neither attorney requests a hearing, the attorneys do not oppose a judicial finding of incompetence, or the judge does not believe a hearing is necessary.[47] The defendant has a right to counsel before any evaluation or proceeding where competency will be determined[48] and the right to a jury trial on the issue of competency, if requested.[49] When competence becomes an issue after the defendant's trial has begun, the court may inquire into competence at any time before sentencing.[50]

Once a person is deemed incompetent to stand trial, the State may attempt to restore the person's competency; the State may commit the defendant to the State mental hospital or similar facility for 60 days in misdemeanor cases or 120 days in felony cases.[51] The State may also choose to dismiss the case.[52]

---

[43] TEX. CODE CRIM. PROC. ANN. art. 46B.004(a)-(c)(1) (West 2016).

[44] TEX. CODE CRIM. PROC. ANN. art. 46B.004(c)(1) (West 2016).

[45] TEX. CODE CRIM. PROC. ANN. arts. 46B.004(d) and 46B.005(a) (West 2016).

[46] TEX. CODE CRIM. PROC. ANN. arts. 46B.021 and 46B.022 (West 2016).

[47] TEX. CODE CRIM. PROC. ANN. art. 46B.005(c) (West 2016).

[48] TEX. CODE CRIM. PROC. ANN. art. 46B.006 (West 2016).

[49] TEX. CODE CRIM. PROC. ANN. art. 46B.051 (West 2016).

[50] TEX. CODE CRIM. PROC. ANN. art. 46B.005(d) (West 2016).

[51] TEX. CODE CRIM. PROC. ANN. art. 46B.073 (West 2016).

[52] TEX. CODE CRIM. PROC. ANN. art. 46B.004(e) (West 2016).

Competency restoration is often accomplished through therapy and medication, and in many cases, an indigent defendant remains incarcerated in the local jail until a bed at one of the State hospitals becomes available. Defendants may remain on bond or receive a bond while they are awaiting restoration.[53] In many cases, one restoration period and the treatment the defendant receives during that period is enough to restore competency. The defendant will return to court, and if deemed competent, the proceedings against the defendant will resume.[54] However, mental health professionals may need more time. It is permissible for the trial court to order subsequent competency commitments.[55]

Any time the defendant spends in jail or in the State hospital awaiting competency restoration is credited to her sentence; she cannot remain in custody regaining mental competency past the maximum sentence she could have received had she been convicted of the charged crime.[56] In rare cases, a defendant may never regain competency. In this instance, prosecutors may be forced to dismiss the defendant's case; if the prosecutor refuses to dismiss the case, the judge may be required to continue to preside over the stayed charge and continue to have jurisdiction over the defendant indefinitely.

———————◆———————

Insanity

You likely learned about the insanity defense in your criminal law class as a first-year law student. You may have examined the defense's history, its development, the Model Penal Code insanity defense, or the common law insanity defense. If you have not learned about it already, it is important that you understand the Texas insanity defense.

The Texas Penal Code states:

> (a) It is an affirmative defense to prosecution that, at the time of the conduct charged, the actor, as a result of severe mental disease or defect, did not know that his conduct was wrong.

---

[53] TEX. CODE CRIM. PROC. ANN. arts. 46B.023 and 46B.072 (West 2016).
[54] TEX. CODE CRIM. PROC. ANN. art. 46B.084 (West 2016).
[55] TEX. CODE CRIM. PROC. ANN. art. 46B.084 et. seq. (West 2016).
[56] TEX. CODE CRIM. PROC. ANN. art. 46B.0095 (West 2016).

(b) The term "mental disease or defect" does not include an abnormality manifested only by repeated criminal or otherwise antisocial conduct.[57]

Courts have interpreted the defense, as the next case illustrates. Pay particular attention to the applicable law section of the next opinion, which further defines the "did not know the conduct was wrong" language in the statute.

Con Manh Pham v. State
463 S.W.3d 660
(Tex. App.—Amarillo 2015, pet. ref'd)

Appellant, Con Manh Pham, appeals the trial court's judgment by which he was convicted of murder and sentenced to 30 years' imprisonment. On appeal, he challenges the legal and factual sufficiency of the jury's rejection of his insanity defense …. We will affirm.

The Day of the Murder

On the morning of September 10, 2010, Dinh Pham came to his church, Our Lady of Vietnam Church, to continue his volunteer work of painting areas of the church. Between 10:00 and 11:00 that morning, appellant, also a member of the congregation, came to the office of the church's pastor, Father John Tran Tinh, and asked for his prayers due to appellant's failing health. Appellant and Father John talked for about ten minutes; the two had what Father John described as a "very normal conversation."

At the suggestion of Father John, appellant joined Dinh in the church basement where Dinh was painting the children's Sunday school rooms. For some time, it seems, the two may have been painting together. However, at some point, the collaboration turned deadly. While the two men were in the basement together, appellant stabbed Dinh several times, sliced his throat, and placed his body on a piece of cardboard in a spread eagle-type pose. Then, appellant called 911 at approximately 1:30 in the afternoon.

Through a translator, the 911 operator was able to understand that there had been a stabbing at the Our Lady of Vietnam Church. The caller, identified as appellant, reported that another man had stabbed him and that

---

[57] TEX. PENAL CODE ANN. §8.01 (West 2011).

he had stabbed that man in return. Police were immediately dispatched to the church.

First to arrive was Corporal Darrell Roberts, who encountered appellant as he came out the side door of the church. Appellant was in a "distraught" state, flailing about and falling to the ground as he held his leg, which showed to have a small amount of blood on it. Roberts communicated as best he could with appellant for a moment, and appellant gestured to him in such a way as to direct Roberts's attention inside the church. Thinking that he was going inside to search for the suspect and that appellant was the apparent victim of the reported stabbing, Roberts went inside the church… [and eventually] discovered Dinh's body lying on the floor in the basement. Roberts radioed upstairs to several other officers who had, by then, responded to the location, indicating that appellant was now the suspect and should be detained. …

Appellant repeatedly reported … that Dinh had stabbed him, so appellant stabbed him back. During the time immediately after the murder, appellant never wavered from this self-defense scenario ….

Appellant's Behavior Leading up to the Murder

From the record, we learn that appellant has had a rather long history of suffering from mental illness. For many years, he was under the care of a doctor and was prescribed medications that would greatly improve his mental and physical well-being. … [A]ppellant stopped taking his medication in the months leading up to the murder and that, at the moment he stopped taking them, his mental and physical health began to deteriorate, a fact that family members noted.

Appellant's mother, Tran Dao, testified that her son … was not well and observed his increasingly erratic behavior. Dao described an incident during which appellant destroyed her couch with a hammer after explaining that he did not like it any longer …. She described him as looking very strange during that episode. She also described an incident during which appellant cut down a tree in her front yard despite her protests and despite the fact that there was nothing apparently wrong with the tree. … She also explained that appellant was afraid of something and, out of fear, covered over all the windows of her house with newspaper. Appellant told her that he was afraid someone would see him and do him harm. Appellant also installed a security camera in her home, but, when he suspected someone had tampered with it, he destroyed the camera by throwing it on the floor. Dao also testified as to appellant's obsession with washing his clothes repeatedly and his growing suspicion that someone—perhaps his brother and/or his wife—was poisoning his food. He would often refuse to eat and, as a result, grew thinner and weaker throughout the summer. Dao explained that when appellant was taking his medication, he looked healthier and acted normally, but, when he did not, he looked "very weird" and could not work.

On the morning of the murder, appellant came to Dao's house to drop off his son for her to watch while he went somewhere. Dao described him as looking "very sick and very weak" that morning. His behavior was "abnormal," and he told her he was going to go to the doctor. She encouraged him to begin taking his medication again.

Appellant's brother, Cang Pham, also testified that, when appellant would cease taking his medication, he would become ill and would often stay at the house with him and their mother. He, too, described appellant as "weak" and not doing well in the weeks before the murder. ... In fact, appellant's appearance and demeanor became so worrisome that Cang called the police to seek help in how to get appellant back on his medication. Either the police or another source directed Cang to application paperwork that would initiate a commitment proceeding by which appellant might be hospitalized. Shortly before the murder, Cang got the application, but, because of a language barrier, was unable to complete that application before the murder occurred. Cang also urged appellant to go back to his doctor who had been treating appellant's mental illness for years, but appellant refused. A month or two before the murder, Cang scheduled an appointment for appellant with a new doctor, but, again, appellant refused to go.

Appellant's wife, Minh Nguyen, ...testified that, after working at his job for over ten years, he quit in March 2010 but returned to that job in August 2010, weeks before the murder. His return to work served to accelerate his physical and mental deterioration, according to Nguyen. She testified that he slept very, very little, and, when he did sleep, he would wake up in the night to wash his feet, telling her that he felt like there was something inside them causing him to itch.

Much like appellant's mother, Nguyen reported a distinct difference between appellant's behavior and appearance when he was properly medicated and when he was not. She testified that he would wear scarves during the hot summer months before the murder. On a whim, he also took a trip to France in July 2010. Nguyen also noticed that appellant would repeatedly wash his clothes. Appellant would frequently hear people inside the house, which caused him a great deal of fear. He also voiced his suspicion to her that their next-door neighbors were hiding dead bodies in their garage.

She testified, too, that appellant … [had] become both verbally and physically abusive. …Nguyen called the police … to try to get … appellant back on his medication. Nguyen testified that appellant believed at times that she was poisoning his food; he would often refuse to eat and lost a lot of weight. The morning of the murder, appellant spoke with Nguyen about the poisoning and discussed divorce. Nguyen made clear that she thought her husband was mentally ill, characterizing him as "a sick man."

Expert Testimony on Appellant's State of Mind, Sanity

The trial court appointed Steven C. Schneider, Ph.D., a neuropsychologist, to conduct an examination on appellant to determine whether appellant was sane or insane at the time of the offense. Schneider examined appellant a little over a year after the incident, after appellant had been medicated. Schneider's testing revealed that appellant had "a significant executive function impairment" as evidenced by imaging of his brain's frontal lobe activity, an impairment which would result in him having less self-control. Based on this "severe frontal lobe impairment," Schneider testified that, unmedicated, appellant would likely experience "some tremendous confusion and distortion." Citing appellant's paranoid schizophrenia, his frontal lobe impairment, and appellant's explanation that he believed that Dinh was a demonic cannibal, Schneider concluded that, at the time of the offense, appellant was not able to distinguish right from wrong and was, therefore, legally insane. Schneider testified that appellant believed that Dinh was going to eat him and stabbed Dinh to prevent him from doing so. In an anachronistic narrative, appellant explained to Schneider why he thought Dinh was a cannibal: appellant saw Dinh the day after the murder when Dinh threw something—perhaps something resembling human remains—in the garbage can while drinking a beer. Schneider explained that, during the examination, the more lucid appellant, who did express remorse for the murder during the evaluation, was aware that his thoughts at the time were confused and disjointed.

Schneider discounted appellant's initial reports that he killed Dinh in self-defense—and his attendant silence regarding his suspicions that Dinh was a cannibal—as appellant's attempts to adjust his behavior and thought pattern to society's norms, to avoid a negative reaction to his suspicions. Schneider expressed a reluctance to interpret appellant's story immediately after the murder as indicative of appellant's ability to distinguish right from wrong. Schneider ... explained that a person suffering from mental illness will, at times, do appropriate things, often depending on their state of mind and level of psychological arousal at the time. Schneider also described some of appellant's bizarre behavior immediately after the incident as atypical for someone who felt guilt about his action, suggesting that appellant was not aware that killing Dinh was wrong.

The State hired its own expert: Dr. James Avery Rush IV, M.D., a psychiatrist, who agreed with Schneider that appellant was suffering from a mental illness, but expressly disagreed that appellant was unable to distinguish right from wrong. Unlike Schneider, Rush cited appellant's fabricated self-defense story and some of appellant's behavior prior to the murder as evidence that appellant knew that killing Dinh was wrong. Rush's conclusion, after reviewing the records, reports, and interviews and his examination of appellant approximately two and one-half years after the incident, was that appellant was sane at the time of the murder.

Rush testified that appellant reported to him that he killed Dinh because he thought Dinh was a cannibal and was going to kill children. Rush noted that nowhere, prior to his examination by Dr. Schneider, did appellant mention killing Dinh to prevent Dinh from cannibalizing anyone. Rush also explained that the fact that appellant called 911 after the killing demonstrated that he knew "something was wrong with what he had just done." In Rush's experience, had appellant been experiencing at the time of the murder the later-reported hallucinations that Dinh was a cannibal who was about to eat appellant, some manifestation of appellant's abnormal thinking and hallucinations of Dinh's [demon] possession and cannibalism would have been revealed the day of the murder or soon thereafter, indicating that an acutely psychotic person experiencing such thought patterns or hallucinations would not be able to suppress them for a sustained period in that situation. ... Ultimately, Rush agreed with Schneider that appellant was suffering from an active mental disease the day of the murder but disagreed that, as a result of that mental disease, appellant was unable to distinguish right from wrong.

By its guilty verdict, the jury rejected appellant's plea of insanity and, consistent with Rush's conclusions, impliedly found that appellant was sane at the time of the offense. ...

Appellant challenges the legal and factual sufficiency of the evidence to support the jury's rejection of his insanity defense, implied by its guilty verdict.

Applicable Law

...Texas law excuses a defendant from criminal responsibility if he proves, by a preponderance of the evidence, the affirmative defense of insanity. The insanity defense focuses on whether the accused understood the nature of his action and whether he knew he should not do it. The insanity defense excuses the person from criminal responsibility even though the State has proved every element of the offense, including the *mens rea*, beyond a reasonable doubt. "The test for determining insanity is whether, at the time of the conduct charged, the defendant—as a result of a severe mental disease or defect—did not know that his conduct was 'wrong.'"[58] Under Texas law, "wrong" in this context means "illegal." Thus, the question for deciding insanity becomes as follows: Does the defendant factually know that society considers this conduct against the law, even though the defendant, due to his mental disease or defect, may think that the conduct is morally justified? If the accused knows that his conduct is "illegal" by societal standards, then he understands that his conduct is wrong, even if, due to a mental disease or defect, he thinks his conduct is morally justified.

"There is a general presumption of sanity and the defendant bears the burden of proving, by a preponderance of the evidence, his insanity at the time of the conduct charged."[59] ... At trial, a defendant bears both the burden of production of evidence and the burden of persuasion for his affirmative defense of insanity. Ultimately, whether the defense of insanity was proved is a decision that lies within the province of the trier of fact, not only as to the credibility of witnesses and the weight of the evidence, but also as to the limits of the defense.

---

[58] *Ruffin v. State*, 270 S.W.3d 586, 592 (Tex. Crim. App. 2008).
[59] *Martinez v. State*, 867 S.W.2d 30, 33 (Tex. Crim. App. 1993).

...Appellant challenges the legal and factual sufficiency of the evidence to support the jury's implied rejection of his affirmative defense of insanity. ...

Analysis

Both experts agreed that appellant was suffering from a severe mental disease or defect at the time of the murder. The evidence certainly supports such a conclusion as well. Neither party challenges that aspect of the evidence. Resolution of appellant's issues will turn on evaluation of the evidence regarding appellant's ability, at the time of the murder, to distinguish right from wrong. One expert concluded that appellant was not able to make such a distinction as a result of his mental disease or defect; the other expert concluded that he was able to do so.

Having searched the record for evidence favorable to the jury's rejection of appellant's claim of insanity, we note Dr. Rush's testimony that certain behaviors preceding the murder and immediately after the murder, appellant's 911 call, his fabricated self-defense story, and his steadfast adherence to that story in the time immediately after the murder all suggest that, at the time he murdered Dinh, appellant was able to distinguish right from wrong. Having found some evidence to support the jury's implied finding that appellant was sane at the time of the murder, we must reject appellant's challenge to the legal sufficiency of the jury's finding.

We next review the factual sufficiency of the evidence to support the jury's finding by evaluating the entirety of the evidence in a neutral light. We have previously outlined in detail both doctors' bases for their conflicting conclusions regarding appellant's sanity at the time of the murder and note that the jury had before it the testimony of both doctors. Again, the determination of whether the insanity defense was proved lies within the province of the trier of fact. Remaining mindful that we are not to "usurp the function of the jury by substituting our judgment in place of the jury's assessment of the weight and credibility of the witnesses' testimony," we cannot state, based on the record before us, that the evidence contrary to the jury's finding so greatly outweighs the evidence supporting the verdict that the verdict is manifestly unjust, conscience-shocking, or clearly biased. We overrule appellant's contention that the evidence supporting the jury's verdict was factually insufficient.

Notes and Questions

1. That the defendant was psychotic and suffering from untreated, paranoid schizophrenia at the time of the murder did not render him legally insane. Why?

2. The Amarillo Court of Appeals and other Texas appellate courts have consistently held that placing a 911 call to report a crime is evidence the defendant knew right from wrong. What are other reasons a person might call 911? Did Mr. Pham call to report that he had committed murder? Do you agree with the Court that Mr. Pham's 911 call was an admission that he recognized he had done something wrong?

3. While mental psychosis can cause incompetency and insanity, other mental impairments can as well. People who suffer from brain injuries, depression, post-traumatic stress, severe stress, and mental developmental or intellectual disabilities have raised competency issues and the insanity defense. The law does not specify that people with psychotic and mood disorders such as schizophrenia, schizoaffective disorder, bipolar disorder, and depression are the only people who can claim incompetence or insanity. The test is still whether the defendant was able to appreciate the wrongfulness of his conduct due to severe mental disease or defect.

Filing Notice of Insanity as a Defense and Appointing Experts

When a defendant plans on raising the issue of insanity, he must file a notice of intent to raise the insanity defense at least 20 days before trial; this notice must be served on the State.[60] When this notice is filed, the court may on any party's motion or *sua sponte* appoint one or more disinterested experts to examine the defendant and testify as to the defendant's insanity at any trial or hearing that involves that issue.[61] You saw this in the case above: two experts testified in the *Pham* case, one appointed by the trial court, the other hired by the State. These experts are psychologists or psychiatrists and must

---

[60] TEX. CODE CRIM. PROC. ANN. art. 46C.051 (West 2016).
[61] TEX. CODE CRIM. PROC. ANN. art. 46C.101 (West 2016).

meet certain qualifications in order to be appointed by the court as an expert on insanity.[62]

Remember from your evidence class that the judge is the gatekeeper for evidence and expert testimony; in insanity cases, the judge can only appoint experts who meet statutorily enumerated qualifications. These appointed experts may also evaluate competency.[63] Within 30 days, the expert must file a written report detailing how she conducted the evaluation.[64] In that report, she will list her observations, findings, and opinions and determine whether the defendant has a severe mental disease or defect.[65]

As stated above, the judge will appoint two neutral experts to evaluate a defendant for insanity. These two experts cost the defendant nothing; the county pays their fees.[66] If the defendant wants to hire experts of his choosing, he may do. The judge must provide the expert an opportunity to evaluate the defendant.[67]

The Factfinder's Role in Determining Insanity

Insanity is an affirmative defense to criminal responsibility such as duress or entrapment. The defendant must prove the defense by a preponderance of the evidence.[68] The defense may be considered by a judge or jury only when it is supported by competent evidence.[69] The factfinder must render a verdict of guilty, not guilty, or not guilty by reason of insanity following a trial when the insanity defense is raised.[70]

Finding of Dangerousness

If the judge or jury finds the defendant not guilty by reason of insanity, it is deemed a legal acquittal, but it is not treated the same as a regular acquittal

---

[62] TEX. CODE CRIM. PROC. ANN. art. 46C.102 (West 2016).
[63] TEX. CODE CRIM. PROC. ANN. art. 46C.103 (West 2016).
[64] TEX. CODE CRIM. PROC. ANN. art. 46C.105 (West 2016).
[65] *Id.*
[66] TEX. CODE CRIM. PROC. ANN. art. 46C.106 (West 2016).
[67] TEX. CODE CRIM. PROC. ANN. art. 46C.107 (West 2016).
[68] TEX. CODE CRIM. PROC. ANN. art. 46C.153(a)(2) (West 2016).
[69] TEX. CODE CRIM. PROC. ANN. arts. 46C.151 and 46C.152 (West 2016).
[70] *Id.*

or not guilty verdict.[71] In a regular acquittal, a person is let go and is free and clear of the charge. Once a person is acquitted by reason of insanity, however, the judge must immediately determine whether the acquittee is dangerous.[72] The acquittee will be deemed dangerous if she caused serious bodily injury to another, placed a person in imminent harm of serious bodily injury, or threatened someone with a deadly weapon that would have caused serious bodily injury.[73]

If the judge finds the insanity acquittee is dangerous, the trial court retains jurisdiction post acquittal.[74] If the judge finds the insanity acquittee is not dangerous but is mentally ill or intellectually disabled, the person may still face civil commitment, placement in a facility, or placement with a person who promises to care for the acquittee.[75] If the judge finds the insanity acquittee is not dangerous and is no longer mentally ill or is not intellectually disabled, the person shall be set free.[76]

Post-Acquittal Commitment

Insanity acquittees found dangerous by a judge are committed to a maximum-security unit for a short evaluation and treatment.[77] A forensic psychologist or psychiatrist will evaluate the acquittee's mental state, assess whether the mental state causes the person to be a danger to self or others, and determine the least restrictive environment for the recommended mental health treatment, if any.[78] All of these findings and recommendations will be included in the mental health professional's report, which is given to the judge. The judge will then hold a hearing and determine whether the person will continue to be under the supervision of the court and, if so, what the treatment will be and whether it should be inpatient or outpatient treatment.[79]

---

[71] TEX. CODE CRIM. PROC. ANN. art. 46C.155 (West 2016).
[72] TEX. CODE CRIM. PROC. ANN. art. 46C.157 (West 2016).
[73] *Id.*
[74] TEX. CODE CRIM. PROC. ANN. art. 46C.158 (West 2016).
[75] TEX. CODE CRIM. PROC. ANN. art. 46C.201 (West 2016).
[76] TEX. CODE CRIM. PROC. ANN. art. 56C.202 (West 2016).
[77] TEX. CODE CRIM. PROC. ANN. art. 46C.251 (West 2016).
[78] TEX. CODE CRIM. PROC. ANN. art. 46C.252 (West 2016).
[79] TEX. CODE CRIM. PROC. ANN. art. 46C.253 (West 2016).

Acquittees may continue to receive treatment or remain in the care of others for years, if not decades. That the mental condition is stabilized is not necessarily enough to terminate supervision.[80] The trial court's jurisdiction is terminated when the person's cumulative time in jail, inpatient care, and outpatient treatment equals the maximum, hypothetical prison sentence.[81]

Key Differences Between Competency and Insanity

Competency and insanity should not be confused or conjoined; they are two separate legal concepts. It may help to illustrate a few key differences between them here:

- *Mental competency* refers to the defendant's ability to understand the legal proceedings against him and communicate with his attorney, whereas insanity refers to a serious mental disease or defect that causes an inability to distinguish between right and wrong at the time the crime was committed;
- Mental competency is assessed at the time of the criminal proceedings (*e.g.*, arraignment, court appearances, trial), whereas insanity is assessed at the time the crime was committed;
- Insanity is an affirmative defense, whereas mental incompetency is not;
- A finding of insanity results in acquittal of the charge(s), whereas a finding of mental incompetency results in a stay of proceedings.

Here are some similarities between the mental competency and insanity:

- Both require proof by a preponderance of the evidence;
- The burden of proof falls on the defendant;
- The defendant in both circumstances must be released when the time spent in custody or on supervision exceeds the maximum hypothetical sentence; and
- Both require evaluation by a qualified, mental health expert (such as a psychologist or psychiatrist).

———————◆———————

---

[80] TEX. CODE CRIM. PROC. ANN. art. 46C.254 (West 2016).
[81] TEX. CODE CRIM. PROC. ANN. art. 46C.269(a) (West 2016).

Subpoenas

Trials require behind-the-scenes coordination. Think for a moment about your own life. What happens when you try to get friends or family together for an event? First, you have to pick a date and notify everyone. Second, the people you invite must clear their calendars. Third, some people may be unable to attend or may ask if you can change the date of the event. The same is true for litigation. It is the judge and the attorneys who agree on a date (after they check their schedules and calendars), and once a date is chosen, all witnesses must appear. Subpoenas serve the purpose of ensuring that witnesses will appear and the trial will take place on the chosen date. This section will discuss the procedures surrounding subpoenas.

Types of Subpoenas

A *subpoena* is a judicial order to appear in court at a specified date and time.[82] There are two types of subpoenas: subpoenas issued to people and subpoenas requesting things or evidence that people need to bring to court. The latter type of subpoena is called a subpoena *duces tecum* (which means "bring with you" in Latin).[83]

Let's use an illustration to see how these subpoenas work in practice. Suppose that you are a prosecutor, and you have a case set for trial against the defendant for unlawfully carrying a weapon. You read the police report in preparation of trial and discover that the defendant, a person with a concealed weapons permit, carried it on the premises of a hospital, in violation of Texas Penal Code §46.035(4).

In the report, you learn that a concerned patient at the hospital notified two nurses that she saw the defendant with a gun sticking out of his waistband. The nurses then confirmed that the defendant, who was at the hospital visiting a sick relative, indeed had a gun. The nurses told a police officer who was working security at the hospital about the situation, and he ultimately arrested the defendant for unlawfully carrying the gun into a hospital. The officer seized the gun as evidence and checked it into the evidence room at the police department, where it remains to this day.

---

[82] TEX. CODE CRIM. PROC. ANN. art. 24.01 (West 2016).
[83] TEX. CODE CRIM. PROC. ANN. art. 24.02 (West 2016).

Who and what would you subpoena for trial? In order to know what to subpoena, it helps to consider what elements you must prove at trial. If you subpoena a thing, you must subpoena the person who has custody of the thing. In the case of evidence that has been submitted to a police evidence room for safekeeping, the person who has authority to bring the evidence to court is the evidence custodian or the officer who seized the evidence who will testify at trial. As you can see, you must know the elements of the law you have to prove before you issue subpoenas as well as the witnesses and evidence you must have in order to prove these elements.

Issuance of Subpoenas

A subpoena may issue to secure a witness's testimony for a hearing, a trial, the grand jury, or "in any other proceeding in which the person's testimony may be required."[84] Anyone over the age of 18 can receive a subpoena.[85] If the witness is a child, the subpoena should be directed to the person who has custody of the child.[86]

Applying for a Subpoena

County and district attorneys' offices and courts usually have subpoena forms in electronically generated or handwritten forms.[87] The attorney must include certain information on the subpoena before it issues (is sent out) from the court. The Code requires the following information:

1. The name of the witness;
2. The address where the witness can be found, if known;
3. The witness's vocation (*e.g.*, police officer, doctor, custodian of records), if known; and
4. An assertion that the testimony the witness will give is material.[88]

If you are requesting the subpoenaed person to bring something to court (*e.g.*, a police officer should bring a copy of his police report to the hearing to refresh his memory, or a witness should bring physical evidence in her

---

[84] TEX. CODE CRIM. PROC. ANN. art. 24.01 (West 2016).
[85] TEX. CODE CRIM. PROC. ANN. art. 24.01(b)(2) (West 2016).
[86] TEX. CODE CRIM. PROC. ANN. arts. 24.01 and 24.011 (West 2016).
[87] TEX. CODE CRIM. PROC. ANN. art. 24.03 (West 2016).
[88] *Id.*

possession to court), you should also include a notation describing the thing the witness should bring to court. By requesting that the person bring an object or document to court, you are filing a subpoena duces tecum. The process for both types of subpoenas is the same; one merely asks witnesses to come to court, and the other asks witnesses to come to court with a listed object.

Once an attorney fills out the subpoena with the above information, he must give it to the court clerk, who places it in the clerk's file for all parties to see.[89] Once the clerk files it, the subpoena is delivered to the witness by the bailiff or process server working in the court. This process server will note whether the subpoena was mailed or hand delivered to the witness, or whether he was unable to locate the witness.[90]

Subpoenas for jailable misdemeanor offenses (Class A and B) and felony offenses are valid statewide.[91] This means that a witness who is served with a subpoena outside the county where the trial is held is required to appear in court. The Code states that the process for serving a subpoena is the same process described above, whether the person being served lives in the county or resides outside of the county.[92]

Subpoenas are a serious matter in criminal practice. Because the State carries the burden of proof, the prosecutor is responsible for proving every element of the charged offense beyond a reasonable doubt. This means the prosecutor must carefully consider the testimony and evidence he needs to prove every element. If an attorney fails to subpoena critical evidence or witnesses, that mistake may result in an acquittal.

Creating, filing, and supervising the issuance of subpoenas can be time consuming. Trials are frequently reset; every time a case is rescheduled, new subpoenas must be drafted and sent out. With each new issuance of a set of subpoenas, witnesses may grow weary or apathetic about coming to court. It is possible for attorneys to seek permission to place witnesses on call, but attorneys must be able to locate witnesses once the trial begins. Until an attorney knows that all of her witnesses are present or available, the potential success of trial is uncertain.

---

[89] *Id.*

[90] TEX. CODE CRIM. PROC. ANN. arts. 24.03, 24.04, and 24.17 (West 2016).

[91] TEX. CODE CRIM. PROC. ANN. art. 24.16 (West 2016).

[92] TEX. CODE CRIM. PROC. ANN. art. 24.03 (West 2016).

Consequences of Disobeying a Subpoena

What happens when a witness was properly subpoenaed but fails or refuses to come to court to testify? The word subpoena means under penalty in Latin; witnesses who fail to appear may face a judicial penalty for doing so. The Code permits the parties through the judge to force the witness to come to court. There are two ways to do this.

First, a judge can enforce a subpoena by issuing a *writ of attachment*.[93] The party who has properly subpoenaed the witness has a right to have the witness attached — taken into custody and delivered to the court immediately.[94] Writs of attachments are also warranted in instances where the attorney believes the witness is about to leave the county.[95] Finally, they can be used for witnesses who are inmates in a corrections facility[96] and for disobedient grand jury witnesses who were subpoenaed.[97] The writ of attachment acts like an arrest warrant in that it gives a law enforcement official the right to seize the person by force and deliver the person to the court (as opposed to jail) to testify.

Second, if a witness refuses to obey a subpoena, the judge may fine the witness: up to $500 for felony cases and up to $100 for misdemeanor cases.[98] The fine may be waived if the witness is able to show cause (a legal term meaning to explain your actions to the court) why she should not be fined[99] or if she ultimately testifies.[100] Waiving the fine is in the discretion of the judge.[101]

———————————◆———————————

Notes and Questions

1. The State carries the burden of proof. As a result, it has a common-law duty to disclose all witnesses it intends to call if the defense requests

---

[93] TEX. CODE CRIM. PROC. ANN. art. 24.11 (West 2016).

[94] *Sturgeon v. State*, 106 S.W.3d 81, 90 (Tex. Crim. App. 2003).

[95] TEX. CODE CRIM. PROC. ANN. art. 24.14 (West 2016).

[96] TEX. CODE CRIM. PROC. ANN. art. 24.13 (West 2016).

[97] TEX. CODE CRIM. PROC. ANN. art. 24.15 (West 2016).

[98] TEX. CODE CRIM. PROC. ANN. art. 24.05 (West 2016).

[99] TEX. CODE CRIM. PROC. ANN. arts. 24.06(3), and 24.07-24.09 (West 2016).

[100] TEX. CODE CRIM. PROC. ANN. art. 24.10 (West 2016).

[101] TEX. CODE CRIM. PROC. ANN. art. 24.05 (West 2016).

witness discovery.[102] The defense, on the other hand, has no obligation to disclose lay witnesses to the State. Therefore, most defense attorneys do not subpoena their own witnesses. What are the benefits to the defense of not subpoenaing a witness? What are the possible detriments of this practice?

———————◆———————

Motions for Continuance

Suppose a witness cannot appear on the trial date due to a conflict that cannot be resolved (*e.g.*, illness, a funeral, an out-of-country vacation). Most court appearances are agreed upon by the court coordinator, the defense attorney (after consulting the defendant about her schedule), and the prosecutor well in advance of trial. Scheduling conflicts may not be known until these witnesses receive their subpoenas.

Either party may attempt to postpone the trial by filing a motion for continuance. There are two ways to receive a continuance: (1) when the parties agree in open court to continue the matter for good cause;[103] or (2) when the parties cannot agree and the moving party establishes sufficient cause.[104] In this second instance, the party who seeks a continuance must file a written motion with the court demonstrating the reason why the continuance is needed.[105] In either instance—agreed or not—the continuance will be granted only for as long as necessary.[106] All motions for continuance must be sworn to by someone who has personal knowledge about the facts that support the request for the continuance.[107]

Continuances Based on Witness Unavailability

While the above requirements apply to any reason for a continuance, the Code specifically addresses a witness who is unavailable on the court date. Some witnesses fear testifying, particularly in violent felony cases. In

---

[102] *Martinez v. State*, 867 S.W.2d 30, 39 (Tex. Crim. App. 1993) ("Notice of the State's witnesses shall be given upon request.").
[103] TEX. CODE CRIM. PROC. ANN. art. 29.02 (West 2016).
[104] TEX. CODE CRIM. PROC. ANN. arts. 29.02 and 29.03 (West 2016).
[105] TEX. CODE CRIM. PROC. ANN. art. 29.03 (West 2016).
[106] TEX. CODE CRIM. PROC. ANN. arts. 29.02 and 29.03 (West 2016).
[107] TEX. CODE CRIM. PROC. ANN. art. 29.08 (West 2016).

domestic violence cases, the victim may be unwilling to testify in an effort to protect the defendant or may avoid process (being served). It could be that the witness merely finds court inconvenient and refuses to appear. There are many reasons why witnesses may be hard, if not impossible, to secure for hearings or trial. The requirements as to what must be satisfied in order to get a continuance based upon the witness's unavailability depend on whether the prosecution or the defense is requesting the continuance.

Prosecution Motions for Continuance

The prosecutor must demonstrate the following things the first time she seeks to get a continuance:

1. The name and place where the witness resides, if known;
2. What the prosecution has done to locate and secure the witness (issuing a subpoena is not enough); and
3. That the witness's testimony is material to the State.[108]

If the court grants the continuance and the witness is again missing at the rescheduled hearing or trial, in addition to proving everything above, the prosecutor must establish the following things in her subsequent request for a continuance:

1. The facts that the prosecutor expects the witness to testify about (the court must find this evidence material);
2. The prosecutor will be able to procure the witness at the next hearing or trial; and
3. That the testimony of this witness is not available through any other source.[109]

Defense Motions for Continuance

If it is defense counsel seeking a continuance based upon an unavailable witness, the requirements are different. The defense must establish the following in its first motion for continuance:

1. The name and place where the witness resides, if known;

---

[108] TEX. CODE CRIM. PROC. ANN. art. 29.04 (West 2016).
[109] TEX. CODE CRIM. PROC. ANN. art. 29.05 (West 2016).

2. What the defense has done to locate and secure the witness (issuing a subpoena is not enough);

3. That the witness's testimony is material to the defense;

4. That the defense has not encouraged or caused the witness to be absent;

5. That the motion is not made for delay; and

6. That there is no reasonable expectation the witness can appear on a different day of the current proceeding[110]

If the matter is continued and the defense seeks a subsequent motion for continuance, in addition to all of the above requisites, the defense must establish that:

1. The testimony of this witness is not available through any other source; and

2. The defense believes that it will be able to procure the witness at the next hearing or trial.[111]

Contesting a Motion for Continuance

When one person is missing from the list of witnesses, the question may be whether this witness's testimony is merely desirable or necessary. If it is the former, opposing counsel may contest the continuance. If opposing counsel wants to contest the continuance, she may file a written, sworn affidavit by a party with personal knowledge who denies the material fact that forms the basis for the motion.[112]

Continuances After Trial Has Begun

Getting a continuance granted once a trial has begun is much more difficult. A party must demonstrate to the satisfaction of the judge that an unexpected occurrence arose after the trial began that no reasonable diligence could have uncovered and that it has taken the party by such surprise that a fair trial is not possible.[113] This continuance would be available

---

[110] TEX. CODE CRIM. PROC. ANN. art. 29.06 (West 2016).
[111] TEX. CODE CRIM. PROC. ANN. art. 20.08 (West 2016).
[112] TEX. CODE CRIM. PROC. ANN. art. 29.09 (West 2016).
[113] TEX. CODE CRIM. PROC. ANN. art. 29.13 (West 2016).

in only the most extreme cases, for example where exculpatory evidence was disclosed after trial began[114] or where one of the lawyers becomes seriously ill or dies during trial.

Denying the Motion for Continuance

The judge may grant or deny any motion for continuance. If the judge denies it, her decision will be reversed on appeal for abuse of discretion only if the party seeking the continuance factually establishes that she was harmed by not having more preparation time and the judge erred by denying the motion.[115] This burden is onerous on the party and deferential to the judge; it will almost never result in a reversal, as the next case illustrates.

Earl Carl Heiselbetz v. State
906 S.W.2d 500
(Tex. Crim. App. 1995)

[Appellant was convicted of capital murder and sentenced to death.]

[A]ppellant claims the trial court erred in denying his motion for continuance. Appellant argues that he had inadequate time to prepare for trial. Specifically, he argues the following: defense counsel is a solo practitioner and had only forty-three days to prepare before the beginning of voir dire; the State included over eighty-seven potential witnesses on its witness list, including fourteen names added only two weeks before trial was set to begin; the State listed over one hundred potential exhibits, ninety-five of which were actually introduced; and counsel could not adequately review medical records which contained potential mitigating evidence. In the affidavit attached to the original motion for continuance, the investigator working with defense counsel indicated that he had not yet had time to report back adequately to counsel on his interviews with the State's witnesses.

Where denial of a continuance has resulted in representation by counsel who was not prepared, we have not hesitated to declare an abuse of discretion . . . Nevertheless, the granting or denial of a motion for continuance is within the sound discretion of the trial court . . . Art. 29.03 (criminal action may be continued upon sufficient cause shown in motion);

---

[114] *O'Rarden v. State*, 777 S.W.2d 455, 459–60 (Tex. App.—Dallas 1989, pet. ref'd).
[115] *Gonzales v. State*, 304 S.W.3d 838, 842–43 (Tex. Crim. App. 2010).

Art. 29.06(6) (sufficiency of a motion for continuance shall be addressed to "sound discretion" of court and "shall not be granted as matter of right"). To find an abuse of discretion in refusing to grant a motion for continuance, there must be a showing that the defendant was prejudiced by his counsel's inadequate preparation time.

Appellant's counsel contends that the denial of the continuance rendered him unable to prepare an adequate defense; however, he does not argue, much less establish, any specific prejudice to his cause arising from the trial court's failure to continue the trial. In *Hernandez*, appointed counsel had less time than appellant to prepare for trial, but we, nevertheless, held:

> Although this is a relatively short time for preparation in a [capital murder trial], no specific, serious matter has been raised by the appellant and the record does not otherwise show that the appellant's defense was prejudiced by counsel not having more time to prepare for trial.[116]

Like Hernandez, appellant does not allege any specific prejudice to his defense. He does not allege that he was unfairly surprised at trial or unable to effectively cross-examine any of the State's witnesses. The bare assertion that counsel did not have adequate time to interview the State's potential witnesses does not alone establish prejudice. The assertion that counsel did not have time to adequately investigate medical records for potential mitigating evidence without any showing of harm likewise fails to establish an abuse of discretion. Absent a showing of prejudice, we cannot hold that the trial court abused its discretion in overruling appellant's motion for continuance. Appellant's ... point of error is overruled.

————————◆————————

Notes and Questions

1. Notice that the continuance in the above case was not sought on the basis of a missing witness but because defense counsel did not have enough time to prepare for a case of this magnitude in the time frame he was given. A motion for continuance may be based upon any number of reasons; it is within the trial court's decision to grant or deny the motion.

2. Based on the *Heiselbetz* case, does a defendant have a right to a continuance?

---

[116] *Hernandez v. State*, 643 S.W.2d 397, 399-400 (Tex. Crim. App. 1983).

3. One of the trial court's roles is to manage dockets, hearings, trials, and all of the other things that happen in the courtroom on a regular basis. This ability to manage proceedings and the trial court's role as fact-finder are two strengths appellate courts defer to. Appellate courts have different strengths: knowing, making, and applying the law. When the expertise of the trial court is higher than the appellate court's, the standard of review is deferential. When the expertise of the appellate court is higher than the trial court's, the standard of review is less deferential and favors the appellate court. The abuse of discretion standard of review, the one used in the above case, is the most deferential to the trial court. Because the act of granting or denying continuances involves credibility determinations and docket management, appellate courts give trial courts much deference and will not overturn the trial judge's decision absent an abuse of discretion.

4. Notice in the rules detailed before the *Heiselbetz* case that the State has to establish the witness's testimony is material when it asks for a subsequent motion for continuance. The defense does not. Why?

5. Why must the defense prove more than the prosecution when it comes to its motion for continuance? Should there be a difference? Why or why not?

———————————◆———————————

Recusal

The Texas Code of Criminal Procedure and the Texas Constitution include a limited number of scenarios that mandate judicial recusal or removal from presiding over a case.[117] Under both, a judge cannot preside over a cause of action in the following instances:

1. When the judge is the injured party;
2. When he previously acted as prosecutor or defense counsel in the present case;[118] or
3. When he is closely related to either party.[119]

---

[117] TEX. CONST. art. V §11; TEX. CODE CRIM. PROC. ANN. art. 30.01 (West 2016).
[118] Although Article 30.01 broadly disqualifies a judge when he has "been of counsel for the State or the accused," courts have narrowed this to mean in the current cause of action. *E.g., Ex Parte Miller*, 696 S.W.2d 908, 910 (Tex. Crim. App. 1985).

Attorneys sometimes seek to get a judge removed for other reasons. In *Gaal v. State*, the defendant was charged with a felony driving while intoxicated offense.[120] After the defendant twice violated bond conditions and twice refused to plead guilty to negotiated, lenient plea agreements, the presiding judge declared in open court, "For the record, I will not accept any plea bargain in this matter, unless it's for the maximum term of ten years."[121] The defendant then filed a motion to recuse the judge on the ground that he was biased against him; the motion was denied by the presiding judge following a hearing.[122] The Court of Criminal Appeals described the bases for recusal:

> A Texas judge may be removed from presiding over a case for one of three reasons: he is constitutionally disqualified; he is subject to a statutory strike; or, he is subject to statutory disqualification or recusal under Texas Supreme Court rules. ... Rule 18b(2) of the Texas Rules of Civil Procedure sets out the law concerning recusal and includes instances in which a judge must step down from hearing a case for reasons other than the disqualifying grounds listed in the constitution. Rule 18b(2) states, in relevant part, that "A judge shall recuse himself in any proceeding in which: (a) his impartiality might reasonably be questioned; [or] (b) he has a personal bias or prejudice concerning the subject matter or a party, or personal knowledge of disputed evidentiary facts concerning the proceeding[.]"

> There is much overlap between these two subsections ... but ... a judge's impartiality might reasonably be questioned "only if it appears that he or she harbors an aversion, hostility or disposition of a kind that a fair-minded person could not set aside when judging the dispute."

> Rule 18b(2)(b) is more specific: It covers how the judge feels and what the judge knows. A Texas court has held, for instance, that a trial judge's feeling of personal bias was evidenced by ex-parte communications with the prosecutor that had the "trial court providing guidance to the prosecutor on the presentation of his case ...." A clear instance of "personal knowledge of disputed evidentiary facts" requiring recusal arose in one unpublished case where, in a suppression hearing, the trial judge interrupted and announced that he himself had observed the conduct that led to the defendant's initial

---

[119] TEX. CONST. art. V §11; TEX. CODE CRIM. PROC. ANN. art. 30.01 (West 2016).
[120] *Gaal v. State*, 332 S.W.3d 448, 450 (Tex. Crim. App. 2011).
[121] *Id.*
[122] *Id.*

detention. Generally, though, recusal is not required when based solely on judicial rulings, remarks, or actions.

... [A] judge's remarks during trial that are critical, disapproving, or hostile to counsel, the parties, or their cases, usually will not support a bias or partiality challenge, although they may do so if they reveal an opinion based on extrajudicial information, and they will require recusal if they reveal "such a high degree of favoritism or antagonism as to make fair judgment impossible." On the other hand, "expressions of impatience, dissatisfaction, annoyance, and even anger, that are within the bounds of what imperfect men and women" may display, do not establish bias or partiality. ... Although intemperate remarks may well violate a rule of judicial conduct, such a violation does not necessarily mean that the judge should be recused.

Recusal has been required, however, when a trial judge revoked a defendant's bond and put him in jail solely because he decided to invoke his right to a jury trial, or when a trial judge arbitrarily, without any evidence before him, refused to consider a portion of the range of punishment. Recusal of the trial judge in a criminal trial was also proper under the reasonable-person standard where the trial judge's remarks evidenced "a degree of anger and hostility toward the government that is in excess of any provocation that we can find in the record," or a personal prejudice against the defendant for successfully appealing his conviction on the basis of the judge's actions during a prior trial.[123]

After considering the bases for recusal, the *Gaal* Court determined that though the judge made intemperate comments, they did not rise to the level of a legal basis for recusal.[124]

If a judge is disqualified from serving for any reason, the case's venue is not changed.[125] Rather, the recused judge must notify the presiding judge of the disqualification, and the case is then transferred to another judge.[126]

———————◆———————

[123] *Id.* at 452-56.
[124] *Id.* at 460.
[125] TEX. CODE CRIM. PROC. ANN. art. 30.02 (West 2016).
[126] *Id.*

Practice Questions

Bar examiners repeatedly group together the following pretrial hearing subjects in bar questions: the time frame for filing pretrial matters, the list of matters to be raised at the pretrial hearing, and the consequences for late filings. They have asked pretrial hearing questions about challenges to venue, motions for discovery, probation applications, discovery, and election on punishment numerous times over the years.

Each of the topics covered in this chapter appear in varying degrees on the bar exam. Topics such as competency, insanity, and subpoenas appear in questions with more regularity whereas the statute of limitations is tested rarely. All told, the topics in this chapter have been tested more than 60 times on bar exams over the years.

Because this chapter has so many separate topics, the practice questions appear with titles in the same order in which their correlating sections appear in the chapter.

Right to Counsel and Duties of Appointed Counsel

1. (J-2011) How soon must appointed counsel visit with Defendant, who is still incarcerated? What can Judge do if Counsel fails to meet Defendant within the specified time frame? Explain.

    _____

    _____

    _____

    _____

    _____

2. (J-2008) Defendant's bail was set at $100,000 by the judge after his examining trial. The judge found probable cause for the offense and appointed him a lawyer. Three months later, Defendant is still unable to make bail, and Defendant's first lawyer has not done any work on the case, much less visit his client in jail. Judge recently replaced Defendant's first lawyer with you, another appointed lawyer.

Did the first lawyer make a timely effort to contact Defendant? Was Judge legally permitted to substitute counsel based on his failure to meet with Defendant during the three-month period following his examining trial? Explain.

_____

_____

_____

_____

_____

3. (F-2005) In preparing for trial, you determine you will need the help of an expert. However, Defendant, who is indigent, cannot afford to hire one. What document can you file to obtain the assistance of an expert and how can you get the funds to pay the expert? Explain.

_____

_____

_____

_____

_____

Pretrial Hearings

4. (F-2016 (motion for probation), F-2015 (motion for discovery), J-2013 (motion for probation), F-2013 (motion for probation), J-2011 (motion to change venue), F-2011 (punishment election), F-2010 (motion for community supervision and punishment election), F-2009 (punishment election), F-2008 (punishment election), J-2007 (motion to suppress, motion for probation, and punishment election), F-2007 (trial election), J-2005 (trial election), J-2004 (trial election), F-2004 (trial election), F-2001 (motion for probation and punishment election), and J-2000 (motion to suppress victim's identification, defendant's post-arrest statements, and trial election):

The Court sets a date for a pretrial hearing. You would like to file a motion for discovery.

When must you file your motion for discovery? What happens if you fail to file the discovery motion by the deadline?

_____

_____

_____

_____

_____

5. (J-2010, J-2006, and F-2002) On the day Defendant is indicted, Judge says you have three days to file any pretrial pleadings.

    Is Judge's order correct? Explain.

_____

_____

_____

_____

_____

6. (F-2009) Judge waits for Defendant to show up at pretrial hearing. You tell Judge Defendant is running 20 minutes late. Judge says he has no more time to wait and starts the hearing in Defendant's absence. You object, but Judge overrules your objection and begins to hear evidence.

    Was the Judge's ruling correct? Does Defendant have a right to be present at his own pretrial hearing? Explain.

_____

_____

_____

_____

_____

7. (J-2007, J-2005, J-2001, and J-2000) You want to suppress Defendant's statement and request a pretrial hearing on the matter. Defendant has expressed concern about testifying at the hearing.

Will Defendant waive his right to remain silent at trial by testifying at the hearing? If he does testify, may Prosecutor ask whether Defendant is guilty of the crime during cross-examination? Explain.

_____

_____

_____

_____

_____

8. (F-2003 and F-2002) Defendant voluntarily testified at a pretrial hearing on his motion to suppress evidence. The trial judge denied his motion.

   Has Defendant waived his right to remain silent at trial by testifying at the pretrial hearing? For example, could Prosecutor call Defendant to the stand on the basis that he has testified before?

_____

_____

_____

_____

_____

Statute of Limitations

9. (J-2016 and F-2010) Three years after committing a forgery, Defendant is arrested. Two months later, the grand jury indicts him. You have been appointed to represent Defendant. Does this time frame bar prosecution? Explain.

_____

_____

_____

_____

_____

Competency and Insanity

Note: Remember that competency and insanity are different legal concepts raised at different stages of the criminal justice process. They should not be confused. However, they are mentioned together here because bar examiners frequently ask about both in a single question or in a series of questions.

10. (J-2013) As you prepare for trial, you realize you should raise the insanity defense in Defendant's trial. Your client cannot afford to hire a mental health expert to testify on his behalf, much less evaluate him independently of the State.

    Is there any way to obtain psychological testimony despite the fact that Defendant cannot afford to hire an expert for trial? Explain.

    _____

    _____

    _____

    _____

    _____

11. (J-2013) Before trial begins, two experts determine Defendant was insane when he committed the crime. You have decided to keep this defense a surprise. At trial, as you begin to introduce evidence of insanity, Prosecutor objects that you had a duty to reveal your defense pretrial. You respond that your defense was privileged information because it was revealed through attorney-client communications before trial.

    How should the Court rule and why? Explain.

    _____

    _____

    _____

    _____

    _____

12. (F-2012) After you review the State's file, you interview Defendant. During the interview, Defendant tells you he cannot remember committing the crime. You see from his file that he has a history of mental blackouts and mental treatment. He knows who you are, and he seems coherent during the interview, but he can offer no details about what happened yesterday or beyond.

As his defense counsel, should you raise incompetency, insanity, or both at trial? Explain.

_____
_____
_____
_____
_____

13. (F-2010, J-2007, J-2005, J-2003, F-2002, and J-2000) At your initial meeting, you begin to doubt that your client is mentally competent to stand trial. He seems confused about who you are and why he is in jail.

Is there a presumption of competency? What must be proven in order to rebut any presumption that exists? Who has the burden of proof and what is it? Explain.

_____
_____
_____
_____
_____

14. (J-2007 and J-2000) What happens after a Defendant is found incompetent to stand trial? Detail your answer.

_____
_____
_____
_____
_____

15. (J-2007, F-2005, and F-2002) List three differences between incompetency and insanity under Texas law.

_____
_____
_____
_____
_____

Subpoenas

16. (J-2015, J-2012, and F-2009) Before trial, Prosecutor tells you Witness did not see Defendant with the murder weapon. What procedural step can you take to ensure that Witness is present at trial to testify? List two things you must state as part of that procedural step?

_____

_____

_____

_____

_____

17. (J-2006, J-2004, F-2004, and J-2001) You subpoena Doctor, who treated Defendant in the hospital following the alleged crime. Doctor's testimony is material. Though Doctor acknowledges she received the subpoena, she refuses to obey it claiming she simply cannot reschedule her patients' appointments, and her work is far more important than this trial.

What procedural step can you take to get Doctor to come to court? Explain.

_____

_____

_____

_____

_____

18. (J-2004) You are preparing for trial and have learned that one of your witnesses has moved 206 miles outside of the county where the trial will be held. Witness refuses to appear, arguing that because he resides outside of the county, there is nothing you can do to force him to appear in court.

Is this witness required to obey the subpoena? What is your remedy? Explain.

_____

_____

_____

Motions for Continuance

19. (F-2014, F-2012, and F-2009) What can you do to buy more time before trial to track down a material witness who is temporarily out of the country? When must you take such a step, and what must you establish in order to accomplish it? Explain.

_____

_____

_____

_____

_____

20. (F-2006, J-2005, F-2003, and J-2001) Name two things you must allege in your first motion for continuance. Do you have a right to one continuance? Must your motion for continuance be sworn?

_____

_____

_____

_____

_____

Recusal

21. (F-2012) When reviewing a video of the crime, you notice Judge was one of the Defendant's victims, though Judge does not yet know it.

What can you do to ensure Defendant has a fair and impartial presiding judge? What would be your legal basis for taking action? Explain.

_____

_____

_____

_____

_____

344 | Texas Criminal Procedure and Evidence

22. (J-2005) Judge prosecuted Defendant seven years ago in another case. Defendant recognizes Judge and requests you seek to remove him from being the judge in his case.

When is a judge disqualified in a criminal case? Is Judge disqualified in this case? Explain.

_____

_____

_____

_____

_____

———————◆———————

Chapter 8
Plea Negotiations

Introduction

Plea bargaining is a necessary part of the criminal justice system. The Amarillo Court of Appeals defines plea bargaining as follows:

> Plea bargaining consists of the prosecutor making concessions regarding specific punishment, lesser charges, the reduction of counts and the like, in exchange for a defendant's agreement to enter a plea of guilty [or] nolo contendere …. This bargaining flows from the mutuality of advantage to the defendant and the prosecution, as each have their own reasons for wanting to avoid trial. The specific terms of the bargain are left to the parties.[1]

Without a significant number of defendants choosing to plead guilty, the system, as it functions today, would break down. Trials require resources and time that governments simply cannot offer every defendant charged with a crime. It is fortunate for governments then that upwards of 90 percent of criminal cases end in a plea of guilty or no contest.[2]

---

[1] *Freeman v. State*, 913 S.W.2d 714, 717-18 (Tex. App.—Amarillo 1995, pet. ref'd).

[2] Stephanos Bibas, *Incompetent Plea Bargaining and Extrajudicial Reforms*, 126 HARV. L. REV. 150, 150 n. 4 (2012) (97 percent of federal cases were resolved through plea bargains and dismissals in 2010, whereas 94 percent of state cases were resolved through plea bargains in 2006).

The plea bargain purports to be a true bargain for all involved. The defendant's bargain is a lowered punishment from the one he could have received from a jury. The prosecutor's bargain stems from the time and effort saved from having to prepare for and sit through a trial. Prosecutors are overworked.[3] Courts are overworked. Courts pressure prosecutors to move cases through the system quickly. Consequently, prosecutors are eager for defendants to plead guilty.

Jury trials are also a risky gamble; any litigator can recount trials that should have had a different result but did not. The certainty a plea offers—the State knows it will obtain a punishment for a law violation, and the defendant knows what punishment to expect—benefits both parties. Finally, it is a bargain to the community as it saves witnesses and victims from having to testify before an audience and finite resources the local government would exhaust on litigation.

A negotiated plea is not ideal. There are downsides for the defendant. For example, the defendant must waive constitutional rights to enter a plea of guilty or no contest. Had she gone to trial, she may have been acquitted, or she may have received a lesser punishment. Many defendants wonder after the fact whether pleading guilty was the right decision.

In felony cases, the plea process involves three components: (1) the waiver of rights; (2) the judge's admonishments; and (3) the introduction of substantiating evidence. The misdemeanor method of pleas differs from the felony process. This chapter will examine the defendant's waiver of the right to a trial, the obligations each participant has in the plea process, the misdemeanor plea process, and the right to appeal following a plea.

———————————◆———————————

---

[3] See generally Adam M. Gershowitz and Laura R. Killinger, *The State (Never) Rests: How Excessive Prosecutorial Caseloads Harm Criminal Defendants*, 105 Nw. U.L. Rev. 261 (2011) (examining the harms that result from overworked prosecutors).

Waiving the Right to a Jury Trial

In order for a defendant to plead guilty or no contest, he must waive the right to a jury trial. There are several requirements to a legally valid waiver.

The Code authorizes a jury trial waiver when

- the defendant is not charged with capital murder and facing a death sentence;
- the defendant appears in person in open court;
- the defendant waives his or her right to a jury trial in writing; and
- the court and the prosecutor consent to the waiver.[4]

A defendant charged with a felony offense cannot waive a jury trial unless he is represented by an attorney, appointed or hired, at the time of his waiver.[5]

◆

The Prosecutor's Role

Assuming the defendant has legally waived his right to trial, he can plead guilty to the charged offense. The next few subsections of this chapter will examine the legal duties and roles each participant plays in the plea process. We will begin with the prosecutor. It may seem odd to start with the prosecutor's role, when it is the defendant's plea, but the plea process begins with the prosecutor.

After the defendant is charged with a crime and the case is assigned to a court, the district attorneys' office creates a file for the case. The prosecutor assigned to the case reviews the information in the file, speaks with victims and witnesses, and determines what punishment to recommend.

No one but the State may offer a plea bargain. The defendant may accept, reject, or counter the offer. Negotiations between the defense counsel and the prosecutor are commonplace, especially as the attorneys learn more about the strengths and weaknesses of the case. What might start off as an offer of eight years in prison may later be reduced to four, if the prosecutor discovers evidentiary weaknesses or the defense attorney successfully argues

---

[4] TEX. CODE CRIM. PROC. ANN. art. 1.13(a) (West 2016).
[5] TEX. CODE CRIM. PROC. ANN. art. 1.13(b) (West 2016).

for mitigation. On the other hand, sometimes a prosecutor may realize the initial offer was too generous, decide to increase it before it has been accepted, or place time constraints on acceptance ("This offer will remain open until May 15th."). It is legally permissible for the State to make changes to the offer before the defendant accepts it.[6]

Once the State and the defendant negotiate and agree upon the punishment, the defendant will plead guilty to the offense in exchange for the punishment. "At its core, a plea bargain is a contract between the state and the defendant. As a contract, once both parties have entered knowingly and voluntarily into a plea bargain, they are bound by the terms of that agreement once it is accepted by the judge."[7] This next case considers a prosecutor who failed to agree by the terms of the plea bargain.

Earl Owen Bitterman v. State
180 S.W.3d 139
(Tex. Crim. App. 2005)

Appellant Earl Owen Bitterman pled guilty to the offense of aggravated sexual assault pursuant to a plea agreement with the State and was sentenced by the court to five years in the Texas Department of Criminal Justice, Institutional Division. Appellant then filed a motion for a new trial, in which he alleged that the State breached the terms of the plea agreement. The trial court denied this motion, and Appellant subsequently filed a timely notice of appeal.

Facts

Appellant pled guilty to the aggravated sexual assault of his twelve-year-old niece. As part of the plea agreement, the State agreed to the following sentencing recommendation:

5 YEARS IN THE TEXAS DEPARTMENT OF CRIMINAL JUSTICE, INSTITUTIONAL DIVISION, AND A FINE OF $0.00; THE STATE NEITHER OPPOSES NOR RECOMMENDS THAT THE COURT

---

[6] *E.g., Wingfield v. State*, 481 S.W.3d 376, 382 (Tex. App.—Amarillo 2015, pet. ref'd) (prosecutor did not act vindictively by departing upwards in plea offer after promising to hold the offer open for a period of time).

[7] *Moore v. State,* 295 S.W.3d 329, 331–33 (Tex. Crim. App. 2009).

GRANT DEFERRED ADJUDICATION PROBATION IN THIS MATTER.

The record reflects that the State agreed to allow Appellant to "make a pitch" for probation, but that it would remain silent as to probation at Appellant's sentencing. At the sentencing hearing, Appellant had several witnesses testify in support of his request for deferred adjudication, and the State cross-examined these witnesses. During cross-examination, the State questioned whether Appellant deserved deferred adjudication, and additionally, called the complainant's counselor as a rebuttal witness who testified that granting Appellant deferred adjudication would send the wrong message to the complainant. The State also argued to the court that Appellant was "not the kind of person that would be deserving of a second chance and an opportunity for probation" and that "it would be very dangerous for the victim to give him probation and send a message to her that in fact it was her fault." The State then recommended that the trial court sentence Appellant to five years in [prison]. The trial court followed the State's recommendation.

Plea Bargains

It is well established that it is a defendant's right to have the State honor a plea bargain entered into by the defendant in exchange for a guilty plea after the judge has accepted the plea bargain in open court. Plea bargains play an extremely important role in the criminal judicial process, and numerous cases in federal and Texas state law emphasize the importance of implementing safeguards to protect the due process rights of defendants who enter into such plea bargains. When a defendant enters into a plea bargain, he waives a number of fundamental constitutional rights, including a trial by jury, the right to confront one's accusers, the right to present witnesses in one's defense, the right to remain silent, and the right to be convicted only by proof beyond a reasonable doubt. There are strict federal and state guidelines and requirements regarding the defendant's ability to enter into such an agreement in order to protect the constitutional rights of the defendant, and among these is the requirement that if a defendant's plea is made based on a promise given by the State, the State must keep up its part of the agreement or the plea will be rendered involuntary. When the prosecution breaches its promise with respect to an executed plea agreement, the defendant pleads guilty on a false premise, and hence his conviction cannot stand. [T]he United States Supreme Court emphasized this point stating that "when a plea rests in any significant degree on a promise or agreement of the prosecutor, so that it can be said to be part of the inducement or consideration, such promise must be fulfilled." Additionally, this Court has previously held that a plea agreement is binding upon all parties once the trial judge has accepted it, and that if the prosecution does not perform its responsibilities under the agreement, the plea bargain is considered involuntary.

IV. Analysis

... While Appellant could have withdrawn his plea at the sentencing hearing, he chose instead to request a new trial in order to compel specific performance of the plea agreement which the State had violated. Due to the flagrant violation of his plea agreement by the State, which rendered his plea involuntary, the court of appeals should have reviewed this issue for abuse of discretion by the trial judge in denying Appellant's motion for a new trial.

Conclusion

Based upon the underlying constitutional due process principles involved when a defendant agrees to plead guilty in return for a promise by the State, as well as upon a long history of Texas cases supporting a defendant's right to withdraw a plea once the State has violated the plea bargain, we hold that Appellant properly preserved the issue of the plea bargain breach by bringing it to the trial court's attention as soon as the error could be cured, in a motion for a new trial. ... [W]e ... remand the cause to the court for further proceedings consistent with this opinion.

————————◆————————

Notice that the State and the defendant in the above case entered into an agreement. It was only after the defendant's open plea—a plea that has no agreed punishment where the judge assesses punishment—and the court's acceptance of his plea of guilt that the State violated the terms of the agreement. Once the State and the defendant have agreed to the terms, and the judge accepts the plea bargain in open court, the defendant has a right to specific performance, if possible, or to withdraw his plea.[8]

---

[8] *Ex parte De Leon*, 400 S.W.3d 83, 91 (Tex. Crim. App. 2013).

Substantiating Evidence

Unlike other jurisdictions, Texas requires that a felony plea of guilt must be supported by evidence. The Code requires the State to offer evidence into the record of the defendant's guilt; this evidence is accepted by the court as the basis for its judgment.[9] The corroborating evidence the State must produce is called "substantiating evidence." The following excerpt explains the purposes for substantiating evidence and the forms it can take.

> Although the United States Constitution does not require substantiation of a guilty plea in state court, Texas ... provide[s] this additional procedural safeguard. Under the article, a court may not enter a conviction in a felony case based on a guilty plea unless evidence is presented establishing guilt in addition to and independent of the plea. The evidence does not have to establish the defendant's guilt beyond a reasonable doubt but must embrace *every element of the offense charged.*
>
> Evidence substantiating a guilty plea can take several possible forms. Article 1.15 itself states that a defendant may consent to the presentation of evidence either by oral testimony or in written form, or to an oral or written stipulation of what the evidence would be, without necessarily admitting to its veracity or accuracy. Additionally, courts have recognized that a defendant may enter a sworn written confession, or may testify under oath in open court, admitting his or her culpability or at least acknowledging generally that the allegations against him or her are in fact true and correct. A deficiency in one form of proof may be compensated for by other competent evidence in the record. Evidence adduced at a sentencing hearing may also suffice to substantiate a guilty plea.[10]

Thus, substantiation can occur through a written judicial confession, an oral judicial confession, or through stipulation of evidence. Failure to comply with these requirements may result in a reversal of the plea itself.[11]

Inadmissibility of Pleas and Negotiations

Sometimes a defendant considers pleading guilty or is in the middle of a plea when he changes his mind. Can the prosecutor use the defendant's plea

---

[9] TEX. CODE CRIM. PROC. ANN. art. 1.15 (West 2016).
[10] *Jones v. State*, 373 S.W.3d 790, 792–93 (Tex. App.—Houston [14th Dist.] 2012, no pet.) (emphasis added).
[11] *Ex parte Duran*, 581 S.W.2d 683, 686 (Tex. Crim. App. 1979).

or statements made during plea negotiations as evidence of guilt at trial? The Texas Rules of Evidence address this dilemma. Rule 410 states that the following pleas and statements cannot be used in legal proceedings as evidence of guilt:

1. a plea of guilty that is later withdrawn;
2. in civil or criminal cases, a plea of nolo contendere that was later withdrawn;
3. in civil cases, a nolo contendere plea;
4. a statement made during plea negotiations in federal court or in any other state court where the plea was later withdrawn; or
5. a statement made to the prosecutor in the course of plea negotiations that did not lead to a plea or that led to a plea that was later withdrawn.[12]

The reason that these withdrawn pleas and statements are inadmissible is simple: pleas are an important part of the criminal justice system, and defendants should not fear their participation in plea negotiations will later be used against them at trial.[13]

There is one exception to the inadmissibility of the statements mentioned in the last two enumerated provisions above:

> In a civil case, the court may admit a statement ... and in a criminal case, the court may admit a statement ... when another statement made during the same plea or plea discussions has been introduced and in fairness the statements ought to be considered together.[14]

This exception applies when the defense "opens the door" to statements made during plea negotiations with the State. When the defense brings in some of the statements the defendant made, the State is permitted, in the interest of fairness, to offer other statements the defendant left out during her testimony.[15]

The admission of a plea in violation of this rule has serious consequences: "[It] is reversible error for the trial court to allow the introduction of

---

[12] TEX. R. EVID. 410.

[13] *Abdygapparova v. State*, 243 S.W.3d 191, 206 (Tex. App.—San Antonio 2007, pet. ref'd).

[14] *Id.*

[15] *Taylor v. State*, 19 S.W.3d 858, 863–64 (Tex. App.—Eastland 2000, pet. ref'd).

evidence of a prior plea of guilty … when [the defendant] has timely changed his plea to one of not guilty."[16]

The State's Duty to Keep the Victim Informed

Crime victims have several rights, one of which is, upon request, to be informed by the prosecutor about the progress of the case.[17] The Code grants victims (1) the right to be informed by the State about plea negotiations and (2) the right to provide pertinent information related to sentencing.[18] To this end, the prosecutor shall assist victims in completing victim impact statements and ensure that the judge has the statement before sentencing or before a plea agreement is accepted.[19]

While these rights permit the victim to be informed about pleas and participate in them, if desired, the Code states that "A victim, guardian of a victim, or close relative of a deceased victim does not have standing to participate as a party in a criminal proceeding or to contest the disposition of any charge."[20]

◆

The Defendant's Role

The defendant has no right to receive a plea bargain; he cannot compel the State to offer him anything in return for a plea of guilt.[21] "It is no more reasonable to argue that the State must enter into a plea bargain with every defendant than to argue that every defendant must plead guilty and enter into a plea bargain."[22]

The defendant's plea must be freely and voluntarily given.[23] He should not plead guilty due to pressure from others, whether it be defense counsel,

---

16 *Childs v. State*, 837 S.W.2d 822, 824–25 (Tex. App.—San Antonio 1992, pet. ref'd).
17 TEX. CODE CRIM. PROC. ANN. art. 56.02(a)(3)(A) (West 2016).
18 TEX. CODE CRIM. PROC. ANN. art. 56.02(a)(4)–(5) (West 2016).
19 TEX. CODE CRIM. PROC. ANN. art. 56.02(12) (West 2016).
20 TEX. CODE CRIM. PROC. ANN. art. 56.02(d) (West 2016).
21 *DeRusse v. State*, 579 S.W.2d 224, 236 (Tex. Crim. App. 1979).
22 *Morano v. State*, 572 S.W.2d 550, 551 (Tex. Crim. App. 1978).
23 TEX. CODE CRIM. PROC. ANN. art. 26.13(b) (West 2016).

family, employers, or friends. He alone is the one who decides which plea to enter.

A defendant who pleads not guilty, without later changing his plea, will proceed to trial, unless the prosecutor dismisses the case. If the defendant does not want a trial and the prosecutor does not dismiss the case, the defendant may plead guilty or nolo contendere (no contest) to the charges.[24] Both of these pleadings have the same legal effect in criminal court, the sole distinction being that a plea of nolo contendere may not be used against the defendant in any civil suit arising from the criminal act.[25] Throughout the rest of the chapter, unless otherwise stated, pleas of guilty and pleas of no contest will be used interchangeably. When the text refers to a plea of guilty, it also could include a plea of no contest.

The defendant has three options when it comes to pleading guilty: (1) negotiate a plea with the State for a set punishment and plead guilty in exchange for that offer; (2) plead and go to the judge without an agreed punishment, letting the judge assess punishment; or (3) plead and go to the jury for punishment, letting the jury determine punishment.[26]

Each of the above options has a name. The first is called a *plea bargain* or a *negotiated plea* because the punishment was negotiated between the State and the defense. The second option is called an *open plea* because the full range of punishment is open to the judge. The third is a jury trial on punishment only, or a unilateral trial.[27]

Normally, Texas criminal trials are bifurcated, meaning the first portion of the trial asks the fact-finder to determine guilt/innocence, and the second portion, if the defendant is found guilty, asks the fact-finder to assess punishment. When the defendant pleads guilty to a jury, there is no reason for the first part of the bifurcated trial; therefore, it is a unitary trial. Unitary trials may look—to the untrained eye—like a bifurcated trial. This is because in order to assess punishment for the crime, the jury has to know the details of the underlying offense.

Jury trials on punishment following a guilty plea are rare. They typically happen when the State and the defendant are unable to agree on a negotiated plea, and the defendant believes jury punishment may be favorable. Of the

---

[24] TEX. CODE CRIM. PROC. ANN. art. 27.02 (West 2016).
[25] *Id.*
[26] TEX. CODE CRIM. PROC. ANN. art. 26.14 (West 2016).
[27] *Wilkerson v. State*, 736 S.W.2d 656, 659 (Tex. Crim. App. 1987).

three options for a plea—a negotiated plea between the State and the defendant, an open plea where the judge assess punishment following a plea of guilt, or a unitary trial on punishment before a jury—negotiated pleas are by far the most common.

What happens when a defendant attempts to withdraw a negotiated plea? The next case addresses this issue. Before you read the *Saldana* case, you need to understand presentence investigation (PSI) reports. The Code permits the judge to request a PSI report from a probation officer when community supervision is a punishment option.[28] The report includes details about the facts of the crime, the amount of restitution owed to the victim, the defendant's social and criminal history, a plan for community supervision if the defendant is eligible for it, and any other recommendations the probation department may have regarding punishment.[29] The purpose of the report is to assist the judge in determining how to sentence the defendant, or in the case of a negotiated plea, whether it is just, or whether conditions should be added to an offer of probation or deferred adjudication. The judge will consult the PSI report in assessing punishment.

Jason Andrew Saldana v. State
150 S.W.3d 486
(Tex. App.—Austin 2004, no pet.)

Appellant Jason Andrew Saldana appeals his conviction for possession of marihuana in an amount less than five pounds but more than four ounces. Appellant waived trial by jury and entered a plea of guilty before the trial court. The trial court assessed punishment at two years' confinement in state jail.

Appellant advances a single point of error—that the trial court abused its discretion when it refused to allow appellant to withdraw his plea of guilty.

Background and Facts

On July 18, 2003, appellant appeared before Judge Martha J. Trudo while represented by retained counsel. He waived trial by jury and entered a plea of guilty to the indictment. Appellant told Judge Trudo that he was freely and voluntarily pleading guilty because he was guilty. The trial court carefully

---

[28] TEX. CODE CRIM. PROC. ANN. art. 42.12 § 9 (West 2016).
[29] *Id.*

admonished appellant of the consequences of his plea, and determined him to be mentally competent. Appellant's judicial confession, tracking the language of the indictment, was entered into evidence. The trial court made a finding that the evidence was sufficient to support the plea of guilty. Appellant requested a presentence investigative report.

On August 28, 2003, appellant appeared with his counsel before Judge Joe Carroll, who had received appellant's presentence investigative report. The State indicated that it had no further evidence to offer. Appellant called his mother, Heather Saldana, as a witness. She related that she was in poor health suffering from multiple sclerosis, had poor vision, and needed appellant for healthcare and financial purposes.

The twenty-six-year-old appellant testified in his own behalf. When asked on direct examination what happened on the day of the offense, appellant unveiled an exculpatory scenario. [After describing a complicated and unbelievable fact scenario, appellant suggested that the drugs he was charged with possessing actually belonged to a man whose name he did not know.]

On cross-examination, appellant admitted that [he gave the] police officer a false name and a false date of birth because he panicked under the circumstances. Appellant acknowledged that all the convictions listed in the presentence report were correct. Appellant stated that he had stolen "a bunch" of motor vehicles in Nevada and "did time there"; that he had two Texas convictions for burglary of a motor vehicle, which he "did." He agreed that he served thirty days in the Coryell County jail for misdemeanor theft, but was framed. When asked about a Texas forgery conviction, appellant related that a woman inquired if he could forge "something" and he said "no," but she got six months' probation, and he served a year in state jail for "forgery by knowledge." When the prosecutor asked if the instant case was like the forgery case—that he was not guilty but knew the marihuana was in the truck—appellant's counsel objected, "Well, your Honor, that's not true. We've pled guilty under the facts and circumstances of the case...." The objection was overruled and the cross-examination continued. Appellant then stated that he was not guilty but knew the marihuana was in the truck, and he was with the wrong person at the wrong time.

Subsequently, when the prosecutor inquired if appellant was guilty of anything, an objection was interposed. At this point, the trial court began an inquiry of appellant as to his plea. In response, appellant told the trial court that he had discussed the indictment's allegations with his attorney and knew that he was pleading guilty to intentionally and knowingly possessing marihuana. In answer to another question, appellant responded: "Yes, sir, I do want to plead guilty."

After further cross-examination, the trial court returned to the subject matter of its earlier interrogation. Appellant assured the trial court that Judge Trudo had admonished him of the consequences of his plea, that he had freely and voluntarily entered his guilty plea, and that he was pleading guilty because he was guilty. The trial court stated that appellant seemed to be pleading guilty but testifying to the contrary. At this point, appellant's counsel asked to withdraw appellant's plea of guilty, stating that "the prosecutor caused it." After a colloquy at the bench, the trial court refused to allow the plea to be withdrawn.

In argument, appellant's counsel stated:

> I think that because of the health of his mother he is deserving of this chance [deferred adjudication] or if you feel that he is not, Your Honor, you do what you want to. But the man has entered his plea freely and voluntarily.

The trial court heard the State's argument and assessed punishment.

A Unitary Trial

The instant trial took on some characteristics of a bifurcated trial but was nevertheless a unitary trial. It is also important to remember in discussing the withdrawal of a guilty plea that the instant case did not involve a jury. When a jury is in the box, different rules are applicable regardless of a defendant's plea. The following discussion of the legal issue of plea withdrawal, however, involves only a plea of guilty before the court in a unitary trial.

Discussion

A liberal practice has prevailed in Texas concerning the withdrawal of a guilty plea. A defendant may withdraw his guilty plea as a matter of right without assigning any reason until the judgment has been pronounced or the case has been taken under advisement.

When, however, a defendant decides to withdraw his guilty plea after the trial court takes the case under advisement or pronounces judgment, the withdrawal of such plea is within the sound discretion of the trial court.

In *Harling v. State*, the court stated:

> It is well-settled law that after a court has admonished the defendant, received the guilty plea and received the evidence, passing the case for a presentence investigation is "taking the case under advisement." Following these cases, we find that here the trial court had taken the case under advisement when it reset the case on November 15, 1993 for a presentence investigation.

Thus, appellant did not have an absolute right to withdraw his guilty plea because his request came too late or was untimely because the case had been taken under advisement at the July 18, 2003, hearing.

Under the circumstances, even if appellant had properly presented the issue for review, we find the trial court did not abuse its discretion in refusing to permit the withdrawal of the plea. The point of error is overruled.

The judgment is affirmed.

---◆---

Notes and Questions

1. In the above case, the court stated that the "defendant may withdraw his guilty plea as a matter of right without assigning any reason until the judgment has been pronounced or the case has been taken under advisement."[30] When has a case been taken under advisement? When the judge has taken the plea and considered punishment evidence before sentencing the defendant.[31] At that point, it is in the discretion of the court to permit the plea to be withdrawn.

2. What happens when the defendant enters a guilty plea, elects to have the jury assess punishment, but then wishes to withdraw his plea during the punishment hearing? When is a plea withdrawal timely in this instance? The defendant may withdraw his guilty plea at any time before the jury retires to deliberate.[32]

When this happens, the jury is instructed to disregard the defendant's earlier plea, which causes the trial to revert from a unitary trial to a bifurcated

---

[30] *Saldana v. State*, 150 S.W.3d 486, 490 (Tex. App.—Austin 2004, no pet.).
[31] *Taplin v. State*, 78 S.W.3d 459, 461 (Tex. App.—Austin 2001, no pet.) (attempt to withdraw plea at the close of the punishment hearing came too late).
[32] *Wilson v. State*, 515 S.W.2d 274, 274 (Tex. Crim. App. 1974).

trial.[33] It seems odd to request the same jury to "unhear" the defendant's guilty plea in open court, but this is the procedure.

3. Unlike most aspects of criminal procedure, which are based in the Code of Criminal Procedure, the timeliness of a plea withdrawal is a common law rule.

The Defense Attorney's Role

Defense attorneys have several roles in the plea process. The first is that of communicator. Defense counsel is ethically obligated to communicate plea offers to the defendant and communicate the defendant's acceptance or rejection of the offers back to the State.[34] When attorneys fail to communicate offers to their clients, it may have terrible consequences. For example, in *Atkins v. State*, a trial prosecutor offered Atkins 12 years in prison, even though he was facing a statutory minimum of 25 years for a habitual felony DWI.[35] His attorney never communicated the offer.[36] Atkins discovered the 12-year offer on the day of trial and communicated to the court he would have accepted it then and wanted to accept it now; however, the State refused to reoffer the 12-year sentence.[37] On appeal, the Beaumont Court of Appeals rendered defense counsel's performance ineffective, reversed the judgment of conviction, and ordered the State to reinstate the 12-year offer.[38]

In another case, defense counsel's failure to convey the State's offer in a timely manner resulted in the State's withdrawal of a 35-year offer and a life sentence.[39] The Court of Criminal Appeals held defense counsel's failure to

---

[33] *Fairfield v. State*, 610 S.W.2d 771, 778 (Tex. Crim. App. 1981).

[34] *Ex parte Wilson*, 724 S.W.2d 72, 73–75 (Tex. Crim. App. 1987) (defense counsel has duty to inform client about plea offers); *Randle v. State*, 847 S.W.2d 576, 579 (Tex. Crim. App. 1993) (defense counsel has duty to convey acceptance of offer to prosecutor).

[35] *Atkins v. State*, 26 S.W.3d 580, 581-83 (Tex. App.—Beaumont 2000, pet. ref'd).

[36] *Id.*

[37] *Id.*

[38] *Id.*

[39] *Randle v. State*, 847 S.W.2d 576, 580–81 (Tex. Crim. App. 1993).

communicate the offer in a timely manner resulted in ineffective assistance of counsel.[40]

Unethical as the practice is, a number of defense attorneys fail to communicate offers to their clients on a regular basis. The reason: there is a financial incentive not to do so. An attorney may fear that by communicating the offer to an accepting defendant, he will lose the chance to receive money the defendant owes him (and will pay over time) or, in the case of appointed attorneys, lose money he would receive from the county by making a future appearance in court. If you ask defense attorneys in the courthouse who engages in this practice, they will tell you. They know. However, it is unethical to do so. It not only damages reputations among peers, it can result in a finding of ineffectiveness and a grievance with the State bar.

Defense counsel's other roles in the plea bargaining process are to negotiate the best possible punishment for her client, know the legal consequences of the plea, and advise the defendant about all available options. Again, the decision to go to trial or enter a plea is solely the defendant's, but the defense attorney should counsel the defendant about the wisdom of entering a plea given the facts and law of the case.

Defense counsel must be aware of the following things when advising a defendant about plea bargaining:

- The punishment range for each level and type of offense;
- Whether the type of punishment the defendant desires (*e.g.*, deferred adjudication or probation) is available given the charged crime; and
- Whether the judge or the jury can award the desired punishment.

These factors are discussed in more detail in Chapter 13.

———————◆———————

Notes and Questions

1. Attorneys must carefully and accurately advise clients and explain the law and rights in the process of their representation. If an attorney passes on

---

[40] *Id.*

erroneous information to the defendant, the resulting plea, if based upon that misinformation, is rendered involuntary.[41]

2. Defense attorneys who represent noncitizens must know immigration law well enough to explain the collateral consequences a plea of guilty or nolo contendere has on the person's status to become a citizen or remain in the United States. Attorneys who do not properly advise a client on these consequences render ineffective assistance of counsel and violate the client's right to counsel under the Sixth Amendment of the U.S. Constitution.[42]

3. Defense attorneys should carefully advise clients about parole time tables. However, there is a difference between when a defendant becomes eligible for parole (*parole eligibility*) and when he actually will be paroled (*parole attainment*).

> Parole attainment is indeed highly speculative, due to various factors associated with circumstances surrounding an individual prisoner's parole application, such as the prisoner's behavior in prison, the composition and attitude of the parole board, the identity and attitude of the governor, the population of the prison system, and regulations governing "good time." The question of parole eligibility, however, elicits a straightforward answer because an applicant's parole eligibility is determined by the law in effect on the date of the offense.[43]

When an attorney gives incorrect advice about parole eligibility that induces a defendant to plead guilty and the client is harmed, the plea is rendered involuntary.[44]

———————————◆———————————

The Judge's Role

The State offers the plea bargain, the defense attorney communicates the offer and advises her client about whether to accept it, the defendant chooses which plea to enter (not guilty, guilty, or no contest), and the judge oversees the process and may render punishment in an open plea or when the terms of the negotiated plea are not acceptable. When it comes to roles, the Code

---

[41] *Rivera v. State*, 952 S.W.2d 34, 36 (Tex. App.—San Antonio 1997, no pet.).
[42] *Ex Parte De Los Reyes*, 392 S.W.3d 675, 678–79 (Tex. Crim. App. 2013).
[43] *Ex Parte Moussazadeh*, 361 S.W.3d 684, 690 (Tex. Crim. App. 2012).
[44] *Id.* at 691-92.

of Criminal Procedure devotes the most attention to the trial court's role in this process. This section will look at the judge's responsibilities in the plea process.

The Judge's Role in a Negotiated Plea

Recall the pleading defendant has three options: pursue a negotiated plea, pursue an open plea, or pursue a jury trial on punishment only. When the State and the defense attorney negotiate a plea bargain and the defendant accepts it, the parties will begin filling out plea papers. These papers are examined by the judge before she takes the plea. Most of the time, the judge approves the negotiated plea, asks the defendant to enter his plea in open court, and sentences the defendant according to the agreement between the State and the defense.

The Corpus Christi Court of Appeals framed the judge's role in a negotiated plea as follows:

> A plea bargain consists of three things: the defendant's plea, the punishment the State offers in exchange for that plea, and the approval by the court of the agreement. Courts view this negotiated plea as a contract. In order for the contract to be binding, the trial judge must approve and accept both aspects of it. When presented with a plea bargain, the court has the right to accept or reject it; however, it may not hold the defendant to his plea of guilty while rejecting the benefit the defendant was to receive. If the court does not approve the entire agreement, the defendant must be allowed to withdraw his plea of guilty.[45]

———————◆———————

Admonishments

The process of pleading guilty is complicated. It involves more than the defendant announcing he is guilty in open court and the judge assessing punishment. The judge must admonish or warn the defendant before taking the plea, ensuring the defendant is aware of the legal consequences and the waived rights he is giving up by pleading to the offense. This section details the admonishments required for felony cases.

---

[45] *Ortiz v. State*, 885 S.W.2d 271, 273 (Tex. App.—Corpus Christi 1994), *aff'd*, 933 S.W.2d 102 (Tex. Crim. App. 1996).

The admonishments' purpose is to protect the due process rights of defendants who enter into plea bargains.[46] Pleading defendants not only waive the right to a jury trial but also waive other fundamental, constitutional rights as well (*e.g.*, the right to make the State prove its case beyond a reasonable doubt and the right to confront witnesses). Moreover, some defendants will face consequences of the plea that may affect them for a lifetime. While the judge is not required by law to provide an exhaustive list of rights lost or consequences to come, before the defendant pleads guilty in a felony case, the judge must admonish the defendant. There are five admonishments required by the Code of Criminal Procedure in a felony case:

- The judge must admonish the defendant on the range of punishment;
- The judge must inform the defendant that the prosecutor's recommendation of punishment is not binding upon the court; however, if the court rejects the agreement, the defendant may withdraw his plea;
- The judge must inform the defendant that he must have the court's permission to appeal following a plea if the negotiated plea is not exceeded, except in matters raised through a written, pretrial motion;
- The judge must inform the defendant about immigration ramifications: if the defendant is not a citizen, a plea of guilty or no contest could result in his deportation, his inability to become a citizen, or his inability to re-enter the country; and
- The judge must inform the defendant about sex offender registration if the defendant is convicted or placed on deferred adjudication for a sexual crime.[47]

The judge is also required to ensure that each pleading defendant is mentally competent and is entering the plea voluntarily; however, these two requirements are not considered admonishments.[48]

Judges are required to ensure that the plea is voluntary.[49] In *Bitterman*, the plea was rendered involuntary when the State failed to comply with the

---

[46] *Bitterman v. State*, 180 S.W.3d 139, 141 (Tex. Crim. App. 2005).
[47] TEX. CODE CRIM. PROC. ANN. art. 26.13(a) (West 2016).
[48] *Id.*

promise that induced the plea. Is a guilty plea, when the defendant maintains his innocence, involuntary? Not necessarily. If the defendant was promised something, induced, or threatened to make the plea, yes, but if the defendant fears a harsher punishment than the one offered by the State, he may choose the certainty of the negotiated punishment in lieu of the uncertainty of trial. A judge is not required to withdraw a plea when there is evidence consistent with innocence, though many judges do.[50]

A judge need only substantially comply with the required admonishments.[51] Once the judge complies substantially with the admonishments, she creates a prima facie case that the defendant entered the plea knowingly and voluntarily.[52] "A defendant may still raise the claim that his plea was not voluntary; however, the burden shifts to the defendant to demonstrate that he did not fully understand the consequences of his plea such that he suffered harm."[53] Finally, the Code prohibits a court from setting aside the conviction for failure to substantially comply with the sex offender admonishment,[54] and appellate courts have found immigration admonishment errors harmless when the record demonstrates the defendant is a U.S. citizen.[55]

The Code permits judges to admonish the defendant either orally or in writing.[56] If the judge admonishes the defendant in writing, the judge must receive a copy of the admonishments signed by the defendant and the defendant's attorney, acknowledging that the defendant understands them

---

[49] *Id.*

[50] *Houston v. State*, 201 S.W.3d 212, 219 (Tex. App.—Houston [14th Dist.] 2006, no pet.).

[51] TEX. CODE CRIM. PROC. ANN. art. 26.13(h) (West 2016).

[52] *Martinez v. State*, 981 S.W.2d 195, 197 (Tex. Crim. App. 1998).

[53] *Id.*

[54] TEX. CODE CRIM. PROC. ANN. art. 26.13(h) (West 2016).

[55] *E.g., Matchett v. State*, 941 S.W.2d 922, 930 (Tex. Crim. App. 1996) ("It would be an absurd result—a result the Legislature could not possibly have intended—to allow a defendant's conviction on a plea of guilty or nolo contendere to be reversed on appeal for failure to give the article 26.13(a)(4) admonishment where the record conclusively shows, as it does in this case, that the defendant is a U.S. citizen and thus the admonishment is legally inapplicable to him. We conclude under the facts of this case that the error was harmless beyond a reasonable doubt").

[56] TEX. CODE CRIM. PROC. ANN. art. 26.13(d) (West 2016).

and the consequences of his plea.[57] If the defendant refuses to sign the written admonishments, the judge shall orally state the admonishments.[58]

Judge Not Bound by Prosecutor's Recommendation

This admonishment is worth discussing in more detail. The judge always has the option to disapprove the negotiated plea. This may happen before the parties begin the plea process, at the bench while the defendant is being admonished, or midway through the plea. The judge was not a party to the contract and is not bound by it. "Any plea of guilty as part of a plea bargain agreement is tentative until the trial court approves or rejects the agreement."[59]

There are reasons the judge may reject the plea bargain. The negotiated punishment may offend the judge's sensibilities. Practitioners refer to this as "busting the plea." When the judge busts the plea, the parties are left with the options of renegotiating the plea, seeking an open plea, or setting the case for trial.

What rights does the defendant have when the judge disagrees with the terms of the contract? The next case answers this question.

Jonathan James Moore v. State
295 S.W.3d 329
(Tex. Crim. App. 2009)

Appellant entered into a plea agreement with the state whereby he would plead guilty to manufacturing methamphetamine in exchange for a recommended sentence of 28 years' imprisonment and the dismissal of two other charges. On January 4, 2006, appellant entered his guilty plea before the trial court at a hearing in which he waived various rights and was admonished by the court verbally and in writing.

During the plea hearing, the court asked if sentencing was to take place at a later date. The state informed the court that a continuance for sentencing was not part of the plea bargain, but that the state had no objections if appellant and the court could come to an agreement on the issue. The court

---

[57] *Id.*

[58] *Id.*

[59] *Ortiz v. State*, 885 S.W.2d 271, 273 (Tex. App.—Corpus Christi 1994), *aff'd*, 933 S.W.2d 102 (Tex. Crim. App. 1996).

offered to postpone sentencing until February 15, 2006, with the condition that either appellant appeared for sentencing or his guilty plea would be converted to an open plea. The trial court then admonished appellant about the results of this agreement: a failure to appear on February 15, 2006, could mean a sentence of up to life and a fine of up to $10,000. Appellant agreed to the court's terms and was found competent. The court then approved the plea bargain with the added conditions, and appellant entered a plea of guilty.

Appellant failed to appear for sentencing on February 15, 2006, and was arrested the next day. At the sentencing hearing on February 27, 2006, the court announced that appellant had made an open plea and sentenced him to 40 years in the Texas Department of Criminal Justice-institutional division.

On appeal, appellant argued that the trial court erred by treating his plea as an open plea without giving him the opportunity to withdraw his plea as required by TEX. CODE CRIM. PROC. art. 26.13(a)(2). The court of appeals held that the trial court exceeded its authority by injecting itself into the plea-bargain negotiations between the state and appellant. The court of appeals reversed the trial court and remanded for further proceedings.

We granted the state's petition for review on two grounds: (1) the court of appeals did not address preservation of the error complained of, and (2) whether the court of appeals is required to conduct a harm analysis of the error alleged by the appellant.

Plea Bargains

Plea bargains are an integral part of the criminal justice system. At its core, a plea bargain is a contract between the state and the defendant. As a contract, once both parties have entered knowingly and voluntarily into a plea bargain, they are bound by the terms of that agreement once it is accepted by the judge. Plea agreements may contain a wide variety of stipulations and conditions that allow the state to tailor conditions in order to reach agreement with the defendant.

The only proper role of the trial court in the plea-bargain process is advising the defendant whether it will "follow or reject" the bargain between the state and the defendant. TEX. CODE CRIM. PROC. art. 26.13(a)(2)("the court shall inquire as to the existence of any plea bargaining agreements between the state and the defendant and, in the event that such an agreement exists, the court shall inform the defendant whether it will follow or reject such agreement in open court and before any finding on the plea."). If the trial court accepts a plea-bargain agreement, the state may not withdraw its offer. If the trial court rejects the plea-bargain agreement, the defendant is, as a matter of right, allowed to withdraw his guilty plea, and the state may then withdraw its offer. TEX. CODE CRIM. PROC. art. 26.13(a)(2)("Should the court reject any such agreement, the defendant shall be permitted to withdraw his plea of guilty or nolo contendere.").

Only the state may offer or withdraw a plea bargain. Because a plea-bargain agreement is solely between the state and the defendant, only the state and the defendant may alter the terms of the agreement; the trial court commits error if it unilaterally adds un-negotiated terms to a plea-bargain agreement.

A trial court may conditionally agree to follow a plea-bargain agreement, but only by delaying the unconditional acceptance or rejection of the agreement until after the condition of acceptance has been fulfilled. If, after a conditional acceptance of a plea bargain, the trial court rejects the plea-bargain agreement, the court must still allow the defendant the opportunity to withdraw his guilty plea.

In this case, the trial court said that it would "approve the plea bargain agreement as stated" and would also, by a separate agreement with appellant, reset for sentencing. The statute uses the word "follow," for which "conform," "abide by," and "adhere to" are synonyms. "Agree to," "adopt," and "concur in" are synonyms for "approve." From these synonyms, we conclude that, by "approving" the plea agreement, the trial court informed appellant that it intended to "follow" the agreement. Because of lack of precision in its language, it is not clear to us whether the trial court intended to alter the state's offer and approve it as altered or to enter into a side agreement with appellant.

In this case, we need not decide whether, by requiring appellant to agree to enter an open plea if he failed to appear at his sentencing hearing, the trial court created its own terms and improperly added them to the state's plea-bargain offer or merely expressed its conditional intent to "approve" the plea agreement, subject to fulfillment of a separate agreement between the trial court and appellant. Whatever its intent, when the trial court rejected the plea agreement during the sentencing hearing, it was required to permit appellant to withdraw his plea of guilty.

Preservation of Error

Preservation of error is a systemic requirement of every appeal. The state has complained that the appellate court failed to address preservation of error, and we granted review to address that issue. TEX. R. APP. P. 33.1 controls the issue of preservation of error for most trial errors. The general rule provides that complaints must be made in the "trial court by a timely request, objection, or motion...."

The state argues that appellant failed to preserve error at trial by neither objecting to the conditions placed on him by the trial court during the plea hearing nor by objecting at the sentencing hearing when the court declared an open plea. Appellant argues that the error presented is systemic and may be raised for the first time on appeal as an admonishment error under TEX. CODE CRIM. PROC. art. 26.13(a). However, the error in this case does not involve ... admonishment requirements. Instead the error arises from the trial court's improper intrusion into the plea-bargaining process. The error at issue is not systemic and may not be brought for the first time on appeal. The record reflects that, despite having the opportunity to object during the plea hearing and again at sentencing, appellant did not do so.

Appellant also argues that he was not allowed to withdraw his guilty plea. The record does not bear out this complaint. Appellant agreed to the terms improperly placed on him by the court and, at sentencing, appellant did not move to withdraw his guilty plea, despite having the opportunity to do so. The rationale of Rule 33.1 is that, if objections are raised before the trial court in a timely manner, those issues may be addressed, and possibly corrected, at trial. "[A]ll but the most fundamental rights are thought to be forfeited if not insisted upon by the party to whom they belong." By failing to object that the trial court's conditions were improper, appellant failed to preserve error. This court has not held that a trial court's intrusion in plea-bargain negotiations is systemic or waivable-only error and declines to make such a determination now.

Conclusion

We hold that, by not raising the error at either the plea hearing or the sentencing hearing, appellant failed to preserve error for review on appeal. We reverse the judgment of the court of appeals and affirm the judgment of the trial court.

Notes and Questions

1. Recall the rule that when a defendant accused of a felony offense waives her right to trial, she must be represented by counsel. Moore was charged with a felony drug offense. His defense attorney should have been by his side during the plea. Who should have objected? Do defendants know about the legal requirements for preserving error? Should the Court have taken that into consideration, or does the saying, "Ignorance of the law is no excuse" apply to Moore?

2. As you see from the above case, the judge must warn the defendant she is not bound by the prosecutor's recommendation. If the judge departs from the negotiated plea, the judge must give the defendant an opportunity to withdraw the plea. This is the rule in a felony case. It is not the rule in a misdemeanor case.[60] If a judge varies from the recommended punishment in a misdemeanor case, the defendant has no right to withdraw the plea.

3. A trial judge should not participate in any plea bargain agreement discussions until an agreement has been reached between the prosecutor and the defendant.[61] The trial judge should always avoid the appearance of any judicial coercion or prejudgment of the defendant since such influence might affect the voluntariness of the defendant's plea.

Unfortunately, some judges improperly insert themselves or their opinions into the plea process or into the punishment decision before the time for the judge's punishment assessment is appropriate. This may happen when a judge wants to move a case forward or seeks to convince the defendant that his punishment opinion is more favorable than the State's or the jury's likely will be. The Court of Criminal Appeals has stated this practice is contrary to public policy:

> Judicial involvement in plea negotiations runs afoul of due process and fundamental fairness in several ways. First, the trial court's role as neutral arbiter between competing parties is compromised as the court seeks to convince the defendant to accept its proffered plea. Second, rejection of the court's offer by a defendant creates the possibility of prejudice against the defendant on the court's part whether or not such prejudice is conscious or intentional. Third, the trial court's power over the defendant gives it an uneven advantage in the negotiations and brings home to the defendant the

---

[60] *McGuire v. State*, 617 S.W.2d 259, 261 (Tex. Crim. App. 1981).
[61] *Ex parte Williams*, 704 S.W.2d 773, 777, n. 6 (Tex. Crim. App. 1986).

possibly unhappy consequences of rejecting the court's offer. Finally, during the course of negotiations between the court and the defendant, the defendant may very well make explicit or implicit admissions or confessions that would not normally be admissible before the court during formal trial.[62]

For all of these reasons and more, the judge must overcome his desire to participate in plea negotiations with the defendant or to interject his own opinion or ideas about punishment before the defendant enters his plea and the time for judicial approval has come.

4. Once a judge accepts the plea, he is bound by the terms of the agreement, and the defendant has the right to demand specific performance. The judge cannot *sua sponte* force a defendant to withdraw his plea.[63] In the *Perkins* case, the defendant was charged with murder. The State entered into plea negotiations—offering 25 years—before talking to the victims and witnesses in the case. The judge took the plea and agreed to sentence the defendant at a later date. Between the date of the plea and the date of sentencing, the prosecutor discovered the defendant was more culpable than previously believed. The State communicated this to the judge at the sentencing hearing, and the judge withdrew the defendant's plea over the defendant's objection. The Court of Criminal Appeals held the judge cannot force a defendant to withdraw his plea over objection. Therefore, the defendant was entitled to specific performance because the judge had already accepted the negotiated plea of 25 years.[64]

5. The Code of Criminal Procedure gives judges additional authority over negotiated pleas for community supervision (probation or deferred adjudication). First, the Code states that "the judge may, after receiving a plea of guilty ... or nolo contendere ... place the defendant on community supervision.[65] Thus, a negotiated plea in exchange for community supervision is not certain—like all other negotiated pleas—until the trial court assents to it.

---

[62] *State ex rel. Bryan v. McDonald*, 662 S.W.2d 5, 8–9 (Tex. Crim. App. 1983).
[63] *Perkins v. Third Court of Appeals*, 738 S.W.2d 276, 280-81 (Tex. Crim. App. 1987).
[64] *Id.* at 278-85.
[65] TEX. CODE CRIM. PROC. ANN. art. 42.12 § 5(a) (West 2016).

Second, the Code gives the judge authority to set conditions of community supervision:

> The judge … shall determine the conditions of community supervision and may, at any time during the period of community supervision, alter or modify the conditions. The judge may impose any reasonable condition that is designed to protect or restore the community, protect or restore the victim, or punish, rehabilitate, or reform the defendant.[66]

In this way, the trial court possesses authority to modify, set, reject, or expand the negotiated conditions of the probation or deferred adjudication. In practice, it is common for the State to suggest conditions to defense counsel and to the court, but these conditions are typically based upon the judge's habit of assigning conditions. Furthermore, it is common practice for the judge to ask the parties about the details of the crime, ask the defendant questions about her personal life during the plea, and to take this gathered information into consideration when fashioning conditions that are meant to punish, deter, and rehabilitate the defendant while restoring the victim and community. Chapter 13 will explore probation, deferred adjudication, and conditions of community supervision in more detail.

———————◆———————

The Judge's Duties to the Crime Victim

While defense counsel is required to zealously represent the defendant, the prosecutor has an obligation to ensure that justice is done. The judge, as neutral overseer of the plea process, must make certain the defendant and the victim are legally protected in the plea process. This means the judge has some duty to safeguard the victim's rights.

Earlier in the chapter, you learned that the prosecutor must keep the victim informed about the status of the case. The judge owes the victim duties too. The judge shall determine whether a victim impact statement was returned to the prosecutor and, if so, ask to see a copy of it during the plea.[67] This happens at the time the plea is taking place. The judge must also inquire as to whether the State has notified the victim or the victim's family about

---

[66] TEX. CODE CRIM. PROC. ANN. art. 42.12 §§ 10(a) and 11(a)(West 2016).
[67] TEX. CODE CRIM. PROC. ANN. art. 26.13(e)(1) (West 2016).

the terms of the plea agreement.[68] In this way, the judge prevents prosecutors and defense attorneys from pleading a case without notifying or attempting to notify the victim about the terms of the negotiated plea.

———————◆———————

Misdemeanor Pleas

The process for pleading guilty or no contest in a misdemeanor case is much less formal and cumbersome than the process for entering felony pleas. These differences are best illustrated through the use of a chart.

Felony Pleas	Misdemeanor Pleas
Plea must be made in open court by the defendant in person with counsel.[69]	Plea must be made in open court by the defendant or his counsel.[70]
Plea must be supported by substantiating evidence of guilt.[71]	Plea is made without substantiating evidence.[72]
The defendant may withdraw his plea if the judge varies from the negotiated plea.[73]	The defendant has no right to withdraw his plea if the judge varies from the negotiated plea.[74]
The judge must substantially comply with admonishments.[75]	General admonishments do not apply. The only admonishment required is to warn family violence defendants of their loss of the right to possess or transfer a firearm.[76]

———————◆———————

[68] TEX. CODE CRIM. PROC. ANN. art. 26.13(e)(2) (West 2016).
[69] TEX. CODE CRIM. PROC. ANN. arts. 1.13 and 27.13 (West 2016).
[70] TEX. CODE CRIM. PROC. ANN. art. 27.14(a) (West 2016).
[71] TEX. CODE CRIM. PROC. ANN. art. 1.15 (West 2016).
[72] TEX. CODE CRIM. PROC. ANN. art. 27.14(a) (West 2016).
[73] TEX. CODE CRIM. PROC. ANN. art. 26.13(a)(2) (West 2016).
[74] *McGuire v. State*, 617 S.W.2d 259, 261 (Tex. Crim. App. 1981).
[75] TEX. CODE CRIM. PROC. ANN. art. 26.13(h) (West 2016).
[76] TEX. CODE CRIM. PROC. ANN. arts. 27.14(e)(1), 42.0131 (West 2016).

Appealing a Plea

Defendants who plead guilty or no contest have a limited right to appeal following their plea. The Court of Criminal Appeals has stated:

> A defendant in any criminal action has a right to appeal. However, a defendant in a non-capital felony case may waive any rights secured to him by law, including the right of appeal. Texas has "long held that a valid waiver of appeal prevents a defendant from appealing without the trial court's consent." A valid waiver of the right to appeal is one that was made voluntarily, knowingly, and intelligently.[77]

If the judge follows the recommendation of the prosecutor in a negotiated plea, the defendant's right to appeal is limited to matters the judge permits to be appealed or matters raised through written, pretrial motions (*e.g.*, a motion to suppress).[78]

Most courts notify a defendant in writing about the waiver of appeal following a plea; the waiver may even be an additional, stand-alone form. In a plea-bargained case, this waiver prohibits the defendant from appealing.[79] However, in an open plea, "the validity of a pretrial waiver of appeal is in question because the waiver cannot be knowing and intelligent when potential errors cannot be anticipated and the consequences of the waiver are unknown."[80]

Though defendants are admonished orally and in writing that by pleading guilty they are waiving their right to appeal, some defendants attempt to appeal anyway. The next case considers the Court of Criminal Appeals' response to a defendant who persistently attempted to appeal following a negotiated plea. Pay close attention to the appellate rules and the policies for them.

---

[77] *Ex parte Delaney*, 207 S.W.3d 794, 796–97 (Tex. Crim. App. 2006).
[78] TEX. CODE CRIM. PROC. ANN. art. 26.13(a)(3) (West 2016).
[79] *Blanco v. State*, 18 S.W.3d 218, 220 (Tex. Crim. App. 2000).
[80] *Ex parte Delaney*, 207 S.W.3d 794, 798 (Tex. Crim. App. 2006).

Terry Wayne Cooper v. State
45 S.W.3d 77
(Tex. Crim. App. 2001)

This case presents the question of whether a plea-bargaining defendant may appeal the voluntariness of the plea. We hold that such an appeal was forbidden by an act of the legislature in 1977, and that our rules do not, and may not, allow such an appeal.

On July 16, 1998, the appellant waived in writing his right to trial by jury and pleaded nolo contendere to an indictment for forgery, a felony. There was a plea-bargain agreement by which the State agreed to recommend punishment of "one year confinement in the state jail facility with credit for 351 days, no fine, and restitution in the amount of … approximately $37,000.00." The court sentenced the appellant according to the terms of that agreement. The appellant was admonished orally, and agreed in writing, that he could not appeal without the permission of the trial court except as to matters raised by written motion filed prior to trial. He filed a written waiver of his right to appeal.

Twelve days later the appellant filed, pro se, a handwritten notice of appeal, which said only that he "files this his notice of appeal." On August 11, represented by counsel, he requested permission to appeal, which was denied the following day. He immediately filed an amended notice of appeal which said, "The substance of this appeal was raised by written motion and ruled on prior to trial."

The appellant's issues on appeal, however, had nothing to do with any pre-trial motions. They were whether his plea was knowing and voluntary, and whether the trial court erred in accepting the plea because the court failed to adequately admonish him about the waiver of his right to appeal.

The court of appeals dismissed the appeal for want of jurisdiction, citing its holdings … that such a defendant may not challenge the voluntariness of his plea if the notice of appeal does not reflect that the trial court granted permission to appeal.

Rule of Appellate Procedure 25.2(b) does not authorize an appeal in a case such as this. The rule reads:

(3) [I]f the appeal is from a judgment rendered on the defendant's plea of guilty or nolo contendere … and the punishment assessed did not exceed

the punishment recommended by the prosecutor and agreed to by the defendant, the notice must:

(A) specify that the appeal is for a jurisdictional defect;

(B) specify that the substance of the appeal was raised by written motion and ruled on before trial; or

(C) state that the trial court granted permission to appeal.

[The statute] limit[s] every appeal in a plea-bargain, felony case....

The main thrust of the [Rule 25.2's predecessor] was to eliminate appeals where the defendant had entered a plea of guilty or nolo contendere before the court as a result of a plea bargain and the punishment assessed did not exceed that agreed upon. The same legislature enacted another amendment to curtail the right to bail pending appeal. Taken together, these two acts were aimed at eliminating, or reducing, the ability of plea-bargaining defendants to delay the execution of their sentences by taking meritless appeals.

There is nothing in the language of the [predecessor] statute that suggests that the voluntariness of a plea was exempt from the limitation on appeal. Indeed, any such exception to the operation of the proviso would have completely frustrated the legislative purpose to eliminate meritless appeals. The only limitation on the ability of an appellant to allege that the plea was involuntary is the limit of the human imagination, which is exactly the evil that the legislation sought to eliminate.

Our conclusion that the [predecessor to Rule 25.2(b)] limits every appeal on every ground in a plea-bargain, felony case is bolstered by the action of the next legislature in enacting article 26.13(a)(3) of the Code of Criminal Procedure. That act required a court to admonish a defendant who was pleading guilty in a felony case of "the fact that if the punishment assessed does not exceed the punishment recommended by the prosecutor and agreed to by the defendant and his attorney, the trial court must give its permission to the defendant before he may prosecute an appeal on any matter in the case except for those matters raised by written motions filed prior to trial." The evident purpose of this act was to inform the defendant of the restrictions on appeal ...so that the defendant could take them into account before making a knowing and voluntary decision to plead guilty.

When we actually consider the issue of whether voluntariness of a guilty plea may be raised on appeal from a plea-bargained, felony conviction, we

376 | Texas Criminal Procedure and Evidence

find that the answer must be that it may not. The first two reasons have been set out above: The legislature forbade it in 1977, and to do so would completely frustrate the statute. Our rule-making authority does not extend to enlarging the right of appeal in this fashion.

Two other reasons support the legislative decision to forbid appeals of voluntariness in such cases. One is a cost-benefit analysis. The number of plea-bargain, felony cases in which a plea was entered involuntarily is very small, compared to the large number of meritless appeals that would be authorized.

It must be remembered that the rule we are construing applies only to plea-bargained, felony cases. In a former era a defendant was expected to plead guilty (often without a lawyer) and throw himself on the mercy of the court with no assurance of the punishment to follow. The defendant's decision to do so was first manifested in court when the plea was entered. At that time it was crucial that the court give the defendant information about the consequences of a plea of guilty so that the decision to do so could be voluntary and knowing. But the practice of plea bargaining, which was made necessary by the lack of judicial resources, shifted the crucial decision in most cases to a plea-bargain agreement that was struck between attorneys for the State and the defendant in a negotiation that took place off the record. Now in a plea-bargain case the defendant knows, and has accepted before the plea is entered, the most important consequence of the plea of guilty: the upper limit on punishment. Even when the record shows that the trial court erred in admonishing a defendant before his plea is accepted, the plea will not be held involuntary on appeal if the defendant knew the punishment he was facing and the trial court followed the plea agreement. In a real sense, therefore, when the legislature identified cases in which the trial court followed the plea-bargain agreement, it identified cases in which the pleas were voluntary.

The number of cases in which the plea is involuntary when the trial court followed the plea agreement is therefore very small, and the number of cases in which the involuntariness would appear in an appellate record is even smaller. Experience has shown us that most cases of involuntary pleas result from circumstances that existed outside the record, such as misunderstandings, erroneous information, impaired judgment, ineffective assistance of counsel, and plea-bargains that were not followed or turn out to be impossible of performance. The legislature reasonably determined to eliminate a small number of meritorious appeals to prevent a much larger number of meritless appeals.

This decision may be seen as even more reasonable when it is remembered that meritorious claims of involuntary pleas may be raised by other procedures: motion for new trial and habeas corpus. These procedures are not only adequate to resolve claims of involuntary pleas, but they are superior to appeal in that the claim may be supported by information from sources broader than the appellate record.

Rule 25.2(b) does not permit the voluntariness of the plea to be raised on appeal. The judgment of the Second Court of Appeals is affirmed.

---◆---

Practice Questions

The bar exam, in general, follows a pattern. The format plays out as follows: the hypothetical defendant is arrested and charged with an offense, he decides he wants to plead guilty, changes his mind, then takes his case to trial. The fictional, short-lived decision to plead guilty typically results in one or two plea questions per exam.

1. (J-2016, J-2013, and F-2010) Prosecutor agrees to be very generous in her plea bargain, which makes Defendant fear the judge will reject the negotiated plea, and he will be stuck with it after giving up his right to a trial.

    What is your response to Defendant's concern? What are his options if the judge rejects the negotiated punishment?

---

2. (F-2016 and F-2010) What similarities and differences exist between a plea of nolo contendere and a plea of guilty? Explain.

_____

_____

_____

_____

_____

3. (J-2015 and F-2009) Client has had a hard time deciding whether to plead guilty or pursue a trial. He finally decides to go forward with the plea agreement. At the bench, the trial court asks:

COURT: What is your plea to the charge in the indictment?

CLIENT: Guilty.

COURT: We will now go through your legal admonishments…

CLIENT: Your Honor, I've changed my mind. I don't want to plead guilty. I want a trial.

Is it too late for the defendant to withdraw his plea at this point in the proceeding? Explain.

_____

_____

_____

_____

_____

4. (F-2015) You negotiate a plea agreement recommending that Defendant be given probation. The judge adds conditions to the community supervision. Is this permissible?

_____

_____

_____

_____

_____

5. (J-2014) Can a defendant enter a guilty plea only before a judge, only before a jury, or before either? Explain.

_____

_____

_____

_____

_____

6. (J-2014 and F-2012) If Defendant pleads guilty, will he be barred from appealing his motion to suppress that the court heard and denied before he entered his plea?

_____

_____

_____

_____

_____

7. (F-2014, F-2013, J-2009, F-2008, J-2007, F-2007, J-2006, F-2006, F-2005, J-2003, F-2002, and F-2001) List three admonishments the court must give to a defendant before accepting a felony plea of guilty.

_____

_____

_____

_____

_____

8. (J-2013, F-2009, J-2006, F-2005, J-2003, F-2003, and J-2001) Defendant pled guilty to the offense before withdrawing her plea and proceeding to trial. Prosecutor calls Victim to the stand to testify about statements he overheard Defendant make during plea negotiations. Prosecutor would like to admit these statements as evidence of guilt. You object to these statements coming into evidence. What is the basis for your objection, and how should Judge rule?

_____

_____

_____

_____

_____

9. (J-2012) Prosecutor knows his case against Defendant has some weaknesses. As a result, he offers her an extremely lenient plea bargain and hopes Victim won't find out about it. Will Prosecutor be able to get through the plea without letting Judge know whether the Victim has been notified about the plea agreement? Explain.

_____

_____

_____

_____

_____

10. (J-2011) Defendant states she would like to plead guilty, but she wants a jury to assess punishment. Is the jury permitted to assess punishment following a guilty plea? Explain.

_____

_____

_____

_____

_____

11. (F-2011) If you and Prosecutor agree to a negotiated plea, is Judge required to impose that sentence? Explain.

_____

_____

_____

_____

_____

12. (J-2008) Defendant has a disability that makes writing impossible. She asks Judge during the plea process whether she must sign the written admonishments. Judge chides her for not taking responsibility before rejecting her plea and setting her case for trial. Can Judge insist on a signed and written list of admonishments? Can Defendant still plead guilty even if she cannot sign the written admonishments? Explain.

_____

_____

_____

13. (J-2007-5) Defendant's statements at the time he committed the crime suggest he is mentally ill. However, he refuses to submit to a psychiatric evaluation and insists on pleading guilty. Should Judge accept his plea? Why or why not?

14. (F-2007, F-2006, J-2003, and F-2001) After fully investigating your client's case, you tell Defendant you believe the plea offer from Prosecutor is much more generous than the punishment he would receive following a trial. You encourage him to accept the offer. However, he suggests you and Prosecutor are in cahoots together and persists in his plea of not guilty. Who decides what plea will be entered? Explain.

Chapter 9
Discovery

Introduction

One of the most significant differences between civil litigation and criminal litigation lies in the process of discovery. Civil trials are rarer than criminal trials. The battle in civil litigation is not usually the trial itself, because most cases never make it to trial, but in the process of discovery. Parties exhaust most of their time and resources on discovery. In criminal law, however, the battle lies in plea negotiations or trial, not discovery.

There are several reasons why discovery in criminal practice is not designed to be a battle ground. First, the prosecutor carries the burden of proof, which means that all of the evidence needed to convict the defendant lies with the prosecution. Thus, discovery is generally one-sided. Second, the primary role of the prosecutor is to seek justice, not convictions.[1] The Code states that prosecutors "shall not suppress facts or secrete witnesses capable of establishing the innocence of the accused."[2] This requires prosecutors to be particularly open about favorable, mitigating, or exculpatory evidence. Third, with only a couple of exceptions, if the defense requests to inspect information and evidence in the State's possession, the law mandates the State to permit inspection as soon as possible.[3] The laws in Texas, therefore, are designed to make discovery straightforward. This chapter will examine the discovery process, the categories of evidence and information that are discoverable and those that are not, and what courts do when there is a discovery violation.

———————◆———————

The Discovery Process

Typically, attorneys who practice criminal law discover evidence and information through the prosecutor's "open file" and through discovery motions. These two methods, along with defense counsel's own investigation, help the defense team learn what evidence will be admitted against the defendant.

When we speak of *discovery* in Texas, we almost always mean the defense's right to discover the evidence and the information the State possesses. Aside from expert witness discovery[4] and the duty to notify the State that the defendant will raise the insanity defense,[5] the State has no right to obtain information or evidence from the defense. This is because the State bears the burden of proof, not the defendant. Therefore, assume discovery means a request by defense counsel to inspect what the State has, not the other way around.

---

[1] TEX. CODE CRIM. PROC. ANN. art. 2.01 (West 2016).
[2] *Id.*
[3] TEX. CODE CRIM. PROC. ANN. art. 39.14 (West 2016).
[4] TEX. CODE CRIM. PROC. ANN. art. 39.14(b) (West 2016).
[5] TEX. CODE CRIM. PROC. ANN. art. 46C.051 (West 2016) (defendant is required to give notice of her intent to raise the insanity defense before the pretrial hearing).

Open File Policies

One method of discovery is facilitated through a statewide mandated "open file policy." Prosecutors create a file for each defendant. A defendant charged with multiple crimes may have multiple files or just one, depending on the prosecutor's organization preference. The prosecutor's file may include the charging instrument, the police report, witness statements, confessions, work product, and the defendant's criminal history. Depending on the type of crime and the volume of reports, records, and evidence connected to the case, the file may be housed within a thin, manila envelope or in several, large boxes.

There was a time when prosecutors restricted access to their files. Some district attorney offices closed their files to the defense bar or crafted policies that limited access. Legislators put an end to that practice in 2014 with the passage of the Michael Morton Act, which is codified in Article 39.14 of the Texas Code of Criminal Procedure. Article 39.14 is the primary discovery statute. The namesake of the Act, Michael Morton, was a man falsely accused, convicted, and sentenced to prison for a murder he did not commit; he served 25 years in prison because his prosecutor failed to reveal exculpatory evidence located in the file to the defense team.[6] The Act ensures defendants have greater access to evidence in the State's possession.[7] The details of the Act will be discussed in more detail below.

Discovery Motions

Motions for discovery provide another method of discovery. Before the Michael Morton Act, apart from *Brady* obligations, which are discussed later in this chapter, the State was not required to turn over anything to the defense until the judge granted the defense's motion for discovery. The law now requires the State to permit defense counsel to examine items within the State's possession "as soon as practicable after receiving a timely request from the defendant."[8] The law does not specify that the request be in writing.

---

[6] See generally Cynthia E. Hujar Orr & Robert G. Rodery, *The Michael Morton Act: Minimizing Prosecutorial Misconduct*, 46 ST. MARY'S L.J. 407 (2015).

[7] *Ex parte Pruett*, 458 S.W.3d 537, 542 (Tex. Crim. App. 2015).

[8] TEX. CODE CRIM. PROC. ANN. art. 39.14(a) (West 2016).

Nevertheless, in practice, most attorneys and courts continue to make use of discovery motions. It is, therefore, important to discuss discovery motions.

When to File a Discovery Motion

When a criminal case is headed to trial, the parties will request a trial date from the judge. Prior to the trial date, the court may schedule a motions or pretrial hearing.[9] Discovery is one of the many topics that may be addressed during this hearing.[10] If the court sets a pretrial hearing, a discovery order must be filed at least seven days before the pretrial hearing date.[11] A discovery motion filed after that time will not be considered by the judge unless the court grants permission for good cause shown.[12]

In practice, most courts schedule a discovery or motions conference, not a formal pretrial hearing. At this informal setting, defense counsel asks and the prosecutor agrees to disclose evidence pursuant to a written discovery motion. The discovery motion may be created by defense counsel, or it may be a standard discovery order created by the judge. A standard discovery order applies to all criminal cases and usually lists items that the defendant has a right to discover pursuant to the Code or other laws of Texas. The parties negotiate the list, line by line, and seek the judge's opinion on items they cannot agree upon.

Discovery Orders

Once all items on the list are resolved, the judge will grant the motion for discovery and sign the attached discovery order, which makes discovery mandatory and enforceable. A motion asks the judge to do something. A judicial order, on the other hand, mandates the parties do what the judge has ordered. Disobeying a judicial order carries consequences. A discovery order requires the parties to comply with discovery by the date listed on the order, which is usually 10 to 20 days before trial. Compliance means turning over, revealing, or disclosing the items agreed upon or ordered by the judge (*e.g.*, the prosecutor must provide a copy of a lab report to defense counsel before

---

[9] TEX. CODE CRIM. PROC. ANN. art. 28.01 §1 (8) (West 2016).
[10] *Id.*
[11] *Id.*
[12] *Id.*

trial, and the police department must permit defense counsel the opportunity to inspect physical evidence being held in the evidence room at the police station).

Defense counsel must ensure there is a date specified on the order. If an order has no date on it, defense counsel is barred from complaining that the prosecutor released the evidence in an untimely fashion.[13]

———————◆———————

Discoverable Evidence

Now that you understand the process of discovery, it is important to discuss what evidence and information is discoverable in Texas. The Code of Criminal Procedure sets out a test to determine what is discoverable and lists items that are discoverable. This section will examine the test and the items that defense counsel is entitled to discover.

Article 39.14

As stated earlier, Article 39.14 is the primary statute on discovery. It was altered in 2014 by the Michael Morton Act. According to Article 39.14, upon request, the State shall produce and permit the inspection and copying of

- any information, writing, or tangible thing,
- that constitutes material evidence,
- that is not otherwise privileged, and
- that is in the possession, custody, or control of the government.[14]

This is the test to determine whether information or an item is discoverable. Any information or item that meets all of the above criteria is discoverable; any information or item that does not meet all of the above criteria is not discoverable unless the State has an independent *Brady* obligation to produce it. Notice that the list refers to items already in the

---

[13] *E.g., Kirksey v. State*, 132 S.W.3d 49, 55 (Tex. App.—Beaumont 2004, no pet.) ("As there was no time, place or manner specified by the trial court for the State to respond to discovery, the prosecutor's production of the photographs immediately prior to the taking of testimony was proper.").
[14] Tex. Code Crim. Proc. Ann. art. 39.14(a) (West 2016).

State's possession, custody, or control. This statement hints at two, basic discovery truths: (1) the State is not generally required to create evidence that does not already exist; and (2) the State is not generally required to provide discovery for information and items that are not within its possession or control.[15] In other words, if defense counsel can obtain discovery without going through the State (*e.g.*, medical records of the defendant that he can access), the State has no duty to provide the requested item or thing.

In addition to providing a test, Article 39.14 includes a list of things the State may be required to produce or permit to be copied:

- offense reports;
- the defendant's written or recorded statements;
- the written or recorded statements of any witnesses;
- the written or recorded statements of any law enforcement officer; or
- any designated documents, papers, books, accounts, letters, or photographs.[16]

Recall from the grand jury chapter that grand jury testimony, which is transcribed by a court reporter, is discoverable only after the defendant demonstrates a particularized need for it.[17] Absent such a showing, he is not entitled to discover it. A defendant who seeks discovery of grand jury testimony must file a petition for disclosure with the district court who presides over that particular grand jury and deliver a copy of the petition to the prosecutor and any other interested parties.[18] All interested parties are entitled to appear before the district court and present arguments in favor of or against the defendant's petition for disclosure.[19]

---

[15] *E.g., In re Watkins,* 369 S.W.3d 702, 706-07 (Tex. App.—Dallas 2012, orig. proceeding) (State was required to produce information about witnesses that it had already developed, but it had no such obligation if the information had not been developed).

[16] TEX. CODE CRIM. PROC. ANN. art. 39.14(a) (West 2016).

[17] TEX. CODE CRIM. PROC. ANN. art. 20.02(d) (West 2016).

[18] TEX. CODE CRIM. PROC. ANN. art. 20.02(e) (West 2016).

[19] *Id.*

Motions for Inspection

The discovery section of the Code states that upon timely request, "the state shall produce and permit the inspection" of non-privileged, material evidence that is in the possession, custody, or control of the State.[20] The defense team is not permitted to remove any item from the State's possession nor is it authorized to inspect the object without a State representative present.[21] No court has yet determined if a motion for inspection is still required after the Michael Morton Act amendments to Article 39.14.[22] Therefore, if the defense wants access to tangible items in the State's custody, a motion for inspection is still required.

What happens when defense counsel wants to inspect a murder weapon that is lawfully seized by police and held in the evidence room of the police department? What procedural steps does the attorney take to examine such evidence? She must file a motion for inspection with the court. Once her motion is signed, the motion becomes an order for inspection and directs the government employee holding the evidence to permit defense counsel the opportunity to inspect it by a date certain;[23] inspection means more than just visual observation.[24] In the case of the murder weapon, the defense attorney can hold it, permit an expert to examine it, or may seek additional steps to have it tested forensically.

Defense Discovery Obligations

The Michael Morton Act liberalized discovery for the defense team. In theory, the defense team can discover more information with greater ease. This fact was a concern to some groups who wanted to prevent the defendant, not the professionals working for the defendant, from seeing this information. These concerned groups lobbied and received provisions that place safekeeping burdens on the defense team and permit prosecutors to redact sensitive information.

The defense team includes the attorney, investigators, experts, or any other agent working for the defense. None of these people have authority to

---

[20] TEX. CODE CRIM. PROC. ANN. art. 39.14(a) (West 2016).

[21] Id.

[22] Cf. Ehrke v. State, 459 S.W.3d 606, 612-14 (Tex. Crim. App. 2015).

[23] E.g., Kirksey v. State, 132 S.W.3d 49, 54-55 (Tex. App.—Beaumont 2004, no pet.).

[24] Detmering v. State, 481 S.W.2d 863, 864 (Tex. Crim. App. 1972).

disclose any evidence to third parties unless the evidence has already been made public, the defense team shows good cause, and the court orders the disclosure after a hearing and after giving notice.[25] The court must balance the security and privacy interests of the victim or the witness with the desire for third-party disclosure.[26]

The defense team may permit the defendant, a witness, or a prospective witness an opportunity to view information and evidence, but it must redact the address, phone number, date of birth, any identifying numbers (*e.g.*, social security number), and bank account information contained within.[27] This requirement protects the witness or the victim from a defendant who may abuse such information. Furthermore, the defense team cannot provide a copy of any documents to the defendant or the witness unless it is a statement the viewing person made.[28]

Prosecutors may redact or withhold non-discoverable information.[29] If the prosecutor withholds information from an otherwise discoverable item, the defendant may request a hearing before the judge to determine whether the information is indeed non-discoverable.[30] The judge will then perform an in camera inspection (a private inspection, usually conducted in the judge's chambers) to determine whether the information is indeed non-discoverable.

Discovery is allowed only following a court order for pro se defendants.[31] Pro se defendants are not permitted to receive electronic copies of evidence.[32]

The Michael Morton Act, codified within Article 39.14, is the result of a compromise between the defense bar, who wanted discovery with greater access and more ease, and prosecutor's offices who wanted to guard sensitive information. The final Act reflects compromise on the part of both groups. Ultimately, it grants prosecutors limited rights to shield sensitive information from disclosure, it places a hedge around what the defendant can see in the State's file, it places the responsibility on defense counsel to shield the

---

[25] TEX. CODE CRIM. PROC. ANN. art. 39.14(e) (West 2016).
[26] *Id.*
[27] TEX. CODE CRIM. PROC. ANN. art. 39.14(f) (West 2016).
[28] *Id.*
[29] TEX. CODE CRIM. PROC. ANN. art. 39.14(c) (West 2016).
[30] *Id.*
[31] TEX. CODE CRIM. PROC. ANN. art. 39.14(d) (West 2016).
[32] *Id.*

defendant from viewing that information, and it asks the judge to referee discovery disagreements between the parties.

————————◆————————

Brady Evidence

A person unfamiliar with criminal law practice might assume that the State possesses only incriminating evidence against the defendant. Making such an assumption would be a mistake. For any number of reasons, while investigating the crime or examining the case, the prosecutor or other government actors may find evidence that is favorable to the accused, exculpatory, or mitigating, or evidence that impeaches the victim or the State's witnesses.

There are many times that the State or its agents might discover this kind of evidence. For example, the investigating detective may have originally suspected someone else of committing the crime. The prosecutor may discover a lie from a witness about what happened on the night of the crime, which diminishes the witness's credibility. A prosecutor's investigator may interview a witness who suggests the defendant was acting in self-defense. All of these hypothetical scenarios have two things in common: (1) they involve government actors or agents (2) who discover favorable, exculpatory, mitigating, or impeachment evidence. This category of evidence is called *Brady* evidence. The best way to understand *Brady* evidence is to read its namesake case.

John L. Brady v. Maryland
373 U.S. 83 (1963)

Petitioner and a companion, Boblit, were found guilty of murder in the first degree and were sentenced to death, their convictions being affirmed by the Court of Appeals of Maryland. Their trials were separate, petitioner being tried first. At his trial, Brady took the stand and admitted his participation in the crime, but he claimed that Boblit did the actual killing. And, in his summation to the jury, Brady's counsel conceded that Brady was guilty of murder in the first degree, asking only that the jury return that verdict "without capital punishment." Prior to the trial, petitioner's counsel had requested the prosecution to allow him to examine Boblit's extrajudicial statements. Several of those statements were shown to him; but one dated July 9, 1958, in which Boblit admitted the actual homicide, was withheld by the prosecution and did not come to petitioner's notice until after he had been tried, convicted, and sentenced, and after his conviction had been affirmed.

Petitioner moved the trial court for a new trial based on the newly discovered evidence that had been suppressed by the prosecution. [His] petition for post-conviction relief was dismissed by the trial court; and on appeal the Court of Appeals held that suppression of the evidence by the prosecution denied petitioner due process of law and remanded the case for a retrial of the question of punishment, not the question of guilt. The case is here on certiorari.

The crime in question was murder committed in the perpetration of a robbery....

We agree with the Court of Appeals that suppression of this confession was a violation of the Due Process Clause of the Fourteenth Amendment. ...

We now hold that the suppression by the prosecution of evidence favorable to an accused upon request violates due process where the evidence is material either to guilt or to punishment, irrespective of the good faith or bad faith of the prosecution.

The principle ... is not punishment of society for misdeeds of a prosecutor but avoidance of an unfair trial to the accused. Society wins not only when the guilty are convicted but when criminal trials are fair; our system of the administration of justice suffers when any accused is treated unfairly. An inscription on the walls of the Department of Justice states the proposition candidly for the federal domain: "The United States wins its point whenever justice is done its citizens in the courts." A prosecution that withholds evidence on demand of an accused which, if made available, would tend to exculpate him or reduce the penalty helps shape a trial that bears heavily on the defendant. That casts the prosecutor in the role of an architect of a proceeding that does not comport with standards of justice....

The question remains whether petitioner was denied a constitutional right when the Court of Appeals restricted his new trial to the question of punishment. In justification of that ruling the Court of Appeals stated:

> There is considerable doubt as to how much good Boblit's undisclosed confession would have done Brady if it had been before the jury. It clearly implicated Brady as being the one who wanted to strangle the victim,

Brooks. Boblit, according to this statement, also favored killing him, but he wanted to do it by shooting. We cannot put ourselves in the place of the jury and assume what their views would have been as to whether it did or did not matter whether it was Brady's hands or Boblit's hands that twisted the shirt about the victim's neck. … (I)t would be "too dogmatic" for us to say that the jury would not have attached any significance to this evidence in considering the punishment of the defendant Brady.

Not without some doubt, we conclude that the withholding of this particular confession of Boblit's was prejudicial to the defendant Brady. …

The appellant's sole claim of prejudice goes to the punishment imposed. If Boblit's withheld confession had been before the jury, nothing in it could have reduced the appellant Brady's offense below murder in the first degree. We, therefore, see no occasion to retry that issue.

[The Supreme Court then affirmed the Court of Appeals by stating that Brady was entitled to only a new punishment portion of the trial.]

———————◆———————

Texas Law on Disclosure of Brady Evidence

One of the reasons prosecutors are required to disclose favorable, exculpatory, or mitigating evidence stems from their duty to seek justice. As stated at the beginning of this chapter, according to the Texas Code of Criminal Procedure, prosecutors "shall not suppress facts or secrete witnesses capable of establishing the innocence of the accused."[33]

The *Brady* Court held that "suppression by the prosecution of evidence favorable to an accused upon request violates due process where the evidence is material either to guilt or to punishment, irrespective of the good faith or bad faith of the prosecution." While the Texas rule encompasses all that *Brady* does, it is more expansive.

The Texas Code of Criminal Procedure states that the prosecutor "shall disclose to the defendant any exculpatory, impeachment, or mitigating document, item, or information in the possession, custody, or control of the state that tends to negate the guilt of the defendant or would tend to reduce the punishment for the offense charged."[34] The duty of the prosecutor to

---

[33] TEX. CODE CRIM. PROC. ANN. art. 2.01 (West 2016).
[34] TEX. CODE CRIM. PROC. ANN. art. 39.14 (West 2016).

disclose *Brady* evidence continues indefinitely.[35] If at any time before, during, or after trial the State discovers *Brady* evidence, it must promptly disclose its existence to the defendant or the court.[36]

There are two key differences between the *Brady* rule and the Code's rule. First, *Brady* mandates disclosure even without a request. This means the defendant need not request disclosure for *Brady* evidence before he is entitled to receive it. The duty is on the prosecutor to disclose it, not on defense counsel to request it. Second, the Code requires the prosecutor to disclose impeachment evidence whereas the *Brady* Court did not.[37]

Another expansion on *Brady* and Article 39.14 can be found in Rule 3.09(d) of the Texas Disciplinary Rules of Professional Conduct. This Rule requires prosecutors to

> make timely disclosure to the defense of all evidence or information known to the prosecutor that tends to negate the guilt of the accused or mitigates the offense, and, in connection with sentencing, disclose to the defense and to the tribunal all unprivileged mitigating information known to the prosecutor, except when the prosecutor is relieved of this responsibility by a protective order of the tribunal.

Rule 3.09(d) thus requires prosecutors to turn over *all* favorable or mitigating evidence, not just admissible evidence, regardless of whether it is material.

The Board of Disciplinary Appeals recently held that a prosecutor violated this ethics rule when he withheld conflicting statements that the victim was unable to identify her attacker's face.[38] The Board stated,

> The ethics rules acknowledge that a prosecutor shall not make a determination of materiality in his ethical obligation to disclose information to the defense. In an adversarial system, it is the role of both parties to develop arguments why certain evidence is irrelevant, immaterial, and inadmissible. It is the prosecutor's role to disclose impeachment information, the defense lawyer's role to present the impeaching

---

[35] TEX. CODE CRIM. PROC. ANN. art. 39.14(k) (West 2016).

[36] *Id.*

[37] In *United States v. Bagley,* 473 U.S. 667, 676 (1985), the United States Supreme Court held that *Brady* evidence included evidence that could be used to impeach the State's witnesses.

[38] *Schultz v. State Bar of Texas,* 2015 WL 9855916, at *2-3 (Tex. Bd. Disciplinary App. Dec. 17, 2015).

information as evidence, and the trial court's role to determine whether the information is admissible evidence. Rule 3.09(d) is specifically intended to advise – and prevent – a prosecutor from making an incorrect judgment call, such as that Maria's "inconsistent statements" did not rise to the level of *Brady*-mandated disclosure. The clarity of Rule 3.09(d) is a safeguard for prosecutors and citizens alike: if there is any way a piece of information could be viewed as exculpatory, impeaching, or mitigating – err on the side of disclosure.[39]

In this way, the Board places all of the burden and risk of violating *Brady* and Ethics Rule 3.09(d) upon the prosecutor.

———————————◆———————————

Witnesses and Experts

The common law, not the Code, requires the State to disclose the names of the witnesses it intends to call at trial.[40] The Code speaks about the prosecutor's duty to list witnesses who testified before the grand jury on the defendant's indictment,[41] but the Code is silent about the defendant's right to see the State's trial witness list.[42] Nevertheless, discovery motions and orders routinely require the State to disclose witnesses it intends to call at trial to defense counsel. Appellate courts have consistently upheld this duty.[43] In practice, prosecutors file a subpoena list in the clerk's file and direct the defense attorney to examine it. The Court of Criminal Appeals has stated this practice is sufficient.[44]

While other jurisdictions have created reciprocal discovery, Texas has not followed suit. There is one exception: both parties are required to disclose any experts they intend to call once the other side files a motion to disclose

---

[39] *Id.* at *6.

[40] *Martinez v. State*, 867 S.W.2d 30, 39 (Tex. Crim. App. 1993) ("Notice of the State's witnesses shall be given upon request.").

[41] TEX. CODE CRIM. PROC. ANN. art. 20.20 (West 2016).

[42] *Curtis v. State*, 519 S.W.2d 883, 887 (Tex. Crim. App. 1975) ("[T]he discovery statute does not provide for the production of such witnesses' names.").

[43] *Henricks v. State*, 293 S.W.3d 267, 274 (Tex. App.—Eastland 2009, pet. ref'd) ("Upon defendant's request or a trial court's order, the State is required to disclose a list of witnesses it intends to use at trial.").

[44] *Bell v. State*, 442 S.W.2d 716, 719 (Tex. Crim. App. 1969) (State's subpoena list was sufficient to satisfy defense request for witness list).

experts and serves opposing counsel with it.[45] The party filing a motion to disclose experts is entitled to the name and address of the expert; disclosure must be made not later than the 30th day before trial begins.[46] This exception only applies to expert witnesses, not lay witnesses. The defense is under no reciprocal duty to disclose nonexpert witnesses to the State.

What happens when a party fails to disclose an expert witness following a request? *De Pena* sets out the analysis appellate courts use to evaluate an expert witness discovery violation.

Darcy Julio De Pena v. State
148 S.W.3d 461
(Tex. App.—Corpus Christi 2004, no pet.)

[Appellant threw the victim from a two story balcony. The victim's spinal cord was severed, which caused paralysis.][47] A jury convicted appellant of [aggravated assault], and assessed punishment at ten years confinement in the Texas Department of Criminal Justice–Institutional Division, and a fine of $10,000. We affirm the judgment of the trial court.

I. Failure to Disclose Witness.

The first point of error contends the trial judge erred in permitting an expert witness to testify during the State's rebuttal case. Specifically, appellant argues Dr. Keith Rose should not have been permitted to testify as an expert witness without prior notice to appellant. The State advances several arguments as to why the trial judge did not err in admitting Dr. Rose's testimony.

A. Factual Summary.

Prior to trial, appellant filed a discovery motion seeking, inter alia, a list of the State's expert witnesses. Specifically, the motion sought "[t]he name, address, and telephone number of any expert witness who may testify for the State either on guilt or innocence or punishment phase of the trial." Under this portion of the motion, the word "granted" is circled, and "agreed" is written. However, the order granting the motion was not signed. The State

---

[45] Tex. Code Crim. Proc. Ann. art. 39.14(b) (West 2016).
[46] *Id.*
[47] *DePena v. State*, 56 S.W.3d 926, 928 (Tex. App.—Corpus Christi 2001, no pet.).

complied with this ruling by filing its notice of expert witnesses, listing eleven possible expert witnesses. Dr. Rose was not on the list. Appellant filed his notice of expert witnesses, listing only James L. Booker, Ph.D.

During its case-in-chief, the defense called Dr. Booker, a toxicologist. The purpose of this testimony was to raise the defense of involuntary intoxication. Dr. Booker testified that he examined the results of a drug screen of appellant's blood which was drawn at 2:00 p.m. on December 31, 2000. The alleged offense occurred thirty-six hours earlier at approximately 2:30 a.m. on December 30, 2000. The sample tested positive for benzodiazepines, a mood altering "class of compounds." Benzodiazepines alter the mental abilities of the individual by causing confusion and memory loss. However, benzodiazepines do not affect one's physical abilities. When taken in combination with alcohol, benzodiazepines could produce unpredictable "exaggerated emotional responses" which would lead to anger and violence. This is also known as "paradoxical rage." A characteristic of benzodiazepines is severe memory loss. Another side effect is urinary retention.

Prior to Booker's testimony, appellant and others testified that appellant exhibited these side effects on the date of the alleged offense. Specifically, appellant testified that on the night of the alleged offense, he had a headache and took two pills which he believed to be Excedrin. The pills were provided by Chris Caldwell, the owner of the home where this incident occurred. Early the next morning, shortly after 2:00 a.m., Caldwell gave appellant two more pills. Appellant took the pills and sat at the kitchen counter with the complainant on his lap, and that is the last thing appellant remembered before the alleged offense. The next thing he remembered was being awakened in the guestroom of his parent's home. Appellant's father, a surgeon, suggested that appellant have a drug screen. On December 30, the night of the alleged offense, at approximately 8:30 p.m., appellant went to the Calallen Minor Emergency Clinic where he attempted to give a urine sample. However, appellant was unable to urinate. The following day, December 31, appellant provided the blood sample which was the subject of Booker's testimony. He also returned to the clinic and gave a urine specimen.

To rebut the defense of involuntary intoxication, the State called Dr. Rose, the owner of Calallen Minor Emergency Clinic, first visited by appellant on the night of December 30, the date of the alleged offense, one day before giving the blood sample analyzed by Booker. Dr. Rose testified appellant provided a urine sample on December 30 which tested negative for benzodiazepines. Medical records were introduced to corroborate Dr. Rose's testimony. There was no indication from these records that appellant was unable to urinate on December 30. Dr. Rose testified it was not possible for the urine test to be negative and the blood sample examined by Dr. Booker to be positive unless appellant had ingested the drug between the two tests.

B. Preservation of Issue for Appellate Review.

As noted above, appellant's pretrial discovery motion was not signed by the trial judge. The State argues that because the trial judge did not sign the order, appellant failed to obtain a ruling on the motions, and the issue is not preserved for appellate review. We reject this argument for two reasons. First, both parties complied with the notations on the motion as if the trial judge had signed the order granting same. Specifically, the State filed the "State's Notice of Expert Witnesses," stating the notice was given "in reply to Defendant's request of said notice." Second, when objecting to Dr. Rose's testimony, defense counsel stated: "The Court ordered the State to disclose expert witnesses ... [T]he court ordered us to disclose experts." These statements were not objected to by the State, or qualified by the trial judge. Therefore, we will consider them as correct assertions that the discovery motion was granted, even though the order was not signed. Accordingly, we hold this issue is preserved for our review.

C. The State's Duty to Disclose Witnesses.

Our law is clear that upon request by the defense, the State must disclose the witnesses who will be used at any stage of the trial. In the context of expert witnesses, this common law duty has been codified by statute, and has been extended to criminal defendants. Therefore, we hold the State had a duty to disclose Dr. Rose as a witness.

Nevertheless, the State argues they were not required to disclose Dr. Rose as a witness because: (a) he was called in rebuttal; and, (b) there was no time for disclosure. We will address these arguments seriatim.

Rebuttal.

...[T]he court of criminal appeals has held the State is not required to disclose the identity of rebuttal witnesses. The rationale for this proposition is that evidence offered in rebuttal cannot be foreseen because the State does not know what theories the defendant will advance at trial. However, this rationale has not been tested in the context of article 39.14(b) which provides:

> On motion of a party and on notice to the other parties, the court in which an action is pending may order one or more of the other parties to disclose to the party making the motion the name and address of each person the other party may use at trial to present [expert testimony]. The court shall specify in the order the time and manner in which the other party must make the disclosure to the moving party, but in specifying the time in which the other party shall make disclosure the court shall require the other party to make the disclosure not later than the 20th day before the date the trial begins.[48]

We are required to apply the "literal text" of this statute unless doing so would lead to an absurd result. Article 39.14(b) does not exempt rebuttal witnesses, and we are not at liberty to engraft such an exemption into the statute. The reason the legislature did not make an exception for rebuttal witnesses is readily apparent — many times the expert's testimony is not relevant unless and until the defendant has raised a defense which requires expert testimony to rebut. The most obvious example of this is in the insanity defense. The State has no burden to establish the defendant's sanity at the time of the commission of the alleged offense. Therefore, only after the insanity defense has been raised by the defense may the State rebut it. Nevertheless, the State may not hide behind the law and not disclose the expert witnesses who are prepared to testify in rebuttal. For these reasons, we hold that article 39.14(b)'s duty to disclose expert witnesses includes rebuttal witnesses.

We are aware of the line of cases holding the State is not bound to disclose witnesses to rebut an unforeseen defensive theory. *Doyle v. State*, 875 S.W.2d 21, 22 (Tex. App.—Tyler 1994, no pet.) (holding it is not reasonable for the State to anticipate needing undisclosed witness to rebut defense testimony that it could not foresee). However, the State cannot successfully rely on those cases in the instant case because appellant disclosed Dr. Booker as his expert witness. Therefore, the defensive theory could not have been "unforeseen."

Accordingly, we hold the State was not excused from its duty to disclose Dr. Rose merely because he was a rebuttal witness.

---

[48] TEX. CODE CRIM. PROC. ANN. art. 39.14(b) (West 2016).

2. Time for Disclosure.

We now consider the State's argument that there simply was no time for the disclosure of Dr. Rose. Appellant was the final witness on December 16, 2002. The next morning, the defense continued with its case-in-chief by calling a medical records custodian and Booker. At the conclusion of Booker's testimony, the defense rested, and the State immediately called Dr. Rose. During the colloquy following appellant's objection to the nondisclosure of Dr. Rose, one prosecutor stated:

> We didn't even know that [Dr. Rose] existed until yesterday when [appellant] took the stand and said that he had tried to have another urine test in Calallen. I found through calls and calls and calls and calls that there was one, and I went at 7:00 o'clock and got everything done and everything taken care of. We didn't know this person existed until [appellant] took the stand. There's no way we could have known.

We accept at face value that the State was not aware of appellant's relationship with Dr. Rose, and his clinic, until appellant testified. Consequently, we find the State was unaware of Dr. Rose at the time its "State's Notice of Expert Witnesses" was filed, and could not have disclosed Dr. Rose as a potential witness before appellant testified. However, we also accept at face value that the State upon becoming aware of Dr. Rose, contacted him, and concluded that he would be a witness in rebuttal, but never disclosed Dr. Rose's identity to appellant. The State has a continuing burden of disclosure after the trial judge grants the defendant's request for witnesses. Under this continuing burden, the State should notify opposing counsel immediately that an additional witness had surfaced who conceivably could be called to testify. Therefore, the State was under a duty to disclose Dr. Rose when the State determined he would be a possible rebuttal witness. Consequently, we hold the State was not excused from its duty to disclose Dr. Rose merely because he was not discovered until the night before his testimony.

D. Abuse of Discretion.

When the trial judge grants a motion for discovery, and the prosecution fails to disclose the evidence ordered disclosed by the trial judge, that evidence should not be admitted into evidence by the State during the trial. If a trial court allows an unlisted witness to testify over objection, the decision is reviewed for an abuse of discretion. Among the factors to be considered by an appellate court are any showing by the defendant of bad faith on the part of the prosecution in failing to disclose, and whether the defendant could have reasonably anticipated that the witness would testify despite the State's nondisclosure. Unless the defendant makes the necessary showing, the trial court's decision to allow the testimony will not be disturbed on appeal.

In determining whether the State acted in bad faith in failing to provide the name of the witness, we consider whether the State intended to deceive, whether the State's notice left adequate time to prepare, and whether the State freely provided the defense with information. In the instant case, the State became aware of Dr. Rose at 7:00 p.m. the night before he testified. However, the State never disclosed Dr. Rose's identity despite its continuing burden to do so. Instead of disclosing Dr. Rose, the State waited until the optimum time to call him as a witness—immediately after Dr. Booker when appellant had no time to prepare for Dr. Rose's testimony. This indicates an intent to deceive. Furthermore, we note that even though appellant disclosed Dr. Booker to the State, the State made no effort prior to trial to contact Dr. Booker to determine the substance of his testimony. The State cannot use its lack of due diligence as a subterfuge to escape its duty to disclose witnesses. Under these circumstances, we hold the State acted in bad faith.

We now turn to whether defense counsel could not have reasonably anticipated Dr. Rose's testimony. This is "only a factor to be considered and is not determinative of whether the trial court abused its discretion." During Dr. Rose's testimony, the State introduced appellant's medical records which showed that appellant successfully submitted a urine sample, and that sample tested negative for benzodiazepines. Attached to those medical records was a "medical records release" executed by appellant permitting defense to review these records. Dr. Rose testified that the records were released to defense counsel prior to trial. This testimony regarding appellant's ability to provide a urine sample was only relevant because the appellant and his brother testified on direct examination that appellant was unable to provide a urine sample. As soon as this testimony was submitted, appellant should have anticipated that someone from the Calallen Minor Emergency Clinic would testify since the medical records from that facility showed appellant was able to provide a urine sample. In other words, this testimony could have been anticipated even before Dr. Booker testified. After Dr. Booker testified, it should have been a foregone conclusion that someone from the Calallen Minor

Emergency Clinic would testify that the urine sample tested negative for benzodiazepines.

Additionally, we note that defense counsel could have requested a recess or continuance had he needed additional time to prepare for Dr. Rose's cross-examination. However, no such request was made.

While we in no way condone the State's breach of its duty to disclose Dr. Rose as a witness, in light of the urine sample testimony being developed on direct examination by defense counsel, and defense counsel's prior knowledge of the medical records from the Calallen Minor Emergency Clinic, we cannot conclude the trial judge abused his discretion in permitting Dr. Rose to testify over appellant's timely objection. Accordingly, the first point of error is overruled.

◆

Rebuttal and Punishment Witnesses

Because the State carries the burden of proof, the State presents its evidence first. The defense presents its evidence second. The State is then given an opportunity to rebut the defense's evidence.

In *De Pena*, the State argued it did not need to disclose the expert called during rebuttal. The court disagreed because the provision regarding expert witnesses includes no exception for rebuttal witnesses. This rule does not apply to a non-expert rebuttal witness.

Aside from expert witnesses, the State has no right to discover the defendant's evidence or witness list. Thus, the State cannot anticipate who it will call as a rebuttal witness until after the defense has rested. For this reason, courts typically exclude rebuttal witnesses from those that are required to be named in the State's witness list. The Tyler Court of Appeals stated,

> Absent a showing of bad faith by the State, bringing a witness for the sole purpose of rebutting unforeseen testimony is proper. Until Appellant testified to facts that were diametrically opposed to the State's understanding of the events, it was not reasonable for the State to anticipate needing the [rebuttal witness's] testimony. It would be impractical for the State to anticipate all scenarios that a defendant might claim and for the State to designate possible rebuttal witnesses for each of them.[49]

---

[49] *Doyle v. State*, 875 S.W.2d 21, 22 (Tex. App.—Tyler 1994, no pet.).

As prosecutor, the safer and better practice is to inform the defense, upon request, about any witnesses you expect to call, regardless of when you expect them to testify.[50]

———————————◆———————————

Witness Statements

When it comes to accessing a written or recorded witness statement, there is a conflict between the Rules of Evidence and the Michael Morton Act. Under the Rules of Evidence, some evidence is discoverable only at trial, not before. Texas Rule of Evidence 615(a) permits opposing counsel discovery of witness statements after the witness testifies on direct examination but before cross-examination begins. Before 2014, this was the rule when it came to witness statements and impeachment through prior inconsistent statements. Rule 615 further restricts discovery to the subject matter of the witness's testimony. The purpose of the Rule is to allow opposing counsel the opportunity to better cross-examine and impeach a witness whose testimony has changed over time.[51]

Rule 615 defines "statement" as:

(1) a written statement that the witness makes and signs, or otherwise adopts or approves;
(2) a substantially verbatim, contemporaneously recorded recital of the witness's oral statement that is contained in any recording or any transcription of a recording; or
(3) the witness's statement to a grand jury, however taken or recorded, or a transcription of such a statement.[52]

Upon request, the court shall order the statement be turned over to opposing counsel.[53] Rule 615 applies to either party, not just the defense.

Rule 615's applicability has been called into question following passage of the Michael Morton Act in 2014. This is because the State's witness statements are discoverable upon request, according to the Act. The State can no longer wait until after direct examination at trial to present the witness

---

[50] *Rainey v. State*, 949 S.W.2d 537, 544 (Tex. App.—Austin 1997, pet. ref'd) ("Upon request, the State should disclose to a defendant prior to trial any witnesses that will be examined by the State during any stage of the trial.").
[51] *Enos v. State*, 889 S.W.2d 303, 305 (Tex. Crim. App. 1994).
[52] TEX. R. EVID. 615(f).
[53] TEX. R. EVID. 615(a).

statement to defense counsel. In January 2016, the Court of Criminal Appeals stated,

> The Michael Morton Act, codified at Texas Code of Criminal Procedure art. 39.14, affords defendants substantial pre-trial discovery, requiring the state, upon request from the defendant, to produce and permit the defendant to inspect and copy various items, including witness statements. In many instances, therefore, art. 39.14 eliminates the need, after the witness testifies on direct examination, for a defendant to request, and the court to order, production of a witness's statement.
>
> But Art. 39.14 does not entirely eliminate the need for in-trial discovery of witness statements. Art. 39.14 does not extend equivalent discovery rights to the prosecution, and so prosecutors will still need to use Rule 615 to obtain witness statements of defense witnesses. Moreover, some defendants may fail to exercise their discovery rights under art. 39.14 and so may wish to obtain a witness statement under Rule 615.
>
> Consequently, Rule 615(a) has been amended to account for the changed pre-trial discovery regime introduced by the Michael Morton Act. If a party's adversary has already produced a witness's statement—whether through formal discovery under art. 39.14 or through more informal means—Rule 615(a) no longer gives a party the right to obtain, after the witness testifies on direct examination, a court order for production of the witness's statement. But if a party's adversary has not already produced a witness's statement, the party may still use Rule 615(a) to request and obtain a court order requiring production of the witness's statement after the witness finishes testifying on direct examination.[54]

Based on this Court of Criminal Appeals order, it appears that Rule 615 applies to defense witness statements, but Article 39.14 applies to State witness statements.

———————◆———————

Extraneous Offense Evidence

If the defendant would like to discover whether the State plans on admitting evidence of extraneous crimes, wrongs, or bad acts against him at

---

[54] 2016 Texas Court Order 0003.

trial, he may request discovery of such evidence before trial. The premise for this rule, like much of discovery, is to avoid surprise at trial.

Like the Federal Rules of Evidence, the Texas Rules of Evidence limit the use of evidence of crimes, wrongs, or bad acts during trial. Rule 404(b) states,

> (1) Evidence of a crime, wrong, or other act is not admissible to prove a person's character in order to show that on a particular occasion the person acted in accordance with the character.

> (2) Permitted Uses; Notice in Criminal Case. This evidence may be admissible for another purpose, such as proving motive, opportunity, intent, preparation, plan, knowledge, identity, absence of mistake, or lack of accident. On timely request by a defendant in a criminal case, the prosecutor must provide reasonable notice before trial that the prosecution intends to introduce such evidence – other than that arising in the same transaction – in its case-in-chief.[55]

Observe a few things about the above provision. First, the defendant must first make a timely request for evidence of extraneous offenses the State plans on using at trial. Second, the State's notice must be reasonable. *Reasonable* refers to the timing of the notice; notice must be given within a reasonable time before trial begins.[56] Notice may be unreasonable if delivered on the day of or the day before trial.[57]

Third, Rule 404(b) does not require that the notice from the State be written.[58] However, the best practice is to put the notice in writing, detail the extraneous offenses the State intends to offer at trial, and verify that defense counsel received the notice. The next case examines the sufficiency of the notice required under Rule 404(b) in more detail.

---

[55] TEX. R. EVID. 404 (b) (emphasis added).
[56] *Hayden v. State*, 66 S.W.3d 269, 272 (Tex. Crim. App. 2001).
[57] *Neuman v. State*, 951 S.W.2d 538, 540 (Tex. App.—Austin 1997, no pet.) (when request for notice was made six weeks earlier and State waited until day of trial, notice was not timely); *Hernandez v. State*, 914 S.W.2d 226, 234 (Tex. App.—Waco 1996, no pet.) (when request was made ten months earlier, notice given the day before trial was to begin was improper).
[58] *Agbogwe v. State*, 414 S.W.3d 820, 836 (Tex. App.—Houston [1st Dist.] 2013, no pet.).

Bobby Ray Hayden v. State
66 S.W.3d 269
(Tex. Crim. App. 2001)

[Appellant was convicted of indecency with a child, whose initials are A.R. The State also sought to introduce evidence at trial of appellant's sexual conduct with two other children: A.R.'s sibling, K.R., and A.R.'s friend, K.S.[59]]

We are called upon to decide whether the notice requirement found in Texas Rule of Evidence 404(b) is satisfied when the State gives to the defense copies of witness statements that describe the extraneous offenses later admitted into evidence at trial. We hold that the trial court did not abuse its discretion in concluding that the State could satisfy Rule 404(b) in this manner and reverse the decision of the Court of Appeals.

A. Background

The defense timely requested from the State notice of extraneous offenses under Rule 404(b). The State served a response designating that a certain witness would testify, but this response did not explain what extraneous offenses would be discussed. The State also gave to the defense copies of several witness statements that involved descriptions of extraneous offenses. The record does not reflect when the State gave copies of these witness statements to the defense. At trial, the following colloquy occurred:

[DEFENSE COUNSEL]: So we object ... to any testimony from K.S. because we have no notice under 404(b) with respect to the State's intention. And with respect to any other extraneous offense we have no notice, not even a suggestion.

[PROSECUTOR]: With the exception of the fact we've provided [defense counsel's] office with the statement, complete statement of [K.S.] as well as the statement of [K.R.] which contains the other matters that were talked about in chambers regarding watching of a pornographic movie and the slapping of the child [A.R.] in connection with the request by the Defendant for her to remove her clothing which of course was the method by which the offense was committed, we anticipate the evidence is going to show that in each and every instance, and I think there's going to be

---

[59] *Hayden v. State*, 13 S.W.3d 69, 71–72 (Tex. App.—Texarkana 2000), *rev'd*, 66 S.W.3d 269 (Tex. Crim. App. 2001).

evidence that there were probably three incidents where [A.R.] was required to remove her clothing and expose her genitals to the defendant, on two of those occasions he exposed himself, but he did not require [A.R.] and [K.S.] to expose themselves to him in the same manner he had done with [A.R.] on several other occasions. Those full and complete statements were provided to [defense counsel's] office. I think he's clearly had notice of those matters and knew that indeed they were part of the State's case.

[THE COURT]: Okay, anything further from the Defendant?

[DEFENSE COUNSEL]: Nothing with respect to that, Your Honor, and I would suggest that discovery does not satisfy 404(b) and I think the case is pretty clear on that, that when a request for notice under 404(b) … is made, the Defendant is entitled to a specific response with respect to what the State intends to use in their case in chief under 404(b) and the punishment phase….

The trial court overruled appellant's objection. The witness statements referenced by the State were never made a part of the appellate record.

[T]he Court of Appeals found that the State had failed to give sufficient notice under Rule 404(b) because giving the defendant witness statements did not inform the defendant of whether the State had any intent to introduce such evidence at trial. The Court of Appeals also held that the State could not rely upon these statements to satisfy the Rule 404(b) notice because the statements were not in the record.

B. Analysis

Rule 404(b) allows admission of certain extraneous offenses, provided that: "upon timely request by the accused in a criminal case, reasonable notice is given in advance of trial of intent to introduce in the State's case-in-chief such evidence other than that arising in the same transaction." In *Buchanan v. State*, we held that an open file policy was not sufficient to comply with the rule.[60] Even if the State's open file contains a document describing the extraneous offense in question, we could not conclude that "the mere opening of its file … satisfies the requirement of giving notice 'of intent to introduce' such evidence."

The question before us is whether the State's delivery to defense counsel of witness statements concerning the extraneous offenses may be sufficient

---

[60] 911 S.W.2d 11, 15 (Tex. Crim. App. 1995).

notice of the State's intent to introduce the extraneous offenses in question. The State contends that the act of delivering such statements may be sufficient conveyance of its intent to introduce the evidence. Appellant disagrees. The trial court's ruling that the act of delivery in this particular case constituted "reasonable notice" of the State's intent to introduce evidence of the extraneous offenses is reviewed for abuse of discretion.

The question is one of first impression before this Court....

Because the purpose of Rule 404(b) notice is to prevent surprise, we agree with the cases indicating that delivery to the defense of witness statements detailing extraneous offenses may, in an appropriate case, satisfy the notice requirements of Rule 404(b). The rule requires "reasonable" notice. Whether the delivery of witness statements constitutes reasonable notice depends in part on the timing of that delivery. If the State gave the statements to the defense shortly after receiving the request for notice, the implicit statement is: "These are the extraneous offenses that we intend to offer in the case-in-chief." The longer the time lapse between the receipt of the notice and the delivery of the witness statements, the less likely that the recipient will conclude, "This is the evidence that responds to my request." ... The record in this case does not reflect how soon after its receipt of the notice the State responded with its delivery of the witness statements. The State claimed at trial that appellant, "... clearly had notice of these matters and knew in fact that they were part of the State's case." When the trial court asked if there was anything further, defense counsel responded, "Nothing with respect to that, Your Honor." He did not dispute the State's claim that he had actual notice. Instead, his claim was that "discovery doesn't satisfy 404(b)." If the defense did not make the connection between its request and the implicit statement by the State, ... it could have and should have communicated that fact to the trial court. Absent such an objection, we cannot conclude that the trial court abused its discretion on finding that the State had provided reasonable notice. In such instance, the State has done more than simply say, "Look in our file and see what you can find." ... The prosecution is not required to make a written response concerning its intent, although this is certainly the recommended procedure. Although the better practice is for the prosecutor to state explicitly the intent to introduce extraneous offense evidence, the trial court did not abuse its discretion in concluding that delivery of witness statements to the defense in this particular case provided appellant with reasonable notice. Conversely, had the trial judge ruled that the State's notice was not reasonable under these circumstances, that factual determination would not have constituted an abuse of discretion.

…[T]he State claimed before the trial court that the witness statements described all of the extraneous offenses. Appellant did not dispute this claim and did not attempt to have the witness statements placed in the record. We assume, therefore, that the witness statements are as the State represented them to be.

The judgment of the Court of Appeals is reversed and the judgment of the trial court is affirmed.

———————◆———————

Notes and Questions

1. The State has a continuing duty to disclose requested evidence. In the context of extraneous offense evidence, the State has an obligation to correct any response to a discovery motion once it realizes the response was false, regardless of who made the error.[61]

2. Rule 404(b) requires notice of extraneous offense evidence if the evidence is offered in the State's case-in-chief. Notice is not required if it is offered in rebuttal.[62]

3. Rule 404(b) does not require notice of same-transaction extraneous evidence.

4. Article 37.07(g) requires that, upon request, the State provide notice of extraneous offense evidence that will be used during the punishment phase of trial. The Waco Court of Appeals explained the basis for the rule and the analysis appellate courts undertake in determining whether to exclude punishment extraneous offense evidence the prosecutor failed to disclose:

> The purpose of article 37.07, section 3(g) is to avoid unfair surprise and to enable a defendant to prepare to answer the extraneous offense evidence. This analysis requires examining the record to determine whether the deficient notice resulted from prosecutorial bad faith or prevented the defendant from preparing for trial. In determining the latter, appellate

---

[61] *Herring v. State*, 752 S.W.2d 169, 172 (Tex. App.—Houston [1st Dist.] 1988, no pet.).

[62] *Id.* (despite State's failure to give notice, extraneous offense was admissible during rebuttal).

courts look at whether the defendant was surprised by the substance of the testimony and whether that affected his ability to prepare cross-examination or mitigating evidence.[63]

Prosecutors routinely deliver combination 404(b) and 37.07(g) notices to defense counsel, expressing their intent to introduce evidence of extraneous offense evidence in both the case-in-chief and punishment phases of trial. The best practice is to deliver written notice and retain proof that it was delivered and received by defense counsel.

5. Extraneous offense evidence admitted during the punishment phase of trial must be proven beyond a reasonable doubt. The Court of Criminal Appeals explained the purpose this evidence serves at this stage of trial:

> Prior crimes or bad acts are introduced to provide additional information which the jury may use to determine what sentence the defendant should receive. The statute requires that such evidence may not be considered in assessing punishment until the fact-finder is satisfied beyond a reasonable doubt that these prior acts are attributable to the defendant. Once this requirement is met, the fact-finder may use the evidence however it chooses in assessing punishment.[64]

------------◆------------

Discovery Violations

What happens when a party fails to comply with a discovery order or request? A party can face a consequence for noncompliance. The Code is silent, but courts have fashioned consequences for violations, depending on the willfulness of the party and the circumstances following the violation. The next case details the analysis courts perform in assessing discovery violations and one remedy available to courts when they happen.

---

[63] *Luna v. State*, 301 S.W.3d 322, 326 (Tex. App.—Waco 2009, no pet.).
[64] *Fields v. State*, 1 S.W.3d 687, 688 (Tex. Crim. App. 1999).

Calin Mugur Oprean v. State
201 S.W.3d 724
(Tex. Crim. App. 2006)

On February 25, 2004, Judge Don Stricklin signed a document entitled "Discovery Order," directing the State "to furnish the items ordered for inspection and copying on or before ten (10) days prior to trial." Those items included, among other things, "[a]ll video and tape recordings that contain the defendant's voice." It is undisputed that no such items were produced before trial.

Oprean's felony DWI jury trial began on April 12, 2004. After hearing evidence and deliberating, the jury found Oprean guilty on April 14 and was recessed for the day.

That evening, Oprean's attorney asked the trial prosecutor what evidence she intended to present on the punishment issue the next morning. She replied that she intended to present only the "judgments and sentences" in Oprean's prior convictions.

Just minutes before the punishment phase began, defense counsel learned that the prosecutor was going to offer a videotape depicting one of Oprean's previous offenses into evidence. The prosecutor informed defense counsel of her intent to offer the video only after defense counsel inquired about the presence of a police officer in the courtroom, who he assumed was present for another case. The prosecutor informed the trial judge and defense counsel that the officer was there to "testify that the video is a fair and accurate depiction."

Outside the presence of the jury, defense counsel objected to the admission of the video, pointing out to the judge that the prosecutor had violated the discovery order by failing to allow the defense ten days to inspect the video and relating the conversation he had with the prosecutor the previous evening. The prosecutor replied that "there was no [Article 37.07(g)] charge in this Court's discovery order and no [37.07] request was ever made by defense counsel, which is required to be made to me to give him this evidence." The trial judge overruled defense counsel's objection to the tape's admission.

Defense counsel then asked the judge to grant a recess so that he could inspect the video and prepare his strategy, but the judge summarily denied his request. The tape was introduced before the jury, and the jury assessed Oprean's punishment at five years' imprisonment and a $5,000 fine.

Oprean appealed, and the First Court of Appeals affirmed his conviction. The court of appeals determined that it could not "conclude that the State's article 37.07, section 3(g) explanation is meritless on it[s] face." As a result, the court stated: "the record does not demonstrate that the State acted with specific intent to willfully disobey the discovery order. We hold that the trial judge did not abuse its discretion in admitting the videotape." We granted Oprean's petition for discretionary review to decide whether the Court of Appeals erred in upholding the trial judge's decision to admit the video over Oprean's objection.

LAW AND ANALYSIS

"Evidence willfully withheld from disclosure under a discovery order should be excluded from evidence." When reviewing a trial judge's decision to admit or exclude evidence, an appellate court must determine whether the judge's decision was an abuse of discretion. Unless the trial judge's decision was outside the "zone of reasonable disagreement," an appellate court should uphold the ruling. When a trial judge makes findings of fact "based on an evaluation of credibility and demeanor," an "appellate court should show almost total deference" to those findings. And when the trial judge fails to enter written or oral findings of fact, an appellate court will "view the evidence in the light most favorable to the trial court's ruling and assume that the trial court made implicit findings of fact that support its ruling as long as those findings are supported by the record." ...

In this case we must determine whether the prosecutor acted with the specific intent to willfully disobey the discovery order by failing to turn over the videotape from Oprean's prior 2002 DWI conviction to the defense. We conclude that she did.

It should be noted at the outset that a visiting judge handled the punishment phase and the hearing immediately preceding it, so he may not have been aware of the pretrial order at issue before Oprean's lawyer called it to his attention. Nevertheless, the order was part of the record before him. And the order unambiguously directed the State to disclose ten days before trial the very item introduced into evidence. The plain wording of the order is clear to anyone who can read.

Two things are particularly unacceptable about the prosecutor's conduct. First, the prosecutor told defense counsel the night before the punishment phase began that she intended to introduce only the judgments and sentences from the previous convictions. She did not dispute the fact that she made that statement. There is no suggestion that later that night or early the next morning she suddenly discovered the videotape's existence. And because her signature appears at the end of the discovery order, it cannot be said that she was unaware of it.

Second, when defense counsel argued that he had not received notice as required by the discovery order, the prosecutor responded by stating that "there was no [37.07] charge in [the] Court's discovery order." … [T]he validity of the explanation offered by the prosecutor is a relevant factor that should be considered when determining willfulness. The discovery order did not mention anything about Article 37.07, and therefore was not limited by that provision. Because the prosecutor knew about the discovery order and chose to invoke Article 37.07 after counsel called her attention to the order, she made a conscious decision to violate the plain directive of the discovery order.

Affording total deference to the trial judge's implicit findings of fact that are supported by the record, we find that the trial judge abused his discretion in admitting the videotape over defense counsel's objection. The record reveals that… the prosecutor's conduct here was a calculated effort to frustrate the defense. Because intent is inferred from acts done and words spoken, we have considered the prosecutor's statements and actions in finding her conduct to be willful.

CONCLUSION

The judgment of the Court of Appeals is reversed, and the case is remanded to that court to determine what harm, if any, was caused by the videotape's admission into evidence during the punishment phase of Oprean's trial.

COCHRAN, J., filed a concurring opinion in which KELLER, P.J., joined.

I join in the Court's judgment, but I cannot join the majority opinion which concludes that the prosecutor "willfully" violated a discovery order. This record certainly would support a factual finding that the prosecutor acted "with the specific intent to willfully disobey the discovery order by

414 | Texas Criminal Procedure and Evidence

failing to turn over the videotape from Oprean's prior 2002 DWI conviction to the defense." Had the trial court made such a finding, I would agree with it. But the trial court did not so rule. Instead, the trial court's ruling is an implicit finding that the prosecutor did not willfully violate the discovery order. I cannot conclude that the trial court was clearly erroneous in making that implicit factual finding. ...

In this particular case, I agree that the trial court abused its discretion in admitting the videotape in violation of the discovery order without also ensuring the defendant's right to due process notice.

Each case must, of course, be examined on its own merits, but here the defendant made a very persuasive showing in the trial court that he was actually "surprised" by the sudden appearance of this scene videotape from an earlier DWI. He should have been given at least a "recess" to view that videotape, discuss that evidence with his client, and formulate a defensive strategy. Defense counsel was affirmatively (though perhaps innocently) misled by the prosecutor into believing that the only evidence that the State would offer about his client's prior DWI conviction would be the written judgment. Counsel devised his punishment stage strategy with this promise in mind. Indeed, the prosecutor did not even have the common courtesy to tell him about the existence of the videotape and its sponsoring witness on the morning of the punishment hearing. Defense counsel fortuitously discovered it moments before the punishment phase began. He had not known of its existence; he had not viewed it; he had relied upon the fact that the State told him that it was not offering any evidence except the written judgment. His claim of "surprise" is not only plausible, it is compelling. Under these circumstances, the trial judge had the discretion to do one of two things: (1) exclude the videotape because it had not been produced in a timely manner to allow the defense to see it and digest its import before the punishment phase started; or (2) declare a short recess for the defense (and the trial judge) to view the videotape and prepare for the State's offer.

In this case, the defense requested, as an alternative to excluding the videotape, a one-day recess. An entire day might not be necessary to assure sufficient notice to the defense of the contents and import of this evidence, but a short delay of an hour or two comports with both the defendant's right to due process notice and the court's interest in the orderly administration of justice. The punishment phase in this case began at 11:54 a.m., a time that many might consider suitable for a lunch hour recess.

Of course it is not always reversible (*i.e.*, harmful) error for the trial judge to refuse to exclude the evidence or grant a short recess, but I agree with the majority that the trial court committed error in this particular case and join in the remand order.

———————◆———————

Notes and Questions

1. The concurring opinion in *Oprean* mentioned that giving the defense a short recess to watch and process the video may have cured the error. Granting the defense team a short recess or continuance following a discovery violation gives the defense attorney time to consult with the defendant, determine how to proceed, and process the evidentiary revelation. However, a more punitive response is required when discovery order violations are deemed willful. Punitive sanctions include holding the offending attorney in contempt of court for violating the discovery order; the judge may order the attorney to serve a short jail sentence or pay a fine after being held in contempt. The most extreme sanction is to suppress the withheld evidence from trial.[65] This remedy is only available for bad-faith or willful violations.[66]

———————◆———————

Non-discoverable Evidence

There are two categories of evidence that are in the State's exclusive possession that are nonetheless non-discoverable: privileged evidence and work product. Sometimes work product is deemed privileged. When defense counsel asks for discovery of items that are non-discoverable, the State will challenge the request by characterizing the evidence as privileged or work product. This section explains these two categories of non-discoverable evidence.

---

[65] *E.g., Peña v. State*, 864 S.W.2d 147, 149 (Tex. App.—Waco 1993, no pet.).
[66] *Id.*

Privileged Evidence

The State may attempt to prevent discovery of privileged information. However, the trial court may be called upon to determine whether the evidence is truly privileged through an in camera hearing.[67] Examples of privileged, non-discoverable evidence have included the identity of a Crime Stoppers tipster,[68] the identity of a confidential informant,[69] and evidence characterized by the Texas Rules of Evidence as privileged. Most of the privileges under the Texas Rules of Evidence work in favor of the defense (*e.g.*, husband-wife privilege, physician-patient privilege, and clergy privileges). These privileges are discussed in more detail in the Chapter 15. This section will highlight the privilege against disclosing a confidential informant, which is a privilege the State may claim when it comes to discovery.

Texas Rule of Evidence 508, titled "Informer's Identity Privilege," gives the government a privilege to refuse to disclose a person's identity if:

(1) The person has furnished information to a law enforcement officer or a legislator who is investigating a possible violation of law; and
(2) The information relates to or assists in the investigation.

The exceptions to the rule permit disclosure if the informant's identity has already been voluntarily disclosed, the informer is called as a witness, or when "the informer can give testimony necessary to a fair determination of guilt or innocence." [70] If defense counsel wishes to contest the privilege, he may ask the judge to have an in camera inspection that requires law enforcement agents to describe the extent of the informant's knowledge of the underlying charges to the judge in chambers or in private without any parties present.[71] Any testimony or evidence the trial court discovers during the in camera inspection is kept confidential.[72]

If the judge orders the informant's identity disclosed because he has knowledge related to the guilt or the innocence of the defendant, several consequences may follow. First, the State can disclose the identity to the

---

[67] *Texas Bd. of Pardons & Paroles v. Miller*, 590 S.W.2d 142, 143-44 (Tex. Crim. App. 1979).

[68] *In re Hinterlong*, 109 S.W.3d 611, 624 (Tex. App.—Fort Worth 2003, no pet.).

[69] TEX. R. EVID. 508.

[70] TEX. R. EVID. 508(c).

[71] TEX. R. EVID. 508(c)(2)(C).

[72] TEX. R. EVID. 508(c)(2)–(3).

defense team. Second, if the State chooses not to disclose the informant's identity, the judge may order disclosure if the informant's testimony is relevant to the issue of guilt/innocence or if the judge finds the informant not credible.[73] Third, the judge could order dismissal of the charges supported by the informant's testimony.[74]

———————◆———————

Notes and Questions

1. Why are the rules for secrecy and disclosure of confidential informants so complex? What are the benefits of using informants when it comes to law enforcement? What defense detriments arise from not knowing the identity of the informant? What dangers do confidential informants whose identities are discovered face? Do you believe Rule 508 balances these competing interests effectively?

———————◆———————

Work Product

Like privileged evidence, work product is not discoverable. What is work product? The Code describes it as "written communications between the state and an agent, representative, or employee of the state" and the State's investigators' reports or notes.[75] Generally speaking, it is anything generated by the prosecutor or its agents in preparation of trial, not evidence that will be admitted at trial against the accused. In practice, work product typically consists of documents, letters, questions, or notes passed between State agents in preparation of trial.

Notice that the Code references only the State in discussing work product. It is rare that work product is raised by the defense. In an unusual case in which the State sought to discover a recorded statement from the defense and the defense successfully claimed the recording was work product, the Texas Court of Criminal Appeals made the following observation about why the work product exception almost always applies to the State:

---

[73] TEX. R. EVID. 508(c)(2)(A) and (3)(B).
[74] TEX. R. EVID. 508(c)(2)(A).
[75] TEX. CODE CRIM. PROC. ANN. art. 39.14(a) (West 2016).

This Court has not been called on to address the issues of the State's right to discovery or the defendant's right to resist discovery by invoking the work-product doctrine in a criminal case. Discovery in Texas criminal cases has been a "one-way proposition," with the focus on requests by defendants for discovery and the State resisting those requests. Criminal defendants do not have a general right to discover evidence in the State's possession, but they have been granted limited discovery by Article 39.14. No similar provision grants the right to discover evidence to the State.[76]

Now that you know the work product exception is almost always claimed by the State and rarely by the defense, it is important to examine what it is. A hypothetical may help explain. Suppose the defendant in a DWI case caused a car accident, performed field sobriety tests at the scene and again at the police station, and provided a breath sample. According to the Code, the defendant can discover the police report, accident report, witness statements, scene and station videos, and breath test result. These things, though collected or created by government actors, are not work product. They are evidence of the crime and will be preserved for and used during trial, but they are not work product.

Imagine this DWI defendant wants a trial. At the moment her attorney informs the prosecutor about the possibility of trial, the prosecutor will begin to evaluate the case for trial. The prosecutor will read the reports more closely, call the witnesses and interview them, and will watch the videos. The prosecutor may write a written report or otherwise document his opinion about the likelihood of success at trial. The prosecutor's personal observations, even if put in writing, are his work product. The questions he wants to ask witnesses at trial and his closing argument are also work product. Thus, they are not discoverable to defense counsel.

The Court of Criminal Appeals described work product as follows:

The scope of the attorney work-product doctrine is sometimes confused with that of the attorney-client privilege. The attorney-client privilege is an evidentiary privilege and protects against the compelled disclosure of confidential communications. This privilege belongs to and protects the client. The attorney work-product doctrine, while not a true evidentiary privilege, belongs to and protects the attorney. Its purpose is to stimulate the production of information for trials, and it rewards an attorney's creative efforts by giving his work product a qualified privilege from being

---

[76] *Washington v. State*, 856 S.W.2d 184, 187 (Tex. Crim. App. 1993).

shared with others. It is premised on the notion that an attorney should not be compelled to disclose the fruits of his labor to his adversary.[77]

Work product also includes work by agents of the attorney, such as investigators or experts.[78] Attorneys cannot claim work product to shield otherwise discoverable evidence from the opposing party. Using the DWI example above, if the prosecutor uncovers *Brady* evidence, this cannot be deemed work product, even if it was discovered in preparation of trial or was discussed between State agents.

◆

Depositions

Though depositions are commonplace in civil practice, in criminal practice, they are a rarity.[79] Nevertheless, the Code provides a procedure to take depositions in criminal cases.

The State or the defendant may request a witness's deposition.[80] Parties who wish to depose a witness must take the following steps: (1) file an affidavit with the clerk that includes "facts necessary to constitute a good reason for taking the witness's deposition;" (2) file an application to take the deposition; and (3) provide notice of the affidavit and the application to the opposing party.[81] Requesting a deposition through a standard discovery order will not suffice.[82]

In practice, "good reason" may mean one of two things. First, it may mean the deposition is necessary because the deposed person will be unavailable at trial due to age, infirmity, death, an out-of-state move, or any other reason. In this way, the deposition seeks to preserve testimony to be used at trial in lieu of the witness's live testimony.[83] Second, "good reason"

---

[77] *Pope v. State*, 207 S.W.3d 352, 357–58 (Tex. Crim. App. 2006).
[78] *E.g.*, *Skinner v. State*, 956 S.W.2d 532, 540 (Tex. Crim. App. 1997) (defense expert's opinion was protected under work product doctrine).
[79] *Janecka v. State*, 937 S.W.2d 456, 468 (Tex. Crim. App. 1996) ("A deposition … is of such an extraordinary nature that little jurisprudence exists to govern its application.").
[80] TEX. CODE CRIM. PROC. ANN. art. 39.02 (West 2016).
[81] *Id.*
[82] *Martinez v. State*, 507 S.W.2d 223, 226 (Tex. Crim. App. 1974).
[83] TEX. CODE CRIM. PROC. ANN. art. 39.01–02 (West 2016).

may apply when a witness who has information critical to the case known only by that witness is unavailable, by choice or otherwise, to speak to the party before trial.[84] A classic example of this second instance is when a critical witness refuses to speak to defense counsel.[85] In this instance, the court may order a deposition, but only if the information the attorney seeks cannot be obtained through other means.[86]

After the party has taken the three steps, the trial court is required to hear the request and determine whether good reason for the deposition exists.[87] The court must base its decision to grant or deny the application upon the facts known at the time of the hearing.[88] Unlike depositions in civil practice, if the application is granted, the attorney who requests the deposition does not take the deposition. Instead, the trial court appoints one of the following persons to depose the witness or victim: a district court judge, a county court judge, a notary public, a district clerk, or a county clerk.[89]

Depositions can be oral or written, or can take the form of written interrogatories.[90] A witness who fails to appear at the designated time and place for the deposition can be held in contempt of court.[91] The defendant has the right to attend the deposition, but the State may take steps to ensure that the deposed person remains safe during the deposition procedure.[92] If the defendant cannot appear at the deposition, her attorney may request a continuance; if the defendant does not appear, she waives her right to be present at the deposition.[93]

While some depositions may be taken as part of discovery, others may be taken to preserve testimony that may not be available at trial due to the health or age of a witness. These depositions have an altogether different procedure. The prosecutor shall depose elderly or disabled victims and witnesses within 60 days from the time the deposition application is filed,

---

[84] *Morrow v. State*, 139 S.W.3d 736, 742–44 (Tex. App.—Texarkana 2004, no pet.).
[85] *Id.*
[86] *Id.*
[87] TEX. CODE CRIM. PROC. ANN. art. 39.02 (West 2016).
[88] *Id.*
[89] TEX. CODE CRIM. PROC. ANN. art. 39.03 (West 2016).
[90] TEX. CODE CRIM. PROC. ANN. art. 39.03, 39.06 (West 2016).
[91] TEX. CODE CRIM. PROC. ANN. art. 39.03 (West 2016).
[92] TEX. CODE CRIM. PROC. ANN. art. 39.025(f) (West 2016).
[93] *Id.*

unless the time period must be extended due to poor health or unavailability.[94]

Appellate courts give the trial court much discretion, finding no abuse of discretion in denying an application where the witness testified at trial and was subject to cross-examination.[95] Attorneys have yet to win an appeal of a trial court's denial of a deposition.

If the State desires to introduce a deposition into evidence at trial, it must safeguard the defendant's right of confrontation at that deposition. In a case of sexual abuse of a child, the Texas Court of Criminal Appeals explained that the use of interrogatories violated the defendant's right to confront the witnesses against him:

> The content of the constitutional rights to confrontation and cross-examination do not depend upon the type of crime charged or the fragility of the witnesses; all accused citizens are entitled to the full protection of the constitution.

> Furthermore, the *Crawford* decision made clear that direct and personal cross-examination, with counsel's ability to ask follow-up questions, is essential "to tease out the truth" at trial. Thus, the *Crawford* Court stated that depositions or other prior testimony could be admitted against an accused only if he was present and had an opportunity to cross-examine *during* that deposition or prior testimony. And, in ringing terms, the Supreme Court declared that, "'under no circumstances'" shall the defendant be deprived of "'seeing the witness face to face, and . . . subjecting him to the ordeal of a cross-examination.'" In the context of battered women, small children, and other fragile witnesses, this is a heavy price to pay, but it is the price that our constitution and our Supreme Court requires. There is no "balancing" the defendant's constitutional right of confrontation and cross-examination against other social policies, even compelling ones.[96]

---

[94] TEX. CODE CRIM. PROC. ANN. art. 39.025(b)-(d) (West 2016).
[95] *Cooks v. State*, 844 S.W.2d 697, 729 (Tex. Crim. App. 1992).
[96] *Coronado v. State*, 351 S.W.3d 315, 328-29 (Tex. Crim. App. 2011) (citing *Crawford v. Washington*, 541 U.S. 36, 57, 67 (2004); *Mattox v. United States*, 156 U.S. 237, 244 (1895)).

Practice Questions

Recent bar exams have included a question or two about discovery. Older bar exams contained as few as zero and as many as four discovery questions per exam. If you are consulting older comments to questions on the Texas Board of Law Examiner's webpage, know that with the passage of the Michael Morton Act, some of the comments are no longer legally accurate. Use caution in consulting comments before 2014, as the Michael Morton Act substantially changed specific areas of discovery law. Always check past questions and answers against current laws.

1. (J-2016, F-2013, F-2010, F-2008, and F-2003) Defendant tells you before trial that he committed the same crime several years ago but was never caught or charged. He doesn't think anyone knows about this. Still, you do not want to be surprised at trial.

   a. (F-2010) What procedural step can you take before trial to ascertain whether Prosecutor knows about this act and, if so, whether she will attempt to admit evidence about it at any time during trial?

   _____

   _____

   _____

   _____

   _____

   b. (F-2004 and F-2003) Assume you took the step above. What, if any, obligation does Prosecutor now have?

   _____

   _____

   _____

   _____

   _____

2. (F-2016, F-2010, F-2009, and F-2008) You ask Prosecutor for a copy of the police offense report. Prosecutor refuses citing the work product privilege.

   Do you have a right to a copy of the offense report?

   _____

   _____

   _____

   _____

   _____

3. (J-2015, J-2008, J-2004, F-2004, and J-2000) You learn that there was a witness to the crime. You want to obtain her testimony before trial.

   What procedural step can you take to try to accomplish this, and what must you show?

   _____

   _____

   _____

   _____

   _____

4. (F-2015 and J-2009-6) Defendant's case is set for a pretrial hearing. You would like to file a motion for discovery.

   When should you file your motion? What happens if you miss the filing deadline?

   _____

   _____

   _____

   _____

   _____

5. (F-2015) There is a material witness statement inside Prosecutor's file that is housed inside a sealed envelope. You request to see it.

    Does the Code require Prosecutor to do anything in response to your request and if so, what? Explain.

    _____

    _____

    _____

    _____

    _____

6. (J-2014, J-2012, J-2009, F-2007, J-2005, J-2003, F-2002, and F-2001) In the course of investigating the case, police officers met Witness who suggested another person committed the offense. Given all of the other evidence they had indicating Defendant was the person who committed the crime, they did not believe Witness. Prosecutor discovers this information a few days before trial. He likewise does not find Witness credible.

    Is Prosecutor required to disclose this information to defense counsel? Would your answer change if defense counsel never filed a discovery motion or requested this kind of information? Explain.

    _____

    _____

    _____

    _____

    _____

7. (F-2014, F-2012, J-2009, F-2007, J-2006, F-2006, J-2004, F-2004, J-2002, F-2001, and J-2000) You file a discovery motion requiring Prosecutor to disclose all witnesses, including expert witnesses. Prosecutor in turn files a motion requesting you to disclose all of your lay and expert witnesses.

How should Judge rule on these motions? Explain.

_____

_____

_____

_____

_____

8. (J-2013 and J-2011) Defendant is charged with murder. You would like to inspect the pistol that he allegedly used to kill Victim. You ask Prosecutor for permission to inspect it, but Prosecutor refuses your request.

    What procedural step can you take to inspect the gun? Explain.

_____

_____

_____

_____

_____

9. (F-2012) Prosecutor's file contains a printed email exchange between Prosecutor and Investigator that includes their opinions about the strength of the case. The printed email is sealed within an envelope. You request that Judge order the State to let you read the email.

    How should Judge rule and why?

_____

_____

_____

_____

_____

10. (F-2009) Prosecutor gives you timely and proper notice that she intends to admit testimony of Defendant's uncharged offense into evidence during the punishment phase of trial.

Under what circumstances, if any, is such evidence admissible during the punishment or sentencing phase of trial? Explain.

_____

_____

_____

_____

_____

11. (J-2006 and F-2006) You discover from Defendant that she gave a signed, written statement to police while she was in jail. You request a copy of the statement. Prosecutor refuses to give you a copy of the statement, claiming it is work product.

Are you entitled to see it? What, if any, step can you take following Prosecutor's refusal? Explain.

_____

_____

_____

_____

_____

12. (J-2006, J-2004, J-2003, F-2002, and J-2000) What remedies or sanctions may a court impose when a party violates a discovery order? Explain.

_____

_____

_____

_____

_____

13. (F-2004) Defendant is charged with manufacturing methamphetamine. Police began investigating Defendant after Informant provided information about Defendant. You would like to know who Informant is, so you file a pretrial motion requesting Prosecutor disclose Informant's identity. Prosecutor refuses. You then file a motion to compel Prosecutor to reveal Informant's identity.

    What procedure follows your motion? Explain.

    _____
    _____
    _____
    _____
    _____

14. (F-2002 and J-2001) You file a written motion for discovery and ask to see the following items, all of which are relevant to the charged offense: (a) video taken at the crime scene; (b) State witness statements; (c) toxicological reports; (d) Defendant's statement; and (e) Grand Jury transcripts.

    How should Judge rule? Explain.

    _____
    _____
    _____
    _____
    _____

————————◆————————

Chapter 10
Statements

Introduction

In any number of crime shows, and sometimes in real-life criminal cases, defendants give a "confession." What comes to mind when you hear that word? Do you think of a written or oral confession? Do you imagine a meticulous explanation of what really happened? Perhaps you envision a confession that contains facts known only by the accused, facts the police had yet to ascertain through their own investigation. Regardless of what the word *confession* invokes in our imaginations, Texas chooses to call written and oral "confessions" something else: statements. *Statement* is a more apt name, as many fail to include confessions. The defendant's statement may include an alibi, it may minimize culpability, it may contain more falsehood than truth, or it may only partly take responsibility for the criminal act. It is rare that a defendant's statement is a full and true confession.

Regardless of the form or the contents of the statement, Texas laws provide more safeguards for defendants than federal laws. Nevertheless, federal constitutional law, Texas common law, and statutory law work together to assign evidentiary weight and admissibility to a statement. For this reason, this chapter will examine both federal and Texas law related to statements.

This chapter will begin with *Miranda v. Arizona*, which lays the foundation for custodial interrogation, which is the primary means by which police obtain statements. This chapter will then examine how courts determine whether statements were voluntarily given, various types of statements and their legal requirements, and exceptions to the requirements for admissibility.

---◆---

Miranda Warnings

Most Americans have heard real or fictional police recite *Miranda* warnings: "You have the right to remain silent. Anything you say can and will be used against you. You have the right to have an attorney present during any questioning. If you cannot afford an attorney, one will be appointed to you. Do you understand these rights?" The wording may vary slightly, but the warnings explain two Constitutional rights—the right against self-incrimination and the right to counsel. The warnings are given in plain English at a time when the accused needs to be reminded of these fundamental constitutional rights.

What most lay people do not realize is that these warnings are triggered when someone is (1) in custody, and (2) being interrogated. *Miranda*, the warnings' namesake case, illustrates why these warnings are critical.

Ernesto A. Miranda v. Arizona
384 U.S. 436 (1966)

The cases before us raise questions which go to the roots of our concepts of American criminal jurisprudence: the restraints society must observe consistent with the Federal Constitution in prosecuting individuals for crime. More specifically, we deal with the admissibility of statements obtained from an individual who is subjected to custodial police interrogation and the necessity for procedures which assure that the individual is accorded his privilege under the Fifth Amendment to the Constitution not to be compelled to incriminate himself.

We dealt with certain phases of this problem recently in *Escobedo v. State of Illinois*, 378 U.S. 478 (1964). There, as in the four cases before us, law enforcement officials took the defendant into custody and interrogated him in a police station for the purpose of obtaining a confession. The police did not effectively advise him of his right to remain silent or of his right to consult with his attorney. Rather, they confronted him with an alleged accomplice who accused him of having perpetrated a murder. When the defendant denied the accusation and said "I didn't shoot Manuel, you did it," they handcuffed him and took him to an interrogation room. There, while handcuffed and standing, he was questioned for four hours until he confessed. During this interrogation, the police denied his request to speak to his attorney, and they prevented his retained attorney, who had come to the police station, from consulting with him. At his trial, the State, over his objection, introduced the confession against him. We held that the statements thus made were constitutionally inadmissible.

... [T]he prosecution may not use statements, whether exculpatory or inculpatory, stemming from custodial interrogation of the defendant unless it demonstrates the use of procedural safeguards effective to secure the privilege against self-incrimination. By custodial interrogation, we mean questioning initiated by law enforcement officers after a person has been taken into custody or otherwise deprived of his freedom of action in any significant way. As for the procedural safeguards to be employed, unless other fully effective means are devised to inform accused persons of their right of silence and to assure a continuous opportunity to exercise it, the following measures are required. Prior to any questioning, the person must be warned that he has a right to remain silent, that any statement he does make may be used as evidence against him, and that he has a right to the presence of an attorney, either retained or appointed. The defendant may waive ... these rights, provided the waiver is made voluntarily, knowingly and intelligently. If, however, he indicates in any manner and at any stage of the process that he wishes to consult with an attorney before speaking there can be no questioning. Likewise, if the individual is alone and indicates in any manner that he does not wish to be interrogated, the police may not question him. The mere fact that he may have answered some questions or volunteered some statements on his own does not deprive him of the right to refrain from answering any further inquiries until he has consulted with an attorney and thereafter consents to be questioned.

Notes and Questions

1.   The right against self-incrimination only protects a defendant from involuntary testimonial incrimination.[1] It does not protect a defendant, who, for example is arrested for DWI, seen on a videotape, and asked to recite the alphabet, even when the defendant's response reveals slurred speech.[2] The Texas Court of Criminal Appeals has ruled that compelling the defendant to provide fingerprint or foot imprints, to provide DNA samples, to stand and speak while participating in a lineup, even to submit to an eye exam during trial, are likewise non-testimonial.[3] None of these are considered testimonial or the functional equivalent of a statement, even if they ultimately led to inculpatory evidence against the accused.

> The Fifth Amendment privilege against self-incrimination protects a defendant "from being compelled to testify against himself, or otherwise provide the State with evidence of a testimonial or communicative nature." ... [T]he Fifth Amendment does not apply to every sort of incriminating evidence – only to testimonial communications that are incriminating. In order to be testimonial, the communication "must itself, explicitly or implicitly, relate a factual assertion or disclose information."[4]

2.   If you have seen a videotape of a DWI suspect taken at the police station, you will notice (regardless of jurisdiction) they follow the same routine. First, the suspect is asked to perform a number of field sobriety tests, some that focus on the person's cognitive impairment (*e.g.*, counting backwards and reciting portions of the alphabet) and some that focus on the person's physical impairment (*e.g.*, balancing on one foot and walking heel to toe on a line). Second, the person is asked to provide a breath or blood sample. Both of these phases include law enforcement requests to provide evidence while the person is in custody. The suspect is not told that she has the right to refuse the tests or have a lawyer present because these requests do not fall under the ambit of *Miranda*. They are requests to provide non-

---

[1] *Chadwick v. State*, 766 S.W.2d 819, 821 (Tex. App.—Dallas 1988), *aff'd*, 795 S.W.2d 177 (Tex. Crim. App. 1990); *Gassaway v. State*, 957 S.W.2d 48, 50-51 (Tex. Crim. App. 1997).

[2] *Id.*

[3] *Olson v. State*, 484 S.W.2d 756, 763 (Tex. Crim. App. 1969); *Guerrero v. State*, 80 S.W. 1001, 1002 (Tex. Crim. App. 1904); *Clement v. State*, ___ S.W.3d ___, 02-14-00267-CR, 2016 WL 3902494, at *2 (Tex. App.—Fort Worth July 14, 2016, no. pet.).

[4] *Williams v. State*, 116 S.W.3d 788, 791 (Tex. Crim. App. 2003).

testimonial evidence, so *Miranda* does not apply. It is only after the suspect performs or refuses to perform these tests that officers read the suspect *Miranda* rights and interrogate the suspect by asking questions that elicit testimonial statements about the events leading up to the arrest.

Can you think of a reason why the non-testimonial evidence is elicited first? Why do officers wait to read *Miranda* warnings until two of these three steps are complete?

--------------------◆--------------------

The *Miranda* Court painted a vivid picture of custodial interrogation: a murder suspect questioned for hours in an interrogation room, handcuffed, mentally and emotionally tormented until he confessed. Not all custodial interrogations are like this. What happens when the person is not handcuffed, is not in jail, or is not in custody when he is questioned? Appellate courts use a totality of the circumstances analysis to determine whether the events should have triggered *Miranda* warnings, as the next case illustrates.

Andrew Ramirez v. State
105 S.W.3d 730
(Tex. App.—Austin 2003, no pet.)

Following the district court's denial of his motion to suppress, appellant Andrew Ramirez pleaded guilty to felony possession of marihuana. The district court sentenced appellant to six months in a state-jail facility. Appellant had moved the court to suppress both an oral statement he made to police and the marihuana obtained when a police officer searched, without a warrant or consent, a closed ice cooler in the appellant's garage. Appellant appeals only the district court's denial of his motion to suppress. We will reverse and remand.

Background

On the afternoon of November 21, 2001, the Austin Police Department ("APD") received a call from a neighbor of appellant, complaining that she was "tired of [appellant] selling mari[h]uana out of his garage." APD Officer Chris Sobieszczyk responded to the call. Sobieszczyk first approached the neighbor's house, speaking with the neighbor for approximately ten to fifteen minutes. Then Sobieszczyk knocked on the front door of appellant's residence, and a young boy answered. Sobieszczyk asked whether an adult was present, and the boy directed him to the garage. When Sobieszczyk reached the garage, he knocked on the garage's closed door. From inside, individuals shouted profanities at Sobieszczyk. The officer then identified himself as "Austin police." Sobieszczyk heard shuffling, and a few moments later, appellant came to the garage door and stepped outside, closing the door behind him. While the door was open, Sobieszczyk noticed a scale with marihuana residue and seeds on it, a set of finger scales, and a large green pipe on a table approximately two feet inside the garage. Sobieszczyk detected a strong odor of fresh marihuana and noticed plastic baggies and rolling papers on the floor. Outside of the garage, in a garbage can, he saw a brick-sized cellophane wrapper containing marihuana residue.

Sobieszczyk talked with appellant and learned that appellant owned the property. During the discussion, a second individual, Pedro Reynosa, left the garage, leaving the door partially open behind him. Sobieszczyk had been at the scene of an aggravated assault involving a shooting the prior week. He knew Reynosa "had been handled for weapons before," and believed that either Reynosa or one of Reynosa's brothers had been involved in the shooting. Sobieszczyk was concerned that Reynosa or appellant might possess weapons.

Both appellant and Reynosa acted nervously, hiding their hands either behind their backs or inside their clothing. Appellant, who wore a gray sweatshirt with a large front pocket, held his hands inside the pocket. Because it was dark behind the garage and because he believed Reynosa might possess weapons, Sobieszczyk called for a backup officer before conducting a safety pat down of appellant and Reynosa. Sobieszczyk continued to talk with the two men until Officer Kenneth Murphy arrived.

Murphy approached Reynosa and requested his permission to pat down Reynosa for weapons. Reynosa told Murphy that he had a knife. During his pat down of Reynosa, Murphy found a double-edged stiletto and a small plastic bag of marihuana in a pocket of Reynosa's pants. Reynosa was immediately placed under arrest and moved away from the garage doorway.

After Murphy secured Reynosa, Sobieszczyk patted down appellant. As he began the pat down, Sobieszczyk told appellant, "[Y]ou are being detained," and placed him in handcuffs. Sobieszczyk also told appellant that he could see drug paraphernalia and drug residue in the garage. Sobieszczyk then asked appellant, "Is there anything else I'm going to find in there that's illegal, any more mari[h]uana?" Appellant hesitated, and Sobieszczyk moved appellant closer to Murphy and Reynosa and stepped into the garage. Appellant then stated that he "guess[ed] there's some pot in the red cooler." Sobieszczyk testified that his main intent for entering the garage was to seize the paraphernalia and to ensure that no other individuals remained inside the garage. He seized the pipe and the cooler. Although the record is not clear as to the precise sequence of events, at the suppression hearing, the State suggested that, based on appellant's admission, Sobieszczyk searched the cooler, seized the marihuana inside the cooler, and then applied for a search warrant. The record does not contain the warrant. In its closing argument at the suppression hearing, the State argued that "we have no idea if the judge would have signed a search warrant had there not been any mari[h]uana seized."

Appellant filed a motion to suppress both his oral statement to Sobieszczyk and the marihuana obtained from the cooler, contending that both were obtained illegally. Specifically, appellant argued that the admission regarding the cooler was the product of a custodial interrogation. Because he had not been read his *Miranda* rights, appellant argued that the statement was inadmissible.

The district court denied appellant's motion, ruling that appellant was temporarily detained and not under arrest at the time and admitted his statement because it was not the product of custodial interrogation.

Custody

Appellant's first point of error asserts that the district court erred in ruling that appellant was merely detained, rather than formally arrested. He argues that, because he had been formally arrested at the time his statement was made, the district court erroneously admitted the [statement] … into evidence. Neither the Fourth Amendment nor article 38.22 of the Texas Code of Criminal Procedure preclude the admission of noncustodial statements. Thus, in order to determine whether appellant's comments to Sobieszczyk are admissible, we must first determine the point at which officers placed appellant in custody.

A determination of custody must be made on an ad hoc basis, in consideration of all of the objective circumstances of the detention. A person is "in custody" only if, under the circumstances, a reasonable person would believe that his freedom of movement was restrained to the degree associated

436 Texas Criminal Procedure and Evidence

with a formal arrest. The "reasonable person" standard presupposes an innocent person. In determining whether custody exists, the subjective intent of law-enforcement officials to arrest is irrelevant, unless the intent is communicated or manifested to the suspect in some way.

On the other hand, a person held for investigative detention is not in "custody." An investigative detention involves detaining a person reasonably suspected of criminal activity in order to determine his identity or to momentarily maintain the status quo in order to garner more information. This sort of *"Terry* stop" must be a temporary detention, must last no longer than necessary to effectuate the purpose of the stop, must involve actual investigation, and must use the least intrusive means possible.

The need for *Miranda* warnings arises when a person being questioned by law-enforcement officials has been "taken into custody or otherwise deprived of his freedom of action in any significant way." An initial determination of custody "depends on the objective circumstances of the interrogation." The following situations may constitute custody: (1) when the suspect is physically deprived of his freedom of action in any significant way, (2) when a law-enforcement officer tells the subject he cannot leave, (3) when law-enforcement officers create a situation that would lead a reasonable person to believe that his freedom of movement has been significantly restricted, or (4) when there is probable cause to arrest and law-enforcement officers do not tell the suspect he is free to leave. For the first three situations, … the restriction of freedom must elevate to the level of arrest, not merely investigative detention. Regarding the fourth situation, the officer's knowledge of probable cause must be manifested to the suspect. This manifestation could occur "if information substantiating probable cause is related by the officers to the suspect or by the suspect to the officers." Probable cause to arrest cannot alone constitute custody; custody is established only if a manifestation of probable cause, paired with other circumstances, would encourage a reasonable person to believe officers were restricting him to the degree associated with arrest.

Curiously, the use of handcuffs does not necessarily constitute arrest or custody. Although an interrogation may begin as noncustodial, police conduct during the encounter may transform a consensual exchange into a custodial interrogation.

In the present case, Sobieszczyk appeared at appellant's residence in response to a disturbance call placed by a neighbor. The neighbor complained that she and appellant had argued because she was "tired of [appellant] selling mari[h]uana out of his garage." Sobieszczyk approached appellant's residence after speaking a few minutes with the neighbor. Initially, appellant voluntarily left his garage and engaged in small talk with Sobieszczyk. Sobieszczyk asked appellant general questions pertaining to the disturbance call. Although the officer testified that, even at the time he was speaking with appellant and Reynosa before the arrival of Murphy, neither suspect was free to leave, the officer's conduct did not elevate the situation beyond an investigative detention. Even when Murphy patted down Reynosa for possible weapons, the situation did not exceed a permissible *Terry* frisk because Reynosa's behavior suggested he might be concealing a weapon.

The key moment comes when Sobieszczyk frisked appellant. The officer handcuffed appellant behind his back either before or during the pat down. At this point, Reynosa was already handcuffed and under formal arrest. The officer testified that, during the pat down, he told appellant, "[Y]ou are being detained. I can see the mari[h]uana in there. I can see residue, the drug paraphernalia." At the time of this statement, Sobieszczyk had probable cause to arrest appellant, had handcuffed him, and did not tell him that he was free to leave. Sobieszczyk then asked appellant, "Is there anything else I'm going to find in there that's illegal, any more mari[h]uana?" When appellant hesitated, Sobieszczyk moved the handcuffed appellant to where Murphy detained Reynosa. Then Sobieszczyk moved to enter the garage. After a couple of seconds, appellant responded, "Well, I guess there's some pot in the red cooler."

[W]e determine that appellant was in custody at the time Sobieszczyk asked him whether he would find any additional illegal items or marihuana in the garage. First, Sobieszczyk physically deprived appellant of his freedom of action in a significant way when he handcuffed him and began patting him down. Second, he told appellant he was being detained, indicating the suspect could not leave. Third, Sobieszczyk's actions in handcuffing appellant and stating that appellant was detained created a situation that would lead a reasonable person in appellant's position to believe that his freedom of movement was significantly restricted. Finally, the officer told appellant he saw drug paraphernalia and drug residue in his garage. He indicated that he knew the items were contraband by asking appellant whether he would find anything else "illegal" in the garage and whether he would find "any more mari[h]uana." These factors, paired with the fact that Sobieszczyk never told appellant he was free to leave, satisfy the ... standards defining custody. We hold that appellant was in custody at the time he made the statement concerning the presence of marihuana in the cooler.

Interrogation

In *Miranda*, the Supreme Court established that custodial interrogation means "questioning initiated by law enforcement officers after a person has been taken into custody or otherwise deprived of his freedom of action in any significant way." The Supreme Court clearly distinguishes between volunteered custodial statements and those made in response to interrogation.

The need for *Miranda* safeguards arises when a person in custody "is subjected to either express questioning or its functional equivalent." "Interrogation," for *Miranda* purposes, refers both to express questioning and to any words or actions by the police—other than those normally attendant to arrest and custody—that police "should know are reasonably likely to elicit an incriminating response."[5] "Incriminating response" refers to both inculpatory and exculpatory responses that prosecutors may seek to introduce at trial. The likelihood of eliciting a response focuses on the perception of the suspect, not the intent of the police. The Court noted that any practice the police should know is "reasonably likely to evoke an incriminating response from a suspect" constitutes interrogation.

We hold that appellant was "interrogated" within the meaning of *Miranda*. Before appellant made any incriminating statements, he was in custody. By asking appellant whether there was "anything else [he was] going to find in [the garage] that's illegal, any more mari[h]uana," Sobieszczyk engaged in express questioning of appellant. The officer did not first provide *Miranda* warnings to appellant.

At a minimum, Sobieszczyk's inquiries were the "functional equivalent" of questioning. When Sobieszczyk asked appellant whether he would find

---

[5] A question that might normally be considered attendant to arrest can still be considered "interrogation" if the interrogating officer should have known that the question was likely to elicit an incriminating response. *Cf. State v. Cruz*, 461 S.W.3d 531, 539-40 (Tex. Crim. App. 2015) (asking defendant for his name and telephone number constituted interrogation because officers informed defendant that they had several names for him, revealing that he had provided a false name, and because a telephone number would tie defendant to the location of his cell phone at or near time of murder).

more marihuana in appellant's garage, he had just informed appellant that he had seen marihuana paraphernalia and residue in the garage. Further, according to his own testimony, Sobieszczyk already had placed appellant in handcuffs and told him that he was being detained. No officer had administered the warnings required by *Miranda*.

A police officer "should know" that asking appellant whether he would find more narcotics in the garage was "reasonably likely to evoke an incriminating response" from appellant. Further, a police officer should know that, if appellant responded in the affirmative, the response would be of the sort prosecutors would seek to introduce at trial. Appellant saw Sobieszczyk begin to enter the garage. He likely believed the officer would find the drugs. Sobieszczyk should have known that the combination of his entry into the garage and his questioning of appellant would encourage the suspect to provide an incriminating response.

The State argues that, even if Sobieszczyk "interrogated" appellant, appellant's statement about marihuana being located in the closed cooler constituted a voluntary statement, rather than an incriminating response to an impermissible interrogation. The State emphasizes the fact that appellant paused and "refused to answer" after the officer asked the question. According to the State, this pause effectively ended the conversation between the officer and appellant. Thus, appellant's admission served as a voluntary statement, making it admissible. The record, however, does not support the State's assertion. Sobieszczyk testified that the pause lasted but "a few seconds"—only enough time for him to take "just a couple of steps."

Voluntary statements generally do not occur in response to a direct question from a police officer. That the suspect was neither expressly nor implicitly questioned by police officers at the time the statement was made often determines the voluntariness of a statement. ...*Sanchez v. State*, 589 S.W.2d 422, 423 (Tex. Crim. App. 1979) (defendant's statement after arrest that officers were lucky they caught him and his inquiries about whether someone "had squealed on him" admissible as voluntary statements because they were not products of interrogation or responses to inquiry by officers); *Earnhart v. State*, 582 S.W.2d 444, 448 (Tex. Crim. App. 1979) (statement of arrested defendant who said, "It's got blood on it. I want to get a clean one," when grabbing shirt to wear was admissible because it was voluntary and not made in response to inquiry or as result of interrogation); *Davis v. State*, 780 S.W.2d 945, 947 (Tex. App.—Fort Worth 1989, pet. ref'd) (finding that suspect's statement, "It's cool. You got me," upon apprehension by police was admissible as res gestae or voluntary statement before interrogation).

Here, appellant's incriminating statement directly responded to an inquiry from Sobieszczyk. Under these facts, we cannot say that the statement was voluntary. We hold that appellant's statement was made pursuant to a custodial interrogation and was thus inadmissible in evidence.

———————————◆———————————

Notes and Questions

1.   There was some debate in the above case whether the officers ever sought or obtained a search warrant. Based upon his observations and knowledge, do you believe Officer Sobieszczyk would have been able to obtain a valid search warrant for the garage? If so, at what point in time? If he could have obtained one, why do you suppose he asked the defendant what he would find inside the garage?

2.   The court defines "incriminating response" as "both inculpatory and exculpatory responses that prosecutors may seek to introduce at trial." Can you think of situations when an exculpatory response may be used against the accused at trial by the State?

———————————◆———————————

Invoking *Miranda*

What happens when a defendant invokes her right to remain silent or she requests a lawyer? The *Miranda* Court stated that once a suspect invokes her right to remain silent or requests an attorney, officers must stop the interrogation.[6] However, in order for officers to know that the defendant has invoked her rights, she must clearly and unambiguously state she wishes to remain silent or speak to a lawyer. This is how the Amarillo Court of Appeals characterizes "clear and unambiguous:"

> [I]nterrogation must immediately cease if the suspect states "that he wants an attorney...." And, like the invocation of the right to remain silent, the request for counsel must also be clear and unambiguous. In other words, the totality of circumstances inherent in the case must illustrate that the

———————————

[6] *Miranda v. Arizona*, 384 U.S. 436, 473–74 (1966).

suspect "actually invoke[d] his right." And, whether he did depends upon whether the "suspect express[ed] a definite desire to speak to someone, and that person be an attorney." For instance, comments like "I can't say more than that[,] I need to rest" and "'[m]aybe I should talk to a lawyer,'" have been found to be too ambiguous. On the other hand, the suspect uttering that he was "'not doing any [field sobriety] tests'" when coupled with "'you are trying to incriminate me and without an attorney'" do exemplify a desire for legal counsel.[7]

What happens when a defendant clearly and unambiguously invokes her Fifth Amendment right to remain silent or speak to a lawyer and officers ignore the request? Texas courts hold that the incriminating statements are subject to suppression.[8] Thus, the procedural step a lawyer must take to keep these statements from being heard by the jury is to file a motion to suppress and request a hearing for the judge to rule on the motion. The basis for the motion to suppress is that the officers violated the defendant's right by interrogating a defendant who clearly and unambiguously invoked that right.

It is common for portions of a videotaped statement to be shown to the jury, particularly in DWI trials where the defendant's level of intoxication may be exhibited physically or verbally, and the jury needs to see the video to determine a fact issue. However, the defendant's invocation of the right to remain silent or to request an attorney should not be heard by the jury because jurors may impermissibly view this as a sign of guilt. "The State may not penalize an individual for exercising his Fifth Amendment rights when he is under police interrogation. Evidence of an individual's invocation of his right to counsel is inadmissible as evidence of guilt."[9] Thus, when the defendant invokes her rights under *Miranda*, that portion of the video can be and should be muted to protect the defendant's presumption of innocence. In order to prevent the jury from hearing the defendant's invocation of rights, defense counsel should file a motion in limine or a motion to suppress.

———————◆———————

---

[7] *Mayes v. State*, 8 S.W.3d 354, 359 (Tex. App.—Amarillo 1999, no pet.) (citations and quotations omitted).

[8] *E.g., id.* at 358–61 (holding officers "transgressed constitutional dictate" by not respecting the defendant's right to remain silent and, as a result, "the ensuing written confession was tainted and subject to suppression.").

[9] *Mathieu v. State*, 992 S.W.2d 725, 729 (Tex. App.—Houston [1st Dist.] 1999, no pet.).

Voluntariness

So far, we have discussed *Miranda* warnings and statements given in response to custodial interrogation. Following an arrest, an officer may request a written statement from the accused or may interview the accused on video. This will lead to a recorded statement, either in writing or through electronic recording.

According to the Code, a "statement of an accused may be used in evidence against him if it appears the same was freely and voluntarily made without compulsion or persuasion...."[10] When a statement is made following threats or promises, it is considered involuntary and inadmissible, regardless of whether the defendant subjectively believed he was coerced into making the statement.[11] The next two cases examine the effect promises and threats have on the voluntariness of a statement.

Mark Edwin Hardesty v. State
667 S.W.2d 130
(Tex. Crim. App. 1984)

The only evidence adduced which connected appellant with the two burglaries for which he was convicted and for which his probation was revoked ... were two written extrajudicial inculpatory statements. Appellant contends those statements should have been excluded because they were obtained as a result of a promise of benefit and were therefore involuntary within the meaning of Article 38.22, ... and the Constitutions of the United States and this State.

On February 21, 1980, at approximately 6:30 a.m., appellant was arrested pursuant to a warrant by Detective Jim Roberts of the Irving Police Department; he was warned and taken to the Irving City Jail. In Detective Roberts' office, appellant was again warned. According to Roberts, appellant,

> ... asked us exactly how many cases we would file against him and we told
> him that he would be filed on for one case if he cleaned up all offenses he

---

[10] TEX. CODE CRIM. PROC. ANN. art. 38.21 (West 2016).
[11] *Oursbourn v. State*, 259 S.W.3d 159, 171 (Tex. Crim. App. 2008) (the issue of voluntariness does not require an assessment of the defendant's actual state of mind at the time he made the statement but an objective evaluation of police behavior).

had committed in Irving. And he agreed to that and he didn't want to talk to an attorney until he had cleaned up his business....

Appellant proceeded to give four consecutive statements concerning four different burglaries, one of which occurred in Irving and underlies the conviction ...; another offense occurred in Grand Prairie and forms the basis for [the other] conviction.... The other two statements were not included in the record.

At the hearing on the motion to suppress, Detective Roberts denied under direct examination that he had promised appellant any reward or benefit in order to obtain the statements. On cross examination of Roberts, the following occurred:

Q: You said also a moment ago that you made no promise of reward or benefit in order to get [appellant] to sign these statements?

A: That's correct.

Q: Didn't you say that you told him if he signed the statements you would only file one case on him?

A: Yes, sir.

Q: Is that a reward or benefit?

A: No, Sir. Because he asked me what Grand Prairie was going to do and I told him, "I have no idea." ...

Q: But you did tell him, though, if he signed it you would only file one case?

A: Yes, sir, on that statement.

...The trial court overruled appellant's motion to suppress ...

Thereafter, a trial on the merits was convened in the three causes before a different judge. The issue regarding the voluntariness of the two confessions was raised by the State without objection by appellant. Detective Roberts testified he promised appellant no reward or benefit in order to obtain four statements. When the prosecutor offered State's Exhibits Nos. 1 and 2, defense counsel requested an opportunity to question the witness before the statements were admitted. Some of that testimony follows:

Q: ... Do you recall having a conversation with this Defendant which you told the Defendant that if he would sign the four statements, you would file only one case?

A: No, Sir, I never told him that. …

Q: All right. Well then, tell us what you did tell him.

A: Mr. Hardesty asked me what I could do for him. … And he told me that what he would tell me would depend on what I could do for him. … And I told him that I could not vouch for any other agency other than my own. … And whatever business he had to clean up in the City of Irving, that I would file one case on him.

Q: All right. And how many pieces of business did he clean up in the City of Irving? …

A: Two or three.

Q: And you took statements on those, didn't you?

A: Yes, Sir, I believe I did.

Q: But you did not file on those?

A: No, Sir, I did not.

Q: And you did not file on those because you told him you would not file on those?

A: I would not file the cases or the crimes he had committed within the City of Irving. … I told him as far as other agencies, that I did not have that authority to make that—any sort of promise or deal with him … that that would be solely up to that department.

Q: But you did, in effect, promise him that if he would make statements and come clean, you would file only one case? …

A: I told him I would only file one case. At that time, Mr. Hardesty then said fine, I will tell you everything that I know.

Q: Okay. But now, this conversation took place before the statements were signed, or before he gave you any information?

A: Yes, Sir.

Q: Okay. You didn't consider that to be a favor to not file cases on a person in exchange for them signing confessions or statements?

… Defense counsel's objection to the admissibility of [the statements because] they "were obtained after promises of leniency made by the officer" was overruled and the statements were admitted into evidence.

We hold the trial court erred in admitting State's Exhibit No. 1 concerning the Irving offense.

Officer Roberts' testimony at trial makes it clear that appellant gave the inculpatory content of that exhibit as a result of Roberts' promise he would file only one Irving case against appellant; this testimony also demonstrates that Roberts in fact did not file two other Irving cases to which appellant had confessed, pursuant to their agreement. The totality of Roberts' testimony belies his repeated denials that he had "promised" appellant anything.

An inculpatory statement obtained as a result of a benefit positively promised to the defendant made or sanctioned by one in authority and of such a character as would be likely to influence a defendant to speak untruthfully is not admissible. State's Exhibit No. 1 falls into that category. The judgment of [that] conviction ... must be reversed.[12]

However, under the same criteria, ... State's Exhibit No. 2 does not fall into the prohibited category. Detective Roberts' testimony was consistently positive and unequivocal that he told appellant he had no authority over offenses committed outside the city limits of Irving and he therefore could neither do nor promise anything regarding offenses committed by appellant in Grand Prairie. Nor did Roberts make his end of the "bargain" contingent upon appellant's making any inculpatory statement about offenses committed outside Irving. Accordingly, appellant's written statement admitting to a burglary committed in Grand Prairie (State's Exhibit No. 2) could not have resulted from the promise of benefit made by Detective Roberts.

We hold the trial court's admission of State's Exhibit No. 2 on the ground that it was voluntarily made did not constitute error.

———————◆———————

Notes and Questions

1. Detective Roberts promised that if Mr. Hardesty admitted to all of the burglaries, he would file only one charge against him in Irving. Mr.

---

[12] *Cf. Penry v. State*, 903 S.W.2d 715, 748-49 (Tex. Crim. App. 1995) (officer's promise that he would not charge defendant with crime that he did not commit did not render defendant's subsequent statements to be inadmissible because promise could not have reasonably induced defendant to confess to crime that he did not commit).

Hardesty admitted to committing a total of four burglaries, three in Irving and one in Grand Prairie. Detective Roberts only filed one case in Irving and made no promise about Grand Prairie. Officer Roberts delivered his promise. What's wrong with that?

———————◆———————

Gerald Christopher Zuliani v. State
903 S.W.2d 812
(Tex. App.—Austin 1995, no pet.)

Appellant Gerald Christopher Zuliani was charged by indictment with intentionally and knowingly causing serious bodily injury to a child younger than fourteen years.

…In his motion to suppress the confession, appellant contended that the confession was the result of custodial interrogation following an illegal arrest and that it was obtained "by coercion and threats by law enforcement personnel without the proper warnings of his constitutional and statutory rights after he had attempted to terminate the questioning." At the suppression hearing (conducted prior to the first trial), it was shown that Sergeant Bruce Boardman of the Austin Police Department received a telephone call and then assigned Sergeants Michael Huckabay and Hector Polanco to investigate a possible child abuse case. [Initially, doctors were told the two-year old child nearly drowned.] Upon arrival at Brackenridge Hospital, Huckabay and Polanco viewed the injured child, who was in critical condition, and were informed by Dr. Jaffe that the injuries were not the result of a drowning. The officers went to the hospital's family room where they encountered appellant, Boutwell, appellant's mother, a neighbor, and a social worker. Since appellant and Boutwell were the only adults present at the time of the injuries, the officers requested that they come to the police station to give statements. They agreed. Polanco testified that at this point, the officers did not have sufficient information about the cause of the injuries to view appellant and Boutwell as suspects or to conclude that a criminal act had occurred.

Upon arrival at the police station at about 1:00 a.m. on January 3, 1990, Boutwell was placed in one interview room and appellant in another. Sergeants Huckabay and Polanco commenced their investigation by interviewing Boutwell. At first, she persisted in repeating the drowning story.

When her interrogators said that they did not believe her, Boutwell began to yell and scream at the officers. At this point, Sergeant Mark Rush was asked by the officers involved to move appellant so that he could not hear Boutwell. Rush placed appellant in a lobby near the elevators. Later, Boutwell incriminated appellant, accusing him of causing the injuries to her two-year-old son.

At about 3:00 a.m., Huckabay went to the lobby area and returned appellant to an interview room. There, Huckabay and Polanco reintroduced themselves and asked appellant what had happened to the child. Appellant repeated the drowning story. Huckabay told appellant "to think about it, get it straight." The officers left the room. Sometime later, Huckabay returned to the room where appellant was seated. Sergeant Huckabay administered the *Miranda* warnings to appellant and informed him that Boutwell was now blaming appellant for the child's injuries. Appellant maintained his innocence, although Huckabay told him that the child's injuries were not consistent with appellant's story and that appellant was lying. Huckabay reported that appellant became angry and began debating with him; he also recalled that appellant had a smirk on his face. Huckabay lost his composure and yelled at appellant, "[T]o hell with you." When Huckabay got up to leave, appellant asked the officer to wait, but Huckabay told appellant that he did not "want to hear what you've got to say."

Sergeant Boardman, who was still working on another case, heard the yelling and went to the interview room. As Huckabay opened the door to leave, appellant asked if he could talk to Boardman. The officer entered the room and shut the door. Appellant continued to protest his innocence. Boardman explained that the child had not drowned, that there was a subdural hematoma, and that the child was now brain dead. Boardman also informed appellant that the police knew the victim had been admitted to the hospital two or three weeks earlier. He rejected each explanation appellant made. The interrogation continued. Boardman described appellant's attitude and demeanor as being inappropriate under the circumstances; he was cocky, unfeeling, uncaring, and had a smirk on his face. When appellant stated that Boardman was saying the same things as Huckabay, Boardman got up to leave. Before leaving, Boardman, a weightlifter, suddenly grabbed appellant by the lapels of his jacket. Boardman described what happened next:

> I shoved him against the wall and I told him that if he didn't take that shit-eating grin off his face, that I was going to pull his head off and shit down

his throat. I then told him that he was—several different things about what I thought about him. Then I asked how it felt—'How do you think little Christopher felt to have someone your size throwing him around?' I said 'How does it feel to be scared?'

Boardman denied that his motive was to obtain a statement. He claimed that he only wished to get appellant's "attention" and change his "attitude" towards the investigation. He thought that appellant "was more stunned than anything" about what happened. The record further reflects on cross examination:

[DEFENSE COUNSEL]: In retrospect you were trying to intimidate him.

A: In retrospect, I was trying to get his attention, make him aware that we weren't talking about a shop-lifting case and we weren't talking about … committing a burglary; we were talking about the murder of a child.

Q: And you threatened him?

A: No sir. I promised him. . . .

Q: But what you were conveying to him was that you were promising physical harm?

A: Yes sir.

Huckabay, who was in an interview room with Boutwell across the hall, heard Boardman "being pretty loud." Huckabay also heard "thumps" and "rumbling on the wall." Huckabay went to the room in question and opened the door. He saw that Boardman had appellant "up against the wall with his feet off the ground." Boardman was yelling and Huckabay heard the statement that Boardman acknowledged making. As Boardman was leaving the room, Huckabay heard Boardman tell appellant, "I don't need anything from you. You can leave. I don't care. I don't have to have you." Huckabay heard appellant respond: "Well, if you don't believe me, don't believe me, but I didn't do it. All I can do is tell you the truth. I don't know what you want me to do." At least, Huckabay thought it was "something to that effect."

As Boardman left, Huckabay entered the room and resumed the interrogation. Huckabay noted that appellant did not complain that Boardman had injured or hurt him. Huckabay apologized for his own previous conduct, told appellant that appellant was "probably a nice guy" who had made a mistake, that appellant really did not mean to hurt the child, that things happened that caused appellant to "lose it," that appellant was still a salvageable human being who, if he hurt the child, "needed to get it off his chest." Appellant again urged his innocence. The interrogation continued. Fifteen or twenty minutes later, Boardman returned and asked if appellant thought that he deserved what Boardman had done to him. Appellant was indignant and replied: "No, I don't think you deserved to do that to me." Boardman responded: "Well, that's fine. Do you think little Christopher deserved what you did to him?" Appellant broke down and began crying. Boardman left the room and had no further contact with appellant.

Huckabay continued the interrogation after Boardman left. According to Huckabay, appellant did not seem afraid of Boardman. After some time, appellant began to cry and admitted orally that he had injured the child on various occasions and on the fatal night. Appellant then indicated that he would give a taped statement. Appellant was again given the *Miranda* warnings and those required by statute. Appellant stated that he understood his rights; he did not request an attorney. He signed a card acknowledging the warnings and waiving his rights. At 5:25 a.m., the officers made an electronic record of appellant's confession. It appears that all the [legal] requirements …were met. The taping concluded about 6:00 a.m. on January 3, 1990. A complaint was then filed, and appellant was formally arrested and jailed. At about 9:30 a.m., appellant was taken before a magistrate and given the magistrate's warnings.

In its findings of fact and conclusions of law, the trial court found that the electronically recorded confession was freely and voluntarily made by the twenty-three-year-old appellant after he had been duly warned of his rights under *Miranda* and article 38.22, and had affirmatively waived those rights. The trial court further found that the taped confession met the statutory requirements for electronically recorded statements. The trial court also found appellant was not induced to make the confession by "any compulsion, threats, promises or persuasion." In its specific findings, the trial court concluded that the incident with Sergeant Boardman "was brief, was not intended to secure a statement from the defendant, had no affect [sic] on the defendant's demeanor or attitude and involved no physical injury to the defendant." Moreover, the trial court found that Sergeant Boardman was not present during the final interrogation resulting in the confession, and that the incident between Boardman and appellant was disconnected with and unrelated to the confession. The trial court concluded that the confession was admissible in evidence as a matter of law.

The Texas Code of Criminal Procedure expressly allows the statement of an accused to be used against him if it appears that the statement was freely and voluntarily made without compulsion or persuasion. Apart from the statutory requirements, the admissibility of a confession is contingent on the accused being accorded "due course of the law of the land." ...[A] confession must not only meet state law requirements, it must not ... [violate] ... the Due Process Clause of the Fourteenth Amendment to the United States Constitution. ...

The United States Supreme Court has long held that certain interrogation techniques, either in isolation or as applied to the unique characteristics of a particular suspect, are so offensive to a civilized system of justice that they must be condemned under the due process clause of the Fourteenth Amendment. ...

...[A] finding of coercion need not depend upon actual violence by a governmental agent; a credible threat is sufficient. As the Court has said: "Coercion can be mental as well as physical and.... the blood of the accused is not the only hallmark of an unconstitutional inquisition." ... [A] defendant in a criminal case is deprived of due process of law if his conviction is founded, in whole or in part, upon an involuntary confession without regard to the truth or falsity of the confession, even though there is ample evidence aside from the confession to support the conviction.

Likewise, Texas courts have held confessions inadmissible as a matter of law when the uncontradicted evidence has shown they were obtained by coercion, threats or fear.

In this case, appellant was interrogated by Officer Huckabay, who admittedly lost his composure and began yelling as appellant continued to protest his innocence.

The "totality of the circumstances" is to be examined to determine whether a confession is voluntary. The State has the burden to prove the voluntariness of a confession. It must satisfactorily negate the accused's allegations of coercion in order to satisfy its burden of proof. Under the "totality of the circumstances" test, "the burden of proving voluntariness after flagrant police misconduct is, properly, substantial."

Whenever an accused's testimony of alleged coercion is undisputed, the resulting confession is inadmissible as a matter of law. Although appellant did not testify, the uncontradicted evidence in the instant case of the coercive acts was elicited from the State's own witnesses, principally the officers in question.

The question to be confronted in each case is whether the accused's will was overborne when he confessed. The confession must be the product of an essentially free and unconstrained choice by its maker. In some cases, the need for such an individual calculus is obviated by the egregiousness of the police conduct. Confessions accompanied by physical violence wrought by law enforcement personnel have been considered per se inadmissible.

Confessions accompanied by physical violence are presumed involuntary both because of their unreliability and because of the great likelihood that the use or threatened use of violence overbears a suspect's will.

> Physical violence or threat of it by the custodian of a prisoner during detention serves no lawful purpose, invalidates confessions that otherwise would be convincing, and is universally condemned by the law. When present, there is no need to weigh or measure its effects on the will of the individual victim. The tendency of the innocent, as well as the guilty, to risk remote results of a false confession rather than suffer immediate pain is so strong that judges long ago found it necessary to guard against miscarriages of justice by treating any confession made concurrently with torture or threat of brutality as too untrustworthy to be received as evidence of guilt.

[P]hysical torture or violence usually produces a confession, not during the actual violence, but afterwards through fear of repetition. A rule, however, that all confessions preceded by violence are inadmissible and incurable, regardless of ameliorative circumstances, is too rigid. It is nevertheless difficult to draw the line between those confessions properly considered coerced because of concurrent violence (in which a conclusive presumption that one's will is overborne is appropriate), and those sufficiently attenuated from such misconduct to justify application of the more lenient "totality of the circumstances" test. An interruption in the stream of events between the initial coercion and the confession has been recognized as significant. A confession is not rendered inadmissible as a matter of law because of an assault upon the defendant which occurred prior to, disconnected with, and apparently unrelated to the subsequent confession.

In this case, appellant was interrogated by Officer Huckabay, who admittedly lost his composure and began yelling as appellant continued to protest his innocence. Appellant invited Sergeant Boardman into the interview room following Huckabay's outburst. The interrogation continued with Boardman rejecting every explanation appellant made. At some point, Boardman threatened to pull appellant's head off, shoved him against the wall and lifted his feet off the ground. Boardman conceded that he was promising appellant physical harm. When Boardman left, Huckabay reentered the room with no break in the interrogation. This time Huckabay was composed and apologized for his earlier outbursts. After a few minutes, Boardman returned to ask if appellant thought that he deserved Boardman's rough treatment. This action alerted appellant to the fact that Boardman was still present, and it was then that he broke down and began crying. By then the twenty-three-year-old appellant had been awake some twenty hours. He had had no prior experience with the police. Within an hour or so, appellant gave an oral statement to Huckabay. Thereafter, the taped confession was taken from appellant. We find no interruption in the stream of events between the undisputed coercion by Sergeant Boardman and the taped confession taken by Huckabay. The police may take certain steps after physical abuse, such as removing the errant officer from the scene, assuring the suspect that he would no longer be harmed, and establishing via colloquy that his fears have been eliminated. Such curative measures might defuse a formerly coercive environment. Here, there is no evidence that the police acted affirmatively to dissipate the coercive environment created by Boardman's actions and his "promise of harm" to appellant.

...[A]n officer's assault does not render a confession inadmissible as a matter of law if the assault was prior to, disconnected with, and apparently unrelated to the subsequent confession. In *Brooks* and *Barton*,[13] the confessions were taken the day after the alleged abuse at a different locale by an official not involved in the abusive behavior. In *Berry*,[14] the assault and threats by a security guard and a police officer clearly had nothing to do with the confession obtained an hour and a half later by another officer.

In the instant case, appellant was being interrogated about the offense when Boardman entered the picture. Boardman continued to question appellant about the injuries to the child and continued to reject appellant's claims of innocence. Boardman insisted that he was not attempting to induce a statement, but rather that his assault on appellant and his promise of harm

---

[13] *Brooks v. State*, 95 S.W.2d 136, 138–39 (Tex. Crim. App. 1936); *Barton v. State*, 605 S.W.2d 605, 607 (Tex. Crim. App. 1980).
[14] *Berry v. State*, 582 S.W.2d 463, 465 (Tex. Crim. App. 1979).

were to change appellant's "attitude" towards the investigation, which was then centered on appellant. While Boardman's assault preceded the confession, the evidence does not show that it was disconnected with and apparently unrelated to the taking of the confession as in *Barton*, *Berry*, and *Brooks*. Appellant broke down emotionally and began crying upon Boardman's last visit to the interrogation room, shortly before he confessed. An individual calculus to determine whether the confession was the product of appellant's essentially free and unconstrained choice is unnecessary because of the egregiousness of the police conduct. We hold that the confession, as a matter of law, was coerced and involuntary and taken in violation of the due process clause of the Fourteenth Amendment, and that the trial court erred in failing to suppress such a confession.

———————◆———————

Notes and Questions

1. The *Zuliani* Court examined the "unique characteristics of a particular suspect" and the role the officers' mental coercion and fear tactics played in the defendant's decision to provide a statement. Individuals who are young, immature, mentally ill, or intellectually challenged may be more susceptible to police misconduct in the confession context than individuals who are older, more mature, or mentally competent.

Consider police interrogation of a person who is mentally ill or intellectually disabled. Does a person's mental state affect voluntariness? This is what the Court of Criminal Appeals had to say when an intellectually disabled man challenged the admissibility of his statement on appeal:

> The totality of the circumstances standard has been held to be sufficiently all-encompassing to protect the rights of juveniles and adults alike, taking into account such factors as intelligence, age, experience, education, maturity, etc. Because a confessor's mental capabilities are but one factor to be evaluated among many, this measure of voluntariness may be applicable to confessions made by anyone, no matter what their IQ happens to be.[15]

> What about someone who gives a statement while he is suffering from mental illness? Again, appellate courts examine the totality of the circumstances. Using that test, the Fort Worth appellate court found a

---

[15] *Delao v. State*, 235 S.W.3d 235, 241 (Tex. Crim. App. 2007).

confession voluntary even when the defendant was undergoing psychiatric treatment at the time he gave the statement.[16] In another case, a man suffering from a severe case of paranoid schizophrenia admitted to police that he stabbed his brother.[17] The defendant was not in custody or being interrogated when he made the statement; nevertheless, at trial his defense attorney objected to the statement by asserting that the defendant's mental state rendered his statement involuntary.[18] The Houston Court of Appeals held,

> While appellant's mental state is relevant to the jury's determination of the accuracy of his pre-arrest admission, it is not determinative of its admissibility. Appellant may have been mentally disturbed at the time of his admission or confession, but the compulsion influencing his admission was internal and not that of custodial interrogation.[19]

> The above statement seems to imply there are cases where officers could take advantage of a suspect's psychosis to extract a statement., However, just because a defendant is mentally ill or retarded does not automatically render a statement involuntary or inadmissible. Appellate courts make it clear that all statements, regardless of who gives them, must be evaluated the same way: by examining all of the facts and circumstances surrounding the taking of the statement.

    2.   There is a distinction between the protection afforded by the Fifth Amendment and that provided under Texas law. The U.S. Supreme Court has emphasized that the "sole concern of the Fifth Amendment, on which *Miranda* was based, is governmental coercion. Indeed, the Fifth Amendment privilege is not concerned 'with moral and psychological pressures to confess emanating from sources other than official coercion.'"[20]

    Texas law, on the other hand, permits a defendant to raise voluntariness even when coercion came from non-government actors or was due to mental

---

[16] *Reed v. State*, 59 S.W.3d 278, 282 (Tex. App.—Fort Worth 2001, pet. ref'd).
[17] *Baker v. State*, 682 S.W.2d 701, 710 (Tex. App.—Houston [1st Dist.] 1984), *rev'd on other grounds*, 707 S.W.2d 893 (Tex. Crim. App. 1986).
[18] *Id.*
[19] *Id.* at 703.
[20] *Colorado v. Connelly*, 479 U.S. 157, 170 (1986).

or cognitive disabilities. Consider what the Court of Criminal Appeals said about the difference between Texas and federal law:

> Under Articles 38.21 and 38.22 and their predecessors, fact scenarios that can raise a state-law claim of involuntariness (even though they do not raise a federal constitutional claim) include the following: (1) the suspect was ill and on medication and that fact may have rendered his confession involuntary; (2) the suspect was mentally retarded and may not have "knowingly, intelligently and voluntarily" waived his rights; (3) the suspect "lacked the mental capacity to understand his rights"; (4) the suspect was intoxicated, and he "did not know what he was signing and thought it was an accident report"; (5) the suspect was confronted by the brother-in-law of his murder victim and beaten; (6) the suspect was returned to the store he broke into "for questioning by several persons armed 'with six-shooters.'"

> In sum, the potential "involuntary" fact scenarios encompassed by Articles 38.21 and 38.22 are broader in scope than those covered by the Due Process Clause or *Miranda*. Although this Court has held that youth, intoxication, mental retardation, and other disabilities are usually not enough, by themselves, to render a statement inadmissible under Article 38.22, they are factors that a jury, armed with a proper instruction, is entitled to consider.[21]

3. The *Zuliani* Court also contemplated "curative measures" the officers could have taken to "defuse a formerly coercive environment." This language hints at the attenuation doctrine discussed in Chapter 2, which is implicated frequently in the context of statements. "The attenuation doctrine provides that the tainted evidence may be admitted if the prosecution can show that the connection between the initial illegality and the evidence has become so attenuated [or removed] so as to dissipate the taint."[22]

The *Zuliani* Court did not consider attenuation given the ongoing and egregious conduct of the police. The Court suggested several facts that could have resulted in attenuation (*i.e.*, a break in the events that would have removed the statement from the threats and force of the officers' actions). Since none of those things happened, however, there was no attenuation, and the confession was deemed a product of the officers' threats and use of physical force.

---

[21] *Oursbourn v. State*, 259 S.W.3d 159, 172-73 (Tex. Crim. App. 2008).
[22] *Reed v. State*, 809 S.W.2d 940, 944-45 (Tex. App.—Dallas 1991, no pet.).

4. When a defendant challenges the voluntariness of his confession, he may request a hearing before the judge.[23] This hearing is referred to as a *Jackson v. Denno* hearing,[24] and it is described as follows:

> When a defendant makes a pretrial challenge to the voluntariness and admissibility of his confession, the prosecution bears the burden of proving voluntariness by a preponderance of the evidence. The court, outside the presence of the jury, must conduct a hearing to determine for itself whether the statement was voluntarily given. Voluntariness is determined by considering the totality of the circumstances.[25]

———◆———

Written Statements

Just because a statement was voluntarily given by an accused does not render it admissible. All written statements require a specified set of warnings before they can be admitted into evidence. The law dictating the admissibility of written statements is triggered when a person makes a statement while he is in custody and being interrogated.[26] A written statement is defined as a statement:

1. made by the accused in his own handwriting or
2. made in a language the accused can read or understand that
    a. the accused signed; or
    b. if the accused is unable to read or write bears his mark, and the mark is witnessed by someone who is not a peace officer.[27]

---

[23] TEX. CODE CRIM. PROC. ANN. art. 38.22 § 6 (West 2016).
[24] *Jackson v. Denno*, 378 U.S. 368, 380 (1964) ("A defendant objecting to the admission of a confession is entitled to a fair hearing in which both the underlying factual issues and the voluntariness of his confession are actually and reliably determined").
[25] *Simpson v. State*, 227 S.W.3d 855, 858 (Tex. App.—Houston [14th Dist.] 2007, no pet.).
[26] TEX. CODE CRIM. PROC. ANN. art. 38.22 § 2 (West 2016).
[27] TEX. CODE CRIM. PROC. ANN. art. 38.22 § 1 (West 2016).

In order for a written statement taken during custodial interrogation to be admissible against him in court, the following criteria must be met:

1. The accused must be given magistrate warnings by a magistrate prior to making his statement; or

2. The person to whom the statement was made must give the accused the following warnings,[28] which appear on the face of the written statement:

    a. You have the right to remain silent and not make any statement at all and any statement you make may be used against you at trial;

    b. Any statement you make may be used as evidence against you in court;

    c. You have the right to have a lawyer present to advise you prior to and during any questioning;

    d. If you are unable to employ a lawyer, you have the right to have a lawyer appointed to advise you prior to and during any questioning; and

    e. You have the right to terminate the interview at any time.[29]

Notice that the rights required on the face of the statement are similar to the *Miranda* warnings with two exceptions: the accused may terminate the interview at any time, and the statement can be used against him not only at trial but also in court.

In order for a statement to be admissible, the accused, prior to and during the making of the statement, must knowingly, intelligently, and voluntarily waive the rights set out above.[30] It is not enough that the statement, on its face, demonstrate the accused acknowledged these rights; it must demonstrate he waived them.[31] The State has the burden of proving by a preponderance of the evidence that the accused knowingly, intelligently, and voluntarily waived these rights.[32]

---

[28] *Dowthitt v. State*, 931 S.W.2d 244, 258 (Tex. Crim. App. 1996) ("this requirement is satisfied so long as the officer taking the confession was present when the warnings were given").

[29] TEX. CODE CRIM. PROC. ANN. art. 38.22 § 2 (a) (West 2016).

[30] TEX. CODE CRIM. PROC. ANN. art. 38.22 § 2 (b) (West 2016).

[31] *Joseph v. State*, 309 S.W.3d 20, 23-24 (Tex. Crim. App. 2010).

[32] *Id.* at 24.

One of the above warnings is worth mentioning further. In the first two required warnings, the following language must appear on the face of the statement: that it "may be used as evidence against you." In the past, officers have suggested, in an effort to encourage an accused to confess, that the defendant's statement may be used "for or against" him. This is what the Eastland Court of Appeals said about this language, which may be viewed as an inducement:

> If the defendant receives proper warnings, but the interrogating officer later promises him that his statement may be used "for or against" him, that promise becomes a factor for the court to consider when determining the voluntariness of the statement but does not render it inadmissible per se.[33]

When it comes to the wording of the statutory warnings, courts have repeatedly held that the language need not track the statutory language verbatim; substantial compliance is sufficient,[34] Nevertheless, the Court of Criminal Appeals has also stated that "without the proper predicate of proper warnings, even a voluntary confession is inadmissible."[35]

---------------◆---------------

Notes and Questions

1. Suppose Matt and Eileen murder Jason. When they are charged and arrested, Matt invokes his right to remain silent. Eileen, however, gives a written statement to police that implicates Matt and herself in Jason's murder. Suppose her statement meets all of the criteria and is admissible. Matt and Eileen are tried together. Eileen refuses to testify at trial. Can the prosecutor use Eileen's statement as evidence at trial? Does admitting the statement into evidence violate Matt's right to confront the witness—in this case, Eileen?

---

[33] *Davila v. State*, 4 S.W.3d 844, 849 (Tex. App.—Eastland 1999, no pet.).
[34] *Nonn v. State*, 41 S.W.3d 677, 679 (Tex. Crim. App. 2001); *Campbell v. State*, 885 S.W.2d 528, 530 (Tex. App.—El Paso 1994, no pet.) (though warnings suffered "from some brevity when compared to the statutory requirements," the accused acknowledged he understood what rights he was giving up in his written statement, which satisfied the legal requirements).
[35] *Clark v. State*, 627 S.W.2d 693, 704 (Tex. Crim. App. 1982).

In *Scott*, co-defendant Robert Springsteen gave a statement implicating the appellant, Michael Scott, in the murder of four girls.[36] The prosecutor admitted Springsteen's redacted statement into evidence.[37] Scott complained this violated his right to confront Springsteen.[38] The Court of Criminal Appeals agreed by saying:

> [S]tatements made during police interrogations are testimonial, and like other testimonial statements, they are admissible under the Sixth Amendment only if the declarant is unavailable and the defendant had a prior opportunity to cross-examine. Springsteen's statement to the police was no less testimonial because it had been redacted to remove all references to Scott. Because Scott had no prior opportunity to cross-examine, the introduction of Springsteen's testimonial statement violated Scott's Sixth Amendment right to confront the witnesses against him.

> A recent opinion by the Fort Worth Court of Appeals is consistent with our holding in this cause. In *Hale*,[39] the defendant unsuccessfully moved to suppress his accomplice's statement to the police on Sixth Amendment grounds. The statement had been redacted to delete the defendant's name, although references to the defendant's conduct remained. Without expressing any opinion regarding the effect of the redaction, the appellate court held that the statement was inadmissible.[40]

Two solutions to this problem include not admitting the confession into evidence or severing the trials by trying the co-defendants separately. Motions to sever are discussed in more detail in Chapter 12.

2. The voluntariness of a statement can be considered by the jury, even if the judge has already found the statement admissible following a pretrial hearing on the defendant's motion to suppress. Consider the following Court of Criminal Appeals description of how the issue of admissibility gets from the judge to the jury:

> ... This is the sequence of events that seems to be contemplated [when voluntariness is an issue]: (1) a party notifies the trial judge that there is an

---

[36] *Scott v. State*, 165 S.W.3d 27, 36-37 (Tex. App.—Austin 2005), *rev'd on other grounds*, 227 S.W.3d 670 (Tex. Crim. App. 2007).

[37] *Id.*

[38] *Id.* at 45.

[39] *Hale v. State*, 139 S.W.3d 418, 420 (Tex. App.—Fort Worth 2004, no pet.).

[40] *Scott*, 165 S.W.3d at 47-48.

issue about the voluntariness of the confession … ; (2) the trial judge holds a hearing outside the presence of the jury; (3) the trial judge decides whether the confession was voluntary; (4) if the trial judge decides that the confession was voluntary, it will be admitted, and a party may offer evidence before the jury suggesting that the confession was not in fact voluntary; (5) if such evidence is offered before the jury, the trial judge shall give the jury a voluntariness instruction. It is only after the trial judge is notified of the voluntariness issue … that a chain of other requirements comes into play, culminating in the defendant's right to a jury instruction.[41]

3.   Law enforcement officers are aware that if they interrogate first and warn later, they are more likely to obtain a statement. This practice is referred to as "a two-step 'question first, warn later' interrogation technique."[42] The Code specifically mandates that warnings be read before questioning begins.[43]

Police obtained the following three-page confession by using this technique.[44] Despite the inappropriate actions of the officers, the Court held its erroneous admission harmless because it was admitted during the punishment phase, its contents related to extraneous offenses, and numerous witnesses testified about these extraneous offenses.[45] Nevertheless, the statement should never have been admitted into evidence due to the unlawful two-step technique, which runs afoul of the Code's requirement to warn an accused before taking his statement.[46]

As you examine the statement, notice the warnings at the beginning, the indicators that the defendant not only knew his rights but waived them, and the other statutory requirements that are evidenced in the copy of the statement itself. Finally, consider the initials that appear throughout the statement and why they appear where they do.

---

[41] *Oursbourn v. State*, 259 S.W.3d 159, 173-75 (Tex. Crim. App. 2008).

[42] *Carter v. State*, 309 S.W.3d 31, 38 (Tex. Crim. App. 2010).

[43] *Martinez-Hernandez v. State*, 468 S.W.3d 748, 758 (Tex. App.—San Antonio 2015, no pet.).

[44] *Jones v. State*, 119 S.W.3d 766, 775-76 (Tex. Crim. App. 2003).

[45] *Id.* at 780.

[46] *See also Missouri v. Seibert*, 542 U.S. 600, 622 (2004) (Kennedy, J., concurring) ("If the deliberate two-step strategy has been used, post-warning statements that are related to the substance of prewarning statements must be excluded unless curative measures are taken before the postwarning statement is made.").

1

VOLUNTARY STATEMENT OF ACCUSED
Officer

State of Texas X

unty of TARRANT X   09-22   19 99

N I, Quinton P. Jones   after being duly warned by
N. I ANE AKIN + Chris RodRiGUEZ   , the person to whom this statement is made, that:

1. I have the right to remain silent and not make any statement at all and that any statement I make may be used against me at my trial;
2. Any statement I make may be used as evidence against me in court;
3. I have the right to have a lawyer present to advise me prior to and during any questioning;
4. If I am unable to employ a lawyer, I have the right to have a lawyer appointed to advise me prior to and during any questioning;
5. I have the right to terminate the interview at any time.

and prior to and during the making of this statement I knowingly, intelligently, and voluntarily waive those rights set forth in this document and having knowingly, intelligently and voluntarily waived those rights I do hereby make the following free and voluntary statement:

My name is Quinton P. Jones , I live at 3521 Baylor Street, Fort Worth

I am 20 years of age. My nearest relative is Elizabeth Hill , whose relation

to me is GRANDMOTHER and who resides at ON DANIELS IN FORT WORTH.

QS Me and Red were heading to my house. The car broke. We walked to my house. Red asked me if I knew someone with money. We had done some business with Little Boo. I beeped Little Boo, Clark Peoples. Red said he was going to hide behind the door. I was hoping that Little Boo was by himself, but Marc Sanders was with him. Little Boo walked in by himself. Marc stayed in the car, a smoked gray Altima. When Little Boo walked in, Red, Ricky, hit him, Little Boo, with a barbell. He hit him more than three times. Little Boo was hollering. He fell to the floor. Red told me grab him and hold him. I held little Boo down while Red choked him with his hands. Red started hitting little Boo harder and harder. Red was hyped from this shit. Red told me to bring a belt to tie little Boo. I took a braided leather belt out of my pants. Red tied little Boo with the belt. Red told me to help move little Boo out of sight. We moved little Boo in the back room. Little Boo was wearing some white shoes, blue Dickey pants and a sky blue shirt. Red told me to holler at Marc and have him come in. I did. Marc came in the house and Red hit him in the head with the barbell. Red was mad because it took Marc a long time to give up. Red kept on QS

Witness N. Neal Allen

Chris Rodriguez - TCSO   Quinton Jones   ACCUSED
Witness

Ra-31 (Rev. 6/85)

2

VOLUNTARY STATEMENT OF ACCUSED
Officer

State of Texas X
County of TARRANT X

09-22-_____ 19 99

I, Quinton P. Jones _____ after being duly warned by
N. Lane Akin + Chris Rodriguez _____, the person to whom this statement is made, that:

1. I have the right to remain silent and not make any statement at all and that any statement I make may be used against me at my trial;
2. Any statement I make may be used as evidence against me in court;
3. I have the right to have a lawyer present to advise me prior to and during any questioning;
4. If I am unable to employ a lawyer, I have the right to have a lawyer appointed to advise me prior to and during any questioning;
5. I have the right to terminate the interview at any time.

and prior to and during the making of this statement I knowingly, intelligently, and voluntarily waive those rights set forth in this document and having knowingly, intelligently and voluntarily waived those rights I do hereby make the following free and voluntary statement:

My name is Quinton P. Jones _____ I live at _____
I am 20 years of age. My nearest relative is Elizabeth P. Jones _____ whose relation
to me is GRANDMOTHER and who resides at _____

hitting Marc until he fell. Red took the barbell
& pushed it down against Marc's neck. He told me
to bring something to tie Marc up with. I brought
him a white extension chord. We tied him up.
Red told me to drive around back in little Boo's
Car. And, I did. I opened the trunk. We put
little Boo in the trunk. Red opened the back door
and we tried to put Marc in the back seat.
Marc was heavy, but we got him in there. We
went in the house and cleaned up. Marc had a
necklace, a Rope, gold. Marc had a ring, gold, and
a pager. Clark had two or three rings. One of them
was gold the other was diamond and gold. And
Clark had a gold and diamond cross necklace.
Clark had a pager. They had two or three hundred
dollars or a little bit more. They had two hundred
dollars or more in Crack Cocaine. After they were
loaded into the car, Red said he knew a place and
he told me to drive. I drove through Lake Worth
and we drove to a river. They had a van there.
So, I didn't know the neighborhood and so Red drove.
We drove around around getting high. Then we came
back and basically we pushed it down a hill into the river. QS

Witness _____
Chris Rodriquez - TCSO
Witness

ACCUSED
Quinton Jones

Ra-31 (Rev. 8/85)

1

3

VOLUNTARY STATEMENT OF ACCUSED
Officer

State of Texas X

County of TARRANT X

09-22 1999

I, Quinten P. Jones _____ after being duly warned by

N. Cane Akin + Chris Rodriquez _____, the person to whom this statement is made, that:

1. I have the right to remain silent and not make any statement at all and that any statement I make may be used against me at my trial;
2. Any statement I make may be used as evidence against me in court;
3. I have the right to have a lawyer present to advise me prior to and during any questioning;
4. If I am unable to employ a lawyer, I have the right to have a lawyer appointed to advise me prior to and during any questioning;
5. I have the right to terminate the interview at any time.

and prior to and during the making of this statement I knowingly, intelligently, and voluntarily waive those rights set forth in this document and having knowingly, intelligently and voluntarily waived those rights I do hereby make the following free and voluntary statement:

My name is Quinton P. Jones _____ I live at _____

I am 20 years of age. My nearest relative is Elizabeth P. Jones _____ whose relation to me is GRANDMOTHER and who resides at _____

I think there was a bridge close by. I walked in the water and pushed them a little father. Then he drove to the other side were there was a trail. We dumped everything in the river, towels, clothes and the barbell. After we dumped all that in the river, he drove to a friends house. He told me to stay in the car. It was like a trailer type home in the area. He came back out and then we headed to the store and bought some cleaning stuff. It was like dusk. It was a hardware type store. We drove to some apartments in the area. We cleaned out the car. We walked to a friends house. We had waited on someone else, but they never came. So, we paid this other friend to drive us back to Fort Worth. He was kind of big and he had a white or gray van. He, Red, pawned the jewelry in Wise County or Azle or Lake Worth.

Chris Rodriquez — TCSO
Witness

N. Cane Akin
Witness

Quinton Jones
ACCUSED

Ra-31 (Rev. 6/85)

Oral Statements

In Texas, oral statements are generally inadmissible. There are several reasons for this rule. Oral, inculpatory admissions may be misquoted or fabricated. Furthermore, once an officer claims the defendant confessed, this evidence is difficult to contradict or disprove. For these reasons and more, oral statements are admissible only when they meet the requirements set out below.

According to the Code, no oral or sign language statement made while the accused is in custody and being interrogated may be used against him in any criminal proceeding unless it meets the following criteria. It must be

1. An electronic, visual recording of the oral statement;
2. The recording must include the legal warnings set out above, and the defendant must waive those rights on the recording;
3. The recording must be true and correct and unaltered;
4. All voices on the recording must be identifiable; and
5. A copy of the full and accurate recording must be provided to defense counsel at least 20 days before trial.[47]

Furthermore, the full recording must be kept until the defendant's conviction is final and all appeals are complete.[48]

There is one limited exception to the above requirements worth mentioning here. Any oral statement that (1) contains assertions of facts or circumstances that (2) are found to be true and (3) which establish the guilt of the accused may be admitted against him over objection if the accused received *Miranda* warnings before giving the statement.[49] In this instance, an otherwise inadmissible oral statement becomes admissible if it led to the discovery of incriminating evidence or information not previously known to or discovered by the State.[50]

———————◆———————

---

[47] TEX. CODE CRIM. PROC. ANN. art. 38.22 §3 (a) (West 2016).
[48] TEX. CODE CRIM. PROC. ANN. art. 38.22 §3 (b) (West 2016).
[49] TEX. CODE CRIM. PROC. ANN. art. 38.22 §3(c)(West 2016); *State v. Ortiz*, 346 S.W.3d 127, 136 (Tex. App.—Amarillo 2011), *aff'd*, 382 S.W.3d 367 (Tex. Crim. App. 2012).
[50] *McGilvery v. State*, 533 S.W.2d 24, 26 (Tex. Crim. App. 1976).

Notes and Questions

1. Any statement, whether written, oral, or sign language, is admissible if it was given out of state and complies with that state's law, Texas's law, or federal law.[51]

————————◆————————

Res Gestae

Res gestae is exempt from the statutory requirements provided for oral statements. What is *res gestae*? It is a statement of the defendant that is "made in response to a startling event, spontaneously or impulsively, without time for reflection or contrivance."[52] In the criminal procedure context, the shocking event is the defendant's detention, the arrest, or the crime itself, as the next case illustrates.

Gordon Kent Davis v. State
780 S.W.2d 945
(Tex. App.—Fort Worth 1989, pet. ref'd)

At about 3:00 a.m. on the morning of Sunday, April 26, 1987, Fort Worth Police Officer Randy Cunningham was on routine patrol on the north side of Fort Worth when his attention was drawn to the parking lot of Trinity Distributors. Two vehicles were parked in the parking lot, one of them a newer model silver Pontiac Fiero, with their doors or hoods open. Two men, both [B]lack males of medium build and height, were carrying something in their hands and moving from a broken glass door at the front of the building toward the vehicles. As Cunningham's patrol car entered the parking lot, the two men got into a vehicle and drove off. Officer Cunningham gave chase to the silver Fiero.

Officer Cunningham did not lose sight of the Fiero during the entire chase. The Fiero came to a halt on a dirt mound at the end of a dead-end street where Davis got out and began running across an open field. Officer Cunningham shouted, "Halt. I'm a police officer." He did not lose sight of Davis although it was Officer Stamp, another police officer who had joined

---

[51] TEX. CODE CRIM. PROC. ANN. art. 38.22 §8 (West 2016).
[52] *Williamson v. State*, 771 S.W.2d 601, 606 (Tex. App.—Dallas 1989, pet. ref'd).

in the chase, who first caught up to Davis a couple of hundred yards into the field. Davis stopped, put his hands up in the air and said, "It's cool. You got me," or "You got me."

Davis first complains the trial court committed reversible error by admitting his oral statement made while under arrest as "res gestae" in violation of ... art. 38.22.

As a general rule, a statement made by an accused during a custodial interrogation before he has been warned of his rights is inadmissible. Under section 5 of article 38.22, however, this rule does not apply to a statement that is res gestae of the arrest before interrogation or to a statement that does not stem from custodial interrogation....

A res gestae statement is a statement made in response to a startling event, spontaneously or impulsively, without time for reflection or contrivance. An arrest may be such a startling event.

A volunteered statement, on the other hand, is a statement not made in response to interrogation. Interrogation includes both express questioning by the police and its functional equivalent, "any words or actions on the part of the police (other than those normally attendant to arrest and custody) that the police should know are reasonably likely to elicit an incriminating response from the subject."

In the present case the statement made by Davis upon being apprehended by the police, "It's cool. You got me." was a res gestae statement before interrogation. The statement was made by Davis just before Officer Stamp apprehended him, immediately following a high-speed car chase where Davis had wrecked his car and was attempting to escape on foot.

Since the discovery and chase were startling events, and appellant's statement was clearly immediate and spontaneous, the statement was admissible as a res gestae statement.

Davis' statement was also admissible as a volunteered statement. As Officers Cunningham and Stamp chased Davis, neither officer asked him any actual questions. Officer Cunningham identified himself as a police officer and yelled for Davis to stop, but we have not found any cases which stand for the proposition that such an identification or command constitutes interrogation likely to elicit an incriminating response. To the contrary, Officer Cunningham's identification and command would appear to be exactly those words considered "normally attendant to arrest and custody" and therefore not interrogation.

Since appellant was not expressly or implicitly questioned by Officers Cunningham and Stamp, his statement was volunteered. ...

Since Davis' oral statement was admissible either as a res gestae statement before interrogation or as a volunteered statement, the trial court did not err in admitting it into evidence. Davis' first point of error is overruled.

————————◆————————

Notes and Questions

1. What is it about res gestae statements that make them worthy of an exception to the general prohibition against oral statements?

2. Res gestae is not the only exception to the prohibition against unrecorded oral statements. The Code lists several exceptions to the mandates for admissible written and oral statements: (1) statements made by the defendant at trial, before a grand jury, or at his examining trial; (2) a statement made outside of a custodial interrogation setting; (3) a voluntary statement that is used to impeach the defendant's credibility at trial; or (4) any other statement that is admissible under law.[53] Statements that fit into any one of these exceptions are admissible.

A case example illustrates the effect the above exceptions have on otherwise inadmissible statements. In *Girndt v. State*, the defendant was charged with driving while intoxicated (DWI).[54] Mr. Girndt testified at trial that he was not the driver of the van; therefore, he was not guilty of DWI.[55] After he testified, the prosecutor called the arresting officer to the stand to testify as a rebuttal witness.[56] The officer said that following Mr. Girndt's arrest, he explained that he stopped Mr. Girndt because he was weaving all over the road; the defendant replied, "Well, I didn't think I was weaving that badly."[57] The Court of Criminal Appeals held that the otherwise inadmissible statement made while the defendant was in custody became admissible

---

[53] TEX. CODE CRIM. PROC. ANN. art. 38.22 § 5 (West 2016).
[54] *Girndt v. State*, 623 S.W.2d 930, 930-31 (Tex. Crim. App. 1981).
[55] *Id.* at 931-32.
[56] *Id.*
[57] *Id.* at 932.

because it impeached the defendant's testimony that he was not the driver of the van.[58] The Court stated,

> Art. 38.22 ... generally prohibits the admissibility of an oral statement if it stems from custodial interrogation, but an oral in-custody statement is not prohibited from being used at trial if it "has a bearing upon the credibility of the accused as a witness." Thus, such a statement becomes admissible only if the accused testifies at his trial. If the accused does not desire an oral custodial statement to be admitted for impeachment purposes, then he may prevent its admissibility by not testifying at his trial. If he does testify and he has made an oral statement that "has a bearing upon his credibility," *e. g.*, one which conflicts with his testimony, then it becomes admissible for impeachment purposes even if made while in custody.[59]

Keep in mind that all of the oral statements mentioned above—impeaching statements, res gestae, and trial testimony—fall under a provision in Article 38.22 that specifically allows them to be admitted against the accused at trial.[60] Finally, statements that are not a product of custodial interrogation are admissible.

———————◆———————

Practice Questions

On average, questions about statements appear on roughly half of all bar exams. Bar examiners typically ask two questions about statements on the exams in which such questions appear.

Question topics address the warnings that must appear on the face of the statement, the rights triggered by custodial interrogation, the requirements for admissibility of oral statements, the *Miranda* warnings, and the res gestae exception. Bar examiners also ask for arguments that can be made for or against a statement's admissibility, the admissibility of a co-defendant's statement, voluntariness, and other topics discussed in this chapter.

---

[58] *Id.*
[59] *Id.*
[60] TEX. CODE CRIM. PROC. ANN. art. 38.22 § 5 (West 2016).

1. (F-2016, F-2013, F-2010, and F-2003) Prosecutor informs you that Officer will testify at trial that after he arrested Defendant, read him his rights, and questioned him, Defendant admitted to committing the crime.

    What procedural step can you take to prevent this testimony from coming in? What will you argue?

    _____

    _____

    _____

    _____

    _____

2. (F-2016) Prosecutor files a motion requesting a DNA sample from your client so his DNA can be compared to the DNA found at the crime scene. You file a written response to Prosecutor's motion, claiming that to do so would violate Defendant's right against self-incrimination.

    How should the Court rule? Explain.

    _____

    _____

    _____

    _____

    _____

3. (F-2012) On the first day of trial, Prosecutor attempts to admit Defendant's taped oral confession into evidence. You object on the grounds that you were never given a copy of the taped statement in violation of the discovery order. Prosecutor hands you a copy after you make your objection and says, "Well, now you have it."

    What is the deadline, if any, that Prosecutor should have made the tape recording available to you, given her desire to admit the oral statement into evidence at trial? Explain.

    _____

    _____

_____

_____

_____

4. (F-2012) Defendant suffers from mental illness. He does not remember anything, including giving his statement. You listen to the recorded oral statement and, from the beginning, hear the Defendant speak about demonic forces and Satan in response to most of Detective's questions. Detective begins to encourage Defendant to waive his *Miranda* rights saying, "Satan will drag you to hell with him if you don't confess your sins to me."

    What procedural step should you take to prevent the statement from coming into evidence? What will you argue? Explain.

_____

_____

_____

_____

_____

5. (J-2011 and F-2009) You represent Defendant, who committed the offense with Co-defendant. After her arrest, Co-defendant gave a written statement to police implicating herself and Defendant in the crime. Co-defendant refuses to testify at trial against Defendant, but Prosecutor wants to admit Co-defendant's statement into evidence.

    What objections or requests, if any, can you make with regard to the admission of Co-defendant's statement? Explain.

_____

_____

_____

_____

_____

6. (F-2010) One year after the act, Defendant believes he must confess to a murder that no one suspects he committed. He walks to the nearest police station and confesses to the first person he sees: Janitor. When Janitor leaves to get a police officer to assist him, Defendant regrets his decision and runs from the station. He is apprehended and is later charged with the crime.

   What procedural step can you take to prevent Janitor from testifying about what Defendant said? What argument(s), if any, can you make?

   _____

   _____

   _____

   _____

   _____

7. (F-2008) You file a motion to suppress the Defendant's statement because it was given involuntarily. The trial court denies the motion at the hearing on the motion to suppress.

   What procedural step can you take and what evidence must you present, if any, to permit the jury to consider the voluntariness of the statement? Explain.

   _____

   _____

   _____

   _____

   _____

8. (F-2008 and J-2003) After Defendant is arrested, he asks to speak to his lawyer. Detective ignores him, continues the custodial interrogation, and eventually wears Defendant down to the point that he obtains a written confession from Defendant.

What procedural step can you take, when can you take it, and what will you argue?

_____

_____

_____

_____

_____

9. (J-2007) Defendant is apprehended after committing armed robbery by holding a teenage boy at gunpoint and demanding his backpack. Moments after Defendant is apprehended, he wails, "He may look like a teenage boy, but he really is an alien from outer space, and his backpack has a bomb in it! He is a danger to us all!"

    What step can you take to exclude defendant's statement? When must you take that step? What argument(s) can you make?

    _____

    _____

    _____

    _____

    _____

10. (F-2006) List three warnings that must appear on the face of a statement in order for it to be admissible? List something other than a warning that must appear on the face of the statement to make it admissible at trial?

    _____

    _____

    _____

    _____

    _____

11. (J-2004 and J-2000) Outside of the presence of the jury, the State tells you that Officer will testify that as he approached Defendant, he

exclaimed, "Thank goodness you caught me red-handed! I'm tired of running from the law!" You object as follows:

DEFENSE LAWYER: Your Honor, we object to this testimony coming in. The Code of Criminal Procedure bars the admission of unrecorded oral statements. Plus, it's hearsay.

COURT: Your objections are overruled. You may proceed.

Is the Court's ruling correct? Explain.

_____

_____

_____

_____

_____

12. (J-2003) List three requirements that must be met before an oral statement can be admitted at trial.

_____

_____

_____

_____

_____

13. (F-2003) You file a pretrial, written motion to suppress Defendant's unrecorded, custodial oral statement. Defendant refused to give a written statement. After conducting a *Jackson v. Denno* hearing on the motion, Judge rules that since Defendant waived his rights, the oral statement is admissible.

Is the Court's ruling correct? Explain.

_____

_____

_____

_____

_____

14. (J-2001) Defendant is arrested for DWI. She is taken to the station, where she is videotaped. After she performs sobriety tests, Officer recites the *Miranda* warnings. When Officer asks if Defendant would like to waive her rights and answer questions, Defendant replies, "No, I want my lawyer." Prosecutor intends to play the entire video to the jury.

Is this permissible? Why or why not? What procedural step, if any, can you take to prevent the jury from seeing the video in its entirety?

_____

_____

_____

_____

_____

———————————◆———————————

Chapter 11
Jury Selection

Introduction

There are two types of jurors in the criminal justice system: (1) grand jurors, who make probable cause determinations in felony cases; and (2) petit jurors, who render verdicts and determine punishments following a criminal trial. This chapter will focus on the second type of juror and the petit jury selection process.

Petit jurors are fundamental to the criminal justice system. While the majority of cases are disposed through dismissal or plea bargain (approximately 97 percent), of those cases tried, jurors serve as fact finders in many of them. According to the Texas Constitution and the Code of Criminal Procedure, "The right of trial by jury shall remain inviolate."[1] In criminal trials, the defendant has a constitutional right to have a jury decide the first phase of trial (guilt/innocence) and a statutory right to have a jury decide the second phase of trial (punishment).[2] The defendant must waive this right in writing if she pleads guilty or desires a bench trial with a judge instead.[3]

While a number of defendants may elect a bench trial, jury trials are quite common in Texas courthouses. Jury service is an opportunity for members of the community to come together and determine what happened in a legal matter and the consequences for criminal actions. Some defendants would rather have the community members make these decisions rather than a judge. This chapter will examine the qualifications jurors must possess and laws related to the jury selection process.

———————◆———————

Juror Qualifications

The Texas Constitution grants the legislature authority to determine who can serve as a juror in a trial and who cannot.[4] The legislature has enacted statutes that qualify or exclude Texas residents from jury service. The judge and attorneys have an obligation to keep unfit jurors from serving.[5]

---

[1] TEX. CONST. art. I, § 15; TEX. CODE CRIM. PROC. ANN. art. 1.12 (West 2016).
[2] *Id.*; TEX. CODE CRIM. PROC. ANN. art. 26.14 (West 2016).
[3] TEX. CODE CRIM. PROC. ANN. art. 1.13 (West 2016) (describing jury trial waiver required for a defendant to plead guilty).
[4] TEX. CONST. art. V, § 14.
[5] TEX. CODE CRIM. PROC. ANN. art. 35.12 (West 2016); *State v. Holloway*, 886 S.W.2d 482, 485-88 (Tex. App.—Houston [1st Dist.] 1994, pet. ref'd).

The Government Code states,

A person is disqualified to serve as a petit juror unless the person:

(1) is at least 18 years of age;
(2) is a citizen of the United States;
(3) is a resident of this state and of the county in which the person is to serve as a juror;
(4) is qualified under the constitution and laws to vote in the county in which the person is to serve as a juror;
(5) is of sound mind and good moral character;
(6) is able to read and write;
(7) has not served as a petit juror for six days during the preceding three months in the county court or during the preceding six months in the district court;
(8) has not been convicted of misdemeanor theft or a felony; and
(9) is not under indictment or other legal accusation for misdemeanor theft or a felony.[6]

Jurors are summoned through voter registration records and through driver's license registries. However, not every citizen of the United States or resident of Texas is qualified to serve. The chart below summarizes those absolutely disqualified from serving and those who may be considered legally unfit for jury service.[7] Anyone who is absolutely disqualified from serving as a juror[8] may not serve, even if both parties consent.[9]

[6] TEX. GOV'T CODE ANN. §62.102 (West 2005).
[7] TEX. CODE CRIM. PROC. ANN. art. 35.16(a) (West 2016).
[8] TEX. CODE CRIM. PROC. ANN. art. 35.19 (West 2016).
[9] TEX. CODE CRIM. PROC. ANN. art. 35.16(a)(11) (West 2016).

Basis for Disqualification[10]	Type of Disqualification
Felony or theft conviction	Absolute Disqualification
Felony or theft charge pending	Absolute Disqualification
Mentally insane	Absolute Disqualification
Not a qualified voter	Basis for Challenge for Cause
Physical disability that renders person unfit for jury service (*e.g.*, blindness, deafness, mental defect, or organ problems)	Basis for Challenge for Cause
Unable to read or write	Basis for Challenge for Cause
Witness in the present case	Basis for Challenge for Cause
Served on the grand jury in the present case	Basis for Challenge for Cause
Served as a petit juror recently	Basis for Challenge for Cause
Related to the defendant, the victim, or the prosecutor	Basis for Challenge for Cause
Served as a petit juror in a former trial of the same case	Basis for Challenge for Cause
Bias towards/against a party (including witnesses)	Basis for Challenge for Cause
Bias for/against guilt or innocence	Basis for Challenge for Cause
Bias towards/against punishment range	Basis for Challenge for Cause
Bias towards/against applicable law	Basis for Challenge for Cause

All of the above disqualifications and challenges for cause come from one article in the Code: 35.16. The Court of Criminal Appeals has held that Article 35.16 "is a complete list of challenges for cause."[11] The Code requires judges to test the qualifications of prospective jurors by asking the jurors on the array the following questions:

- Are you qualified to vote in this county and State?
- Have you ever been convicted of theft or any felony?
- Are you under accusation or indictment for theft or any felony? [12]

---

[10] TEX. CODE CRIM. PROC. ANN. art. 35.16 (West 2016).
[11] *Butler v. State*, 830 S.W.2d 125, 130 (Tex. Crim. App. 1992).
[12] TEX. CODE CRIM. PROC. ANN. art. 35.12 (West 2016).

The attorneys should raise an objection to an unfit juror as soon as they are aware of a disqualification, which in most cases is before the jury is picked and sworn. After all, no unfit juror should be sworn and empaneled.[13] What happens when someone unfit to serve nevertheless becomes a juror? This could happen when a prospective juror misunderstands one of the above questions or does not reply honestly to them.

> A conviction in a criminal case may be reversed on appeal on the ground that a juror in the case was absolutely disqualified from service … only if: (1) the defendant raises the disqualification before the verdict is entered; or (2) the disqualification was not discovered or brought to the attention of the trial court until after the verdict was entered and the defendant makes a showing of significant harm by the service of the disqualified juror.[14]

When the circumstances fall under the second category above, an attorney can raise the issue through a motion for new trial.[15] Attorneys should be aware of what one appellate court calls "laying behind the log."[16] This happens when an attorney knows a juror is disqualified, fails to bring it to the court's attention, gambles on a favorable verdict, and raises the objection for the first time on appeal.[17] Attorneys who fail to raise a timely disqualification may waive error.[18] If at all possible, attorneys must raise the issue of a juror's qualifications before jury selection is over or, if discovered later, before the verdict is entered.

———————◆———————

Juror Exemptions

An otherwise qualified prospective juror may ask to be relieved from jury service for any number of reasons. A person may be exempted from jury duty if she

(1) is over 70 years of age;

---

[13] TEX. CODE CRIM. PROC. ANN. art. 35.19 (West 2016).

[14] TEX. CODE CRIM. PROC. ANN. art. 44.46 (West 2016).

[15] *State v. Holloway*, 886 S.W.2d 482, 485 (Tex. App.—Houston [1st Dist.] 1994, pet. ref'd).

[16] *Id.* at 487-88.

[17] *Id.*

[18] *Id.* at 488.

(2) has custody of a child under 12 who would be left without adequate supervision;

(3) is a student of a secondary school;

(4) is enrolled in and attending college;

(5) is a member of the legislature;

(6) has served as a petit juror in the past 24 months;

(7) is the primary caretaker of someone who cannot take care of himself;

(8) is a member of the military forces serving on active duty outside the person's county of residence;[19] or

(9) is observing a religious holiday.[20]

Prospective jurors fill out exemption forms, which are mailed in; no court appearance is needed.[21] A juror may also claim an exemption for the first time in the courtroom. When this happens, the prospective juror shall be discharged from service immediately.[22] Excusing a person from jury service is largely within the judge's discretion.[23]

———————◆———————

Number of Jurors

In a district court, when the case is a felony, the jury consists of 12 members.[24] In the county courts and in district courts trying a misdemeanor offense, the jury consists of six jurors.[25]

A judge may select alternate jurors in lengthy cases or as a matter of personal preference for the practice. Jurors may get sick or die during their service, may have an emergency arise, or may otherwise be unable to complete their service. For this reason, cautious judges may pick alternate jurors in case a regular juror is unable to complete her service.

In district courts, judges may impanel as many as four alternates; in county courts, judges may impanel up to two.[26] Alternates must replace

---

[19] TEX. GOV'T CODE ANN. §62.106 (West 2015).

[20] TEX. CODE CRIM. PROC. ANN. art. 35.03 § 3 (West 2016).

[21] TEX. CODE CRIM. PROC. ANN. art. 35.04 (West 2016).

[22] TEX. CODE CRIM. PROC. ANN. art. 35.03 § 1 (West 2016).

[23] E.g., Sayyadi v. State, 40 S.W.3d 722, 724 (Tex. App.—Austin 2001, no pet.) (juror was not disqualified due to illiteracy, but judge did not err by dismissing juror after he asked to be excused due his limited knowledge of English).

[24] TEX. CODE CRIM. PROC. ANN. art. 33.01 (West 2016).

[25] Id.

[26] TEX. CODE CRIM. PROC. ANN. art. 33.011 (West 2016).

regular jurors in the order in which they were called from the array. An alternate juror has all of the same powers and privileges as a regular juror, but if he does not replace a regular juror by the time the verdict is rendered, he will be discharged.[27]

───────────◆───────────

Jury Shuffles

Once the jury array is assembled but before voir dire begins, both parties are entitled to see a list of the prospective jurors.[28] The clerk of the court prepares the list by randomly selecting the jurors in the array and listing them in the order in which they will be organized and seated in the courtroom.[29]

The list contains identifying information—name, age, race, gender, employer, and religious affiliation. It is rare that jurors answer questionnaires in criminal cases, but if they do, both parties have an opportunity to review them before voir dire begins. Voir dire officially begins when the judge or either lawyer begins to ask questions, not when the parties review the lists, jurors' personal information, or questionnaires.[30]

A party may request a jury shuffle before voir dire begins. In order to understand why shuffles are requested, it is important to discuss a fundamental truth: prospective jurors sitting near the front of the panel are more likely to serve at trial.

Consider the following diagram:

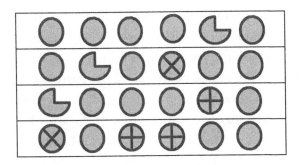

───────────────────

[27] *Id.*

[28] Tex. Code Crim. Proc. Ann. art. 35.11 (West 2016).

[29] *Id.*

[30] *Garza v. State*, 7 S.W.3d 164, 166 (Tex. Crim. App. 1999).

Imagine each symbol represents a prospective juror seated on the benches of a county courtroom for a misdemeanor trial. Jurors are numbered. The circle on the bottom, left corner represents prospective juror number 1, and the circle on the top right corner represents prospective juror number 24. Because this is a misdemeanor case, only six jurors will ultimately serve.

We will discuss challenges for cause and peremptory strikes later in this chapter. For now, know that in a misdemeanor case, each side is given three peremptory strikes (*e.g.*, strikes without any reason), and there are unlimited challenges for cause (*e.g.*, strikes due to bias or disqualification). If the State peremptorily strikes only two potential jurors (marked by an X), the defense peremptorily strikes three (marked by a +), and the judge grants three challenges for cause (the C-shaped symbols), which prospective jurors will actually serve? The first six jurors who were not struck or challenged will make up the petit jury. Notice that the jurors in the front are more likely to serve, and the jurors in the back are less likely to serve on the petit jury.

With this reality in mind, lawyers pay closer attention to the jurors seated near the front of the array. Conversations between the attorneys, the judge, and the prospective jurors lead to strikes, but body language, clothing, age, or other factors may provide indicia of bias before voir dire begins.

Say, for example, you are a defense attorney representing a defendant in a misdemeanor possession of marijuana case. You believe younger people are more accepting of marijuana use while older people are not; this is obviously a generalization, but there may be some truth behind your theory. Assume in your array that all of the younger jurors are seated at the back and all of the older jurors are seated at the front. After conferring with your client, you decide to request a shuffle. Your hope is that by reordering the prospective jurors, a larger number of younger jurors will be seated in the front, and a greater number of older jurors will be seated in the back.

Jury shuffles are unique to Texas. Either party is permitted to request a shuffle. The clerk who randomly selected the seating order of the array the first time will rearrange the seating order of the array by shuffling the juror information cards electronically or manually. The jurors will stand up, will move to the hallway outside the courtroom, will be reordered by the bailiff, and will return to the courtroom to be seated once again in their new, reshuffled order.

There are a number of goals behind an effective voir dire. One set of goals is to impanel jurors who can be impartial, consider all of the evidence, follow the law, and render a true and just verdict. Another goal is to educate potential jurors about the law and the facts of the case without directly speaking about the facts of the present case. Finally, lawyers attempt to establish a rapport with potential jurors. During voir dire, many jurors decide which attorney or party they are more likely to believe moving forward.

Once the jury array is seated, the judge may introduce herself, address the array, and ask questions related to qualifications to serve. Once the judge is finished, she will turn questioning over first to the prosecutor and then to defense counsel. Questions may be directed to the entire panel or to individual jurors. In all cases except capital murder cases, attorneys must pose questions to the entire array.[42] In capital murder trials, the jurors will be asked questions collectively on basic legal principles but individually, if either side requests, when it comes to specific or directed questions.[43]

Role of Court Reporter During Voir Dire

The Texas Rules of Appellate Procedure state that a court reporter must, unless excused by agreement of the parties, attend court proceedings and make a full record of the trial.[44] To ensure that the court reporter is present during voir dire, most defense attorneys file a written pretrial motion requesting the court reporter to transcribe the entire trial, including voir dire. An attorney who fails to object to the absence of the court reporter at voir dire or the recording of any testimony waives any error that happened during voir dire on appeal.[45] This is because appeals are limited to the record; if an issue is not included in the record, it cannot be appealed. It is the burden of the appellant to make sure a record for appeal exists.[46] For this reason,

---

[42] TEX. CODE CRIM. PROC. ANN. art. 35.17 (West 2016).

[43] *Id.*

[44] TEX. R. APP. PROC. 13.1(a).

[45] *Ham v. State*, 355 S.W.3d 819, 823 (Tex. App.—Amarillo 2011, pet. ref'd) ("'[A] party should not be permitted to ignore at the time a court reporter's dereliction of duty and later rely on that dereliction to challenge a conviction' . . . The appellate record contains no objection presented to the trial court complaining of any matter related to the court reporter or the taking of the record.").

[46] *Davis v. State*, 345 S.W.3d 71, 77 (Tex. Crim. App. 2011).

defense counsel should always request that voir dire be transcribed by the court reporter.

Role of the Judge and Attorneys During Voir Dire

In this section, you will read two cases that examine the role of the judge and the attorneys during voir dire. These two cases focus on types of questions attorneys ask prospective jurors and the role the judge plays in the jury selection process. In this next case, you will learn about commitment or contracting questions.

James David Wingo v. State
143 S.W.3d 178
(Tex. App.—San Antonio 2004)
aff'd, 189 S.W.3d 270 (Tex. Crim. App. 2006)

[Appellant was a San Antonio police officer who falsified an offense report and was subsequently indicted and convicted for tampering with a government record.]

In his first issue on appeal, Wingo contends that the trial court erred in overruling his objection to the State's improper commitment questions during the specific voir dire of venire member Carreon. The State responds that the challenged questions were not commitment questions and that Wingo was not harmed by the alleged error.

The general rule is that an attorney cannot attempt to bind or commit a venire member to a verdict based on a hypothetical set of facts. Questions that commit prospective jurors to a position, using a hypothetical or otherwise, are improper and serve no purpose other than to commit the jury to a specific set of facts before the presentation of any evidence at trial. To determine if the voir dire question calls for an improper commitment, we must determine (1) whether the question is a commitment question, and (2) whether the question includes only those facts that lead to a valid challenge for cause. If the answer to the first question is "yes" and the answer to the second question is "no," then the voir dire question is an improper commitment question.

Commitment questions "commit a prospective juror to resolve, or to refrain from resolving, an issue a certain way after learning a particular fact." These questions tend to require a "yes" or "no" answer, in which one or both of the possible answers commits the jury to resolving an issue a certain way. Commitment questions may contain words such as "consider," "would," and "could."

A commitment question can be proper or improper, depending on whether the question leads to a valid challenge for cause. The law requires jurors to make certain commitments. Therefore, attorneys may ask the prospective jurors whether they can follow the law in that regard. Additionally, to be proper, "a commitment question must contain only those facts necessary to test whether a prospective juror is challengeable for cause." Thus, commitment questions are improper when (1) the law does not require a commitment; or (2) the question adds facts beyond those necessary to establish a challenge for cause.

Although the trial court may exercise discretion in conducting voir dire, the allowance of an improper question represents an abuse of discretion.

During the State's specific voir dire of venire member Carreon, the following exchange and ruling took place:

> Q. What about tampering with a government record? And [another venire member] brought out that police officers do write police reports. Do you believe there's anything wrong with putting false information in a police report?
>
> [Defense Counsel]: Objection, Judge. That's the same line of questioning as before.
>
> The COURT: Overruled. He just asked him—
>
> [Defense Counsel]: Anything wrong with that type of offense.
>
> The COURT: Right. Overruled.
>
> [Defense Counsel]: Note my objection.
>
> Q. Do you have any problem with a police officer putting false information in a police report?
>
> A. Yes.
>
> Q. Okay.

The questioning of the other venire member referenced by defense counsel included the question, "And on a police report, if they put something false in there, which would be tampering with a government record, would you have a problem finding someone guilty if the State proves a case beyond

488 | Texas Criminal Procedure and Evidence

a reasonable doubt?" Wingo objected to the question, and the trial court sustained the objection.

Wingo argues that the question "Do you believe there's anything wrong with putting false information in a police report?" was a commitment question. The Court of Criminal Appeals recently addressed an improper voir dire question in *Lydia v. State*, where the prosecutor asked, "Do each of you feel as though you could evaluate a witness and his testimony and decide if he's being truthful without automatically dismissing his testimony because of some criminal history?" The Court held that the question was a commitment question because it asked the jurors to resolve witness credibility (issue) based on the knowledge that the witness had a criminal history (particular fact). The Court held that the prosecutor did not ask whether the venire members could impartially evaluate testimony, but instead asked the venire members to resolve an issue in the case based on a particular fact.

Similarly, the question in this case is a commitment question. The State sought a commitment on an issue in the case (*i.e.* culpability of conduct) from the venire member based on a particular fact (*i.e.* an officer putting false information in a police report). Although the State asked whether the venire member believed there was "anything wrong" with this particular kind of falsehood, direct committal language is not necessary.

Additionally, the question is improper because it does not include only those facts necessary to test whether a venire member is challengeable for cause. The State did not ask whether the venire member could impartially apply the law, which is a proper commitment question that would give rise to a valid challenge for cause. Furthermore, even if the question was construed to give rise to a challenge for cause, the State's question was rendered improper by the use of facts beyond those necessary to sustain a challenge for cause. The [tampering with a government record] law refers to a "person" and a "government record," while the State's question unnecessarily included "police officer" and "police report." Therefore, the trial court abused its discretion in allowing the State's improper commitment question.

———————◆———————

Notes and Questions

1. It is permissible to ask jurors whether they can commit to following the law. For example, an attorney may ask, "Would you consider the full range of punishment in a murder case?" or "Could you base your verdict on the testimony of a single, credible witness?" Both of these questions get at legal duties: to consider the full range of punishment and to base decisions on credible testimony, but asking, "if I prove X, Y, and Z facts, will you find the defendant guilty?" is impermissible. The former category commits them to following the law, not to render a verdict on a specific set of facts. The Court of Criminal Appeals had this to say about the distinction between the two:

> The defendant has a constitutional right to a trial "by an impartial jury." Thus, the purpose for prohibiting improper commitment questions by either the State or the defendant is to ensure that the jury will listen to the evidence with an open mind—a mind that is impartial and without bias or prejudice—and render a verdict based upon that evidence. Commitment questions require a venireman to promise that he will base his verdict or course of action on some specific set of facts before he has heard any evidence, much less all of the evidence in its proper context. It is this prejudgment of the value and importance of certain evidence that is the evil to be avoided unless the law requires such a commitment.
>
> An improper commitment question attempts to create a bias or prejudice in the venireman before he has heard the evidence, whereas a proper voir dire question attempts to discover a venireman's preexisting bias or prejudice.[47]

———————◆———————

Once again, consider the judge the gatekeeper of questions and the manager of time in all proceedings on the Judge's docket. In these capacities, the judge may place time limits on voir dire. The next case examines the difficult job appellate courts have in balancing the trial court's need for expedient trials with the defendant's right to a fair and impartial jury.

---

[47] *Sanchez v. State*, 165 S.W.3d 707, 712 (Tex. Crim. App. 2005).

Donovan Keith Wappler v. State
183 S.W.3d 765
(Tex. App.—Houston [1st Dist.] 2005, pet. struck)

A jury found appellant, Donovan Keith Wappler, guilty of the misdemeanor offense of driving while intoxicated (DWI). The trial court, in accordance with an agreement between appellant and the State, assessed appellant's punishment at 42 days in jail. On appeal, appellant argued that the trial court erred in imposing a 15-minute time limit on voir dire. We reverse the cause and remand for a new trial.

[Appellant rear-ended another driver and was arrested for DWI after failing a field sobriety test at the scene and exhibiting physical symptoms of intoxication. Appellant admitted to drinking alcohol, but refused to provide a breath sample or perform additional field sobriety tests at the station while being videotaped. He was ultimately arrested, charged, and convicted of DWI.]

Procedural History

During jury selection at appellant's trial, the jury panel initially consisted of 20 people. The trial judge, [Janice Law,] conducted preliminary voir dire of the venire members. The trial judge introduced herself and had the attorneys stand and introduce themselves. She asked the panel members if anyone knew either herself or the attorneys. She asked the panel if they were qualified voters in Harris County; if anyone had ever been convicted of theft or any felony; if anyone was under indictment or legal accusation for theft or any felony; if anyone had ever been arrested; if anyone … or … someone close to him [had previously] been arrested or charged with DWI; if everyone could read English; and if anyone had anything private to discuss with the Court. The trial judge instructed the venire members that she would speak individually to anyone who had any information on these topics.

At the bench, for about an hour, the trial court and the attorneys each questioned the jurors who had information concerning the topics addressed by the Court. Of the panel of 20 venire members, nine people had information concerning the trial court's voir-dire questions. The trial court and both the State's and the appellant's attorneys each individually questioned venire members 1, 2, 4, 7, 10, 11, 12, 15, and 18. The trial court granted six challenges for cause on venire members 1, 2, 4, 10, 12, and 15 and excused them from the courtroom.

The trial court then asked each of the remaining 14 venire members to stand up individually and state his name and occupation. The remaining jurors then individually stated their names and described their occupations. The trial court explained to the jury that each side would conduct voir dire for 15 minutes. Neither the State nor appellant's attorney voiced any objections to the court's time limit.

The State's attorney questioned members of the venire panel concerning the elements of the DWI offense, their feelings about police officers, ways jurors could tell whether a driver or person was intoxicated, and the jurors' willingness to convict based on the testimony of one witness. The trial court granted the State an additional minute and one-half to finish its voir dire when time was called, on the grounds that the court had made a few comments from the bench during the State's voir dire.

Appellant's attorney then conducted his voir dire. He asked how many people were missing work to be in court, whether the jurors believed that people were innocent until proven guilty, whether the jurors wondered what appellant had done, and whether anyone had served on a grand jury; he then explained the concept of "beyond a reasonable doubt." Appellant's attorney also asked the venire members whether they could think of any reason why a sober person might not want to take a breath test and whether any of the venire members had experienced any bad interactions with police officers. Appellant's attorney then discussed reasons people might choose not to testify in their own defense at their trial.

When time was called, appellant's counsel requested additional time for voir dire, stating that he had more issues to cover. The court would not allow him any more time and told him that he could read the questions he wanted to ask the venire members into the record at the break[, as part of a bill of exceptions], after the parties had exercised their peremptory strikes.

Appellant argued that he should be allowed to make his bill of exceptions before making his strikes and before the jury was impaneled, but the trial judge denied this request. ...After the jury was seated, appellant renewed his objection to the limitation on voir dire and made a bill of exceptions about the questions he would have asked had he been given additional time. The trial court left the courtroom shortly after defense counsel began to make his bill, but counsel for the State remained in court.

The gist of the questions counsel contended he did not have time to ask included: (1) whether the venire could consider the full range of punishment; (2) whether any venire members were members of Mothers Against Drunk Drivers (MADD); (3) whether any of the venire members had been affected by alcohol and whether those experiences would cause them to favor the State; (4) whether any of the venire members would believe a police officer simply because of his occupation and whether any of the venire members were related to or knew police officers, resulting in a bias for the State; (5) whether the venire members could disregard incriminating, but illegally obtained statements; and (6) whether the venire members would find appellant guilty simply because he had been in an accident.

Limitation of Voir Dire

Appellant argues that, because he was not able to explore the questions in his bill of exceptions with the venire, he could not intelligently exercise his peremptory strikes. Jury selection and the laws governing it are designed to ensure that juries in criminal cases are fair to both sides; of paramount concern is the defendant's right to exercise peremptory challenges intelligently. The purpose of voir dire is to (1) elicit information that would establish a basis for a challenge for cause because the venireman is legally disqualified from serving or is biased or prejudiced for or against one of the parties or some aspect of the relevant law; (2) facilitate the intelligent use of peremptory challenges that may be "exercised without a reason stated, without inquiry and without being subject to the court's control"; and (3) indoctrinate the jurors on the party's theory of the case and to establish rapport with the prospective jury members. Texas trial courts have broad discretion over the jury-selection process. The trial court's right to dispatch its business expeditiously must be justly balanced against society's interest in seating fair juries.

A trial court may impose reasonable restrictions on the exercise of voir-dire examination, including reasonable limits on the amount of time each party can question the jury panel. No bright-line rule identifies what amount of time allowed for voir dire is too short. The amount of time allotted is not, alone, conclusive. A reasonable time limitation for one case may not be reasonable for another case; thus, each case must be examined on its own facts.

Standard of Review

The trial court does not err in restricting voir dire unless the court abuses its discretion. Absent an abuse of discretion, we will not reverse the trial court's refusal to allow defense counsel additional voir-dire time. A trial court abuses its discretion when it prohibits defense counsel from asking proper voir-dire questions. When a party complains of an inability to question the venire collectively, the following two-part test applies: (1) whether the complaining party attempted to prolong the voir dire by asking questions that were irrelevant, immaterial, or unnecessarily repetitious and (2) whether the questions the party was not permitted to ask were proper voir-dire questions. When a party's voir dire is terminated as he attempts to question venire members individually, we must also consider a third factor—(3) whether the party was prevented from examining a prospective juror who actually served on the jury. Here, appellant's voir dire was terminated while his counsel was asking questions of a venire member. Therefore, we apply the three-part [*McCarter*] test[, described above]. *McCarter v. State*, 837 S.W.2d 117, 120 (Tex. Crim. App. 1992).

Propriety of Questions

A "proper" voir-dire question is one that seeks to discover a venire member's views on issues relevant to the case. An otherwise proper question is impermissible, however, if it attempts to commit the juror to a particular verdict based on particular facts. In addition, a voir-dire question that is so vague or broad in nature as to constitute a global fishing expedition is not proper and may be prohibited by the trial court.

Counsel's first intended question, regarding the range of punishment, was an appropriate question on a topic that had not been previously covered. ...Counsel's second intended question, concerning membership in MADD and the impact of alcohol on the venire member's lives, was a proper question because it was not overly broad and addressed an issue relevant to the case. His third intended question, regarding bias toward police officers, was also a proper one. His fourth and fifth intended questions, concerning "illegally" obtained statements and *Miranda* warnings, were also proper questions. Counsel's sixth question, however, was simply a variation of his first question regarding the impact of alcohol on the lives of individual venire members. ... Counsel's seventh intended question—whether the venire members would conclude that appellant was guilty simply because he was involved in an automobile accident—was improper because it sought a commitment from the venire members.

Of the intended questions that appellant complains about on appeal, we have concluded that five were proper questions. Appellant, therefore, satisfied the second prong of the *McCarter* test. Accordingly, we turn to the [first prong] of whether, had counsel adequately managed his time during voir dire, he would have had sufficient time to question the venire members concerning their ability to consider the full range of punishment, membership in MADD, whether they could disregard incriminating, but illegally obtained statements, the impact of alcohol on their lives, and the issue of bias toward police officers.

Time Management

Counsel's use of time during voir dire was neither a model of efficiency nor an egregious attempt to prolong the voir dire. Although counsel repeated questions on the same topics already discussed by the trial court ...and the ...State..., we cannot conclude that counsel's repetition ... was the result of an attempt to prolong voir dire unduly. Our review of the record shows that counsel discussed a few matters in a somewhat repetitive manner, but the overall tenor and content of his voir dire does not show that the questions posed to the venire members were irrelevant, immaterial, or unnecessarily repetitious. ..."[D]efense counsel may not be precluded from the traditional voir-dire examination simply because the questions asked are repetitious of those asked by the court and the prosecutor." Therefore, appellant satisfied the first prong of the *McCarter* test

We hold that appellant has satisfied the three-part test in *McCarter* and that the trial court abused its discretion by prohibiting defense counsel from asking proper voir-dire questions. ...

The trial court was not present in the courtroom when appellant's attorney made his bill of exception on the record. The trial court also refused to allow appellant's attorney to present his bill of exception until after the venire panel was excused and a jury was seated. By refusing to consider appellant's attorney's bill of exception through her mere presence in the courtroom and before the attorneys made their peremptory strikes, the trial court deprived herself of the opportunity to evaluate whether appellant's proposed voir-dire questions were proper at a time when the error could have been cured by allowing the questions before the dismissal of the venire. We hold that the trial court abused its discretion by terminating voir dire and seating the jury without hearing and evaluating the questions defense counsel was not permitted to ask. ... We turn, therefore, to whether the error was harmless.

Harm Analysis

The Sixth Amendment guarantees the right to a trial before an impartial jury. The right to question venire members to exercise peremptory challenges intelligently is an essential part of that Sixth Amendment guarantee. ... *Gonzales v. State*, 994 S.W.2d 170, 171 (Tex. Crim. App. 1999) ("[T]he right to pose proper questions during voir-dire examination is included within the right to counsel under Article I, § 10, of the Texas Constitution."). If the trial court abuses its discretion by denying a defendant the right to propound a proper question to prospective jurors, we must conduct a harm analysis.

[W]hile not every error in the selection of a jury violates the constitutional right of a trial by an impartial jury, we conclude that the error in this case did violate that right.

The Sixth Amendment guarantees the right to a trial before an impartial jury. Part of the constitutional guarantee of the right to an impartial jury includes adequate voir dire to identify unqualified jurors. And we have consistently held that essential to the Sixth Amendment guarantees of the assistance of counsel and trial before an impartial jury "is the right to question venire members in order to intelligently exercise peremptory challenges and challenges for cause."

[After conducting a harm analysis, examining all evidence admitted during the trial and the court's jury charge, the appellate court held that it was possible the appellant was harmed by Judge Law's refusal to grant him more time during voir dire.]

We reverse the judgment of the trial court and remand the cause for a new trial.

———————◆———————

Notes and Questions

1. In order to appeal an alleged error made at the trial-court level, there must be evidence of the alleged error in the record. One way of making that

record is through a bill of exceptions. The complaining attorney makes the bill by speaking the questions he would have asked the jury into the record and any other information that must be satisfied on appeal to establish error; this is done outside of the presence of the jury. In the voir dire context, a bill of exception essentially contrasts the strategies and the wishes the attorney had in seating the jury with the hindrances the attorney faced. This record is what the appellate court will evaluate on appeal, as evidenced in the above case.

2. The defendant has a federal and a state right to be present at his own trial, which includes voir dire.[48] In *Sumrell v. State*, the defendant's behavior during voir dire concerned the trial court and prospective jurors; the judge excused the defendant from the courtroom so he could ascertain whether the worrisome behavior had created bias amongst the potential jurors.[49] It was unclear from the record how much of the voir dire the defendant missed, but his lawyer exercised three challenges for cause and two peremptory strikes in his absence.[50] The Dallas Court of Appeals held that the trial court violated the defendant's right to be present at trial by excluding the defendant from the courtroom during voir dire.[51]

---◆---

Challenging Jurors

The concept of fairness is fundamental to jury selection. Both parties— the State and the defense—have a right to a jury trial. That right is rendered meaningless when jurors have been unfairly selected or struck, or when jurors express bias against the State or the defendant and nevertheless are seated on the jury. Being able to gather information about jurors and challenge those who cannot be impartial or are otherwise unfit for service furthers the constitutional right to a fair trial.

---

[48] *Sumrell v. State*, 326 S.W.3d 621, 623 (Tex. App.—Dallas 2009) *pet. dism'd as improvidently granted*, 320 S.W.3d 338 (Tex. Crim. App. 2010) (*per curiam*).
[49] *Id.* at 623-24.
[50] *Id.*
[51] *Id.* at 627.

Challenging the Array

Recall the grand jury selection process mentioned in an earlier chapter. Just as a defendant is permitted to challenge the way grand jurors were selected, a defendant may challenge the way petit jurors are selected. Before voir dire questions begin, either the State or the defendant may challenge the array on the ground that they were selected with the express desire to secure a conviction or an acquittal.[52]

When a party raises an objection to the array, the challenge must be in writing setting forth the reasons for the challenge, it must be supported by affidavit, if made by the defendant, and the judge must then have a hearing.[53] Challenges are rarely brought under this provision, but if they are raised and sustained, the judge must discharge the first array of jurors and bring in a new array.[54]

Challenges for Cause

During voir dire, the attorneys get to know the prospective jurors and usually find them more or less desirable as questioning continues. Once an attorney hears the comments and the answers to her questions, she has three options: accept the juror, challenge the juror for cause, or exercise a preemptory challenge. This section will explore the second option: challenges for cause.

The Code defines a *challenge for cause* as "an objection made to a particular juror, alleging some fact which renders the juror incapable or unfit to serve on the jury."[55] Either party may raise a challenge for cause. The judge may even strike a prospective juror on her own motion.

Challenges for cause can be made on several grounds. Recall the chart that appeared earlier in the chapter that listed all reasons for a valid challenge for cause. The most common reason for a challenge for cause may be bias or prejudice towards a party or the law itself.[56] For example, imagine a prospective juror states he has reached a conclusion about guilt before hearing any evidence because the defendant "looks guilty." Imagine another

---

[52] TEX. CODE CRIM. PROC. ANN. arts. 35.06 and 35.07 (West 2016).
[53] TEX. CODE CRIM. PROC. ANN. art. 35.07 (West 2016).
[54] TEX. CODE CRIM. PROC. ANN. art. 35.08 (West 2016).
[55] TEX. CODE CRIM. PROC. ANN. art. 35.16(a) (West 2016).
[56] TEX. CODE CRIM. PROC. ANN. art. 35.16(a)-(b) (West 2016).

juror says she must be convinced beyond all doubt, not just a reasonable doubt, before she could convict a defendant. Both of these jurors can be challenged for cause. The first juror will be challenged by the defense because he has expressed bias against the defendant whereas the second juror will be challenged by the prosecutor because she wants to hold the prosecutor to a higher burden than the law requires. Remember that the fundamental concern in voir dire is that all jurors ultimately seated need to be fair and impartial, willing and able to follow the law. The next case illustrates the difficulties lawyers and judges face in selecting jurors.

James Vernon Allridge III v. State
850 S.W.2d 471
(Tex. Crim. App. 1991)

[Appellant was convicted of capital murder after robbing and murdering a convenience store clerk. The jury convicted him and sentenced him to death.]

In his first point of error, appellant argued the trial court erred by excusing venireperson Martin Osborn for cause. According to appellant, Osborn's opinion of the death penalty merely involved his emotions and would only affect his view of the seriousness of his task as a capital juror. Appellant argued that Osborn's answers on voir dire implied that he could follow the law and not be controlled by his feelings.

The State replied that Osborn was a venireperson whose beliefs about the death penalty would substantially impair his performance as a capital juror. The State explained that Osborn's entire voir dire revealed strong feelings that would impair him from fairly and impartially carrying out his oath as a capital juror. Also, the State alleged that Osborn's scruples indicate he would hold the State to a higher burden of proof than required by law.

In order to assess Osborn's capacity to obey his oath and follow the trial court's instructions, we will not focus on only one answer or passage from his voir dire. This Court must examine Osborn's testimony as a whole. We will review the entire record of Osborn's voir dire to determine if it shows that Osborn's opposition to the death penalty would prevent or substantially impair his performance of his duties as a juror in accordance with his instructions and oath.

This review is an assessment of whether the record of voir dire supports the trial court's decision that a venireperson was substantially impaired in his or her ability to perform the duties of a juror in accordance with their instructions and oath, rather than an analysis of whether or not this Court would have excused the venireperson for cause. This is a task which a trial court is uniquely capable of performing.

When the record of voir dire is unclear, as it is in the instant case with venireperson Osborn, "there will be situations where the trial judge is left with the definite impression that a prospective juror would be unable to faithfully and impartially apply the law." This results in a finding by the trial court concerning the venireperson's state of mind. This finding will be based upon many factors, including determinations of the credibility and demeanor of the venireperson. If the entire record contains sufficient evidence to support a trial court's determination that a juror would be prevented or substantially impaired from obeying his oath and following his instructions, deference must be paid to that determination.

In the instant case, Venireperson Osborn explained that as a result of his experiences in Viet Nam, he did not believe that he could make a decision on the death penalty. Osborn stated that he had a "gut" feeling that he could not assess the death penalty, and that he'd be very uncomfortable casting the final vote of "yes." He acknowledged his feelings were strong and would tend to prevent him from answering the special issues affirmatively. He also stated that he could not sign the verdict as foreman. The state then submitted Osborn to the trial court to be excused for cause. Appellant requested an opportunity to rehabilitate Osborn.

Appellant's trial counsel asked Osborn if he could follow the oath and answer the questions honestly. Osborn replied that he would be as honest as he possibly could, but that it would be tempered by his "basic instincts that it is wrong for one person to take another's life." When the trial court asked Osborn if he would answer the special issues "no" just to avoid the death penalty, he responded, "I don't honestly know . . . I can't say." The trial court then denied the state's challenge. The trial court permitted the state to resume its voir dire of Osborn.

The state asked Osborn about the burden of proof at the punishment phase of appellant's trial. Osborn replied that he would have to have "little or no doubt" that the answers to the special issues were "yes" before he could answer them affirmatively. Osborn later said there could be some doubt and he would still vote "yes." The state asked Osborn whether his feelings about the death penalty would bias him. He replied that his feelings would tend to bias him against the death penalty and for the saving of a life. Osborn said that he did not think he could honestly take the oath and not "do violence" to his strong feelings. Realizing the severe consequences of a yes vote on the special issues, Osborn responded that he thought his feelings might change how he viewed the evidence at trial. The trial court then granted the state's resubmission of Osborn to be excused for cause.

Appellant requested another opportunity to rehabilitate Osborn. Initially, the trial court denied the request. When appellant pointed out that Osborn had been re-submitted for cause, the trial court granted his request to ask Osborn more questions. After listening to Osborn explain how his strong feelings about the consequences of his vote would affect his decisions, the trial court stopped the voir dire of Osborn and granted the state's challenge for cause.

In a capital case, the State is entitled to jurors who "will consider and decide the facts impartially and conscientiously apply the law as charged by the court." From his responses on voir dire, it appears that Osborn was torn between the obligation to honestly comply with his oath as a juror and his strong feelings in opposition to the death penalty. Osborn's answers that those feelings would influence his assessment of the evidence at punishment and affect his ability to comply with his oath support the trial court's determination that Osborn was substantially impaired in his ability to perform his duties as a capital juror in accordance with his instructions and oath. Osborn's answers that he would have to have little or no doubt that an answer to a special issue should be yes for him to vote that way indicate he would hold the state to a greater burden of proof at the punishment phase of trial than required by statute. This also supports the trial court's decision to excuse Osborn for cause. Appellant's first point of error is overruled.

———————◆———————

Notes and Questions

1. A judge or an attorney may attempt to rehabilitate a juror. You saw that in the above case. The prosecutor wanted to strike the anti–death penalty juror, whereas defense counsel wanted to save him. After the prosecutor established bias through questioning, the defense attorney asked

for permission to ask additional questions. His questions probably emphasized putting personal feelings aside and committing to follow the law. When a juror expresses bias and the judge or an attorney gets that juror to state that he can put his bias aside and follow the law, the juror has been rehabilitated. At this point, the attorney who wanted the juror struck for cause must use a peremptory strike on the juror to remove him from the array.

———————◆———————

How Many Challenges for Cause Are Attorneys Given?

Unlike peremptory challenges, challenges for cause are unlimited in number. Think of it this way: a challenge for cause dismisses a prospective juror for legal reasons. There is thus no limit to the number of strikes for cause in any case for any party.

Timing of Challenges for Cause

The Code is silent about when challenges for cause must be made. In practice, judges ask that strikes for cause be raised as soon as they become obvious, or that all strikes for cause be made at the conclusion of voir dire but before peremptory strikes are made.[57] Parties must comply with whichever time frame the trial court sets. It is not an abuse of discretion for the trial judge to disallow challenges for cause when an attorney waits to make them outside of the specified time frame.[58]

How to Preserve Error for Appeal

In order for a defendant to claim harm from a denial of a challenge for cause, she must follow several steps during voir dire.

> To preserve error for a trial court's denial of a valid challenge for cause, … the record [must show] that appellant asserted a clear and specific challenge for cause, that he used a peremptory challenge on that juror, that all his

---

[57] *Contreras v. State*, 56 S.W.3d 274, 277 (Tex. App.—Houston [14th Dist.] 2001, pet. ref'd) (challenges for cause are timely when they are made before peremptory strike lists are submitted by the parties).
[58] *Id.* at 278.

peremptory challenges were exhausted, that his request for additional strikes was denied, and that an objectionable juror sat on the jury.[59]

Unless and until a party can prove all of the above, an appellate court will find no harm.

———————————◆———————————

Peremptory Challenges

Challenges for cause are not the only way to remove a prospective juror from service; jurors can also be removed through peremptory challenges or strikes. The Code defines a *peremptory challenge* as a strike made to a juror without reason.[60] In 1921, the Court of Criminal Appeals described the peremptory strike and its importance as follows:

> It is the privilege of [the] accused to exclude from service one whom, in his judgment is unacceptable to him. In conferring it, the law gives effect to the natural impulse to eliminate from the jury list not only persons who are rendered incompetent for some of the disqualifying causes named in the statute, but persons, who, by reason of politics, religion, environment, association, or appearance, or by reason of the want of information with reference to them, the accused may object to their service upon the jury to which the disposition of his life or liberty is submitted. In other words, the law fixes the number of challenges and confers upon the accused the right to arbitrarily exercise them. This right having been denied the appellant in the instant case … and having been forced to try his case before jurors who were objectionable and whom he sought to challenge peremptorily, the verdict of conviction rendered by the jury so selected cannot, we think, with due respect to the law, be held to reflect the result of a fair trial by an impartial jury, which it is the design of our law shall be given to those accused of crime.[61]

Peremptory strikes are at the heart of the right to an impartial jury and a fair trial. Even though the court opinion above referenced the defendant's rights to a fair trial and an impartial jury through use of peremptory strikes, the State shares these rights as well.[62]

---

[59] *Green v. State*, 934 S.W.2d 92, 105 (Tex. Crim. App. 1996).
[60] TEX. CODE CRIM. PROC. ANN. art. 35.14 (West 2016).
[61] *Kerley v. State*, 230 S.W. 163, 164–65 (Tex. Crim. App. 1921).
[62] TEX. CODE CRIM. PROC. ANN. art. 35.15 (West 2016).

One of the purposes of voir dire is indoctrinating the panel with the lawyers' views of the case. In practice, this indoctrination begins with establishing a rapport between the lawyers and the prospective jurors. As attorneys question the panel, they may notice a specific juror reacting positively towards one party and negatively towards the other. Body language, career choice, opinions, education, personality, and demeanor may give juror preferences away, even if these things do not lead to a valid strike for cause. For example, once you become an attorney, you will discover that other attorneys do not want you serving on their jury. Perhaps lawyers are afraid other lawyers know too much or that the other empaneled jurors will give a lawyer's vote more credence during deliberations. Regardless, when a party senses a prospective juror is unfavorable or undesirable, that party is likely to exercise a peremptory strike.

The Code assigns a number of peremptory challenges to both sides equally (*i.e.*, no party ever gets more than another to begin with) as follows:

Type of Case	Single Defendant Trials — Peremptory strikes allotted to each attorney (prosecution and defense)	2+ Defendant Trials — Peremptory strikes allotted per defendant; State's strikes equal combined defendants' strikes
Capital Murder (death penalty sought)	15	8
Felony cases	10	6
Misdemeanor tried in district court (*e.g.*, official oppression)	5	3
Misdemeanors tried in county court	3	3

Judges may elect to seat alternate jurors. Typically, judges select alternates as a matter of practice or for particularly lengthy cases. When a judge determines that alternates will be selected, attorneys are granted additional peremptory strikes:

Number of Alternate Jurors	Number of Additional Peremptory Strikes Given to Each Side
1-2	1
3-4	2

The process of selecting alternate jurors and striking them is unique. The Code states that "additional peremptory challenges ... may be used against an alternate juror only, and the other peremptory challenges allowed by law may not be used against an alternate juror."[63] The Court of Criminal Appeals explains this process a little more clearly:

> Selection of alternate jurors is treated as distinct and separate from selection of the primary panel. Following selection of the required number of jurors for the panel, the parties' unused peremptory strikes are essentially wiped out and each party is given the designated number of strikes for use in selecting one or more alternate jurors.[64]

Exhausting or "Busting" the Panel

Assume in a misdemeanor driving while intoxicated case, 20 jurors are summoned to the courtroom for voir dire. Of the 20, 10 are struck for cause. This leaves 10 jurors. A misdemeanor jury panel must consist of at least six jurors. What if both sides exercise the three peremptory challenges allotted them? This would leave only four jurors, which is not enough. The Code provides a remedy for this: "In any criminal case ... in which the venire has been exhausted by challenge or otherwise, the court shall order additional veniremen in such numbers as the court may deem advisable."[65] This may result in more than one voir dire with more than one array for a single case.

———————————— ◆ ————————————

---

[63] TEX. CODE CRIM. PROC. ANN. art. 35.15(d) (West 2016).
[64] *Cooks v. State*, 844 S.W.2d 697, 721 (Tex. Crim. App. 1992).
[65] TEX. CODE CRIM. PROC. ANN. art. 34.02 (West 2016).

Notes and Questions

1. In practice, challenges for cause are made at the bench, while peremptory challenges are made privately, usually at the lawyers' tables in the courtroom. The attorneys or the judge may call up each juror who is being challenged for cause, have a quiet, brief conversation with the juror to affirm the basis for the challenge, try to rehabilitate the juror, and either re-seat or dismiss the juror. After all challengeable jurors meet with the judge and the attorneys at the bench, the clerk prepares a list of the remaining jurors. Each attorney then decides which, if any, of the prospective jurors to peremptorily challenge. The attorneys exercise their challenges by striking through the names of undesirable jurors. This explains why lawyers describe peremptory challenges as "strikes." The lists and the strike marks, initialed or signed by each party, become a part of the clerk's record on appeal.

The first 6 jurors in a misdemeanor case, or 12 jurors in a felony case, who have not been challenged or struck become the petit jury.[66] For this reason, it is a misnomer to refer to this process as "jury selection," since the jurors who serve are not really selected, but are those who remain after the others have been eliminated.

———————————— ◆ ————————————

Batson Challenges

Peremptory challenges are made because the attorneys or the defendant, for whatever reason, do not want the prospective juror to serve in that case. Peremptory challenges may be exercised for almost any reason. Unless the strikes are impermissible, "a party need not assign a reason for exercising his peremptory strikes."[67] In other words, attorneys are not required to explain the basis for peremptorily challenging a juror. However, there are two exceptions to this principle: attorneys cannot strike jurors based upon race or gender.

When a party suspects opposing counsel exercised a peremptory challenge based on race or gender, he may raise a *Batson* challenge, named after the well-known case, *Batson v. Kentucky*, 476 U.S. 79 (1986), in which an

---

66 TEX. CODE CRIM. PROC. ANN. art. 35.26 (West 2016).
67 *Lewis v. State*, 911 S.W.2d 1, 4 (Tex. Crim. App. 1995).

African-American defendant successfully challenged the prosecutor for striking the only four African-American jurors on the array, which resulted in an all-white jury deciding his case. The next case explains the test for determining whether there has been a *Batson* violation. Pay particular attention to the analysis used to test a *Batson* challenge.

Hermalando Ulloa Lopez v. State
940 S.W.2d 388
(Tex. App.—Austin 1997, no pet.)

Appellant complains the trial court erred by denying his *Batson* challenge to the State's peremptory strike of the only African–American on the jury panel. Appellant argues that the prosecutor used this strike in a racially discriminatory manner, excluding the African–American veniremember from service on the jury because of his race[, which] violates the Equal Protection Clause of the Fourteenth Amendment to the United States Constitution.

[T]he analysis used to test a *Batson* challenge consists of three steps. First, the defendant must establish a prima facie showing of discrimination by the State against eligible veniremembers. To make such a case, the defendant must show that relevant circumstances raise an inference that the State made a race-based peremptory strike. All that is needed to support a rational inference is a "minimum quantum of evidence." Accordingly, the burden of establishing a prima facie case is not onerous.

Second, if a prima facie case is made, the State then has the burden to come forward with a race-neutral reason for exercising the strike. A prosecutor's explanation must be "clear and reasonably specific" and contain "legitimate reasons" for the strike that are related to the case being tried at the moment.

Finally, once the State offers a neutral explanation, the burden shifts back to the defendant to persuade the trial court that the State's purported reasons for its peremptory strikes are mere pretext and are in fact racially motivated.

If, after reviewing all the evidence, we cannot say that the district court's ruling was clearly erroneous, we must uphold the district court's ruling even if this Court would have weighed the evidence differently.

In the instant case, a factual issue of deliberate exclusion was fairly raised by the evidence when the State exercised a peremptory challenge against the only African–American member of the jury panel. *See Salazar v. State*, 795

S.W.2d 187, 193 (Tex. Crim. App. 1990) (striking the only Hispanic veniremember constitutes a prima facie case). The State's use of peremptory challenges to dismiss all or most Black jurors is illustrative of the type of evidence that can be used to raise the inference of discrimination. The State did not ask any questions of or receive any answers from the excluded juror about issues raised during voir dire. The type and manner of questions directed to the challenged juror, including a lack of questions, can also be considered evidence leading to an inference of discrimination. Because appellant satisfied the first step of a *Batson* challenge by establishing a prima facie case of discrimination, it then became the State's burden to come forward with a race neutral reason for the strike.

Without expressly ruling on whether the appellant had met his burden of establishing a prima facie case, the trial judge asked the State if it wanted to respond to appellant's *Batson* challenge. The prosecutor stated that the strike was based on information provided by law enforcement officers who commented that this panel member would not make a good juror. Appellant responded that the State's explanation was not a valid answer. After a brief exchange between the State and appellant about the racial composition of law enforcement officers in Burnet County, the trial court denied appellant's motion.

We agree with appellant that the State failed to meet its burden of providing a race-neutral reason for striking the only African-American from the jury panel. The State did not present any evidence that could be used to overcome the presumption of discrimination and show neutrality. The State's only response was that its strike was based on information provided by law enforcement officers. Merely identifying the source of the information did not provide the district court with a legitimate, race-neutral reason for the State's strike. The law enforcement officers may have had racially motivated reasons or race-neutral reasons for advising the State to exclude the African-American jury panelist. From this record, we cannot tell. The State could have met its burden by establishing that the officers' reasons were race-neutral. Although the State offered to provide this information, it never did. Accordingly, the State gave no race-neutral reason for its strike and, therefore, failed to meet its burden. We hold that the district court's implied conclusion that the State's peremptory challenge was exercised for race-neutral reasons is clearly erroneous because it is not supported by the record.

Because the exclusion of even one member from the jury panel for racial reasons denies due process in the jury selection process, appellant is entitled to a new trial.

———————◆———————

In the above case, the fact that the struck juror was the only African-American raised an inference that the strike was racially motivated, which satisfied the first prong of the three-part test. A pattern of strikes against all or most of a particular race or gender generally satisfies the first prong of a *Batson* challenge.[68] In order for the *Batson* claim to succeed, all three parts of the test must be satisfied, as the next case illustrates.

Christopher McGee v. State
342 S.W.3d 245
(Tex. App.—Amarillo 2011, pet. ref'd)

We first consider appellant's *Batson* challenge. The focus of that challenge lies upon the State's use of a peremptory challenge against an African–American venireman named Shepherd. The latter was struck, according to the prosecutor, because he was asleep during voir dire. We overrule the issue.

One levying a *Batson* challenge must make a prima facie showing of racial discrimination. If that happens, the burden then shifts to the State to offer a race-neutral explanation for the strike. Should such an explanation be proffered, then the burden shifts back to the defendant to show the explanation was really a pretext for discrimination. And, in reviewing the trial court's decision, we must allow it to stand unless it is clearly erroneous.

In explaining his decision to challenge the particular venireman, the prosecutor informed the trial court that, "when I called on him and asked him [about] punishment or rehabilitation he was startled and woken up [sic] before he answered the question, so Mr. Shepherd was sleeping during my portion of the voir dire and that's why I cut him." Appellant did not dispute that or question the prosecutor.

———————

[68] *Dewberry v. State*, 776 S.W.2d 589, 591 (Tex. Crim. App. 1989) ("the defendant may establish a prima facie case by showing that the State has struck most or all of the members of the identified group from the venire, or has used a disproportionate number of peremptories against the group").

Sleeping during voir dire is a race-neutral reason for using a peremptory challenge. [T]hat the prosecutor called out Shepherd's name twice to garner the venireman's attention while all other members answered the particular question after the prosecutor called their name once lends support to the contention that Shepard may have been sleeping. *See Roberson v. State*, 866 S.W.2d 259, 261–62 (Tex. App.—Fort Worth 1993, no pet.) (...when the State strikes a juror on a basis that cannot be easily determined by a reviewing court, that basis must be substantiated by something other than the prosecutor's statement). Finally, we note that appellant did not dispute the contention below. Therefore, we lack a basis to conclude that the trial court's rejection of the *Batson* challenge was clearly erroneous. *See Moore v. State*, 265 S.W.3d at 82 (stating that the [trial] court is in the best position to determine if the prosecutor was correct that the juror was inattentive, and noting that the defendant did not dispute the contention thereby resulting in the conclusion that the record supported it).

───────────◆───────────

Notes and Questions

1. Before *Batson*, the reasons for peremptory strikes remained confidential; not even the judge could inquire into them. Consider the following excerpt from a Texas Court of Criminal Appeals case decided just two years after the *Batson* decision:

> [T]he *Batson* decision calls for a new procedure not heretofore familiar to daily trial practice—that of demanding of a party the reasons for their exercise of peremptory strikes.... "The trial judge's task is extremely difficult. One doubts that a prosecutor will admit that his decision to challenge a particular member of the venire was based on race. The court is left with determining from the totality of the circumstances whether an articulated neutral explanation is but an excuse for improper discrimination. *Batson* thus requires the trial judge to embrace a participatory role in voir dire, noting the subtle nuance of both verbal and nonverbal communication from each member of the venire and from the prosecutor himself."[69]

─────────────

[69] *Keeton v. State*, 749 S.W.2d 861, 865 (Tex. Crim. App. 1988) (quoting *Missouri v. Antwine*, 743 S.W.2d 51, 64–65 (Mo. 1987)).

2. The party complaining of the *Batson* violation need not be of the same race as the prospective jurors struck.[70] For example, an Asian defendant could raise a *Batson* challenge claiming that the prosecutor impermissibly struck Hispanics from the jury array.

3. *Batson* was later extended to include gender[71] and to include impermissible strikes made by defense attorneys.[72] It has not, however, been extended to include religious affiliation,[73] age,[74] national origin,[75] or any other characteristic. The Court of Criminal Appeals explained its refusal to apply *Batson* to protect against religious discrimination in jury selection:

> To hold … that a veniremember may not be excluded on account of his religious preference is tantamount to a holding that he may not be struck on account of his beliefs. If pursued to its logical conclusion, such a holding would undercut the essential features of our jury selection system altogether because our form of government protects not only religious belief, but all manner of political, moral, social, and scientific conviction as well. The treatment of religious creed as an inappropriate basis for peremptory exclusion cannot rationally be distinguished from a similar treatment of persons on account of their Libertarian politics, their advocacy of communal living, or their membership in the Flat Earth Society.[76]

4. If the basis for exercising peremptory strikes involves both permissible and impermissible reasons, it will likely not pass muster under *Batson*. For example, in *Fritz v. State*, the Court of Criminal Appeals found

---

[70] *Green v. State*, 880 S.W.2d 198, 201 (Tex. App.—Texarkana 1994, no pet.).

[71] *Guzman v. State*, 85 S.W.3d 242, 245 (Tex. Crim. App. 2002).

[72] *Georgia v. McCollum*, 505 U.S. 42, 49–50 (1992) ("Just as public confidence in criminal justice is undermined by a conviction in a trial where racial discrimination has occurred in jury selection, so is public confidence undermined where a defendant, assisted by racially discriminatory peremptory strikes, obtains an acquittal.").

[73] *Casarez v. State*, 857 S.W.2d 779, 784 (Tex. App.—Fort Worth 1993), *aff'd*, 913 S.W.2d 468 (Tex. Crim. App. 1994) ("we decline to apply an expanded version of *Batson* to peremptory challenges made on the basis of a venireperson's religious affiliation").

[74] *Brown v. State*, 925 S.W.2d 1, 3 (Tex. App.—Tyler 1994), *rev'd on other grounds*, 913 S.W.2d 577 (Tex. Crim. App. 1996) (age listed as a permissible, race-neutral reason for striking a juror).

[75] *Wamget v. State*, 67 S.W.3d 851, 859 (Tex. Crim. App. 2001) (juror struck on basis that she was born in Liberia was a race-neutral reason).

[76] *Casarez v. State*, 913 S.W.2d 468, 491 (Tex. Crim. App. 1994).

that striking seven male jurors who were "under the age of 30 upon the assumption that such male veniremembers would possess a 'potential bias' or 'common ground' with the defendant" was not an entirely gender-neutral basis.[77] The Court reasoned that the Sixth Amendment guarantees a jury that represents the community, and negative stereotypes based on race and gender have no place in jury selection.[78]

   5.   What protections exist to ensure non-discriminatory intent when it comes to peremptory strikes that are not present when it comes to jury shuffles? If a party wants to challenge a jury shuffle based upon the possibility of racial discrimination, can he force opposing counsel to offer a race-neutral explanation before the shuffle commences?

   Jury shuffle critics believe it permits race and gender discrimination, or at least the potential for it. There is no *Batson*-like procedure for a jury shuffle. The jury shuffle allows parties to mix up the seating order based solely on juror appearance before a single question has been asked. While appearance includes factors beyond race and gender, those two elements must have played a role, albeit a silent one, in any number of jury shuffles over the years.

———————————◆———————————

Batson Hearing Procedure

   After the lawyers have returned the list of prospective jurors with their peremptory strikes to the clerk, the clerk calls the jurors to be seated in the jury box. It is at this time that both sides are made aware of whom the other side struck peremptorily. If no objection to the jury is made, the jurors are sworn in, and the trial begins. If either side wishes to object to the peremptory strikes based on *Batson*, the time to lodge the objection is before the jury is sworn in and empaneled. If an objection is made, the judge stops the proceedings and has a *Batson* hearing outside of the presence of the jury. *Batson* hearings are held in open court, not behind closed doors or in private.[79] Furthermore, the attorney who raises the *Batson* objection has the right to cross-examine the attorney who allegedly violated *Batson*.[80] The court

---

[77] *Fritz v. State*, 946 S.W.2d 844, 847 (Tex. Crim. App. 1997).
[78] *Id.* at 846.
[79] *Salazar v. State*, 795 S.W.2d 187, 192 (Tex. Crim. App. 1990).
[80] *Id.*

and the parties proceed with the three-step test, but the burden begins and ends with the party who raised the *Batson* challenge.[81]

Remedy for *Batson* Violations

There are multiple remedies for *Batson* violations. If the court determines that the party accused of violating *Batson* did, in fact, strike jurors on a discriminatory basis, the court shall call a new array in the case.[82] This remedy is a statutory one. There are common law remedies too.

The *Batson* Court stated, "we express no view on whether it is more appropriate in a particular case, upon a finding of discrimination against black jurors, for the trial court to discharge the venire and select a new jury from a panel not previously associated with the case ... or to disallow the discriminatory challenges and resume selection with the improperly challenged jurors reinstated on the venire."[83] In this way, the *Batson* Court considered the statutory remedy above and a common-law remedy of disallowing the impermissible strikes. The Court of Criminal Appeals followed *Batson's* suggestion by upholding a trial judge's reinstatement of two African-American jurors who were impermissibly struck by the prosecutor.[84] In doing so, the Court of Criminal Appeals stated:

> The potential juror excluded by a racial generality suffers a profound personal humiliation heightened by its public character. ...[D]enying a person participation on a jury – the quintessential governing body, on account of his race unconstitutionally discriminates against the excluded juror. "Regardless of who invokes the discriminatory challenge, there can be no doubt that the harm is the same – in all cases, the juror is subjected to open and public racial discrimination." Therefore, a *Batson* violation is not merely harmful to the parties involved but to the individual veniremember as well. If the only remedy is dismissal of the array, the affected veniremember is still not allowed to participate in the process. Indeed, the sole [statutory] remedy, [dismissing the array,] may defeat the purpose of the protection.[85]

---

[81] TEX. CODE CRIM. PROC. ANN. art. 35.261(a) (West 2016).

[82] TEX. CODE CRIM. PROC. ANN. art. 35.261(b) (West 2016).

[83] *Batson v. Kentucky*, 476 U.S. 79, 99 (1986).

[84] *State ex rel. Curry v. Bowman*, 885 S.W.2d 421, 425 (Tex. Crim. App. 1993).

[85] *Id.*

Which remedy do you think is more just?

———————◆———————

Practice Questions

Jury selection is a popular bar exam topic. In recent years, one or two jury selection questions have appeared on each exam, but examiners have asked as few as zero (only once) and as many as four questions (also only once) in the past. The questions tend to focus on a few key areas: challenges for cause, peremptory strikes, jury shuffles, *Batson*, the propriety of specific types of voir dire questions, and voir dire procedure.

1. (J-2016, F-2016, F-2015, F-2011, F-2007, F-2006, F-2005, and J-2001) In a single-defendant felony trial, how many peremptory challenges does each side have? How many jurors will ultimately be selected to serve? If Defendant were tried with Co-defendant instead, how many peremptory challenges would Defendant, Co-defendant, and Prosecutor each have?

_____

_____

_____

_____

_____

2. Prosecutor views the jury array and wishes to change the seating order.

   a. (J-2016, J-2011, J-2008, J-2006, F-2005, J-2003, and F-2002) What procedural step can she take to change the seating order of the array? When must she take this step?

_____

_____

_____

_____

_____

b. (F-2014) After Prosecutor takes the above procedural step, you decide you want to change the order of the array again. Judge denies your request.

Was the Court's ruling correct? Explain.

_____

_____

_____

_____

_____

3. (J-2015) During voir dire, a prospective juror says she thinks Defendant's case sounds familiar. Through more questioning, you discover she indicted Defendant when she served as a member of the grand jury.

Is there something you can do to prevent this person from serving as a petit juror and what is the basis for your action? Explain.

_____

_____

_____

_____

_____

4. (J-2015) In Defendant's trial, Judge decides two alternate jurors will be chosen. Consequently, Judge gives you and Prosecutor one additional peremptory challenge. You exercise only one peremptory challenge in choosing the jury.

How many peremptory challenges may you use when you select alternate jurors? Explain.

_____

_____

_____

_____

_____

5. (F-2015, F-2007, F-2006, F-2003, and J-2001) Defendant is charged with the felony offense of injuring a child.

    What is a challenge for cause, and how many do you have? What is a peremptory challenge, and how many of those do you have?

    _____

    _____

    _____

    _____

    _____

6. (J-2014) Defendant elects to have a jury trial. Judge unexpectedly schedules Defendant's case for trial early without notifying you. The court coordinator calls to tell you that jury selection will begin in three hours. Unfortunately, Defendant is out of town and cannot make it back in time. You appear in court and object to picking a jury in Defendant's absence. Judge overrules your objection, and a jury is selected.

    Was Judge correct in moving forward with voir dire?

    _____

    _____

    _____

    _____

    _____

7. (J-2014 and J-2012) Judge informs you that the attorneys will not be asking any questions during voir dire, that only she will ask the prospective jurors questions. You propose asking just three questions of the panel, which the Judge acknowledges are relevant questions. Nevertheless, Judge refuses your request.

Is Judge's practice correct? Explain.

_____

_____

_____

_____

_____

8. (F-2014 (juror read about case in newspaper and believes Defendant is guilty), J-2013 (juror would not convict Defendant of charged crime), J-2009 (juror believes Defendant is guilty based on fact he was indicted), F-2009 (juror cannot consider probation for this type of offense), J-2008 (juror would not question truthfulness of witness), F-2007 (juror would only consider maximum punishment), J-2005 (same), F-2004 (same), J-2003 (juror has strong feelings against people charged with this crime), and J-2001 (juror believes Defendant is guilty)):

   During voir dire in a drug possession case, a prospective juror reveals he would not consider the maximum punishment for anyone convicted of a drug offense, and he is not even sure that he could convict someone for a victimless crime like this.

   What must the State establish to challenge this prospective juror for cause?

_____

_____

_____

_____

_____

9. (F-2013 and J-2010) During jury selection, Prosecutor strikes all male prospective jurors so that only women are seated on the jury.

How can you challenge her action? Can Prosecutor rebut this challenge? What must you show to be successful? Explain.

_____

_____

_____

_____

_____

10. (F-2013 and F-2012) Defendant faces a jury trial in Brazos County, Texas. During jury selection, you discover the following things about three prospective jurors: (1) Juror A is qualified to vote in Brazos County, Texas, but is not registered to vote; (2) Juror B has a prior conviction for misdemeanor theft; and (3) Juror C has been charged with, but not convicted of, a felony offense. Prosecutor attempts to use three challenges for cause on these jurors, but you oppose them.

How should Judge rule on Prosecutor's challenges for cause of each juror? Explain.

_____

_____

_____

_____

_____

11. (J-2012) After the jury has been selected and empaneled, you discover one of the jurors is disqualified to serve.

What, if anything, can you do to preserve error for appeal, and when should you take action? Explain.

_____

_____

_____

518 | Texas Criminal Procedure and Evidence

_____

_____

12. (F-2012) Defendant is charged with aggravated robbery, a second-degree felony. Judge gives eight peremptory challenges to you and Prosecutor. You use your seventh and eighth peremptory challenges to strike two prospective jurors because they are wearing T-shirts with slogans you don't like. The Court asks you to explain why you made these two peremptory challenges.

Did the Court allot the correct number of peremptory challenges? Were you entitled to use your peremptory challenges to strike jurors based on their T-shirts? Are you obligated to explain why you peremptorily struck these jurors? Explain.

_____

_____

_____

_____

_____

13. (J-2011) During voir dire, Prosecutor asks the following question: "Imagine the evidence, in a hypothetical case, showed that the defendant robbed a store, using a gun, and threatened to shoot the cashier if she withheld the money. Would any of you hesitate to find the defendant guilty of aggravated robbery?" You object to this question because it is remarkably similar to the underlying facts of Defendant's case.

Should the Court overrule or sustain your objection and if so, on what grounds? Explain.

_____

_____

_____

_____

_____

14. (F-2011, J-2006, and J-2002) During voir dire, you discover there are several unfit prospective jurors. You wish to challenge them for cause.

List five challenges for cause that may be made by either party.

_____

_____

_____

_____

_____

15. (J-2010 and J-2004) What three questions must the Court ask to determine whether a prospective juror is legally qualified to serve on a petit jury?

_____

_____

_____

_____

_____

16. (F-2010 and F-2008) During voir dire in a felony insurance fraud case, one potential juror relays that though he is a retired police chief, he would be fair and impartial as a juror and follow the law. Nevertheless, Defendant does not like him.

Can you prevent this man from serving on the jury? If so, what kind of challenge can you make, and how many of that type of challenge are you entitled to receive? Explain.

_____

_____

_____

_____

_____

17. (F-2008, F-2007, F-2006, J-2005, F-2004, J-2003, F-2003, F-2002, F-2001, and J-2000) In a misdemeanor case, the Judge requests 24 jurors. Of the 24, six are African-Americans. As defense counsel, you like each of these six jurors. After voir dire, the prosecutor challenges all six for cause, but the Judge only grants three of those challenges. The prosecutor then uses all three of his peremptory strikes on these veniremen, leaving no African-Americans in the array.

What can you do to challenge the actions of the prosecutor and when should you take this procedural step? What is the remedy you will request from the Judge?

_____

_____

_____

_____

_____

18. (J-2002 and J-2000) When Judge begins to ask the jury panel questions, you notice there is no court reporter present.

What should you do and when to guarantee the court reporter transcribes voir dire? What are the consequences if you fail to do so?

_____

_____

_____

_____

_____

19. (J-2001) Defendant has been charged with misdemeanor driving while intoxicated.

What is the number of challenges for cause that each side gets? Does the number of peremptory strikes differ depending on whether the case is tried in a county or district court? Explain.

_____

_____

_____

_____

_____

—————————————◆—————————————

Chapter 12
Trial

Introduction

Relatively few criminal cases are resolved through trial. However, attorneys who practice criminal law litigate much more frequently than civil litigators. Many of you have participated in mock trial or have observed an actual trial. From this experience, you learned there is an order to trial and that this order is consistent, no matter the parties or case. This chapter will discuss the rights of the defendant, the order of criminal trials in Texas, and other trial-related matters.

———————◆———————

Bifurcation

In Texas, criminal trials for all but Class C misdemeanors are bifurcated. *Bifurcated* is a Latin word meaning "divided in two forks" or "two-pronged." Bifurcated criminal trials have two phases: guilt/innocence and punishment.[1] However, when a jury acquits a defendant, the first phase ends, and the second phase never begins, Consequently, there are only two phases of trial if the defendant is found guilty.

Most states do not have a bifurcated system like the one in Texas. Why then does Texas have bifurcated criminal trials? It is a better trial procedure. Before trials were bifurcated in Texas, prejudicial evidence related to punishment enhancements had to be admitted into evidence during trial while other prejudicial evidence useful for assessing punishment—prior bad acts and extraneous offense evidence—was deemed inadmissible. As a result, both the defendant and the jury were prejudiced to some extent. In 1965, that changed. Here is how the Court of Criminal Appeals characterized the change:

> One of the innovations wrought by the 1965 Code of Criminal Procedure was the bifurcated trial. As originally enacted, the procedure was ... entitled "alternate procedure" as though it was to be experimental only, but ... it became *the* procedure in all applicable cases.
>
> The procedure involved splitting the trial on the issues of guilt and punishment and provided that at the penalty stage of the proceedings whether the assessor of punishment be ...the jury or the judge, either side

---

[1] TEX. CODE CRIM. PROC. ANN. art. 37.07 §1 (b) and § 2(a)-(b) (West 2016).

could offer evidence of the defendant's prior criminal record, his character or reputation. Such procedure was obviously designed to take the blindfolds off the judge or jury when it came to assessing punishment. It authorized the introduction of evidence on punishment not heretofore held to be generally admissible. It did, however, limit such introduction to the penalty stage to prevent the accused from being tried as a criminal generally prior to the determination of the issue of guilt. It thus allowed evidence critical to an enlightened determination of punishment but avoided the possibility of prejudice on the issue of guilt.

Further, it had long been recognized that jury verdicts of the unitary system were often the product of compromise, *i.e.*, a finding of guilty in exchanging for moderate punishment, or a finding of not guilty because of the severity of the punishment. Some commentators also believed that a constitutional due process question was involved in the practice of reading the allegations of the indictments as to prior convictions and permitting proof of the same before the determination of guilt or innocence. ... In order to remedy this and other defects, Article 37.07... was amended in 1967 to provide for bifurcated trials in all criminal cases, other than [Class C] misdemeanor trials....[2]

At the same time these revisions were being made in the 1960s, Article 36.01 was also revised. This Article mandates that when prior convictions are used to enhance a defendant's punishment, the enhancement paragraphs, which appear in the charging instrument, should not be read in open court by the prosecutor until the punishment of trial begins.[3]

———————◆———————

Election

Recall that a criminal defendant has a statutory and constitutional right to a jury trial.[4] Texas grants the right to have a jury trial for every type and level of criminal offense, even Class C misdemeanor offenses. However, a

---

[2] *Brumfield v. State*, 445 S.W.2d 732, 737-38 (Tex. Crim. App. 1969) (emphasis added).

[3] TEX. CODE CRIM. PROC. ANN. art. 36.01(a)(1) (West 2016). This does not apply to jurisdictional enhancements that are used to elevate a misdemeanor offense to a felony offense due to repeat criminal acts. *Id.*

[4] TEX. CODE CRIM. PROC. ANN. art. 1.12 (West 2016).

defendant may file a written waiver to a jury trial and elect to have a bench trial before the judge instead.[5]

If the defendant wishes to proceed with a bench trial, the State must consent to the waiver.[6] On rare occasions, the prosecutor refuses to waive a jury trial, forcing a defendant who wants a bench trial to have a jury trial instead.[7] This usually happens when the State fears the judge will acquit the defendant or be lenient in punishment. Remember that both the defendant and the State have a right to a jury trial.

Not only must the defendant make an election regarding the guilt/innocence phase, she must also elect who will assess punishment in the event she is found guilty. If the defendant wants the jury to assess punishment, she must file an election before the pretrial hearing,[8] or before voir dire begins, if there is no pretrial hearing.[9] What happens when the defendant fails to timely file an election to have the jury assess punishment? The trial judge will, by default, become the punishment assessor.[10] In the event the defendant wants to change his election after a timely election has been made, the State must consent to that change.[11]

———————◆———————

Joinder and Severance

In Chapter 4, you learned that a prosecutor can join more than one charge in a single indictment, which is referred to as *joinder*. The term *joinder* is used in another procedural context as well. It means to consolidate or join several offenses into one trial, regardless of whether those offenses stem from multiple charging instruments or one.[12] In this chapter, we will discuss joinder of criminal trials.

---

[5] TEX. CODE CRIM. PROC. ANN. art. 45.025 (West 2016).
[6] TEX. CODE CRIM. PROC. ANN. art. 1.13 (West 2016).
[7] *E.g., State ex rel. Curry v. Carr*, 847 S.W.2d 561, 562 (Tex. Crim. App. 1992).
[8] TEX. CODE CRIM. PROC. ANN. art. 27.02(7), and 28.01(2) (West 2016).
[9] TEX. CODE CRIM. PROC. ANN. art. 37.07 §2 (West 2016); *Postell v. State*, 693 S.W.2d 462, 464–65 (Tex. Crim. App. 1985).
[10] TEX. CODE CRIM. PROC. ANN. art. 37.07 §2(b) (West 2016).
[11] *Id.*
[12] *LaPorte v. State*, 840 S.W.2d 412, 415 (Tex. Crim. App. 1992).

When multiple crimes arise out of the same criminal episode, a defendant can be tried for multiple offenses in one trial.[13] If a prosecutor wants to try a defendant on multiple charges arising from the same criminal episode in a single trial, she must give the defendant written notice at least 30 days before trial.[14] The 30-day notice gives the defendant enough time to decide whether to proceed with the joined trial or whether to contest it through a motion to sever.[15]

Once the State joins offenses in a single trial, the defendant must choose whether to sever them, and thus face a separate trial for each offense, or proceed with a single trial on all charges.[16] A defendant who agrees to have the offenses consolidated obtains a reward for fostering judicial economy: if he is found guilty on more than one charge, the sentences for the crimes run concurrently.[17] If the defendant files a motion to sever the offenses into multiple trials, on the other hand, the judge has the option of ordering the sentences to run concurrently or consecutively, also known as a "stacked" sentence.[18] The Court of Criminal Appeals characterizes joinder as a "trade-off" for the prosecutor who can clear cases more quickly and a defendant who benefits from a consecutive sentence.[19]

A defendant's motion to sever crimes must be made seven days before the pretrial hearing.[20] However, not all crimes are severable. Some crimes (*e.g.*, intoxication manslaughter, sexual crimes against children, and possession of child pornography) cannot be severed without a showing of unfair prejudice. Even when these crimes are joined together in a single trial, the judge has the option of running the sentences concurrently or consecutively. In other words, certain categories of crimes are exempted from the general rule that a defendant who faces a single trial with joined offenses faces concurrent rather than consecutive sentences.

Not only may a single defendant be tried for multiple offenses in a single trial, but co-defendants can be tried in a single trial for offenses that arose

---

[13] TEX. PENAL CODE ANN. §3.02(a) (West 2011).
[14] TEX. PENAL CODE ANN. §3.02(b) (West 2011).
[15] *LaPorte v. State*, 840 S.W.2d 412, 415 (Tex. Crim. App. 1992).
[16] TEX. PENAL CODE ANN. §3.04(a) (West 2011).
[17] TEX. PENAL CODE ANN. §3.03(a) (West 2011).
[18] TEX. PENAL CODE ANN. §3.04(b) (West 2011).
[19] *LaPorte v. State*, 840 S.W.2d 412, 414-15 (Tex. Crim. App. 1992).
[20] *Thornton v. State*, 986 S.W.2d 615, 617-18 (Tex. Crim. App. 1999).

from the same criminal episode. The Code of Criminal Procedure states that "[t]wo of more defendants who are jointly or separately [charged] for the same offense or any offense growing out of the same transaction may be, in the discretion of the court, tried jointly or separately."[21]

However, there is also an exception to this rule. Where trying co-defendants is prejudicial to one of the defendants, that defendant may file a motion to sever his trial from the others' trial.[22] Normally, the judge has discretion to sever co-defendants' trials,[23] but in some instances, the prejudiced defendant has a right to a severance:

- When one co-defendant has an admissible prior conviction whereas the other does not, which produces "'guilt by association' from the jury's exposure to the co-defendant's previous crime";[24] or

- A joint trial would prejudice the moving defendant.[25]

This last prong is difficult to meet. The Texas Court of Criminal Appeals has stated,

> To establish prejudice, the defendant must show a serious risk that a specific trial right would be compromised by a joint trial, or that a joint trial would prevent the jury from making a reliable judgment about guilt or innocence, and that the problem could not be adequately addressed by lesser curative measures, such as a limiting instruction.[26]

If a severance is granted, the defendants can agree upon the order in which they will be tried, and if they cannot agree, the judge will decide.[27]

———————————◆———————————

[21] TEX. CODE CRIM. PROC. ANN. art. 36.09 (West 2016).
[22] *Id.*
[23] *Id.*
[24] *Qualley v. State*, 206 S.W.3d 624, 637 (Tex. Crim. App. 2006).
[25] TEX. CODE CRIM. PROC. ANN. art. 36.09 (West 2016).
[26] *Qualley v. State*, 206 S.W.3d 624, 636 (Tex. Crim. App. 2006).
[27] TEX. CODE CRIM. PROC. ANN. art. 36.10 (West 2016).

Defendant's Rights at Trial

Texas's Constitution and its statutory laws grant the defendant several trial-related rights.[28] The Code of Criminal Procedure grants the defendant the rights to a speedy trial by an impartial jury, to testify or not to testify, to confront witnesses,[29] to be presumed innocent,[30] and to be present at trial.[31] Those rights will be discussed in this section. Other trial rights, such as the rights to an impartial jury, to a public trial and a jury trial, to be adequately represented by an attorney, and to not face double jeopardy appear elsewhere in this chapter or in this book.

◆

Right to a Speedy Trial

The Sixth Amendment of the U.S. Constitution grants the defendant the right to a speedy trial: "In all criminal prosecutions, the accused shall enjoy the right to a speedy … trial."[32] The Texas Code of Criminal Procedure echoes these exact words [33] but also discusses this right in two other statutory provisions:

- "This Code … seeks [t]o insure a trial with as little delay as is consistent with the ends of justice."[34]
- "Insofar as is practicable, the trial of a criminal action shall be given preference over trials of civil cases, and the trial of a criminal action against a defendant who is detained in jail pending trial of the action shall be given preference over trials of other criminal actions."[35]

---

[28] *E.g.*, TEX. CONST. art. 1 §10 (rights to a speedy trial, an impartial jury, to demand accusation against him and to have a copy, the right to or not to testify, the right to confront witnesses, the right to compel witnesses to testify on his behalf, and the right to an indictment).

[29] TEX. CODE CRIM. PROC. ANN. arts. 1.05 and 38.08 (West 2016).

[30] TEX. CODE CRIM. PROC. ANN. art. 38.03 (West 2016).

[31] TEX. CODE CRIM. PROC. ANN. art. 33.03 (West 2016).

[32] U.S. CONST. amend. VI.

[33] TEX. CODE CRIM. PROC. ANN. art. 1.05 (West 2016).

[34] TEX. CODE CRIM. PROC. ANN. art. 1.03 (West 2016).

[35] TEX. CODE CRIM. PROC. ANN. art. 32A.01 (West 2016).

The timing of this right, like the federal right, is triggered when a defendant is formally charged.[36] Texas also uses the four-part, balancing test that federal courts use to determine whether the right has been violated: "The factors to be weighed in the balance include, but are not limited to, the length of the delay, the reason for the delay, the defendant's assertion of the right, and the prejudice to the defendant resulting from the delay."[37] There is no set time used to determine speediness; courts balance these four factors to determine whether the defendant's right to a speedy trial was violated.

If the defendant believes her right to a speedy trial has been violated, she may raise the issue by filing a motion for a speedy trial or a motion to set aside the indictment.[38] The remedy for the violation is dismissal of the charging instrument with prejudice, which acts as a bar to future prosecution.[39]

———————◆———————

Right to Be Presumed Innocent

All defendants are presumed innocent until the prosecutor proves every element beyond a reasonable doubt.[40] The State bears this burden of proof. Unless an accused is raising an affirmative defense, the defendant is not required to prove anything during his trial. That a defendant "has been arrested, confined, or indicted for, or otherwise charged with, the offense gives rise to no inference of guilt at his trial."[41] This provision, or some variation of it, appears in the jury charge and is usually discussed with potential jurors during voir dire. When potential jurors cannot presume a defendant guilty, they may be struck for cause, which was discussed in Chapter 11.

———————◆———————

---

[36] *Fewell v. State*, 687 S.W.2d 807, 811 (Tex. App.—Houston [14th Dist.] 1985, no pet.).
[37] *Harris v. State*, 827 S.W.2d 949, 956 (Tex. Crim. App. 1992).
[38] *Ex parte Jones*, 449 S.W.2d 59, 60 (Tex. Crim. App. 1970).
[39] *Cantu v. State*, 253 S.W.3d 273, 281 (Tex. Crim. App. 2008).
[40] TEX. CODE CRIM. PROC. ANN. art. 38.03 (West 2016).
[41] *Id.*

Right to Be Present at Trial

The defendant has a right to be present for his own trial. This right stems from the U.S. Constitution's and Texas Constitution's rights of confrontation.[42]

> In all prosecutions for felonies, the defendant must be personally present at the trial, and he must likewise be present in all cases of misdemeanor when the punishment … is imprisonment in jail; provided, however, that in all cases, when the defendant voluntarily absents himself after pleading to the indictment or information, or after the jury has been selected when trial is before a jury, the trial may proceed to its conclusion.[43]

Why would a defendant voluntarily choose to be absent from his own trial? This usually occurs when a defendant does not like the way trial is going and decides not to return to court, thereby violating his bond.

Whether the trial can go on in his absence depends on when the defendant leaves. Once the jury has been selected, which occurs when both sides submit their peremptory strike lists, the trial may continue in the defendant's absence.[44] If, on the other hand, the defendant has not entered a plea in a bench trial or in a jury trial when jury selection is ongoing, the trial must stop if the defendant leaves. A judge who decides to continue at these early stages without the defendant present, which is prohibited by the statute above, will be reversed by an appellate court.[45]

Right to Confront Witnesses

The Confrontation Clause of the Sixth Amendment of the U.S. Constitution,[46] the Texas Code of Criminal Procedure,[47] and the Texas Constitution,[48] guarantee the defendant's right to be confronted with the

---

[42] U.S. CONST. amend. VI; TEX. CONST. art. I, § 10.
[43] TEX. CODE CRIM. PROC. ANN. art. 33.03 (West 2016).
[44] *Miller v. State*, 692 S.W.2d 88, 93 (Tex. Crim. App. 1985).
[45] *E.g.*, *Kerr v. State*, 83 S.W.3d 832, 833–34 (Tex. App.—Texarkana 2002, no pet.).
[46] U.S. CONST. amend VI ("In all criminal prosecutions, the accused shall enjoy the right to . . . be confronted with the witnesses against him.").
[47] TEX. CODE CRIM. PROC. ANN. art. 1.05 (West 2016).
[48] TEX. CONST. art. I, §10("In all criminal prosecutions the accused shall have . . . the right to . . . be confronted by the witnesses against him . . . .").

witnesses against him through cross-examination and to have inadmissible hearsay evidence offered by unavailable witnesses excluded from trial.[49]

The Confrontation Clause protects against any number of violations. In *Romero v. State*, the prosecutor permitted a witness, who was afraid to testify against the defendant, to wear a baseball cap pulled down low, sunglasses, and a jacket with the collar pulled up to hide the lower half of his face.[50] The defendant appealed claiming a violation of his right to confront this witness.[51] On discretionary review, the Court of Criminal Appeals held that the defendant's right to confrontation was compromised, stating:

> The Sixth Amendment's Confrontation Clause reflects a strong preference for face-to-face confrontation at trial.
>
> …[T]he reliability of the testimony … turns upon the extent to which the proceedings respect the four elements of confrontation: physical presence, oath, cross-examination, and observation of demeanor by the trier of fact. In *Maryland v. Craig*,[52] the Supreme Court found sufficient assurance of reliability in a procedure that denied one of these elements—physical presence—where the remaining three elements were unimpaired. In that case, a child witness testified in front of a one-way closed-circuit monitor that prevented her from seeing the defendant but permitted the judge, jury, and defendant to see the witness. Because the witness was under oath, subject to contemporaneous cross-examination, and her demeanor was on display before the trier of fact, the Supreme Court found that the procedure adequately ensured that the testimony was "both reliable and subject to rigorous adversarial testing in a manner functionally equivalent to that accorded live, in person testimony."
>
> In this case, as with *Craig*, the presence element of confrontation was compromised. Although the physical presence element might appear, on a superficial level, to have been satisfied by Vasquez's taking the witness stand, it is clear that Vasquez believed the disguise would confer a degree of anonymity that would insulate him from the defendant. The physical presence element entails an accountability of the witness to the defendant.

[49] *E.g., Boutang v. State*, 402 S.W.3d 782, 786–87 (Tex. App.—San Antonio 2013, pet. ref'd) ("Out-of-court testimonial statements by witnesses are barred under the Confrontation Clause unless the witnesses are unavailable and defendant had a prior opportunity to cross-examine the witness.").
[50] *Romero v. State*, 173 S.W.3d 502, 503-05 (Tex. Crim. App. 2005).
[51] *Id.* at 504-05.
[52] *Maryland v. Craig*, 497 U.S. 836, 845-850 (1990).

The ... presence requirement is motivated by the idea that a witness cannot "hide behind the shadow" but will be compelled to "look [the defendant] in the eye" while giving accusatory testimony. In the present case, accountability was compromised because the witness was permitted to hide behind his disguise.

But unlike *Craig*, the present case also involves a failure to respect a second element of confrontation: observation of the witness's demeanor. Although Vasquez's tone of voice was subject to evaluation and some body language might have been observable, the trier of fact was deprived of the ability to observe his eyes and his facial expressions. And while wearing a disguise may itself be an aspect of demeanor that jurors could consider in assessing credibility, that fact cannot by any stretch of the imagination be considered an adequate substitute for the jurors' ability to view a witness's face, the most expressive part of the body and something that is traditionally regarded as one of the most important factors in assessing credibility. To hold otherwise is to remove the "face" from "face-to-face confrontation."

Consider another common Confrontation Clause violation: hearsay. Do you remember the hearsay rule and all of its exceptions from your Evidence class? Why are there so many rules and exceptions to hearsay? Hearsay is generally excluded because hearsay implicates the Confrontation Clause. Consider this hearsay statement from a witness, "I don't know the defendant that well, but my friend Jenny says he's violent." If Jenny is not at trial and that statement is offered to prove the truth of the matter asserted, the defendant is left without an opportunity to cross-examine Jenny, test the veracity of Jenny's opinion about him, or discover what facts led Jenny to reach this conclusion.

Another Confrontation Clause violation occurs in the context of admitting a co-defendant's statement into evidence against the defendant. In the Joinder and Severance section, you learned that a defendant may have a right to sever his trial from a co-defendant's trial if he can establish "prejudice." A defendant can establish prejudice by demonstrating that there is a "serious risk that a specific trial right would be compromised by a joint trial."[53] The Confrontation Clause may be implicated in this context. A fictional case helps illustrate this point.

Alex and Brian committed aggravated robbery together. Both were subsequently arrested and charged with the offense. Following the arrest,

---

[53] *Qualley v. State*, 206 S.W.3d 624, 636 (Tex. Crim. App. 2006).

Alex invoked his right to remain silent, but Brian gave the police a legally valid, written statement admitting he and Alex were responsible for the crime. Prosecutor joined their trials together. If Brian's statement is admitted as evidence of both his and Alex's guilt at trial and Brian invokes his right not to testify, then Alex will be unable to confront the veracity of Brian's testimonial statement. This will result in a violation of Alex's right to confront the witnesses against him.

Recall in the Joinder and Severance section that the Court of Criminal Appeals has advocated using "lesser curative measures" before granting a severance based on prejudice.[54] In the hypothetical case, appropriate measures may include redacting parts of the statement that implicate Alex or not permitting the State to admit the statement into evidence at all. If these remedies are not available, Alex could successfully argue that to proceed with a joint trial would prejudice him by violating his right to confront Brian, and the judge would be required to grant Alex a severance.

———————————◆———————————

Right to Testify or Not Testify

The Fifth Amendment of the U.S. Constitution grants the defendant the right against being "compelled in any criminal case to be a witness against himself."[55] While this right speaks to the defendant's right not to testify, the Code permits the defendant the right to testify at his own trial.[56] Thus, the defendant may freely choose whether or not he wants to testify.

Rights against self-incrimination at trial are an extension of the right to remain silent that *Miranda* guarantees. From the moment a person becomes a suspect, he has the right to remain silent. This right continues throughout the criminal justice process. He will be reminded of this right and the fact that anything he says may be used against him by police officers during custodial interrogation, by the magistrate at the preliminary hearing, by the judge during arraignment, by the grand jury should he choose to testify, and by the judge at his examining trial. By the time he takes his case to trial, he will have heard these rights at least once, perhaps multiple times.

---

[54] *Id.*
[55] U.S. CONST. amend V.
[56] TEX. CODE CRIM. PROC. ANN. art. 38.08 (West 2016).

The Code states that, "the failure of any defendant to … testify shall not be taken as a circumstance against him, nor shall the same be alluded to or commented on by counsel" in his case.[57] This right and the dangers stemming from its exercise arise in two trial contexts: one is with the jury and the other is with prosecutors. Jurors may falsely believe that innocent people speak in their defense while guilty people remain silent in the face of accusation. These beliefs fly in the face of the defendant's constitutional and statutory right to remain silent at trial. As a result, this topic is a commonly explored during voir dire.

Appellate courts are asked (too frequently) to determine whether a prosecutor has crossed the line by directly or indirectly commenting on the defendant's refusal to testify. Direct comments by a prosecutor (*e.g.*, "Why didn't the defendant testify? He's the only one who could tell us what really happened that night.") amount to a violation of the defendant's right against self-incrimination. Indirect comments may also violate the defendant's rights. For example, appellate courts have supported the defendant's request for a mistrial when the prosecutor argued that the non-testifying defendant lacked remorse[58] or when the prosecutor turned during closing arguments to the non-testifying defendant, pointed, and asked if he heard his victim's screams at night?[59] The best course of action for prosecutors is to avoid any overt or implicit reference at trial to the defendant's failure to testify.

The right to testify, the right not to testify, and the right to be free from comments about exercising these rights are equally enforceable at the guilt/innocence and punishment phases of trial.[60] Just because a defendant testifies during the first phase of trial does not waive his right to refuse to testify during the punishment phase of trial.[61] A comment by the prosecutor

---

[57] *Id.*

[58] *Snowden v. State*, 353 S.W.3d 815, 823-24 (Tex. Crim. App. 2011) ("the prosecutor's remark about the appellant's lack of remorse in the courtroom was an objectionable comment on the appellant's failure to testify because it highlighted for the jury the appellant's failure to take the stand and claim present remorse").

[59] *Archie v. State*, 340 S.W.3d 734, 740 (Tex. Crim. App. 2011) ("asking of these questions, coupled with the prosecutor's act of turning from the jury to face the defense counsel table, pointing, and taking a step or two towards the appellant, directly highlighted the fact that the appellant did not personally take the stand to testify").

[60] *Randolph v. State*, 353 S.W.3d 887, 891-92 (Tex. Crim. App. 2011).

[61] *Id.*

during the punishment phase is as inappropriate as it would be at the guilt/innocence phase of trial.[62] Again, prosecutors are wise to avoid any questions or comments on the defendant's right to remain silent, regardless of the stage of trial.

Suppose a prosecutor does comment on the defendant's right to remain silent before trial, during trial, or during closing arguments. What must defense counsel do to remove the taint of the comment and preserve her objection for appeal? In order to preserve error for appeal, defense counsel must object, state the grounds for objection, ask the judge to instruct the jury to disregard the prosectuor's improper comment, and then ask the judge for a mistrial.[63] Defense counsel must object until he receives an adverse ruling or a mistrial. Consider what the Tyler Court of Appeals said about the trial court's discretion in these instances:

> When the trial court sustains an objection and instructs the jury to disregard, but denies appellant's motion for a mistrial, the question is whether the trial court erred in denying the mistrial. Only when it is apparent that an objectionable event at trial is so emotionally inflammatory that curative instructions are not likely to prevent the jury from being unfairly prejudiced against the defendant may a motion for mistrial be granted. The asking of an improper question, by itself, will seldom call for a mistrial. Further, an instruction to disregard an improper comment on appellant's post-arrest silence is generally sufficient to cure any harm, and will be presumed effective unless the facts of the case suggest the impossibility of removing the impression produced on the minds of the jury. The effectiveness of a curative instruction is determined on a case-by-case basis.[64]

Thus, the relief granted following an improper comment on the defendant's failure to testify or right to remain silent depends on how egregious the comment was. Nevertheless, defense counsel has a duty to preserve error on appeal by obtaining an adverse ruling from the trial court. This is true for any rights violation or harm committed against the accused.

———————————◆———————————

---

[62] *Id.*

[63] *E.g., Little v. State*, 853 S.W.2d 179, 181-82 (Tex. App.—Corpus Christi 1993, no pet.).

[64] *H.J. Ross v. State*, 12-01-00299-CR, 2003 WL 21088124, at *5 (Tex. App.—Tyler May 14, 2003, no pet.).

Motions in Limine

So far we have discussed the structure of trials in Texas and the defendant's trial rights. Now it is time to begin discussing the order of trials. Before trial begins, parties may file a motion in limine. These motions are used to keep the jury from hearing objectionable evidence. They may be made in writing or orally before or during trial. The motion is used to notify the judge in advance that there is objectionable evidence and the reason why the evidence is objectionable. It also allows the judge an opportunity to cure any evidentiary errors before they occur.

The Court of Criminal Appeals described the motion in limine as follows:

> The purpose of a motion in limine is to prevent particular matters from coming before the jury. It is, in practice, a method of raising objection to an area of inquiry prior to the matter reaching the ears of the jury through a posed question, jury argument, or other means. As such, it is wider in scope than the sustaining of an objection made after the objectionable matter has been expressed. However, it is also, by its nature, subject to reconsideration by the court throughout the course of the trial. This is because it may not be enforced to exclude properly admissible evidence.[65]

A motion in limine asks the judge to prohibit the other party from mentioning or eliciting the objectionable evidence until a hearing is held outside the presence of the jury to determine the admissibility of the evidence.[66] A hypothetical illustrates how a motion in limine works.

Suppose a defense attorney believes that the victim in a domestic violence case will testify that there were many instances of abuse before this one. Evidence of that nature is certainly prejudicial to the defendant, and it may amount to inadmissible prior bad acts or character conformity evidence. To prevent the jury from hearing the testimony, the defense attorney will make a motion in limine requesting the prosecutor to approach the bench before asking the victim any questions about past assaults or abuse. If the judge grants the motion, the prosecutor must approach the bench and notify the judge when the objectionable evidence is about to be admitted.

The judge, up to this point, has been listening to the testimony, has determined whether the proper foundation has been laid for the admission of

---

[65] *Norman v. State*, 523 S.W.2d 669, 671 (Tex. Crim. App. 1975).
[66] *Geuder v. State*, 115 S.W.3d 11, 14 (Tex. Crim. App. 2003).

evidence, and may decide to hear more about the testimony covered by the motion in limine and the context for its admission outside of the presence of the jury. Once the judge excuses the jury, hears the objectionable testimony, and listens to the arguments from both parties, the judge will determine whether the evidence should be admitted or excluded. If the evidence is admitted, the party who objects to its admission must object on the record in order to preserve error for appeal. The Court of Criminal Appeals explained why a motion in limine alone does not preserve error:

> [R]eliance on a motion in limine will not preserve error. A defendant must object on the proper grounds when the evidence is offered at trial. The reason for this rule is that a judge is often not in a position to decide on the admissibility of evidence prior to the beginning of trial. This is particularly true when the objection is based on grounds such as the failure to prove a proper predicate. Counsel could ask in the motion in limine that before a suspect area is entered into at trial, the opposing counsel be required to approach the bench and inform the court so that the jury may be excluded. By that procedure the evidence may be challenged at the proper time without risk of prejudicing the jury. Whatever the procedure chosen, defense counsel must object before the evidence is admitted during trial in order to properly call the court's attention to the matter and preserve the error for appeal.[67]

In sum, every time objectionable evidence is sought to be admitted, opposing counsel must object at the time that evidence is offered. When a party fails to object to the introduction of objectionable evidence, he waives error on appeal regardless of whether he filed a motion in limine.

───────────◆───────────

Order of Trial

For the rest of the chapter, assume a defendant has elected to have a jury trial, and the jury has been selected, sworn, and empaneled. What happens next? This section of the chapter will analyze each stage of a criminal trial in sequential order.

───────────◆───────────

---

[67] *Romo v. State*, 577 S.W.2d 251, 252 (Tex. Crim. App. 1979).

Reading the Indictment and Entering the Plea

After the jury is empaneled, the prosecutor reads the charging instrument aloud in the courtroom with the jury present.[68] The defendant then responds by entering her plea of "not guilty" before the jury.[69] The Code indicates these steps are mandatory with "shall" language.[70] The Texas Court of Criminal Appeals explained why this portion of the trial is critical:

> The reading of the indictment has long been held to be mandatory. The rationale for the rule is to inform the accused of the charges against him and to inform the jury of the precise terms of the particular charge against the accused. Without the reading of the indictment and the entering of a plea, no issue is joined upon which to try.[71]

In other words, a trial is supposed to resolve a factual issue in dispute; the factual issue for every criminal trial is whether the defendant is guilty, as the State alleges, or not guilty, as the defendant alleges. The jury is called upon to resolve this dispute, and the reading of the charge and the entering of the plea place the factual dispute before the jury.

What happens if the parties and the judge forget this mandatory step, which should take place as soon as the trial begins? There is a procedure that can cure the error if it is caught before the trial has ended: the prosecutor must read the indictment to the jury, the defendant must enter her plea, and then the trial may resume.[72] If the parties do not catch the error until after trial, this procedure does not cure the error.[73] For post-verdict discoveries of this error, an appellate court engages in harm analysis to determine whether violations of this procedure warrant reversal.[74]

———————————◆———————————

[68] TEX. CODE CRIM. PROC. ANN. art. 36.01(a)(1) (West 2016).
[69] TEX. CODE CRIM. PROC. ANN. art. 36.01(a)(2) (West 2016).
[70] TEX. CODE CRIM. PROC. ANN. art. 36.01(a)(1) and (a)(2) (West 2016).
[71] *Warren v. State*, 693 S.W.2d 414, 415 (Tex. Crim. App. 1985).
[72] *Id.* at 416.
[73] *Id.*
[74] *Turner v. State*, 897 S.W.2d 786, 789 (Tex. Crim. App. 1995) (prosecutor must strictly comply with this procedure); *Linton v. State*, 15 S.W.3d 615, 620 (Tex. App.— Houston [14th Dist.] 2000, pet. ref'd) (36.01 violations are subject to harm analysis based on more recent Court of Criminal Appeals' opinions).

Opening Statement

After the charge is read to the jury in open court and the defendant has entered her plea of not guilty, the prosecutor gives his opening statement, if he chooses to make one. The purpose of the prosecutor's opening statement is to reveal the nature of the crime and the facts the State will prove in its case-in-chief. For the defense, opening statement permits defense counsel the opportunity to reveal the nature of the defenses and the facts it expects to prove. Think of opening statement like a movie preview in relation to a movie; in a matter of minutes, the opening statement reveals what the jury is about to see unfold in the courtroom over the next few hours, days, or weeks, depending on the length and complexity of the trial.

Opening statement is optional for both sides. If the State chooses to make an opening statement, the State presents its opening immediately before calling its first witness to testify.[75] If the prosecutor makes an opening statement, the defense attorney has one of two options: (1) make an opening statement following the prosecutor's opening statement;[76] or (2) wait for the State to present all of the evidence, rest its case, and then present opening statement at the beginning of the defense's case-in-chief.[77] What does defense counsel do when the prosecutor chooses not to make an opening statement? In this instance, defense counsel must wait until the beginning of his case-in-chief to make his opening statement.[78]

---◆---

The State's Case

The State next presents its witnesses and evidence to support the charge.[79] The State calls witnesses, asks questions, and then passes the witnesses to defense counsel for cross-examination. If the prosecutor wants to follow the defense attorney's cross-examination with rebuttal, she may do so. Witnesses will be directed and cross-examined until the parties are finished asking questions of the witness. The prosecutor must present

---

[75] TEX. CODE CRIM. PROC. ANN. art. 36.01(a)(3) (West 2016).
[76] TEX. CODE CRIM. PROC. ANN. art. 36.01(b) (West 2016).
[77] TEX. CODE CRIM. PROC. ANN. art. 36.01(a)(4)-(5) (West 2016).
[78] *Moore v. State*, 868 S.W.2d 787, 791 (Tex. Crim. App. 1993).
[79] TEX. CODE CRIM. PROC. ANN. art. 36.01(a)(4) (West 2016).

enough evidence to support every element of the charge and venue. She must prove each element of the offense beyond a reasonable doubt.[80] When the prosecutor has finished presenting evidence, she will announce in open court, "The State rests."

———————————◆———————————

Proving Identification

The State must prove that the person present at trial is the person who committed the charged offense. Aside from a case where DNA or other forensic evidence links the defendant to the crime, identification requires the victim, witnesses, or police officers—whoever was an eyewitness to the crime or present at the crime scene—to identify the defendant in open court. These identifications are called *in-court identifications*.

There is another type of identification: *out-of-court identifications*. Out-of-court identifications take several forms:

- a lineup, where (usually six) similar looking suspects stand in a line for identification purposes (a lineup may also rely on voice recognition by requiring the people in the lineup to verbalize words a witness heard a suspect say during the crime);
- a show-up, where the suspect alone is brought to the victim immediately following the crime; or
- a photo array, where the photos of similar looking suspects (usually six) are shown to the victim or witnesses.

The law prohibits police officers from making an out-of-court identification impermissibly suggestive.[81] After all, we want witnesses to recall a face, a voice, or a body type based on their own recollection, not based upon someone else's suggestion. Unfortunately, officers may nevertheless suggest who the "right" suspect is, intentionally or inadvertently. Once an impermissibly suggestive out-of-court identification takes place, it taints the in-court identification.[82] "Reliability is the 'linchpin' in determining admissibility of … identification testimony. If indicia of reliability outweigh

---

[80] TEX. CODE CRIM. PROC. ANN. art. 38.03 (West 2016).

[81] *E.g., Barley v. State*, 906 S.W.2d 27, 32-33 (Tex. Crim. App. 1995).

[82] *Loserth v. State*, 963 S.W.2d 770, 771 (Tex. Crim. App. 1998).

suggestiveness then an identification is admissible."[83] When the witness's identification is tainted, suggested, or otherwise unreliable,[84] the defense attorney may take the procedural step of filing a motion to suppress either or both the out-of-court and in-court identifications.[85]

————————◆————————

Motion for Directed Verdict

If the State has failed to prove an element of the offense, the jurisdiction, or that the defendant in the courtroom is the person who committed the crime by the close of its case, the defense will make a motion for directed verdict. This motion is made outside of the presence of the jury. Once the jury is excused, the judge will hear the defendant's motion, both parties' arguments, and rule on the motion. If the judge denies the motion, the trial continues. If the judge grants the defendant's motion, the jurors come back into the courtroom, and the judge orders the jury to find the defendant not guilty. In this way, the judge directs or orders the jury's verdict, which explains the name of this motion. A directed verdict results in an acquittal of the charges; the State may not retry the defendant for the crime without running afoul of the double jeopardy clause, which is discussed later in this chapter.[86]

————————◆————————

The Defense's Case

If the defense did not make an opening statement—either because the State did not make one at the beginning of trial or because the defense chose to wait—it can make one at the start of its case-in-chief. The defense will next call witnesses and put on any evidence it may have, though it is not required to prove anything aside from affirmative defenses.[87] The defendant may or may not choose to testify.[88] All defense witnesses, like State witnesses,

---

[83] *Barley v. State*, 906 S.W.2d 27, 34 (Tex. Crim. App. 1995).
[84] *Ibarra v. State*, 11 S.W.3d 189, 195 (Tex. Crim. App. 1999).
[85] *Loserth v. State*, 963 S.W.2d 770, 771 (Tex. Crim. App. 1998).
[86] *State v. Moreno*, 294 S.W.2d 594, 601 (Tex. Crim. App. 2009).
[87] TEX. CODE CRIM. PROC. ANN. art. 36.01(a)(5) (West 2016).
[88] TEX. CODE CRIM. PROC. ANN. art. 38.08 (West 2016).

are subject to cross-examination. Once the defense has put on all of its evidence, it will announce in open court, "The defense rests."

———————◆———————

Rebuttal

After the defense has rested, the State may rebut any testimony offered in the defense's case. This part of the trial is referred to as rebuttal. The Code states that "[r]ebutting testimony may be offered on the part of each party," which indicates the defense may rebut the State's rebuttal as well.[89] "The purpose of rebuttal evidence is to directly counter testimony from another source. As a general proposition, when a party introduces matters into evidence, it invites the other side to reply to that evidence."[90] In other words, rebuttal evidence is limited in scope in that it rebuts what the other side most recently raised.[91]

———————◆———————

The Jury Charge

While the jury is the exclusive arbiter of the facts at trial,[92] the judge must instruct the jury on the relevant law.[93] Applicable law appears in a document known as the jury instruction or the jury charge. These two names are used interchangeably to refer to a single document. The document instructs the jury about the law (hence the name *jury instruction*), and the judge charges or orders the jury to follow the law in the instructions during deliberations (hence the name *jury charge*). The instructions contain legal definitions and the law related to the charged offense, applicable defenses, and other laws raised by the testimony, evidence, or circumstances of the trial.

The charge is written neutrally. The Code states the charge must not

---

[89] TEX. CODE CRIM. PROC. ANN. art. 36.01(a)(7) (West 2016).

[90] *Martin v. State*, 151 S.W.3d 236, 239 (Tex. App.—Texarkana 2004, pet. ref'd).

[91] *E.g.*, *Laws v. State*, 549 S.W.2d 738, 741 (Tex. Crim. App. 1977) ("The prosecution is entitled on rebuttal to present any evidence that tends to refute the defensive theory of the accused and the evidence introduced in support of it.").

[92] TEX. CODE CRIM. PROC. ANN. art. 36.13 (West 2016).

[93] TEX. CODE CRIM. PROC. ANN. art. 36.14 (West 2016).

- express any opinion about the weight of evidence;
- summarize the evidence;
- discuss the facts; or
- arouse the sympathy or emotions of the jury.[94]

The charge must reflect the judge's neutral position during trial. The instructions cannot comment on the weight of the evidence or characterize the evidence in a biased way. The instructions must not favor or disparage any party or evidence.

How does the charge come about? Once the State and the defense have rested, the jury is excused while the parties work on the jury instructions: this informal hearing is called a *charge conference*. During the conference, the parties read the judge's proposed instructions, object and argue for or against the instructions, object and argue for or against the inclusion of additional instructions, or agree to the instructions as written.[95] Any objections to the charge or suggested instructions that a party wants to include should be made and read to the court reporter at the conference or submitted in writing to preserve error for appeal.[96] Though the parties may make objections or suggestions regarding the contents of the charge, it is the judge who determines the charge's content.

Once the charge conference is over, the judge prints the jury instructions and asks the jury to return to the courtroom. The judge then reads the instructions to the jury in open court before closing arguments and charges the jury to follow the laws contained within the instructions when it retires to deliberate.[97] When the jury leaves the courtroom, it will bring the jury instructions to the deliberation room to read and consider during its deliberations.[98]

There are a few specific areas of jury instruction law that are also important to address here. The first is the structure of the jury charge. The jury charge has three main parts:

- The abstract portion, which tells the jury the applicable law;

---

[94] *Id.*

[95] *Id.*; TEX. CODE CRIM. PROC. ANN. arts. 36.15 and 36.16 (West 2016).

[96] TEX. CODE CRIM. PROC. ANN. art. 36.15 (West 2016).

[97] TEX. CODE CRIM. PROC. ANN. art. 36.16 (West 2016).

[98] TEX. CODE CRIM. PROC. ANN. art. 36.18 (West 2016).

- The application portion, which applies the law to the facts; and
- The verdict form, filled out by the jury during deliberations, which indicates its decision on guilt/innocence or punishment.[99]

The abstract portion includes the law and legal definitions that apply to the case. The Court of Criminal Appeals describes the next portion, the application paragraph, as follows:

> The application paragraph is that portion of the jury charge that applies the pertinent penal law, abstract definitions, and general legal principles to the particular facts and the indictment allegations. Because that paragraph specifies the factual circumstances under which the jury should convict or acquit, it is the "heart and soul" of the jury charge.[100]

A jury charge that fails to include an application section will be held erroneous on appeal.[101] The verdict form and verdict in general will be discussed in more detail below.

Another issue with jury instructions is whether the charge should define beyond a reasonable doubt. While legal definitions commonly appear in the abstract portion of the jury charge, courts in Texas believe the jury should decide what "beyond a reasonable doubt" means. In 2000, the Court of Criminal Appeals stated that it was "ill-advised for us to require trial courts to provide the jury with a redundant, confusing, and logically flawed definition when the Constitution does not require it" and "the better practice is to give no definition of reasonable doubt at all to the jury."[102] However, the Court held that if both sides want to define beyond a reasonable doubt, it would not be reversible error for the trial court to do so.[103] Nevertheless, it is common practice to leave that definition out of the instruction.

---

[99] The jury charge also includes the language of the charging instrument, defenses raised by the evidence, lesser-included offenses, evidentiary instructions, applicable constitutional rights, other instructions raised by the evidence or nature of the case, and instructions on the conduct of the jury (*e.g.*, what the jury can consider or who may communicate with the jury). *See e.g.*, TEX. CODE CRIM. PROC. ANN. arts. 35.23, 36.13, 36.22, 36.25-36.28, 37.04, 37.07-37.08, 37.11, 38.03-38.04, 38.075, 38.08, 38.14, 38.21-38.23(a) (West 2016).

[100] *Vasquez v. State*, 389 S.W.3d 361, 366-67 (Tex. Crim. App. 2012).

[101] *Gray v. State*, 152 S.W.3d 125, 127-28 (Tex. Crim. App. 2004).

[102] *Paulson v. State*, 28 S.W.3d 570, 573 (Tex. Crim. App. 2000).

[103] *Id.*

Finally, recall the defendant has a right to testify or not to testify at her own trial. The Code states, "the failure of any defendant to so testify shall not be taken as a circumstance against him."[104] The defendant has a right if he does not testify to a "no-adverse-inference instruction," which informs jurors they are not to infer guilt from the defendant's failure to testify.[105] When the defendant requests such an instruction, it is error for the trial court to refuse to include such an instruction.[106]

> [W]here a request is made to the trial court to add to its charge ... an instruction on the failure of the defendant to testify, or an objection is made to the omission of such charge, it is reversible error if the trial court fails to honor that request or objection.... "[M]embers of the jury, unless instructed otherwise, may well draw adverse inferences from a defendant's silence" at the punishment phase of the trial, just as they could from the defendant's silence at the guilt-innocence stage of the trial. "No judge can prevent jurors from speculating about why a defendant stands mute ..., but a judge can, and must, if requested to do so, use the unique jury instruction to reduce that speculation to a minimum."[107]

Again, the constitutional right against self-incrimination at any stage of the criminal justice process must be protected. Jurors shall be advised in the charge that they cannot speculate or draw negative inferences from the defendant's failure to testify.

---◆---

Lesser-Included Offenses

Another subset of law addressed by the jury instruction is the lesser-included offense. A lesser-included offense is a crime with a lesser punishment than the charged offense that:

1. requires proof of the same or less than all the facts required to establish the charged offense;
2. results in a less serious injury or risk of injury than the charged offense;

[104] TEX. CODE CRIM. PROC. ANN. art. 38.08 (West 2016).
[105] *De La Paz v. State*, 901 S.W.2d 571, 578 (Tex. App.—El Paso 1995, pet. ref'd).
[106] *Id.*
[107] *Brown v. State*, 617 S.W.2d 234, 238 (Tex. Crim. App. 1981).

3. requires a less culpable mental state than the charged offense; or

4. consists of an attempt to commit the charged offense.[108]

When the defendant would like the jury to consider a lesser-included offense, he must request a jury instruction permitting the jurors to consider convicting the defendant of the lesser-included offense.

> "A defendant is entitled to an instruction on a lesser-included offense where the proof for the offense charged includes the proof necessary to establish the lesser-included offense and there is some evidence in the record that would permit a jury rationally to find that if the defendant is guilty, he is guilty only of the lesser-included offense." … [A]nything more than a scintilla of evidence may be sufficient to entitle a defendant to a lesser charge. In other words, the evidence must establish the lesser-included offense as "a valid, rational alternative to the charged offense."[109]

If the judge agrees that the defendant has met the two criteria above, she will instruct the jury that it may consider finding the defendant guilty of the lesser-included offense. The jury will then have the option of finding the defendant not guilty, guilty of the charged offense, or guilty of the lesser-included offense.[110]

───────────── ◆ ─────────────

Closing Arguments

After the judge has instructed the jury, each side will be given time to deliver closing arguments. "The purpose of closing argument is to assimilate the evidence to assist the fact-finder in drawing proper conclusions from the evidence."[111]

Both sides are given the same amount of time for argument.[112] Though the Code states that the order of argument may be regulated by the judge, the

---

108 TEX. CODE CRIM. PROC. ANN. art. 37.09 (West 2016).

109 *Hall v. State*, 225 S.W.3d 524, 536 (Tex. Crim. App. 2007) (quoting *Bignall v. State*, 887 S.W.2d 21, 23 (Tex. Crim. App. 1994) and *Forest v. State*, 989 S.W.2d 365, 367 (Tex. Crim. App. 1999)).

110 TEX. CODE CRIM. PROC. ANN. art. 37.08 (West 2016).

111 *Gaddis v. State*, 753 S.W.2d 396, 400 (Tex. Crim. App. 1988).

112 Appellate courts rarely hold that a judge abused her discretion by limiting closing argument time. Nevertheless, the Court of Criminal Appeals has provided a non-exclusive list of factors to consider when assessing whether time for closing

prosecutor has the right to make the last argument to the jury.[113] In practice, the State usually delivers a portion of closing argument first, defense counsel then delivers the entirety of its closing argument, and the State uses its remainder of time to rebut the defense's closing argument. However, the State could also choose to use all of its time to go first or all of its time to go last. Regardless, the State always has the right to have the first word and the last word during closing arguments. When either party—the State or the defendant—is represented by more than one attorney, the court must permit at least two arguments (so at least two attorneys will be permitted to argue).

In many ways, trial feels like an emotional or mental battle. At the end of trial, attorneys may feel battered, and their emotions may run high. As a result, closing arguments are ripe for highly charged comments and arguments. Fortunately, the law places boundaries on closing arguments.

"The general rule is that proper jury argument by the State involves: summation of the evidence, deductions from the evidence, an answer to the defendant's argument, and a plea for law enforcement."[114] Anything that does not fit into those four areas is in theory outside of the scope of permissible closing argument. This section will focus on those topics.

Personal Opinion and Personal Attacks

Attorneys must avoid testifying during closing arguments by inserting their own opinions about the credibility of witnesses. They must also demonstrate professionalism in the courtroom by not implying opposing counsel is unethical or a liar. It is the jurors, not the attorneys, who are the exclusive judges of facts and credibility. This next case outlines the law on two areas of improper closing arguments—personal opinion and personal attacks—and the proper procedure for objecting to inappropriate closing argument.

---

arguments was reasonable: the amount of the evidence, length of the trial, number of the testimony conflicts, severity of the crime, complexity of the case, and whether counsel used time efficiently and explained on the record arguments he was not able to make due to the time constraints. *Dang v. State*, 154 S.W.3d 616, 621 (Tex. Crim. App. 2005). Some of these factors mirror those discussed in Chapter 11 regarding the reasonableness of time constraint for voir dire.

[113] TEX. CODE CRIM. PROC. ANN. arts. 36.07-36.08 (West 2016).

[114] *Lopez v. State*, 838 S.W.2d 758, 760 (Tex. App.—Corpus Christi 1992, no pet.).

Del Eugene Lange v. State
57 S.W.3d 458
(Tex. App.—Amarillo 2001, pet. ref'd)

[Appellant was convicted for sexually assaulting his seven-year-old daughter, A.L., on two separate occasions. The jury found him guilty and assessed punishment at 35 years for each charge. He appealed on several grounds, arguing that the State made improper jury arguments.]

Appellant … objects to the State's closing argument in his third issue, alleging the prosecutor interjected his personal opinion regarding the veracity of the alleged victim. This portion of the closing argument, the subject of appellant's second issue, which immediately preceded the argument under appellant's second issue, is as follows:

[The State:] You also have to believe that if [A.L.] is lying that she's capable of sustaining that lie for 15 months and fooling all these people, Nicole Lacowski, Detective Stautzenberger, of the Bryan Police, the first person to take the report, Nick Canto at Scotty's House, Jane Riley at Scotty's House—

Defense Counsel: Objection—

The State: Detective Kinard—

The Court: Do I have an objection?

Defense Counsel: Could we approach the bench?

The Court: You may.

Defense Counsel: There's a list up there of about 12 different people that he's saying that she's fooled. Now, the implied in that, Judge, is that all of these people have the conclusion that she was molested and it was Del. There's been no testimony of a number of these names as far as them reaching any conclusion. To put the prosecutor's name up there is a personal opinion by him that the child has been—

The Court: I don't think that evidence is before the jury. The objection is overruled.

…The State: (Continuing.) …Detective Kinard talked to her afterwards, Lila Belitz who was a counselor, the prosecutors, and finally you. Because I took an oath and I resent his allusions that I'm trying to do a perversion of justice—

Defense Counsel: Judge, now that—

The State: —in coaching that witness.

Defense Counsel: There's no evidence of that.

The State: It's invited argument, your Honor.

Defense Counsel: I object to that as outside the record, what his personal opinion is about this case.

The Court: Objection overruled.

The gist of the argument is that, because the prosecutor's name was included in a list of people that the victim had to fool if she was lying, he was offering his personal opinion that the victim told the truth and also implying that the other witnesses believed the victim was truthful. When the prosecutor attaches a personal belief to the credibility of a witness, the effect is to bolster the credibility of the witness with unsworn testimony, which is improper. It has also been held error to suggest to the jury that they should defer to any other person's assessment of the truthfulness of a witness, no matter how experienced that person may be. However, if the State's argument falls within one of the four permissible categories previously enumerated, it does not constitute error. Remarks of counsel must be considered within the context of the entire argument.

In contending the argument was proper, the State relies on *Wylie v. State*, 908 S.W.2d 307 (Tex. App.—San Antonio 1995, pet. ref'd), in which the defendant, who was convicted of aggravated sexual assault of a child, raised a claim of ineffective assistance of counsel because his attorney failed to object to jury argument in which the prosecutor attempted to uphold the credibility of the child complainant and inferred that the child had "convinced" a number of witnesses. Because the defense strategy was to attack the complainant's credibility by suggesting she had a tendency to fabricate and was influenced by the prejudices of others, the arguments of the State were found to be a response to the defense and reasonable deductions from the evidence.

In *Kelly*, the prosecutor made the statement he would "put every bean I have got on Mathew Jackson" in response to argument from defense counsel that the witness had misidentified the defendant. We found that the State's argument was a response to defense counsel's argument and also a reasonable deduction of the evidence in light of testimony from the witness of four separate opportunities he had to observe the defendant.

Similarly, in *Richards v. State*, 912 S.W.2d 374 (Tex. App.—Houston [14th Dist.] 1995, pet. ref'd), the prosecutor argued that "... the only person who testified completely truthfully in this case and did not make a single mistake was Bernard Phearse. He is the only person in my opinion." The court noted that the defense strategy was to disprove the complainant's credibility by implying the testimony was influenced by others, particularly the prosecutor. The court concluded that the statement was not an improper attempt to bolster the testimony because it was a reasonable deduction from the evidence and a summation of the evidence.

Defense counsel attempted during the trial and closing argument to attack the complainant's credibility by showing inconsistencies in her story and that she had been manipulated by others into bringing the allegations. During cross-examination, she was specifically questioned as to each person she had spoken to about the alleged incidents, including the prosecutors. The State's response was to attempt to demonstrate consistency in her story by referring the jury to those witnesses to whom she had relayed the incidents. The prosecutor never directly stated that he believed the complainant. He stated that if the jury believed she was lying, they also had to believe that she had fooled the witnesses who testified at trial as to her version of the events. The prosecutor also included himself as one of the persons the complainant would have had to fool.

Similarly, in *Wylie*, two of the witnesses mentioned did not testify at trial, but because their names were brought out in the testimony of other witnesses, it was a reasonable deduction from the evidence for the prosecution to refer to them again. In this case, although the prosecutors were not witnesses, the complainant was questioned regarding her discussions with the prosecutors about her allegations. In light of the defense argument that the complainant had been influenced in her testimony by others, including the prosecutor, we believe the prosecutor's statement was a proper response to that argument. Appellant's third issue is overruled.

In his fourth issue, appellant attacks the trial court's overruling of his objections to the State's argument that he attempted to divert the jury from the truth. Appellant cites us to two separate occurrences in the record. The first exchange was as follows:

The State: Well, they can hardly smear a 7–year–old can they? I mean, it would be ludicrous to try to smear a 7–year–old. So they do the next best thing. They find the closest person to the victim, and they do their best to drag her down into the mire. And the hope is that it can generate enough dust and smoke—

Defense Counsel: Objection, Judge—

The State: —from the truth of this case.

Defense Counsel: Same objection.

The State: Judge—

The Court: Objection overruled.

The second exchange occurred shortly thereafter:

The State: (Continuing.) Well, ladies and gentlemen, I think we can all agree that there's a lot of different defenses you can throw out; but there's only one truth. And they've thrown out a lot of different defenses. And you can ask yourself: Do they really intend for us to follow all these defenses? Did they argue them all the same? Can they all be true, or are they really just an effort to distract us from the truth?

Defense Counsel: Objection. Same objection, Judge.

The Court: Objection overruled.

The State: (Continuing.) Let's talk about some of these rabbit trails.

Defense Counsel: Objection. Rabbit trails again. Same objection.

The Court: Objection sustained.

Defense Counsel: Ask for instruction to disregard.

The Court: Jury is instructed to disregard.

Defense Counsel: Move for mistrial.

The Court: Denied.

The State: (Continuing.) The first of these so-called offenses—so common prosecutors have an acronym for it—some other dude did it. And Mr. Bryan appears to have abandoned that in his closing argument. During the trial there were allusions to Allen Hickman and there were allusions to Jerry. There were allusions to his friend, Brian. Fortunately, we could clear that up when he took the stand; and there's other people that could have done that.

And the Defendant's actions indicate that there's no other person that did it. Imagine a father falsely accused and believing that his daughter at least might have been molested—

Defense Counsel: Judge, got "rabbits" written at the top of his chart: and that is case law and specifically held that that is improper. We object.

The Court: The jury has been instructed to disregard that comment.

Defense Counsel: Could we have the chart taken down or at least that part of it, Judge?

The Court: No. The jury has been instructed to disregard it. Ladies and gentlemen, you'll abide by my instructions. Do you understand that? Very well.

Appellant contends that this argument was an uninvited accusation of improper conduct on his part. As we noted in *Howard v. State*, 896 S.W.2d 401 (Tex. App.—Amarillo 1995, pet. ref'd), it is important to differentiate between comments which facially appear aimed at defense counsel but actually strike at his argument. Counsel runs the risk of improper argument when it is made in terms of defense counsel personally and explicitly impugns his character. In *Howard*, the State analogized the defense tactic to a "bunny trail" and charged defense counsel with presenting false issues, but it did not charge the defense with actually manufacturing false evidence. We held that given its brevity, its de minimis derogatory content, and its direct relationship to the defendant's argument, the statements were permissible.

…During closing argument, defense counsel here had asserted that the complainant's mother was bitter about her divorce, was trying to get back at appellant and his family and she had manipulated her daughter into making false accusations. There was also trial testimony that the complainant had been alone with other males who may have had an opportunity to assault her. We therefore believe that the State's argument was in response to defense counsel's closing argument and evidence presented at trial. Moreover, even assuming the references to "rabbit trails" were improper, reversible error is shown only if substantial rights have been affected. In making that determination with respect to improper argument cases, courts generally look to the severity of the misconduct, measures adopted to cure the misconduct, and the certainty of conviction absent the misconduct. In this instance, the State did not charge that defense counsel had manufactured evidence and the court sustained the objection to the use of "rabbit trails" and instructed the jury to disregard it, as well as the chart where the phrase appeared. While the veracity of the complainant was hotly contested at trial, given the mild effect of the conduct and the court's instruction, we do not believe reversible error occurred. Appellant's fourth issue is overruled.

————————◆————————

Notes and Questions

1.   The general rule is that the attorneys may not inject personal opinions or testify during closing argument.[115]   If that is so, why was the prosecutor permitted to respond in closing argument that he was not fooled by the victim? Defense counsel invited the argument because he suggested the victim was lying and the witnesses were fooled by her. This is known as the *invited argument rule*. If one party invites improper argument, the other party's response, even if improper, may be excused. One Court of Criminal Appeals judge disfavored this rule by suggesting that it is "akin to reasoning that two wrongs make a right."[116] Nevertheless, it is commonly employed by judges to waive error in improper argument claims.

2.   What is a prosecutor who alleges defense counsel has led the jury on a rabbit trail implying? Is it one thing to say the accused's defense is not credible and another to suggest defense counsel is intentionally misleading the jury? Where should judges draw the line?

3.   Recall the following portion of argument from the *Lange* case:

"The State: Let's talk about some of these rabbit trails.

Defense Counsel: Objection. Rabbit trails again. Same objection [as before].

The Court: Objection sustained.

Defense Counsel: Ask for instruction to disregard.

The Court: Jury is instructed to disregard.

Defense Counsel: Move for mistrial.

The Court: Denied."

---

[115] *E.g., Lookingbill v. State*, 855 S.W.2d 66, 76 (Tex. App.—Corpus Christi 1993, pet. ref'd).
[116] *Wilder v. State*, 560 S.W.2d 676, 678 (Tex. Crim. App. 1978) (Roberts, J., concurring).

In order to preserve error for review, the record must show that the objecting party made a specific request, objection, or motion that made the trial court aware of the complaint, and the trial court ruled on the request, objection, or motion.[117] Next, the objecting party must pursue the objection to an adverse ruling (*i.e.*, until the judge denies or overrules the party's request). This requires the party to "(1) object and, if the objection is sustained, (2) request an instruction to disregard, and (3) if an instruction is given, move for a mistrial."[118] In the case above, the judge sustained the objection and instructed the jury to disregard the argument but denied defense counsel's request for a mistrial. Denying the request for a mistrial was an adverse ruling. Therefore, defense counsel preserved the issue for appeal.

———————◆———————

Pleas for Law Enforcement and the Community

One of the four proper areas for closing arguments is a plea for law enforcement. This means that attorneys (usually prosecutors, in this instance) can ask that the jury respect the law, enforce the law, and send a message to the community that our laws and their enforcement are important. However, it is improper for an attorney to request the jury render a specific verdict or suggest to the jury that the community demands a specific punishment in the present case. The following case examines this type of closing argument.

John Fitzgerald Smith v. State
966 S.W.2d 111
(Tex. App.—Beaumont 1998, pet. ref'd)

John Fitzgerald Smith appeals from a conviction for aggravated robbery, where the jury found Smith to be a repeat offender and sentenced him to thirty years of imprisonment in the Texas Department of Criminal Justice, Institutional Division. The sole point of error presents the issue: "Whether the State's jury argument induced the jury to assess punishment based on community desire or expectation so as to prevent Appellant from having a fair trial."

---

[117] TEX. R. APP. P. 33.1(a).
[118] *Harris v. State*, 784 S.W.2d 5, 12 n. 4 (Tex. Crim. App. 1989).

Proper jury argument falls into four categories: (1) summation of the evidence, (2) reasonable deduction from the evidence, (3) response to opposing counsel's argument, and (4) plea for law enforcement. An improper argument based upon community expectations has been rather eloquently expressed as "asking the jury to lend an ear to the community rather than a voice."

Defense counsel objected to two statements made by the prosecutor during her closing arguments to the jury on punishment:

[State:] [D]o you remember when there was a time when kids could ride their bikes in the streets? There was a time when kids could go to the store for their moms. ... Parents would let their kids go visit the next door neighbor. Because of this man and people like him, parents can't do that anymore. Parents can't even go to a convenience store— ...

[T]hat's what you're here for, to punish. You've got to make his sentence tough enough that he is punished and he knows he cannot get away with this in Jefferson County. Because as you notice, he stays in this county. He keeps committing these crimes in this county.

Ladies and gentlemen, it's your job to protect society, to keep us safe, to keep your children safe from people like him—

Cases holding an argument impermissibly pressured a jury to assess punishment to meet the expectations of the community invariably refer directly to the demands or expectations of the community for a particular verdict. Examples of improper demands to meet community expectations include: "Now, the only punishment that you can assess that would be any satisfaction at all to the people of this county would be life [imprisonment]." ... "So I ask you, this is a hard decision that you have to make, but I will tell you on behalf of the State of Texas, an aggravated sexual assault such as this, probation is not what this community and what the State would want."

On the other hand, a reference to the community which asks the jury to represent the community is a plea for law enforcement which does not exceed the bounds of proper argument. Included within this category are such arguments as: "I am asking you to enforce it. I'm asking you to do what needs to be done to send these type of people a message to tell them we're not tolerating this type of behavior in our county."; "... I think you will want to give them an answer you can be proud of, that your friends and neighbors can be proud of."; "You know, you're here because you have been chosen by the community to make the decision, and that's it"; …"[I]f you want to find somebody like this innocent of the charge, you may do it, but you will have to explain your actions to the community."; … "Probation, in this case, members of the jury, would be a slap on the wrist to the Defendant, would be a slap in the face to law enforcement in this community."; "consider the community effect of your verdict."; ….

The State's jury argument did not unequivocally refer to community expectations of a particular punishment. Read in context, both arguments were clearly pleas for law enforcement. The trial court did not err in overruling Smith's objections to the arguments. We overrule the point of error. The judgment and sentence of the trial court are affirmed.

———————◆———————

Jury Deliberations

Once the jury receives the charge and hears closing arguments, it takes the charge to the jury room and begins to deliberate.[119] The jury is given a room to use for deliberations.[120] Like the grand jury, no one is permitted to be in the room with the petit jury at this time.[121] A sheriff's deputy or a bailiff escorts the jury to and from the room and attends to the jury's needs (*e.g.*, takes them to lunch and brings evidence to them upon request).[122] Any communication the jury has with the bailiff or the judge regarding the case must be in writing, and these communications become part of the record for purposes of appeal.[123]

If the jurors disagree with the statement of any witness, they may ask the court to have the testimony of that witness, which was taken down by the court reporter at trial, read back to them.[124] The jurors must be specific about which portion of the testimony they question; only that portion may be read back to them.[125]

---

[119] TEX. CODE CRIM. PROC. ANN. art. 36.18 (West 2016).
[120] TEX. CODE CRIM. PROC. ANN. art. 36.21 (West 2016).
[121] TEX. CODE CRIM. PROC. ANN. art. 36.22 (West 2016).
[122] TEX. CODE CRIM. PROC. ANN. art. 36.24 (West 2016).
[123] TEX. CODE CRIM. PROC. ANN. art. 36.27 (West 2016).
[124] TEX. CODE CRIM. PROC. ANN. art. 36.28 (West 2016).
[125] *Id.*

The Verdict

A verdict is a written declaration by a jury of its decision on the issues the judge submitted to it.[126] Recall that in Texas, we have bifurcated criminal trials for jailable offenses. When the case is "tried before a jury on a plea of not guilty, the judge shall, before argument begins, first submit to the jury the issue of guilt or innocence of the defendant … without authorizing the jury to pass upon the punishment to be imposed."[127] The jury may find the defendant not guilty or guilty of the charged crime. Even though this phase is called the *guilt/innocence phase,* the jury never has the option of finding the defendant innocent, just "not guilty." Only if the jury finds that the defendant is guilty in the first phase of trial does the second phase of trial, the punishment phase, begin. Both of these phases require a verdict.

Once the jury has decided its verdict, the jury returns to the courtroom with a verdict form, which is signed by the jury foreperson.[128] The verdict is then read aloud in the courtroom by the judge, the foreperson of the jury, or the clerk.[129] In felony cases, the defendant must be present at the time the verdict is read unless he is voluntarily absent, but in misdemeanor cases, the verdict may be received and read without the defendant's presence in the courtroom.[130]

In felony cases, all 12 jurors must agree upon and return a verdict of guilty, and all six must agree upon and return a verdict of guilty in misdemeanor cases.[131] The verdict for the first phase of trial must be unanimous. "The unanimity requirement is a complement to and helps in effectuating the 'beyond a reasonable doubt' standard of proof."[132]

Sometimes unexpected things happen to jurors during trial. For instance, a juror may become seriously ill or die while the trial is ongoing. Does the trial go on without the juror, or must the court declare a mistrial? If the trial court selected alternate jurors, this is when an alternate juror would replace

[126] TEX. CODE CRIM. PROC. ANN. art. 37.01 (West 2016).
[127] TEX. CODE CRIM. PROC. ANN. art. 37.07 §2(a) (West 2016).
[128] TEX. CODE CRIM. PROC. ANN. art. 37.04 (West 2016).
[129] *Id.*
[130] TEX. CODE CRIM. PROC. ANN. art. 37.08 (West 2016).
[131] TEX. CODE CRIM. PROC. ANN. arts. 36.29(a) and 37.03 (West 2016).
[132] *Ngo v. State*, 175 S.W.3d 738, 745 n. 23 (Tex. Crim. App. 2005).

the disabled[133] or deceased juror.[134] What happens when there are no alternates? If a juror dies or becomes disabled from sitting before the jury is charged in a felony case, the remaining 11 jurors are given legal authority to render the verdict; when this happens, all jurors, not just the foreperson, must sign the verdict.[135] If there are no alternate jurors and a juror becomes disabled or dies after the charge is read, the jury must be discharged unless the defendant, defense counsel, and the prosecutor agree on the record to continue with the remaining 11 jurors.[136] Again, in this instance, all jurors must sign the verdict form.[137]

———————————◆———————————

Mistrials

Many juries have no difficulty reaching a unanimous verdict, but some do not. A jury may deliberate for minutes, hours, or days depending on the complexity of the evidence and the thoroughness of the jury. If the jury cannot agree on the verdict—for example, two believe the defendant is not guilty, whereas ten believe he is guilty—the jury will send a note to the judge stating it is deadlocked. When this happens, the judge may declare a mistrial.[138]

When encountered with a verdict that is not unanimous, judges may wait to declare a mistrial. It is common practice for the judge to bring the jurors back into the courtroom and to admonish them using an "*Allen* charge"[139] or "dynamite charge":

> A "dynamite" or "*Allen*" charge is typically used in an attempt to break a deadlocked jury by instructing that the result of a hung jury is a mistrial and that jurors at a retrial would be faced with essentially the same decision, and

---

133 "Disabled" in this context means "the juror was physically or mentally impaired in some way which hindered his ability to perform his duty as a juror." *Brooks v. State*, 990 S.W.2d 278, 286 (Tex. Crim. App. 1999).
134 TEX. CODE CRIM. PROC. ANN. art. 36.29(b) (West 2016).
135 TEX. CODE CRIM. PROC. ANN. art. 36.29(a) (West 2016).
136 TEX. CODE CRIM. PROC. ANN. art. 36.29(c) (West 2016).
137 TEX. CODE CRIM. PROC. ANN. art. 36.29(d) (West 2016).
138 TEX. CODE CRIM. PROC. ANN. art. 37.07 § 2(a) (West 2016).
139 *Allen v. United States*, 164 U.S. 492, 501-02 (1896).

by encouraging the jurors to try to resolve their differences without coercing one another.[140]

Once the judge reads the charge to the jury, the jury retires to deliberate again. The jury may then reach a unanimous verdict. However, if it sends a note to the judge stating it is still deadlocked, the judge has a couple of options:

> The court may discharge a hung jury under two circumstances: when the jury cannot agree and the parties consent to the jury's discharge; or when the jury cannot agree and the parties do not consent but the jury has "been kept together for such time as to render it altogether improbable that it can agree."[141]

When a jury has been discharged without rendering a verdict, the case may be tried again without running afoul of double jeopardy.[142]

———————◆———————

Witnesses

Witnesses are an essential component of trials. This section will examine several important aspects of witnesses and witness testimony: the Rule, whether judges can testify, what evidence must accompany accomplice witness testimony at trial, and witness competency.

———————◆———————

The Rule

A witness's testimony should be based solely upon what she saw, heard, or experienced. Her testimony should not be influenced by others' testimony. To ensure the integrity of witness testimony, any party or the court on its own motion may exclude a witness or witnesses from the courtroom until they are called to testify. This is referred to as "invoking the Rule." The Rule refers to Texas Rule of Evidence 614. It permits the trial judge to order the witnesses to leave the courtroom until they testify so they do not hear the

---

[140] *Broussard v. State*, 163 S.W.3d 312, 316 (Tex. App.—Beaumont 2005, no pet.).
[141] *Galvan v. State*, 869 S.W.2d 526, 528 (Tex. App.—Corpus Christi 1993, pet ref'd).
[142] TEX. CODE CRIM. PROC. ANN. art. 36.33 (West 2016).

other witnesses' testimony. The Rule can be invoked at any time during the trial, but it is more commonly invoked at the start of trial, before a single witness testifies.

> When the Rule is invoked, a witness should not hear testimony in the case or talk to any other person about the case without the court's permission. While the trial court is obligated to exclude witnesses from the courtroom during other witnesses' testimony, the court's decision to allow testimony from a witness who has violated the Rule is discretionary.[143]

The Rule applies to any person who the State or the defense intends to call as a witness; it does not apply to the defendant, however, who is permitted to remain in the courtroom for the duration of the trial. The Code also states that witnesses placed under the Rule shall be instructed not to speak with other witnesses, unless given permission by the judge, not to read about the case, and not to comment about their own testimony to others while under the Rule.[144]

Victims who testify are typically required to leave the courtroom as well, unless the judge determines their testimony would not be materially altered by hearing the other witnesses' testimony.[145] It is within the judge's discretion to exempt experts from the Rule; they are permitted to listen to and testify about the other side's expert and the expert's opinion.[146]

The court has two possible sanctions for violating the Rule: (1) holding the witness in contempt; or (2) refusing to allow the witness to testify.[147] Most judges verbally scold witnesses and attorneys without resorting to implementing either of these two sanctions, but these measures are available.

———————◆———————

Judge as Witness

Texas Rule of Evidence 605 states, "The judge presiding at the trial may not testify in that trial as a witness. No objection need be made in order to preserve the point." This is not to say that a judge can never be a witness in a

---

[143] *Minor v. State*, 91 S.W.3d 824, 829 (Tex. App.—Fort Worth 2002, pet. ref'd).
[144] TEX. CODE CRIM. PROC. ANN. art. 36.06 (West 2016).
[145] TEX. CODE CRIM. PROC. ANN. art. 36.03 (West 2016).
[146] *Lewis v. State*, 486 S.W.2d 104, 106 (Tex. Crim. App. 1972).
[147] *Bell v. State*, 938 S.W.2d 35, 50 (Tex. Crim. App. 1996).

trial or legal proceeding that she does not preside over,[148] but the judge may not be a witness in trials over which she presides.

———————◆———————

Accomplice as Witness

An accomplice is a person who participates in the commission of the crime with the defendant and can be prosecuted for the same crime or a lesser-included offense.[149] A conviction cannot rest solely on the testimony of an accomplice "unless corroborated by other evidence tending to connect the defendant with the offense committed."[150] In addition, the corroboration must do more than merely prove the commission of the offense.[151]

The Austin Court of Appeals explained the policy reasons for this rule:

> [A]ccomplice testimony implicating another person should be viewed with a measure of caution, because accomplices often have incentives to lie, such as to avoid punishment or shift blame to another person. The accomplice's motives in testifying against the accused may well include malice or an attempt to curry favor from the state in the form of a lesser punishment, or perhaps, no punishment. The Texas legislature has determined that because the testimony of an accomplice is inherently untrustworthy and should be viewed with caution, uncorroborated testimony of an accomplice, standing alone, is not enough to support a criminal conviction.
>
> The court of criminal appeals has described an accomplice as a discredited witness. No matter how complete a case may be established by an accomplice witness, a conviction is not permitted unless the accomplice's testimony is corroborated. The testimony of an accomplice witness is untrustworthy and should be received and acted on with caution. It should be carefully scrutinized not only because of the potential self-interest of the accomplice, but because such testimony is evidence from a corrupt source.[152]

In sum, without more, testimony from an accomplice is not enough to sustain a conviction against the defendant.

---

[148] *Hensarling v. State*, 829 S.W.2d 168, 170-71 (Tex. Crim. App. 1992).
[149] *Medina v. State*, 7 S.W.3d 633, 641 (Tex. Crim. App. 1999).
[150] TEX. CODE CRIM. PROC. ANN. art. 38.14 (West 2016).
[151] *Id.*
[152] *Wincott v. State*, 59 S.W.3d 691, 698 (Tex. App.—Austin 2001, pet. ref'd).

Witness Competency

In Chapter 7, you read that defendants must be competent in order to stand trial. *Competent* was used in the context of a defendant who, due to mental disease or defect, was unable to understand the proceedings against her or communicate with attorneys. Competency in the witness context does not mean the same thing. Insane persons—whether presently insane or insane at the time they witnessed the events they're testifying about—and a child or any other person "whom the court examines and finds lacks sufficient intellect to testify concerning the matters in issue" is incompetent as a witness and prohibited from testifying.[153]

This does not mean that all children are incompetent witnesses. Instead, the law requires the judge to gauge "the sufficiency of the child-witness's cognitive ability to relate relevant facts … [and] inquire whether the child-witness possesses the capacity to appreciate the obligations of the oath – or can at least distinguish the truth from a lie."[154] The judge may permit the parties to ask the child questions to help the judge determine whether the child witness is competent.[155]

———◆———

Double Jeopardy

The Fifth Amendment of the U.S. Constitution,[156] the Texas Constitution,[157] and the Texas Code of Criminal Procedure[158] protect defendants from double jeopardy. The Code states, "No person for the same offense shall be twice put in jeopardy of life or liberty; nor shall a person be again put upon trial for the same offense, after a verdict of not guilty …."[159]

What does "twice put in jeopardy" mean? Imagine that you represent a client charged with a crime who takes her case to trial. The jury acquits her.

---

153 TEX. R. EVID. 601.
154 *Gilley v. State*, 418 S.W.3d 114, 120-21 (Tex. Crim. App. 2014).
155 *Id.*
156 U.S. CONST. amend V ("nor shall any person be subject for the same offense to be twice put in jeopardy of life or limb").
157 TEX. CONST. art. I, §14.
158 TEX. CODE CRIM. PROC. ANN. art. 1.10 (West 2016).
159 *Id.*

She is elated; she thanks you for doing an excellent job and leaves the courthouse to go home. The next day she calls you from jail and says she has just been arrested for committing the offense for which she was acquitted yesterday. You think she must be mistaken, so you go to the courthouse and speak to the prosecutor who tried the case. The prosecutor states she refiled the case and would like a different jury to convict the same defendant for the same crime because she did not like the outcome of the first trial. Under these circumstances, the defendant could successfully raise a double jeopardy claim because she is at risk for punishment a second time for the same offense.

"Same offense" does not necessarily mean the exact same offense. Double jeopardy claims arise in a number of scenarios: (1) when a person faces a subsequent prosecution for the same offense following an acquittal, like the instance above; (2) when a person faces a subsequent prosecution for the same offense following a conviction; or (3) when a person faces multiple punishments for the same offense. [160] The following two cases explain the analysis courts conduct to determine whether an offense is the same for purposes of double jeopardy. The first case highlights the *Blockburger* test, [161] which is used by federal and Texas courts to determine whether two separate charges are actually the same offense for purposes of double jeopardy. The second case identifies "units of prosecution," which is another way of identifying double jeopardy violations.

State v. William David Kelley
866 S.W.2d 650
(Tex. App.—Houston [14th Dist.] 1993, no pet.)

Pursuant to a plea bargain whereby the State abandoned the enhancement paragraphs, appellee pled nolo contendere to the charge of aggravated kidnapping with intent to violate and abuse the complainant sexually. Appellee was assessed twenty years confinement. The State subsequently charged appellee with burglary of a building with intent to commit sexual assault. The aggravated kidnapping and burglary of a building offenses arose out of the same transaction. Prior to trial on the second charge, the trial court granted appellee's request to quash the indictment on

---

[160] TEX. CODE CRIM. PROC. ANN. art. 1.11 (West 2016).
[161] *Blockburger v. United States*, 284 U.S. 299 (1932).

grounds that prosecution for the offense was barred by the double jeopardy protections of the United States Constitution and our State Constitution. In a single point of error, the State asserts that the trial court erred in granting appellee's plea in jeopardy.... We reverse.

In determining whether a successive prosecution is barred by double jeopardy, we apply the "same-elements" test, sometimes referred to as the "*Blockburger*" test. *See ... Blockburger v. United States*, 284 U.S. 299 (1932). The *Blockburger* test inquires whether each offense contains an element not contained in the other; if not, they are the "same offense" and double jeopardy bars successive prosecution. Texas courts have consistently followed *Blockburger*.

Appellee's prosecution on the burglary charge following his conviction on the aggravated kidnapping charge is not barred under *Blockburger* because both offenses contain an element the other does not contain. Under the facts of this case, a charge of aggravated kidnapping required the State to prove that appellee intentionally or knowingly abducted another person with the intent to violate or abuse her sexually. To convict appellee of the subsequent charge of burglary of a building with intent to commit sexual assault, the State would be required to prove that appellee, with the intent to commit sexual assault, entered a building not then open to the public, without the effective consent of the owner. Each of these offenses obviously consists of dissimilar elements, and each offense requires proof of elements not required by the other. Accordingly, we sustain the State's sole point of error.

The judgment of the trial court is reversed and remanded for further proceedings not inconsistent with this opinion.

———————◆———————

Jimmy Jack Lozano v. State
860 S.W.2d 152
(Tex. App.—Austin 1993, pet. denied)

... In five separate indictments, appellant was charged with crimes arising out of a fire that killed four people and caused serious bodily injury to a fifth person. Each indictment alleged that appellant used a lighter to ignite combustible material. [One] indictment ... charged that appellant committed arson resulting in the bodily injury of the victim. The other four indictments charged appellant with the murder of four victims committed in the course of arson. The court granted the State's motion to consolidate the charges, and appellant pleaded not guilty in each cause.

In a bench trial, one witness testified that appellant knocked on the door of a house, was told by the occupants to go away, walked around the house to a room at the back, then started a fire with his lighter. Shortly thereafter, appellant departed, leaving the house ablaze. One witness testified that appellant stated he burned the house because the people inside owed him money. Four people inside the house died and one person was seriously burned.

Under the indictments, the trial court could have found appellant guilty of four acts of murder as well as the crime of arson. It did not. Instead, it found him guilty of arson in each cause. ...

DISCUSSION

In his third point of error, appellant complains that the trial court erred in finding him guilty of five separate arson offenses. It is undisputed that the four deaths and the fifth person's injuries all were caused by a single fire. Appellant argues that under section 28.02 of the Penal Code, death or injury is not an element of arson giving rise to multiple offenses. Instead, he asserts, any number of deaths or bodily injuries only enhances arson from a second-degree felony to a first-degree felony.

Appellant's point of error raises double jeopardy concerns. The United States Constitution provides that no person shall "be subject for the same offense to be twice put in jeopardy of life or limb." Article I, section 14 of the Texas Constitution provides similar protection. The federal and state double jeopardy clauses protect an individual against multiple prosecutions for the same offense after acquittal or conviction and against multiple punishments for the same offense. Both the United States Constitution and the Texas Constitution speak of double jeopardy in terms of the "same offense" rather than the "same transaction." Appellant complains he was convicted five times of the same offense, a single act of arson.

...Double jeopardy does not bar multiple convictions where separate and distinct offenses occur during the same transaction. ... In *Rathmell*, the accused drove his vehicle while intoxicated, causing an accident in which two persons were killed. He was convicted of the involuntary manslaughter of one victim. When the State attempted to obtain an additional conviction based upon another victim's death, the accused sought to have the second indictment dismissed, claiming a second trial would expose him to double jeopardy. The Court of Criminal Appeals determined that each individual death constituted a separate and distinct offense and held that a second trial was not barred by double jeopardy.

In *Phillips*, the defendant was convicted for the aggravated assault of two individuals arising out of a single automobile collision. On appeal, he raised double jeopardy objections. Citing *Rathmell*, the court held that his actions constituted two separate offenses against two separate people. The relevant involuntary manslaughter statute in *Rathmell* and the aggravated assault statute in *Phillips* state in pertinent part:

> (a) A person commits [involuntary manslaughter] if he:
> (1) recklessly causes the death of an individual; or
> (2) by accident or mistake when operating a motor vehicle, airplane, helicopter, or boat while intoxicated and, by reason of such intoxication, causes the death of an individual.

> (a) A person commits [aggravated assault] if the person commits assault as defined in Section 22.01 of this code and the person:
> (1) causes serious bodily injury to another.

The court held that these statutes clearly reflect that the Legislature intended that the offenses of involuntary manslaughter and aggravated assault, both offenses against the person, are complete upon the death or assault of a single person. Each individual death or assault constitutes a complete and distinct offense and, as such, each offense constitutes a separate "allowable unit of prosecution."

In contrast, arson is an offense against property. The Penal Code defines arson as occurring when a person starts a fire or causes an explosion with intent to destroy or damage property. An arson offense is complete when the fire is started, not when bodily injury or death occurs as a result. The occurrence of such damage is not an element to be proven. When bodily injury or death occurs as a result of arson, the statutory offense against property remains unaffected, although the degree of the chargeable felony increases.

We hold that appellant committed a single offense, allowing a single unit of prosecution, when he committed arson by setting a single house on fire. Appellant's constitutional rights under the Double Jeopardy clauses of the United States and Texas constitutions protecting him from multiple punishments for the same offense were violated by the multiple convictions for first-degree arson.

———————————◆———————————

When Jeopardy Attaches

In order to determine whether someone has twice been placed in jeopardy, it is important to determine when they were first placed in jeopardy. The time differs depending on whether the first trial was before a jury or judge. Jeopardy attaches in a jury trial when the jurors are empaneled and sworn.[162] The jury is empaneled and sworn after jury selection but before the prosecutor reads the indictment in open court. "The reason for holding that jeopardy attaches when the jury is empaneled and sworn lies in the need to protect the interest of an accused in retaining a chosen jury."[163]

For a bench trial, "jeopardy attaches when both sides have announced ready, and the defendant has pled to the charging instrument."[164] The rationale for jeopardy attaching at this stage is that "[o]nce a defendant has pled 'not guilty,' the issue between the State and the defendant has formed and he has a right to have the trier of fact decide that issue."[165]

If the defendant was tried and acquitted, the first trial was terminated due to prosecutorial or judicial misconduct, or the appellate court found the evidence legally insufficient resulting in an acquittal on appeal, the defendant may raise a claim of double jeopardy if the State charges him a second time for the same offense.[166] This is done through a special plea.[167] A defendant may also claim double jeopardy when he has been convicted of a lesser-included offense and he is subsequently re-tried for the greater offense to which he was acquitted by the first jury,[168] or when he is convicted of both the greater offense and its lesser-included offense.[169] The reason the latter

---

[162] *Hill v. State*, 90 S.W.3d 308, 313 (Tex. Crim. App. 2002).

[163] *Crist v. Bretz*, 437 U.S. 28, 35-37 (1978).

[164] *State v. Torres*, 805 S.W.2d 418, 421 (Tex. Crim. App. 1991).

[165] *State v. Torres*, 780 S.W.2d 513, 516 (Tex. App.—Corpus Christi 1989), *aff'd*, 805 S.W.2d 418 (Tex. Crim. App. 1991).

[166] TEX. CODE CRIM. PROC. ANN. art. 27.05 (West 2016).

[167] *Id.*

[168] TEX. CODE CRIM. PROC. ANN. art. 37.14 (West 2016).

[169] *Ex Parte Denton*, 399 S.W.3d 540, 547 (Tex. Crim. App. 2013).

example violates double jeopardy is because the defendant is being punished multiple times for committing the same offense.

What happens when the defendant is accused of the same offense in both state and federal court? For example, it is common for felons in possession of weapons to be prosecuted by both federal and state prosecutors. Federal and state prosecutions for the same offense are allowed by both judicial systems because the defendant violates "the statutes of two separate sovereigns and thus commit[s] two separate offenses."[170]

Finally, as discussed earlier in this chapter, a subsequent prosecution following a mistrial due to a hung jury, whether in the guilt/innocence stage or at the punishment stage of trial, does not result in a double jeopardy violation.[171] If the jury cannot agree at the guilt/innocence stage, the jury is dismissed without a final verdict. Therefore, the prosecutor can pursue a second trial with a new jury.

◆

Practice Questions

Bar examiners ask between two and five questions about trial on each bar exam. Evidence is the only other topic that is tested this frequently. While this chapter has the most questions of any chapter in this book, consider practicing them all; many of these questions have appeared on numerous bar exams.

In most chapters, practice questions are organized in chronological order. However, because there are so many areas of law addressed in this chapter, the questions for this topic are organized differently. They track the organization of this chapter. The questions within each subtopic are not organized by the date they appeared on the bar exam. They are either organized in the way the subtopics appear within the chapter, or they are organized in a common-sense way. For example, in the Mistrials subsection, a question about guilt/innocence phase mistrials appears before a question

---

[170] *Ex parte Gary*, 895 S.W.2d 465, 468 (Tex. App.—Amarillo 1995, pet. ref'd); *Hill v. Beto*, 390 F.2d 640, 641 (5th Cir. 1968).
[171] TEX. CODE CRIM. PROC. ANN. art. 36.33 (West 2016); *Ellis v. State*, 99 S.W.3d 783, 787 (Tex. App.—Houston [1st Dist.] 2003, pet. ref'd).

about punishment phase mistrials. Each subsection of questions is labeled by topic to make answering the questions easier.

Bifurcation

1. (F-2013) Defendant is charged with a felony offense. Prosecutor has a funeral to attend tomorrow. To save time, Prosecutor requests Judge combine the evidence from both phases of trial into one phase, rather than two. He also suggests the jury render its decisions on one verdict instead of two. The Court denies his request.

    Did the Court make the correct ruling? Explain.

    _____

    _____

    _____

    _____

    _____

Trial Election

2. (F-2015, F-2007, J-2005, J-2004, F-2004, and J-2000) Defendant decides she wants a trial and asks you whether the case will be tried before a judge or a jury.

    a. What procedural step must you take to make this choice and who makes it? When must the step be taken? Does the decision have to be the same for both phases of trial? Explain.

    _____

    _____

    _____

    _____

    _____

b. (F-2009 and J-2003) Can Defendant change her punishment election midway through trial? May Prosecutor object to this change?

_____

_____

_____

_____

_____

Note: Remember that questions about the time to file elections for both phases of trial, discussed in Chapter 7, have been asked on a number of past exams: F-2011 (punishment election), F-2010 (punishment election), F-2009 (punishment election), F-2008 (punishment election), J-2007 (punishment election), F-2007 (trial election), J-2005 (trial election), J-2004 (trial election), F-2004 (trial election), F-2001 (punishment election), and J-2000 (trial election).

Joinder and Severance

3. (F-2015 and J-2010) Defendant is charged with three crimes arising out of the same transaction. You are concerned he will be unfairly prejudiced if a single trial is held on all three charges.

   What procedural step, if any, can you take to obtain separate trials for the three charges? Could taking this procedural step affect Defendant's sentence? Explain.

_____

_____

_____

_____

_____

4. (F-2016, F-2014, J-2012, and F-2009) Your client, Defendant, has no criminal record. Co-defendant, however, has a lengthy criminal record. Prosecutor wants to try both defendants together. Judge ruled Prosecutor will be allowed to admit Co-defendant's criminal record into evidence at the joint trial.

What procedural step, if any, can you take to avoid the introduction of these records, what will you argue, and how should Judge rule? Explain.

_____

_____

_____

_____

_____

5. (F-2016) Defendant A and Defendant B are charged with robbing a store clerk together on May 12.

    May Prosecutor try them jointly, even though they are charged in two separate indictments?

_____

_____

_____

_____

_____

Defendant's Rights at Trial

a. Speedy Trial

6. (J-2002) Nine months after the grand jury indicts Defendant, the case has not been set for trial, and the State has not yet announced that it is ready to try the case.

    What procedural step should you take? What will you argue? Explain.

_____

_____

_____

_____

_____

b. Presumption of Innocence

7. (J-2010) Prosecutor asserts, during closing argument:

"Members of the jury, you heard the State's witnesses. We proved our case. The presumption of innocence exists to protect only the innocent, and it disappeared once I offered some evidence of Defendant's guilt. Proof beyond a reasonable doubt likewise exists only in cases where people are innocent. It doesn't apply in this case because Defendant is clearly guilty."

Should you object to this argument? If so, on what ground(s) will you object?

_____

_____

_____

_____

_____

Note: Bar examiners have asked questions related to strikes for cause on the grounds of presumption of innocence on the following exams: F-2014 (juror read about case in newspaper and believes Defendant is guilty), J-2009 (juror believes Defendant is guilty based on fact he was indicted), and J-2001 (juror believes Defendant is guilty). The presumption of innocence as it relates to prospective juror bias is discussed in more detail in Chapter 11.

c. The Defendant's Presence at Trial

8. (J-2014, F-2010, F-2007, and J-2002) Defendant, who is charged with a felony offense, is dissatisfied with the progress of trial. As a result, Defendant, who is on bond, fails to appear in court on the third day of trial, which is a day when several witnesses for the State are testifying.

What is the general rule regarding the presence of the accused in a felony case and in a misdemeanor case? Can the trial proceed in the Defendant's absence under these circumstances?

_____

_____

_____

_____

_____

d. Confrontation Clause

9. (F-2016 and F-2013) Co-defendant gave a statement implicating himself and your client, Defendant, in a burglary. Defendant did not give a statement to the police. Prosecutor would like to admit Co-defendant's statement as evidence of both defendants' culpability.

    What remedies will you seek and what will you argue?

_____

_____

_____

_____

_____

e. Right to Testify or Not Testify

10. (J-2009, J-2009, F-2009, F-2007, J-2006, F-2006, F-2005, J-2003, F-2003, F-2002, and F-2001) During trial, Prosecutor stands up to call her next witness, and says, "We call Defendant to the stand." You object.

    What are the reasons for your objection, and how should Judge rule?

_____

_____

_____

_____

_____

Motions in Limine

11. (J-2016, F-2014, J-2010, J-2008, F-2007, J-2005, F-2005, J-2004, J-2001, and F-2001) Before trial begins, Prosecutor tells you she wishes to introduce evidence of Defendant's extraneous acts of misconduct through Witness. You are concerned Prosecutor will refer to these acts during her opening statement.

    What procedural step, if any, can you take to prevent Prosecutor from mentioning them? What must you do to preserve the issue for appeal? Explain.

    _____

    _____

    _____

    _____

    _____

Order of Trial

a. Reading the Indictment and Plea

12. (J-2016, F-2012, and F-2005) After the jury is empaneled, what are the next two things that happen during trial? If these two steps are skipped, can the error be fixed later during trial? Explain.

    _____

    _____

    _____

    _____

    _____

b. Opening Statement

13. (J-2015, J-2013, J-2009, J-2006, J-2004, F-2004, J-2001, and J-2000) Prosecutor announces she will make an opening statement after the jury is empaneled.

a. Are you required to make your opening statement immediately after Prosecutor's opening statement? Explain.

_____

_____

_____

_____

_____

b. If Prosecutor changes her mind and decides not to make an opening statement, can you make one before the State calls its first witness?

_____

_____

_____

_____

_____

c. **Proving Identification**

14. (J-2015, J-2010, J-2007 and J-2000) Prosecutor intends to call Victim to testify during Defendant's trial. You have concerns about the identification in this case. Officer showed Victim a photo of Defendant, told Victim Defendant was arrested for the crime, and then asked whether Defendant was the perpetrator. Victim replied he was.

What procedural step can you take to prevent Victim from identifying the Defendant? What will you argue to support this procedure?

_____

_____

_____

_____

_____

d. Jury Instructions

15. Explain whether the following jury instructions are legally permissible:

    a. (J-2015 and F-2010) "You are not bound to follow the State's DNA expert's opinion that Defendant's DNA was found at the scene. You are the ultimate judges of the credibility and reliability of that opinion. Remember that expert was paid by the State who wants to convict Defendant."

    _____

    _____

    _____

    _____

    _____

    b. (J-2014 and F-2009) Prosecutor's proffered definition of reasonable doubt, which is offered over your objection.

    _____

    _____

    _____

    _____

    _____

    c. (F-2006) An instruction to the jury regarding Defendant's right to remain silent in a case where Defendant did not take the stand.

    _____

    _____

    _____

    _____

    _____

16. (J-2012 and J-2000) You would like the jury to consider an acquittal based upon the defense you raised at trial: self-defense. What procedural

step should you take to allow the jury to consider this option? What additional step must you take to preserve the issue for appeal if Judge denies the jury this option? Explain.

_____

_____

_____

_____

_____

17. (F-2001) What must Judge do with the jury charge: read it to the jury, give a copy to the jury, neither, or both? If he must do any of these things, when must he do them? Explain.

_____

_____

_____

_____

_____

18. (J-2009) Judge prepares the jury charge. You examine it and notice that it contains statutory law, definitions, and a verdict form but no way for the jury to understand how to apply these legal concepts to the facts of the case. You ask Judge in writing to include a section that does this, but Judge denies your request. Is Judge correct?

_____

_____

_____

_____

_____

e. Lesser Included Offenses

19. (J-2010 and J-2008) At the close of evidence, you believe Prosecutor, at most, proved a lesser-included offense of the original charged offense. If the jury agrees, it could convict Defendant of a lower level crime. What

procedural step can you take to give the jury the option of convicting Defendant of the lesser crime? When and how can you take that step?

_____

_____

_____

_____

_____

f. Closing Arguments

20. (J-2008, J-2004, and J-2002) What is the order and number of closing arguments permitted in Texas criminal cases? Explain.

_____

_____

_____

_____

_____

21. Prosecutor makes the following arguments. Are these arguments appropriate? If not, on what grounds, if any, can you object to them?

a. (J-2010, J-2009, and F-2008) "Members of the jury, you have heard all of the testimony and know beyond a reasonable doubt that Defendant is guilty. Do you think I would risk my legal career by putting forth a case if I didn't believe it to be true? I know for a fact that each one of my witnesses told the truth on the stand. Defense counsel, on the other hand, has put forth a bunch of smoke and mirrors in an effort to trick you. Do not fall for his tricks."

_____

_____

_____

_____

_____

b. (F-2002) "We all know that crime is a serious problem in our community. The community has given you, members of the jury, the opportunity to do something about it today. Do not let your fellow citizens down."

_____

_____

_____

_____

_____

g. Motion for Directed Verdict

22. (F-2014, J-2007, F-2005, F-2004, F-2002, and F-2001) After Prosecutor rests his case, you realize he failed to prove the offense occurred in El Paso County.

What procedural step can you take to bring this to Judge's attention? When must you take this step, and should you perform this step within the presence of the jury? Explain.

_____

_____

_____

_____

_____

h. Jury Deliberations

23. (J-2011) The jury retires to deliberate. After two hours of deliberation, the jurors disagree about what Witness said on cross-examination.

What can the jury do, if anything, to settle this dispute? Explain.

_____

_____

_____

i. Verdict

24. (J-2009, J-2007, and J-2003) What is the burden of proof required to support a guilty verdict and who has it? How many jurors must agree to support a guilty verdict? What number is required to support a not guilty verdict? What happens if the verdict is not unanimous as to guilt/innocence? Explain.

_____

_____

_____

_____

_____

Mistrials

25. (F-2010) Following opening statements in a felony case, one of the jurors suffers a stroke and is admitted to the hospital. The prosecutor makes a motion for a mistrial, stating that in Texas, no fewer than 12 jurors can return a verdict in a felony trial.

    Is Prosecutor correct? Explain.

_____

_____

_____

_____

_____

26. (F-2005 and J-2001) Following the charge and the closing arguments during the guilt/innocence phase of trial, the jury begins to deliberate. After two days of deliberating, the jury announces that it is deadlocked. You move for a mistrial, but Prosecutor opposes.

Must Prosecutor agree with you before Judge grants a mistrial? Explain.

_____

_____

_____

_____

_____

27. (F-2013, F-2008, and F-2001) The jury cannot agree on punishment for Defendant. You request a mistrial, asking Judge for a retrial of both the guilt/innocence and punishment phases.

What should Judge do? Explain.

_____

_____

_____

_____

_____

Witnesses

   a. The Rule

28. (F-2009 and J-2000) As defense counsel, you realize several minutes into the testimony of the State's first witness that you forgot to invoke the Rule. You then announce to the judge you wish to do so.

What is the Rule? Under these circumstances, is it too late to invoke it? Name two possible sanctions that can be imposed if the Rule is violated.

_____

_____

_____

_____

_____

b. Judge as Witness

29. (J-2005, F-2005, and J-2001) You would like to call the presiding Judge as a witness during trial to testify that Defendant arrives to court on time and is well behaved during docket. Can Defendant call Judge as a witness? Explain.

_____

_____

_____

_____

_____

c. Accomplice Witnesses

30. (F-2016, F-2014, F-2013, F-2011, and F-2008) Co-defendant, who pled guilty, is the State's first witness to testify at Defendant's trial. Though the State has physical evidence and law-enforcement testimony to corroborate Co-defendant's account of the events, Co-defendant's testimony is so compelling that Prosecutor is tempted to rest her case after the Co-defendant testifies. Is Co-defendant's testimony alone enough to convict Defendant? Explain.

_____

_____

_____

_____

_____

d. Witness Competency

31. (F-2015, J-2007, and J-2002) During trial, Prosecutor announces that he will be calling Child, a six-year-old witness to the crime. You object on the grounds that children are not competent witnesses.

How should Judge rule? What can Judge do, if anything, to test Child's competency? Explain.

_____

_____

_____

_____

_____

Double Jeopardy

32. (F-2012) Defendant is charged with being a felon in possession of a weapon, which is a crime under federal and Texas law.

Does the double jeopardy clause prohibit his prosecution in Texas if he is also under indictment in a federal court for the exact same offense? Explain.

_____

_____

_____

_____

_____

33. (J-2008) Does it violate the double jeopardy clause for a grand jury to indict Defendant for a lesser-included offense after he has been convicted of the greater offense? Explain.

_____

_____

_____

_____

_____

34. (F-2008) Is it a violation of the double jeopardy clause for Judge to retry Defendant on the issue of punishment after a jury has returned a guilty verdict but was hung on punishment? Explain.

_____

_____

_____

_____

_____

———————————◆———————————

Chapter 13
Punishment

Introduction

Following a conviction, a defendant faces punishment. There are long-standing policies for punishing individuals who violate criminal laws. In theory, criminal punishment serves the following goals: (1) deterring future criminal activity by the present defendant and others who aim to commit future crimes; (2) rehabilitating the present defendant; (3) restoring the victim; (4) seeking vengeance against the defendant on behalf of the victim or the victim's family; and (5) incapacitating the defendant by incarcerating him.

In Texas, guilt is decided before punishment.[1] Once a defendant has pled guilty or no contest or has been found guilty following a trial, the question becomes, "What punishment fits this crime and this defendant?" This chapter examines the punishment process.

————————◆————————

---

[1] TEX. CODE CRIM. PROC. ANN. art. 37.07 §2 (West 2016).

Punishment Election

A criminal defendant has a statutory and constitutional right to have a jury assess punishment in all Texas criminal cases.[2] This is highly unusual; the federal system does not permit jury sentencing, nor do most states. In most jurisdictions across the nation and the world, it is the judge alone who assesses punishment following a trial.

In Texas, all but Class C misdemeanor trials are bifurcated. In Class C misdemeanor trials, the judge or the jury simultaneously determines guilt/innocence and punishment during deliberations. In all other criminal trials, the fact finder first determines whether the defendant is guilty or not guilty. If there is a verdict of guilt, the punishment phase of trial follows.

In Chapter 12, you learned the defendant must choose whether her trial will be heard by a judge or a jury. This is called *election*. The defendant must elect which fact finder—judge or jury—will hear the first and second phases of trial. If the defendant wants the jury to assess punishment, she must file an election seven days before the pretrial hearing,[3] or before voir dire begins, if she does not have a pretrial hearing.[4] If the defendant does not file an election to have the jury assess punishment, the judge will assess punishment.[5]

Sometimes a defendant may wish to change the election after trial has begun or after the fact finder reaches the verdict. The Code allows a defendant the opportunity to untimely change her punishment election following a guilty verdict only if the State consents to the change.[6]

———————◆———————

Punishment Evidence

The fact finder's role during the guilt/innocence stage is to determine whether there is proof beyond reasonable doubt that the defendant committed the charged offense. The fact finder's role during the punishment

---

[2] TEX. CODE CRIM. PROC. ANN. art. 1.12 (West 2016).

[3] TEX. CODE CRIM. PROC. ANN. arts. 27.02(7), and 28.01(2) (West 2016).

[4] TEX. CODE CRIM. PROC. ANN. art. 37.07 §2 (West 2016); *Postell v. State*, 693 S.W.2d 462, 464–65 (Tex. Crim. App. 1985).

[5] TEX. CODE CRIM. PROC. ANN. art. 37.07 §2(b) (West 2016).

[6] *Id.*

phase is entirely different. The judge or jury must determine, given the facts of the present crime, the facts of charged or uncharged extraneous offenses (*i.e.*, other crimes committed during, before, or after the charged crime), and the facts of bad acts how this defendant should be punished. Is it possible to rehabilitate the defendant? Is this crime the first offense the defendant has committed? Is this defendant a danger to the community, a habitual criminal, or someone who has been given numerous opportunities to rehabilitate herself to no avail? Is there mitigating evidence that suggests the defendant was less culpable than others or the circumstances were less serious? How has this crime impacted the victim and the community? Should the defendant remain in the community or be incarcerated? Does the defendant have a family he supports financially, and how will his punishment affect them? There are many fact-specific and defendant-specific questions that must be resolved by the judge or jury during the punishment phase of trial.

The fact finder may consider the evidence admitted during the guilt/innocence and punishment phases of trial in determining what punishment is appropriate. Different types of evidence may be offered during each phase. The Code permits the following evidence to be considered during the punishment phase of trial:

> [E]vidence may be offered by the state and the defendant as to any matter the court deems relevant to sentencing, including but not limited to the prior criminal record of the defendant, his general reputation [which is an exception to the hearsay rule], his character, an opinion regarding his character, the circumstances of the offense for which he is being tried, and, notwithstanding Rules 404 and 405, Texas Rules of Evidence, any other evidence of an extraneous crime or bad act that is shown beyond a reasonable doubt by evidence to have been committed by the defendant or for which he could be held criminally responsible, regardless of whether he has previously been charged with or finally convicted of the crime or act. A court may consider as a factor in mitigating punishment the conduct of a defendant while participating in a program ... as a condition of release on bail. Additionally, ... evidence may be offered by the state and the defendant of a [juvenile] adjudication of delinquency based on a violation by the defendant of a ... felony ... or ... a misdemeanor punishable by confinement in jail.[7]

---

[7] TEX. CODE CRIM. PROC. ANN. art. 37.07 §3 (a)(1) (West 2016).

As you see, the law requires that extraneous conduct and bad acts be proven beyond a reasonable doubt before they can be considered by the fact finder.

The evidence that is admitted during the punishment phase differs from the evidence admitted during the guilt/innocence phase of trial. The Court of Criminal Appeals explained the evidentiary basis for Texas's bifurcated, guilt-first-punishment-second criminal procedure:

> ...[S]plitting the trial on the issues of guilt and punishment ... [allows] either side [to] offer evidence of the defendant's prior criminal record, his character or reputation. Such procedure was obviously designed to take the blindfolds off the judge or jury when it came to assessing punishment. It authorized the introduction of evidence on punishment not heretofore held to be generally admissible. It did, however, limit such introduction to the penalty stage to prevent the accused from being tried as a criminal generally prior to the determination of the issue of guilt. It thus allowed evidence critical to an enlightened determination of punishment but avoided the possibility of prejudice on the issue of guilt.[8]

The guilt/innocence phase requires the fact finder to answer a specific question: did the State prove the defendant committed the charged crime beyond a reasonable doubt? Evidence that is relevant to that question will be admitted, but the question in the punishment phase is more ambiguous: what punishment is fitting? As a result, determining what evidence is relevant during the punishment phase can be difficult, as the next case illustrates.

Raul Rodriguez v. State
203 S.W.3d 837
(Tex. Crim. App. 2006)

Appellant pled guilty to escape and providing implements for escape and elected to have a jury determine his sentence. He was sentenced to 10 years for escape and 5 years for providing implements for escape and fined $10,000 for each of the convictions. Appellant appealed the sentence, claiming that evidence of the crimes of others was improperly admitted. The court of appeals held that the trial court did not err in admitting evidence regarding the post-escape crimes of the escapees. We granted review to determine whether evidence of crimes committed by others is relevant to a

---

[8] *Brumfield v. State*, 445 S.W.2d 732, 738 (Tex. Crim. App. 1969).

defendant's sentence, and if relevant, whether such evidence is admissible under Rule of Evidence 403.

We hold that the trial court did not err in admitting evidence of the crimes committed by persons other than the defendant at the defendant's sentencing and affirm the judgment of the court of appeals.

FACTS

Appellant's son, Michael Rodriguez, was convicted of murder and sentenced to life in prison, which he was serving at the maximum security Connally Unit prison in Kennedy. On one Sunday while Appellant was visiting him in prison, Michael told Appellant that a guard was going to help him escape and give him a ride to the nearby Wal-Mart. Michael asked Appellant if he would help him flee by getting him a car and leaving it in the Wal-Mart parking lot on Tuesday morning. Appellant initially told his son that he was unsure about helping him, but he said that if he could he would get a car and leave it in the parking lot with a red bow in the dashboard and the key in the muffler. When Appellant left the prison that day, he went to the convenience store he owned and went through the classified section of the newspaper looking for a car to buy. He found a Suburban for sale for $3700 and cut out the advertisement. The next day, Appellant gave the newspaper clipping and $4000 to his friend, Patsy Gomez, and asked her to go buy the car for him. Patsy purchased the car that evening. The following morning, she went to Appellant's convenience store, and Appellant told her that his friend, Ernesto Perez, was going to take the Suburban to the Wal-Mart in Kennedy and Patsy was to follow Ernesto and bring him back to San Antonio in her car. Ernesto believed that they were taking the Suburban to Kennedy to meet someone who wanted to purchase the car from Patsy and was not informed of the plan to leave it there for Michael. Appellant gave Patsy a red bow to place in the dashboard so that his son could identify the car and gave her a magnetic key holder to use to hide the key in the muffler. He also gave her a bag containing $300 and instructed her to place the cash and the title to the car under the floor mat.

On December 13, 2000, Michael and six other inmates escaped from prison by assaulting multiple guards, threatening them with shanks, tying them up, stealing their clothes, and stealing 14 pistols and one shotgun from the prison armory before fleeing in a State pickup truck. The inmates drove to the Wal-Mart where they abandoned the State pickup truck and found the

Suburban furnished by Appellant. The escapees, who were referred to as the Connally Seven [or Texas Seven], committed several crimes over the next month, including multiple armed robberies and the murder of a police officer, before being apprehended in Colorado.

Because his son was one of the escapees, officers questioned Appellant several times during their investigation and asked him if he had any knowledge of the escape. Due to the media coverage, Appellant was aware of the crimes being committed by the escapees, however he did not inform investigators of the Suburban he provided or aid law enforcement in any way during the pursuit of the Connally Seven, despite the repeated requests for information leading to their arrest.

After the escapees were arrested, investigators learned of Appellant's role in the escape. Appellant pled guilty to two charges, second-degree felony escape and third-degree felony of providing implements for escape, and elected to have a jury determine his sentence. At the punishment phase of his trial, the State offered evidence relating to the crimes committed by the escapees as well as the penitentiary packets of the escapees, which described their criminal histories, including the crimes for which they were incarcerated in the Connally Unit. The trial judge admitted the evidence over the objections of the defense. Appellant testified that, other than what Michael said regarding the guard driving him to the Wal–Mart, he did not know about the events that were supposed to take place the day of the escape. He stated that prior to the news reports of the escape, he never knew about the six other inmates who escaped with his son, and he had never heard the names of any of the other escapees. Before summation, the defense filed its Special Requested Jury Instruction Number One, which sought to have the jury disregard the evidence of the crimes committed by the escapees, contending that it was erroneously admitted. The trial court refused to give the instruction offered by the defense and, instead, gave its own instruction that the jury could not consider the other crimes evidence unless it found beyond a reasonable doubt that Raul Rodriguez "intended that such bad acts or offenses would be committed by the other persons, or that he should reasonably have anticipated that such bad acts or offenses would be committed by the other persons."

Appellant asked the jury to consider his application for probation, but instead the jury sentenced him to 10 years for escape and 5 years for providing implements for escape, as well as a fine of $10,000 for each of the convictions.

COURT OF APPEALS

Appellant appealed his sentence, claiming that the evidence admitted at his sentencing hearing was irrelevant, was substantially more prejudicial than probative, and violated the Due Process Clause of the Fourteenth Amendment to the United States Constitution. The court of appeals held that the trial court could reasonably determine that the evidence showed Appellant's character and moral blameworthiness and therefore, was helpful to the jury in deciding the appropriate sentence. Additionally, the court determined that the proper review is whether the trial court abused its discretion and held that the trial court's decision to admit the evidence over Appellant's Rule 403 objections was not outside the zone of reasonable agreement. Finally, the court held that the admission of the evidence did not deny Appellant a fair trial.

ANALYSIS

Because trial courts are in the best position to decide questions of admissibility, we review a trial court's decision regarding the admissibility of evidence under an abuse of discretion standard. *See Montgomery*, 810 S.W.2d [at] 391 (trial court "has the best vantage from which to decide" admissibility questions). This standard requires an appellate court to uphold a trial court's admissibility decision when that decision is within the zone of reasonable disagreement. An appellate court would misapply the appellate abuse of discretion standard of review to reverse a trial court's admissibility decision solely because the appellate court disagreed with it.

Relevance

Appellant first contends that evidence of crimes committed by other persons is not relevant to his sentence when Appellant himself did not commit the other crimes, was not criminally responsible for their commission, did not intend their commission, and could not have reasonably anticipated their commission.

Article 37.07, § 3(a)(1) of the Texas Code of Criminal Procedure states that during the sentencing phase, the State may offer evidence "as to any matter the court deems relevant to sentencing." The term "relevant" is not defined, however the statute also provides that evidence relevant to sentencing includes, but is not limited to: (1) the prior criminal record of the defendant; (2) the defendant's general reputation; (3) the defendant's general character; (4) an opinion regarding the defendant's character; (5) the circumstances of the offense being tried; and (6) notwithstanding Texas Rules of Evidence 404 and 405, any other evidence of an extraneous crime or bad act that is shown beyond a reasonable doubt by evidence to have been committed by the defendant or for which the defendant could be held criminally responsible, regardless of whether the defendant has previously been charged with or finally convicted of the crime or act.

In *Murphy v. State*, 777 S.W.2d 44, 63 (Tex. Crim. App. 1988), we noted that the admissibility of evidence at the punishment phase of a non-capital felony offense is a function of policy rather than relevance. We discussed this in *Miller–El v. State*, and stated that:

> This is so because by and large there are no discreet factual issues at the punishment stage. There are simply no distinct "facts ... of consequence" that proffered evidence can be said to make more or less likely to exist. Rather, "deciding what punishment to assess is a normative process, not intrinsically factbound." What evidence should be admitted to inform that normative decision is not a question of logical relevance, but of policy. Apart from Article 37.07, § 3(a), however, the Legislature has not set a coherent policy to guide courts in discerning what evidence is appropriate to the punishment deliberation. Moving to fill the policy void, this Court has declared that, subject to limitations imposed by Article 37.07, § 3(a), evidence of "the circumstances of the offense itself or ... the defendant himself" will be admissible at the punishment phase.[9]

Determining what is relevant then should be a question of what is helpful to the jury in determining the appropriate sentence for a particular defendant in a particular case. In a non-capital felony punishment hearing, the jury has discretion to assess whatever punishment it sees fit, within the prescribed range.

It is also noteworthy that, for the offense of escape, Appellant was charged as a party. Texas Penal Code section 7.02(a)(2) allowed Appellant to be charged as a party to the offense of escape although he was not present

---

[9] *Miller–El v. State*, 782 S.W.2d 892, 894–95 (Tex. Crim. App. 1990) (footnotes and citations omitted).

during the actual commission of the crime. As a party to an offense, a person is criminally responsible for the conduct of the other parties to the offense. Thus, because Appellant aided in the commission of the escape, he could be held criminally responsible for the offense.

Evidence that the escapees were on a month-long crime spree while evading the police is relevant to show that Appellant was aware that more crimes were being committed as a result of the escape he had aided, but he still failed to go to the police to assist in the recapture. And, due to the nature of the offense of escape, the penitentiary packets of the escapees are relevant to help the jury determine whether the crimes committed between the escape and recapture were foreseeable. While Appellant was not present at the crimes introduced at his sentencing phase, in determining Appellant's moral blameworthiness, a jury may reasonably consider the offenses that occurred as a result of Appellant's conduct of aiding in the escape. The evidence of extraneous crimes committed by others was relevant to Appellant's sentencing.

Rule 403

Next, Appellant contends that Rule 403 of Texas Rules of Evidence does not permit a large amount of damaging misconduct evidence at his sentencing trial when the defendant did not commit the misconduct, was not criminally responsible for it, and could not reasonably have anticipated that others would do so.

As stated above, the trial court's decision on questions of relevance in sentencing is broad. And, the evidence of the crimes of the escapees was relevant to show the circumstances of the offense for which Appellant was charged. However, under Texas Rule of Evidence 403, even relevant evidence may be excluded if its probative value is substantially outweighed by the danger of unfair prejudice, confusion of issues, misleading the jury, considerations of undue delay, or needless presentation of cumulative evidence. We have held that a Rule 403 analysis may include considerations of: (1) the probative value of the evidence; (2) the potential of the evidence to impress the jury in some irrational, but nevertheless indelible way; (3) the time the proponent needs to develop the evidence; and (4) the proponent's need for the evidence. For this Court to overrule the trial court's Rule 403 analysis, we would have to say that the evidence lay outside the "zone of reasonable disagreement."

The evidence did not take an inordinate amount of time to present, and there is little danger that the evidence confused the issues or misled the jury. The evidence of the crimes committed by the escapees who were aided by Appellant had significant value in giving the jury the complete information regarding the offense for which Appellant was charged. Rather than confusing the issues, the evidence served to further the jury's understanding of the issues by explaining the circumstances surrounding the escape. The penitentiary packets of the escapees explain why they were in prison and lay the foundation for the discussion of the offense of escape. The past crimes of the escapees are also probative to help the jury determine the foreseeability of the crimes the escapees committed between the escape and the recapture. It would be extremely confusing to the jury if the circumstances surrounding the offense of escape were not explained to them.

Appellant is correct that, although he was charged as a party to the escape, he could not be charged as a party to the aggravated robberies or the capital murder committed by the escapees. However, the evidence regarding the post-escape crimes of the escapees was highly probative of Appellant's moral blameworthiness for not assisting the police in the recapture of the escapees. Testimony indicated that it would have been easier to find the escapees if they had been using a stolen car because the police would have had a description and license number of the stolen vehicle to search for. Appellant watched the television coverage of the crimes being committed by the Connally Seven, yet rather than informing the investigators of the Suburban he provided the escapees, he continued to lie to the police.

We disagree with Appellant that he could not have reasonably anticipated the commission of the crimes committed by the escapees. After Appellant pled guilty as a party to the escape, the jury could reasonably conclude that in facilitating the offense, he should have anticipated the events and circumstances surrounding the escape, including that additional crimes would be committed by the escapees in an attempt to evade police and prevent recapture. We also disagree that the evidence was unfairly prejudicial to Appellant. The evidence regarding the crimes committed by the escapees consisted of their penitentiary packets and testimony from officers who were searching for them after the escape. This evidence was not shocking or gruesome and is not the type of evidence that would impress the jury in some irrational way. The jury was informed that Appellant could not be charged with the post-escape crimes of the escapees, and the sentence assessed by the jury was within the prescribed range for the offenses with which Appellant was charged.

The court of appeals correctly determined that the trial court did not abuse its discretion in admitting the evidence of the crimes committed by the escapees for the jury to consider during the punishment phase of Appellant's trial.

CONCLUSION

[The] Texas Code of Criminal Procedure allows evidence regarding the circumstances of the offense being tried to be admitted at a defendant's sentencing hearing. In the case before us, admitting evidence of crimes committed by others was well within the trial court's discretion and it was not error for the jury to use the evidence to determine Appellant's moral blameworthiness for punishment purposes. Furthermore, the trial court did not err in conducting its Rule 403 analysis and concluding that the probative value of the evidence in explaining the circumstances of the charged offense was not substantially outweighed by the danger of unfair prejudice.

The judgment of the court of appeals is affirmed.

———————◆———————

Notes and Questions

1. If the defense makes a timely request for notice of intent to introduce evidence of bad acts or uncharged crimes during the punishment phase of trial, the prosecuting attorney must provide reasonable notice to the defendant.[10] The State's notice is reasonable if it includes the date, county, alleged crime or bad act, and victim.[11]

What happens if defense counsel timely files a request for notice of extraneous conduct and bad acts, and the State fails to provide notice? "The logical and proper consequence of [notice] violations ... is that the evidence is inadmissible."[12] Cautious prosecutors send notice of extraneous conduct evidence in every case whether or not the defense requests it. By doing this,

---

[10] TEX. CODE CRIM. PROC. ANN. art. 37.07 § 3(g) (West 2016).
[11] *Id.*
[12] *Roethel v. State*, 80 S.W.3d 276, 281 (Tex. App.—Austin 2002, no pet.).

the prosecutor is not prohibited from admitting extraneous conduct evidence during the punishment phase of trial.

2. The State can offer evidence of the defendant's prior criminal history during the punishment phase. This evidence is used for two distinct reasons. First, the State may ask the jury to enhance the defendant's punishment. Prior convictions, if included in the charging instrument, serve as enhancements, elevating the level of punishment the defendant could receive. For example, a defendant who has been convicted of multiple crimes may be considered a habitual offender, which carries a more severe punishment.[13] An offender who commits multiple crimes of the same type may face a harsher punishment on subsequent convictions (e.g., theft offenses).

Not only do these enhancements affect punishment, they may also be jurisdictional by permitting a lower-level offense to be heard in a higher-level court (e.g., following two misdemeanor-level DWI convictions, a third DWI charge becomes a felony offense).[14] While jurisdictional enhancements must be proven during the guilt-innocence phase, punishment enhancements and prior criminal convictions are admissible during the punishment phase.

The defendant must enter a plea for these enhancements of true or not true; a not true plea requires the fact-finder to find the enhancement true before using it to assess a harsher punishment.[15] If the fact finder finds the enhancement true or if the defendant pleads true to the enhancing offense, the punishment range is elevated.

There is another reason why a defendant's criminal history is admissible. Even if the crimes do not legally enhance the punishment, they are still admissible as evidence the jury can consider in assessing the defendant's punishment. This is because the punishment phase asks the fact-finder to evaluate the person the defendant is, both past and present, in assessing punishment.

How does the prosecutor prove these past criminal convictions? One of the most common methods is by introducing a penitentiary packet, which was referenced in the case above. This is a group of documents produced by the Texas Department of Corrections, which is the agency that oversees Texas penitentiaries. These documents include a set of the defendant's

---

[13] E.g., TEX. PENAL CODE ANN. §§12.42 and 12.43 (West 2011).
[14] TEX. CODE CRIM. PROC. ANN. art. 36.01(a)(1) (West 2016).
[15] Id.

fingerprints and photos that were taken when he entered the prison, information about the type of crime for which he was convicted, and the date the sentence began. Another way to prove extraneous offenses is to call witnesses and victims of the defendant's old crimes to testify during the punishment phase of trial. In this way, the punishment phase may resemble a trial within a trial. Although the prosecutor may prove these crimes using business records or other forms of evidence, using "pen packets" and calling witnesses are the two most common ways to prove extraneous offenses.

3. One form of admissible punishment evidence is reputation or opinion evidence. Texas Rule of Evidence 405(a) describes this evidence as follows:

> When evidence of a person's character or character trait is admissible, it may be proved by testimony about the person's reputation or by testimony in the form of an opinion. On cross-examination of the character witness, inquiry may be made into relevant specific instances of the person's conduct.

Furthermore, Texas Rule of Evidence 608 permits bolstering of the witness's reputation for truthfulness or untruthfulness, but only after the witness's character for truthfulness has been attacked.

Questions that inquire about reputation seek to reveal the defendant's character. Sometimes a more general reputation trait, such as being a law-abiding citizen, is the subject of inquiry during the punishment phase of trial. The character trait that underlies the reputation or opinion inquiry must be relevant. For example, in an aggravated assault case, the defendant's reputation for violence (from the prosecutor's standpoint) or peacefulness (from the defense's position) is relevant. This kind of reputation evidence would not be relevant in a shoplifting trial. Reputation evidence can be used to confirm that the defendant's behavior during the crime was typical or out of the ordinary.

4. Mitigating evidence may be offered during the punishment phase. In capital murder cases, the jury is instructed to determine whether favorable evidence mitigates against a death sentence.[16] In murder cases, evidence the defendant acted under sudden passion mitigates punishment by reducing punishment from a first-degree level to a second-degree level.[17] Because

---

[16] TEX. CODE CRIM. PROC. ANN. art. 37.071 (d)(1) (West 2016).
[17] TEX. PENAL CODE ANN. §19.02(d) (West 2011).

sudden passion affects the punishment range, evidence of sudden passion is admitted during the punishment phase of trial. However, any type of relevant mitigating evidence is admissible during the punishment phase of trial.

Community Supervision

Most defendants would like to avoid incarceration or a conviction because they carry negative long-term economic and social consequences for defendants. A defendant who successfully completes community supervision may be able to avoid incarceration and perhaps even a conviction, depending on the type of community supervision she receives.

The Code defines community supervision as "the placement of a defendant by a court under a continuum of programs and sanctions, with conditions imposed by the court for a specified period."[18] Community supervision is thus a contract between the court and the defendant that requires the defendant to fulfill the conditions in order to live freely in the community. The judge must consider the safety of others and the ability of the defendant to fulfill these conditions in determining whether he should remain free. "The judge may impose any reasonable condition that is designed to protect or restore the community, protect or restore the victim, or punish, rehabilitate, or reform the defendant."[19]

The Code lists several community supervision conditions, but this list is not exhaustive; so long as the conditions are reasonable, they are permissible.[20] Community supervision conditions may include rehabilitative programs, drug treatment, mental health treatment, behavior modification, community service hours, and employment, education, and living conditions. In addition, the defendant may be required to pay restitution to the victim, abstain from alcohol and drug use, avoid association with disreputable people or places, and support dependents. All of these conditions and more are codified within the community supervision statute.[21] If the defendant

---

[18] TEX. CODE CRIM. PROC. ANN. art. 42.12 §2 (West 2016).
[19] TEX. CODE CRIM. PROC. ANN. art. 42.12 §11(a) (West 2016).
[20] *Id.*
[21] TEX. CODE CRIM. PROC. ANN. art. 42.12 §11 (West 2016).

completes all conditions and refrains from committing new crimes, he will successfully complete community supervision.

When a defendant is placed on community supervision, the judge assesses both a sentence, which is to be served if the defendant's community supervision is revoked, and a community supervision period. The sentence is the incarceration time the defendant will serve if the community supervision is revoked. The community supervision period is how long the person will be on probation or deferred adjudication. The length of community supervision does not need to match the length of the sentence. For example, the judge could sentence a defendant to five years in prison that is probated for ten years. This means the defendant will be on probation for ten years, but if that probation is revoked, the defendant will serve five years in prison. It is the judge who determines the length of both terms.

A prosecutor may recommend or bargain with the defendant for a specific sentence and probation length. When a defendant elects jury punishment and the jury recommends probation, the judge must follow the jury's recommendation and order probation.[22] However, the judge is not bound by the jury's recommended period of probation length.[23] In other words, if the jury recommends the defendant's sentence of five years be probated for five years, the judge may change the term of probation to eight years.

———————◆———————

---

[22] TEX. CODE CRIM. PROC. ANN. art. 42.12 §(4)(a) (West 2016) (the judge shall suspend the imposition of the sentence and place the defendant on community supervision if the jury makes that recommendation in the verdict). However, in a misdemeanor DWI case in which the defendant did not want probation, the jury assessed jail time, but the trial court nevertheless suspended the sentence by placing the defendant on probation. *Ivey v. State*, 277 S.W.3d 43, 45 (Tex. Crim. App. 2009). The Court of Criminal Appeals held that the trial court was permitted to suspend the sentence. *Id.*

[23] TEX. CODE CRIM. PROC. ANN. art. 42.12 §(4)(b) (West 2016); *Fuentez v. State*, 196 S.W.3d 839, 845 (Tex. App.—Eastland 2006, no pet.) (judge's probation term of ten years was permissible even though jury recommended probation term of five years).

Deferred Adjudication and Probation

The two most common forms of community supervision are probation and deferred adjudication.[24] Although the word *probation* no longer appears in the Code—it has been replaced by *community supervision*—most practitioners and even the Texas Court of Criminal Appeals still use this word to describe a form of community supervision.[25] Therefore, this chapter will use *probation* to refer to a specific form of community supervision and *community supervision* to refer to community supervision in general.

Probation and deferred adjudication bring about different outcomes. Probation results in a conviction, but it suspends imprisonment so long as the defendant complies with the conditions of probation.[26] If the defendant completes probation successfully, she will not face incarceration. However, she will have a conviction for the crime. Deferred adjudication, on the other hand, does not result in a conviction; rather, it defers (or postpones) a finding of guilt so long as the defendant complies with conditions and does not commit any new law violations.[27] If the defendant completes the deferred adjudication successfully, the defendant's plea of guilt is not entered. [28] Therefore, he does not have a conviction.

The Code grants judges the authority to place a defendant on community supervision when it best serves justice, the community, and the defendant.[29] However, the defendant has no right to receive community supervision as punishment. Probation can be bargained for with the State, recommended by a jury,[30] or ordered by a judge,[31] depending on the defendant's crime and criminal history.[32] Deferred adjudication can only be bargained for with the State or ordered by the judge.[33] It can never be granted by a jury.[34] Though

---

[24] See generally TEX. CODE CRIM. PROC. ANN. art. 42.12 (West 2016).

[25] *E.g., State v. Crook*, 248 S.W.3d 172, 173 (Tex. Crim. App. 2008) ("The jury assessed punishment on each count at ten years' confinement with a recommendation of community supervision (probation) for this portion of appellee's sentence.").

[26] TEX. CODE CRIM. PROC. ANN. art. 42.12 §2 (2)(B) (West 2016).

[27] TEX. CODE CRIM. PROC. ANN. art. 42.12 §5(a) (West 2016).

[28] TEX. CODE CRIM. PROC. ANN. art. 42.12 §3(g) (West 2016).

[29] TEX. CODE CRIM. PROC. ANN. art. 42.12 §3(a) (West 2016).

[30] TEX. CODE CRIM. PROC. ANN. art. 42.12 §4 (West 2016).

[31] TEX. CODE CRIM. PROC. ANN. art. 42.12 §3 (West 2016).

[32] TEX. CODE CRIM. PROC. ANN. art. 42.12 § 4 (West 2016).

[33] TEX. CODE CRIM. PROC. ANN. art. 42.12 §5(a) (West 2016).

the Code permits the jury to recommend probation,[35] it prohibits a jury from recommending deferred adjudication following a guilty plea or verdict.[36] The reason is that once the fact finder enters a guilty verdict, the verdict can no longer be deferred. As a result, no jury can recommend that a defendant be placed on deferred adjudication.[37]

Eligibility for Community Supervision

The Code requires that the defendant meet three eligibility requirements in order to be placed on probation:

1. The defendant must file a written sworn motion for probation with the judge before trial begins or seven days before the pretrial hearing, if there is one;
2. The motion for probation must state that the defendant has not previously been convicted of a felony in this or any other state; and
3. The fact finder must enter in the verdict form that the information in the defndant's motion is true.[38]

The fact finder must determine whether the sworn motion declaring the defendant has no prior felony convictions is true. If so, the defendant may receive probation.

In most cases, the prosecutor is well aware of the defendant's criminal history and whether she is eligible for community supervision. However, sometimes a defendant may have a prior felony conviction the prosecutor has not uncovered. A defendant who attempts to hide prior felony convictions yet swears under oath that she has no prior felony conviction in

---

[34] *Id.*

[35] TEX. CODE CRIM. PROC. ANN. art. 42.12 §3(a) (West 2016) ("A judge . . . after conviction or a plea of guilty or nolo contendere, may suspend the imposition of the sentence and place the defendant on community supervision . . . .").

[36] TEX. CODE CRIM. PROC. ANN. art. 42.12 §5(a) (West 2016) ("the judge may, after receiving a plea of guilty or plea of nolo contendere . . . defer further proceedings without entering an adjudication of guilt").

[37] *Id.*

[38] TEX. CODE CRIM. PROC. ANN. arts. 27.02, 28.01, and 42.12 §4(e) (West 2016).

her motion for probation can be prosecuted for aggravated perjury.[39] When a client confides in her lawyer that she has a prior felony conviction but would like to nevertheless file a sworn motion for probation claiming she has never been convicted of a felony offense, the lawyer must refuse to do so. The lawyer cannot ethically reveal the defendant's criminal history to the prosecutor, as it arose from privileged communication, but the lawyer also cannot suborn perjury by filing the motion knowing the defendant's sworn testimony is false.

Additional Limitations to Community Supervision Eligibility

The Austin Court of Appeals has described the community supervision statute as follows: "Article 42.12 is an 'amendment-abused' statute and it is difficult for judges and others to keep abreast of the frequent legislative changes and of the temporary retention of former laws found only in the historical and statutory notes following a codified statute."[40] Not only is Article 42.12 the longest and most complex statute in the Texas Code of Criminal Procedure, but it contains a long list of exclusions for probation and deferred adjudication consideration that are best illustrated by the following bulleted points:

- Defendants convicted of any state jail felony offense can only receive probation from a judge, not a jury.[41]

- Defendants whose recommended punishment term exceeds ten years are ineligible for community supervision.[42]

- Defendants who are found guilty of the following crimes cannot be placed on probation by a judge: murder; capital murder; indecency with a child; aggravated kidnapping; aggravated sexual assault; aggravated robbery; using a child to assist with

---

[39] *Butler v. State*, 936 S.W.2d 453, 460 (Tex. App.—Houston [14th Dist.] 1996, pet. ref'd); *Smith v. State*, 84 S.W.3d 36, 38-39 (Tex. App.—Texarkana 2002, no pet.) (defendant committed aggravated perjury by signing a sworn application for probation claiming he had no prior felony convictions when he had ten prior felony convictions).

[40] *Haith v. State*, 03-97-00518-CR, 1998 WL 644138, at *3 (Tex. App.—Austin Sept. 17, 1998, no pet.).

[41] TEX. CODE CRIM. PROC. ANN. art. 42.12 §15(a) (West 2016).

[42] TEX. CODE CRIM. PROC. ANN. art. 42.12 §4(d)(1) (West 2016).

manufacturing or delivering drugs; committing a drug offense in a drug-free zone when the defendant has been convicted of the same offense previously and the punishment was enhanced; sexual assault; intentional injury to a child, disabled person, or elderly person that resulted in serious bodily injury; sexual performance of a child; solicitation of capital murder; burglary of a habitation where the felony the defendant intended to commit was not theft; or in a case where the defendant used a deadly weapon to commit the offense and the factfinder entered a deadly weapon finding.[43]

Each of these offenses are listed under section 3(g) of Article 42.12; these crimes are referred to by practitioners as "3g offenses." They are considered aggravated crimes that carry harsher penalties, fewer community supervision opportunities, and longer incarceration periods.

If a defendant wishes to receive community supervision for any 3g offense, he may have two options to receive it. If the State offers a plea bargain recommending deferred adjudication and the judge accepts the negotiated plea, the defendant may receive it. If the defendant elects the jury to assess punishment, rather than the judge, the jury can recommend probation but not deferred adjudication, for most 3g offenses. The jury cannot recommend probation if the defendant is convicted for the following 3g offenses: committing a drug offense in a drug-free zone when the defendant has been convicted of the same offense previously and the punishment was enhanced; a sexual crime against a child under the age of 14; forced prostitution or human trafficking; and murder.[44]

- Defendants who plead no contest or guilty to any of the following crimes are ineligible for deferred adjudication: intoxication crimes;[45] manufacturing or delivery of drugs in a drug-free zone; indecency with a child, sexual assault, or aggravated sexual assault, regardless of the victim's age, when the

---

[43] TEX. CODE CRIM. PROC. ANN. art. 42.12 §(3)(g) (West 2016).
[44] TEX. CODE CRIM. PROC. ANN. art. 42.12 §4 (West 2016).
[45] TEX. PENAL CODE ANN. §49.09(d) (West 2011).

defendant has previously received community supervision; continuous sexual assault of a child; aggravated sexual assault of a child; and most murder cases.[46]

—————————◆—————————

Notes and Questions

1. Another form of community supervision mentioned in the Code is "shock probation." The eligibility requirements are the same as other forms of community supervision. However, this type of community supervision includes a condition that the defendant be incarcerated as a condition of probation. The Code permits a judge to incarcerate a defendant for no more than 180 days for a felony offense and no more than 30 days for a misdemeanor offense.[47] Judges may order shock probation when the defendant has committed a more egregious offense or is likely to violate a condition of probation, or when the judge wants to get the defendant's attention or correct the defendant's poor attitude. Judges hope the shock of life behind bars, if only temporary, motivates the defendant to follow the conditions of community supervision upon release.

2. Finally, one more form of community supervision exists that is hardly referenced in statutory law:[48] pretrial intervention, also known as pretrial diversion. This form of community supervision is not ordered by a judge or recommended by a jury. Instead, it is an agreement for community supervision that is entered into between the prosecutor and the defendant.

Pretrial intervention is like deferred adjudication in that the defendant's plea will not be entered, the defendant must fulfill all conditions, and the defendant must avoid committing new offenses. However, unlike deferred adjudication, which if completed successfully results in the judge dismissing the charge, when the defendant successfully completes pretrial intervention, the prosecutor will dismiss the charge. The defendant has no right to request or receive pretrial intervention; whether it is offered is entirely in the discretion of the prosecutor.

———————————

[46] TEX. CODE CRIM. PROC. ANN. art. 42.12 §5(d) (West 2016).
[47] TEX. CODE CRIM. PROC. ANN. art. 42.12 §12 (West 2016).
[48] TEX. CODE CRIM. PROC. ANN. art. 102.012 (West 2016); TEX. GOV'T CODE ANN. §76.011 (West 2013).

Unlike the offense limitations that exist for probation and deferred adjudication eligibility, pretrial intervention has no such offense restrictions. However, prosecutors generally offer pretrial intervention to defendants who are young, defendants with little or no criminal history, or to defendants whose offenses are minor or involve strong mitigating circumstances. In some district or county attorney offices, pretrial intervention is used rarely, whereas in others it may be customarily offered to certain types of offenders or offenders who commit specific categories of offenses.

<hr>

Revocation of Community Supervision

In Texas, when and if the defendant violates the conditions of community supervision or commits a new crime, the judge will schedule a revocation hearing. Depending on the severity of the violations, the judge has the authority to impose additional conditions, modify the community supervision, or revoke it and consider punishment.[49] The judge is authorized to issue a warrant and detain the defendant until the hearing.[50] A defendant who violates conditions of community supervision retains some of the same rights she had before punishment: the right to due process, the right to counsel, and the right to appeal.[51] The hearing is adversarial; it resembles a trial. The prosecutor will attempt to prove the violations by calling witnesses and admitting evidence. Defense counsel has the right to cross-examine witnesses and present mitigating evidence on the defendant's behalf.[52]

If the judge decides after the hearing to revoke the defendant's community supervision, the punishment range the judge may consider differs, depending on whether the defendant received probation or deferred adjudication. Consider the following Fort Worth Court of Appeals case, in

---

[49] TEX. CODE CRIM. PROC. ANN. art. 42.12 §10 (West 2016).

[50] TEX. CODE CRIM. PROC. ANN. art. 42.12 §21 (West 2016).

[51] *Id.* (defendant has the right to appeal revocation of deferred adjudication and a right to a hearing); TEX. CODE CRIM. PROC. ANN. art. 42.12 § 23(b) (West 2016) (right to appeal revocation of community supervision); *Issa v. State*, 826 S.W.2d 159, 161 (Tex. Crim. App. 1992) (defendant has the right to present evidence).

[52] *Issa v. State*, 826 S.W.2d 159, 161 (Tex. Crim. App. 1992) ("the defendant is entitled to a punishment hearing after the adjudication of guilt, and the trial judge must allow the accused the opportunity to present evidence").

which the prosecution argued the trial court should be authorized to consider the original, full range of punishment following probation revocation:

> [T]he State argues that once community supervision is revoked, ... [the] trial court [has] authority to increase the punishment originally assessed when the defendant was first convicted. According to this rationale, the trial court should be able to consider the full range of punishment in the revocation hearing, and should not be confined to the punishment originally assessed. While that option is available when a trial court revokes a defendant's deferred adjudication probation, the same is not true for traditional probation. ...
>
> A fundamental distinction between traditional and deferred adjudication probation is that the later does not involve a "conviction." Because deferred adjudication involves neither an adjudication of guilt nor assessment of punishment, the trial court must pursue prosecution of guilt/innocence following revocation of community supervision. In that instance, article 42.12 provides "[a]fter an adjudication of guilt, all proceedings, including assessment of punishment, ... continue as if the adjudication of guilt had not been deferred." Having previously deferred sentencing the defendant, the trial court is therefore free to consider the full range of offense-appropriate punishment, and is not confined to a prior order, as in this case with traditional probation.[53]

To illustrate this point, assume a defendant is convicted of a second-degree drug offense, and the judge grants community supervision following the punishment phase of trial. If this defendant received a term of probation that lasts for ten years with a probated sentence of five, he will serve five years in prison if that probation is revoked. The judge may not decrease or increase the term of incarceration.

Suppose instead of receiving probation following a trial, the defendant pled guilty and received deferred adjudication. Assume the judge set the term of deferred adjudication at ten years. If the defendant committed a new law violation or otherwise violated a condition, the deferred adjudication would be adjudicated. Once this happens, the full punishment range is open for consideration. This means the judge could consider a sentence of 2 to 20 years in prison, which is the punishment range for a second-degree felony, regardless of the original length of deferred adjudication. This is yet another

---

[53] *Weed v. State*, 891 S.W.2d 22, 24-25 (Tex. App.—Fort Worth 1995, no pet.).

difference that exists between the two forms of community supervision that the defendant and his attorney must consider before asking for probation or deferred adjudication.

Reduction and Termination of Community Supervision

A defendant who satisfactorily complies with the conditions of community supervision may seek to have the period of community supervision reduced.[54] Reduction does not apply to all crimes.[55] Furthermore, the decision to reduce the term is entirely within the judge's discretion.[56]

A defendant who satisfactorily completes community supervision may seek to have its length shortened. This is called early termination.[57] If the defendant was on probation, successful completion of probation still results in a conviction. "[A] person who successfully completes all of the terms and conditions of community supervision must be discharged from community supervision. This is not a discretionary matter."[58]

————————◆————————

Presentence Investigations

When a judge assesses punishment, he must order the probation department to perform a presentence investigation (PSI) and write a report based upon the findings of the PSI.[59] The purpose of the PSI is to inform the judge about the facts of the charged offense, any restitution that is owed the victim, the defendant's criminal record and social history, and any other relevant information that will assist the judge in determining the appropriate punishment.[60]

The PSI report writer does not recommend a specific punishment to the judge[61] but provides the judge with facts that may be taken into consideration

---

54 TEX. CODE CRIM. PROC. ANN. art. 42.12 §20 (West 2016).
55 *Id.*
56 *Id.*
57 *Id.*
58 *Cuellar v. State*, 70 S.W.3d 815, 820 (Tex. Crim. App. 2002).
59 TEX. CODE CRIM. PROC. ANN. art. 42.12 §9 (West 2016).
60 *Id.*
61 *Id.* ("It is not necessary that the report contain a sentencing recommendation.").

when assessing punishment. The purpose of these facts is to paint a full picture of the crime and the person who committed the crime. If the defendant is eligible for community supervision, "the report must contain a proposed client supervision plan describing programs and sanctions that the community supervision and corrections department would provide the defendant" if he is placed on probation or deferred adjudication.[62]

If sentencing is done by the judge, PSI reports are mandatory in noncapital felony cases following a timely request by a defendant who is eligible for community supervision.[63] In misdemeanor cases, the judge is not required to request a PSI if (1) the defendant requests no report be made and the judge agrees, or (2) there is enough information in the record for the judge to render a meaningful discretion of punishment, and the judge explains this in the record.[64] In felony cases, the judge is not required to request a PSI (1) when the jury will be assessing punishment, (2) the charge is capital murder, (3) the only punishment available is imprisonment, or (4) the defendant is entering a plea in exchange for imprisonment, and the judge intends to follow the State's recommendation.[65]

———————————◆———————————

Verdicts, Judgments, and Sentences

Recall from Chapter 12, that the word *verdict* is defined as "a written declaration by a jury of its decision of the issue submitted to it in the case."[66] Like the guilt/innocence verdict, the punishment verdict must be unanimous.

> In the event the jury shall fail to agree on the issue of punishment, a mistrial shall be declared only in the punishment phase of the trial, the jury shall be discharged, and no jeopardy shall attach. The court shall impanel another jury as soon as practicable to determine the issue of punishment.[67]

---

[62] *Id.*
[63] TEX. CODE CRIM. PROC. ANN. art. 42.12 §9(g) (West 2016).
[64] TEX. CODE CRIM. PROC. ANN. art. 42.12 §9(a)–(b) (West 2016).
[65] TEX. CODE CRIM. PROC. ANN. art. 42.12 §9(g) (West 2016).
[66] TEX. CODE CRIM. PROC. ANN. art. 37.001 (West 2016).
[67] TEX. CODE CRIM. PROC. ANN. art. 37.07 (West 2016).

However, in capital murder cases, if the jury disagrees about whether the defendant should be put to death, given a life sentence, or life without parole, the defendant will receive a default sentence of life imprisonment.[68]

The Code requires that unless the punishment is fixed by law, a punishment verdict must contain the jury's sentence.[69] Once a jury agrees upon a sentence, the punishment verdict is read in open court in the defendant's presence and entered into the court's minutes, which are kept in the clerk's file.[70] If the defendant elects the judge to assess punishment, the judge does not render a verdict but merely announces the punishment in open court.[71] Regardless of whether punishment follows a negotiated plea, a jury's verdict, or a judge's oral pronouncement, the punishment will result in a final judgment.

The Code defines *judgment* as "the written declaration of the court signed by the trial judge and entered [into the] record showing the conviction or acquittal of the defendant. The sentence served shall be based on the information contained in the judgment."[72] The judgment will contain the case number, the names of the parties, the charged offense, the defendant's plea, whether the case was heard by a judge or jury, the punishment assessed, the date the verdict or judgment was entered, the date the sentence was imposed, and the defendant's thumb print, among other things.[73] The judgment is essentially a record of the trial and its outcome after the fact. The judgment can be used as proof to enhance or establish as punishment evidence the criminal conviction in future trials. A defendant begins serving his sentence once the judgment and sentence is pronounced in open court.[74]

———————◆———————

[68] *Lawton v. State*, 913 S.W.2d 542, 558 (Tex. Crim. App. 1995), *overruled on other grounds, Mosley v. State*, 983 S.W.2d 249, 272 n. 18 (Tex. Crim. App. 1998).
[69] TEX. CODE CRIM. PROC. ANN. art. 37.07(b) (West 2016).
[70] TEX. CODE CRIM. PROC. ANN. arts. 37.04 and 37.05 (West 2016).
[71] TEX. CODE CRIM. PROC. ANN. art. 37.07 §(3)(d) (West 2016).
[72] TEX. CODE CRIM. PROC. ANN. art. 42.01 §1 (West 2016).
[73] *Id.*
[74] TEX. CODE CRIM. PROC. ANN. art. 42.03 (West 2016).

Victim Impact Statements

Victims and guardians or relatives of victims are permitted to make an oral victim impact statement about "the person's views about the offense, the defendant, and the effect of the offense on the victim."[75] The statement is not designed to question or elicit responses from the defendant.[76] The next case addresses how and when a victim impact statement is made and the policy reasons for victim impact statement procedures.

Ivan Johnson v. State
286 S.W.3d 346
(Tex. Crim. App. 2009)

Appellant asks whether a trial judge has the discretion to impose jail time as a condition of community supervision immediately after he has heard unsworn, un-cross-examined victim-allocution statements that they wanted appellant to go to jail. The answer is no. The pertinent statute is both clear and explicit: Article 42.03 requires that the victim-allocution statement be read after the sentence has been imposed and "after the court has announced the terms and conditions of the sentence." This error was not harmless. We therefore reverse the court of appeals, which had held that error, if any, was harmless because the trial court retained authority to modify and amend the conditions of probation at any time during the period of community supervision.

In this case, appellant was charged with two counts of indecency with a child. The jury acquitted him of the count involving Savannah, but convicted him of the count involving Brittany. The jury then assessed his punishment at five years' imprisonment and a fine of $5,000, but further recommended that both the fine and the imprisonment be probated and that appellant be placed on community supervision. The trial judge accepted the jury's punishment verdict and imposed the "standard" conditions of community supervision, including sex-offender registration. After the judge completed his oral pronouncement of the sentence and community supervision conditions, he permitted the mothers of both children to give an oral allocution statement in open court pursuant to Article 42.03, § 1(b).

---

[75] TEX. CODE CRIM. PROC. ANN. art. 42.03 §1(b) (West 2016).
[76] *Id.*

Brittany's mother also read Brittany's statement out loud. Then the trial judge read a statement written by Savannah out loud, even though appellant had been acquitted of molesting her.

Immediately thereafter, the trial judge imposed additional conditions of probation, including the requirement that appellant sell his home and that he serve 180 days in the county jail. Appellant objected; he filed a bill of exceptions because Article 42.03 prohibits the court reporter from recording victim-allocution statements; and he obtained an adverse ruling from the trial court. He properly preserved error.

The court of appeals correctly noted that Article 42.03 allows "a victim statement only after sentencing in order to alleviate any risk that the statement might affect the partiality of the fact finder at the punishment phase." This statute is not ambiguous or difficult to understand. The statute says that the victim's statement "must be made ... after the court has announced the terms and conditions of the sentence; and after sentence is pronounced." Only after the entire sentencing procedure is complete –when it is not possible for anyone to think that unsworn, uncross-examined testimony could affect the trial judge's sentencing – may the victim deliver a statement to the defendant, the court, and the public. The term "after sentence is pronounced" does not mean that a first sentencing is a prelude to a second sentencing after the victim-allocution statement.

It is widely acknowledged by commentators that victim-allocution statements are to have "no effect" upon the jury or judge's decision making. What does "no effect" mean? Does it mean that the trial judge may not increase the literal sentence, but he may add whatever new terms and conditions he thinks appropriate based upon the unsworn, uncross-examined victim-allocution statements? No. The whole purpose of requiring that these statements be made after the sentencing stage is complete is to protect the trial judge and the justice system from charges of partiality or any suggestion that these unsworn, uncross-examined statements can or will sway the sentencing authority in any respect whatsoever.

... Although four members of the Court have previously stated that a trial judge commits error if he changes, modifies, or alters his sentence or the conditions of community supervision immediately after hearing a victim-allocution statement, this is an issue of first impression for the Court as a whole.

The court of appeals avoided this issue by holding that it was at most harmless error because the trial court retained authority to modify or amend the conditions of probation at any time during the period of community supervision. There are two problems with this conclusion.

First, the trial judge did not modify or amend the conditions of community supervision. Indeed, the trial judge said that he was "imposing" jail time as a part of the "terms and conditions of probation;" he did not state that he was "amending" or "modifying" his original probation conditions. ... The only intervening event between the original pronouncement of sentence and conditions of community supervision and the pronouncement of the "180 days in jail" condition was the victim-allocution statements asking for the appellant to go to jail. ...

Second, the court of appeals's "no harm, no foul" reasoning fails to acknowledge the "any reason except a prohibited one" rule. The trial court does indeed retain authority to impose confinement in jail as a condition of community supervision "at any time during the supervision period." Unless prohibited by law, he may do so for any reason and perhaps for no reason. But just as a judge may not impose jail time as a condition of community supervision solely because of the defendant's race, he may not impose jail time as a condition of community supervision for any other statutorily prohibited reason. ... If the trial judge is not permitted to amend the conditions of probation based on the victim's allocution statements, it is of no moment that he could have later amended those same conditions based on a valid reason.

We do not doubt the sincerity of the trial judge in this case. He stated, on the record, that he did not modify appellant's sentence because of any influence caused by the reading of the victim-allocution statements. But the purpose of article 42.03, § 1(b) is to protect the trial judge from any implicit or explicit accusations that he could be or would be influenced by the victim-allocution statement. It is the appearance of possible influence, as much as the possible fact of influence that the statute guards against.

Although the trial judge erred by violating the express terms of article 42.03, we are confident that the honorable judge will do what he promised to do if he knew that his imposition of the "180–days–in–jail" condition was illegal: Delete it from the judgment. If the trial judge finds that appellant is a less than perfect probationer, he may always amend the conditions of community service to include jail time as long as that condition is not inextricably connected to the victims' allocution statements asking for jail time.

We therefore reverse the judgment of the court of appeals and remand this case to the trial court for further proceedings consistent with this opinion.

————————◆————————

Notes and Questions

1.   There is a difference between an oral victim impact statement, which was considered in the above section, a written victim impact statement, and victim impact evidence. The oral victim impact statement is made in open court by the victim or the victim's family member after punishment has been pronounced.

A written victim impact statement is actually a form, sent out to the victim by the victim assistance coordinator, who may work with the district or county attorney's office.[77] Victims or family members are asked to answer the questions on the form, which seek any of the following information:

- economic loss suffered as a result of the crime;
- physical or psychological injury suffered as a result of the crime;
- psychological counseling or services required as a result of the crime;
- any changes in the personal welfare of the person making the statement;
- the effect on familial relationships as a result of the crime; or
- any other pertinent information related to the impact the crime has had on the person making the statement.[78]

The judge is required to inquire about this form at sentencing.[79] The form is subject to discovery when it contains exculpatory material.[80] It can also be

---

[77] Tex. Code Crim. Proc. Ann. art. 56.03 (b) (West 2016).
[78] *Id.*
[79] Tex. Code Crim. Proc. Ann. art. 26.13 (e) (West 2016).
[80] Tex. Code Crim. Proc. Ann. art. 56.03 (g) (West 2016).

used by the parole board in determining whether the defendant should be paroled.[81]

Victim impact evidence, on the other hand, is admissible during the punishment phase if it is relevant to the defendant's personal responsibility or moral guilt on the charged offense.[82] It may include evidence of psychological injury to the victim[83] or the fact that the defendant transmitted a sexual disease to a sexual assault victim.[84]

2. Just as a victim may not advocate for a particular punishment while delivering a victim impact statement, neither a witness nor an expert may suggest a particular sentence during the punishment phase of trial.[85] This is because these witnesses have "no more expertise for suggesting the proper punishment than any member of the jury."[86] This testimony is outside the scope of lay witness opinion or expert testimony.

Relatedly, the prosecutor is not bound to offer the victim's preferred punishment during plea bargaining. Victims are given a voice in the criminal justice process but cannot dictate punishment, regardless of who is assessing or offering it.

———————◆———————

Parole

In Texas, most individuals incarcerated for felony offenses will be paroled before they serve their full sentences.[87] The prevalence of parole is not lost on jurors. Jurors have improperly taken parole into consideration

---

[81] TEX. CODE CRIM. PROC. ANN. art. 56.03 (d) and (i) (West 2016).
[82] E.g., *Miller-El v. State*, 782 S.W.2d 892, 895 (Tex. Crim. App. 1990) (doctor's testimony about victim's paralysis was admissible during punishment phase because it was a consequence of the offense).
[83] *Stavinoha v. State*, 808 S.W.2d 76, 79 (Tex. Crim. App. 1991).
[84] *Hunter v. State*, 799 S.W.2d 356, 360 (Tex. App.—Houston [14th Dist.] 1990, no pet.).
[85] E.g., *Simpson v. State*, 119 S.W.3d 262, 272 (Tex. Crim. App. 2003) (victim's family members' wishes on punishment were inadmissible during punishment phase); *Sattiewhite v. State*, 786 S.W.2d 271, 290 (Tex. Crim. App. 1989) (defense expert not permitted to testify that in her opinion, defendant should receive a life sentence in a capital murder case).
[86] *Hughes v. State*, 787 S.W.2d 193, 196 (Tex. App.—Corpus Christi 1990, pet. ref'd).
[87] TEX. CODE CRIM. PROC. ANN. art. 37.07(a) (West 2016).

when assessing punishment. This is a flawed practice for several reasons. First, parole laws change frequently. Second, the use of parole fluctuates with the number of current inmates and the cost of and room needed to house any incarcerated population. When prisons are operating at full capacity, they must release more inmates on parole. When State funds are depleted, the legislature reduces budgets, which results in a greater number of inmates who are released on parole. It is thus difficult to ascertain when prison overcrowding will lead to higher incidences of parole.

Parole is also specifically variable. The Court of Criminal Appeals characterized the ability to make parole for a specific inmate as unpredictable:

> Parole attainment is indeed highly speculative, due to various factors associated with circumstances surrounding an individual prisoner's parole application, such as the prisoner's behavior in prison, the composition and attitude of the parole board, the identity and attitude of the governor, the population of the prison system, and regulations governing "good time."[88]

For all of these reasons and more, jurors are not to consider parole in assessing a sentence.[89] The Code contains a jury instruction that advises jurors that while they may consider the existence of parole and good conduct time, they are not permitted to consider how it may be applied towards the defendant in the future.[90] The instruction is designed to quell the jurors' erroneous applications of parole laws and good conduct time.

Lawyers at trial are prohibited from introducing evidence regarding parole and good conduct time at trial.[91] Furthermore, lawyers are not permitted to encourage jurors to violate the instruction forbidding their application of parole laws to a defendant in their closing arguments.[92] In *Mendoza*, the prosecutor improperly argued the following during the punishment phase of a murder trial:

> As to how much time, that's up to you. But I think in no situation should it be less than 45 years because she's not going to serve 45 years. Look at the

[88] *Ex Parte Moussazadeh*, 361 S.W.3d 684, 690 (Tex. Crim. App. 2012).
[89] TEX. CODE CRIM. PROC. ANN. art. 37.07 §4 (a)–(d) (West 2016).
[90] TEX. CODE CRIM. PROC. ANN. art. 37.07 §4 (a)–(c) (West 2016).
[91] TEX. CODE CRIM. PROC. ANN. art. 37.07 §4 (d) (West 2016).
[92] *Clark v. State*, 643 S.W.2d 723, 725 (Tex. Crim. App. 1982) ("While it is common knowledge that inmates are frequently paroled before serving their full sentence, a jury in a felony case is not authorized to consider or apply parole law in assessing punishment. Uninvited argument urging them to do so constitutes error.").

charge. It tells you she's not going to serve 45 calendar years. It's going to be reduced.

You know what they have now in Huntsville is a revolving door. I mean by the time you all get home some will have already been let out that were sentenced yesterday. So keep that in mind. No probation for sure. Whatever you want to do, but in no case less than 45.[93]

The Corpus Christi Court of Appeals held this argument was improper and harmful.[94] It reversed and remanded the case for a new punishment phase of trial.[95] In other cases, appellate courts have found that the defendant waived error by failing to object or that an instruction to disregard cured the error.[96] Regardless, asking the jury to consider how parole eligibility and good conduct time will apply to a specific defendant is improper.

———————◆———————

Practice Questions

On average, examiners ask one punishment question per exam. However, examiners have asked as few as none and as many as five on past bar exams. Bar examiner comments to punishment questions indicate that students frequently fail to answer these questions correctly. As a result, students who master these topics may be able to earn points that many examinees miss.

1. (J-2016 and F-2009) Not only did Defendant commit the present burglary of a habitation, but law enforcement officers have evidence he committed other burglaries, though he was never charged or convicted. Prosecutor gave you timely and proper notice that, at the punishment

---

[93] *Mendoza v. State*, 840 S.W.2d 697, 701–02 (Tex. App.—Corpus Christi 1992, no pet.).

[94] *Id.* at 702.

[95] *Id.*

[96] *E.g., Cockrell v. State*, 933 S.W.2d 73, 91 (Tex. Crim. App. 1996) (defendant's failure to object waived error of improper argument on application of parole laws); *Brown v. State*, 769 S.W.2d 565, 567 (Tex. Crim. App. 1989) ("although the complained of argument was improper in that it was a call for the jury to consider and apply the parole law to this appellant, it was not of such a nature that the curative instruction did not remedy the error").

phase of trial, she would attempt to introduce evidence of the uncharged burglaries.

Are these uncharged crimes admissible against Defendant during the punishment phase of trial? Explain.

_____

_____

_____

_____

_____

2. (F-2016, F-2015, J-2013, J-2011, F-2011, and F-2001) Defendant is charged with a third-degree felony offense. Defendant would like the jury to assess punishment.

   a. What procedural steps, if any, should you take to give the jury the option of assessing punishment and imposing probation? When should you take them?

   _____

   _____

   _____

   _____

   _____

   b. (F-2012) If you fail to take the steps above, what will happen?

   _____

   _____

   _____

   _____

   _____

3. (J-2015, J-2007, and F-2002) In exchange for his plea of guilty, the State offers Defendant deferred adjudication. Defendant asks you to explain the differences between deferred adjudication and probation.

   List two ways in which deferred adjudication differs from probation?

   _____

   _____

   _____

   _____

   _____

4. (F-2014, J-2009, J-2006, and J-2002) List three prerequisites for probation eligibility.

   _____

   _____

   _____

   _____

   _____

5. (F-2013) Following the punishment phase of trial, the jury announces it is deadlocked. You request that the Judge grant a mistrial and ask for new guilt-innocence and punishment phases for Defendant. The Court grants your request.

   Is this a proper ruling? Explain.

   _____

   _____

   _____

   _____

   _____

6. (J-2011, J-2007, F-2007, and F-2005, J-2004, and F-2001) Defendant wants probation. She has a prior felony conviction in Maryland, but the State does not know about it.

   Should you file a motion for probation? If you do not, are you required to disclose this conviction to the State? Explain.

   _____

   _____

   _____

   _____

   _____

7. Defendant is charged with aggravated robbery. He is hoping for community supervision if he is convicted.

   a. (J-2012, F-2011, and J-2008) Should the judge or jury assess punishment? Explain.

   _____

   _____

   _____

   _____

   _____

   b. (F-2011 and F-2003) Assume he is convicted. Can the judge or jury place him on deferred adjudication? Explain.

   _____

   _____

   _____

   _____

   _____

8. (F-2011) List two times when a judge is not required to direct a probation officer to prepare a presentence investigation (PSI) report in a felony case?

_____

_____

_____

_____

_____

9. (F-2011 and F-2004) Before Judge assesses punishment, Judge permits Victim to appear in person and present a statement in open court about the effects the offense had on Victim. You object to this procedure, but Judge overrules your objection. After Victim makes his statement, Defendant is sentenced to serve ten years in prison.

   Was the Court's ruling appropriate? Explain.

_____

_____

_____

_____

_____

10. (F-2010) The jury convicts Defendant of arson. The jury assesses Defendant's punishment at five years' incarceration but recommends to the Court that it suspend the imposition of the sentence and place Defendant on community supervision.

   May the Court ignore the jury's recommendation of community supervision and incarcerate Defendant instead? Explain.

_____

_____

_____

_____

_____

11. (J-2007 and F-2001) The jury finds Defendant guilty after only five minutes of deliberation. Based upon the quick decision, Defendant wants to change his punishment election from the jury to the judge. Prosecutor objects.

    Is it too late for Defendant to change his election under these circumstances? Explain.

    _____

    _____

    _____

    _____

    _____

12. (J-2005) List three legal precepts (from common law or statutes) about deferred adjudication.

    _____

    _____

    _____

    _____

    _____

13. (J-2002) During the punishment phase, the following exchange takes place:

    PROSECUTOR: Do you know Defendant's reputation for being a peaceful and law-abiding man?

    WITNESS: Yes.

    PROSECUTOR: And is his reputation good or bad?

    WITNESS: It's really, really bad.

    Is this kind of evidence admissible? Why or why not? Explain.

    _____

    _____

    _____

| Texas Criminal Procedure and Evidence

_____

_____

14. (F-2002) Does the judge or jury set punishment in a Texas criminal case? Is this different or similar to the way it happens in a federal criminal case? Explain.

_____

_____

_____

_____

_____

15. (F-2001) Defendant committed an aggravated felony offense. Judge's punishment jury charge informs jury that Defendant will not be parole eligible until he serves half of his sentence. During closing argument, Prosecutor argues:

Ladies and gentlemen of the jury, read the jury charge. Whatever punishment you give Defendant, he will only serve half of it. Therefore, give him double whatever you wish him actually to serve so he can't harm anyone else.

Was this appropriate? Why or why not? Explain.

_____

_____

_____

_____

_____

16. (F-2001) During the punishment phase of trial, Prosecutor asks Witness whether she has an opinion on Defendant's punishment, and if so, what it is.

Is testimony of this nature admissible? Explain.

_____

_____

_____

_____

_____

———————————◆———————————

Chapter 14
Post-Conviction Relief

Introduction

When a defendant is found guilty at trial, her attorney may seek to avoid the conviction and its consequences through post-conviction relief. Every post-conviction remedy in this chapter—motions for new trial, appeals, and ineffective assistance of counsel claims—relies heavily, if not entirely, on the record at trial. Therefore, this chapter will begin by examining the importance of the record.

◆

The Record

The basis for all forms of post-conviction relief begins with the record. When a defendant appeals his conviction to an appellate court immediately following his conviction (this is called a direct appeal), if the error does not appear in the record, it is as if the error did not happen. Consider what the Waco Court of Appeals said in a case where defense counsel invoked a *Batson* claim with an insufficient record on appeal:

> Unless reflected by the evidence, an appellate court does not judicially "know" where jurors were seated on the venire, which jurors were peremptorily struck by the parties, jurors' ethnicity, ages, occupations, styles

of dress, religious preferences, or a myriad of other factors which may support or negate a charge that the state has used its peremptory challenges in a racially discriminatory manner. The most elaborately constructed, fact-based argument on appeal is for naught unless it is supported by evidence in the record.[1]

This leads to the following question: what is "the record?" The record on appeal consists of the clerk's record and the reporter's record.[2] The clerk's record includes the charging instrument, written and filed motions, waivers, stipulations, pleas, the court's docket sheets related to the case, arrest and search warrants, the attorneys' lists of peremptory strikes, subpoenas, the jury charge, the judgment and sentence, the notice of appeal, and any other documents filed with the court clerk before, during, or after trial.[3] Each attorney has a file containing documents that pertain to the case; likewise, the court clerk keeps a record of documents filed in the court related to the case. These documents comprise the clerk's record.

The record on appeal also includes the court reporter's record.[4] The court reporter's record includes the court reporter's stenographic recording of testimony and proceedings that took place within the court room during trial.[5] It also includes any exhibits admitted into evidence at trial.[6] Together, the clerk's record and the reporter's record comprise the record on appeal.

If the defendant wants to complain about anything on appeal, the basis for that complaint, whether it occurred before trial, during the guilt/innocence stage, during the punishment stage, or at sentencing after trial, must appear in the record. If it does not appear in the record, it is the duty of the attorney who is complaining on appeal to find a way to include it in the record.

Records of error usually make their way into a record through testimony or objections that are transcribed by the court reporter or through motions or other written documents included in the case file by the clerk. How does an attorney include something in the record when the trial court refuses to admit it, whether it is a question, a piece of evidence, or something else?

---

[1] *Shields v. State*, 820 S.W.2d 831, 834 (Tex. App.—Waco 1991, no pet.).
[2] TEX. R. APP. P. 34.1.
[3] TEX. R. APP. P. 34.5.
[4] TEX. R. APP. P. 34.6.
[5] *Id.*
[6] *Id.*

When the trial court excludes evidence at trial, the attorney attempting to admit it can make an offer of proof outside of the presence of the jury.[7] This offer explains what the evidence is, why it should have been admitted, and how its exclusion harms the complaining party.[8] Offers of proof may also be used during jury selection to explain attempts to exclude or keep potential jurors. An offer of proof is timely if it is filed before the jury charge is read to the jury.[9]

Another way to include alleged error in the record is to file a formal bill of exception.[10] There is no specified form to the bill, but it must contain the party's objection to a court ruling in specific enough form to make the trial court aware of the complaint, and it must contain a transcription of the proffered evidence certified by the court reporter.[11] The bill is then submitted to the trial court judge who files it with the court clerk, which becomes part of the clerk's record.[12] A bill of exception is timely if it is filed no later than 60 days after the sentence is imposed or 90 days, if a motion for new trial is filed.[13] Formal bills of exception are rarely used; offers of proof are more common in practice.

———————————— ◆ ————————————

Appeals

The Code of Criminal Procedure sets out the parameters of the State's right and the defendant's right to appeal. The State is limited to appeals when the trial court does any of the following:

1. dismisses, in part or in whole, the entire charging instrument;
2. modifies or arrests the judgment;
3. grants the defendant a new trial;
4. sustains a double jeopardy claim; or

---

[7] TEX. R. EVID. 103(b).
[8] *Id.*
[9] *Id.*
[10] TEX. R. APP. P. 33.2.
[11] TEX. R. APP. P. 33.2(b) and (f).
[12] TEX. R. APP. P. 33.2(c).
[13] TEX. R. APP. P. 33.2(e).

5. grants a motion to suppress evidence.[14]

The State is also permitted to raise issues on appeal when the defendant appeals the case.[15] This kind of appeal is referred to as a cross appeal.[16] The Court of Criminal Appeals described a cross appeal as follows: "A 'cross-appeal' asserts that, once the court of appeals has dealt with the defendant's claim of 'X' error, it should ...also address a separate legal ruling by the trial judge—ruling 'Y'—that the State claims is erroneous."[17] In the five instances listed above, the State has 20 days to file its own appeal following the order, ruling, or sentence the State wishes to appeal.[18] The 20-day deadline does not apply to cross appeals, which may be raised in the State's appellee brief.[19]

Notice that the appealable items in the list above effectively kill or seriously injure the State's case. The State is not permitted to appeal acquittals, unfavorable rulings, or any other matter not included in the list above. Consider the taxpayer's expense, wasted court resources, violations of rights to the acquitted defendant, and the denigrated value of the jury's decision to acquit were the State permitted to appeal an acquittal.

In fewer ways, the defendant's right to appeal is also limited. He generally has the right to appeal unless it is from a plea of guilty or no contest where the terms of the plea bargain were followed; in those instances, he must have the permission of the trial court or he must be appealing matters raised by written, pretrial motions.[20] A defendant generally does not have the right to an interlocutory (pretrial) appeal, but he may be able to bring an appeal from a trial court's denial of relief on an application for a pretrial writ of habeas corpus.[21]

---

[14] TEX. CODE CRIM. PROC. ANN. art. 44.01(a) (West 2016). Remember from earlier chapters that if a motion to suppress is granted, the State must certify to the trial court that the interlocutory appeal is not taken for purposes of delay and that the suppressed evidence is of substantial importance to the case. *Id.* at art. 44.01(a)(5).

[15] TEX. CODE CRIM. PROC. ANN. art. 44.01(c) (West 2016).

[16] *Pfeiffer v. State*, 363 S.W.3d 594, 601 (Tex. Crim. App. 2012).

[17] *Id.*

[18] TEX. R. APP. P. 26.2(b).

[19] TEX. CODE CRIM. PROC. ANN. art. 44.01(a)(6) (West 2016).

[20] TEX. CODE CRIM. PROC. ANN. art. 44.02 (West 2016).

[21] *See Ex parte Smith*, 178 S.W.3d 797, 801-02 (Tex. Crim. App. 2005); *Apolinar v. State*, 820 S.W.2d 792, 794 (Tex. Crim. App. 1991).

A defendant who wishes to appeal must file a timely, written notice of appeal.[22] The notice must be filed with the trial clerk 30 days after the sentenced is imposed, suspended, or another appealable order has been entered.[23] When a motion for new trial is filed, the notice deadline extends to 90 days.[24]

It is possible to get an extension beyond these time limits if the defendant (1) files a notice of appeal in the trial court within 15 days of the deadline, and (2) files a motion to extend time with the appellate court.[25] The motion to extend time must state the original deadline, facts that explain the need for an extension, and must provide the appellate court with the trial court, the date of judgment, the name of the case, and the case number.[26] The Texas Rules of Appellate Procedure do not specify the length of the extension; that presumably is within the appellate court's discretion, depending on the circumstances.

————————◆————————

Notes and Questions

1.   One of the more common issues raised on appeal is a challenge to the legal sufficiency of the evidence. This claim asserts the evidence to support the defendant's conviction is legally insufficient. In other words, despite the jury's decision, the evidence in the case is too weak to support the jury's finding of guilt. The standard of review the appellate court must use is whether "[c]onsidering all of the evidence in the light most favorable to the verdict, was a jury rationally justified in finding guilt beyond a reasonable doubt?"[27] Why is the standard of review as to the legal sufficiency of the evidence viewed in the light most favorable to the verdict? Who is in the better position to have viewed that evidence: the fact finder who observed the trial, or the appellate judges who are examining a "cold" record?

2.   Trial counsel, whether appointed or paid, is statutorily obligated to consult with and advise the defendant about her right to file a motion for

---

[22] TEX. R. APP. P. 25.2(c).
[23] *Id.*; TEX. R. APP. P. 26.2.
[24] TEX. R. APP. P. 26.2.
[25] TEX. R. APP. P. 26.3.
[26] TEX. R. APP. P. 10.5(b)(2).
[27] *Brooks v. State*, 323 S.W.3d 893, 899 (Tex. Crim. App. 2010).

new trial and a notice of appeal.[28] Furthermore, trial counsel must not only advise the defendant but must file the motion and/or notice.[29] If, after filing the proper notices and motions, trial counsel is not interested or equipped to assist the defendant in post-trial matters, he may withdraw from the case and ask that appellate counsel be appointed or hired to replace him.[30]

———————◆———————

Motions for New Trial

There are three reasons why attorneys file a motion for new trial: (1) to ask for a new guilt/innocence or punishment phase; (2) to extend the deadline to file a notice of appeal or an appellate brief; or (3) to supplement the record on appeal with facts, testimony, or evidence that is not currently in the record but is needed on appeal.

The Texas Rules of Appellate Procedure define a new trial as "the rehearing of a criminal action after the trial court has, on the defendant's motion, set aside a finding or verdict of guilt."[31] This motion does exactly what it sounds like it does: it asks the trial court for a new trial after the defendant's conviction. The Texas Rules of Appellate Procedure authorize motions for new trials in the following instances:

1. When the defendant has been tried in absentia or when he has been denied counsel;

2. When the judge has wrongly instructed the jury about the law or has committed another material error that may injure the defendant's rights;

3. When the verdict has been decided by lot or in another way that does not reflect a juror's fair opinion of guilt/innocence;

4. When a juror has been bribed to convict or has engaged in other corrupt conduct;

---

[28] TEX. CODE CRIM. PROC. ANN. art. 26.04(j)(3)(A) (West 2016); *Ex parte Axel,* 757 S.W.2d 369, 374 (Tex. Crim. App. 1988).
[29] *Id.*
[30] TEX. CODE CRIM. PROC. ANN. art. 26.04(j)(2)-(3) (West 2016).
[31] TEX. R. APP. P. 21.1(a).

5. When a material witness for the defense has been prevented from testifying or when exculpatory evidence has been intentionally destroyed or withheld;

6. When, after retiring to deliberate, the jury has received other evidence, talked with someone about the case, or become intoxicated and that intoxication probably influenced the juror's verdict;

7. When the jury engaged in misconduct that resulted in an unfair trial or an impartial jury; or

8. When the verdict is contrary to the law or evidence.[32]

9. Finally, the Texas Code of Criminal Procedure provides, "A new trial shall be granted an accused when material evidence favorable to the accused has been discovered since trial."[33] This refers to *Brady* evidence.

A motion for new trial must be filed within 30 days after the court entered its judgment and sentence.[34] If the defendant wants to amend his original motion for new trial or file an additional motion for new trial, he must do so within 30 days after judgment and sentence and before the judge rules on the original motion for new trial.[35]

Not only must the defendant file his motion for new trial, he must also present it. A motion is filed when it is given to the court clerk to include in the clerk's record. Presentment, on the other hand, puts the trial judge "on actual notice that a defendant desires the trial court to take some action on the motion for new trial such as a ruling or a hearing on it."[36] The judge does not err when he fails to rule on the motion for new trial or hold a hearing if the motion was never presented to him.[37]

The defendant must present the motion to the trial court within ten days after filing it.[38] The trial court, in its discretion, can permit it to be presented and can schedule a hearing within 75 days from the date the court renders

---

[32] TEX. R. APP. P. 21.3.

[33] TEX. CODE CRIM. PROC. ANN. art. 40.001 (West 2016).

[34] TEX. R. APP. P. 21.4(a).

[35] TEX. R. APP. P. 21.4(b).

[36] *Carranza v. State*, 960 S.W.2d 76, 78 (Tex. Crim. App. 1998).

[37] *Gardner v. State*, 306 S.W.3d 274, 306 (Tex. Crim. App. 2009) ("Because appellant did not show that he timely presented his motion for new trial to the trial judge or that he requested a hearing on that motion, the trial judge did not abuse his discretion in failing to conduct a hearing.").

[38] TEX. R. APP. P. 21.6.

the sentence.[39] If the judge does not rule on the motion or schedule a hearing within that 75-day period, the motion is considered overruled by operation of law.[40]

A motion for new trial may be granted for the entire trial—guilt/innocence and punishment—or for the punishment phase only.[41] Whether and what type of new trial is granted depends on the alleged error and when that error occurred. For example, if a defendant discovered after the verdict that jurors were bribed to render a guilty verdict, he would be entitled to a new guilt/innocence and punishment phase. If a judge instructed the jury in error during the punishment phase of trial, the defendant would only be entitled to a new punishment phase.

There is another reason for requesting a motion for new trial. Like offers of proof and formal bills of exception, a motion for new trial offers a chance to enter into the record what would otherwise be kept out. The law states, "A motion for new trial is a prerequisite to presenting a point of error on appeal only when necessary to adduce facts not in the record."[42] The motion hearing may resemble a mini-trial with live witnesses, affidavits, and evidence admitted into the record. Attorneys who do not use a motion for new trial to get all testimony and facts before the appellate court through the record place corresponding appellate claims in jeopardy, as the next case illustrates. The case below also illustrates the appellate court's careful review of the record, its reluctance to assume facts not in the record, and its review of legal sufficiency on appeal.

Larry Dale Baxter v. State
66 S.W.3d 494
(Tex. App.—Austin 2001, pet. ref'd)

Appellant Larry Dale Baxter was convicted, in a jury trial, of the offenses of engaging in organized criminal activity and of gambling promotion.

Appellant asserts that the evidence is insufficient to support the jury's verdicts and that the trial court erred in ... refusing to allow a sitting juror to be interrogated. The judgments will be affirmed.

---

[39] *Id.*
[40] TEX. R. APP. P. 21.8.
[41] TEX. R. APP. P. 21.1.
[42] TEX. R. APP. P. 21.2.

Sufficiency of Evidence

In his sixth and seventh points of error, appellant insists that the evidence is insufficient to support the jury's verdicts. In reviewing the legal sufficiency of the evidence, the relevant question is whether, after viewing the evidence in the light most favorable to the prosecution, any rational trier of fact could have found the essential elements of the crime beyond a reasonable doubt. *Jackson v. Virginia*, 443 U.S. 307, 319 (1979).

A person commits the offense of engaging in organized criminal activity if, with the intent to establish, maintain, or participate in a combination or the profits of a combination, he commits or conspires to commit any gambling offense punishable as a Class A misdemeanor. "Combination" means three or more persons who collaborate in carrying on criminal activities. A person commits the Class A misdemeanor offense of gambling promotion if he intentionally or knowingly operates or participates in the earnings of a gambling place. "Gambling Place" means any real estate, building, room, tent, vehicle, boat, or other property whatsoever, one of the uses of which is the making or settling of bets. "Bet" means any agreement to win or lose something of value solely or partially by chance.

In appellate cause number 3–01–00061–CR, the indictment charged that on or about May 6, 1999, appellant

> did then and there, with intent to establish, maintain, or participate in a combination or in the profits of a combination, said combination consisting of LARRY DALE BAXTER, SHANNON CARPENTER, CINDY RICHARDS, AND JERRY DEAN CLEMENTS, who collaborated in carrying on the hereinafter described criminal activity, commit the offense of Gambling Promotion, to-wit: by operating and participating in the earnings of a gambling place, namely: a building located at 1601 Harrison, San Angelo, Texas, by then and there making and settling of bets.

A San Angelo Police SWAT team executed a search warrant and searched the house located at 1601 Harrison, in the city of San Angelo. When they entered the house, the officers found a craps table, dozens of dice, thousands of dollars in cash, and a notebook keeping account of debts. One of the windows was boarded up so the craps table could not be seen from outside the house. Signs posted inside the home declared "no checks, no credit, cash only."

Evidence shows that appellant assisted by Clements, Carpenter, and Richards conducted craps games in the building located at 1601 Harrison in San Angelo, where bets were made and settled. Appellant furnished free drinks and barbecue to those who participated in the dice games. Appellant used a dice table similar to those used in well-known casinos. Many citizens in the community participated in the dice games conducted by appellant and the other alleged individuals. Large amounts of money—thousands of dollars—were bet and lost. To prove appellant guilty of the offense charged, it was not necessary to show that he profited from the games. However, there is ample evidence that he did.

The jury as the trier of fact could rationally find from the direct and circumstantial evidence, viewed in the light most favorable to the prosecution, that appellant was guilty, beyond a reasonable doubt, of intentionally participating in a combination with Clements, Carpenter, and Richards to commit the Class A misdemeanor gambling offense of gambling promotion by intentionally and knowingly using the place alleged where bets were made and settled. The evidence is sufficient to support the jury's verdict finding appellant guilty of engaging in organized criminal activity. Appellant's sixth point of error is overruled.

In appellate cause number 3–01–00062–CR, it was charged that on or about March 31, 1999, appellant,

> did then and there, with intent to establish, maintain, or participate in a combination or in the profits of a combination, said combination consisting of LARRY DALE BAXTER, JERRY DEAN CLEMENTS, AND ROBERT FAIRCHILD, who collaborated in carrying on the hereinafter described criminal activity, commit the offense of GAMBLING PROMOTION, to-wit: by operating and participating in the earnings of a gambling place, namely: a building located at 1122 E. 22nd, San Angelo, Texas, by then and there making and settling of bets.

This case was tried jointly with cause number 3–01–00061–CR. The jury found appellant guilty of the lesser included offense of gambling promotion. The evidence is amply sufficient for the jury to rationally find beyond a reasonable doubt that appellant used a building located at 1122 E. 22nd in San Angelo to intentionally or knowingly operate a gambling place where bets were made and settled. Appellant's seventh point of error is overruled.

Juror Not Questioned

In his fifth point of error, appellant insists that the trial court erred in denying his "request to question a juror who indicated that the fact he knew several witnesses was 'affecting' him as a juror." On the second day of trial, the trial court told counsel that the bailiff had informed the court that one of the jurors had told the bailiff that "he [the juror] knows the witnesses ... and that it is affecting him as a juror." Defense Counsel asked to have the juror questioned. The trial court refused counsel's request. On appeal, appellant contends that "[a]ppellant's timely request to interrogate the juror to determine whether his knowledge of the State's witnesses was 'affecting him as a juror' called into question his ability to be fair and impartial...." Appellant argues: "During voir dire, the prosecutor asked if anyone knew any State's witnesses. While several panelists noted they knew some State's witnesses, none indicated their ability to be fair and impartial was affected by their knowledge." Appellant is mistaken. On the pages of the record indicated, the prospective jurors were not asked if they knew the witnesses who might testify. On the pages of the record indicated, the prospective jurors were asked whether they knew Jerry Dean Clements, Shannon Carpenter, or Robert Fairchild. These three individuals were alleged to have collaborated with appellant in committing the offense of gambling promotion, but none of these three individuals testified in the trial of these cases. Also, on the pages of the record designated, prospective jurors were asked by the prosecutor whether they knew attorneys Adam Morriss and Melvin Gray. Although Gray's name was mentioned during trial, he was not called as a witness and did not testify. Morriss did not testify before the jury; Morriss was called as a witness by defense counsel and testified out of the presence of the jury on a bill of exception for the defense.

We have examined the record made on jury voir dire and have been unable to find where either the prosecutors or defense counsel informed the prospective jurors who might be witnesses. The prospective jurors were never asked whether the witnesses who might testify would affect the juror's fairness and impartiality. Not having used diligence during voir dire to determine whether the witnesses expected to testify would cause any prospective juror to be prejudiced or biased, appellant cannot now complain.

The State, in its brief, argues that the juror who said he was "affected" by the witnesses who had testified was the same juror who had told the trial court after he had been selected as a juror that his service on the jury would interfere with his planned vacation. From our inspection of the record, we cannot determine whether this was true or not. Counsel has not designated where we can find, and we cannot find, the name or any identification of either the juror whose vacation plans would be interfered with or the juror who said he was "affected" by the witnesses who had testified.

It is also important to note that appellant did not file a motion for new trial and obtain a hearing in an attempt to complete the record on the issue he has now presented on appeal. A motion for new trial is not a requisite for raising a point on appeal; however, a motion for new trial is sometimes a necessary step to adduce facts of a matter not otherwise shown in the record. This is especially necessary when there is a claim of jury misconduct. Because of the state of the record before us, we are unable to say that the trial court abused its discretion in refusing to allow defense counsel to interrogate the juror. Appellant's fifth point of error is overruled.

The judgments are affirmed.

———————◆———————

Notes and Questions

1. Assume the State was correct in its identification of the complained-of juror. If there was nothing in the record substantiating this truth, the appellate court must disregard the State's assertion entirely. Both parties at trial must anticipate claims of error on appeal and prepare the record accordingly. Trial counsel's failure to supplement the record impedes appellate counsel's ability to do her job. When an appellate attorney receives a record that is incomplete, it narrows the issues she can raise on appeal. It is frustrating when appellate attorneys know a fact through their investigation of the case (*e.g.*, by talking with their client or interviewing trial counsel), but the fact is not evidenced anywhere in the record. As stated before, when this happens, the appellate court must assume it never happened.

2. One of the benefits of filing a motion for new trial, as mentioned earlier, is that it extends the time for the appellant to file his brief from 30 days after the judgment and sentence is pronounced to 90 days. For this reason alone, many defense attorneys file a motion for new trial, even when they do not anticipate having a motion for new trial hearing or using the motion to expand the record.

Investigating Juror Misconduct

When an attorney has reason to believe that jurors engaged in misconduct, she may request from the trial court the jurors' personal information in an effort to contact them and investigate.[43] The Code of Criminal Procedure states that a party who wishes to do this must make an application for disclosure to the trial court; however, the trial court may not disclose this information unless the party makes a "showing of good cause."[44] The following case explains what this showing requires.

Brian Pak Cyr v. State
308 S.W.3d 19
(Tex. App.—San Antonio 2009, no pet.)

[Appellant, Brian Cyr, was convicted of murdering Corey Baxter after a cell phone video emerged depicting Cyr's involvement in the revenge killing. Cyr was sentenced to ninety-nine years' imprisonment and given a $10,000 fine. In the trial court below, he was unsuccessful in his attempts to get a motion for new trial hearing or to obtain the juror's contact information.]

Juror Information Cards and Motion for New Trial Hearing

In two separate issues, Cyr argues that the trial court erred in denying his request to review juror information cards and in denying his motion for new trial without conducting a hearing. We disagree.

After the trial, Cyr filed a motion for new trial and a motion to view juror information. Attached to Cyr's motion for new trial was his counsel's affidavit in which his counsel affirmed the following:

> I was informed that one of the jurors in this case approached the media and alleged that she "was not comfortable with her verdict." I confirmed the information with a representative of the media who substantiated that the information was true. Additionally, I was informed that the juror believed that the defendant was not guilty but later changed her verdict during jury deliberations for an unknown reason. A hearing is necessary to determine if that individual juror's verdict was changed for any reason contrary to the

---

[43] TEX. CODE CRIM. PROC. ANN. art. 35.29(b) (West 2016).
[44] Id.

instructions of this Court or law. Such a verdict would therefore not be a fair expression of that juror's opinion.

Emphasizing the information contained within his counsel's affidavit, Cyr argued in his motion for new trial that the jury's verdict was decided in a manner other than a fair expression of a juror's opinion. In his request to view juror information, Cyr argued that he needed the juror information cards "to fully identify the juror and confer with the juror, if she is willing to communicate with counsel." According to Cyr, "[t]he communication with the jury is necessary for counsel to determine if any reversible error occurred and if a new trial may be necessary." The trial court denied both motions without holding a hearing.

Article 35.29 of the Texas Code of Criminal Procedure prohibits personal information about jurors from being disclosed after trial unless good cause is shown. "On a showing of good cause, the court shall permit disclosure of the information sought." Here, Cyr failed to show good cause. In his request for disclosure, Cyr argued that a juror had told a member of the media that she "was not comfortable with her verdict," and that the member of the media had been able to identify the juror only as "Lisa." Thus, Cyr argued the "information contained on the juror's information cards tendered to counsel at the time of voir dire is necessary for counsel to fully identify the juror and confer with the juror, if she is willing to communicate with counsel." Such allegations, however, are not sufficient to show good cause.

What constitutes good cause must be based upon more than a mere possibility that jury misconduct might have occurred; it must have a firm foundation. That a juror was "uncomfortable" with her verdict does not constitute a firm foundation that jury misconduct occurred. *See Castellano v. State*, No. 04–06–00524–CR, 2007 WL 2935399, at *3 (Tex. App.—San Antonio 2007, no pet.) (holding that defendant had "reason to believe" juror misconduct had occurred was not sufficient to show good cause); *Garza v. State*, No. 04–02–00599–CR, 2003 WL 23008845, at *10 (Tex. App.—San Antonio 2003, pet. ref'd) (holding that testimony of defendant's mother that juror was distant relative of defendant and was prejudiced against him was insufficient to show good cause because mother also admitted that she could not remember juror's first name, did not know how juror was related to defendant, and had no personal knowledge of the juror's feelings toward defendant). Therefore, the trial court did not err in denying Cyr's request for juror information.

Cyr also argues that the trial court erred in denying his motion for new trial without holding a hearing. We review the trial court's denial of a hearing on a motion for new trial for abuse of discretion.

The purpose of a hearing on a motion for new trial is to (1) decide whether a cause should be retried and (2) prepare a record for presenting appellate issues if the motion is denied. Such a hearing is not an absolute right and is not required when the matters raised in the motion for new trial are determinable from the record. Here, Cyr has alleged juror misconduct, which is a matter not determinable from the record. However, even though Cyr has raised a matter not determinable from the record, because requiring a hearing on all matters not determinable from the record could lead to "fishing expeditions," he would not be entitled to a hearing on his motion for new trial unless he established the existence of "reasonable grounds" showing that he could be entitled to relief.

Because Cyr must show reasonable grounds exist for a new trial, as a prerequisite to a hearing, his motion had to be supported by an affidavit, either of himself or someone else, specifically setting out the factual basis for the claim. The affidavit need not establish a prima facie case, or even reflect every component legally required to establish the relief requested. "It is sufficient if a fair reading of it gives rise to reasonable grounds in support of the claim."

The State argues that the affidavit in support of Cyr's motion for new trial, affirmed by Cyr's counsel, is insufficient because it does not reflect that Cyr's counsel had personal knowledge and was instead based on hearsay. "It is well established that a motion for new trial complaining of jury misconduct must be supported by the affidavit of a juror, or some other person who was in a position to know the facts, or must state some reason or excuse for failing to produce the affidavits." Counsel's affidavit does not reflect that he was in a position to know the facts. Instead, his affidavit affirms that a member of the media told him that a juror had told him that she was "uncomfortable" with the verdict. Thus, the affidavit was deficient, and the trial court did not err in failing to hold a hearing.

Moreover, even if the affidavit had been sufficient, the trial court still did not err in failing to hold a hearing because the affidavit did not establish the existence of reasonable grounds showing Cyr could be entitled to relief based on jury misconduct. To demonstrate jury misconduct, a defendant must show that (1) the misconduct occurred and (2) the misconduct resulted in harm to the movant. The affidavit at issue here merely states that a juror "was not comfortable with her verdict" and … "believed that the defendant was not guilty but later changed her verdict during jury deliberations for an unknown reason." Being uncomfortable with the verdict and changing your vote during jury deliberations for an unknown reason does not establish that reasonable grounds existed for Cyr to be entitled to a new trial based on jury misconduct. Therefore, the trial court did not err in denying Cyr's motion for new trial without holding a hearing.[45]

Ineffective Assistance of Counsel

The right to counsel necessarily encompasses the right to effective representation. Unfortunately, not all representation is effective. An attorney who fails to render effective assistance may harm a defendant at trial to such an extent that the error warrants a new trial or a new punishment hearing. That the defendant does not like the result of the trial is not enough to establish an ineffective assistance claim. That defense counsel could have or should have done things differently is not enough either. In fact, courts are reluctant to second-guess an attorney's decision-making process, even when another strategy may have led to a better outcome. The next case illustrates the test and the proper analysis a reviewing court uses to determine whether counsel's assistance was ineffective.

---

[45] Even if defense counsel were able to access the jurors' personal information, and even if the trial court held a hearing on the defendant's motion for new trial, it is not clear that the defense would have been able to present admissible evidence in support of a claim of juror misconduct. TEX. R. EVID. 606(b) prevents a juror from testifying about anything that occurred during deliberations, anything that affected a juror's vote, or any juror's mental processes concerning the verdict. The only exceptions to that rule is if an outside influence was improperly brought to bear upon a juror or if there was a need to rebut a claim the juror was not qualified to serve. Compare *Colyer v. State,* 428 S.W.3d 117, 125-30 (Tex. Crim. App. 2014) with *McQuarrie v. State,* 380 S.W.3d 145, 139-50 (Tex. Crim. App. 2012).

Lonnie Ray Andrews v. State
159 S.W.3d 98
(Tex. Crim. App. 2005)

In this case, during closing arguments, the prosecutor made a misstatement of the law that was detrimental to the appellant. The appellant's counsel failed to object to this misstatement of law. In a published case, the Court of Appeals overruled the appellant's point of error because there was no evidence of trial counsel's motive for failing to object to the prosecutor's misstatement. Because we conclude that, under the unusual circumstances of this case, there could be no legitimate trial strategy in failing to object to the prosecutor's misstatement, we reverse the judgment of the Court of Appeals.

I. Facts

The appellant was charged with three counts of sexual assault and one count of indecency with a child. On the day that voir dire began, the State filed a written motion to cumulate [or stack] the sentences under Penal Code Section 3.03. The State hand delivered a copy of the motion to defense counsel. At the close of the guilt phase of the trial, the jury found the appellant guilty of all four counts. Defense counsel did not request, and the charge during the punishment phase of the trial did not contain, an instruction explaining that the trial court may, in its discretion, stack the appellant's sentences.

Six days after filing the motion to cumulate sentences the same prosecutor who had filed the motion argued at the end of the punishment phase that the sentences could not be cumulated:

> So you have to come up with an amount. You've got four charges. They don't add up, by the way. You give him 20 years in each case, it's still just 20 years. It's still not 80. You can give different amounts if you want. You can give 20, 10, 10, five, it's still just 20. And you can forget about the fine. We're talking about keeping him off the streets, keeping him away from other people, for other victims, for the future and for what he did here.

This argument left the jury with the incorrect impression that the appellant's sentences could not be stacked and that the appellant would serve no more than twenty years in prison for all four counts. Defense counsel failed to object to this incorrect argument. The jury assessed punishment at 20 years' imprisonment and a fine of $10,000 for each of the three sexual assault counts and 18 years' imprisonment and a $5000 fine for the indecency count. In the presence of defense counsel, the trial court granted the State's motion to cumulate the sentences and imposed a combined prison sentence of 78 years.

On direct appeal, the appellant complained that his trial counsel was ineffective for failing to object to the prosecutor's misstatement of the law. The Court of Appeals affirmed the appellant's conviction, holding that it would not find counsel's performance deficient without a record that indicated counsel's reasons for failing to object.

The appellant filed a petition for discretionary review, which we granted, complaining that the Court of Appeals erred by rejecting his claim of ineffective assistance of counsel.

II. The Law

In *Strickland v. Washington*,[46] the Supreme Court articulated a two-prong test to be used when analyzing a claim of ineffective assistance of counsel. To have his conviction reversed on the grounds of ineffective assistance of counsel, an appellant must show that (1) counsel's representation fell below an objective standard of reasonableness and (2) the deficient performance prejudiced the appellant. Unless the appellant makes both showings, it cannot be said that his conviction is rendered unreliable by a breakdown in the adversarial process. In *Hernandez v. State*,[47] we adopted the *Strickland* two-prong test for criminal cases in Texas.

Our review of counsel's performance must be highly deferential. There is a strong presumption that counsel's conduct falls within a wide range of reasonable professional assistance, and the defendant must overcome the presumption. We determine the reasonableness of counsel's challenged conduct in context, and view it as of the time of counsel's conduct.

We have said that we commonly assume a strategic motive if any can be imagined and find counsel's performance deficient only if the conduct was so outrageous that no competent attorney would have engaged in it. The policy behind this course is that "[i]ntensive scrutiny of counsel and rigid requirements for acceptable assistance could dampen the ardor and impair the independence of defense counsel, discourage the acceptance of assigned

---

[46] 466 U.S. 668, 694 (1984).
[47] 726 S.W.2d 53 (Tex. Crim. App. 1986).

cases, and undermine the trust between attorney and client." This standard balances the protection of these important policy interests with the protection of each defendant's fundamental Sixth Amendment rights.

As a result, we have said that the record on direct appeal is in almost all cases inadequate to show that counsel's conduct fell below an objectively reasonable standard of performance and that the better course is to pursue the claim in habeas proceedings. But, when no reasonable trial strategy could justify the trial counsel's conduct, counsel's performance falls below an objective standard of reasonableness as a matter of law, regardless of whether the record adequately reflects the trial counsel's subjective reasons for acting as she did.

To satisfy the second prong of the *Strickland* test, we do not require that the appellant show that there would have been a different result if counsel's performance had not been deficient. The defendant must show only that "there is a reasonable probability that, but for counsel's unprofessional errors, the result of the proceeding would have been different. A reasonable probability is a probability sufficient to undermine confidence in the outcome."

III. Deficient Performance

The Supreme Court in *Strickland* said that our review of counsel's performance must be highly deferential. But, in the statement immediately preceding that one, the Supreme Court said that, "In making [its] determination, the [reviewing] court should keep in mind that counsel's function, as elaborated in prevailing professional norms, is to make the adversarial testing process work in the particular case." Counsel failed to do so in this case when he failed to object to the prosecutor's misstatement of the law, even though counsel had received a copy of the State's motion to cumulate sentences on the day that voir dire began. Defense counsel has a duty to correct misstatements of law that are detrimental to his client. This duty derives from counsel's function "to make the adversarial testing process work in the particular case." There can be no reasonable trial strategy in failing to correct a misstatement of law that is detrimental to the client.

The State argues that, because the record is silent about counsel's reasons for failing to object, we should not conclude that counsel's performance was deficient. It says that counsel should be given an opportunity to explain his reasons and claims that this case is no different than *Freeman v. State*,[48] in which we held that, absent an explanation of trial counsel's reasons for failing to file a motion to recuse the trial judge, we could not presume that counsel's performance was deficient.

...Our conclusion regarding the first prong of the *Strickland* test is not a departure from our holding that generally a claim of ineffective assistance of counsel may not be addressed on direct appeal because the record on appeal usually is not sufficient to conclude that counsel's performance was deficient. We ordinarily need to hear from counsel whether there was a legitimate trial strategy for a certain act or omission. Frequently, we can conceive potential reasonable trial strategies that counsel could have been pursuing. When that is the case, we simply cannot conclude that counsel has performed deficiently.

That is not the situation that we are dealing with in this case. Under the extremely unusual circumstances of this case, the record contains all the information that we need to make a decision. Trial counsel failed to object to the prosecutor's misstatement of the law regarding whether the appellant's sentences could be stacked, even though he knew that the State had filed a motion to cumulate the sentences. There can be no reasonable trial strategy in failing to correct this false impression that was harmful to the appellant.

IV. Prejudice

The record also supports the conclusion that the second prong of the *Strickland* test has been satisfied. The State's argument left the jury with the false impression that the maximum sentence that the appellant would serve was twenty years when the maximum sentence was really eighty years. In fact, the appellant was sentenced to a total of 78 years. The jury had incorrect information from which to assess the appropriate sentence for the appellant. The prosecutor told the jury that, after assessing a twenty-year sentence on the first count, it would not matter what sentence the jury assessed for the remaining three counts.

Had defense counsel objected on the basis that the prosecutor's argument was a misstatement of the law, the trial court could have corrected the misstatement and told the jury not to consider whether the court could or would cumulate the sentences. Because the jury received incorrect information about the appellant's punishment, the record supports the

---

[48] 125 S.W.3d 505, 506-07 (Tex. Crim. App. 2003).

conclusion that there is a reasonable probability that the result would have been different.

V. Conclusion

This is a rare case. This is a case in which the appellant has raised a claim of ineffective assistance of counsel on direct appeal and the record is sufficient for us to make a decision on the merits. Because we conclude that the record is sufficient to conclude that counsel's performance was deficient and that the appellant was prejudiced by counsel's failure to object to the prosecutor's misstatement of law, we reverse the judgment of the Court of Appeals and remand for a new punishment hearing.

———————◆———————

Notes and Questions

1. The *Andrews* Court repeatedly emphasizes the extremely unusual circumstances of the case. It is likewise extremely unusual for an appellate court to render counsel's performance ineffective without an explanation from defense counsel through testimony or affidavits presented at a motion for new trial hearing. The *Andrews* Court simply believed there could not be any strategy for an omission of this magnitude. The important takeaways of this case are the two-part *Strickland* test, its application, and the policy reasons for the law.

2. In the *Andrews* case, the defendant's ineffective assistance of counsel (IAC) claim was based upon defense counsel's failure to object to the prosecutor's misstatement of the law. This is not the only basis for an IAC claim. IAC claims may relate to a failure to investigate defenses or call witnesses or present evidence at trial.

Another IAC claim arises when defense counsel gives bad legal advice to a defendant who is about to enter a plea of guilty. Perhaps defense counsel incorrectly said his client was eligible for probation when he was not. Maybe defense counsel was confused about the punishment ranges or level of offense and indicated the defendant would serve a lighter sentence. What usually happens in these scenarios is the defendant rejects a plea bargain only to learn later that his attorney's advice was erroneous. In the end, had he accepted the State's offer, he would have received a lighter punishment. This is when the defendant pursues an IAC claim based upon bad legal advice.

The Texas Court of Criminal Appeals uses the following test to determine whether an attorney has rendered IAC in the plea context:

> [T]o establish prejudice in a claim of ineffective assistance of counsel in which a defendant is not made aware of a plea-bargain offer, or rejects a plea-bargain because of bad legal advice, the applicant must show a reasonable probability that: (1) he would have accepted the earlier offer if counsel had not given ineffective assistance; (2) the prosecution would not have withdrawn the offer; and (3) the trial court would not have refused to accept the plea bargain.[49]

This is the same standard the federal courts use.[50] It essentially requires the defendant to establish he would have taken the plea offer but for the bad advice, the State would not have changed its mind about the negotiated plea, and the judge would have accepted the negotiated plea.[51] This is a difficult hurdle few defendants can overcome.

Having said that, some courts do sustain an IAC claim for bad legal advice given during plea bargaining. When a claim is sustained, the appellate court orders the State to re-offer the plea bargain so the defendant can accept it, placing the defendant in the same position before he received and acted upon defense counsel's bad advice.[52]

———————◆———————

Practice Questions

Post-conviction relief questions do not appear on every exam, but when they do, they ask about appeals, motions for new trial, preserving the record, and IAC claims. In recent exams, one question has been devoted to the topics in this chapter.

In the comments to these questions, examiners frequently state that few examinees knew the answers to the questions. Perhaps post-conviction relief

---

[49] *Ex parte Argent*, 393 S.W.3d 781, 784 (Tex. Crim. App. 2013).

[50] *Id.* at 783 (relying on *Missouri v. Frye*, 132 S. Ct. 1399, 1409 (2012); *Lafler v. Cooper*, 132 S. Ct. 1376, 1376 (2012)).

[51] *Id.*

[52] *Rodriguez v. State*, 470 S.W.3d 823, 829 (Tex. Crim. App. 2015) ("Because Appellant was prejudiced by counsel's ineffective assistance in pre–trial plea bargaining, the first trial judge followed the remedy outlined in *Lafler* and ordered the State to reoffer the ten–year plea.").

is not widely taught in Texas Criminal Procedure courses. Maybe students are tired near the end of the exam; this topic almost always appears in the last or next-to last question. Regardless, this is the least diverse area of questions, which means students who know the topics in this chapter well could easily score points on the final question(s).

1. (F-2016, J-2010, J-2007, and J-2003) The jury convicts Defendant. After her conviction, Defendant complains that Defense Counsel failed to investigate her alibi and evidence that could have exonerated her.

    If Defendant's claims are true, how can she attack her conviction? What legal standard must she meet to prevail?

    _____

    _____

    _____

    _____

    _____

2. (J-2015) Immediately following Defendant's plea of guilt and conviction, she writes Judge complaining that you improperly advised her on the punishment range when she pled guilty to the charged offense. As a result, she is serving a significantly longer sentence.

    If Defendant's claim is true, how can she attack it following her conviction? What is her remedy?

    _____

    _____

    _____

    _____

    _____

3. (F-2015) Defendant is acquitted of all charges. Prosecutor files an appeal within the required time. In it, she asserts the evidence of Defendant's guilt is legally sufficient and asks the Court to reverse the jury's finding of not guilty.

How should the appellate court rule on Prosecutor's appeal?

_____

_____

_____

_____

_____

4. (J-2013 and F-2006) After the State rests, you present your case. You call Expert to the stand to rebut the State's expert testimony. Prosecutor objects to Expert's testimony as cumulative, and Judge sustains the objection. You believe Judge's ruling is erroneous and prejudicial to Defendant's case.

    What must you do in order to preserve this evidentiary issue for appeal and when must you do it? Explain.

    _____

    _____

    _____

    _____

    _____

5. (J-2012 and J-2009) Defendant is convicted following a high-publicity trial, which is covered by the local media. Following the trial, a newspaper reporter interviews the jurors. One of the jurors tells the reporter, "During deliberations, I used my cell phone to call my friend, who is a police officer. She said the Defendant was definitely guilty. After I told the other jurors what my friend said, we voted to convict him."

    What procedural step can you take to bring this matter to the judge's attention? When should you take this step? Explain.

    _____

    _____

    _____

_____

_____

6. (J-2011) What is the standard of review for challenging the legal sufficiency of the evidence following a conviction? Explain.

_____

_____

_____

_____

_____

7. (F-2010) You explore the possibility of filing a motion for new trial, but decide against it. Defendant would nevertheless like to appeal his conviction.

What procedural step must you take to perfect his appeal, and when must you take this step?

_____

_____

_____

_____

_____

8. (J-2007, F-2006, and J-2002) You suspect juror misconduct following the jury's guilty verdict. You ask your investigator to interview the jurors to discover whether your suspicions are correct. However, the court clerk refuses to give you the jurors' personal contact information.

What procedural step, if any, can you take to obtain this information? If you do obtain the information, what procedural step will you take with it to establish juror misconduct? Explain.

_____

_____

_____

_____

_____

9. (J-2000) Defendant is convicted at trial. Defendant informs you that she would like to appeal. You announce orally in open court that you hereby appeal the verdict and state the reasons for appeal.

Is this enough to preserve Defendant's right to appeal? If you decide to file a motion for new trial, within what time period must you file it? May the court grant you an extension beyond that time to file your motion for new trial? Explain.

_____

_____

_____

_____

_____

—————————————◆—————————————

Chapter 15
Evidence

Introduction

Many of you took an evidence course in law school. It is an important class for at least two reasons. First, evidence is a big component of civil and criminal litigation. Second, it is tested on the first and second days of the Texas bar exam. On the first day of the exam, Texas Rules of Evidence (TRE) are tested on the Texas Civil and Texas Criminal Procedure and Evidence portions of the bar exam. On the second day of the bar exam, examinees are tested by the Multi-State Bar Exam (MBE) on the Federal Rules of Evidence (FRE). There are similarities and differences between these evidentiary rules. This chapter examines the TREs in the context of criminal trials.

While this chapter is titled "Evidence," quite a few evidentiary rules were addressed in other chapters. For example, it was appropriate to discuss Texas Rule of Evidence 410, which addresses the inadmissibility of plea negotiations evidence, in Chapter 8. The evidentiary rules that are tested on the bar exam that were not discussed in other chapters are included in this chapter.

In recent years, bar examiners have asked three or four evidence questions on each bar exam. However, there have been as few as zero questions and as many as eight evidence questions on a single exam. Trial and evidence questions are the two categories of most frequently asked questions.

The structure of this chapter is different from the others. This chapter topically groups evidentiary rules, any applicable common or statutory law, and practice questions. The practice questions do not appear at the end of the text but rather in the text of the chapter within their correlating topic. This chapter addresses big evidentiary topics such as impeachment evidence, character evidence, hearsay and hearsay exceptions, privileges, and several smaller topics related to evidence in the criminal litigation context.

Impeachment Evidence

In a trial, the judge or jury is asked to determine what happened. This process requires fact finders to decide who to believe as both parties present a different version of events. The law permits attorneys to discredit witnesses through impeachment. Criminal convictions, negative reputations and opinions, biases, and prior statements all serve to impeach witnesses.

Impeachment through criminal conviction is probably the most common way attorneys attempt to discredit a witness's testimony. In Texas Rule of Evidence 609, only some crimes may be used to impeach a witness: felonies and crimes of moral turpitude. What are crimes of moral turpitude? The rule does not say, but courts have held the following crimes impugn a person's character: felony offenses, theft, male-on-female assault, abuse of children, lying to an officer (as opposed to remaining mute) when he asks a person to identify himself, and misdemeanor sexual crimes (*e.g.*, prostitution, public lewdness, and indecent exposure).[1]

Observe below that the more probative than prejudicial balancing test applies when the conviction is less than ten years old. When the conviction is more than ten years old (practitioners call this a "remote" conviction), the offering party must meet a more onerous test. The language of the rule does not ban these convictions from being used, but it does limit their admission.

Rule 609. Impeachment by Evidence of a Criminal Conviction

(a) In General. Evidence of a criminal conviction offered to attack a witness's character for truthfulness must be admitted if:

(1) the crime was a felony or involved moral turpitude, regardless of punishment;

(2) the probative value of the evidence outweighs its prejudicial effect to a party; and

(3) it is elicited from the witness or established by public record.

(b) Limit on Using the Evidence After Ten Years. This subdivision (b) applies if more than ten years have passed since the witness's conviction or release from confinement for it, whichever is later. Evidence of the conviction is admissible only if its probative value, supported by specific facts and circumstances, substantially outweighs its prejudicial effect.

---

[1] *E.g., Campos v. State*, 458 S.W.3d 120, 149 (Tex. App.—Houston [1st Dist.] 2015), *judgment vacated on other grounds*, 466 S.W.3d 181 (Tex. Crim. App. 2015) (assaults on women and children are crimes of moral turpitude); *Polk v. State*, 865 S.W.2d 627, 630 (Tex. App.—Fort Worth 1993, pet. ref'd) (indecent exposure is a crime of moral turpitude); *Martin v. State*, 265 S.W.3d 435, 444 (Tex. App.—Houston [1st Dist.] 2007, no pet.) (felony drug convictions, theft, and failure to identify are crimes of moral turpitude, but driving while intoxicated is not); *Hardeman v. State*, 868 S.W.2d 404, 405 (Tex. App.—Austin 1993, pet. granted) (prostitution); *Escobedo v. State*, 202 S.W.3d 844, 848 (Tex. App.—Waco 2006, pet. ref'd) (public lewdness).

(c) Effect of a Pardon, Annulment, or Certificate of Rehabilitation. Evidence of a conviction is not admissible if:

(1) the conviction has been the subject of a pardon, annulment, and the person has not been convicted of a later crime that was classified as a felony or involved moral turpitude, regardless of punishment; or

(2) probation has been satisfactorily completed for the conviction, and the person has not been convicted of a later crime that was classified as a felony or involved moral turpitude, regardless of punishment. ...

(e) Pendency of an Appeal. A conviction for which an appeal is pending is not admissible under this rule.

Finally, though a witness or a defendant may be impeached with convictions stemming from felony offenses or crimes of moral turpitude, the impeaching party may not discuss the underlying facts or details of those convictions.[2] "This is because evidence of prior convictions and extraneous bad acts 'is inherently prejudicial, tends to confuse the issues in the case, and forces the accused to defend himself against charges which he had not been notified would be brought against him.'"[3]

1. (J-2015, F-2015, F-2014, F-2014, J-2010, J-2006, J-2004, F-2004, J-2003, J-2001, F-2001, and J-2000) Before trial, you learn that the State's Witness has three prior convictions. The first is a felony drug conviction from 1995; probation was revoked, and Witness served two years in prison. The second is a misdemeanor driving while intoxicated charge from 2004; Witness was sentenced to ten days in jail. The third conviction is a 2016 felony theft conviction with a sentence of five years' imprisonment, but the case is on appeal.

---

[2] *Mays v. State*, 726 S.W.2d 937, 953 (Tex. Crim. App. 1986).
[3] *Arebalo v. State*, 143 S.W.3d 402, 407 (Tex. App.—Austin 2004, pet. ref'd) (quoting *Albrecht v. State*, 486 S.W.2d 97, 100 (Tex. Crim. App. 1972)).

What, if any, of these convictions can be used for impeachment purposes? Explain.

_____

_____

_____

_____

_____

2. (J-2008) Prosecutor, during cross-examination of Defendant asks, "Isn't it true that you were convicted of aggravated assault with a deadly weapon six years ago and in that assault, you broke the Victim's jawbone, cheekbone, and nose even though the Victim had retreated and was begging you to stop the assault?"

If you object to Prosecutor's question, what is your basis? Explain.

_____

_____

_____

_____

_____

Rule 608. A Witness's Character for Truthfulness or Untruthfulness

(a) Reputation or Opinion Evidence. A witness's credibility may be attacked or supported by testimony about the witness's reputation for having a character for truthfulness or untruthfulness, or by testimony in the form of an opinion about that character. But evidence of truthful character is admissible only after the witness's character for truthfulness has been attacked.

(b) Specific Instances of Conduct. Except for a criminal conviction under Rule 609, a party may not inquire into or offer extrinsic evidence to prove specific instances of the witness's conduct in order to attack or support the witness's character for truthfulness.

3. (J-2011) During cross examination of Witness, you ask: "Didn't you cheat on an exam in college once?" Prosecutor objects to your question on the grounds that it is improper impeachment.

    How should the Court rule? Explain.

    _____

    _____

    _____

    _____

    _____

Rule 613. Witness's Prior Statement and Bias or Interest

(a) Witness's Prior Inconsistent Statement.

(1) *Foundation Requirement.* When examining a witness about the witness's prior inconsistent statement—whether oral or written—a party must first tell the witness:

> (A) the contents of the statement;
> (B) the time and place of the statement; and
> (C) the person to whom the witness made the statement.

(2) *Need Not Show Written Statement.* If the witness's prior inconsistent statement is written, a party need not show it to the witness before inquiring about it, but must, upon request, show it to opposing counsel.

(3) *Opportunity to Explain or Deny.* A witness must be given the opportunity to explain or deny the prior inconsistent statement.

(4) *Extrinsic Evidence.* Extrinsic evidence of a witness's prior inconsistent statement is not admissible unless the witness is first examined about the statement and fails to unequivocally admit making the statement....

(b) Witness's Bias or Interest.

(1) *Foundation Requirement.* When examining a witness about the witness's bias or interest, a party must first tell the witness the circumstances or statements that tend to show the witness's bias or interest. If examining a witness about a statement—whether oral or written—to prove the witness's bias or interest, a party must tell the witness:

     (A) the contents of the statement;
     (B) the time and place of the statement; and
     (C) the person to whom the statement was made.

(2) *Need Not Show Written Statement.* If a party uses a written statement to prove the witness's bias or interest, a party need not show the statement to the witness before inquiring about it, but must, upon request, show it to opposing counsel.

(3) *Opportunity to Explain or Deny.* A witness must be given the opportunity to explain or deny the circumstances or statements that tend to show the witness's bias or interest. And the witness's proponent may present evidence to rebut the charge of bias or interest.

(4) *Extrinsic Evidence.* Extrinsic evidence of a witness's bias or interest is not admissible unless the witness is first examined about the bias or interest and fails to unequivocally admit it.

(c) Witness's Prior Consistent Statement. Unless Rule 801(e)(1)(B) provides otherwise, a witness's prior consistent statement is not admissible if offered solely to enhance the witness's credibility.

Rule 607. Who May Impeach a Witness

Any party, including the party that called the witness, may attack the witness's credibility.

4. (J-2012, F-2007, and F-2006) After the State rests, you call Cousin of Defendant to testify. Cousin's testimony differs from what he told you in the past.

    Can you impeach the credibility of your own witness? If you can do so, describe the means of impeaching someone whose testimony has changed.

    _____

    _____

    _____

    _____

    _____

5. (J-2011, J-2009, and F-2004) Co-defendant has agreed to testify against Defendant in return for a lesser punishment. You represent Defendant. On cross-examination, you ask Co-defendant, "Isn't it true that in exchange for your testimony today, Prosecutor has agreed to reduce your sentence?" Prosecutor objects to this question.

    How should Judge rule and why?

    _____

    _____

    _____

    _____

    _____

----------------◆----------------

Character Evidence

Many defendants have committed extraneous offenses or prior bad acts. These offenses and acts are usually excluded from evidence for fear jurors may convict for the wrong reasons. Nevertheless, they may come into evidence for limited purposes. When you answer practice or bar questions about character evidence, it is important that you know the underlying facts and charge and consider why the admitting party is attempting to offer the character evidence. First, let us examine the limitations Texas places on character evidence.

Rule 403. Excluding Relevant Evidence for Prejudice, Confusion, or Other Reasons

The court may exclude relevant evidence if its probative value is substantially outweighed by a danger of one or more of the following: unfair prejudice, confusing the issues, misleading the jury, undue delay, or needlessly presenting cumulative evidence.

Rule 404. Character Evidence; Crimes or Other Acts

(a) Character Evidence.

(1) *Prohibited Uses.* Evidence of a person's character or character trait is not admissible to prove that on a particular occasion the person acted in accordance with the character or trait.

(2) *Exceptions for an Accused.*

(A) In a criminal case, a defendant may offer evidence of the defendant's pertinent trait, and if the evidence is admitted, the prosecutor may offer evidence to rebut it.

(3) *Exceptions for a Victim.*

(A) In a criminal case, subject to the limitations in Rule 412,[4] a defendant may offer evidence of a victim's pertinent trait, and if the evidence is admitted, the prosecutor may offer evidence to rebut it.

(B) In a homicide case, the prosecutor may offer evidence of the victim's trait of peacefulness to rebut evidence that the victim was the first aggressor.

 (4) *Exceptions for a Witness.* Evidence of a witness's character may be admitted under Rules 607, 608, and 609 [which are rules that address impeachment through opinion and reputation evidence and impeachment by evidence of criminal conviction].

(b) Crimes, Wrongs, or Other Acts.

(1) *Prohibited Uses.* Evidence of a crime, wrong, or other act is not admissible to prove a person's character in order to show that on a particular occasion the person acted in accordance with the character.

(2) *Permitted Uses; Notice in Criminal Case.* This evidence may be admissible for another purpose, such as proving motive, opportunity, intent, preparation, plan, knowledge, identity, absence of mistake, or lack of accident.

---

[4] Texas Rule of Evidence 412 deems reputation or opinion evidence about a sexual assault victim's past sexual behavior inadmissible in a sexual assault case. The rule permits the use of evidence of specific instances of the victim's past sexual behavior, but only if the probative value outweighs the danger of unfair prejudice and only then when the evidence is used to explain or rebut scientific evidence (*e.g.*, a DNA result), bias or motive, or consent.

Character Evidence Balancing Test and Burden of Proof

As you see from Rule 403, character evidence admissible under Rule 404 must still meet the Rule 403 balancing test.[5] This balancing process takes place outside of the presence of the jury.[6] The jury is excused, and the judge hears arguments from both parties. Suppose the prosecutor seeks to admit a prior offense through Rule 404. Defense counsel will object, usually arguing it is improper character conformity evidence. "After the opponent objects to the evidence under Rule 404, the proponent has the burden to satisfy the court the evidence is relevant beyond character conformity."[7] The opponent may argue that even if the character evidence is being admitted for proper purposes, the evidence is more prejudicial than probative under Rule 403.[8] In the end, the proponent must satisfy Rules 403 and 404 before the evidence is deemed admissible.

6. (J-2015 and F-2015) Defendant testifies at trial that he struck his Wife accidentally and that he would never hit a woman intentionally. Prosecutor seeks to admit evidence that Defendant pled guilty five years ago and served a jail sentence for assaulting a woman he dated. You object to this evidence on the grounds that it is improper character evidence admitted to show character conformity.

   How should Judge rule? Explain.

   _____

   _____

   _____

   _____

   _____

---

[5] *E.g., Martin v. State*, 144 S.W.3d 29, 33 (Tex. App.—Beaumont 2004), *aff'd*, 173 S.W.3d 463 (Tex. Crim. App. 2005) (extraneous sexual assault evidence admissible in rape case because victim's consent was an issue, and judge conducted 403 balancing test before permitting introduction of extraneous offense evidence).
[6] *Self v. State*, 860 S.W.2d 261, 264 (Tex. App.—Fort Worth 1993, pet. ref'd).
[7] *Grider v. State*, 69 S.W.3d 681, 687 (Tex. App.—Texarkana 2002, no pet.)
[8] *Montgomery v. State*, 810 S.W.2d 372, 389 (Tex. Crim. App. 1990).

7. (F-2012, J-2009, J-2007, F-2006, F-2005, F-2003, J-2002, J-2001, and F-2001) During Prosecutor's case, she calls Officer to testify about all of the times he has arrested Defendant over the years. You request that Judge consider the admissibility of Officer's testimony in a hearing outside the presence of the jury.

What will you argue to exclude Officer's testimony? Who bears the burden of proof at this hearing? Explain.

_____

_____

_____

_____

_____

◆

Experts and Expert Opinions

Most criminal trials do not require expert testimony. In the event an expert is called to testify, the Texas Rules of Evidence address the scope of testimony, qualifications of the witness, and procedures required before the expert's testimony or opinion are admitted into evidence. This section will address those rules.

This first section examines who may testify as an expert and what an expert may testify about. You will see Texas Rule of Evidence 702 address these issues and a case that brings in two additional evidentiary rules that speak to an expert witness's qualifications.

Rule 702. Testimony by Expert Witnesses

A witness who is qualified as an expert by knowledge, skill, experience, training, or education may testify in the form of an opinion or otherwise if the expert's scientific, technical, or other specialized knowledge will help the trier of fact to understand the evidence or to determine a fact in issue.

Martha Aracely Richter v. State
482 S.W.3d 288
(Tex. App.—Texarkana 2015, no pet.)

The Texas Rules of Evidence set out three separate conditions regarding admissibility of expert testimony. First, Rule 104(a) requires that "[p]reliminary questions concerning the qualification of a person to be a witness ... be determined by the court...." Second, Rule 702 states: "If scientific, technical, or other specialized knowledge will assist the trier of fact to understand the evidence or to determine a fact in issue, a witness qualified as an expert by knowledge, skill, experience, training, or education may testify thereto in the form of an opinion or otherwise." And third, Rules 401 and 402 render testimony admissible only if it "tend[s] to make the existence of any fact that is of consequence to the determination of the action more probable or less probable than it would be without the evidence."

These rules require a trial judge to make three separate inquiries, which must all be met before admitting expert testimony: "(1) the witness qualifies as an expert by reason of his knowledge, skill, experience, training, or education; (2) the subject matter of the testimony is an appropriate one for expert testimony; and (3) admitting the expert testimony will actually assist the fact-finder in deciding the case." These conditions are commonly referred to as (1) qualification, (2) reliability, and (3) relevance.

8. (J-2014) You call Expert to the stand to testify about the breathalyzer results. Expert is a former toxicologist who worked for the Department of Public Safety. When you ask Expert whether the breath test result in this case is reliable, Prosecutor objects that Expert is not qualified to give her opinion about this evidence.

   How should Judge assess whether Expert is qualified to testify about the State's evidence?

   _____

   _____

   _____

   _____

   _____

Judges are not the only ones responsible for testing an expert's qualifications. Attorneys have an opportunity to test an expert's qualifications and the basis for any opinion he gives at trial based upon his expertise or analysis of the evidence.

Rule 705. Disclosing the Underlying Facts or Data and Examining an Expert about Them

> **(b) Voir Dire Examination of an Expert About the Underlying Facts or Data.** Before an expert states an opinion or discloses the underlying facts or data, an adverse party ... in a criminal case must ... be permitted to examine the expert about the underlying facts or data. This examination must take place outside the jury's hearing.

Pay attention to the "must" language above. This rule permits opposing counsel the right to voir dire the expert. In Chapter 11, you learned that *voir dire* literally means "to see to speak" in French. This phrase is used not only to describe the attorneys' right to see and speak with potential jurors, it also describes the attorneys' right to test an alleged expert's expertise before the witness is permitted to testify at trial. Following voir dire, if the trial court finds the expert witness is, in fact, qualified to render an opinion—using the three steps above—the testimony will be admitted. The judge has discretion following voir dire to allow the expert to continue with his testimony.[9]

9. (F-2014, F-2010, J-2006, F-2005, J-2004, J-2003, F-2003, and J-2001) Prosecutor calls Expert to testify. You suspect Expert is not really an expert on the subject matter in question. You request an opportunity to question Expert before he testifies in front of the jury. How should Judge rule? Explain.

_____

_____

_____

_____

_____

---

[9] *Rodgers v. State*, 205 S.W.3d 525, 528 (Tex. Crim. App. 2006).

The next case discusses the criteria for determining if evidence derived from a scientific theory is reliable and the factors that help a trial court assess reliability. The criteria and the factors are bolded in the text below for a reason: bar examiners have asked questions requesting examinees to list the three criteria *and* questions requesting examinees to list at least five of the factors. Examinees must keep the two lists separate and be ready to list either set after closely assessing which list (criteria or factors) is the basis for the answer.

Barry Dean Kelly v. State
824 S.W.2d 568
(Tex. Crim. App. 1992)

How does the proponent of novel scientific evidence prove it to be reliable? As a matter of common sense, **evidence derived from a scientific theory, to be considered reliable, must satisfy three criteria** in any particular case: (a) the underlying scientific theory must be valid; (b) the technique applying the theory must be valid; and (c) the technique must have been properly applied on the occasion in question. Under Rule 104(a) and (c) and Rule 702, all three criteria must be proven to the trial court, outside the presence of the jury, before the evidence may be admitted. **Factors that could affect a trial court's determination of reliability include,** but are not limited to, the following: (1) the extent to which the underlying scientific theory and technique are accepted as valid by the relevant scientific community, if such a community can be ascertained; (2) the qualifications of the expert(s) testifying; (3) the existence of literature supporting or rejecting the underlying scientific theory and technique; (4) the potential rate of error of the technique; (5) the availability of other experts to test and evaluate the technique; (6) the clarity with which the underlying scientific theory and technique can be explained to the court; and (7) the experience and skill of the person(s) who applied the technique on the occasion in question. ...

[B]efore novel scientific evidence may be admitted under Rule 702, the proponent must persuade the trial court, by clear and convincing evidence, that the evidence is reliable and therefore relevant.

10. (J-2013) Prosecutor calls Expert to offer bite mark testimony based upon forensic science theories. After reading recent news articles about the unreliability of such evidence, you object that the testimony should be prohibited because it is untrustworthy .

What three criteria must evidence derived from a scientific theory meet before it is deemed reliable?

_____

_____

_____

_____

_____

11. (J-2007, J-2005, and F-2002) You call Expert to testify about the problems with eyewitness identification. Prosecutor objects on the basis that this evidence is unreliable and not relevant. Judge then excuses the jurors to have a hearing.

List five factors Judge should consider in determining whether the evidence based on a scientific theory is reliable.

_____

_____

_____

_____

_____

Handwriting Comparisons

In some cases—for example, financial crimes—the fact finder is called upon to determine whether handwriting or a signature belongs to the defendant. Evidence of suspected handwriting may be compared to a known sample of handwriting by an expert, a layperson, or the fact finder.[10] However, the Texas Code of Criminal Procedure states that if a defendant

_____

[10] TEX. CODE CRIM. PROC. ANN. § art. 38.27 (West 2016).

denies the handwriting is hers under oath, proof by comparison is not sufficient to establish the handwriting in fact belongs to her.[11] Without additional corroborating evidence in the face of denial, the handwriting comparison cannot be considered by the factfinder.[12]

12. (J-2010) Can Expert's handwriting comparison alone be sufficient to establish Defendant forged Victim's signature on the check? Explain.

_____

_____

_____

_____

_____

Lay Witness Opinion Evidence

Experts are limited to give opinions about subjects in their expertise that are reliable and relevant. Similarly, law witness opinions are limited by Rule 701.

Rule 701. Opinion Testimony by Lay Witnesses

If a witness is not testifying as an expert, testimony in the form of an opinion is limited to one that is … rationally based on the witness's perception; and … helpful to clearly understanding the witness's testimony or to determining a fact in issue.

13. (J-2011) Prosecutor calls Victim to testify about his identity being stolen. Victim testifies that he discovered his identity was stolen when he was contacted by the Internal Revenue Service. He has no idea how his Social Security number was obtained, and he has never met Defendant before. At the conclusion of his testimony, Prosecutor asks Victim, "Do you

---

[11] *Id.*
[12] *Camacho v. State*, 765 S.W.2d 431, 432-33 (Tex. Crim. App. 1989).

have an opinion about whether Defendant is guilty of knowingly and intentionally stealing your identity as charged in the indictment?"

On what basis, if any, can you object to Prosecutor's question and Victim's opinion? Explain.

_____

_____

_____

_____

_____

———————————◆———————————

Privileges

Whether communications between two people are privileged varies considerably between the Federal and Texas Rules of Evidence. As a result, bar examiners frequently ask bar examinees privilege questions. This section will examine Texas law on lawyer-client, spousal, and clergy privileges as well the very narrow physician-patient privilege.

Rule 503. Lawyer-Client Privilege

(b) Rules of Privilege.

(1) General Rule. A client has a privilege to refuse to disclose and to prevent any other person from disclosing confidential communications made to facilitate the rendition of professional legal services to the client:

(A) between the client or the client's representative and the client's lawyer or the lawyer's representative;

(B) between the client's lawyer and the lawyer's representative;

(C) by the client, the client's representative, the client's lawyer, or the lawyer's representative to a lawyer representing another party in a pending action or that lawyer's representative, if the communications concern a matter of common interest in the pending action;

(D) between the client's representatives or between the client and the client's representative; or

(E) among lawyers and their representatives representing the same client.

(2) Special Rule in a Criminal Case. In a criminal case, a client has a privilege to prevent a lawyer or lawyer's representative from disclosing any other fact that came to the knowledge of the lawyer or the lawyer's representative by reason of the attorney-client relationship.

Who is a client, for the purposes of this privilege? She is a person who is either represented by an attorney who is providing professional legal services or a person who consults with an attorney in the hopes of obtaining legal services.[13] There are policy reasons for extending the word *client* for purposes of the attorney-client privilege beyond someone who has actually paid for and is receiving legal services:

> [A]llowing the privilege only after a contractual attorney-client relationship had already been established is not only contrary to the wording of the evidentiary rule, but it would also be unsound public policy. Such a policy would have a chilling effect on defendants' willingness to be candid with the lawyers whose services they seek to obtain. Moreover, such a lack of candor on the potential client's part would not be in the lawyer's best interest either, because the lawyer would then have to decide whether to represent a person before that person could feel free to give him or her all the information necessary to make that decision. Thus, public policy as well as normal rules of statutory construction dictate our holding today: that once [attorney] Heckler started to elicit from appellant such incriminating information that a person would feel free to share only with his lawyer, he

---

[13] *Mixon v. State*, 224 S.W.3d 206, 208 (Tex. Crim. App. 2007).

was bound by the same duties of confidentiality that a lawyer owes a client that he has agreed to represent, even though Heckler eventually decided not to represent appellant.[14]

14. (J-2015, J-2006, and F-2002) Prosecutor calls Witness to the stand. Witness testifies she saw Defendant meeting his lawyer for lunch just before trial, and she overheard them talking about this case. You object to Witness's testimony and any further testimony about that conversation, but Prosecutor replies that it is admissible as evidence of guilt. The Court overrules the objection.

Was the Court's ruling correct? Explain.

_____

_____

_____

_____

_____

Rule 504. Spousal Privileges

(a) Confidential Communication Privilege.

(1) *Definition.* A communication is "confidential" if a person makes it privately to the person's spouse and does not intend its disclosure to any other person.

(2) *General Rule.* A person has a privilege to refuse to disclose and to prevent any other person from disclosing a confidential communication made to the person's spouse while they were married. This privilege survives termination of the marriage.

(3) *Who May Claim.* The privilege may be claimed by:

---

[14] *Id.* at 211-12.

(A) the communicating spouse;

(B) the guardian of a communicating spouse who is incompetent; or

(C) the personal representative of a communicating spouse who is deceased.

The other spouse may claim the privilege on the communicating spouse's behalf—and is presumed to have authority to do so.

(4) *Exceptions.* This privilege does not apply ... in a proceeding in which a party is accused of conduct that, if proved, is a crime against the person of the other spouse, any member of the household of either spouse, or any minor child; or ... [in a] criminal proceeding involving a charge of bigamy ....

(b) Privilege Not to Testify in a Criminal Case.

(1) *General Rule.* In a criminal case, an accused's spouse has a privilege not to be called to testify for the state. But this rule neither prohibits a spouse from testifying voluntarily for the state nor gives a spouse a privilege to refuse to be called to testify for the accused.

(2) *Failure to Call Spouse.* If other evidence indicates that the accused's spouse could testify to relevant matters, an accused's failure to call the spouse to testify is a proper subject of comment by counsel.

(3) *Who May Claim.* The privilege not to testify may be claimed by the accused's spouse or the spouse's guardian or representative, but not by the accused.

(4) *Exceptions.* This privilege does not apply: In a criminal proceeding in which a spouse is charged with a crime against the other spouse, any member of the household

of either spouse, or any minor child; or bigamy; or if the spouse is called to testify about matters that occurred before the marriage.

15. (F-2014, J-2007, F-2005, and J-2001) Defendant is charged with embezzlement. Prosecutor calls Defendant's Wife to the stand. You object that Prosecutor cannot call this witness because she is married to Defendant, and he is claiming spousal privilege. Wife tells Judge she wants to testify against Defendant because she hates him and wants him to go to prison.

How should Judge rule? Explain.

_____

_____

_____

_____

Note: When answering spousal privilege questions, it is important to take note of the crime the defendant is charged with committing and who is claiming the spousal privilege. Rule 504 exempts certain offenses from the privilege and permits only the testifying spouse the right to claim the privilege, not the accused.

16. (F-2010, F-2007, J-2005, F-2003, and J-2001) Defendant is charged with driving while intoxicated. Wife does not want to testify against Defendant, who is her husband. Nevertheless, Prosecutor wants to call Wife to testify because Wife was drinking with Defendant just before the accident.

a. Can Wife be compelled, over her objection, to testify for the State? Explain.

_____

_____

_____

_____

_____

b. (J-2003 and F-2003) Assume that instead of being charged with
    driving while intoxicated, Defendant was charged with assaulting his
    Wife after the two became intoxicated and he attacked her.

    How should Judge rule if Wife invokes her spousal privilege and
    refuses to testify, but Prosecutor nevertheless calls her to the witness
    stand to testify?

_____

_____

_____

_____

_____

Rule 505. Privilege for Communications to a Clergy Member

(a) **Definitions**. In this rule:

   (1) A "clergy member" is a minister, priest, rabbi, accredited
       Christian Science Practitioner, or other similar functionary of a
       religious organization or someone whom a communicant
       reasonably believes is a clergy member.

   (2) A "communicant" is a person who consults a clergy member in
       the clergy member's professional capacity as a spiritual adviser.

   (3) A communication is "confidential" if made privately and not
       intended for further disclosure except to other persons present to
       further the purpose of the communication.

(b) **General Rule**. A communicant has a privilege to refuse to disclose and
to prevent any other person from disclosing a confidential communication by

the communicant to a clergy member in the clergy member's professional capacity as spiritual adviser.

(c) **Who May Claim**. The privilege may be claimed by:

  (1) the communicant;
  (2) the communicant's guardian or conservator; or
  (3) a deceased communicant's personal representative.

The clergy member to whom the communication was made may claim the privilege on the communicant's behalf—and is presumed to have authority to do so.

17. (J-2010, J-2008, F-2005, and J-2002) Prosecutor calls Priest to the stand and the following exchange occurs:

State: Would you please introduce yourself?

Priest: Hello. I'm Defendant's Priest. He regularly attends Mass and confession on Saturdays.

State: Has he ever discussed the facts that led to his arrest for this crime with you during confession?

What is the proper objection, if any, to this testimony? How should Judge rule based upon such an objection? Explain.

_____

_____

_____

_____

_____

Rule 509. Physician-Patient Privilege

(a) **Definitions**. In this rule:

(1) A "patient" is a person who consults or is seen by a physician for medical care.

(2) A "physician" is a person licensed, or who the patient reasonably believes is licensed, to practice medicine in any state or nation.

(3) A communication is "confidential" if not intended to be disclosed to third persons other than those:

(A) present to further the patient's interest in the consultation, examination, or interview;

(B) reasonably necessary to transmit the communication; or

(C) participating in the diagnosis and treatment under the physician's direction, including members of the patient's family.

(b) **Limited Privilege in a Criminal Case**. There is no physician-patient privilege in a criminal case. But a confidential communication is not admissible in a criminal case if made:

(1) to a person involved in the treatment of or examination for alcohol or drug abuse; and

(2) by a person being treated voluntarily or being examined for admission to treatment for alcohol or drug abuse.

18. (J-2008, F-2008, F-2007, F-2006, and F-2003) Prosecutor informs you that she intends to call Defendant's medical doctor, psychiatrist, and drug

treatment counselor to testify about what Defendant told them about this crime.

Can you argue Defendant's communications with any of these witnesses were protected, privileged, and, therefore, inadmissible? Explain.

———————————————————————————————

———————————————————————————————

———————————————————————————————

———————————————————————————————

———————————————————————————————

—————————————— ◆ ——————————————

Hearsay and Hearsay Exceptions

Many evidence questions, both in the Texas Civil Procedure and Evidence and Texas Criminal Procedure and Evidence portions of the bar exam, are based on hearsay, non-hearsay, or hearsay exceptions. While there are dozens of rules that apply to hearsay, bar examiners have asked questions about only a few topics: hearsay, non-hearsay statements made by party-opponents, non-hearsay admissions by co-conspirators, statements made in the course of medical diagnosis or treatment, statements against interest, dying declarations, and outcry statements. This section will analyze each of these rules beginning with hearsay and non-hearsay statements.

Rule 801. Definitions That Apply to This Article; Exclusions from Hearsay

(d) Hearsay. "Hearsay" means a statement that:

(1) the declarant does not make while testifying at the current trial or hearing; and

(2) a party offers in evidence to prove the truth of the matter asserted in the statement.

When a witness testifies that someone else told her something, and that "something" is meant to prove the truth of what was said, the testimony may be hearsay. Of course, there are non-hearsay statements and exceptions to hearsay statements. Furthermore, hearsay statements are admissible when a statement is not offered to prove the truth of the matter asserted. Nevertheless, a somebody-told-me-something statement should raise hearsay red flags.

19. (J-2013, F-2008, F-2007, F-2006, J-2005, J-2002, and F-2002) During the State's case in chief, Prosecutor asks Officer, who is called to testify about his investigation, the following:

Prosecutor:	After you arrested Defendant, did you speak with any of the people standing around the crime scene?
Officer:	Yes, I spoke to Bystander.
Prosecutor:	What did Bystander say?
Officer:	She said she heard Defendant say …
Defense Counsel:	Objection.

What is the basis of your objection? How should Judge rule? Explain.

_____

_____

_____

_____

_____

Non-Hearsay Statements

In Texas Rule of Evidence 801, hearsay is defined and several statements are identified as "statements which are not hearsay."[15] Included in that are

---

[15] TEX. R. EVID. 801 (e).

prior statements of a witness, admissions by party opponents, and co-conspirator statements.[16]

Rule 801. Definitions that Apply to this Article; Exclusions from Hearsay

(e) Statements that are not Hearsay. A statement that meets the following conditions is not hearsay:

(2) *An Opposing Party's Statement.* The statement is offered against an opposing party and:

> (A) was made by the party in an individual or representative capacity;
>
> (B) is one the party manifested that it adopted or believed to be true;
>
> (C) was made by a person whom the party authorized to make a statement on the subject;
>
> (D) was made by the party's agent or employee on a matter within the scope of that relationship and while it existed; or
>
> (E) was made by the party's coconspirator during and in furtherance of the conspiracy.

20. (J-2016, F-2004, and J-2002) Consider the previous question. Imagine that instead of Officer testifying about Bystander's statement at trial, Prosecutor calls Bystander to the stand to testify about what she heard Defendant say. Would your answer to the previous question remain the same? Why or why not?

_____

_____

_____

[16] TEX. R. EVID. 801 (e)(1)-(2).

_____

_____

_____

Note: Pay close attention to the wording of hearsay scenarios. Sometimes one or two words can make a statement hearsay or non-hearsay. This has been true for hearsay questions on more than one exam. There is a big difference between a witness testifying about what another person said and a witness testifying about what the defendant said. Oftentimes, inculpatory statements offered against defendants at trial are both a statement against interest and an admission by a party opponent. List all exceptions or exclusions in your answer that apply to the fact scenario given in the question.

21. (J-2016 and F-2011) Prosecutor intends to call Shorty, who will testify at Defendant Johnny's trial, as a witness against him. Shorty will testify as follows:

"Johnny, me, and Slim decided to break into her house to steal her big screen TV. It was Johnny's idea, since he's always wanted one of them big plasma screen TVs. So, the three of us waited until she went to work, then we walked around to the back door and kicked it in. I unhooked the TV while Johnny watched the front door, and Slim ran through the rest of the house to see if anything else was worth stealin'. Somebody musta called the cops because when we were puttin' the TV in Slim's truck, the cops pulled up."

You object to Shorty's statement on the basis of hearsay. How should Judge rule? Explain.

_____

_____

_____

_____

_____

Exceptions to Hearsay

Not only are some statements not considered hearsay under the rules of evidence, but some statements that are considered hearsay are exempted from exclusion. Texas Rule of Evidence 803 includes many exceptions that apply regardless of the declarant's availability at trial. Texas Rule of Evidence 804 exceptions apply only when the declarant is not available to testify at trial. Both sections are discussed below insofar as they have appeared on bar exams.

Rule 803. Exceptions to the Rule against Hearsay Regardless of Whether the Declarant Is Available as a Witness

(4) Statement Made for Medical Diagnosis or Treatment. A statement that:

(A) is made for—and is reasonably pertinent to—medical diagnosis or treatment; and

(B) describes medical history; past or present symptoms or sensations; their inception; or their general cause.

22. (J-2012) Prosecutor calls Doctor to testify about Victim's injuries. Doctor testifies that when she asked how Victim received her injuries, Victim said Defendant pushed her down to the ground after an argument and she received cuts to her lip and the side of her face. You object on the ground that what Victim told Doctor is hearsay. How should Judge rule? Explain.

_____

_____

_____

_____

_____

Note: Medical statement hearsay questions and doctor-patient privilege questions are easy to confuse. Both types of questions involve a doctor testifying about what someone else said. The key is to look at the objection being lodged. If the objection is "Hearsay," then the examiners are likely asking whether the statement made for purposes of medical diagnosis/treatment exception applies. If the objection is "privileged communication," then the examiners are likely asking about whether the doctor-patient privilege applies. Again, a correct or incorrect answer comes down to a few specific words in the question. Pay close attention.

> **(24) Statement Against Interest.** A statement that:
>
> (A) a reasonable person in the declarant's position would have made only if the person believed it to be true because, when made, it was so contrary to the declarant's proprietary or pecuniary interest or had so great a tendency to invalidate the declarant's claim against someone else or to expose the declarant to civil or criminal liability or to make the declarant an object of hatred, ridicule, or disgrace; and
>
> (B) is supported by corroborating circumstances that clearly indicate its trustworthiness, if it is offered in a criminal case as one that tends to expose the declarant to criminal liability.

The Texas Court of Criminal Appeals has created a two-part test based on this exception:

> Any determination regarding the admissibility of a statement in accordance with rule 803(24) requires a two-step inquiry. First, the trial court must determine whether the statement in question tends to expose the declarant to criminal liability. Second, the trial court must determine if there are corroborating circumstances that clearly indicate the trustworthiness of the statement. If both these criteria are met, then rule 803(24) is satisfied.[17]

23. (J-2016, F-2013, F-2004, and J-2002) Prosecutor calls Witness to the stand. Witness testifies that he spoke with Defendant after he bonded out of jail: "I asked whether he really tried to shoot that dude with a gun

---

[17] *Bingham v. State*, 987 S.W.2d 54, 57 (Tex. Crim. App. 1999).

like the cops said. That's when he said, 'Yeah, I tried to shoot that little punk. He's a snitch. He needs to learn a lesson or two, and if I'm the one who has to teach him the hard way, it is what it is.'" You object on hearsay grounds.

How should Judge rule? Explain.

_____

_____

_____

_____

_____

Rule 804. Exceptions to the Rule against Hearsay When the Declarant Is Unavailable as a Witness

(b) The Exceptions. The following are not excluded by the rule against hearsay if the declarant is unavailable as a witness:

[The above language is confusing because of the double negatives ("not" and "against"). What it means put simply is that what follows in subsection (b) are hearsay exceptions that apply when the declarant is unavailable to testify.]

(2) *Statement under the Belief of Imminent Death.* A statement that the declarant, while believing the declarant's death to be imminent, made about [the impending death's] cause or circumstances.

24. (J-2014) Prosecutor calls Nurse to testify that when Victim was brought to the hospital, she was aware that she was "bleeding out" and only had moments to live. Nurse testified, "She grabbed my uniform, pulled me close to her face, and said, 'My sister has always been jealous of me. I guess she finally got what she wanted: for me to die. It's going to break my parents' heart, but please tell them she's the one who stabbed me.' After that, she closed her eyes and breathed her last breath." You object

on hearsay grounds and request that the testimony be stricken and the jury instructed to disregard.

How should the judge rule? Explain.

_____

_____

_____

_____

_____

———————————◆———————————

Outcry Notice

One hearsay exception that is probably not discussed in any Federal Evidence class is the outcry statement. Outcry statements are hearsay statements made by a child to an adult about child abuse.[18] The reason for exempting such statements is that children should be saved from the trauma of testifying about physical or sexual abuse in a courtroom.[19] The outcry statement exception to hearsay is not found in the Texas Rules of Evidence but in the Texas Code of Criminal Procedure.[20]

In child abuse cases, there may be an outcry statement and an outcry witness. A child who is abused, or an adult with a mental disability, may tell an adult—a grandparent, school counselor, Sunday School teacher, or any other adult—about the abuse. The first adult told is known as the "outcry witness." This person is permitted to testify about what the child said. In order to allow the outcry witness to testify, the State must meet three statutory requirements:

> (1) on or before the 14th day before the date the proceeding begins, the party intending to offer the statement:
>
> (A) notifies the adverse party of its intention to do so;

---

[18] TEX. CODE CRIM. PROC. ANN. § art. 38.072 (West 2016).
[19] *Bays v. State*, 396 S.W.3d 580, 595 (Tex. Crim. App. 2013).
[20] TEX. CODE CRIM. PROC. ANN. § art. 38.072 (West 2016).

(B) provides the adverse party with the name of the witness through whom it intends to offer the statement; and

(C) provides the adverse party with a written summary of the statement.[21]

If these requirements are met, the trial court must have a hearing outside of the jury's presence to determine whether the details of the statement (the timing, content, and facts) are reliable, and the child is available to testify.[22] This does not mean the child will be required to testify, but the child must be available to do so. If all of these requirements are met, the outcry witness may testify about the child's outcry statement.

25. (F-2003) Before trial, you receive a notice from Prosecutor indicating he intends to call Witness to testify about Child's outcry statement. List three statutory requirements that must be met before this testimony can be admitted at trial.

_____

_____

_____

_____

_____

———————————◆———————————

Records and Reports

You may not have considered reports and records as exceptions to hearsay, but they are indeed, provided the correct foundation is established by the party seeking to admit them into evidence.[23] Records and reports frequently play a role in criminal cases. Medical records, forensic lab reports, phone records, and business records may be admitted into evidence to prove

---

[21] *Id.*
[22] *Id.*
[23] TEX. R. EVID. 803(6).

an element of a charge or a defense, but just because they're relevant does not mean they are admissible. The attorney seeking to admit the record or the report must lay a proper foundation before the contents of the document are made known to the jury.

There are two ways to admit these reports or records. The first is through the person in charge of making or keeping the reports or records, known as the *custodian of records*. The person, through direct examination, lays the foundation to get the document admitted into evidence. The second is through a self-authenticating affidavit made by the custodian of records. You will see both procedures described in more detail below.

Police reports are excluded from being considered admissible business records because they, "'in criminal cases, tend to be one-sided and self-serving. They are frequently prepared for the use of prosecutors, who use such reports in deciding whether to prosecute.'"[24] Not only are reports written by police officers deemed inadmissible hearsay, but so too are other law enforcement employees' reports, like chemists' and jailers' reports.[25] When a chemist or professional does not work for a law enforcement agency, the report or record is admissible assuming the proper predicate is laid.[26]

Rule 803. Exceptions to the Rule against Hearsay Regardless of Whether the Declarant Is Available as a Witness

> The following are not excluded by the rule against hearsay, regardless of whether the declarant is available as a witness: …
>
> (6) *Records of a Regularly Conducted Activity*. A record of an act, event, condition, opinion, or diagnosis if:

---

[24] *Cole v. State*, 839 S.W.2d 798, 811-12 (Tex. Crim. App. 1990), *decision clarified on reh'g* (Oct. 21, 1992) (quoting a member of the U.S. Senate).
[25] *Bermen v. State*, 798 S.W.2d 8, 12 (Tex. App.—Houston [1st Dist.] 1990, pet. granted) (trial court erred in admitting jailer's report on escapee as business record); *Davenport v. State*, 856 S.W.2d 578, 579 (Tex. App.—Houston [1st Dist.] 1993, no pet.) (chemist report was prepared by law enforcement and was thus not admissible).
[26] *Burris v. State*, 06-13-00039-CR, 2014 WL 576209, at *7 (Tex. App.—Texarkana Feb. 12, 2014, pet. ref'd) ("there is no indication that the company that collected records of persons buying pseudoephedrine was associated with law enforcement or that the records were gathered as part of any adversarial process").

(A) the record was made at or near the time by—or from information transmitted by—someone with knowledge;

(B) the record was kept in the course of a regularly conducted business activity;

(C) making the record was a regular practice of that activity;

(D) all these conditions are shown by the testimony of the custodian or another qualified witness, or by an affidavit or unsworn declaration that complies with Rule 902(10); and

(E) the opponent fails to demonstrate that the source of information or the method or circumstances of preparation indicate a lack of trustworthiness. "Business" as used in this paragraph includes every kind of regular organized activity whether conducted for profit or not.

(7) *Absence of a Record of a Regularly Conducted Activity.* Evidence that a matter is not included in a record described in paragraph (6) if:

(A) the evidence is admitted to prove that the matter did not occur or exist;

(B) a record was regularly kept for a matter of that kind; and

(C) the opponent fails to show that the possible source of the information or other circumstances indicate a lack of trustworthiness.

(8) *Public Records.* A record or statement of a public office if:

    (A) it sets out:

    (i) the office's activities;

(ii) a matter observed while under a legal duty to report, but not including, in a criminal case, a matter observed by law-enforcement personnel; or

(iii) in a civil case or against the government in a criminal case, factual findings from a legally authorized investigation; and

(B) the opponent fails to demonstrate that the source of information or other circumstances indicate a lack of trustworthiness.

Rule 902. Evidence that is Self-Authenticating

The following items of evidence are self-authenticating; they require no extrinsic evidence of authenticity in order to be admitted: ...

(10) *Business Records Accompanied by Affidavit.* The original or a copy of a record that meets the requirements of Rule 803(6) or (7), if the record is accompanied by an affidavit that complies with subparagraph (B) of this rule and any other requirements of law, and the record and affidavit are served in accordance with subparagraph (A). For good cause shown, the court may order that a business record be treated as presumptively authentic even if the proponent fails to comply with subparagraph (A).

    (A) *Service Requirement.* The proponent of a record must serve the record and the accompanying affidavit on each other party to the case at least 14 days before trial. ...

(B) *Form of Affidavit.* An affidavit is sufficient if it includes the following language, but this form is not exclusive. The proponent may use an unsworn declaration made under penalty of perjury in place of an affidavit. [Subsection B includes a sample affidavit.]

26. Prosecutor calls hospital's custodian of records to introduce medical records that establish the extent of Victim's injuries in an aggravated assault case. You object that the records are hearsay.

    a. (F-2015, F-2011, F-2007, F-2003, and F-2001) For the records to be admissible under the Texas Rules of Evidence, what must the testimony of the custodian of records show?

    _____

    _____

    _____

    _____

    _____

    b. (J-2008, F-2006, J-2005, and J-2003) Suppose the custodian of records isn't available to testify at trial.

    Is there another way to admit the records into evidence? If so, explain the process.

    _____

    _____

    _____

    _____

    _____

27. (J-2014) Prosecutor attempts to admit the police report of Officer through Police Department's custodian of records. You object that the report is inadmissible hearsay, but Prosecutor replies that it is an admissible public record.

How should Judge rule? Explain.

_____

_____

_____

_____

_____

————————◆————————

Polygraph Evidence

Polygraph examinations and results, though frequently employed by law enforcement agencies for investigative purposes, are inadmissible at trial. "The ban on polygraph evidence is comprehensive … [It] applies even when both the State and defense agree to admit the evidence.[27] This is because polygraph evidence is deemed inherently unreliable, yet overly persuasive to jurors.[28]

28. (J-2014) You believe Defendant is innocent of the charged crime. To bolster the evidence you have admitted, you call Expert, a polygraph examiner, to testify that Defendant passed a polygraph exam and is telling the truth when he says he is not guilty. Prosecutor objects to Expert's testimony.

   How should the judge rule? Explain.

_____

_____

_____

_____

_____

————————◆————————

---

[27] *Leonard v. State*, 315 S.W.3d 578, 580 (Tex. App.—Eastland 2010), *aff'd*, 385 S.W.3d 570 (Tex. Crim. App. 2012).
[28] *Banda v. State*, 727 S.W.2d 679, 681 (Tex. App.—Austin 1987, no pet.).

Evidence Authentication

One major concern about admitted evidence is whether it is an accurate representation of what it purports to be. There is sometimes a concern that evidence has been altered to favor a party and this alteration distorts the evidence in some way.

Rule 901. Authenticating or Identifying Evidence

In General. To satisfy the requirement of authenticating or identifying an item of evidence, the proponent must produce evidence sufficient to support a finding that the item is what the proponent claims it is.

Rule 901 then goes onto list ways to authenticate evidence.[29] Evidence may be authenticated through testimony by a witness with knowledge, comparisons, opinions, records, documents, systematic evidence, or some other way proscribed by statute or rules.[30]

Waylon Chaz Standmire v. State
475 S.W.3d 336
(Tex. App.—Waco 2014, pet. ref'd)

[Mr. Standmire, a jail inmate, was convicted of aggravated assault with a deadly weapon for cutting Mr. Fedrick's face with a knife as he slept in the jail cell. A surveillance video depicting the assault was admitted against him at trial.]

Standmire's first issue is that the trial court erred in admitting the video recording from the jail surveillance camera because the sponsoring witness[, jailer Parten,] ... did not have sufficient knowledge to authenticate the exhibit. Specifically, Standmire argues that because the detention officer sponsoring the exhibit did not see the assault take place and because he could not show the recording process accurately produced the resulting video, no one with personal knowledge could testify that the images on the exhibit were an accurate portrayal of what occurred. ...

---

[29] TEX. R. EVID. 901 (b).
[30] *Id.*

There are at least two ways, if not more, to authenticate photographic evidence including videos. The most common is by testimony that the photo or video is an accurate representation of the object or scene in question. ... In this situation, the sponsoring witness is not required to be the person who operated the camera or video equipment. Another slightly less common but equally permissible way is by testimony that the process or system that produced the photo or video is reliable. Reliability of the system or process is most often used when there is no witness that was present at the scene or event depicted in the photograph or video. This is common with security videos; such as those used after hours in convenience stores and freestanding automatic teller machines. For authentication of such photographic or video evidence, the sponsoring witness usually 1) describes the type of system used for recording and whether it was working properly; 2) testifies whether he reviewed the video or photos; 3) testifies whether he removed the video or device that stores the photos; and 4) testifies whether the video or photos have been altered or tampered with. But if the sponsoring witness was present when the photographs or video were taken or has personal knowledge of what the photographs or video depict, it is unnecessary for the sponsoring witness to also testify regarding the reliability of the system.

In this instance, Parten was present and is, in fact, shown in the video. He certainly was able to testify whether the video was an accurate portrayal of the events depicted. While he may not have seen the event depicted at the beginning of the video of Standmire's contact with Fedrick while Fedrick was lying on his bunk, Parten did personally witness the events depicted only seconds later and then appeared on the video himself.

Parten's testimony was certainly sufficient to authenticate the video. Because the admission of the exhibit was based on Parten's personal knowledge of the facts depicted in the video, it was unnecessary for the State to authenticate the video by any other means or methods such as proving the reliability of the system or process. Accordingly, the trial court did not abuse its discretion in admitting the video over Standmire's objection; and Standmire's first issue is overruled.

29. (F-2016) Defendant is charged with shoplifting. Prosecutor calls Witness, a theft prevention employee of the store, to testify about the surveillance video, which depicts the theft. Witness testifies that he watched the tape immediately after the theft and just before trial. It has not been altered, it

694 | Texas Criminal Procedure and Evidence

accurately depicts the theft, and the camera was working properly when it recorded the theft. However, Witness did not observe the theft firsthand, as it occurred. You object to the tape coming in on the ground that it has not properly been authenticated.

How should Judge rule on the objection? Explain.

_____

_____

_____

_____

_____

———————————◆———————————

Optional Completeness

You may have learned about the rule of optional completeness in Evidence. It permits a party the option of introducing evidence that would complete evidence submitted by opposing counsel. This usually happens when one attorney offers only partial evidence and by doing so, leaves out beneficial evidence to the opposing party.

Rule 106. Remainder of or Related Writings or Recorded Statements

If a party introduces all or part of a writing or recorded statement, an adverse party may introduce, at that time, any other part—or any other writing or recorded statement—that in fairness ought to be considered at the same time.

Rule 107. Rule of Optional Completeness

If a party introduces part of an act, declaration, conversation, writing, or recorded statement, an adverse party may inquire into any other part on the same subject. An adverse party may also introduce any other act, declaration, conversation, writing, or recorded statement that is necessary to explain or allow the trier of fact to fully understand the part offered by the opponent.

30. (J-2004 and J-2001) During the presentation of the State's case, Prosecutor offers into evidence part of a letter written by Defendant. You believe the omitted portion of the letter is favorable evidence for Defendant.

What, if anything, can you do to get the other part admitted into evidence? Explain.

_____

_____

_____

_____

_____

—————————◆—————————

Preservation of Error

When a criminal case is tried and the defendant is convicted, often the case is then appealed. It is important that any mistakes or errors that happen in the trial court be preserved for appeal. The most common way to preserve error is to make an evidentiary objection. While this topic could have nicely fit into Chapter 14, error must be preserved before the appeal is filed. In most cases, preservation of error takes place before or during trial, and most of the time, the subject of the objection is evidence. Therefore, this topic will be discussed in the context of evidence.

The process for preserving error is found in the Texas Rules of Appellate Procedure. Rule 33.1 states:

As a prerequisite to presenting a complaint for appellate review, the record must show that:

(1) the complaint was made to the trial court by a timely request, objection, or motion that:

(A) stated the grounds for the ruling that the complaining party sought from the trial court with sufficient specificity to make the trial court aware of the complaint, unless the specific grounds were apparent from the context; and

(B) complied with the requirements of the Texas Rules of ... Evidence or the Texas Rules of ... Appellate Procedure; and

(2) the trial court:

(A) ruled on the request, objection, or motion, either expressly or implicitly; or

(B) refused to rule on the request, objection, or motion, and the complaining party objected to the refusal.[31]

The Court of Criminal Appeals explains the reason why a specific objection is essential:

> The purpose of requiring a specific objection in the trial court is twofold: (1) to inform the trial judge of the basis of the objection and give him the opportunity to rule on it; (2) to give opposing counsel the opportunity to respond to the complaint. Although there are no technical considerations or forms of words required to preserve an error for appeal, a party must be specific enough so as to "let the trial judge know what he wants, why he thinks himself entitled to it, and do so clearly enough for the judge to understand him at a time when the trial court is in a proper position to do something about it." The parties, not the judge, are responsible for the correct application of evidentiary rules; in order to preserve a complaint for appeal, the complaining party must have done everything necessary to bring the relevant evidentiary rule and its precise and proper application to the trial court's attention.[32]

---

[31] TEX. R. APP. PROC. 33.1.
[32] *Resendez v. State*, 306 S.W.3d 308, 312-13 (Tex. Crim. App. 2009).

One of the Houston Courts of Appeals summed up the above requirements as follows: "Simply stated, to preserve error, an objection must be timely, specific, and pursued to an adverse ruling."[33]

Texas courts require parties to object each time the objectionable evidence is offered by opposing counsel.[34] If a party does not object each time, the party waives error on appeal. There are two exceptions to this rule, however:

1. When the objectionable evidence is heard outside of the jury's presence and the judge rules it admissible, the objecting party is not required to preserve error by renewing the objection when it is admitted.[35]

2. A party may ask for a "running objection" instead of having to object every time.[36]

Sometimes a party or witness makes an inadmissible or improper statement before the jury. Opposing counsel must cure the error of the jury by (1) objecting and if the objection is sustained, (2) requesting an instruction to disregard, and if the instruction is granted, (3) moving for a mistrial.[37] Again, the party must pursue the objection to an adverse ruling in order to preserve it for appeal.

An attorney who fails to object, does not pursue an objection to an adverse ruling, or fails to state the reason for the objection may waive the right to raise the issue on appeal.

31. (F-2014, F-2009, J-2006, F-2006, F-2005, J-2003, F-2002, and F-2001) During closing arguments, Prosecutor argues, "When Defendant was arrested and read his *Miranda* rights, he kept his mouth shut and said nothing. If he were really innocent, he would have spoken up and declared his innocence from the rooftops, but he didn't. That in itself shows he is guilty." You reply, "Objection!"

---

[33] *Kennedy v. State*, 264 S.W.3d 372, 380 (Tex. App.—Houston [1st Dist.] 2008, pet. ref'd).

[34] *Martinez v. State*, 98 S.W.3d 189, 193 (Tex. Crim. App. 2003).

[35] TEX. R. EVID. 103.

[36] *Ethington v. State*, 819 S.W.2d 854, 858 (Tex. Crim. App. 1991).

[37] *Harris v. State*, 784 S.W.2d 5, 12 n. 4 (Tex. Crim. App. 1989).

Is this enough to protect defendant's rights at trial and preserve error on appeal? If not, what else must you do?

_____

_____

_____

_____

_____

———————————◆———————————